Kickstart

Python Programming Fundamentals

Real-world Projects and Hands-on Exercises to Cement Every Python Programming Concept

Jit Sinha

www.orangeava.com

First Published: June 2025

Published By: Orange Education Pvt Ltd, AVA®

Address: 9, Daryaganj, Delhi, 110002, India

275 New North Road Islington Suite 1314 London,
N1 7AA, United Kingdom

ISBN (PBK): 978-93-49888-65-4

ISBN (E-BOOK): 978-93-49888-55-5

Scan the QR code to explore our entire catalogue

www.orangeava.com

Dedicated To

To My Son, Caesar,
You Are Just Three Now, Full of Wonder, Laughter, and Light.
One Day, When You're Older, I Hope This Book Shows You How
Curiosity Can Lead to Creation, and How Learning Something
New Can Open Many Doors.
This Book is for You—and Because of You

About the Author

Jit Sinha is a seasoned IT professional with over 14 years of experience in the tech industry. He currently works at a leading global IT company, where he plays a key role in designing smart and reliable technology solutions. As a certified Solution Architect in platforms such as Splunk, AWS, Azure, and Google Cloud, Jit has built a strong reputation for creating powerful IT systems for clients in banking, telecom, and healthcare.

His work has helped banks stay secure, supported telecom companies with strong and scalable networks, and improved the way healthcare systems manage and protect sensitive data. Jit has a deep passion for cybersecurity and data analytics, and he is especially known for his expertise in using Splunk to spot threats and strengthen security in complex IT environments.

Lately, he has stepped into the exciting world of Generative AI, combining new AI technologies with traditional IT to build innovative solutions. He actively shares his knowledge through workshops, training sessions, and speaking events. As a Udemy instructor, he has also created a course on Generative AI to help others learn about this fast-growing field.

In addition, Jit is the author of another well-received book on Splunk and cybersecurity, where he explores how to strengthen digital defenses using data-driven insights.

Beyond the tech world, Jit has a love for mythology, geopolitics, and storytelling. His gift for explaining complex ideas in a simple and engaging way makes him a popular speaker and educator. Whether in the classroom, on stage, or online, he is passionate about inspiring and mentoring the next generation of IT professionals.

About the Technical Reviewer

Madhur Yadav brings over seven years of experience in machine learning, deep learning, and software development. He has worked across MNCs and startups with global assignments in the USA, UK, Australia, and India. His expertise spans across statistical analysis, AI/ML model development, and building scalable data solutions. Madhur has a passion for problem-solving and a proven track record of delivering impactful AI-driven applications.

Throughout his career, Madhur has contributed to diverse industries, including healthcare, finance, and enterprise software. His experience includes developing classification and ranking models to reduce hospital readmissions, building custom NLP pipelines for processing medical text, and creating data-driven dashboards for KPI monitoring. He has also worked on multi-label classification models for healthcare applications and built NLP platforms for Named Entity Recognition (NER) and document classification.

Madhur has been recognized for his excellence in AI and ML. He has secured top positions in several ML and DL hackathons. He has also led technical initiatives, worked on AI-driven automation, and built intelligent decision-making systems using modern ML frameworks.

Currently, Madhur is focused on AI, automation, and large-scale data solutions. Passionate about continuous learning, he actively engages in research, upskilling, and mentoring. His work reflects a commitment to leveraging AI and data science to drive business value, optimize operations, and build intelligent applications.

Acknowledgements

There are many people I want to thank for their support and encouragement during the writing of this book.

To my mother, whose strength, love, and constant encouragement gave me the courage to write this book. She has always believed in me, and that belief helped me believe in myself.

To my son, Caesar, whose smile, laughter, and curiosity remind me every day why I strive to create and share. This book is a small gift for his future, written with love and hope.

I am also deeply grateful to the many students, hobbyists, and curious learners whose feedback helped shape this book into a simple, practical guide for beginners. They challenged me to make coding feel less scary and more like an everyday superpower.

I thank my friends and colleagues in the tech world for their insights, ideas, and support. And to the open-source community, whose tools make it possible for anyone to learn and grow. Their work is a gift to the world.

Thank you all for being part of this journey.

Preface

This book covers many different aspects of Python programming, starting from the absolute basics and gradually introducing more advanced topics in a friendly and structured way. It is designed for complete beginners, especially students and self-learners who want to start their coding journey. The content is written in simple English, making it easier for non-native speakers to follow and enjoy the process of learning to code.

Python is one of the most popular programming languages in the world. It is used in web development, data science, automation, machine learning, and more. This book aims to build a strong foundation in Python, helping you learn the core ideas clearly and practically. Each chapter includes small challenges and real-world examples so that you can apply what you have learned in meaningful ways.

This book is divided into **20 chapters**, grouped into different sections. It begins with the fundamentals, moves into advanced Python topics, and ends with practical applications and real-world projects. The goal is to not only teach Python but also to prepare you to use it in real-life situations and even build your own portfolio.

Chapter 1. Beginning with Python: This chapter introduces Python and its importance. It explains how to install Python, set up the coding environment, and run your first program.

Chapter 2. Introduction to Algorithms and Flowcharts: This chapter focuses on algorithms and flowcharts. It helps you understand how to plan before writing a code and turn those plans into working Python programs.

Chapter 3. Basic Python: This chapter explains Python basics such as variables, data types, and operators. By the end, you will be able to write small Python programs confidently.

Chapter 4. Making Choices and Repeating Actions: This chapter teaches you how to make choices and repeat actions using conditional statements and loops.

Chapter 5. Creating Functions: This chapter introduces functions and explains how to write reusable blocks of code that make your programs cleaner and more efficient.

Chapter 6. Organizing Data: This chapter covers Python's built-in data structures such as lists, tuples, dictionaries, and sets–important tools for organizing data.

Chapter 7. Understanding OOP in Python: This chapter gives a gentle introduction to object-oriented programming, a modern way to structure larger and more complex programs.

Chapter 8. Using Modules and Packages: This chapter shows how to use and create Python modules and packages, which help you reuse code and organize large projects.

Chapter 9. Error Handling: This chapter teaches you how to handle errors in your code, so your programs do not crash unexpectedly.

Chapter 10. File Handling and String Manipulation: This chapter explores file handling and string manipulation, showing how to read and write data in files and work with text.

Chapter 11. Dates and Times: This chapter helps you work with dates and times—something very useful in real applications such as calendars or scheduling.

Chapter 12. Working with JSON and XML: This chapter shows you how to handle structured data formats such as JSON and XML, which are commonly used in web and API data.

Chapter 13. Math in Python: This chapter explores Python's math capabilities, including arithmetic, complex numbers, statistics, and linear algebra with NumPy.

Chapter 14. Managing Packages with PIP: This chapter teaches you about managing packages using pip and working with virtual environments for cleaner project management.

Chapter 15. Building Web Apps: This chapter introduces web app development using Flask and Django, two popular Python frameworks.

Chapter 16. Python and Databases: This chapter explains how Python interacts with databases such as SQLite and MongoDB. You will learn how to store and retrieve data.

Chapter 17. Analyzing Data: This chapter covers data analysis using Pandas and visualizations with Matplotlib and Seaborn.

Chapter 18. Python in Artificial Intelligence: This chapter introduces artificial intelligence and machine learning using Python libraries such as scikit-learn.

Chapter 19. Conclusion and Next Steps: This chapter is a conclusion that shares tips on applying your skills, building a Python portfolio, and staying motivated.

Chapter 20. Real-World Project: This chapter presents real-world projects that bring together everything you have learned in the book.

This book was created to be your first friendly companion on your Python journey. It is not just about code—it is about building the confidence to solve problems, create something meaningful, and explore a future full of possibilities.

Downloading the code bundles and colored images

Please follow the links or scan the QR codes to download the
Code Bundles and Images of the book:

https://github.com/ava-orange-education/Kickstarter-Python-Programming-Fundamentals

The code bundles and images of the book are also hosted on
https://rebrand.ly/dbnnik8

In case there's an update to the code, it will be updated on the existing GitHub repository.

Errata

We take immense pride in our work at **Orange Education Pvt Ltd,** and follow best practices to ensure the accuracy of our content to provide an indulging reading experience to our subscribers. Our readers are our mirrors, and we use their inputs to reflect and improve upon human errors, if any, that may have occurred during the publishing processes involved. To let us maintain the quality and help us reach out to any readers who might be having difficulties due to any unforeseen errors, please write to us at :

errata@orangeava.com

Your support, suggestions, and feedback are highly appreciated.

DID YOU KNOW

Did you know that Orange Education Pvt Ltd offers eBook versions of every book published, with PDF and ePub files available? You can upgrade to the eBook version at **www.orangeava.com** and as a print book customer, you are entitled to a discount on the eBook copy. Get in touch with us at: **info@orangeava.com** for more details.

At **www.orangeava.com**, you can also read a collection of free technical articles, sign up for a range of free newsletters, and receive exclusive discounts and offers on Print Books and eBooks.

PIRACY

If you come across any illegal copies of our works in any form on the internet, we would be grateful if you would provide us with the location address or website name. Please contact us at **info@orangeava.com** with a link to the material.

ARE YOU INTERESTED IN AUTHORING WITH US?

If there is a topic that you have expertise in, and you are interested in either writing or contributing to a book, please write to us at **business@orangeava.com**. We are on a journey to help developers and tech professionals to gain insights on the present technological advancements and innovations happening across the globe and build a community that believes Knowledge is best acquired by sharing and learning with others. Please reach out to us to learn what our audience demands and how you can be part of this educational reform. We also welcome ideas from tech experts and help them build learning and development content for their domains.

REVIEWS

Please leave a review. Once you have read and used this book, why not leave a review on the site that you purchased it from? Potential readers can then see and use your unbiased opinion to make purchase decisions. We at Orange Education would love to know what you think about our products, and our authors can learn from your feedback. Thank you!

For more information about Orange Education, please visit **www.orangeava.com**.

Table of Contents

CHAPTER 1
Beginning with Python

Introduction

Welcome to the world of programming! This chapter will help you take your first steps in learning Python, a language that is easy to start with and super useful. You will learn how programming works in everyday life, what makes Python special, and how to set up everything on your computer to get started. By the end of this chapter, you will even write your first Python program! Do not worry if you are new to all this. Everyone starts somewhere, and with a little practice, it becomes easier and more fun. Let us begin this exciting journey and turn your interest into real skills!

Structure

In this chapter, we will cover the following topics:

- Welcome to Programming
    - Understanding Programming
    - The Role of Programming in Our Lives
    - High-Level versus Low-Level Languages: A Brief Overview
- Introduction to Python
    - Brief History of Python
    - Python's Popularity and Versatility
- Significance of Python in Programming
    - Overview of Python's Strengths and Applications
    - Python's Thriving Community and Ecosystem
    - Comparison with Other Programming Languages
- Setting Up Python Environment
    - Prerequisites Before Installing Python
    - Installing Python: A Step-by-Step Guide
    - Introducing IDEs: Your Coding Command Centers
    - Understanding Virtual Environments
- Understanding Package Managers and pip
- Writing and Executing Your First Python Program
    - The "Hello, World!" Program
    - Understanding What You Did
- Exercises and Challenges: Practice Problems and Solutions

Welcome to Programming

Programming is like opening the door to a world where your ideas can come to life. Think of it as turning your "what if" thoughts into "let me show you" solutions. Every line of code you write gets you closer to creating something useful, exciting, or even life-changing.

Understanding Programming

Imagine having a magical notebook where anything you write becomes real. Need a cake? Write the recipe in this notebook, and the cake appears! This might sound magical, but programming works in a similar way. Instead of a notebook, we use code to tell computers what to do.

Fundamentally, programming is the art of training a computer to perform specific tasks. These challenges vary in complexity, from flying a drone to adding two digits. The computer follows these instructions exactly, operating as a very obedient genie that can conduct calculations, data manipulation, and even robot control.

Many people think that learning to program can be as frightening as learning a new language at first. And it is, in a way. However, understanding the fundamentals—a few words and some basic grammar rules—is the first stage in learning any language, followed by forming sentences. Before you know it, you are creating your own software programs or having full-fledged discussions about programming languages.

Remember that all expert programmers started from where you are today. Their first "Hello, World!" program was also their small step into a big universe. Thus, be patient with yourself and keep an open mind as we embark on this journey together. Writing code is just one component of programming; another is utilizing imagination to solve problems. Making mistakes is normal; in fact, they often serve as our best lessons. Every error, every malfunction, brings you one step closer to understanding. You are not just learning to program; you are also learning as you solve problems.

Welcome to the amazing world of programming. Your journey has just begun!

The Role of Programming in Our Lives

Programming plays a huge role in our daily lives, often in ways we do not even notice. From waking up in the morning to going to bed at night, programming shapes the technology we rely on. Consider how we navigate traffic using apps such as Waze or Google Maps. These are not static maps; they are dynamic tools that show us the shortest routes by analyzing real-time data from many sources, allowing us to avoid traffic and save time. Is this magic? Everything is done via code.

Some of the most noteworthy instances are from the healthcare industry. Wearables that can track heart rates, sleep habits, and even predict potential health issues have been developed, thanks to sophisticated programming. These devices utilize carefully created code to collect data, analyze it, and provide insights that can be used to improve our quality of life.

Even education has been transformed by programming. Platforms such as Khan Academy and Duolingo adapt to your pace and style of learning, making education more personalized and effective.

And let us not forget entertainment! From streaming platforms such as Netflix recommending your next favorite show to video games providing immersive experiences, programming brings endless enjoyment.

Programming is not just about creating apps or systems, it is about making life easier, solving real-world problems, and opening up new possibilities. By learning to program, you are not just gaining a technical skill. You are gaining the ability to create, innovate, and make a meaningful impact on the world around you.

Welcome to the world of programming, the hidden force behind much of our modern lives!

High-Level versus Low-Level Languages: A Brief Overview

Programming languages are of two main types: high-level and low-level. Think of it as giving directions to a friend. If you say, "Take the second left after the supermarket, then turn right at the library," it is easy to understand. This is like a high-level language. But if you give exact GPS coordinates, it is harder to follow without special tools. This is like a low-level language.

High-Level Languages are easier to read, write, and understand because they are closer to human language. They handle most of the technical details for you, so you do not need to worry about how the computer's hardware works. Examples include Python, Java, and JavaScript. These languages are versatile and great for things, such as creating websites, apps, or even AI models.

Low-Level Languages, such as machine code and assembly language, work directly with the computer's hardware. They give you more control over how the computer operates but are harder to learn and use. These are used for tasks such as creating operating systems, device drivers, and software that needs maximum performance.

Here is a simple example:

- High-Level Language: "Turn on the light."
- Low-Level Language: "Connect pin 22 to the power source for 0.5 seconds."

Where Does Python Fit In?

Python is a high-level language. It is simple, beginner-friendly, and works on almost any computer. It is widely used in web development, data analysis, machine learning, and more. With Python, you can focus on solving problems without getting stuck in the technical details of the computer's hardware. That is why it is a great first language for anyone starting their programming journey.

Introduction to Python

Python is one of the most loved programming languages today. It is known for being simple, easy to learn, and extremely powerful. But how did Python become so popular? Let us explore its journey.

Brief History of Python

Python's story started in the late 1980s when Guido van Rossum, a Dutch programmer, began working on it during his Christmas break. He wanted to create a language that was simple and solved some issues with ABC, another language he had worked on at CWI in the Netherlands. Guido also took ideas he liked from other programming languages, and his goal was to design something easy to use and powerful.

In 1991, Python was released to the public as version 0.9.0. Even in this early stage, it had many important features, such as functions, exception handling, and classes based on inheritance. It also had simple core data types that made programming easy to understand. Interestingly, Guido named Python after "Monty Python," a British comedy group, as he wanted programming with Python to be fun and enjoyable.

Python grew over time. In 1994, Python 1.0 came out, introducing useful tools, such as lambda, map, filter, and reduce. Then, in 2000, Python 2.0 was released with exciting features such as list comprehensions, garbage collection for cleaning up unused memory and a support for Unicode, which made it more versatile. These updates helped Python gain popularity among programmers worldwide.

The release of Python 3 in 2008 was a big moment. It fixed some old issues in the language but was not backward compatible with Python 2. Python 3 focused on making the language more consistent and easier to use, with features such as better Unicode handling, updated ways to write divisions, and improved type handling. Today, Python 3 is the standard, and Python 2 officially retired in 2020.

Guido van Rossum led Python's development as the "Benevolent Dictator For Life" (BDFL) until 2018. After he stepped down, a steering council was formed to guide Python's future. This ensured that Python remained community-driven, growing and adapting to new challenges and opportunities.

The core values of Python, readability, simplicity, and flexibility, have remained the same. These qualities have made Python a favorite for developers, whether they are building websites, working on software, or doing data science and machine learning. Its huge standard library and countless third-party packages make it even more powerful.

Python's journey is more than just its versions and updates. It is a story of how a programming language became a tool for people around the world to solve problems while keeping things simple and accessible. As technology changes, Python continues to evolve, staying true to its values and leading the way in software development.

Python's Popularity and Versatility

There are numerous reasons why Python is so popular. Because of its simple syntax, which closely mimics plain English, both new and experienced programmers may readily understand it. Python is also extremely versatile, with applications ranging from data analysis to scientific computing, web development, artificial intelligence, and beyond. With the help of a significant ecosystem of third-party packages and an extensive standard library, developers may achieve a wide range of tasks with little to no code.

Furthermore, Python has a strong developer and enthusiast community that actively participates in forums, conferences, and collaborative projects to support the language's development and maintenance. This community is constantly pushing the language's evolution to meet the changing demands of the IT industry while also providing an invaluable resource for learning and troubleshooting.

Python has established itself as a language capable of handling almost any programming task, from simple scripts to complex machine learning algorithms, thanks to its design, philosophy, and welcoming community. Its position as an essential tool for modern developers has been further bolstered by its role in the revolutionary advancement of areas like data science and machine learning.

Python's guiding ideals, as well as the explanations for its versatility and broad use, will become clearer as we progress through this book. Python is a way of thinking about problem solving that emphasizes practicality, clarity, and simplicity. It is not simply a computer language.

Significance of Python in Programming

Python is not just another programming language; it stands out as one of the most popular and versatile tools used by developers worldwide. Python's adaptability and simplicity have made it a leading choice for diverse applications, from web development to scientific computing. Its readability ensures a lower barrier for beginners, while its powerful libraries cater to professionals. Its simplicity, adaptability, and extensive ecosystem make it a preferred choice across a variety of industries. The following is an organized breakdown of Python's strengths, applications, and its thriving community.

Overview of Python's Strengths and Applications

The following table highlights key areas where Python excels, along with examples of its real-world applications.

Aspect	Details
Versatility and Fields of Application	Python's wide range of uses has confirmed its position as a go-to language for solving modern technological challenges. Following are key areas where Python excels.
Web Development	Powers websites and online apps using frameworks such as Flask and Django.
	Example: Instagram uses Django to efficiently manage millions of users and their data.
Data Science and Analysis	Thrives in data visualization, numerical computation, and analysis through tools such as Matplotlib, NumPy, and Pandas.
	Example: Businesses use Python for analyzing consumer patterns and financial forecasting.
Artificial Intelligence and Machine Learning	Facilitates the development of intelligent systems through libraries such as TensorFlow and PyTorch.
	Example: Netflix and Spotify use Python to create personalized recommendation systems for their users.
Scientific Computing	Used in fields such as astronomy, chemistry, and biology for simulations and complex analysis.
	Example: LIGO utilized Python to detect gravitational waves, a discovery recognized with the Nobel Prize in Physics in 2017.
Automation and Scripting	Simplifies repetitive tasks in system administration and software development.
	Example: IT professionals use Python to automate tasks such as server deployments, file processing, and batch activities, reducing errors.
Education	A favored choice for teaching programming due to its simple syntax and readability.
	Widely adopted in introductory programming courses to help students focus on fundamentals.
Game Development	Libraries such as Pygame make Python a fun and effective tool for developing small-scale games and educational projects.
	Often used in independent game development for rapid prototyping.

Table 1.1: *Overview of Python's strengths and applications*

Python's Thriving Community and Ecosystem

This table explains how Python's community and ecosystem play a crucial role in its widespread adoption and growth.

Aspect	Details
Community and Support	Python has a large, active, and welcoming community that has helped it grow and be used widely in many industries.
Open-Source Contribution	Python's open-source nature allows anyone to contribute to its improvement.
	Community-driven frameworks such as Django, Flask, and TensorFlow make it accessible for diverse applications.
Forums and Support Channels	Platforms such as Stack Overflow, Reddit, and Python.org are hubs of active discussion, troubleshooting, and knowledge sharing.
	These resources cater to both beginners and advanced users.

Conferences and Meetups	Events such as PyCon, DjangoCon, and local PyDays foster collaboration and networking.
	These gatherings help promote diversity and encourage contributions to open-source projects.
Educational Resources	Extensive learning materials, from beginner-friendly tutorials to advanced guides, are widely available.
	The official Python documentation and community-created content make learning accessible to everyone.
Mentorship and Inclusion	Programs such as Django Girls and PyLadies work to make Python more inclusive, offering workshops and mentorship opportunities.
	These initiatives help less-involved groups enter the tech field and learn Python programming.

Table 1.2: *Python's thriving community and ecosystem*

Comparison with Other Programming Languages

Python stands apart from other popular programming languages such as Java, C, and C++ due to its unique design. All of these languages have strengths and areas of expertise, but Python provides distinct advantages that have helped it become so popular. Let us look at the comparison between Python and Java and C and C++ in a few important areas.

Aspect	**Python**	**Java**	**C**	**C++**
Readability and Syntax	Easy-to-understand syntax; similar to natural languages	Readable but requires boilerplate code	Strong system resource control but complex for beginners.	Object-oriented version of C
	Suitable for beginners; makes it easy to express ideas clearly and briefly	Influenced by C++, with solutions for memory management issues	Requires understanding of pointers, memory, and so on	More challenging due to advanced concepts such as memory allocation and pointers
Performance	Slower due to being interpreted	Executed via JVM, adding overhead but ensuring portability	High performance due to direct compilation to machine code	Similar to C in terms of performance
	Compensated by a rich standard library and third-party modules	JIT compilation improves performance	Suitable for real-time applications	Ideal for high-performance systems and gaming applications
Application Domains	Ideal for web development, data mining, automation, AI, and scripting	Best for large-scale systems, enterprise solutions, and Android apps	Commonly used for OS, embedded systems, and hardware manipulation	Used in systems programming, gaming, and performance-critical applications
	Supported by a rich library ecosystem	Reliable, portable, and maintainable	Low-level capabilities	Allows hardware optimization

Community and Ecosystem	Diverse ecosystem with extensive libraries and frameworks	Supported by major corporations	Long-standing community with tools and resources	Similar to C with a focus on gaming and systems programming
	Strong and supportive community	Rich in libraries and frameworks, particularly in enterprise domains	Strong in scientific computing and systems programming	Vibrant development community

Table 1.3: *Comparison with other programming languages*

In conclusion, Python is an intriguing alternative for many programmers due to its exceptional combination of usability, adaptability, and a thriving community. Python is particularly appealing for new and seasoned developers working in web development, data science, and artificial intelligence, but Java, C, and C++ each have their specific purposes.

Setting Up Python Environment

One of the most exciting aspects of learning Python is transitioning from theory to actual application. The first practical action you will do is to set up your Python environment, which will serve as the foundation for all of your future projects. Let us go over how to install Python on Windows, macOS, and Linux platforms, as well as select the necessary interpreters and integrated development environments.

Prerequisites Before Installing Python

Before you install Python and begin your programming adventure, be sure you have everything you need to succeed. This section describes the requirements for installing Python to make the setup procedure as simple as possible for you.

Basic Computer Skills

Familiarity with Your Operating System: You should be able to perform fundamental tasks such as browsing the file system, making and managing folders, and downloading and launching software, regardless of whether you are using Windows, macOS, or Linux.

System Requirements

Before diving into the world of Python programming, it is crucial to ensure your system meets the necessary requirements for a smooth setup and operation. The following are the key system requirements to consider when preparing to work with Python, especially if your focus is on a Windows environment.

- **Supported Operating System:** Verify that the most recent version of Python is compatible with your operating system and that it is current. While Python works well on Linux and macOS, this book focuses on Windows.
- **Administrator Access:** Installing Python and changing system path settings, particularly on Windows and macOS, may require administrator access.
- **Internet Connection:** To download the Python installer and any other programs or tools you might require, you must have an active internet connection.

Hardware Requirements

When setting up your environment for Python development, it is important to consider the hardware specifications of your system to ensure it can efficiently handle your programming tasks. Here are the key hardware requirements that will help you run Python applications smoothly, ranging from simple learning exercises to more complex projects.

- **Processor:** For learning purposes and running simple Python applications, a processor clocked at 1 GHz or above should be adequate.
- **Memory:** Python can operate with less RAM, but it is advised to have at least 2GB available. More memory could be useful for more complicated tasks or ones involving data analysis.
- **Disk Space:** To install Python, you will need at least 100MB of free disk space. You will also need space for libraries, development tools, and your own projects.

Software Tools

In the world of Python development, selecting the right software tools can significantly enhance your coding experience, efficiency, and access to resources. Here, we will dive into essential software tools that every Python developer should consider, including text editors, Integrated Development Environments (IDEs), and web browsers.

- **Text Editor:** IDLE is the built-in editor for Python, but for a more comprehensive coding experience, you might want to look into more advanced text editors or Integrated Development Environments (IDEs). Visual Studio Code, PyCharm, and Atom are notable choices because of their advanced features, which include debugging, code completion, and syntax highlighting. In the part that follows, we will go into these tools' specifics.
- **Web Browser:** In order to access community forums, tutorials, and documentation, a web browser is necessary. Any browser will work, including Edge, Firefox, Safari, and Chrome.

Mental Preparation

Embarking on the journey of learning programming, particularly with Python, requires more than just understanding syntax and memorizing commands. Equally important is preparing yourself mentally for the challenges and opportunities that come with acquiring a new skill. Here are some key mental attributes to cultivate that will support your learning process and enhance your problem-solving capabilities.

- **Patience and Curiosity:** Although learning to program can be difficult, the rewards can be enormous. Take a patient approach to this journey and be open to trying new things, failing, and growing from your mistakes.
- **Problem-Solving Mentality:** At its core, programming is the art of problem-solving. Your learning process will be substantially improved by developing a mindset that takes pleasure in taking on problems and discovering answers.

Now that you have these requirements met, you can get started by installing Python and learning the basics of programming. Recall that learning to program is a marathon, not a sprint. Enjoy the process, take your time, and do not be afraid to ask for help or support from the community at any point.

Installing Python: A Step-by-Step Guide

Your first step into the world of programming is to install Python. Regardless of whether you are running Linux, macOS, or Windows, here is a thorough, step-by-step tutorial to ensure that Python is installed on your computer correctly. Let us try to make things go as smoothly as we can.

Download Python:

- To download Python, begin by navigating to the official Python website at https://www.python.org/. This site serves as the central hub for Python information, downloads, and documentation.
- Once there, hover your mouse over the "**`Downloads`**" tab. Based on your operating system, the website should automatically suggest the most recent version of Python that is compatible with your OS. This feature simplifies the process by selecting the best version for your system.

Figure 1.1: *Python download page*

- To initiate the download, simply click on the version that is recommended for Windows. This action will start the download of the Python installer, which you will use in the following steps to install Python on your computer.

For Windows Users

For individuals utilizing Windows as their operating system and wanting to get started with Python, the first step is to download and install Python itself. Here, we detail the straightforward approach to guarantee you have the most recent version of Python ready on your system.

1. **Run the Installer:**
    a. To begin the installation process, find the installer file (typically in your Downloads folder) and double-click it.
    b. There are two settings in the setup's first window that you should not overlook:
        i. Select the "**`Add Python 3.x to PATH`**" check box. The ability to execute Python from the Command Prompt makes this step essential.
        ii. Press the "**`Install Now`**" button.

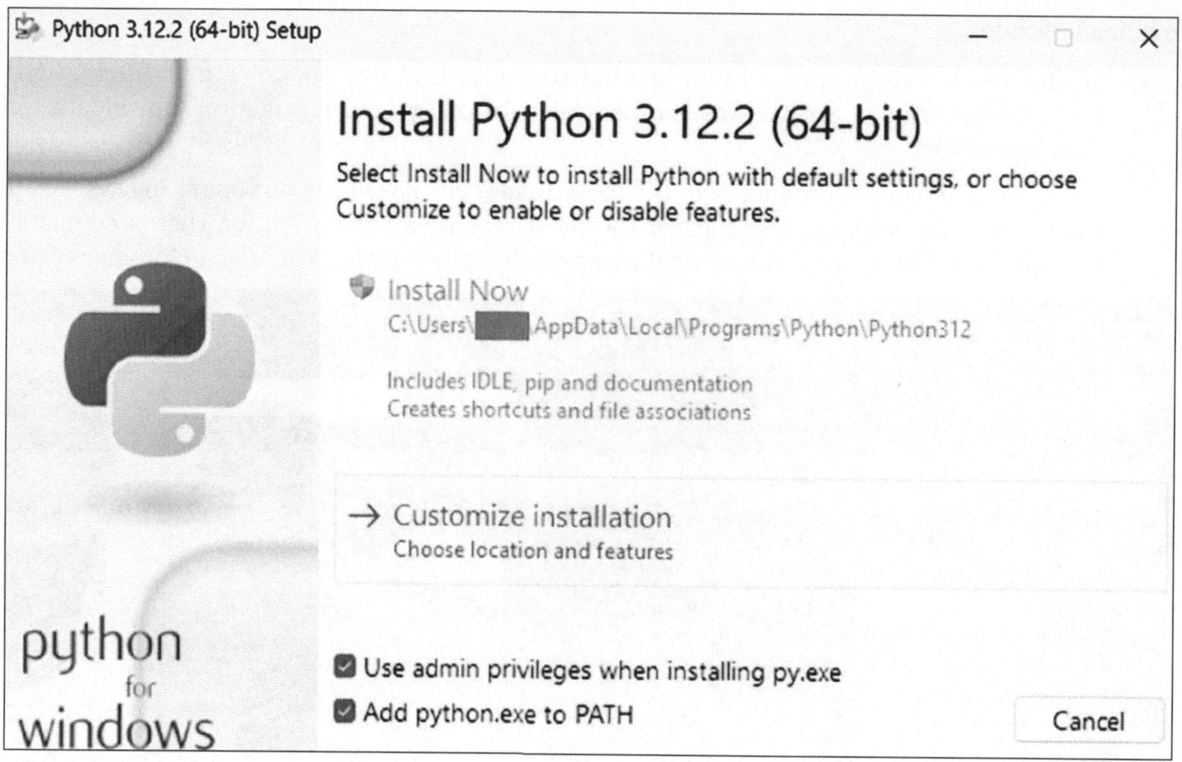

Figure 1.2: *Python installer screen*

2. **Verify the Installation:**

   a. Locate the Command Prompt by looking for it in the start menu once the installation is finished.

   b. Input **`python --version`** and hit **`Return`**. If Python is installed correctly, the version number will appear.

For macOS Users

Setting up Python on macOS differs from Windows. In that it requires particular tasks after the download. After downloading Python from python.org, follow these MacOS-specific steps:

1. **Run the Installer:**

   Open the downloaded installer by double-clicking the **`.pkg`** file and follow the on-screen instructions. macOS may prompt you to enter your administrator password to authorize the installation.

2. **Verify the Installation:**

   Open Terminal (use *Cmd* + *Space* for Spotlight search, type "**`Terminal`**", and hit *Enter*).

   Type **`python3 --version`** and press *Enter* to confirm Python 3.x is installed.

   This process ensures Python is installed and ready for use on your macOS system, with the primary difference being the use of the Terminal and the python3 command for verification.

For Linux Users

The majority of Linux distributions have Python installed by default. You may use it to find out whether Python is installed and what version it is:

1. **Open a Terminal Window:**

   You can usually open the terminal by pressing *Ctrl* + *Alt* + T.

2. **Check for Python:**

   a. Input `python3 –version` and hit `Return`. If Python is installed, the version number will be visible to you.

   b. Using the package manager in your distribution, you can install Python if it is not already installed or if you require a newer version.

3. **Installing Python (if necessary):**

   a. Use `sudo apt-get update` and `sudo apt-get install python3` on Debian/Ubuntu.

   b. Use `sudo dnf install python3` on Fedora.

   c. To finish the installation, adhere to any on-screen instructions.

4. **Verify the Installation:**

   Run `python3 --version` again to verify the version after installation. The Python version that is installed should now be visible.

Introducing IDEs: Your Coding Command Centers

Congratulations! You have successfully installed Python on your system. Now, you might be wondering: **Where do I write my Python code?** While you can use simple text editors such as Notepad or the built-in Python shell, as you progress, you will need a more powerful tool to help you write, test, and debug your programs efficiently.

This is where **Integrated Development Environments (IDEs)** come in. Imagine entering a contemporary airplane's cockpit. Everywhere one looks are buttons, screens, and controls, each with a distinct function to aid the pilot in navigating the sky. Similar to a command center for coding, an Integrated Development Environment (IDE) is used by programmers.

When you are first getting started, the wide world of coding can seem like an uncharted territory. An IDE is comparable to your reliable plane, complete with all the instruments required for a successful and safe flight. However, what is an IDE exactly? Let us dissect it.

Understanding IDE Components in Simple Terms

IDE, or integrated development environment, is a term you will hear a lot when you first start programming. Consider it your one-stop workstation for developing software. Let us put its essential components into very basic language:

Code Editor

This is the code-writing area; it is similar to creating a document in a word processor, but much more awesome. It benefits you in:

- **Text Colorization**: The code editor can color your code to make it easier to understand and identify errors, much as how you may highlight different sections of a text with different colors.

- **Concluding Sentences**: Do you recall how certain phone keyboards offer suggestions for words to finish sentences? Similar actions are taken with your code by the code editor, which helps you save time and effort.
- **Finding Your Way**: The code editor contains a capability similar to the search function you may have used to quickly locate specific words in a document. It facilitates jumping between sections of your code without having to scroll endlessly.
- **Cleaning Up**: Let us imagine you have a lengthy essay that you later feel needs more organization. You can neatly rearrange your code using the code editor's capabilities without affecting its functionality.

Compiler/Interpreter

These function as your code's translators. They convert your writing into a language that is understood by your computer.

- **Compiler:** This is used for translating all of your code at once; it functions similarly to composing and mailing a letter.
- **Interpreter:** Sending messages line by line is more akin to texting. When it executes, it translates your code one segment at a time, which is useful for fast inspections.

Debugger

Your code investigator is here. Similar to using a magnifying glass to seek for clues, the debugger allows you to pause and study your code at multiple points when something goes wrong. It assists you in figuring out where and why an error is occurring.

Build Automation Tools

These are the aides designed to aid you personally. If you had to perform the same tedious chores every day, you would probably want assistance. These tools take care of tedious chores, such as structuring your code or automatically inspecting it for errors, saving you the trouble.

Version Control

Consider this your code's time machine. It records every modification you make, allowing you to revert to an earlier version in case something goes wrong. It is also excellent for collaboration, enabling each person to focus on their own portion of the code without interfering with the work of others.

An IDE makes writing, checking, fixing, and managing code easier. It is like having a large, friendly toolbox at your disposal. Its purpose is to facilitate your transition into programming by taking care of the technical details so you can concentrate on making amazing things. As you practice coding, you will gradually learn how to use these tools, so do not worry about mastering everything at once.

Usage of IDE

An IDE can be thought of as a copilot for those who are new to coding. It does a lot of the tedious or repetitive work for you, so you can concentrate on learning to code. What an IDE adds to your educational process is as follows:

- **Makes Coding Process Simplified:** Syntax suggestions and auto-completion can help you learn the language's syntax while you code more quickly.
- **Maintains Organization:** An IDE allows you to easily transition between all of the project-related files that are housed in one location.

- **Facilitates Debugging:** IDE can direct you directly to the problem's cause, saving you the trouble of manually looking for problems.
- **Simplifies the Testing Process:** There are built-in features in many IDEs that allow you to test your code and ensure that it works as intended.

Popular IDEs for Python

- **IDLE:** This is the user-friendly IDE with built-in Python for beginners. If you are new to coding, this is a fantastic place to start because it is straightforward and unpretentious.
- **PyCharm:** Consider PyCharm to be the cutting-edge IDE equivalent of an aircraft. Professionals use it because it is more feature-rich and specifically made for Python development. There is a commercial version (Professional Edition) with additional features and a free version (Community Edition).
- **VS Code, or Visual Studio Code:** This editor is like a chameleon; it is powerful, flexible, and free. It is extensible and may be tailored to nearly any development requirement you may have. It supports Python.
- **Jupyter Notebooks:** Visualize a real-time journal where you can write, execute, and view the output of your Python code in one location while also taking notes. Because Jupyter Notebooks allow for real-time scripting and visualization, they are ideal for data science and analysis projects.

Finding an environment where you feel comfortable learning and making mistakes is crucial when selecting the ideal IDE for a novice programmer. It is your virtual sandbox, your personal lab where you may practice and develop. So inhale deeply, select your IDE, and get ready to dive into the world of coding!

Navigating Your IDE Without Stress

It is normal to feel a little intimidated at first after learning about the many parts of an Integrated Development Environment (IDE), which range from the complex code editor to compilers/interpreters, debuggers, build automation tools, and version control. Each of these parts adds a degree of complexity to the coding experience with the intention of improving and streamlining your development process.

But it is crucial to keep in mind that you do not have to become an expert at everything right away. Learning to program is a process that takes steps, and the same is true for mastering your IDE. This is a comforting idea:

When you notice all these elements and qualities, do not become anxious. All of these will be discussed in this book.

We will introduce increasingly sophisticated features and concepts gradually, starting with the fundamentals. The following will help you get comfortable with an IDE without getting overwhelmed:

- **Begin with Fundamentals:** At first, concentrate on creating and executing basic programs. Utilize the code editor and become acquainted with its fundamental features, such as auto-completion and syntax highlighting.
- **Gradual Education:** Once you have mastered the fundamentals, go over each new feature one at a time. To fix a straightforward bug, try utilizing the debugger; to manage your changes, use version control.

  The more you use these tools, the more intuitive they will get. Practice makes perfect. Allocate a certain amount of time to explore various functionalities, even in the absence of a particular undertaking.

- **Use Resources:** Make use of your IDE's tutorials, documentation, and community forums. These can be really helpful tools when you are stuck or want to pick up new skills.
- **Have patience:** Keep in mind that all experts were once novices. It is acceptable to feel uncertain or to make errors; these are all necessary components of learning.

Setting Up Visual Studio Code for Python Development: A Beginner's Guide

Now that you understand what an IDE is and why it is essential for efficient programming, it is time to roll up your sleeves and set up **Visual Studio Code (VS Code)** for Python development. In this hands-on guide, we will take you step by step through configuring VS Code, turning it into your powerful and beginner-friendly coding environment. Let us get started!

Note: Why Visual Studio Code?

Visual Studio Code (VS Code) has been chosen as the IDE for this book because it strikes the perfect balance between simplicity and power, making it ideal for both beginners and advanced developers. It is lightweight, free, and packed with features that enhance productivity, such as intelligent code suggestions, debugging tools, and seamless integration with Python. Moreover, its flexibility to work across Windows, macOS, and Linux ensures that every reader, regardless of their operating system, can follow along with ease. With its intuitive interface and beginner-friendly setup, VS Code is the perfect tool to kickstart your Python programming journey.

Step 1: Welcome to the World of VS Code

Initially, we must install Visual Studio Code on your computer.

a. **Download VS Code:**

   Visit the website for Visual Studio Code. The treasure map pointing to the VS Code installer may be found at the following web address:

   https://code.visualstudio.com/

   When you select the appropriate download link for Windows, macOS, or Linux, the download will begin on its own.

b. **Install with a Click:**

   Launch the installer after the download is finished. Like unlocking a door to a whole new world. Click `Install` after following the on-screen directions and accepting the terms (which you should have read first). You will have VS Code installed on your machine before you realize it.

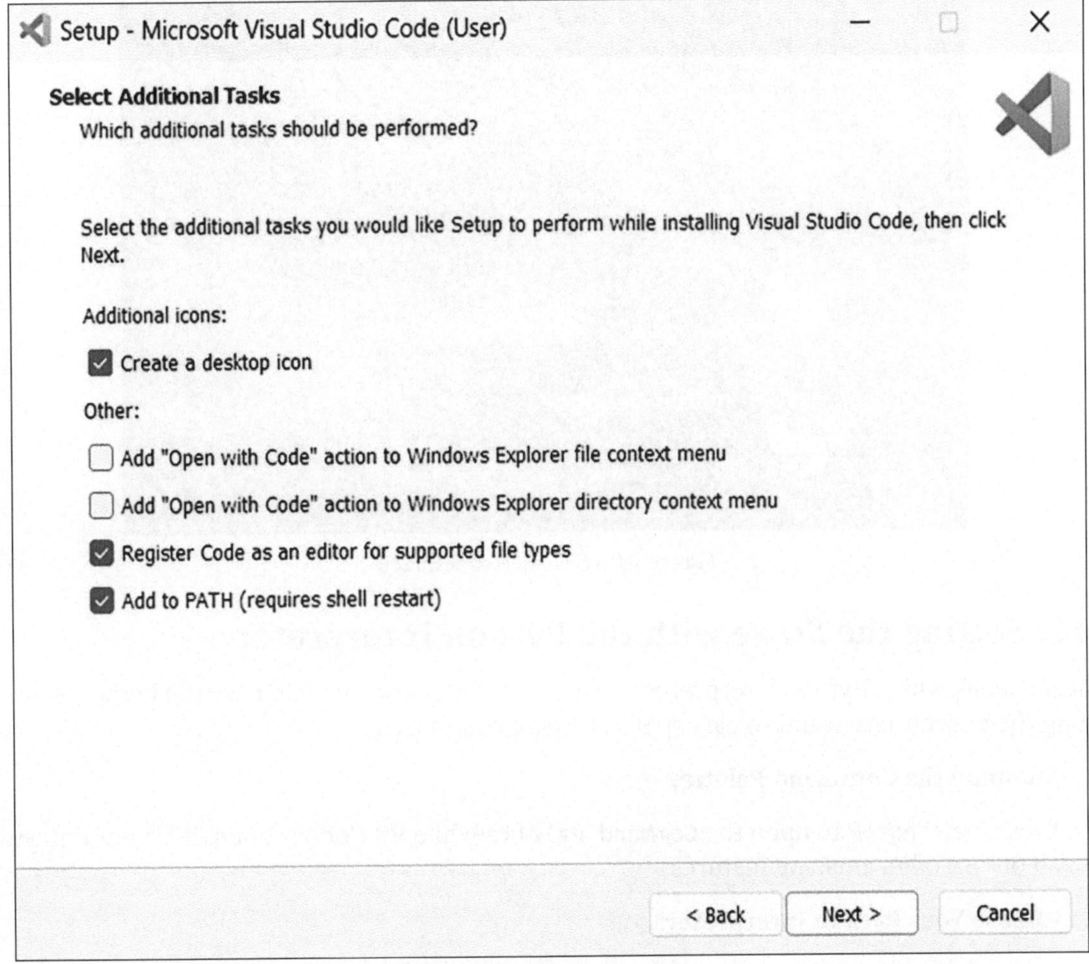

***Figure 1.3:** VS Code installer*

Step 2: Discover the Python Extension

Now that VS Code is installed, let us use Python's power to improve it. Here is where the Python extension helps, offering features and tools that make Python coding a snap.

a. **Open the Extensions Marketplace:**

   Open VS Code and locate the Extensions icon (it appears as four smaller squares stacked on top of each other) in the sidebar. Press *Ctrl+Shift+*X or click on it to launch the Extensions Marketplace. It resembles unwrapping a treasure trove of coding gems.

b. **Search for the Python Treasure:**

   Type "`Python`" into the search field at the top of the Extensions window and hit *Enter*. You are searching for the official Python extension from Microsoft, a wonderful tool that allows VS Code to support the Python language.

c. **Install the Python Extension:**

   Select the green `Install` button after locating the Python extension. This amazing procedure gives VS Code Python-specific features, such as linting, debugging, and IntelliSense (auto-completion).

Figure 1.4: *VS Code Marketplace*

Step 3: Setting the Stage with the Python Interpreter

You must specify which Python interpreter to use in VS Code now that you have the Python extension. Selecting the appropriate wand to cast spells is analogous to this.

a. **Summon the Command Palette:**

   Press *Ctrl+Shift+P* to open the **`Command Palette`** while VS Code is open. It is your entryway to all of VS Code's amazing features.

b. **Choose Your Python Interpreter:**

   In the Command Palette, type "**`Python: Select Interpreter`**" and click on it. A list of the Python interpreters available on your system will appear. This is where Python should appear if you installed it using our prior instructions. Choose the interpreter you want to work with.

Step 4: Optional Enhancements

Although your setup is almost finished, there is always space for more equipment and gadgets, just like in any great adventure.

Consider More Extensions:

Please look into other extensions that could fit your needs, such as Jupyter to work with Jupyter Notebooks directly within VS Code or Pylance for enhanced Python language support.

Congratulations! You have successfully configured Python development with Visual Studio Code. With this, you have access to a robust coding environment that can tackle complex coding tasks while remaining user-friendly for beginners. Remember that every great programmer started somewhere as you set out on this voyage, and with VS Code at your side, you will be well on your way to crafting your own epic tales of programming adventure.

Understanding Virtual Environments

With your IDE set up and ready, it is time to explore **virtual environments**, a key concept for managing your Python projects effectively.

Assume you are an artist, and every painting you do calls for a different combination of colors. Obviously, mixing all of your paints on one palette would not be a good idea. Colors would merge in unexpected places, creating a jumble that would make it difficult to match exactly when creating a painting in the future.

A virtual environment in programming functions as a unique palette for every project you work on. All the paints (or, in our case, libraries and packages) needed for a project are kept in this self-contained directory. You can work on several Python projects at once without having to worry about one project's library requirements getting in the way of another's by employing virtual environments.

Benefits of Virtual Environments:

Benefit	Description
Isolation	Each project may have its own set of dependencies that are separate from those of other projects, much as various artworks call for distinct color palettes.
Control	Just like when selecting a certain color for your artwork, you may control the version of a library your project utilizes.
Simplicity	You will not have to worry about the receiver having the necessary tools installed when you need to share your project. It would be as simple as providing them with a list of the precise paint colors they will require. All they have to do is create a corresponding virtual environment.
Stability	Because installing and testing new tools will not interfere with current installations, your system stays clear and organized. Consider it as maintaining your workspace organized to reduce the possibility of inadvertently toppling a paint can.

Table 1.4: *Benefits of virtual environments*

Creating a Virtual Environment in VS Code

For any aspiring developer, knowing how to create a virtual environment in Visual Studio Code (VS Code) is crucial. It guarantees that any project you work on has a separate, segregated area for dependencies; it is like having a workstation just for every kind of craft you could do. This is a detailed tutorial on configuring a virtual environment in Visual Studio Code.

Step 1: Open Your Terminal in VS Code

Once VS Code is open, use the keyboard shortcuts *Ctrl+{{* (backtick) on Windows or *Cmd+{* (backtick) on macOS to open the terminal. Alternatively, click on **`Terminal`** in the top menu and choose **`New Terminal`**.

Step 2: Move to Your Project Folder

Locate the folder where your Python project is saved or where you intend to save it. In the terminal, use the **`cd`** command to change to this directory.

```
cd myFirstPythonProgramDirectory
```

Note: *In this section, we will be using pip, Python's package manager, to create and manage virtual environments. If you are not familiar with pip yet, do not worry, it will be explained in the next section.*

Step 3: Install the `virtualenv` Package (if not already installed)

Type **`pip install virtualenv`** in the terminal and press *Enter*. This command installs the **`virtualenv`** package, which is used to create virtual environments in Python.

```
C:\myFirstPythonProgramDirectory>pip install virtualenv
Collecting virtualenv
  Obtaining dependency information for virtualenv from https://files.pythonhosted.org/packages/16/65
/0d0bdfdac31e2db8c6d6c18fe1e00236f0dea279f9846f94a9aafa49cfc9/virtualenv-20.25.1-py3-none-any.whl.me
tadata
  Downloading virtualenv-20.25.1-py3-none-any.whl.metadata (4.4 kB)
Collecting distlib<1,>=0.3.7 (from virtualenv)
  Obtaining dependency information for distlib<1,>=0.3.7 from https://files.pythonhosted.org/package
s/8e/41/9307e4f5f9976bc8b7fea0b66367734e8faf3ec84bc0d412d8cfabbb66cd/distlib-0.3.8-py2.py3-none-any.
whl.metadata
  Downloading distlib-0.3.8-py2.py3-none-any.whl.metadata (5.1 kB)
Collecting filelock<4,>=3.12.2 (from virtualenv)
  Obtaining dependency information for filelock<4,>=3.12.2 from https://files.pythonhosted.org/packa
ges/81/54/84d42a0bee35edba99dee7b59a8d4970eccdd44b99fe728ed912106fc781/filelock-3.13.1-py3-none-any.
whl.metadata
  Downloading filelock-3.13.1-py3-none-any.whl.metadata (2.8 kB)
Requirement already satisfied: platformdirs<5,>=3.9.1 in c:\users\gargi\appdata\local\programs\pytho
n\python311\lib\site-packages (from virtualenv) (3.10.0)Downloading virtualenv-20.25.1-py3-none-any.
whl (3.8 MB)
   ---------------------------------------- 3.8/3.8 MB 12.0 MB/s eta 0:00:00
Downloading distlib-0.3.8-py2.py3-none-any.whl (468 kB)
   ---------------------------------------- 468.9/468.9 kB ? eta 0:00:00
Downloading filelock-3.13.1-py3-none-any.whl (11 kB)
Installing collected packages: distlib, filelock, virtualenv
Successfully installed distlib-0.3.8 filelock-3.13.1 virtualenv-20.25.1

[notice] A new release of pip is available: 23.2.1 -> 24.0
[notice] To update, run: python.exe -m pip install --upgrade pip

C:\myFirstPythonProgramDirectory>
```

Figure 1.5: *Installing virtual environment*

Step 4: Create the Virtual Environment

Upon entering your project directory, use the **virtualenv venv** command. The virtual environment folder is named **venv**, though you are free to give it whatever name you choose.

```
C:\myFirstPythonProgramDirectory>virtualenv venv
created virtual environment CPython3.11.5.final.0-64 in 6313ms
  creator CPython3Windows(dest=C:\myFirstPythonProgramDirectory\venv, clear=False, no_vcs_ignore=Fal
se, global=False)
  seeder FromAppData(download=False, pip=bundle, setuptools=bundle, wheel=bundle, via=copy, app_data
_dir=C:\Users\gargi\AppData\Local\pypa\virtualenv)
    added seed packages: pip==24.0, setuptools==69.1.0, wheel==0.42.0
  activators BashActivator,BatchActivator,FishActivator,NushellActivator,PowerShellActivator,PythonA
ctivator

C:\myFirstPythonProgramDirectory>
```

Figure 1.6: *Creating virtual environment*

Step 5: Activate the Virtual Environment

a. To start using the virtual environment, you will need to activate it with the following command:

   On Windows, **venv\Scripts\activate**

   On macOS or Linux, use source **venv/bin/activate**

b. You should see the name of the virtual environment in parentheses in your terminal prompt, indicating that it is now active.

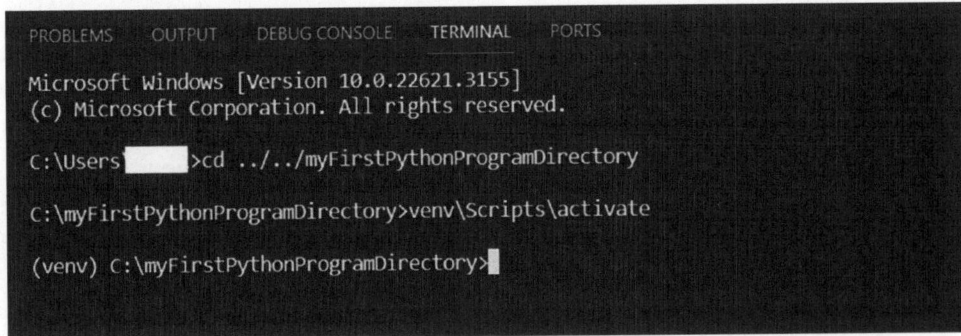

***Figure 1.7:** Activating virtual environment*

Step 6: Verify the Virtual Environment

Using the commands for Python on macOS/Linux or Python on Windows, you may check the Python interpreter path and confirm that you are operating within the virtual environment. The Python executable located in the **venv** directory should be referenced by the output.

```
C:\myFirstPythonProgramDirectory>venv\Scripts\Activate

(venv) C:\myFirstPythonProgramDirectory>deactivate
C:\myFirstPythonProgramDirectory>
```

***Figure 1.8:** De-activating virtual environment*

Step 7: Work on Your Project

Python packages installed by pip will be isolated to this virtual environment as long as it is active. This separation keeps your global Python environment clean and avoids conflicts between projects.

Step 8: Deactivate the Virtual Environment

To return to the global Python environment after working in your virtual environment, just type deactivate into the terminal and hit *Enter*. The virtual environment name will vanish from the terminal prompt, signifying that it is not in use.

Step 9: Re-activating Your Virtual Environment

If you need to work on your project once more, launch Visual Studio Code, go to your project directory via the console, and use the same command you used in Step 5 to activate the virtual environment.

Step 10: Configuring VS Code to Use the Virtual Environment

The active virtual environment's Python interpreter can be automatically detected and used by VS Code. Click on the Python version that appears in VS Code's status bar to choose an interpreter, or open the **`Command Palette`** and search for "**`Python: Select Interpreter`**." Select the translator that matches your vehicle.

You have successfully set up a virtual environment in VS Code by following these steps, which paves the way for a tidy and hassle-free Python development process. Recall that handling your development environments well from the beginning can prevent several possible problems later on, so stop and enjoy the tidy, contained workspace you have set up for your project.

Understanding Package Managers and pip

With your Python environment set up and Visual Studio Code ready to go, you now have a powerful coding workspace at your fingertips. In the previous section, we briefly used **pip**, Python's default package manager, to set up a virtual environment. Now, let us dive deeper into understanding **package**

managers and how **pip** allows you to install and manage additional tools and libraries to enhance your Python projects. It is essential to understand how it works, as we will be using pip quite frequently in the upcoming chapters. Let us break this down step by step.

Understanding Package

A **package** is like a boxed item in a store that contains everything you need to perform a specific task. For example:

- A cake mix box has the ingredients, instructions, and tools needed to bake a cake.
- Similarly, a Python package contains code and instructions that help you solve problems or add features to your program.

Note: *We will explore packages in greater detail in one of the upcoming chapters. For now, think of them as bundles of tools you can add to your programming toolkit.*

Role of a Package Manager:

A **package manager** helps you find, install, and organize these tools (packages) with ease. Imagine having to bake a cake without knowing where to get the ingredients or how to mix them. A package manager like pip makes this process simple and efficient. Here is how:

- **Finds the Tools for You**: Instead of searching online for the right tools, pip gets them for you with a single command.
- **Handles Everything Automatically**: Some tools depend on other tools to work. pip figures this out and installs everything you need.
- **Keeps Things Updated**: pip ensures you are using the latest versions of your tools for better features and security.

Think of pip as your personal shopping assistant. It gets everything you need for your program quickly and easily.

Importance for Beginners:

A package manager is very helpful for someone who is just starting out with programming since it:

- **Reduces Complexity**: It takes the mystery out of software administration so you can concentrate on learning programming instead of worrying about installing and maintaining software.
- **Saves Time**: The amount of time needed to set up and configure development environments is greatly decreased.
- **Enhances Learning**: Having quick access to a variety of libraries and tools can improve learning by enabling new users to explore various packages and learn how they work.

In conclusion, a package manager facilitates your exploration and management of the wide world of software libraries and applications as you begin your programming career by acting as a bridge between you and them.

Understanding pip:

Within the Python ecosystem, pip is the name of this assistance. It installs and maintains extra libraries that are not part of the basic Python installation. It is the default package manager for Python. These libraries can be used to create sophisticated graphical user interfaces or handle data more effectively.

Imagine you are baking a cake and realize you need a whisk. You would go to the store to get one, right? Similarly, in Python, if your program needs a specific tool or library (such as one for making

HTTP requests), you can use pip to get it easily. For example, to install the requests library, you just need to run a single command with pip.

Checking if pip is Installed:

Most of the time, pip is pre-installed on Python computers, so you can use it as soon as you install Python. To see whether pip is set up:

1. Launch a terminal or command line.
2. On some systems that have both Python 2 and Python 3 installed, type **`pip --version`** or **`pip3 --version`** and hit *Enter*.
3. Should pip be installed, a version number will be displayed. If not, an error notice will appear in the terminal, and you will have to manually install it.

```
C:\Windows\System32\cmd.e

Microsoft Windows [Version 10.0.22621.3155]
(c) Microsoft Corporation. All rights reserved.

C:\>pip --version
pip 23.2.1 from C:\Users\     \AppData\Local\Programs\Python\Python311\Lib\
site-packages\pip (python 3.11)

C:\>
```

Figure 1.9: *Checking pip version*

Installing Packages with pip:

Once pip installation has been verified, you may start populating your Python environment with libraries. For instance, all you would need to do is run **`pip install pandas`** into your terminal to install the **`pandas`** library, along with any dependencies, as it will be downloaded and installed by pip. Similarly, to install the **`pandas`** library, you would use the command **`pip install pandas`**, as demonstrated in the following screenshot.

```
C:\Windows\System32\cmd.e

Microsoft Windows [Version 10.0.22621.3155]
(c) Microsoft Corporation. All rights reserved.

C:\>pip install pandas
Collecting pandas
  Obtaining dependency information for pandas from https://files.pythonhosted.org/packages/61/11/181
2ef6cbd7433ad240f72161ce5f84c4c450cede4db080365d371d29117/pandas-2.2.1-cp311-cp311-win_amd64.whl.met
adata
  Downloading pandas-2.2.1-cp311-cp311-win_amd64.whl.metadata (19 kB)
Requirement already satisfied: numpy<2,>=1.23.2 in c:\users\     \appdata\local\programs\python\pyth
on311\lib\site-packages (from pandas) (1.25.2)
Requirement already satisfied: python-dateutil>=2.8.2 in c:\users\     \appdata\local\programs\pytho
n\python311\lib\site-packages (from pandas) (2.8.2)
Requirement already satisfied: pytz>=2020.1 in c:\users\     \appdata\local\programs\python\python31
1\lib\site-packages (from pandas) (2023.3.post1)
Requirement already satisfied: tzdata>=2022.7 in c:\users\     \appdata\local\programs\python\python
311\lib\site-packages (from pandas) (2023.3)
Requirement already satisfied: six>=1.5 in c:\users\     \appdata\local\programs\python\python311\li
b\site-packages (from python-dateutil>=2.8.2->pandas) (1.16.0)
Downloading pandas-2.2.1-cp311-cp311-win_amd64.whl (11.6 MB)
   ---------------------------------------- 11.6/11.6 MB 36.4 MB/s eta 0:00:00
Installing collected packages: pandas
Successfully installed pandas-2.2.1

[notice] A new release of pip is available: 23.2.1 -> 24.0
[notice] To update, run: python.exe -m pip install --upgrade pip

C:\>
```

Figure 1.10: *pip install*

Well done on configuring your Python environment and learning about pip! You are now prepared to explore the world of programming with Python and pip. Keep in mind that the Python community is an enormously helpful and resourceful network as you begin to build and explore. There exists a large community available to assist you in overcoming any obstacles you may face in the event that you experience difficulties or have inquiries.

Note on the Operating System Used in This Book:

Windows will be the main operating system used for all examples, exercises, and demos in this book. The decision was made since Windows is widely used and well-known to a large number of people. With a few slight tweaks or variations in execution, the fundamental Python ideas and code we will examine are applicable to many platforms, including Linux and macOS.

Most of the Python-related instructions, especially those pertaining to syntax, libraries, and frameworks, will still apply to readers using macOS or Linux. To ensure that all readers can follow along regardless of their operating system, any procedures that are peculiar to Windows, especially those that involve the command line or system settings, will be mentioned, and whenever possible, similar commands for macOS and Linux will be provided.

This method leverages Python's cross-platform capabilities to make studying the language accessible and useful for all users, allowing you to apply the information you acquire here to any programming environment you choose to work in.

Writing and Executing Your First Python Program

Now that you have Visual Studio Code installed and your virtual environment configured, you are all prepared to begin your coding journey. The creation and operation of the "Hello, World!" program is the first custom on this voyage. It is a straightforward rite of passage that teaches you how to write and run code. Now let us get started.

The "Hello, World!" Program

Step 1: Create Your Python File

a. In Visual Studio Code, with your virtual environment activated, go to the **`File`** menu and select **`New File`**.

b. Save this new file with a **`.py`** extension, which tells VS Code that it is a Python file. You might name it **`hello_world.py`**.

Step 2: Write the "Hello, World!" Code

In the hello_world.py file, type the following line of code:

```
print("Hello, World!")
```

This line of code is a Python print statement that outputs the text within the parentheses and quotes to the screen.

Step 3: Run Your Program

a. It is now necessary to activate your code. You have multiple options for running your program in VS Code:

b. To launch a Python file in the terminal, right-click anywhere in the text editor.

c. For macOS, use *Cmd+F5* instead of *Ctrl+F5* to run the file without debugging.

d. In the upper-right corner of the editor, there may be a green play button that you can click to launch the program if you have the Python extension installed and enabled.

Step 4: See the Magic Happen

a. After running the program, look at the terminal pane at the bottom of VS Code. You should see the output:

```
(venv) C:\myFirstPythonProgramDirectory>python hello_world.py
Hello, World!

(venv) C:\myFirstPythonProgramDirectory>
```

***Figure 1.11**: "Hello World!" code output*

b. The terminal is where your program's output, or any messages such as errors or prompts for input, will appear when you run it.

Understanding What You Did

Congratulations! Your computer just listened to your command to do something! You can think of the **`print("Hello, World!")`** command as your introduction to the world of coding. It seems as though you have mastered the art of waving and uttering your first hello in Python.

Here is the simple breakdown:

- **`print()`** is a built-in Python function that says, "Hey, show this on the screen!"
- Inside the parentheses, **`"Hello, World!"`** is the message you want to display. The quotation marks tell Python that it is a string of text, a sequence of characters that should be taken literally as is.

It feels as though you have penned a note and posted it for everyone to see on the community bulletin board. This is a historic day in the programming community since all seasoned programmers can recall their very first **`"Hello, World!"`** moment. It is not simply a custom; it is the beginning of a confident relationship as you learn to communicate with computers and give them instructions.

You have created and run your first Python program with success. This is a crucial beginning for any programmer. Savor every moment because there are a ton of fascinating challenges and lessons to come as you delve deeper into the expansive and imaginative realm of programming. Welcome to the programming community! Keep in mind that all seasoned programmers started off by typing **`"Hello, World!"`**

Exercises and Challenges: Practice Problems and Solutions

It is time to put your newfound knowledge to the test after delving into the foundations of Python and configuring your programming environment. The practice questions that follow are meant to test your programming skills and reinforce the concepts you have studied. Your initial attempts at putting the ideas discussed in this chapter into practice are these activities.

Practice Problems

Practice Problem 1: Verify Your Installation

a. **Task**: Confirm that Python is installed on your system.

b. **Challenge**: Open your command line tool, type **`python --version`** (or **`python3 --version`**), and ensure that the system returns the version of Python you installed.

Practice Problem 2: Create and Run a Simple Script

a. **Task**: Write your first Python script.

b. **Challenge**: Use a text editor to create a file named `greet_me.py` that prints `"Hello, Python! My name is [Your_Name]."` Replace `[Your_Name]` with your actual name. Save the file and run it through your command line.

Practice Problem 3: Getting to Know IDLE

a. **Task**: Familiarize yourself with Python's IDLE.

b. **Challenge**: Launch IDLE, create a new file, and write a script that prints out `"IDLE is Python's Integrated Development and Learning Environment."` Execute this script within IDLE.

Practice Problem 4: Mastering Virtual Environments

a. **Task**: Practice setting up a virtual environment.

b. **Challenge**: In your command line, navigate to a new project directory called `PythonChallenges`. Create a virtual environment named `env_challenge` within this directory. Activate the environment, and then deactivate it once you have confirmed it is active.

Practice Problem 5: Personalizing "Hello, World!"

a. **Task**: Add a personal touch to the classic "Hello, World!" program.

b. **Challenge**: Inside the `PythonChallenges` directory (ensure that your virtual environment is active), write a script named `personal_hello.py`. The script should print out `"Hello, World! My journey in Python starts today, [Current_Date]."` Replace `[Current_Date]` with the actual current date. Run the script and see your personalized message.

These practice questions are intended to gently introduce you to the world of coding while being approachable and thought-provoking. They will reinforce your comprehension of the Python environment and the delight of watching your code execute. Recall that the core of programming is experimentation and problem-solving as you go through these problems. If you do not get everything perfect the first time, do not worry. Writing code is only one aspect of learning; the other is debugging. Approach these difficulties one step at a time, as given here:

a. **Reflect on What You Have Learned:** After completing each activity, give some thought to what went well, what did not, and why. You will gain a deeper understanding of Python and the development process by doing this reflection.

b. **Look for Solutions:** If you run into problems, utilize the error messages as hints to help you find a solution. Looking up these messages online frequently yields answers and solutions from the Python community.

c. **Experiment:** After finishing the tasks, try incorporating your own changes. Modify the messages, experiment with alternative commands, or observe the results of purposefully introducing mistakes. Every experiment you do will impart new knowledge.

You are not just learning how to code by solving these practice problems; you are also beginning to develop your programming logic. Additionally, when you conquer obstacles, you are gaining self-assurance and competence that will help you in the future to do more difficult tasks. Continue studying and moving forward while having fun on the trip!

Solutions to Practice Problems

Here are the solutions to the practice problems provided. Use these as a guide to check your work or to help you understand where you might have gone wrong if you encountered any issues.

Solution to Practice Problem 1: Verify Your Installation

1. Open your command line tool (Command Prompt on Windows, Terminal on macOS or Linux).
2. Type **`python --version`** or **`python3 --version`**.
3. Verify that the output displays the version of Python you installed, such as "**`Python 3.8.5.`**"

```
Microsoft Windows [Version 10.0.22621.3155]
(c) Microsoft Corporation. All rights reserved.

C:\>python --version
Python 3.11.5

C:\>
```

Figure 1.12: *Solution to practice problem 1*

Solution to Practice Problem 2: Create and Run a Simple Script

1. Open your text editor and create a new file named **`greet_me.py`**.
2. Write the following line of code:
   `print("Hello, Python! My name is [Your_Name].")`
3. Replace **`[Your_Name]`** with your actual name.
4. Save the file and run it from your command line by navigating to the directory where your file is and typing python **`greet_me.py`** or python3 **`greet_me.py`**.

```
(venv) C:\myFirstPythonProgramDirectory>python greet_me.py
Hello, Python! My name is Jon Doe.

(venv) C:\myFirstPythonProgramDirectory>
```

Figure 1.13: *Solution to practice problem 2*

Solution to Practice Problem 3: Getting to Know IDLE

1. Open IDLE from your start menu or applications folder.
2. Create a new file by selecting **`File`** -> **`New File`** from the IDLE menu.
3. Write the following line of code in the new file:
   `print("IDLE is Python's Integrated Development and Learning Environment.")`
4. Run the script by selecting **`Run -> Run Module`** or by pressing F5.

Solution to Practice Problem 4: Mastering Virtual Environments

1. Open your command line tool and navigate to the **`PythonChallenges`** directory:

   ```
   mkdir PythonChallenges
   cd PythonChallenges
   ```

2. Create the virtual environment:

   ```
   virtualenv env_challenge
   ```

3. Activate the virtual environment:
   a. On Windows:
      `env_challenge\Scripts\activate`
   b. On macOS/Linux:
      `source env_challenge/bin/activate`
4. Deactivate the virtual environment by typing deactivate.

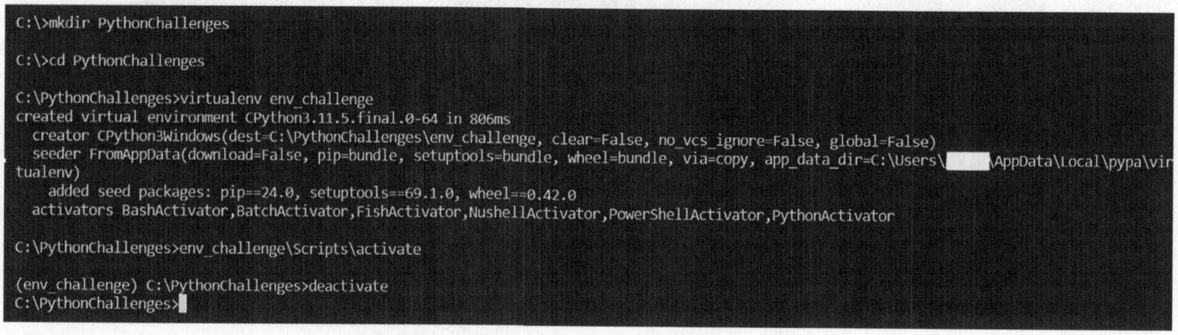

```
C:\>mkdir PythonChallenges

C:\>cd PythonChallenges

C:\PythonChallenges>virtualenv env_challenge
created virtual environment CPython3.11.5.final.0-64 in 806ms
  creator CPython3Windows(dest=C:\PythonChallenges\env_challenge, clear=False, no_vcs_ignore=False, global=False)
  seeder FromAppData(download=False, pip=bundle, setuptools=bundle, wheel=bundle, via=copy, app_data_dir=C:\Users\     \AppData\Local\pypa\virtualenv)
    added seed packages: pip==24.0, setuptools==69.1.0, wheel==0.42.0
  activators BashActivator,BatchActivator,FishActivator,NushellActivator,PowerShellActivator,PythonActivator

C:\PythonChallenges>env_challenge\Scripts\activate

(env_challenge) C:\PythonChallenges>deactivate
C:\PythonChallenges>
```

Figure 1.14: *Solution to practice problem 3*

Solution to Practice Problem 5: Personalizing "Hello, World!"

1. Ensure your virtual environment **`env_challenge`** is activated.
2. Create a new file named **`personal_hello.py`** in the **`PythonChallenges`** directory.
3. Write the following line of code:

```
from datetime import date
print(f"Hello, World! My journey in Python starts today, {date.today()}.")
```

4. Save the file and run it from your command line within the virtual environment by typing `**python personal_hello.py**` or `**python3 personal_hello.py**`.
5. Confirm the output displays the message with the current date.

```
(env_challenge) C:\PythonChallenges>python personal_hello.py
Hello, World! My journey in Python starts today, 2024-02-28.

(env_challenge) C:\PythonChallenges>
```

Figure 1.15: *Solution to practice problem 4*

You have now practiced critical tasks, including managing virtual environments, running Python programs, and checking installs by finishing these solutions. Every task enhances your basic understanding of Python, positioning you for success as you study and create increasingly intricate applications. Recall that learning programming requires a process of trying, failing, and trying again. Every mistake that is fixed is one more step toward mastering Python. Continue to code, maintain your curiosity, and savor each moment of your coding journey!

Conclusion

Congratulations on completing the first chapter of your Python journey! You have taken the first steps into the world of programming by setting up Python, understanding its significance, and even running your first program. These foundational skills set the stage for everything you will achieve as a programmer.

Remember, programming is a journey. Every step you take builds your confidence and skills. Mistakes are part of the process. They help you learn and grow. Keep practicing, stay curious, and do not be afraid to experiment.

In the next chapter, we will dive deeper into Python's basics, exploring variables, data types, and more. You are building a strong foundation for solving real-world problems and creating exciting projects.

Keep Calm and Let us Tame the Python!

Multiple-Choice Questions

1. What is the command to check your installed version of Python in the command line?
   a. `python --check`
   b. `python --version`
   c. `check_python_version`
   d. `python_version`
2. Which of the following is a popular IDE for Python development?
   a. Microsoft Word
   b. PyCharm
   c. Adobe Photoshop
   d. Spotify
3. What is the purpose of a package manager such as pip in Python?
   a. To compile Python programs into machine code
   b. To install, update, and manage Python libraries and packages
   c. To create virtual environments for projects
   d. To debug Python code
4. Which of the following is NOT a valid file extension for Python scripts?
   a. .py
   b. .pyw
   c. .pyt
   d. .pyc
5. In Python, what is a virtual environment?
   a. A 3D simulation space for game development
   b. An isolated workspace for a specific Python project
   c. A social media platform for developers
   d. A version control system

6. The "`Hello, World!`" program in Python is typically used to:
   a. Test if Python is installed correctly
   b. Create a new Python IDE
   c. Increase the speed of the Python interpreter
   d. Hack into the mainframe
7. What does the print function do in Python?
   a. It sends a text message to the default printer
   b. It displays a message in the command line or terminal
   c. It saves a string to a file
   d. It creates a new text document
8. Which command is used to activate a virtual environment on Windows?
   a. `source venv/Scripts/activate`
   b. `activate venv`
   c. `.\venv\Scripts\activate`
   d. `start venv`
9. What is the term for a pre-written piece of code that you can incorporate into your program to perform common tasks?
   a. Algorithm
   b. Library
   c. Interpreter
   d. Compiler
10. When comparing programming languages, Python is considered:
    a. A low-level language
    b. A high-level language
    c. A machine language
    d. An assembly language

Answers

1. b
2. b
3. b
4. c
5. b
6. a
7. b

8. c
9. b
10. b

Points to Remember

- Writing instructions for computers to follow is known as programming, and it makes it possible to create software systems and applications.
- Because programming is essential to the operation of many contemporary conveniences and technologies, it has a substantial impact on our daily lives.
- While low-level languages offer more hardware control and efficiency, high-level languages, such as Python, are more user-friendly and readable.
- Python is well-known for being easy to learn and adaptable, making it a great choice for both novices and experts in a variety of industries, including AI, data science, and web development.
- Python's philosophy places a strong emphasis on readability and simplicity, which helps programmers create concise and effective code.
- Python's large library and active community contribute to its widespread use in a variety of applications, making it a highly sought-after expertise in the tech sector.
- To manage dependencies neatly and prevent conflicts between projects, setting up a Python environment entails installing Python and utilizing virtual environments.
- IDEs that offer robust Python development tools, such as syntax highlighting, code completion, and debugging features, are IDLE, PyCharm, and Visual Studio Code.
- A well-known introductory coding exercise, "Hello, World!" teaches you how to print text to the terminal and provides an overview of Python syntax.
- Participating in the Python community and working through practice issues are crucial for strengthening concepts, improving analytical abilities, and overcoming programming obstacles.

Further Reading

If you are curious to learn more, here are two helpful resources:

1. **Python Official Documentation**: https://docs.python.org/3/- A great way to dive deeper into Python's features and capabilities.
2. **W3Schools Python Tutorial**: https://www.w3schools.com/python/- Beginner-friendly tutorials with interactive examples.

CHAPTER 2
Introduction to Algorithms and Flowcharts

Introduction

Now that you have set up your Python environment and written your first program, it is time to take the next step: learning how to think like a programmer. Before writing code, programmers first plan out their solutions. This is where algorithms and flowcharts come in.

An algorithm is just a step-by-step set of instructions to complete a task. You use algorithms every day without realizing it, whether you are making a cup of tea, tying your shoelaces, or following a recipe. In programming, algorithms help you break down problems into clear, logical steps.

A flowchart is a visual way to represent an algorithm. It uses symbols and arrows to show the sequence of actions, making it easier to understand and follow a process before converting it into code.

In this chapter, you will practice creating your own algorithms and flowcharts for different tasks. These exercises will help you think systematically, plan your programs effectively, and build confidence in problem-solving. By the end, you will be able to turn your ideas into structured steps and even write Python code based on them! Let us get started.

Structure

In this chapter, the following topics will be covered:

- Introduction to Algorithms
    - Everyday Examples of Algorithms
    - Importance of Algorithms in Programming
    - Practice: Identify a Simple Daily Task and Break it Down into an Algorithm
- Breaking Down Problems
    - Step-by-Step Thinking
    - Example of a Simple Algorithm in Python
    - Practice: Write a Step-by-step Algorithm for Calculating the Area of a Rectangle.
- Introduction to Flowcharts
    - Definition of a Flowchart
    - Basic Flowchart Symbols
    - Visualizing Algorithms Using Flowcharts

    - Practice: Create a Flowchart for Choosing an Outfit Based on the Weather
- Designing Effective Flowcharts
    - Step-by-Step Guide to Creating a Flowchart
    - Example: Deciding Whether to Go for a Walk
    - Practice: Create a Flowchart for a Daily Routine
- Converting Flowcharts to Python Code
    - Translating Flowcharts into Code
    - Example: Checking if a Number is Even or Odd
    - Step-by-Step Explanation of the Corresponding Python Code
    - Practice: Convert a Flowchart for a Simple Task into Python Code
- Exercises and Challenges: Practice Problems and Solutions

Introduction to Algorithms

In programming, just like in everyday life, you will follow steps to complete tasks. Whether it is making a cup of tea, solving a math problem, or organizing files on a computer, everything follows a sequence of steps. This step-by-step process is called an algorithm.

Think of an algorithm as a recipe; it tells you exactly what to do and in what order. A recipe takes ingredients (input), follows instructions (processing), and gives you a finished dish (output). Similarly, an algorithm takes data, follows a set of instructions, and produces a result.

Everyday Examples of Algorithms

Algorithms are not just for computers; they are part of your daily routines! Here are some simple examples:

Making a Sandwich:

1. Take two slices of bread.
2. Spread butter on one side of each slice.
3. Add a filling (such as cheese or ham).
4. Place the slices together with the filling inside.
5. Cut the sandwich in half and enjoy!

Tying Your Shoes:

1. Place your shoe in front of you.
2. Cross the laces over each other.
3. Loop one lace under the other and pull to tighten.
4. Make a loop with each lace.
5. Cross the loops over each other.
6. Pull one loop through the hole and tighten the knot.

As you can see, an algorithm is simply a set of instructions that guides you step by step to complete a task.

Importance of Algorithms in Programming

Just like following the right steps makes cooking or tying shoes easier, a well-designed algorithm makes programs more efficient.

- A good algorithm solves a problem quickly and correctly.
- A poorly designed algorithm might still work, but it could be slow or inefficient.

For example, imagine you need to find a specific contact in a long phone list. A smart algorithm can help you search efficiently instead of checking each contact one by one.

Learning how to create and use algorithms makes you a better programmer. It helps you break down complex problems into smaller, manageable steps, just like the way you break down everyday tasks.

Practice: Identify a Simple Daily Task and Break It Down into an Algorithm

Now, let us try creating an algorithm! Think of a simple daily task, like brushing your teeth, and break it into clear, step-by-step instructions, just like the sandwich and shoe-tying examples.

Brushing Your Teeth:

1. Pick up your toothbrush.
2. Apply toothpaste.
3. Rinse the toothbrush with water.
4. Put the toothbrush in your mouth.
5. Brush the top teeth in circles for 30 seconds.
6. Brush the bottom teeth for 30 seconds.
7. Spit out the toothpaste.
8. Rinse your mouth with water.
9. Rinse and store the toothbrush.

Thinking in steps like this helps train your brain to think like a programmer! The more you practice, the easier it will be to design algorithms for real coding problems.

Breaking Down Problems

Now that you understand what algorithms are and how they guide both everyday tasks and programming, let us take it a step further. Before solving a problem, you need to break it down into smaller, manageable steps. This approach makes problem-solving simpler and more effective.

Step-by-Step Thinking

One of the most important skills in programming is learning to think step by step. Instead of jumping straight to the final solution, you should divide a big problem into smaller parts. This ensures that every step is clear and can be easily converted into code.

Let us connect this to what you learned about algorithms. Just like following the steps to make a sandwich, you can break complex problems into smaller tasks.

For example, suppose you need to find the largest number in a list. Instead of scanning the entire list randomly, you can follow a step-by-step process:

1. Start with the first number in the list.
2. Compare it to the next number.
3. If the next number is larger, update the largest number.
4. Repeat this until all numbers are checked.
5. The largest number left at the end is the solution.

This structured way of thinking helps programmers design solutions that are clear, efficient, and easy to troubleshoot.

Example of a Simple Algorithm in Python

Let us apply step-by-step thinking to a simple coding problem: adding two numbers.

Algorithm: Add Two Numbers

1. Ask the user to enter the first number.
2. Ask the user to enter the second number.
3. Add both numbers together.
4. Display the result.

Now, let us translate this into Python code:

```
# Step 1: Ask the user to input the first number
number1 = float(input("Enter the first number: "))

# Step 2: Ask the user to input the second number
number2 = float(input("Enter the second number: "))

# Step 3: Add the two numbers together
result = number1 + number2

# Step 4: Display the result
print("The sum of the two numbers is:", result)
```

Each line of this code matches a step in your algorithm, making it easier to understand. By following this structured approach, you will find it much easier to write, read, and debug your programs.

Practice: Write a Step-by-Step Algorithm For Calculating the Area of a Rectangle

Now it is your turn! Let us break down another problem: finding the area of a rectangle.

Task Description:

You want to create a Python program that:

- Asks the user for the length and width of a rectangle.
- Calculates the area using the formula: Area=Length×Width\text{Area} = \text{Length} \times \text{Width}Area=Length×Width
- Displays the final result.

Steps for the Exercise:

Step 1: Define the Problem

a. **Inputs**: The length and width of the rectangle.

b. **Output**: The calculated area.

Step 2: Write the Algorithm

a. Ask the user to enter the length of the rectangle.

b. Ask the user to enter the width of the rectangle.

c. Calculate the area by multiplying length and width.

d. Display the result.

Step 3: Convert the Algorithm to Python Code

```
# Step 1: Ask the user to input the length of the rectangle
length = float(input("Enter the length of the rectangle: "))

# Step 2: Ask the user to input the width of the rectangle
width = float(input("Enter the width of the rectangle: "))

# Step 3: Calculate the area
area = length * width

# Step 4: Display the calculated area
print(f"The area of the rectangle is: {area}")
```

Understanding the Code:

- **Input Length and Width**: Use `input()` to take user input and convert it to a decimal (float) so that you can handle both whole and decimal numbers.
- **Calculate the Area**: Multiply length and width.
- **Display the Result**: The f-string `(f"The area is {area}")` makes it easy to print the output in a clean format.

This exercise reinforces the habit of breaking problems into steps. As you practice, this structured way of thinking will make programming much easier and more enjoyable!

Key Takeaways:

- Breaking down problems into steps makes programming easier.
- Algorithms help organize your approach before writing code.
- Python programs follow a step-by-step execution, just like real-life instructions.
- Practice is key. The more you break down problems, the better you will get at coding!

Now, try breaking down a simple problem from your daily life into steps, just like you did with the rectangle example. The more you practice, the better you will get at thinking like a programmer!

Introduction to Flowcharts

Now that you have learned how to break down problems into step-by-step algorithms, let us explore another useful tool that helps programmers organize their thoughts: flowcharts.

A flowchart is a visual representation of an algorithm. Instead of writing out steps in text, you use shapes and arrows to show how a process flows. Flowcharts make it easier to understand complex logic, especially when solving problems or explaining ideas to others.

Think of a flowchart like a map for a road trip. It shows where to start, what turns to take, and different paths based on decisions. In programming, flowcharts help plan how a program should work before writing the actual code.

Definition of a Flowchart

A flowchart is a diagram that shows the sequence of steps in a process. Each step is represented by a different shape, and arrows indicate the order in which the steps occur.

For example, if you wanted to make a sandwich, a flowchart might start with "Get two slices of bread," then "Spread butter," and so on. This step-by-step structure makes the process easy to follow.

Flowcharts are widely used in programming, business, and engineering because they provide a clear and organized way to represent how things work.

Basic Flowchart Symbols

To create flowcharts, you need to know a few basic symbols:

- **Oval (Start/End):** Represents the beginning or end of a flowchart. Every flowchart starts and ends with an oval.
- **Rectangle (Process):** Represents an action or step in a process. Example: "Spread butter on bread" or "Calculate total price."
- **Diamond (Decision):** Represents a yes/no or true/false decision. Example: "Is it raining?" If yes, take an umbrella; if no, continue without one.
- **Arrows:** Indicate the direction of the flow. They show how the process moves from one step to the next.

These simple symbols are enough to start designing your own flowcharts!

Visualizing Algorithms Using Flowcharts

Flowcharts are especially helpful for understanding complex algorithms. Instead of reading long paragraphs of text, you can see how the logic flows at a glance.

For beginners, flowcharts help:

- Plan programs before coding.
- Spot mistakes before writing code.
- Explain logic to others more easily.

Whether you are working alone or on a team, flowcharts make problem-solving easier and more structured.

Practice: Create a Flowchart for Choosing an Outfit Based on the Weather

Let us put your knowledge to the test by creating a simple decision-based flowchart. Imagine you are getting dressed and need to decide what to wear based on the weather.

Steps to Create the Flowchart:

1. **Start**: Begin with an oval labeled "Start."
2. **Decision**: Is it raining? Use a diamond.
    a. **Yes**: "Take an umbrella" (rectangle).
    b. **No**: Move to the next decision.
3. **Decision**: Is it cold? Use another diamond.
    a. **Yes**: "Wear a coat" (rectangle).
    b. **No**: "Wear a light jacket" (rectangle).
4. **End**: Finish with an oval labeled "Ready to go!"

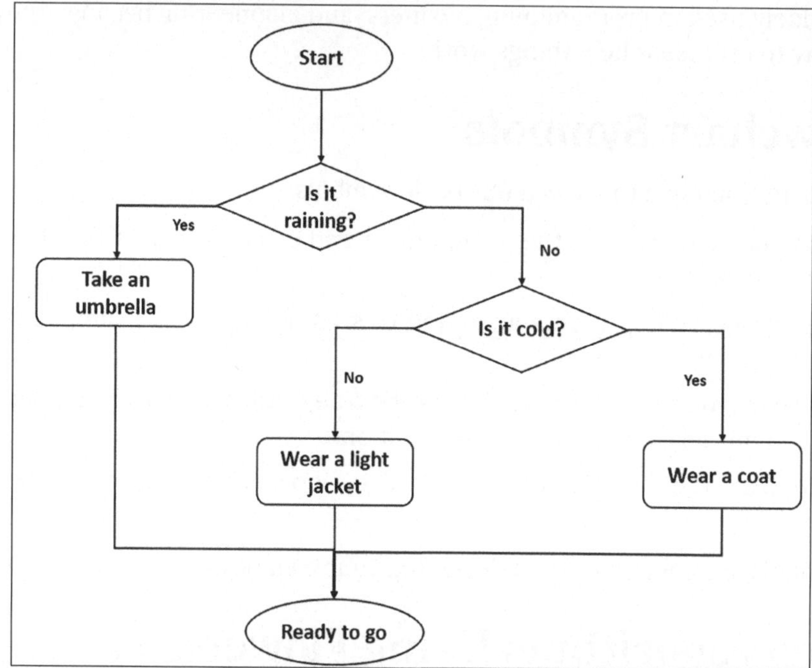

Figure 2.1: *Flowchart demonstration*

This simple flowchart visually maps out your decision process and ensures you are prepared for the weather.

Understanding the Flowchart

This flowchart breaks down a simple real-life decision into steps. It shows,

- **Decision points**: Where choices are made.
- **Actions**: What happens based on decisions.
- **Flow of logic**: How different paths lead to different outcomes.

By practicing with simple flowcharts, you will develop a structured way of thinking, making it easier to plan and write Python programs!

Designing Effective Flowcharts

Now that you have explored flowcharts and their role in organizing algorithms, let us refine your skills by designing them more effectively. This section will guide you through best practices for creating clear and structured flowcharts, using a simple example to illustrate the process.

Step-by-Step Guide to Creating a Flowchart

Creating a flowchart is an easy process when broken down into a few simple steps. This method helps visually organize your ideas, making it easier to plan your algorithms before coding.

1. **Identify the Task or Process**

   The first step in creating a flowchart is to define the task you want to illustrate.

   - What are the steps involved?
   - Are there any decisions to make along the way?

   For example, let us say you want to decide whether to go for a walk based on the weather.

2. **List the Steps**

   Write down each step in order. This should include:

   - **Actions**: What needs to be done?
   - **Decisions**: Where do you need to make a choice?

   For the walk decision, the steps might include:

   a. Check the weather.

   b. If it is raining: Stay inside.

   c. If it is not raining: Check if it is cold.

   d. If it is cold: Wear a coat.

   e. If it is not cold: Go for a walk.

3. **Choose the Right Symbols**

   To design the flowchart, use the correct symbols:

   - **Oval**: Start/End of the process.
   - **Rectangle**: Process/Action, such as "Check the weather."
   - **Diamond**: Decision point, such as "Is it raining?"
   - **Arrows**: Show the flow of actions.

4. **Draw the Flowchart**

   Start with an oval labeled "Start" at the top. Then, add each step in order, connecting them with arrows.

   - Use a diamond for decision points (like "Is it raining?").
   - If the answer is Yes, follow one path; if No, follow another.

5. **Review and Refine**

   Go through your flowchart and check:

   - Are all steps included?
   - Do decisions lead to clear outcomes?
   - Does the flow make sense?

Example: Deciding Whether to Go for a Walk

Let us break this process into a simple flowchart:

Steps:

- Start
- Check the weather.
- Is it raining?
    - **Yes**: Stay inside.
    - **No**: Is it cold?
        - **Yes**: Wear a coat.
        - **No**: Go for a walk.
- End

Flowchart representation:

- **Oval**: Start
- **Rectangle**: Check the weather
- **Diamond**: Is it raining?
    - **Yes - Rectangle**: Stay inside
    - **No - Diamond**: Is it cold?
        - **Yes - Rectangle**: Wear a coat
        - **No - Rectangle**: Go for a walk
- **Oval**: End

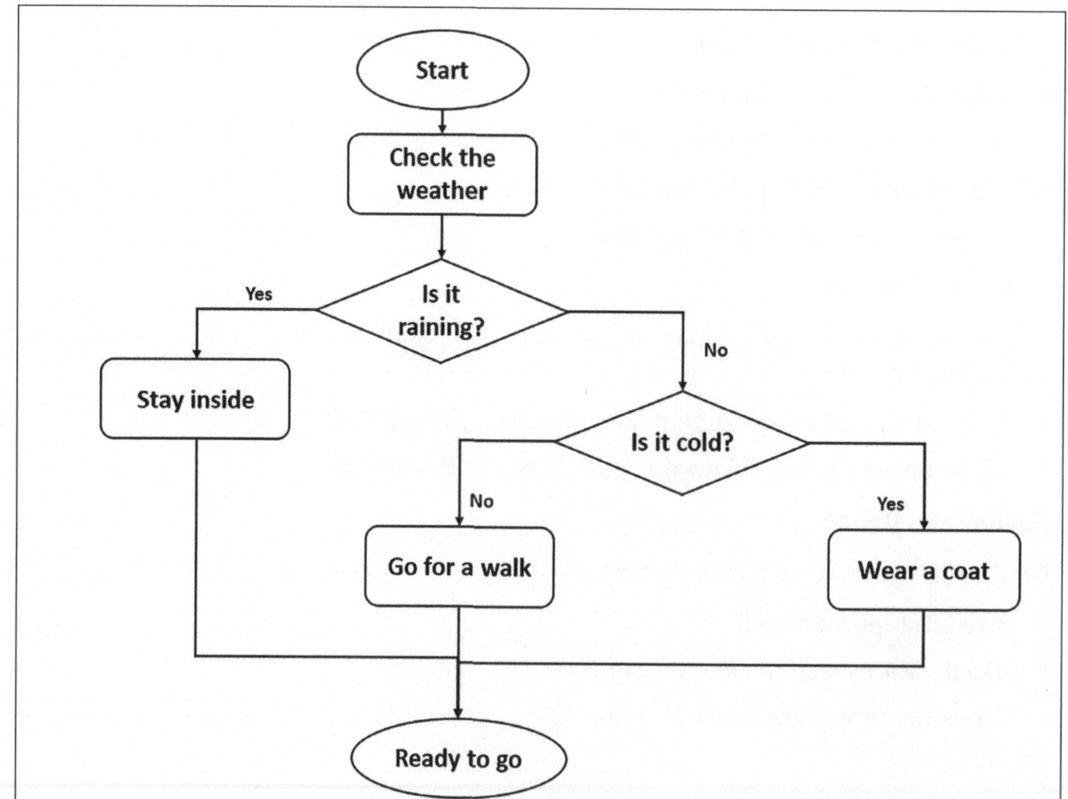

Figure 2.2: *Example flowchart - deciding whether to go for a walk*

Practice: Create a Flowchart for a Daily Routine

Now, let us apply what you have learned by creating a flowchart for your morning routine!

Task: Designing a Morning Routine Flowchart

Think about the steps you take every morning. A good flowchart should include:

- Basic actions (for example, waking up, brushing your teeth)
- Decisions (for example, "Do I have time for breakfast?")

Steps to Create the Flowchart:

1. **Identify the Task**: What does your morning routine look like?
2. **List the Steps**: Write down each action and decision in the order you do them.
3. **Choose Symbols**: Use ovals for start/end, rectangles for actions, and diamonds for decisions.
4. **Create the Flowchart**: Arrange the steps in order, connecting them with arrows.

Morning Routine Flowchart

1. Start
2. Wake up
3. Decide: Get out of bed or snooze the alarm?
    a. Snooze: Go back to step 2.
    b. Get out: Move to the next step.
4. Brush your teeth
5. Eat breakfast
6. Get dressed
7. Ready to go
8. End

Flowchart Representation:

1. **Oval**: Start
2. **Rectangle**: Wake up
3. **Diamond**: Snooze the alarm?
    a. **Yes**: Loop back to "Wake up"
    b. **No**: Move to the next step
4. **Rectangle**: Brush your teeth
5. **Rectangle**: Eat breakfast
6. **Rectangle**: Get dressed
7. **Oval**: Ready to go! (End)

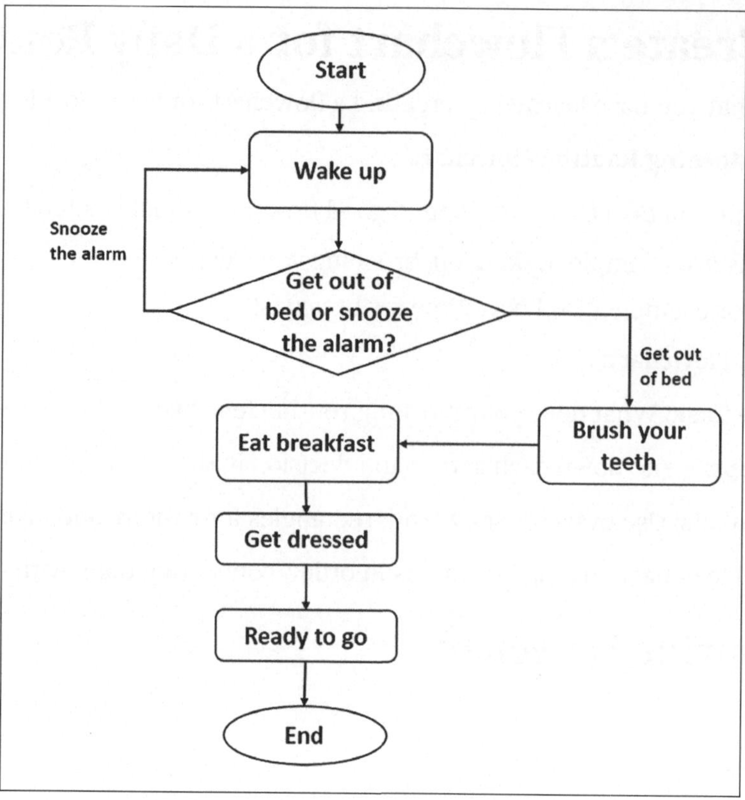

Figure 2.3: *Flowchart for morning routine*

Creating flowcharts for simple tasks like this builds your problem-solving skills and prepares you for more complex programming challenges!

Key Takeaways:

- Flowcharts help break down tasks into clear steps.
- Using the right symbols makes flowcharts easy to understand.
- Practicing with simple examples (such as a morning routine) builds problem-solving skills.
- Flowcharts are useful for both everyday tasks and planning Python programs!

Now that you have created your first flowchart, try designing one for another daily task, such as making a cup of tea or planning a study session!

Converting Flowcharts to Python Code

Now that you understand how to create flowcharts to visualize algorithms, the next step is to bring them to life through coding. Flowcharts are valuable tools for planning a process, but their real power lies in their ability to be translated into executable code. In this section, you will learn how to convert a flowchart into Python code systematically, allowing a computer to follow the steps and perform the intended task automatically.

Translating Flowcharts into Code

Each shape in a flowchart represents a specific type of action in Python code:

- **Ovals (Start/End):** Represent the beginning and end of the process. In Python, these are implied rather than explicitly written.
- **Rectangles (Processes):** Represent actions or calculations. These directly translate into Python statements, such as calculations or function calls.

- **Diamonds (Decisions):** Represent decision points (Yes/No or True/False). In Python, these are written as if statements or loops.

By following the flowchart's steps, you can easily write Python code that performs the same logical actions.

A Quick Note Before You Start Writing Code

So far, you have focused on visualizing logic using flowcharts. Now, you are taking the next step, translating a flowchart into Python code.

At this point, you may not be familiar with Python syntax yet, and that is completely okay!

The goal here is not to fully understand the Python code right away but to see the connection between a flowchart and code.

Think of it as a sneak peek! As you progress through the book, you will gradually learn the Python concepts needed to write and understand this code.

For now, just follow along and focus on how each step in a flowchart translates into an equivalent action in Python.

With that in mind, let us see how a flowchart can be converted into code!

Example: Checking if a Number is Even or Odd

Let us take a simple decision-based flowchart and convert it into Python code.

Flowchart Steps

1. **Start**
2. **Input**: Get a number from the user.
3. **Decision**: Is the number divisible by 2?
   a. **Yes**: Print "The number is even."
   b. **No**: Print "The number is odd."
4. **End**

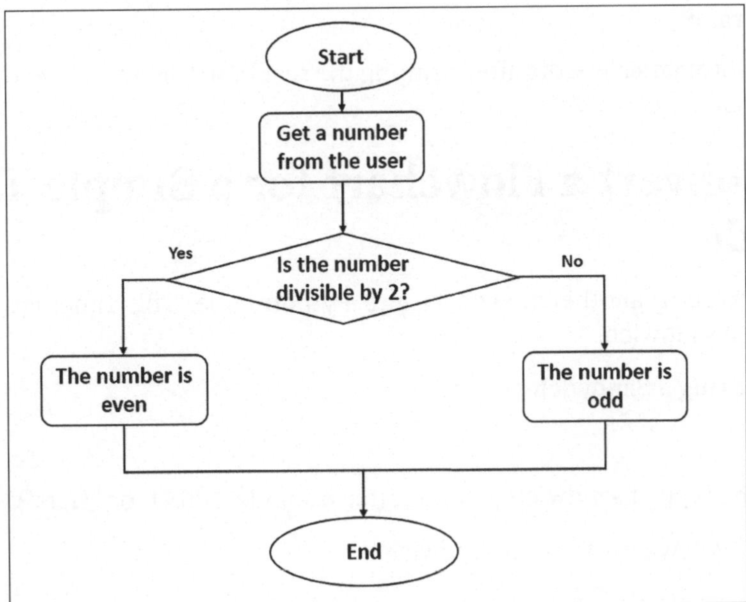

Figure 2.4: *Flowchart for checking if a number is even or odd*

Python Code for the Flowchart

```
# Step 2: Get user input
number = int(input("Enter a number: "))

# Step 3: Check if the number is even or odd
if number % 2 == 0:
    # If remainder is 0, the number is even
    print("The number is even.")
else:
    # Otherwise, the number is odd
    print("The number is odd.")
```

Step-by-Step Explanation of the Corresponding Python Code

1. **Input Step:**

   `number = int(input("Enter a number: "))`

   - The **`input()`** function asks the user to enter a number.
   - The **`int()`** function converts the input into an integer so you can perform calculations.

2. **Decision Step:**

   `if number % 2 == 0:`

   - The modulus operator (%) finds the remainder when dividing the number by 2.
   - If the remainder is 0, the number is even.

3. **Output Step:**

   `print("The number is even.")`

   - If the number is even, this message is displayed.

4. **Else Condition:**

   ```
   else:
       print("The number is odd.")
   ```

   - If the number is not divisible by 2, it must be odd.

5. **End of Program:**

   - Python automatically exits after printing the result, so there is no need for an explicit "**`End`**" command.

Practice: Convert a Flowchart for a Simple Task into Python Code

Now, let us try converting another flowchart into Python code. This time, let us create a simple program for making a sandwich!

Flowchart Steps: Making a Sandwich

1. **Start**
2. **Input**: Get the type of sandwich you want (for example, “PB&J” or “Ham”).
3. **Decision**: Do you want a toasted sandwich?

- **Yes**: Toast the bread.
- **No**: Skip to the next step.

4. **Process**: Add the ingredients (for example, peanut butter and jelly or ham and cheese).
5. **Output**: Print "Your sandwich is ready!"
6. **End**

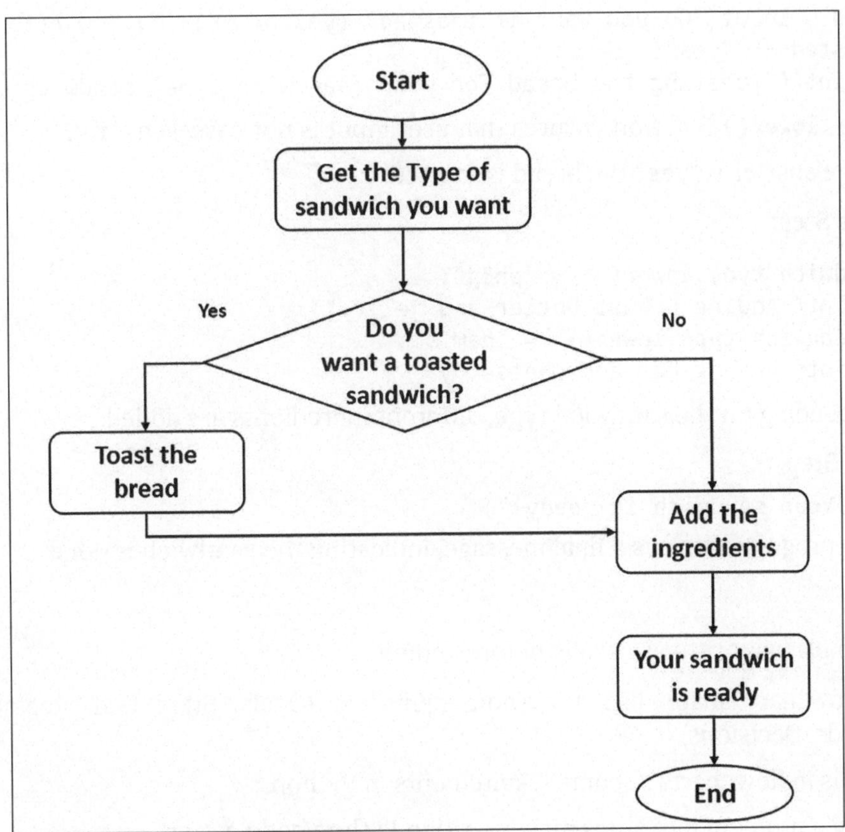

***Figure 2.5**: Flowchart for making a sandwich*

Python Code for the Flowchart

```
# Step 2: Ask for the type of sandwich
sandwich_type = input("What type of sandwich do you want? (PB&J or Ham): ")

# Step 3: Ask if they want it toasted
toasted = input("Do you want it toasted? (yes or no): ").lower()

# If the user wants their sandwich toasted
if toasted == "yes":
    print(f"Toasting the bread for your {sandwich_type} sandwich...")

# Step 4: Add ingredients based on the sandwich type
if sandwich_type.lower() == "pb&j":
    print("Adding peanut butter and jelly.")
elif sandwich_type.lower() == "ham":
    print("Adding ham and cheese.")

# Step 5: Print the final message
print("Your sandwich is ready!")
```

Step-by-Step Breakdown of the Code

1. **Input Step:**

```
sandwich_type = input("What type of sandwich do you want? (PB&J or Ham): ")
```

   - This asks the user what type of sandwich they want.

2. **Decision Step:**

```
toasted = input("Do you want it toasted? (yes or no): ").lower()
if toasted == "yes":
    print(f"Toasting the bread for your {sandwich_type} sandwich...")
```

   - The **.lower()** function ensures that user input is not case-sensitive.
   - If the answer is "**yes**," the bread is toasted.

3. **Process Step:**

```
if sandwich_type.lower() == "pb&j":
    print("Adding peanut butter and jelly.")
elif sandwich_type.lower() == "ham":
    print("Adding ham and cheese.")
```

   - Depending on the sandwich type, different ingredients are added.

4. **Output Step**:

```
print("Your sandwich is ready!")
```

   - The program displays a final message, indicating the sandwich is done.

Key Takeaways

Flowcharts help plan algorithms visually before coding.

- Each flowchart shape has a Python equivalent (Ovals: Start/End, Rectangles: Actions, Diamonds: Decisions).
- Decisions in flowcharts become if statements in Python.
- Breaking a problem into steps makes writing Python code easier!

Now, try choosing another simple task, creating a flowchart and converting it into Python code!

Exercises and Challenges: Practice Problems and Solutions

Now that you have learned how to create flowcharts and convert them into Python code, it is time to put that knowledge into practice!

The following exercises will test your understanding by having you design flowcharts for different real-world scenarios. As an extra challenge, you will also get a chance to translate a flowchart into Python code!

Practice Problem 1: Morning Routine Flowchart

Task: Create a flowchart depicting your entire morning process, from waking up to leaving the house.

Challenge: Create a flowchart that depicts every phase of your morning routine. Consider the weather when making decisions such as whether to have breakfast or what to wear.

Steps:

1. Identify the beginning and end of your routine.
2. List all steps in order, such as waking up, brushing teeth, and getting dressed.
3. Include decision points, such as checking the weather before deciding what to wear.
4. Use appropriate flowchart symbols to indicate each action and choice.

Practice Problem 2: Grocery Shopping Flowchart

Task: Create a flowchart to represent the process of planning a grocery shopping trip.

Challenge: Create a flowchart to help you plan what to buy depending on what you have at home and what meals you intend to prepare.

Steps:

1. Begin with an empty shopping list.
2. Determine what ingredients you already have.
3. Choose which meals you wish to prepare.
4. Add any missing ingredients to your shopping list.
5. Check for additional necessities, such as housekeeping products.
6. Create a detailed shopping list to take to the store.

Practice Problem 3: Event Planning Flowchart

Task: Make a flowchart for organizing an event, such as a birthday party or a team meeting.

Challenge: Create a flowchart outlining the procedures necessary to prepare for the event, such as mailing invitations, selecting a venue, and preparing the schedule.

Steps:

1. Decide on the event type and date.
2. Make a guest list.
3. Select a venue according to the number of visitors.
4. Send invites and confirm attendance.
5. Plan the event schedule (including activities and meals).
6. Create a checklist of things to perform before the event.
7. Conclude with a successfully prepared event.

Solution to Practice Problem 1: Morning Routine Flowchart

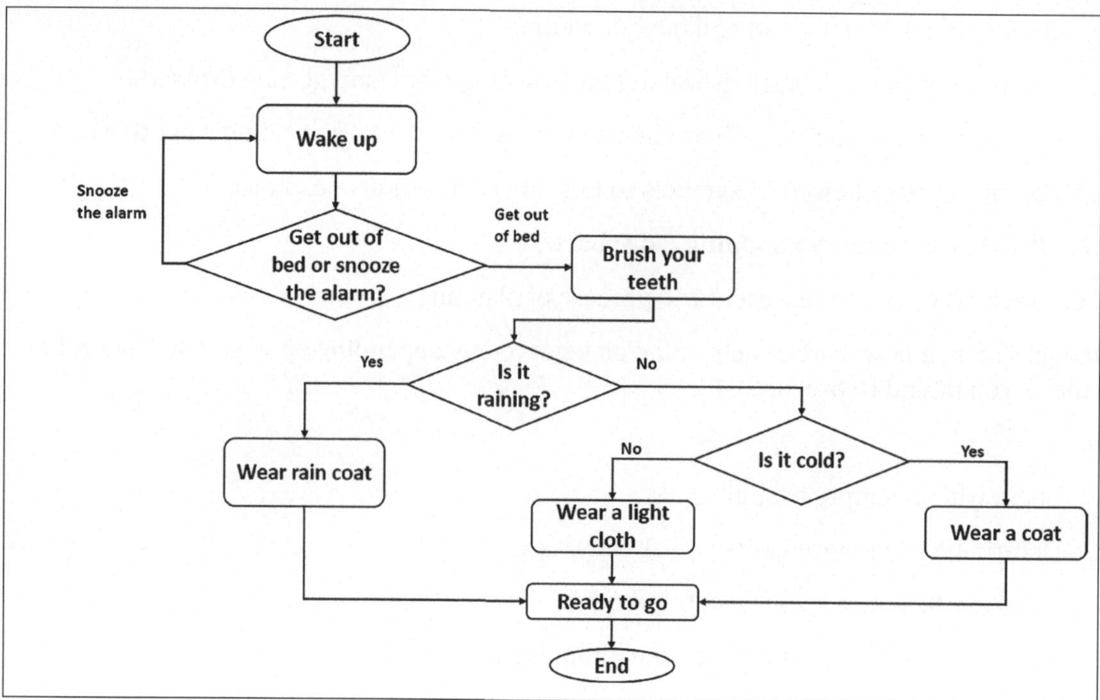

Figure 2.6: *Solution to practice problem 1: morning routine flowchart*

Solution to Practice Problem 2: Grocery Shopping Flowchart

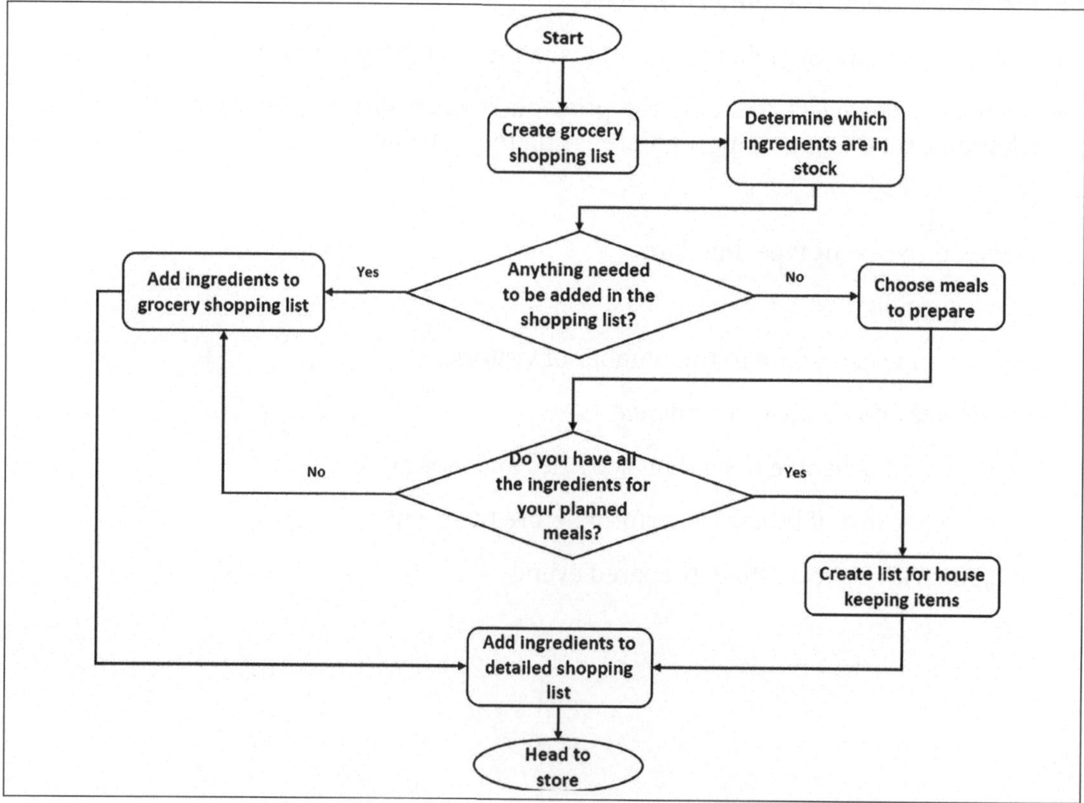

Figure 2.7: *Solution to practice problem 2: grocery shopping flowchart*

Solution to Practice Problem 3: Event Planning Flowchart

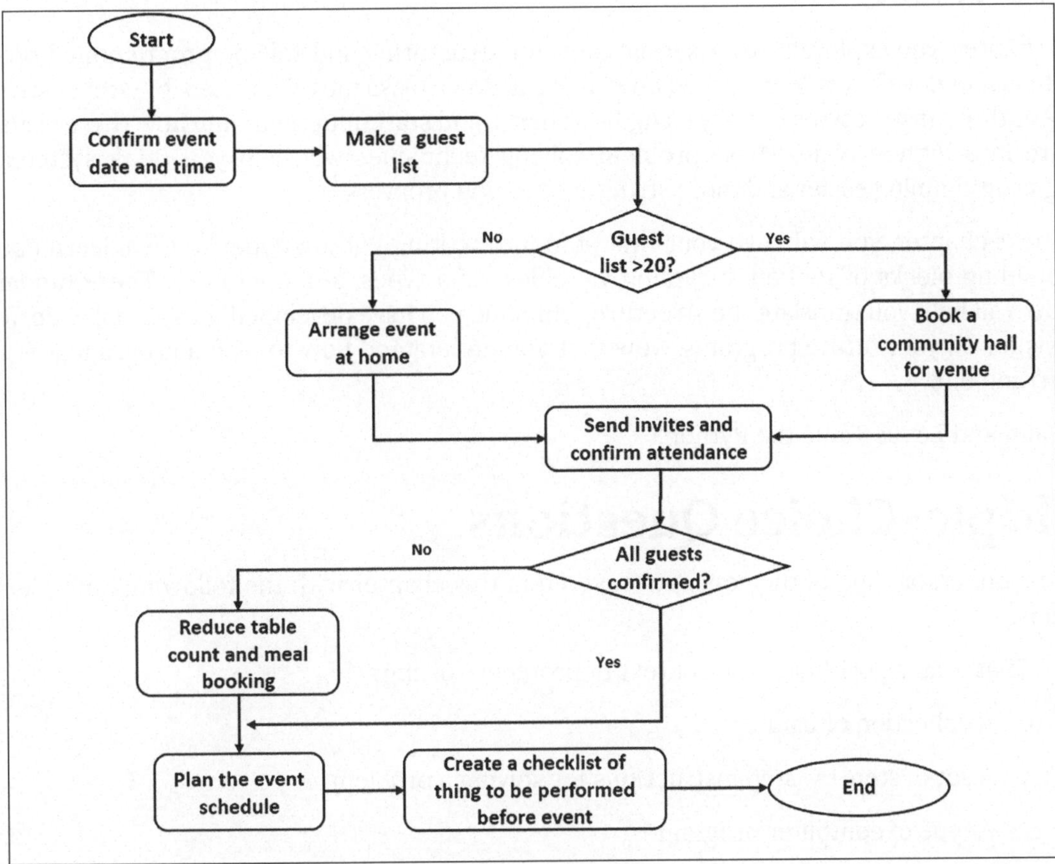

Figure 2.8: *Solution to practice problem 3: event planning flowchart*

Bonus Challenge: Convert a Flowchart into Python Code

Now that you have created your flowcharts, let us take them one step further!

Choose any of the preceding flowcharts you created and translate it into Python code. This will help you understand how visual logic transforms into real programming.

Keep in mind:

- You do not need to write a perfect program. Just focus on translating each step into Python syntax.
- You may not yet know all Python concepts (which is okay!). The idea is to get comfortable thinking like a programmer.
- Use if statements for decision points and `print()` statements for actions.

Example: If you created a morning routine flowchart, try writing Python code that:

- Asks the user if they snooze their alarm or get up.
- Prints different outputs based on their choices.
- Lists the next morning tasks in order.

By completing these exercises, you will feel more confident designing flowcharts and translating them into Python, preparing you for more advanced programming tasks in the future.

So, grab a pen and paper (or a flowchart tool) and start creating!

Conclusion

In this chapter, you explored two essential tools for structuring and solving programming problems: algorithms and flowcharts. You learned how to break down tasks into clear, step-by-step instructions, represent those instructions visually using flowcharts, and start understanding how these visual plans translate into Python code. These problem-solving techniques will help you think systematically, making programming easier and more structured as you progress.

In the next chapter, you will take your first step into writing Python code. You will learn about the basic building blocks of Python, including variables, data types, and operators. These fundamental concepts will help you translate the structured thinking you have developed into actual code, forming the basis for all your future programs. Now that you understand how to plan a program, it is time to start writing one.

Keep Calm and Let us Tame the Python!!

Multiple-Choice Questions

Test your understanding of the concepts covered in this chapter with the following multiple-choice questions.

1. What is an algorithm in the context of problem-solving?
   a. A collection of data
   b. A set of step-by-step instructions for solving a problem
   c. A type of computer program
   d. A method of storing data
2. Which symbol is used in a flowchart to represent the start or end of a process?
   a. Oval
   b. Rectangle
   c. Diamond
   d. Arrow
3. What is the primary purpose of a flowchart?
   a. To store data
   b. To visually represent the steps of an algorithm
   c. To execute a program
   d. To create a user interface
4. Which symbol in a flowchart represents a decision point?
   a. Oval
   b. Rectangle
   c. Diamond
   d. Circle

5. In a flowchart, what does the rectangle symbol typically represent?
   a. Start/End
   b. Process or Action
   c. Decision
   d. Data Storage
6. Why are flowcharts useful before coding?
   a. They help visualize the logic and sequence of actions in an algorithm
   b. They eliminate the need for comments in code
   c. They reduce the complexity of the code
   d. They automatically generate code
7. What should be the first step when creating a flowchart for a process?
   a. Drawing all possible decision points first
   b. Identifying the start and end points of the process
   c. Writing down the code first
   d. Testing the flowchart with data
8. Which of the following is true about flowcharts?
   a. They are used only in computer science
   b. They cannot represent decisions
   c. They help in planning and organizing the logic of a process
   d. They replace the need for any coding
9. How does a flowchart help in problem-solving?
   a. It shows the final output directly
   b. It provides a visual way to organize the steps and decisions in a process
   c. It speeds up the execution of code
   d. It reduces the need for debugging
10. Which part of a flowchart shows the flow of control from one step to another?
    a. Oval
    b. Arrow
    c. Diamond
    d. Rectangle

Answers

1. b
2. a
3. b
4. c
5. b
6. a
7. b
8. c
9. b
10. b

Points to Remember

- Algorithms give clear and efficient instructions for issue solutions. They are crucial to programming and can also be used in everyday tasks.
- Flowcharts visualize algorithm steps, facilitating understanding, communication, and debugging of process logic.
- The most popular symbols in flowcharts are ovals for start/end points, rectangles for processes or actions, and diamonds for decision points. Arrows are used to illustrate the flow of control from one step to the next.
- Flowcharts organize process logic and provide a clear path for coding. They also assist in detecting potential concerns early on in the design phase.
- Creating effective algorithms and flowcharts requires breaking down challenges into simple, achievable steps. This thorough approach ensures that all aspects of the problem are addressed and resolved correctly.
- Regularly designing and translating flowcharts into code improves problem-solving skills and confidence in addressing tough programming challenges.

Further Reading

If you would like to explore algorithms and flowcharts further, here are two great resources:

1. **Introduction to Algorithms - GeeksforGeeks**:

   https://www.geeksforgeeks.org/fundamentals-of-algorithms/
   A beginner-friendly introduction to algorithms, covering basic concepts, types of algorithms, and their real-world applications.

2. **Flowchart Tutorial - Lucidchart**:

   https://www.lucidchart.com/pages/what-is-a-flowchart-tutorial
   A simple guide to understanding and creating flowcharts, including symbol meanings and best practices for designing clear and effective diagrams.

Chapter 3
Basic Python

Introduction

Now that you understand how to break down problems using algorithms and flowcharts, it is time to start writing real Python code. In this chapter, you will learn the basic building blocks of Python, including variables, data types, operators, and syntax rules. These will help you turn your problem-solving ideas into actual programs.

You will see how Python stores and processes data, how to perform calculations, and how to write clean and structured code. The logical thinking skills from the previous chapter will now help you write clear and efficient programs.

By the end of this chapter, you will be able to write and run simple Python programs with confidence. This is your first big step toward building more advanced projects. Let us start coding!

Structure

In this chapter, the following topics will be covered:

- Understanding Variables
- Basic Data Types
    - Integers (int)
    - Floating-Point Numbers (float)
    - Strings (str)
    - Booleans (bool)
- Exploring Basic Operators
    - Arithmetic Operators
    - Comparison Operators
    - Logical Operators
    - Assignment Operators
- Syntax and Program Structure
    - Basic Syntax Rules
    - Case Sensitivity
    - Naming Conventions
    - Indentation
    - Comments and Documentation
- Exercises and Challenges: Practice Problems and Solutions

Understanding Variables: The Basics

When learning Python, one of the first things you will come across is variables. But what exactly are they? Let us break it down in simple terms.

A variable is like a storage box with a name. You can put different types of data inside this box, that is, numbers, words, or even more complex information. The special thing about variables is that their contents can change, which is why they are called "variables."

Imagine you have a notebook where you track your daily expenses. Each page is labeled with a category, like "Food," "Transport," or "Entertainment." You can write new amounts, erase old ones, and update the totals as needed. In programming, a variable works the same way. It has a name, holds information, and can be updated anytime.

Importance of Variables in Programming:

Variables make programs dynamic and interactive. They allow a program to store, change, and retrieve information while running.

For example, imagine a shopping app that calculates the total cost of your cart. Each time you add or remove an item, the app updates the total. This is possible because the app uses a variable to keep track of the total cost. Without variables, programs would not be able to remember or adjust information.

Naming Variables:

Just like labeling pages in your notebook helps you find information quickly, giving clear names to your variables makes your code easier to read and understand.

In Python, variable names should describe the data they store. For example:

- **`user_age`** (stores a person's age)
- **`game_score`** (keeps track of a score in a game)
- **`total_price`** (holds the total cost of items in a cart)

Using meaningful names makes your code easier for you and others to understand.

The Power of Variables

Variables make programming flexible. Instead of using fixed values, you can work with changing data that updates based on user input, program conditions, or real-time events. This ability to store and modify information is what makes programming so powerful!

Understanding variables is one of the most important steps in learning Python. They allow you to store, update, and manage data inside your programs. As you continue your coding journey, you will see how variables play a key role in bringing your code to life!

Basic Data Types

Now that you understand how variables store information, let us explore the different types of data they can hold. In Python, every piece of information has a specific data type that defines how it can be used. Think of it like organizing ingredients in a kitchen. Some are solid, some are liquid, and each serves a different purpose. Similarly, Python's data types allow you to work with numbers, text, and logical values efficiently.

Let us go over the most commonly used data types in Python.

Overview of Basic Data Types:

- **Integers (int)**: Whole numbers, including positive numbers, negative numbers, and zero. Used for counting and operations that do not require fractions.
- **Floating-Point Numbers (float)**: Numbers with decimal points. Used for precise calculations such as measurements and currency.
- **Strings (str)**: Sequences of characters used to store text, names, or sentences.
- **Booleans (bool)**: Can have only two values: True or False. Used to make decisions in programs.

Importance of Data Types:

Each data type has specific operations it supports. Choosing the right data type is important for writing efficient and error-free code.

For example:

- You can add and multiply integers and floating-point numbers.
- But if you try to add a number to a piece of text without converting it first, Python will throw an error.

Understanding data types helps you avoid bugs, write cleaner code, and choose the right tools for the task, just like using the correct appliance in your kitchen (you would not use a blender to make toast!).

Now, let us take a closer look at each data type.

Integers (`int`)

Integers, or whole numbers, are one of the simplest and most commonly used data types in Python. They include positive numbers, negative numbers, and zero.

Understanding Integers:

Integers are used in many real-world scenarios, such as

- Counting items (**`students_in_class = 50`**)
- Tracking age (**`user_age = 25`**)
- Representing years (**`year_of_independence = 1947`**)

In Python, you do not need to declare the type; just assign a number to a variable:

```
days_in_week = 7
temperature = -10
year = 2023
```

Python automatically understands these as integers.

Importance of Integers

Integers are essential because they are used in:

- Loops (repeating actions multiple times)
- Indexing (accessing elements in lists)
- Counting and calculations

Since Python allows very large numbers, you do not have to worry about running out of space; integers can grow as much as your computer's memory allows!

Using Integers Effectively

Use integers when working with:

- Whole numbers (counting objects, days, or quantities)
- Calculations that do not need decimals
- Repetitive operations such as loops

Integers are a fundamental part of Python programming. Whether you are calculating a bill, running a loop, or keeping track of scores in a game, you will use integers all the time.

Floating-Point Numbers (float)

In Python, floating-point numbers (or "floats") are numbers that include a decimal point. They are used when you need more precision than whole numbers (integers).

Understanding Floating-Point Numbers:

A float represents numbers with decimals, such as

2.5, -0.01, 10.75

Floats can also be written using scientific notation for very large or very small numbers:

1.2e-5 (which means 0.000012)

The Importance of Floating-Point Numbers:

Floats are essential when you need precise calculations, such as

- Measurements (for example, temperature, distance, weight)
- Scientific calculations
- Currency calculations

Using Floats:

Assigning a float to a variable is easy:

```
temperature = 23.5
earth_radius_km = 6371.0
```

Python automatically recognizes these as floating-point numbers.

Things to Keep in Mind:

- Floats are not always 100% precise due to how computers store them. For example, 0.1 + 0.2 might not exactly equal 0.3.
- For financial or high-precision calculations, Python provides the Decimal module, which handles decimals more accurately.

Floats are crucial in programming because they allow you to work with real numbers and perform complex calculations. You will use them in everything from math operations to scientific computing!

Strings (str)

A string is a sequence of characters used to store text. Whether it is a single letter, a word, or an entire paragraph, Python treats all text as strings.

Understanding Strings:

Strings can contain letters, numbers, symbols, and spaces. You can create them using single (') or double (") quotes:

```
greeting = "Hello, World!"
name = 'Python Programmer'
```

Both are valid ways to define strings in Python.

Key Features of Strings:

- **Immutable:** Once created, a string cannot be changed directly. Any modification creates a new string instead.
- **Indexable:** You can access individual characters using their position (index).
- **Iterable:** You can loop through each letter in a string easily.

Common String Operations:

Python provides many ways to work with strings:

- Concatenation (joining strings together)

```
first_name = "John"
last_name = "Doe"
full_name = first_name + " " + last_name
print(full_name)  # Output: John Doe
```

- Slicing (extracting a part of a string)

```
word = "Python"
print(word[0:4])  # Output: Pyth
```

- Modifying Strings

```
text = "hello"
print(text.upper())  # Output: HELLO
print(text.replace("h", "H"))  # Output: Hello
```

Importance of Strings:

Strings are everywhere in programming!

- User input (for example, asking for names or messages)
- Displaying text on a website or an app
- Storing and processing large text files

Understanding how to manipulate strings is essential for working with text-based data in Python.

Booleans (bool)

A Boolean (or bool) is the simplest data type in Python. It can only have two values:

- True
- False

Booleans are used in decision-making and logical operations.

Functioning of Booleans:

Booleans come from logic, where things are either true or false. You can directly assign a Boolean value:

```
is_raining = False
is_sunny = True
```

Or, they can be the result of a comparison:

```
x = 10
y = 5

print(x > y)  # Output: True
print(x == y)  # Output: False
```

Common Uses of Booleans:

- Conditions (if, elif, else statements)
- Loops (to control how long a loop runs)
- Logical operations (and, or, not)

Using Booleans:

```
is_python_fun = True

if is_python_fun:
    print("Python is amazing!")
```

Booleans help programs make decisions and control program flow, making them an essential part of coding!

Exercise: Exploring Basic Data Types

Now you have learned about Python's four fundamental data types, integers (int), floating-point numbers (float), strings (str), and booleans (bool). It is time to put them into practice. In this exercise, you will write a simple Python script to define and print variables of each type.

Objective:

Write a Python script that:

- Defines a variable for each basic data type
- Prints each variable's value to the console

Instructions:

1. **Open Visual Studio Code**: Launch VS Code on your computer.
2. Create a New Python File
    a. Click **`File`** > **`New File`** or use the shortcut *Ctrl* + N to create a new file.
    b. Save the file with a **`.py`** extension, for example, **`data_types_demo.py`**.
    c. To save, go to **`File`** > **`Save As`** or use the shortcut *Ctrl* + S.
3. **Write the Python Script**

    In the newly created file, enter the following Python code:

```
# Define an integer variable
my_integer = 42
print("Integer example:", my_integer)

# Define a floating-point variable
my_float = 3.14
print("Floating-point example:", my_float)

# Define a string variable
```

```
my_string = "Hello, Python!"
print("String example:", my_string)

# Define a boolean variable
my_boolean = True
print("Boolean example:", my_boolean)
```

4. **Run the Script**
   a. Open the integrated terminal in VS Code by going to **`View`** > **`Terminal`** or pressing *Ctrl* + `.
   b. Type the following command in the terminal and press *Enter*:
   `python data_types_demo.py`
5. **Observe the Output**
   a. Your terminal should display the following:

```
Integer example: 42
Floating-point example: 3.14
String example: Hello, Python!
Boolean example: True
```

```
(env_challenge) C:\PythonChallenges>python data_types_demo.py
Integer example: 42
Floating-point example: 3.14
String example: Hello, Python!
Boolean example: True

(env_challenge) C:\PythonChallenges>
```

Figure 3.1: *Output of exercise: exploring basic data types in Python*

Exploring Basic Operators

Now that you understand variables and how they store data, let us explore how you can manipulate that data using operators. Operators in Python act like tools in a toolbox, helping you perform calculations, compare values, and control the flow of programs.

Just as a chef uses different utensils for chopping, stirring, and measuring, programmers use different types of operators for various tasks:

- **Arithmetic Operators**: Perform mathematical operations
- **Comparison Operators**: Compare values to make decisions
- **Logical Operators**: Combine conditions for complex decision-making
- **Assignment Operators**: Assign and update variable values

Now, let us start with the arithmetic operators, which allow you to perform basic mathematical calculations in Python.

Arithmetic Operators

Arithmetic operators are used for basic mathematical calculations such as addition, subtraction, multiplication, and division. These operations are essential for finance, data analysis, game development, and general programming.

Operator	Symbol	Description	Example	Output
Addition	+	Adds two numbers	10 + 5	15
Subtraction	-	Subtracts one number from another	20 - 7	13
Multiplication	*	Multiplies two numbers	4 * 3	12
Division	/	Divides one number by another (always returns a float)	2-Oct	5
Integer Division	//	Divides and rounds down to the nearest whole number	10 // 3	3
Modulus	%	Returns the remainder of a division	10 % 3	1
Exponentiation	**	Raises one number to the power of another	2 ** 3	8

Table 3.1: *Arithmetic operators in Python*

Examples of Arithmetic Operators in Action:

- **Addition (+):** Used for adding numbers

```
a = 10 + 5
print(a)  # Output: 15
```

- **Subtraction (-):** Finds the difference between numbers

```
b = 20 - 7
print(b)  # Output: 13
```

- **Multiplication (*):** Multiplies values together

```
c = 4 * 3
print(c)  # Output: 12
```

- **Division (/):** Returns a float even if dividing whole numbers

```
d = 10 / 2
print(d)  # Output: 5.0
```

- **Integer Division (//):** Rounds down to the nearest integer

```
e = 10 // 3
print(e)  # Output: 3
```

- **Modulus (%):** Finds the remainder of a division

```
f = 10 % 3
print(f)  # Output: 1
```

- **Exponentiation (**):** Raises a number to a power

```
g = 2 ** 3
print(g)  # Output: 8
```

Using Arithmetic Operators Effectively:

- Performing calculations (for example, finding totals, differences, and averages)
- Checking if a number is even or odd (% 2 can tell you if a number is even)
- Scaling values up or down (for example, pricing in finance or graphics programming)
- Using exponents in scientific calculations

Arithmetic operators form the foundation of Python programming. Whether you are building a calculator, a financial app, or a game, you will be using them all the time!

Simplified Party Planning Scenario with Arithmetic Operations

Planning a party requires budgeting and calculations, and Python's arithmetic operators can help! Let us break it down step by step using addition, subtraction, multiplication, division, integer division, modulus, and exponentiation.

Scenario Overview

You are planning a birthday party with a limited budget. Here is what you need to buy:

- Decorations
- Food (snack packs for each guest)
- A birthday cake
- Party hats (packs of 5)
- Balloons (sets with exponential growth to create a festive mood)

Your goal is to manage the budget and calculate the right quantities for everything!

Budget and Costs:

Item	Cost / Quantity
Total budget	$150
Cost of decorations	$40
Cost per snack pack	$5
Number of guests	10
Cost of birthday cake	$20
Balloons per set	2^2 = 4

Table 3.2: *Party planning scenario – budget and costs*

Python Script for Party Planning:

Let us write a Python script to calculate expenses and required items efficiently:

```
# Budget and costs
total_budget = 150
decor_cost = 40
snack_cost_per_pack = 5
cake_cost = 20
guests = 10

# Calculate remaining budget after buying decorations and a cake
remaining_budget = total_budget - (decor_cost + cake_cost)

# Determine the number of snack packs to buy (one per guest)
snack_packs_needed = guests
total_snack_cost = snack_cost_per_pack * snack_packs_needed

# Update remaining budget after buying snacks
remaining_budget -= total_snack_cost

# Party hats calculation (packs of 5)
hats_per_pack = 5
```

```
packs_needed = guests // hats_per_pack + (guests % hats_per_pack > 0)  #
Ensuring every guest gets a hat

# Balloons calculation (using exponentiation)
balloon_sets_needed = 2  # Deciding on 2 sets for simplicity
balloons_per_set = 2**2  # Each set contains 2^2 = 4 balloons
total_balloons = balloon_sets_needed * balloons_per_set

# Display results
print(f"Remaining budget after purchases: ${remaining_budget}")
print(f"Total snack packs needed: {snack_packs_needed}")
print(f"Total packs of party hats needed: {packs_needed}")
print(f"Total balloons for decoration: {total_balloons}")
```

```
(env_challenge) C:\PythonChallenges>python Party_planning.py
Remaining budget after purchases: $40
Total snack packs needed: 10
Total packs of party hats needed: 2
Total balloons for decoration: 8

(env_challenge) C:\PythonChallenges>
```

Figure 3.2: *Output of planning scenario – budget and costs*

Expected Outcome and Key Calculations:

This script efficiently manages expenses and determines item quantities using Python's arithmetic operators:

Calculation	Python Operator Used	Result
Remaining Budget	- (subtraction)	$150 - (40 + 20) = $90
Total Snack Cost	* (multiplication)	10 guests × $5 = $50
Final Budget After Snacks	-= (subtraction & assignment)	$90 - $50 = $40
Packs of Party Hats	// (integer division) & % (modulus)	10 // 5 + (10 % 5 > 0) = 2
Total Balloons	** (exponentiation) & * (multiplication)	2 sets × (2^2) = 8

Table 3.3: *Party Planning scenario – expected outcome and key calculations*

Key Takeaways:

- Arithmetic operators help with real-life budgeting
- Python makes planning and calculations efficient
- You can easily modify values for different scenarios

This example demonstrates Python's power in everyday situations, making party planning both fun and efficient!

Comparison Operators

Comparison operators are used to compare values in Python. They evaluate conditions and return a Boolean result (True or False). These operators help programs make decisions based on comparisons.

Types of Comparison Operators:

Python provides six key comparison operators that are frequently used in decision-making and logic-based programming.

Operator	Symbol	Description	Example	Output
Equal to	==	Checks if two values are equal	5 == 5	TRUE
Not equal to	!=	Checks if two values are not equal	5 != 3	TRUE
Greater than	>	Checks if the left value is greater than the right value	10 > 3	TRUE
Less than	<	Checks if the left value is smaller than the right value	2 < 7	TRUE
Greater than or equal to	>=	Checks if the left value is greater than or equal to the right value	4 >= 4	TRUE
Less than or equal to	<=	Checks if the left value is smaller than or equal to the right value	6 <= 8	TRUE

***Table 3.4**: Comparison operators in Python*

Example: Comparing Two Books:

Imagine you have two books on your reading list:

- "Journey Through Python" – 350 pages
- "Data Science Expedition" – 250 pages

You want to compare them with the average programming book length (300 pages). Let us use Python's comparison operators to analyze their lengths.

```
# Define book page counts
book1_pages = 350
book2_pages = 250
average_pages = 300

# Is "Journey Through Python" longer than the average?
print(f"Is 'Journey Through Python' longer than the average programming book?
{book1_pages > average_pages}")

# Is "Data Science Expedition" shorter than the average?
print(f"Is 'Data Science Expedition' shorter than the average programming
book? {book2_pages < average_pages}")

# Do both books have the same number of pages?
print(f"Do both books have the same number of pages? {book1_pages == book2_
pages}")

# Are the books different in length?
print(f"Are the books different in length? {book1_pages != book2_pages}")

# Is "Journey Through Python" at least as long as "Data Science Expedition"?
print(f"Is 'Journey Through Python' as long or longer than 'Data Science
Expedition'? {book1_pages >= book2_pages}")

# Is "Data Science Expedition" as short or shorter than "Journey Through
Python"?
print(f"Is 'Data Science Expedition' as short or shorter than 'Journey Through
Python'? {book2_pages <= book1_pages}")
```

```
(env_challenge) C:\PythonChallenges>python books_example.py
Is 'Journey Through Python' longer than the average programming book? True
Is 'Data Science Expedition' shorter than the average programming book? True
Do 'Journey Through Python' and 'Data Science Expedition' have the same number of pages? False
Are 'Journey Through Python' and 'Data Science Expedition' different in length? True
Is 'Journey Through Python' as long or longer than 'Data Science Expedition'? True
Is 'Data Science Expedition' as short or shorter than 'Journey Through Python'? True

(env_challenge) C:\PythonChallenges>
```

Figure 3.3: *Output of Python code: comparing two books*

Effective Use of Comparison Operators:

- **Making Decisions**: Used in if statements to execute different code blocks
- **Validating User Input**: Ensuring values meet required conditions
- **Sorting and Filtering Data**: Organizing values in lists
- **Loop Control**: Managing iterations in while loops

Comparison operators help Python evaluate conditions and return useful results, making them essential in programming logic.

Logical Operators

Logical operators allow you to combine multiple conditions to make more complex decisions in Python. These operators help control how your program evaluates multiple conditions together.

Python has three logical operators:

Operator	Symbol	Description	Example	Output
AND	and	Returns True if **both** conditions are true	True and True	TRUE
OR	or	Returns True if **at least one** condition is true	True or False	TRUE
NOT	not	Reverses the result (True becomes False, and vice versa)	not True	FALSE

Table 3.5: *Logical operators in Python*

Real-Life Example: Planning a Movie Night

Imagine you are planning a movie night at your home. You want everything to be perfect, so two conditions must be met:

- There must be enough snacks for everyone.
- The weather must be clear since you are projecting the movie outdoors.

If both conditions are met, the movie night will happen. Otherwise, it will be canceled.

Python Code for Decision-Making

Let us translate this real-life scenario into Python using logical operators.

```
# Conditions for movie night
have_enough_snacks = True
weather_is_clear = False

# Using logical operators to decide if movie night can happen
can_have_movie_night = have_enough_snacks and weather_is_clear
```

```
# Using the 'not' operator to check if movie night cannot proceed
cannot_have_movie_night = not can_have_movie_night

# Display the results
print(f"Can we have movie night? {can_have_movie_night}")
print(f"Cannot have movie night? {cannot_have_movie_night}")
```

```
(env_challenge) C:\PythonChallenges>python movie_night_planning.py
Can we have movie night? False
Cannot have movie night? True

(env_challenge) C:\PythonChallenges>
```

Figure 3.4: *Output of Python code: planning a movie night*

Understanding the Code

- The **and** operator ensures both conditions (**have_enough_snacks** and **weather_is_clear**) must be True for the movie night to happen.
- Since **weather_is_clear** is False, the entire condition becomes False.
- The not operator is used to reverse the result, checking if the movie night cannot happen.

Effective Use of Logical Operators

- **Combining Conditions**: Example - Checking if a user is logged in and has admin access
- **Filtering Data**: Example - Selecting customers who are over 18 or have a premium subscription
- **Controlling Program Flow**: Example - Running a function only if multiple conditions are met

Logical operators help your programs think and make decisions like humans do! They allow Python to combine multiple conditions into one decision-making step, making your programs smarter and more dynamic.

Assignment Operators

Assignment operators in Python are used to assign values to variables. While the basic = (equals sign) is the most common, Python also provides compound assignment operators that combine arithmetic operations with assignment.

These compound operators make code simpler and easier to read by performing calculations and updating the variable in one step.

Operator	Symbol	Description	Example	Equivalent To
Basic Assignment	=	Assigns a value to a variable	x = 10	-
Add and Assign	+=	Adds a value to the variable and stores the result	x += 5	x = x + 5
Subtract and Assign	-=	Subtracts a value and stores the result	x -= 3	x = x - 3
Multiply and Assign	*=	Multiplies the variable and stores the result	x *= 2	x = x * 2
Divide and Assign	/=	Divides the variable and stores the result as a float	x /= 4	x = x / 4
Modulus and Assign	%=	Finds the remainder and stores the result	x %= 3	x = x % 3

Table 3.6: *Logical operators in Python*

Examples of Assignment Operators in Action:

```
x = 10  # Basic assignment
print(x)  # Output: 10

x += 5  # Equivalent to x = x + 5
print(x)  # Output: 15

x -= 3  # Equivalent to x = x - 3
print(x)  # Output: 12

x *= 2  # Equivalent to x = x * 2
print(x)  # Output: 24

x /= 4  # Equivalent to x = x / 4
print(x)  # Output: 6.0

x %= 3  # Equivalent to x = x % 3
print(x)  # Output: 0
```

The Purpose of Assignment Operators:

- **Saves time**: Instead of writing x = x + 5, you can just write x += 5
- **Makes code cleaner**: Shortens repetitive operations
- **Improves readability**: Easier to understand at a glance

Assignment operators help streamline code while keeping it clear and efficient. You will use them frequently in loops, calculations, and real-time data updates!

Real-Life Example: Saving Money for a New Laptop

Imagine you are saving up for a new laptop. Each month, you set aside a fixed amount, but sometimes you might:

- Get a bonus and save extra
- Have an unexpected expense and need to adjust savings
- Decide to increase your savings goal

Python's assignment operators make it easy to manage and update your savings efficiently!

Python Code: Managing Your Savings

Let us simulate this scenario in Python using assignment operators:

```
# Initial savings and monthly saving goal
savings = 0
monthly_saving = 200

# January: Basic assignment for initial savings
savings = monthly_saving
print(f"Savings after January: ${savings}")

# February: Add and assign to include February's savings
savings += monthly_saving  # Equivalent to: savings = savings + monthly_saving
print(f"Savings after February: ${savings}")

# March: Received a bonus, deciding to save more
bonus_saving = 300
```

```
savings += bonus_saving
print(f"Savings after March with bonus: ${savings}")

# April: Unexpected expense, need to adjust the saving goal
unexpected_expense = 100
savings -= unexpected_expense  # Subtracting unexpected cost
print(f"Savings after April with expense: ${savings}")

# May: Decide to double the monthly savings
savings *= 2  # Equivalent to: savings = savings * 2
print(f"Savings after May with double saving: ${savings}")
```

```
(env_challenge) C:\PythonChallenges>python savings_for_laptop.py
Savings after January: $200
Savings after February: $400
Savings after March with bonus: $700
Savings after April with expense: $600
Savings after May with double saving: $1200

(env_challenge) C:\PythonChallenges>
```

Figure 3.5: *Output of Python code: saving money for a new laptop*

Month	Operation	Python Code	New Savings Balance
January	Start saving	savings = monthly_saving	$200
February	Add savings	savings += monthly_saving	$400
March	Add bonus	savings += bonus_saving	$700
April	Subtract expense	savings -= unexpected_expense	$600
May	Double savings	savings *= 2	$1,200

Table 3.7: *How assignment operators help in this example*

Key Takeaways:

- Assignment operators make tracking savings easier – No need to manually rewrite calculations.
- Real-world use case – Managing personal finance becomes simpler with Python.
- Improves code readability – Instead of writing savings = savings + monthly_saving, you can just write savings += monthly_saving.

This example shows how Python simplifies financial planning. Whether you are saving for a laptop, a vacation, or even tracking expenses, assignment operators help keep them organized and efficient!

Syntax and Program Structure

Now that you have explored how operators help manipulate data, it is time to focus on how to organize and structure your code. Just like a well-organized recipe ensures a dish turns out perfectly, Python follows a set of syntax rules and structural guidelines to keep code readable, efficient, and error-free.

Just like human languages have grammar and sentence structure, Python has syntax and program structure. Writing clear and structured code is essential for:

- Ensuring the Python interpreter understands and runs your code correctly
- Making your programs readable and maintainable

- Preventing errors and simplifying debugging

Understanding Python's syntax is the first step in writing efficient and error-free code!

The Importance of Syntax and Program Structure:

Aspect	Why It Matters
Readability	Clean and structured code is easier to understand and modify.
Functionality	Following Python's syntax ensures the program runs without errors.
Maintainability	Well-organized code is easier to debug, expand, and improve over time.

Table 3.8: *Importance of syntax in programming*

Real-Life Example: Building a House:

Think of writing Python code like building a house:

- **Syntax is like building codes**: If you do not follow them, the house will not stand.
- **Structure is like architecture**: It defines how the house is designed and arranged.

If you ignore construction rules, the house may collapse. Similarly, if you do not follow Python's syntax, the program will not run properly. A well-structured program is like a well-designed house. It is easier to navigate, modify, and maintain!

Basic Syntax Rules

Python is known for its simplicity and readability. Its syntax is designed to be clear and beginner-friendly while also powerful enough for advanced programmers.

Here are some key characteristics of Python syntax:

- Uses indentation instead of brackets (helps with readability)
- Requires proper spacing between elements
- Uses simple keywords for common tasks

Before diving deep, you might encounter examples that use advanced concepts such as classes and functions. Do not worry! These will be introduced gradually in later chapters. For now, focus on understanding the basics!

Python's syntax is designed to make programming easy to learn and enjoyable, ensuring a smooth learning journey as you progress.

Case Sensitivity

Python is case-sensitive, meaning it treats uppercase and lowercase letters as different. This applies to variable names, function names, class names, and other identifiers.

Being aware of case sensitivity is essential to avoid naming conflicts and ensure your code runs correctly.

How Case Sensitivity Affects Your Code:

In Python, two names that differ only in capitalization are considered completely different.

Example: Case Sensitivity in Variable Names:

```
myVariable = 10
MyVariable = 20
myvariable = 30
```

```
print(myVariable)  # Output: 10
print(MyVariable)  # Output: 20
print(myvariable)  # Output: 30
```

Here, **myVariable**, **MyVariable**, and **myvariable** are three different variables.

Case Sensitivity in Function and Class Names:

The same rule applies to functions and class names.

Example: Case Sensitivity in Function Names:

```
def calculate_distance():
    return "Calculating distance using the first function."

def Calculate_Distance():
    return "Calculating distance using the second function."

print(calculate_distance())  # Calls the first function
print(Calculate_Distance())  # Calls the second function
```

Here, **calculate_distance()** and **Calculate_Distance()** are two separate functions.

```
(env_challenge) C:\PythonChallenges>python case_sensitivity_in_func_name.py
Calculating distance using the first function.
Calculating distance using the second function.

(env_challenge) C:\PythonChallenges>
```

Figure 3.6: *Output of Python code case sensitivity in function and class names*

Example: Case Sensitivity in Class Names:

```
class Myclass:
    pass

class MyClass:
    pass

# `Myclass` and `MyClass` are two different classes.
```

Myclass and **MyClass** are treated as separate classes.

The Significance of Case Sensitivity:

Reason	Why It is Important
Avoiding Conflicts	Names that differ only by case can cause confusion, especially in large codebases.
Maintaining Readability	Python's naming conventions (for example, snake_case for variables, CapWords for classes) rely on case sensitivity.
Ensuring Consistency	Using a consistent naming style makes code easier to read and understand.

Table 3.9: *Importance of case sensitivity*

Key Takeaways:

- Python is case-sensitive, meaning Variable, variable, and VARIABLE are all different.
- Function and class names follow case rules, so **calculate_distance()** is not the same as **Calculate_Distance()**.
- Follow Python's naming conventions to avoid confusion and write cleaner code.

By being consistent and intentional with uppercase and lowercase letters, you can avoid common errors and write more readable and efficient Python programs!

Naming Conventions

Naming conventions in Python help maintain clear, readable, and organized code. They define how to name variables, functions, classes, constants, modules, and packages.

Following these conventions:

- Improves readability for yourself and others
- Ensures consistency across projects
- Prevents confusion when working with multiple functions and variables

Identifier	Convention	Example
Variables	snake_case (lowercase with underscores)	`my_variable = 10`
Functions	snake_case (lowercase with underscores)	`def calculate_total(): pass`
Constants	UPPER_CASE (uppercase with underscores)	`MAX_SIZE = 100`
Classes	CapWords (PascalCase / CamelCase)	`class ShoppingCart: pass`
Modules and Packages	Short, lowercase (optional underscores)	`import serializer`

Table 3.10: *Importance of naming conventions*

Variable Names:

- Use lowercase with underscores (snake_case)
- Choose descriptive names

```
my_variable = 10
total_cost = 200
```

Function Names:

- Use lowercase with underscores (snake_case)
- Make function names descriptive

```
def calculate_total():
    pass

def fetch_user_data():
    pass
```

Constants:

- Use all uppercase letters (`UPPER_CASE`)
- Separate words with underscores

```
MAX_SIZE = 100
DEFAULT_COLOR = "blue"
```

Class Names

- Use CapWords (also known as PascalCase or CamelCase)
- Capitalize each word without underscores

```
class ShoppingCart:
    pass

class UserProfile:
    pass
```

Module and Package Names

- Use lowercase names
- Use underscores only if needed for clarity

```
# Good module names
import serializer
import json_parser
```

The Importance of Naming Conventions

- Increases code readability and makes collaboration easier
- Maintains a standard coding style across teams and projects
- Prevents confusion in large codebases

Python does not enforce naming conventions, but following them helps you write cleaner and more professional code!

Indentation

Python uses indentation (whitespace at the start of a line) to group statements. Unlike other languages that use {} brackets, Python relies on indentation for structuring code.

- Proper indentation improves readability
- Incorrect indentation causes errors

The Importance of Indentation:

Aspect	Why It Matters
Structure and Scope	Defines code blocks, such as loops, functions, and conditionals
Readability	Makes code cleaner and easier to understand
Syntax Requirement	Python enforces indentation; wrong indentation leads to errors

Table 3.11: *Importance of indentation*

Indentation Rules:

- Use 4 spaces per indentation level
- Be consistent; do not mix spaces and tabs
- Nested blocks require additional indentation

Example of Correct Indentation:

```
def my_function():
    for i in range(5):
        print(i)
    print("Done")
```

Both **`print(i)`** and **`print("Done")`** are inside **`my_function()`**, but only **`print(i)`** is inside the loop.

Indentation in Conditional Statements:

- Indent blocks inside if, elif, and else

```
if x > 0:
    print("x is positive")
    if x >= 10:
        print("x is also greater than or equal to 10")
    else:
```

```
        print("x is positive but less than 10")
else:
    print("x is non-positive")
```

- Indentation helps visualize the logic of your code

Key Takeaways:

- Python is case-sensitive: Variable, variable, and VARIABLE are different
- Follow naming conventions: Use snake_case for variables/functions, CapWords for classes
- Indentation is mandatory: Use 4 spaces per level and keep it consistent
- Well-structured code improves readability, maintainability, and avoids errors

By following proper naming conventions and indentation rules, you will write clean, professional, and error-free Python code!

Comments and Documentation

Comments and documentation help explain code, making it easier for you and others to understand. Since Python ignores comments, they do not affect how the program runs, but they are essential for readability, debugging, and collaboration.

Types of Comments:

Python supports two main types of comments:

Type	Syntax	Usage
Single-line Comment	# Comment text	Used for short explanations on a single line
Multi-line Comment / Docstring	""" Multi-line text """	Used for longer explanations or documentation

Table 3.12: *Types of comments in Python*

Single-line Comments

- Use # at the beginning of a line to write a comment.
- Helps explain a specific line of code.

```
# This is a single-line comment
x = 5  # This comment follows a statement on the same line
```

Multi-line Comments (Docstrings)

- Python does not have a specific syntax for multi-line comments, but you can use triple quotes (""" or ''').
- Often used for documentation at the beginning of functions, classes, or modules.

```
"""
This is an example of a multi-line comment.
It can span multiple lines.
"""
```

Docstrings in Functions:

Docstrings describe the purpose of a function, class, or module.

```
def my_function():
    """This function does something useful."""
    pass
```

Tip: *Use docstrings for functions and classes, but # comments for inline explanations.*

The Role of Comments in Code:

Benefit	Why It Matters
Improves Readability	Helps programmers understand the purpose of a function or block of code
Simplifies Maintenance	Makes it easier to update and modify the code in the future
Aids Collaboration	Useful for teams working on the same project

Table 3.13: *Importance of comments*

Best Practices for Writing Comments:

- **Keep comments relevant and updated**: Outdated comments can be misleading.
- **Be concise**: Explain the why, not the what (the code itself shows what it does).
- **Use docstrings for documentation**: Reserve # comments for short explanations.

Key Takeaways:

- Single-line comments (#) are best for brief explanations.
- Multi-line comments (""" """) are used as docstrings for documentation.
- Well-commented code is easier to read, maintain, and collaborate on.

By following best practices, you ensure your code remains accessible and understandable, making future work easier for yourself and others!

Exercises and Challenges: Practice Problems and Solutions

Now that you have learned Python's syntax, structure, and basic operations, it is time to apply your knowledge through these hands-on exercises.

Practice Problem 1: Working with Variables and Data Types

- **Task**: Create variables to store details about your favorite movie.
- **Challenge**: Define variables for the movie's title (string), year released (integer), rating (float), and whether it is a sequel (boolean). Print a sentence using these variables to describe the movie.

Practice Problem 2: Arithmetic Operations Practice

- **Task**: Calculate the area of a rectangle.
- **Challenge:** Create two variables, length and width, with numerical values. Use multiplication to calculate the area and print the result.

Practice Problem 3: Using Basic Operators

- **Task**: Manage a shopping budget.
- **Challenge**: You have a budget of $100. Subtract the cost of items worth $25, $15, and $30 and display how much of the budget remains.

Practice Problem 4: Practicing with Integer Division and Modulus

- **Task**: Organize a classroom into groups.
- **Challenge**: You have 23 students and need to divide them into groups of four. Use integer

division to find how many full groups you can form, and the modulus operator to determine how many students will be left without a group. Print both results.

Practice Problem 5: Experimenting with Exponentiation

- **Task**: Simulate exponential growth.
- **Challenge**: A social media challenge starts with 1 participant. Each day, every participant convinces two new people to join. Use exponentiation (**) to calculate how many participants there will be after five days.

Practice Problem 6: Syntax Practice with Indentation

- **Task**: Fix indentation errors.
- **Challenge**: Given a snippet of Python code with incorrect indentation, correct the errors to ensure the code runs properly.

Practice Problem 7: Enhancing Code with Comments

- **Task**: Document a simple Python script.
- **Challenge**: Write a Python script that calculates the sum of three numbers. Add single-line comments to explain different parts of the code and include a multi-line comment at the beginning to describe the script's purpose.

These exercises are designed to boost your confidence in writing Python scripts and understanding fundamental programming concepts. Approach each problem carefully, and remember, practice is key to becoming a proficient coder!

Solutions to Practice Problems

The following are the solutions to the practice problems. Use these to check your answers or understand the approach if you run into difficulties.

Solution to Practice Problem 1: Working with Variables and Data Types

```
# Define variables for a favorite movie
title = "Inception"
year_released = 2010
rating = 8.8
is_sequel = False

# Print a sentence describing the movie
print(f"{title}, released in {year_released}, has a rating of {rating}.
Sequel: {is_sequel}.")
```

```
(env_challenge) C:\PythonChallenges>python exercise.py
Inception, released in 2010, has a rating of 8.8. Sequel: False.

(env_challenge) C:\PythonChallenges>
```

Figure 3.7: *Output of practice problem 1*

Solution to Practice Problem 2: Arithmetic Operations Practice

```
# Define variables for the dimensions of the rectangle
length = 10  # Example value
width = 5  # Example value

# Calculate the area of the rectangle
area = length * width
```

```
# Print the result
print(f"The area of the rectangle is: {area}")
```

```
(env_challenge) C:\PythonChallenges>python exercise.py
The area of the rectangle is: 50

(env_challenge) C:\PythonChallenges>
```

Figure 3.8: *Output of practice problem 2*

Solution to Practice Problem 3: Using Basic Operators

```
# Starting budget
budget = 100

# Subtract the cost of items from the budget
budget -= 25  # Item 1
budget -= 15  # Item 2
budget -= 30  # Item 3

# Display the remaining budget
print(f"Remaining budget: ${budget}")
```

```
(env_challenge) C:\PythonChallenges>python exercise.py
Remaining budget: $30

(env_challenge) C:\PythonChallenges>
```

Figure 3.9: *Output of practice problem 3*

Solution to Practice Problem 4: Practicing with Integer Division and Modulus

```
# Total number of students
students = 23

# Determine groups and remaining students
groups = students // 4
remaining_students = students % 4

# Print the results
print(f"Number of groups: {groups}")
print(f"Students without a group: {remaining_students}")
```

```
(env_challenge) C:\PythonChallenges>python exercise.py
Number of groups: 5
Students without a group: 3

(env_challenge) C:\PythonChallenges>
```

Figure 3.10: *Output of practice problem 4*

Solution to Practice Problem 5: Experimenting with Exponentiation

```
# Initial participant
participants = 1

# Each participant convinces 2 new people for 5 days
growth_factor = 2
```

```
days = 5

# Calculate total participants after 5 days
total_participants = participants * (growth_factor ** days)

# Print the result
print(f"Total participants after 5 days: {total_participants}")
```

```
(env_challenge) C:\PythonChallenges>python exercise.py
Total participants after 5 days: 32

(env_challenge) C:\PythonChallenges>
```

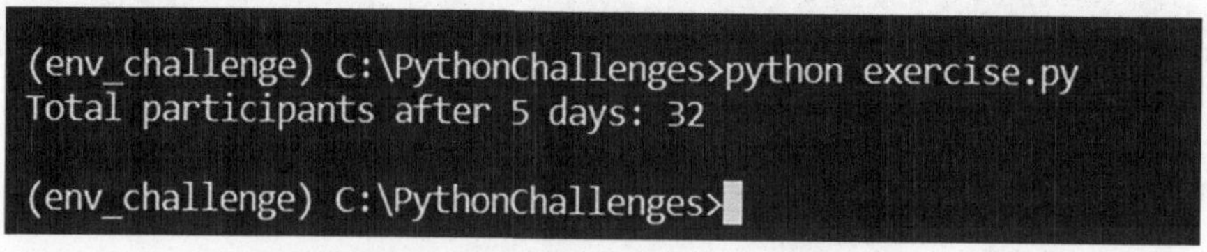

Figure 3.11: *Output of practice problem 5*

Solution to Practice Problem 6: Syntax Practice with Indentation

The solution depends on the provided code, but the key is ensuring all statements within the same block are properly indented.

```
if True:
    print("This is correctly indented.")

if False:
    print("This is also correctly indented.")
```

```
(env_challenge) C:\PythonChallenges>python exercise.py
This is correctly indented.

(env_challenge) C:\PythonChallenges>
```

Figure 3.12: *Output of practice problem 6*

Solution to Practice Problem 7: Enhancing Code with Comments

```
"""
This script calculates the sum of three numbers.
It demonstrates the use of comments in Python scripts.
"""

# Define three numbers
num1 = 5
num2 = 10
num3 = 15

# Calculate the sum of the numbers
total_sum = num1 + num2 + num3

# Print the total sum
print(f"The total sum is: {total_sum}")
```

```
(env_challenge) C:\PythonChallenges>python exercise.py
The total sum is: 30

(env_challenge) C:\PythonChallenges>
```

Figure 3.13: *Output of practice problem 7*

Conclusion

Congratulations on completing this chapter! You have now built a strong foundation in Python programming by learning about variables, data types, operators, and syntax rules. These concepts are essential for writing clear, efficient, and structured programs.

By practicing how to store and manipulate data, perform calculations, and follow Python's syntax, you have taken the first step toward writing real programs. The problem-solving skills from the previous chapter on algorithms and flowcharts have now been applied to actual Python code, making your programs both logical and functional.

With variables, operators, and syntax in your toolkit, you are now ready to add logic to your programs. In the next chapter, you will explore control structures such as loops and conditionals and key tools for writing dynamic and interactive programs!

Till then, Keep Calm and Let us Tame the Python!!

Multiple-Choice Questions

1. Which of the following is a valid variable assignment in Python?
   a. `3x = "Hello"`
   b. `my-variable = 123`
   c. `greeting_message = "Hello, World!"`
   d. `float = 3.14`
2. What data type does the value 22.5 belong to in Python?
   a. int
   b. float
   c. string
   d. double
3. Which operator is used for exponentiation in Python?
   a. ^
   b. **
   c. %%
   d. //
4. Given x = 5 and y = 2, what is the result of x // y?
   a. 2.5
   b. 2
   c. 3
   d. None of the above
5. Which of the following correctly checks if a is not equal to b?
   a. a != b
   b. a <> b

   c. a =! b

   d. a not= b

6. How do you add a single-line comment in Python?

   a. Using <!-- -->

   b. Using /* */

   c. Using #

   d. Using //

7. Which of the following demonstrates compound assignment for subtraction?

   a. x = x - 5

   b. x -= 5

   c. x--

   d. x =- 5

8. What does the % operator calculate?

   a. Percentage

   b. Exponentiation

   c. Modulus (remainder of division)

   d. Multiplication

9. Which data type would you use to represent the value True or False in Python?

   a. String

   b. Boolean

   c. Int

   d. Float

10. In Python, how do you indicate that a block of code is part of the same function?

    a. By placing the code in brackets { }

    b. By using the keyword block

    c. By indenting the code uniformly

    d. By separating the code with a semicolon ;

Answers

1. c
2. b
3. b
4. b
5. a

6. c
7. b
8. c
9. b
10. c

Points to Remember

- Variables allow you to label and reuse data values in your code, making it more dynamic and versatile.
- Python has four core data types: integers (int), floating-point numbers (`float`), strings (`str`), and booleans (`bool`), each with a specific purpose for describing information.
- Python's arithmetic operators, such as addition (+), subtraction (-), multiplication (*), and division (/), allow for direct mathematical operations on data.
- Python's modulus operator (%) and exponentiation operator (**) demonstrate its ability to handle complex calculations.
- Comparison operators like equal to (==) and greater than (>) help make decisions in programs by comparing values.
- Logical operators (and, or, not) combine Boolean expressions to form complicated conditional statements that guide execution based on numerous criteria.
- Assignment operators (=) and compound assignments (+=, -=) simplify code and improve maintainability.
- Python relies on indentation to define blocks of code, highlighting the need for a clear and consistent coding style.
- Python is case-sensitive, which affects how variable names are defined and called in code.
- Comments, both single-line (#) and multi-line (""" """), play a significant role in documenting and explaining your code for others and yourself in the future.

Further Reading

If you would like to explore Python programming and data types in more detail, here are two excellent resources:

1. **Python Data Types – W3Schools:**

   https://www.w3schools.com/python/python_datatypes.asp

   A beginner-friendly guide that provides an in-depth look at Python data types, with examples and interactive tutorials.

2. **Python Syntax and Basics – Real Python:**

   https://realpython.com/python-first-steps/

   An easy-to-follow introduction to Python's syntax, including variables, data types, and how to write clean and readable code.

CHAPTER 4
Making Choices and Repeating Actions

Introduction

Now that you have learned how to work with variables, data types, and operators, it is time to make your programs more dynamic. So far, your code has followed a fixed sequence of instructions, but real-world situations often require decisions and repetition.

So far, you have learned how to write simple programs that follow a fixed set of instructions from start to finish. But real-world scenarios are not always that straightforward. Decisions need to be made, actions get repeated, and situations change based on different conditions.

Think about a self-checkout machine at a grocery store. It does not treat every customer the same way. It scans items, applies discounts, requests payment, and even reminds you if you forget your change. Or consider a fitness tracker; it does not just display numbers; it reacts to your steps, adjusts your goals, and notifies you when you have hit a milestone.

In this chapter, you will start writing programs that can do the same: make choices, repeat actions when needed, and adapt to different situations.

Structure

In this chapter, the following topics will be covered:

- Control Structures Overview
- Understanding Conditional Statements
    - If Statements
    - Else and Elif Statements
    - Combining If, Elif, and Else for Multi-Way Decisions
    - Understanding Nested If-Else Statements
- Exploring Loop Structures
    - For Loops
    - While Loops
- The Essence of Loop Flow Control
    - Real-Life Examples of Loop Flow Control
    - Concept Introduction: Mastering Flow Control with Continue and Break
    - Practical Exercise: Text-based Menu with Exit/Continue Options
- Nested Loops and Conditions
    - Understanding Nested Loops: The Clock Analogy

Control Structures Overview

Imagine you are following a morning routine. If it is cold, you wear a jacket; if it is warm, you wear a t-shirt. You also brush your teeth every day, repeating the action until it is done. Programs work the same way; they make decisions and repeat tasks using control structures.

Control structures guide how a program runs. Think of them like traffic lights. They tell the program when to stop, when to go, and which way to turn.

- Conditional Statements help a program make decisions. It chooses what to do based on a condition, like deciding what to wear based on the weather.
- Loops allow a program to repeat a task many times, such as brushing each tooth until your whole mouth is clean.

Control structures help programs think and act like real-world systems. Understanding them will make your code smarter and more efficient.

Python makes it easy to write programs that make decisions and repeat actions. Instead of following a fixed set of instructions, a program can choose what to do based on different situations or repeat a task until it is done.

In the upcoming sections, you will dive into conditional statements and loops, learning how they help programs become more flexible and efficient.

Understanding Conditional Statements

In programming, conditional statements allow a program to make decisions. They help the program decide what to do next based on the current situation, just like how people make choices in everyday life. When a program checks a condition, it chooses the next step based on whether that condition is true or false.

Importance of Conditional Logic:

Conditional logic is at the heart of programming because it helps programs react to different situations. Just like you decide what to do based on the weather, wearing a jacket if it is cold and shorts if it is hot. Programs also follow different paths depending on conditions. This ability makes programs adaptable and responsive to changes in data and user input.

Understanding Conditions:

Conditions are questions the program asks to decide what to do. For example, a program might check:

- Is the user's password correct?
- Is the temperature above 30°C?
- Did the player win the game?

If the answer is true, one action happens. If it is false, a different action happens. Conditions can be simple comparisons (like checking if one number is bigger than another) or complex decisions involving multiple factors.

Making Multiple Decisions:

Sometimes, a program needs to make several decisions in a row. For example, a self-driving car does not just check if there is a red light; it also looks for pedestrians, speed limits, and road signs before deciding whether to stop or keep moving. Similarly, programs often check many conditions together to find the best action to take.

Handling More Than Two Choices:

While many decisions are yes/no (binary choices), real-world problems often require more options. A food delivery app, for example, does not just check if an order is "delivered" or "not delivered;" it may also track if the order is "preparing," "on the way," or "delayed." Programming allows for more complex decision-making, helping programs handle different situations smoothly.

Significance of Conditional Statements:

Conditional statements make programs smart, flexible, and useful. Without them, a program would follow the same steps every time, unable to react to changes. Learning how to use conditions effectively is key to building programs that can solve real-world problems and make intelligent decisions.

If Statements

In the previous section, you explored how conditional statements help programs make decisions, just like how you make choices in everyday life. Now, you will look at the most basic and essential conditional statement: the if statement.

Imagine you are driving to a friend's house for dinner. Before leaving, you check a traffic app on your phone. If the main road is clear, you take it because it is the fastest route. But if the app shows heavy traffic, you choose an alternate route to avoid delays. This is exactly how an if statement works in programming: it helps a program make decisions based on certain conditions.

Understanding the If Statement

In Python, the if statement is the foundation of decision-making. It allows a program to check a condition and decide whether to execute a specific block of code. This makes programs dynamic and responsive to different situations.

Writing an If Statement in Python

The **basic structure** of an if statement in Python is:

if condition:

```
    # Code to execute if the condition is true
```

- The if keyword starts the statement.
- The condition is checked (it must evaluate to True or False).
- If the condition is true, the indented code block runs.
- If the condition is false, the code block is skipped.

Example: Checking the Weather

```
temperature = 30  # Temperature in degrees Celsius

if temperature > 25:
    print("It's a hot day! Stay hydrated.")
```

Since temperature > 25 is **true**, the message is printed. If the temperature were **lower than 25**, nothing would happen.

Breaking Down the Decision Process

This decision follows a simple pattern, just like in programming:

- **Checking the Condition:** Looking at the traffic app is like a program checking a condition. The program examines data to decide what to do next.
- **Making a Decision:** If the road is clear, take the fastest route. This is like an if statement executing a block of code when a condition is true.
- **Choosing an Alternative:** If the road is blocked, take another route. In programming, this is like using else to run a different set of instructions when the first condition is false.

Executing an If Statement

When a program encounters an if statement, it follows a simple process:

- If the condition is true, the program runs the indented block of code under the if statement.
- If the condition is false, the program skips the if block and continues with the rest of the code.

Importance of Conditional Logic

Just like you use information to make decisions in daily life, computers use if statements to decide which actions to take.

If statements are used in many real-world programming tasks, such as:

- Checking if a user entered the correct password
- Displaying different messages based on user input
- Adjusting game difficulty based on a player's score

They make programs smarter and more interactive, allowing them to respond dynamically to different situations.

Practical Exercise: Identifying Positive or Negative Numbers

Now that you have seen how if statements help programs make decisions, let us apply this concept in a simple Python program. Just like checking traffic conditions before choosing a route, the program will check if a number is positive or negative and respond accordingly.

Task Overview:

Write a Python script that determines whether a number is positive or negative. However, instead of using an else clause, you will use two separate if statements. This approach ensures that each condition is checked independently, reinforcing the concept of conditional logic.

Steps to Follow:

1. **Define a Number:** Store a number in a variable. You can choose any number for this exercise.
2. **Check for Positivity:** Use an if statement to check if the number is greater than zero. If true, print "`The number is positive`."
3. **Check for Negativity:** Use another if statement (instead of else) to check if the number is less than zero. If true, print "`The number is negative`."
4. **What About Zero?** This exercise does not specifically handle the case where the number is exactly zero. Since zero is neither positive nor negative, neither of the conditions will run, showing how programs handle cases that do not match a given condition.

```
# Define the number to check
number = -5

# Check if the number is positive
if number > 0:
    print("The number is positive.")

# Check if the number is negative
if number < 0:
    print("The number is negative.")
```

Understanding the Code:

In this example, the program first stores a number and then uses two separate if statements to check whether it is positive or negative. Since each condition is evaluated on its own, there is no else statement, which means if the number is zero, neither condition will be met, and nothing will be printed.

This method helps reinforce how if statements work independently, allowing programs to evaluate multiple conditions separately. Understanding this logic is an important step in learning how programs make decisions and respond to different situations.

Else and Elif Statements

So far, you have seen how if statements allow programs to make decisions. But in many situations, you need more than just two possible outcomes. This is where else and elif (short for "else if") come in, allowing programs to handle multiple conditions in a clear and organized way.

Understanding Else and Elif Statements

An if statement works well for simple yes/no decisions, but real-world scenarios often involve more choices. For example, when deciding what to wear, you do not just check if it is cold, you also consider if it is raining, warm, or windy. In programming, else and elif statements help structure these types of decisions clearly and efficiently.

Writing an Else Statement in Python:

The else statement acts as a backup plan; it runs only if none of the previous conditions are met. Think of it as a default option that ensures the program always has an action to take.

Functioning of Else Statements:

- It does not require a condition, it simply runs when all previous conditions are false.
- It must be placed at the end of an if-elif structure.

Example: Checking the Temperature

```
temperature = 10

if temperature > 30:
    print("It's a hot day!")
else:
    print("It's not a hot day.")
```

If the temperature is greater than 30, the program prints "`It's a hot day!`". Otherwise, it prints "`It's not a hot day`."

Writing an Elif Statement in Python

The elif statement allows you to check multiple conditions in sequence. Instead of writing multiple separate if statements, elif helps structure the decision process clearly and efficiently.

Functioning of Elif Statements:

- It follows an if statement and comes before the else statement (if one is used).
- Each elif has its own condition, and Python checks them one by one in order.
- As soon as Python finds a true condition, it executes that block of code and skips the rest.

Example: Checking the Temperature with Multiple Conditions

```
temperature = 10

if temperature > 30:
    print("It's a hot day!")
elif temperature > 20:
    print("It's a warm day.")
elif temperature > 10:
    print("It's a cool day.")
else:
    print("It's a cold day.")
```

Understanding the code:

- If the temperature is above 30, it prints "`It's a hot day!`".
- If not, it checks if it is above 20, printing "`It's a warm day.`".
- If not, it checks if it is above 10, printing "`It's a cool day.`".
- If none of the conditions are met, it defaults to the else block, printing "`It's a cold day.`".

Combining If, Elif, and Else for Multi-Way Decisions

Using if, elif, and else together allows programs to handle multiple possibilities efficiently. This works just like making layered decisions in daily life.

For example, deciding what to wear could involve several factors:

- If it is raining, wear a raincoat.
- If it is cold but not raining, wear a jacket.
- If it is warm, wear shorts.
- If none of these apply, just wear jeans.

In programming, else and elif help structure such decisions in a clear and readable way.

Importance of Else and Elif Statements:

- They make programs more flexible and efficient by grouping multiple conditions together.
- They improve readability by organizing decision-making logically instead of using separate if statements.
- They allow programs to respond dynamically to real-world situations, making them more intelligent and interactive.

By mastering if, elif, and else, you will be able to write smarter programs that can handle complex decision-making and user inputs effectively.

Practical Exercise: Categorizing Age Groups

Now that you have explored how if, elif, and else statements help programs make decisions, let us apply this concept to a real-world example. Just like how you decide what to wear based on the weather, programs can also categorize information based on conditions. In this exercise, you will assign a person to an age group based on their age.

Task Overview:

Create a Python program that asks the user for their age and categorizes them into one of four groups:

- Child: 0–12 years
- Teenager: 13–19 years
- Adult: 20–64 years
- Senior: 65 years and older

This will help you see how if, elif, and else work together to handle multiple conditions in a single decision-making process.

Steps to Follow:

1. **Ask for the User's Age**: Use `input()` to collect the user's age. Since input values are stored as text (strings) by default, you need to convert the value to an integer.
2. **Use Conditional Statements**: Start with an if statement to check if the person is 12 or younger. Then, use elif statements for teenagers and adults. Finally, use an else statement for seniors.
3. **Print the Age Group**: Display the correct age category based on the condition met.

```
# Ask for the user's age
age = int(input("Please enter your age: "))

# Determine the age group
if age <= 12:
    print("You are a child.")
elif age <= 19:
    print("You are a teenager.")
elif age <= 64:
    print("You are an adult.")
else:
    print("You are a senior.")
```

Understanding the Code:

This program checks the age step by step, moving through different categories:

- The if statement checks if the person is 12 or younger and labels them as a child.
- If the first condition is false, the elif statement checks if they are 19 or younger, categorizing them as a teenager.
- If both previous conditions are false, another elif statement checks if they are 64 or younger, labeling them as an adult.
- If none of the above conditions are met, the else statement automatically classifies the person as a senior.

This exercise shows the power of elif and else statements in organizing multiple conditions clearly. Instead of using separate if statements, structure the decision-making process logically so that only one condition runs per input.

By mastering conditional statements, you can build programs that respond dynamically to different situations, making them more efficient and user-friendly. In the next section, you will explore more complex ways to refine decision-making and improve program logic.

Understanding Nested If-Else Statements

So far, you have learned how if, elif, and else statements allow a program to make decisions. However, some situations require more than a simple yes/no decision. Nested if-else statements help handle multiple conditions within a single block, allowing for more detailed and specific decision-making.

Purpose of Nested If-Else Statements

Sometimes, a decision depends on a previous decision. For example, if you are choosing a movie, you might first check its age rating and then look at its genre before deciding if it is suitable. In programming, nested if-else statements allow this kind of step-by-step decision-making.

Example: Movie Classification Based on Age Rating and Genre

Let us write a Python program that classifies movies based on age rating and genre:

```
# Ask the user for the movie's age rating and genre
age_rating = input("Enter the age rating (G, PG, PG-13, R): ")
genre = input("Enter the genre (Action, Comedy, Drama, Documentary): ")

# First decision: Check the age rating
if age_rating == "G" or age_rating == "PG":
    print("This movie is suitable for younger audiences.")

    # Nested decision: Check the genre
    if genre == "Action":
        print("Expect some mild action scenes.")
    elif genre == "Comedy":
        print("Prepare for laughs suitable for all ages.")
    else:
        print("A wholesome film for family viewing.")

elif age_rating == "PG-13":
    print("This movie is suitable for teens and above.")

    # Nested decision: Check the genre
    if genre == "Action":
        print("Moderate action scenes with minimal sensitive content.")
    elif genre == "Drama":
        print("Mature themes with strong storytelling.")
    else:
        print("Some material may not be suitable for children under 13.")

else:
    print("This movie is restricted to adult audiences.")

    # Nested decision: Check the genre
    if genre == "Documentary":
        print("Insightful content with mature themes.")
    else:
        print("Content strictly for adults.")
```

Breaking Down the Code:

1. The first if statement checks the age rating to determine general suitability.
2. Within each age category, a nested if-else block provides additional details based on the genre.
3. This layered approach helps the program make more specific decisions rather than just a simple yes/no classification.

Significance of Nested If-Else Statements

Nested if-else statements allow programs to handle complex decision-making in an organized way. Instead of checking conditions separately, group related conditions together, making the logic clearer and easier to manage.

A Quick Note on User Input

In the preceding example, you used user input to allow the program to accept information from the user. Although you have not discussed input handling in depth yet, let us take a brief look at it.

Understanding User Input:

User input allows programs to interact dynamically with users instead of running with fixed values. This makes programs more flexible and personalized.

Functioning of User Input:

In Python, the **`input()`** function is used to capture user input:

```
user_name = input("Please enter your name: ")
print(f"Hello, {user_name}!")
```

Here, the program asks the user for their name and then prints a greeting using the entered value.

Converting User Input:

By default, **`input()`** returns a string. If you need to work with numbers, you must convert the input:

```
age = input("Please enter your age: ")
age = int(age)  # Convert input from string to integer
```

Without this conversion, Python would treat the input as text instead of a number, which could cause errors in calculations.

Looking Ahead:

You will explore user input in greater detail in a future chapter, covering best practices, error handling, and interactive program design. For now, knowing how to capture and process user input is a great starting point as you continue learning how to build dynamic and user-friendly applications.

Exploring Loop Structures

So far, you have learned how programs make decisions using conditional statements. But in many cases, you also need programs to repeat actions multiple times. This is where loops come in. Loops allow you to automate repetitive tasks, making programs more efficient and dynamic.

To understand loops better, let us look at some real-life examples of repetition that you encounter every day.

Repetition in Daily Life: The Morning Routine

Think about your morning routine. Waking up, brushing your teeth, eating breakfast, and checking messages. You repeat these actions every day. Each step is like a loop iteration, continuing until your morning routine is complete. In programming, loops work the same way, running a set of instructions until a certain condition is met.

Decision-Making and Repetition: Choosing What to Wear

Every morning, you decide what to wear based on the weather, the occasion, or your mood. This is another example of a loop: you check conditions, go through different options, and repeat the process every day. Similarly, in programming, loops evaluate conditions and repeat actions until the desired outcome is reached.

Practice and Improvement: Learning a Skill

When learning a new skill, such as playing an instrument or a sport, you practice repeatedly to improve. You might repeat the same drills until you reach a certain skill level. This is just like a loop in programming; it keeps running until a specific goal is achieved.

Importance of Loops in Programming

Loops are essential in programming because they help:

- Automate repetitive tasks, reducing manual effort and errors
- Process large amounts of data, allowing efficient handling of information
- Enhance user interaction, making programs more dynamic and responsive
- Implement algorithms, enabling structured and logical execution of tasks
- Optimize resource usage, improving efficiency and performance

Loops in Programming: A Natural Concept

As you explore different types of loops, keep in mind that looping is not a difficult or abstract concept; it is something you experience every day. Understanding loops helps you build smarter programs that can handle repetitive tasks efficiently, just like you do in real life.

In the next sections, you will dive into the specific types of loops and their real-world applications, making it easier to see how they bring programs to life.

For Loops

In programming, it is often required to repeat an action multiple times. Instead of writing the same code over and over, you will use loops to handle repetition efficiently. One of the most commonly used loops in Python is the for loop, which iterates through a sequence and performs an action for each item.

Real-Life Example: Baking Cookies

Imagine you are baking cookies. You have enough dough to make 48 cookies, but your tray can hold only 12 cookies at a time. To bake all the cookies, you:

1. Place 12 cookies on the tray.
2. Bake them.
3. Remove the baked cookies and repeat the process until all 48 cookies are done.

This is just like a for loop in programming. You know in advance that you need to repeat the baking process 4 times (48 cookies : 12 per batch). Similarly, a for loop repeats an action for a fixed number of times or for each item in a sequence.

Understanding For Loops

A for loop makes it easy to perform an action on each item in a sequence, such as a list, tuple, or string. It is a key tool for automation and repetitive tasks in programming.

Functionalities of a For Loop:

A for loop consists of four key components:

- **The `for` keyword**: Starts the loop
- **The iteration variable**: Stores the current value in the sequence
- **The sequence**: The collection of items the loop goes through (for example, a list or a range of numbers)
- **The code block**: The set of instructions that runs for each item in the sequence

Writing a For Loop

The basic structure of a for loop in Python is:

```
for variable in sequence:
    # Code to execute in each iteration
```

Each time the loop runs, the variable takes the next value from the sequence, and the code inside the loop is executed.

Example: Printing Numbers Using a For Loop

```
# A simple for loop that prints numbers from 0 to 4
for i in range(5):
    print(i)
```

Output:

```
0
1
2
3
4
```

Each number is printed one at a time, showing how the loop iterates through the sequence.

Breaking Down the Code:

1. **Starting the Loop:**
   a. The **`for`** keyword starts the loop, and i is the iteration variable.
   b. The **`range(5)`** function generates a sequence of numbers from 0 to 4 (5 numbers total).
2. **Executing the Loop:**
   a. In the first iteration, **`i = 0`**, and the code inside the loop (**`print(i)`**) runs.
   b. The loop moves to the next number, updating **`i`** to **`1`**, and prints it.
   c. This continues until **`i`** reaches **`4`**.

3. **Ending the Loop:**
    a. Once all numbers in the sequence are processed, the loop stops automatically, and the program moves on.

Importance of For Loops:

For loops help automate repetitive tasks and make code shorter and more efficient. They are commonly used for:

- Processing lists of data (for example, printing each student's name from a list)
- Repeating an action a set number of times (for example, sending five reminder emails)
- Analyzing data (for example, summing up numbers in a list)

By mastering for loops, you can write smarter and more efficient programs that handle repetition automatically instead of manually repeating the same steps.

Practical Exercise: Printing Squares of Numbers

Now that you understand for loops, let us apply them to a real-world task. Loops are great for handling repetitive calculations, and in this exercise, you will use a for loop to calculate and print the squares of numbers in a given range.

Task Overview:

Write a Python program that:

1. Defines a range of numbers (for example, 1 to 10).
2. Uses a for loop to go through each number in the range.
3. Calculates the square of each number by multiplying it by itself.
4. Prints the result in a clear format.

This will help you see how for loops automate calculations, making repetitive tasks much easier.

Steps to Follow:

1. Set a start and end point for the range of numbers.
2. Use a for loop to iterate through the numbers in that range.
3. Calculate the square of each number inside the loop.
4. Print the result, showing the original number and its square.

```
# Define the range of numbers
start = 1
end = 10

# Iterate through each number in the range
for number in range(start, end + 1):
    # Calculate the square of the number
    square = number * number
    # Print the square of the number
    print(f"The square of {number} is {square}.")
```

Understanding the Code:

1. **Defining the Range**:
    a. Set **`start = 1`** and **`end = 10`**, meaning this loop will cover numbers from 1 to 10.

   b. The `range(start, end + 1)` function generates numbers from start to end (inclusive).

2. **Using the For Loop**:
   a. The loop goes through each number in the range one at a time.
   b. The iteration variable (number) takes on each value in the sequence.

3. **Calculating and Printing the Square**:
   a. The square is calculated using `number * number`.
   b. Print a message for each number in the range, showing both the original number and its square.

Example Output:

```
The square of 1 is 1.
The square of 2 is 4.
The square of 3 is 9.
The square of 4 is 16.
The square of 5 is 25.
The square of 6 is 36.
The square of 7 is 49.
The square of 8 is 64.
The square of 9 is 81.
The square of 10 is 100.
```

This exercise demonstrates how loops can process sequences efficiently. Instead of writing 10 separate calculations manually, automate the process with just a few lines of code.

For loops are widely used for:

- Mathematical calculations (like this exercise)
- Processing lists of data (for example, analyzing test scores)
- Automating repetitive tasks (for example, generating reports)

Mastering loops will help you write smarter and more efficient programs. In the next section, you will explore while loops, which offer another way to handle repetition in programming.

While Loops

In programming, while loops are used to repeat a task as long as a condition remains true. Unlike for loops, which iterate over a fixed sequence, while loops continue running until a condition is no longer met. This makes them useful for situations where the number of repetitions is unknown in advance.

Real-Life Example: Filling a Glass of Water

Imagine filling a glass of water. You do not decide beforehand to pour three or four times. Instead, you keep pouring until the glass is full.

Here is how this mirrors a while loop:

- **Condition:** The glass is not full.
- **Action:** Pour water into the glass.
- **Repetition:** Keep pouring as long as the condition is true.
- **Termination:** Stop pouring when the glass is full (condition becomes false).

Similarly, in programming, a while loop keeps running until a certain condition is false.

Understanding While Loops

While loops allow a program to repeat a task without knowing in advance how many times it will run. This makes them useful for:

- Waiting for user input (for example, waiting for a correct password)
- Monitoring data (for example, checking for changes in a stock price)
- Running background operations (for example, a game running until the player loses)

Functionalities of a While Loop:

A while loop consists of three key components:

- **The `while` keyword**: Starts the loop.
- **The condition**: A logical test that is checked before each iteration.
- **The loop body**: The indented block of code that runs while the condition is true.

Writing a While Loop in Python:

The basic structure of a while loop in Python is:

```
while condition:
    # Code to execute while the condition is true
```

Each time the loop runs, the condition is checked before executing the code inside the loop. If the condition is false, the loop stops.

Example: Countdown Timer

Let us write a simple countdown timer using a while loop:

```
# Initiation: Set the starting point of the countdown
counter = 5

# The while loop runs as long as counter is greater than 0
while counter > 0:
    print(counter)  # Print the current countdown number
    counter -= 1  # Reduce counter by 1 in each loop iteration

# When the loop ends, print the final message
print("Countdown finished!")
```

Output:

```
5
4
3
2
1
Countdown finished!
```

Breaking Down the Code

1. **Initiation:**
    a. The variable counter starts at 5.
    b. This value sets the starting point for the countdown.
2. **Execution:**
    a. The while loop checks if **`counter > 0`**.

   b. If true, the loop prints the number and moves to the next step.

3. **Progression:**

   a. `counter -= 1` reduces the value of counter by 1 in each loop cycle.

4. **Re-evaluation:**

   a. The loop checks the updated value of counter.

   b. If counter is still greater than 0, the loop repeats.

5. **Conclusion:**

   a. When counter reaches 0, the condition (`counter > 0`) becomes false, and the loop stops.

   b. The program then prints "Countdown finished!".

Importance of While Loops:

While loops are useful in many situations where the number of repetitions is not known beforehand. They are widely used in:

- **User interactions**: Waiting for user input until a correct response is given.
- **Data processing**: Running calculations until a certain result is reached.
- **Real-time applications**: Continuously monitoring conditions, such as a stock price or game state.

While loops help programmers write flexible and dynamic programs that adapt to different situations, making them essential for building interactive applications.

Practical Exercise: Number Guessing Game

Now that you understand while loops, let us put them into practice by creating an interactive number guessing game. This game will use a while loop to repeatedly ask the user to guess a randomly generated number until they get it right.

Exercise Objective:

The goal of this exercise is to build a Python program that:

- Generates a random number within a specified range
- Continuously asks the user to guess the number using a while loop
- Provides hints if the guess is too high or too low
- Repeats the process until the correct number is guessed
- Congratulates the user once they guess correctly

This exercise will help you see how while loops handle repeated user input while making the program interactive.

Steps to Follow:

1. **Set up the game**: Import the random module and generate a random number.
2. **Start a while loop**: Keep asking the user for a guess until they get the correct answer.
3. **Get user input**: Read the user's guess.
4. **Check the guess**:
   - If the guess is too low, tell the user to try again.

- If the guess is too high, tell the user to try again.
- If the guess is correct, end the loop and congratulate them.

5. **Provide feedback**: After every incorrect guess, help the user adjust by telling them if the number is too high or too low.

```
import random

# Initialize the game
start, end = 1, 100
secret_number = random.randint(start, end)
guess = None

# Start the guessing game loop
while guess != secret_number:
    # Get user input
    guess = int(input(f"Guess the number between {start} and {end}: "))

    # Evaluate the guess
    if guess < secret_number:
        print("Too low, try again!")
    elif guess > secret_number:
        print("Too high, try again!")
    else:
        # The guess is correct, congratulate the user
        print("Congratulations! You guessed the correct number!")

# Game over
print("Thank you for playing the guessing game.")
```

Breaking Down the Code:

1. **Generating the Random Number:**
    a. Use **`random.randint(start, end)`** to generate a secret number between 1 and 100.
2. **Starting the While Loop**:
    a. The loop keeps running as long as **`guess != secret_number`**.
3. **Handling User Input:**
    a. The program asks the user to input a guess.
    b. The input is converted to an integer so you can compare it to the secret number.
4. **Checking the Guess:**
    a. If the guess is too low, the user is told to guess higher.
    b. If the guess is too high, the user is told to guess lower.
    c. If the guess is correct, the loop ends, and a congratulatory message is displayed.
5. **Game Over:**
    a. Once the user guesses correctly, the program prints "**`Thank you for playing the guessing game.`**"

This game demonstrates how while loops allow programs to continuously take user input and provide feedback. Such loops are commonly used in:

- Interactive applications that require user engagement

- Game development, where conditions change dynamically
- Data validation, ensuring the correct input before proceeding

By mastering while loops, you can build interactive, dynamic, and user-friendly programs. In the next section, you will explore how to choose between for loops and while loops, helping you apply them effectively in different scenarios.

The Essence of Loop Flow Control

So far, you have explored for and while loops, which allow programs to repeat tasks efficiently. However, just like in real life, you sometimes need to adjust your path while repeating an action. This is where loop control mechanisms come into play, helping programs skip certain iterations or exit loops early based on changing conditions.

Loops are not just about repetition. They are about smart repetition, ensuring that only the necessary steps are performed while avoiding unnecessary ones.

Real-Life Examples of Loop Flow Control

Following are a few real life examples where loop flow control can be realized.

Curating a Music Playlist:

Imagine you are making a road trip playlist. You start with a list of songs, but as you listen, you skip certain tracks because they do not match your mood. Instead of stopping the playlist, you jump to the next song.

This is just like using loop control in programming. You might want to skip certain loop iterations without stopping the whole loop.

Planning a Road Trip:

Now, consider a road trip with multiple stops. If you see a roadblock, you might choose to skip a planned stop and continue to the next one. In extreme cases, you might even end the trip early if something urgent comes up.

This mirrors loop control in programming, where you can:

- Skip certain iterations (such as skipping a stop but continuing the trip)
- End the loop entirely (such as deciding to cut the trip short)

Significance of Loop Control:

In programming, loop control mechanisms help:

- **Adaptability**: Adjust loops dynamically based on real-time input, just like rerouting a trip.
- **Efficiency**: Avoid unnecessary iterations, like skipping songs on a playlist.
- **Robustness**: Handle unexpected conditions smoothly without crashing the program.

By controlling loops effectively, you optimize performance and improve user experience, making programs more responsive and intelligent.

Concept Introduction: Mastering Flow Control with `continue` and `break`

Just like in real life, sometimes you need to:

- Skip a step and move on (continue).

- Stop the process completely when a certain condition is met (break).

In Python, use the continue and break statements to control loop execution with precision.

Understanding `continue`

Imagine reading a book but skipping an uninteresting chapter to continue reading the next one. That is what continue does in a loop; it skips the current iteration and moves to the next one.

Understanding `break`

Now, imagine you are at a boring party. Instead of staying until the end, you leave early. That is what break does in a loop. It stops the loop immediately, regardless of the original condition.

Enhancing Programs with `continue` and `break`

Using continue and break in loops makes programs:

- **More adaptive**: Respond to changing inputs dynamically.
- **More efficient**: Avoid unnecessary processing, improving performance.
- **Easier to read**: Clearly define when to skip or exit a loop.

Navigating Complexity with Smart Loops

In programming, loops often deal with complex data, user inputs, and real-time decisions. By using continue and break, you ensure that loops are not just repetitive but also intelligent and efficient.

Mastering loop control allows you to write code that adapts, optimizes, and responds dynamically, whether it is filtering data, handling user interactions, or making real-time decisions in applications.

Practical Exercise: Text-based Menu with Exit/Continue Options

So far, you have learned how loops and conditional statements help control the flow of a program. Now, let us apply these concepts by building an interactive text-based menu. This exercise will demonstrate how while loops and conditional logic work together to create a simple yet dynamic program that continuously interacts with the user.

Exercise Objective:

Create a Python program that:

- Displays a menu with two options:
  - Show a greeting message
  - Exit the program
- Repeats the menu until the user chooses to exit.
- Responds to user input dynamically using a while loop and conditional statements.
- Handles invalid inputs gracefully, prompting the user to enter a valid choice.

This will help you see how loop control and conditional logic make programs more interactive and user-friendly.

Understanding Program Execution:

Think of this program as a simple menu system:

- The user is presented with options:
  - Press 1 to display a greeting message.
  - Press 2 to exit the program.
- The program waits for user input and responds based on their choice.
- If the user selects an invalid option, they are asked to try again.
- The program continues running until the user chooses to exit.

Python Code: Implementing the Text-Based Menu

```
while True:
    # Displaying the menu
    print("\nMenu:")
    print("1. Display a greeting message")
    print("2. Exit")

    # Getting user input
    choice = input("Please enter your choice (1 or 2): ")

    # Handling user choices
    if choice == '1':
        print("Hello, world!")  # Option 1: Display greeting
    elif choice == '2':
        print("Goodbye!")  # Option 2: Exit program
        break  # Exit the loop
    else:
        print("Invalid choice, please choose 1 or 2.")  # Handling invalid
input
```

Breaking Down the Code:

1. **Displaying the Menu**:
   a. The program shows a list of options inside the loop.
   b. It runs continuously until the user chooses to exit.
2. **Taking User Input:**
   a. The program asks for user input using **`input()`**.
   b. The input is stored in the variable choice.
3. **Processing the User's Choice**:
   a. If the user enters "1," the program prints "**`Hello, world!`**"
   b. If the user enters "2," the program prints "**`Goodbye!`**" and exits using break.
   c. If the user enters anything else, an error message is shown, and the menu repeats.

This exercise demonstrates:

- **Conditional Logic in User Interaction**: The program makes decisions based on user input.
- **Loop Control for Repetition**: The menu repeats until the user chooses to exit.
- **Graceful Exit Handling**: The break statement ensures the program ends cleanly when needed.

By using loops and conditional statements, create a simple but interactive program that reacts to user choices.

Now that you have built an interactive menu, you can extend this concept to more complex applications, such as:

- User authentication systems
- Automated data entry menus
- Dynamic chatbot interactions

In the next section, you will explore `continue` and `break` statements in more detail, showing how they help refine loop behavior in different scenarios.

Nested Loops and Conditions

As you progress in programming, you often face complex problems that require handling multiple levels of data or decision-making. This is where nested loops and conditions become essential. Just like a Matryoshka doll (Russian nesting doll), where smaller dolls fit inside larger ones, nested loops allow you to perform repetitive tasks within other repetitive tasks, and nested conditions help you make layered decisions.

These structures are powerful tools for solving problems that involve multiple layers of logic, such as data processing, searching, and organizing information efficiently.

Understanding Nested Loops: The Clock Analogy

Nested loops work like a clock:

- The hour hand moves once for every full cycle of the minute hand.
- Similarly, in programming, the outer loop runs once, and the inner loop completes all its iterations before the outer loop moves to the next step.

This concept is useful when dealing with grids, tables, or comparing multiple sets of data.

Understanding Nested Conditions: The Decision Tree Analogy

Nested conditions are like a decision tree:

- Suppose you are planning a tennis tournament.
- You first decide the type of match (singles or doubles).
- Then, within each type, you divide matches into men's, women's, and mixed categories.
- If it rains, you check whether the match needs to be moved indoors.

Each level of decision depends on the previous choice, just like in nested conditions, where one condition leads to another until the final decision is reached.

Bringing It All Together:

Nested loops and conditions allow you to:

- Handle large amounts of data efficiently (for example, analyzing rows and columns in a spreadsheet)
- Automate complex tasks that require multiple levels of repetition (for example, processing every pixel in an image)

- Make logical decisions step by step, just like event planning or match scheduling.

These structures mirror real-life problem-solving, helping programmers build efficient and intelligent programs.

In the next section, you will apply nested loops and conditions in a practical example, showing how they work in real-world programming tasks.

Practical Exercise: Multiplication Table Printer Using Nested Loops

Now that you have explored nested loops, let us put them into practice with a multiplication table printer. This exercise will demonstrate how one loop can exist inside another, making it easier to handle multiple layers of iteration in programming.

Exercise Objective:

The goal of this exercise is to create a Python program that:

- Generates multiplication tables for a range of numbers
- Uses a nested loop, where the outer loop iterates through base numbers and the inner loop iterates through multipliers
- Formats the output clearly, making it easy to read

This exercise will help you understand how nested loops work in real-world applications.

Steps to Follow:

1. Ask the user for input: Get the range of base numbers (for example, from 1 to 3) and the maximum multiplier (for example, up to 5).
2. Implement nested loops:
   a. The outer loop will go through each base number.
   b. The inner loop will calculate and print the product of the base number with each multiplier.
3. Format the output for clarity.

Python Code: Multiplication Table Printer

```
# Get user input for the range of base numbers
start_number = int(input("Enter the start number for the multiplication
tables: "))
end_number = int(input("Enter the end number for the multiplication tables:
"))

# Get user input for the maximum multiplier
max_multiplier = int(input("Enter the maximum multiplier: "))

# Outer loop: Iterates through each base number
for base in range(start_number, end_number + 1):
    print(f"\nMultiplication Table for {base}:")  # Formatting output for
readability

    # Inner loop: Iterates through each multiplier
    for multiplier in range(1, max_multiplier + 1):
        print(f"{base} x {multiplier} = {base * multiplier}")  # Printing the
result
```

```
# Completion message
print("\nMultiplication tables complete.")
```

Breaking Down the Code:

1. **Getting User Input:**
    a. The user enters the range of base numbers and the maximum multiplier.
    b. These values determine how many multiplication tables are printed and how many times each number is multiplied.
2. **Using Nested Loops:**
    a. The outer loop (for base in range(`start_number`, `end_number + 1`)) iterates through each base number.
    b. The inner loop (for multiplier in `range(1, max_multiplier + 1`)) calculates the product for each base number and multiplier.
3. **Printing the Results:**
    a. Inside the inner loop, the program prints each multiplication result in a structured format.
    b. Each multiplication table is clearly labeled, making the output easy to read.
4. **Completing the Process:**
    a. Once all calculations are done, the program prints "Multiplication tables complete."

Example Output (for base numbers 1 to 3, up to multiplier 5):

```
Multiplication Table for 1:
1 x 1 = 1
1 x 2 = 2
1 x 3 = 3
1 x 4 = 4
1 x 5 = 5

Multiplication Table for 2:
2 x 1 = 2
2 x 2 = 4
2 x 3 = 6
2 x 4 = 8
2 x 5 = 10

Multiplication Table for 3:
3 x 1 = 3
3 x 2 = 6
3 x 3 = 9
3 x 4 = 12
3 x 5 = 15

Multiplication tables complete.
```

This exercise demonstrates how nested loops help in structured data processing, making it easier to:

- Process multiple layers of data efficiently
- Handle repetitive calculations with minimal code

- Format output for better readability, improving the user experience

Nested loops are essential in many real-world applications, such as:

- Processing spreadsheets (iterating through rows and columns)
- Game development (handling objects in grids or maps)
- Data visualization (generating tables and structured reports)

By mastering nested loops, you gain the ability to solve more complex problems with structured and optimized code.

Now that you have seen nested loops in action, you can explore more advanced use cases, such as:

- Using nested conditions inside loops for filtered processing.
- Applying nested loops in search algorithms and sorting techniques.

In the next section, you will build on this foundation by applying nested loops to real-world data structures for even more efficient programming solutions.

Common Mistakes and Best Practices

When working with loops and control flow, it is essential to avoid common mistakes that can lead to errors or inefficiencies. The following are key pitfalls and best practices to keep your code clean and effective.

Common Mistakes

- **Forgetting to Update the Loop Variable in While Loops:**
    - **Mistake**: A missing update creates an infinite loop.
    - **Fix**: Always modify the loop variable inside the loop.

    ```
    counter = 5
    while counter > 0:
        print(counter)
        counter -= 1  # Ensures the loop eventually stops
    ```
- **Incorrect Use of break and continue:**
    - **Mistake**: Misusing break can exit a loop too early.
    - **Fix**: Use continue to skip an iteration and break to exit only when needed.
- **Nested Loops Without Proper Control:**
    - **Mistake**: Using too many nested loops can slow execution.
    - **Fix**: Optimize loops with better logic or list comprehensions.

Best Practices

- **Optimize Loop Execution:** Use list comprehensions for efficiency:

    ```
    squares = [x**2 for x in range(10)]
    ```
- **Use else in Loops When Needed:** The else clause runs only if the loop completes normally.

```
for num in range(3):
    print(num)
else:
    print("Loop completed!")
```

- **Keep Conditions Simple:** Instead of complex conditions:

  ```
  if 18 <= age <= 60:
      print("Eligible")
  ```

By following these best practices, you will write cleaner, more efficient loops while avoiding common pitfalls.

Exercises and Challenges: Practice Problems and Solutions

Now that you have explored conditional statements and loops, it is time to put your knowledge into practice. The following exercises will reinforce your understanding of these concepts, helping you build real-world problem-solving skills.

Each challenge focuses on control structures such as if-elif-else statements, for loops, while loops, break, continue, and nested loops.

Practice Problem 1: Simple Calculator with Basic Operations

Task: Create a simple calculator that performs basic arithmetic operations based on user choice.

Challenge:

- Ask the user for two numbers and an operation (addition, subtraction, multiplication, or division).
- Use if-elif-else statements to execute the chosen operation and display the result.
- Ensure division by zero is handled gracefully with an error message.

Practice Problem 2: Sum of Even Numbers

Task: Calculate the sum of even numbers within a user-defined range.

Challenge:

- Prompt the user to enter a start and end range.
- Use a for loop and conditional statements to sum only even numbers in that range.
- Print the final sum.

Practice Problem 3: Password Attempts Counter

Task: Implement a system that limits the number of password attempts.

Challenge:

- Use a while loop with a break condition to allow up to three attempts.
- If the user enters the correct password (hard-coded for now), print a success message and exit.
- After three failed attempts, print a lock-out message and terminate the program.

Practice Problem 4: Finding Prime Numbers

Task: Identify and print all prime numbers within a given range.

Challenge:

- Ask the user for a range (start and end numbers).
- Use nested for loops:
  - The outer loop iterates through numbers in the range.

    - The inner loop checks for factors of the current number.
- Use continue and break to manage loop execution efficiently.

Practice Problem 5: Custom Multiplication Table

Task: Print multiplication tables for numbers up to a user-specified limit, but skip a user-specified number.

Challenge:

- The user enters two numbers: n (range limit) and skip (the number to exclude from tables).
- Use nested loops:
    - The outer loop generates multiplication tables.
    - The inner loop prints products from 1 to 10.
- Use an if condition to skip the table for the specified number.

Practice Problem 6: Leap Year Checker

Task: Determine whether a user-input year is a leap year.

Challenge:

- A year is a leap year if:
    - It is divisible by 4 but not divisible by 100 (unless also divisible by 400).
- Use if-elif-else statements to check the conditions and display the result.

Practice Problem 7: Fibonacci Sequence Generator

Task: Generate the Fibonacci sequence up to a user-specified number of terms.

Challenge:

- Use a while loop to generate Fibonacci numbers.
- The sequence starts with 0 and 1, and each subsequent number is the sum of the previous two.
- Stop the sequence when the user-defined limit is reached.

Now that you have real-world problems to solve, try coding them yourself! In the next section, you will provide step-by-step solutions with explanations, helping you compare your approach with best practices.

Solutions to Practice Problems

Here are the solutions to the specified practice problems. These will help you check your work or guide you in solving the exercises if you encounter any difficulties.

Solution to Practice Problem 1: Simple Calculator with Basic Operations

```
# Ask the user for two numbers. These will be the operands for the arithmetic
operation.
num1 = float(input("Enter the first number: "))
num2 = float(input("Enter the second number: "))
# Ask the user to choose an arithmetic operation. The options are addition,
subtraction, multiplication, and division.
operation = input("Choose the operation (+, -, *, /): ")
# Depending on the operation chosen by the user, perform the corresponding arithmetic
operation.
if operation == '+':
    # If the user chooses addition, add num1 and num2, and display the result.
```

```
    print(f"{num1} + {num2} = {num1 + num2}")
elif operation == '-':
    # If subtraction is chosen, subtract num2 from num1, and display the
result.
    print(f"{num1} - {num2} = {num1 - num2}")
elif operation == '*':
    # For multiplication, multiply num1 by num2, and display the result.
    print(f"{num1} * {num2} = {num1 * num2}")
elif operation == '/':
    # Before division, check if num2 is zero to avoid division by zero error.
    if num2 == 0: print("Error: Cannot divide by zero.")
    else:
        # If num2 is not zero, proceed with the division and display the result.
        print(f"{num1} / {num2} = {num1 / num2}")
else:
    # If the operation entered does not match any of the expected symbols, inform the
user.
    print("Invalid operation selected.")
```

Solution to Practice Problem 2: Sum of Even Numbers

```
# Request the user to specify the starting and ending numbers of a range. The program
will find even numbers within this range.
start_range = int(input("Enter the start of the range: "))
end_range = int(input("Enter the end of the range: "))
# Initialize a variable to keep track of the sum of even numbers.
sum_even = 0
# Loop through each number in the user-defined range.
for number in range(start_range, end_range + 1):
    # Check if the current number is even.
    if number % 2 == 0:
        # If the number is even, add it to the sum_even variable.
        sum_even += number
        # After looping through the range, print the total sum of even numbers found.
print(f"The sum of even numbers from {start_range} to {end_range} is {sum_even}.")
```

Solution to Practice Problem 3: Password Attempts Counter

```
# Define the correct password. In a real application, this might be stored more se-
curely or checked against a database.
correct_password = "secret"
# Initialize a counter to keep track of the number of password attempts made by the
user.
attempts = 0
# Start a loop that allows the user up to 3 attempts to enter the correct password.
while attempts < 3:
    # Ask the user to input their password.
    user_password = input("Enter password: ")
    # Increment the counter for each attempt made.
    attempts += 1 # Compare the entered password against the correct password.
    if user_password == correct_password:
        # If the password is correct, grant access and exit the loop.
        print("Access Granted.")
        break
    else:
        # If the password is incorrect, notify the user.
        print("Wrong password.")
    # After 3 failed attempts, lock the account and exit the loop.
        if attempts == 3:
```

```
            print("Account locked. Too many attempts.")
```

Solution to Practice Problem 4: Finding Prime Numbers

```
# Ask the user to define the range within which they want to find prime numbers.
start = int(input("Enter the start of the range: "))
end = int(input("Enter the end of the range: "))
print(f"Prime numbers between {start} and {end} are:")
# Loop through each number in the defined range.
for num in range(start, end + 1):
    # Only consider numbers greater than 1, as prime numbers are greater than 1.
    if num > 1:
        # Use a nested loop to try dividing the number by all smaller numbers.
        for i in range(2, num):
            # If the number is divisible by any number other than 1 and itself, it›s
not prime.
            if (num % i) == 0:
                break
            else:
                # If the loop completes without finding any factors, num is prime.
                print(num)
                break
```

Solution to Practice Problem 5: Custom Multiplication Table

```
# Get the range within which the multiplication tables are to be printed and the num-
ber to skip.
n = int(input("Enter the range of numbers: "))
skip = int(input("Enter the number to skip: "))
# Start the outer loop to iterate through each number in the range for creating their
multiplication tables.
for base in range(1, n + 1):
    # If the current number is the one to skip, use continue to skip its multiplica-
tion table.
    if base == skip:
        continue
    print(f"Multiplication table for {base}:")
    # Inner loop to go through each multiplier from 1 to 10 for the current base num-
ber.
    for multiplier in range(1, 11):
        # Print the product of the current base number and the multiplier.
        print(f"{base} x {multiplier} = {base * multiplier}")
        # Print a newline after each table for better readability.
        print("")
```

Solution to Practice Problem 6: Leap Year Checker

```
# Prompt the user to enter a year to check if it's a leap year.
year = int(input("Enter a year to check if it's a leap year: "))
# Check if the year is a leap year. A year is a leap year if it's divisible by 4 but
not by 100,
# except if it is also divisible by 400.
if (year % 4 == 0 and year % 100 != 0) or (year % 400 == 0):
    print(f"{year} is a leap year.")
else: print(f"{year} is not a leap year.")
```

Solution to Practice Problem 7: Fibonacci Sequence Generator

```
# Prompt the user for the number of terms in the Fibonacci sequence they wish to
generate.
n_terms = int(input("How many terms? "))
```

```
# Initialize the first two terms of the Fibonacci sequence.
n1, n2 = 0, 1
count = 0
# Validate the number of terms.
if n_terms <= 0:
    print("Please enter a positive integer")
elif n_terms == 1:
    # If only one term is requested, print it directly.
    print("Fibonacci sequence up to", n_terms, ":")
    print(n1)
else:
    # Generate the Fibonacci sequence for the requested number of terms.
    print("Fibonacci sequence:")
    while count < n_terms:
        print(n1)
        # Update the terms for the next iteration.
        nth = n1 + n2
        n1 = n2
        n2 = nth
        count += 1
```

Conclusion

In this chapter, you explored the decision-making and repetition structures that form the backbone of dynamic programming. You learned how to use if, elif, and else statements to guide a program's flow based on conditions and how for and while loops help automate repetitive tasks efficiently. The chapter has also introduced nested loops and conditions, allowing for multi-layered logic that can handle more complex problem-solving scenarios.

The next step in your Python journey is functions, a key concept that allows for modular, reusable, and well-organized code. In the next chapter, you will explore how to define functions, pass values to them, and return results. Functions will enable you to structure your programs more effectively, reducing repetition and improving readability.

So, Keep Calm and Let us Tame the Python!

Multiple-Choice Questions

1. Which statement is used in Python to make a decision?
   a. select
   b. if
   c. decide
   d. choice
2. What will the following code print?
   `if not True: print("1") elif not (1 + 1 == 3): print("2") else: print("3")`
   a. 1
   b. 2
   c. 3
   d. Nothing

3. Which of the following is the correct way to write a conditional statement to check if x is less than 10?

    a. `if x < 10:`

    b. `if x =< 10:`

    c. `if x => 10:`

    d. `if x ==> 10:`

4. For loops are ideal for:

    a. Running a block of code a specific number of times

    b. Running a block of code indefinitely until stopped

    c. Running a block of code only once

    d. Skipping iterations in a loop

5. What does the continue statement do?

    a. Pauses the iteration and resumes

    b. Stops the loop immediately

    c. Skips the rest of the code inside the loop for the current iteration

    d. None of the above

6. Which loop structure is typically used when the number of iterations is unknown beforehand?

    a. For loop

    b. While loop

    c. Do-While loop

    d. Until loop

7. How many times does the inner loop run in a nested loop if the outer loop runs 3 times and the inner loop runs 5 times?

    a. 8

    b. 15

    c. 5

    d. 3

8. What will be the output of the following code?

    ```
    x = 10 while x > 0: x -= 3 print(x, end=" ") if x == 4: break
    ```

    a. 7 4

    b. 7 4 1

    c. 10 7 4

    d. 7 4 1 -2

9. Given the following code, what is the purpose of the elif statement?

   `if condition1: # block of code elif condition2: # block of code else: # block of code`

   a. To specify a new condition if the first condition is true

   b. To specify a new condition if the first condition is false

   c. To end the conditional statement

   d. To create a loop

10. Which scenario is best suited for using a nested loop?

    a. When you need to execute a block of code a single time

    b. When you need to perform a task repeatedly on a collection of items

    c. When you are required to check each item in a list against every other item

    d. When you need to exit a loop based on a condition

Answers

1. b
2. b
3. a
4. a
5. c
6. b
7. b
8. a
9. b
10. c

Points to Remember

- Python's conditional statements (if, elif, else) facilitate decision-making by executing code blocks based on specific criteria.
- If statements are essential for branching logic as they examine a condition and execute code if true.
- Elif allows for numerous sequential condition checks within the same if structure, whereas else gives an alternative path of execution if the if fails.
- For loops automate iterating over items in a sequence or object by running a piece of code for each one.
- While loops execute until a condition is met, making them ideal for repeating activities when the number of iterations is unknown ahead of time.
- The break statement allows you to quit a loop early when a specific condition is met, even if the loop's primary condition remains true.

- The continue statement skips the current iteration of a loop and moves to the next iteration, providing for more precise control over its execution.
- Using nested loops allows for easier handling of sophisticated conditional logic and several levels of data.

Further Reading

For additional insights into control structures and loop handling, explore these resources:

1. **Python Control Flow - Real Python:**

   https://realpython.com/python-conditional-statements/

   A comprehensive guide to conditional statements, explaining how if, elif, and else work in Python with practical examples.

2. **Loops in Python - W3Schools:**

   https://www.w3schools.com/python/python_for_loops.asp

   A beginner-friendly resource covering for and while loops, with interactive tutorials to practice iteration concepts.

Chapter 5
Creating Functions

Introduction

In the last chapter, you learned how to control the flow of a program using loops and conditionals. These tools helped your code make decisions and repeat actions when necessary, allowing you to create dynamic and efficient programs. However, as your programs grow, you may find yourself repeating similar blocks of code, making it harder to manage and update.

In this chapter, you will take the next big step in Python programming by learning about functions. So far, you have worked with loops and conditionals to control the flow of your programs. Now, you will focus on making code more organized, reusable, and efficient by using functions.

Think of functions like a recipe in a cookbook. Instead of writing the same steps repeatedly, you can group them into a function and use them whenever needed. This makes your code cleaner, easier to manage, and more efficient.

By the end of this chapter, you will be able to write smarter code by breaking down complex tasks into smaller, reusable functions. This will help you create programs that are more powerful, adaptable, and easier to read. Let us dive in and discover the magic of functions in Python.

Structure

In this chapter, the following topics will be covered:

- Introduction to Functions
  - Functions in Everyday Life
  - Understanding Functions Through Pseudocode
  - The Concept of Functions in Programming
- Importance of Function Calls
  - Code Reusability
  - Improving Code Readability
  - Simplifying Complex Problems
- Basic Structure of a Function
  - Defining a Function
  - Function Parameters and Arguments
  - The Return Statement
  - Practical Exercise: Basic Calculator Function
- Understanding Variable Scope
  - Local Variables
  - Global Variables
  - Modifying Global Variables Inside a Function

    - Practical Exercise: Tracking a High Score
- Advanced Function Concepts
    - Default Parameter Values
    - Variable-length Arguments (*args and **kwargs)
    - Practical Exercise: Customizable Greeting Card Generator
- Common Mistakes and Best Practices
- Exercises and Challenges: Practice Problems and Solutions

Introduction to Functions

A function in programming is like a specialized tool designed to perform a specific task. It takes input, processes it, and returns an output. Think of it as a small program within a larger one that can be reused whenever needed. Functions help keep code organized, reduce repetition, and make programs easier to manage and understand.

Learning about functions is a key milestone in programming. They allow you to break complex tasks into smaller, reusable parts, making your code more efficient and modular. To make this concept easier, you will first look at everyday examples before applying them to programming.

Functions in Everyday Life

Functions are not just used in programming; they are part of daily life. For example, consider a vending machine and a coffee maker. These machines follow a process similar to how functions work in programming.

The Vending Machine Analogy:

Imagine you are using a vending machine to get a snack. You press a button (input), the machine processes your request, and delivers your selected item (output).

- **Input**: Pressing a button to choose a snack.
- **Processing**: The machine identifies your choice and retrieves the item.
- **Output**: The snack is dispensed.

Similarly, in programming, when you call a function, you provide input, the function executes a set of instructions, and then produces an output.

The Coffee Maker Analogy:

A coffee maker works the same way. You add water and coffee grounds (inputs), the machine processes them to brew coffee, and the final product (output) is a freshly brewed cup.

- **Input**: Water, coffee grounds, and selection of coffee type.
- **Processing**: The machine heats the water, filters it through the coffee, and brews the drink.
- **Output**: A cup of coffee.

This is exactly how functions work in programming. The inputs act as function arguments, the brewing process represents the function's internal logic, and the final coffee is the function's return value.

Using real-world examples makes it easier to understand how functions work. Just like vending machines and coffee makers process inputs and provide outputs, functions in programming help perform specific tasks efficiently.

Connecting Everyday Processes to Programming:

By recognizing how real-world machines function, you can see the connection between physical actions and digital operations. A vending machine encapsulates the process of selecting and dispensing a product, just as a function in programming groups a set of instructions into a reusable block.

The transition from pressing a button on a machine to writing a function in code may seem abstract, but the core idea remains the same. When you call a function with certain inputs, you expect a predictable output, just as you expect a vending machine to give you the snack you choose.

Understanding functions through everyday examples helps bridge the gap between the real and digital worlds, making programming concepts feel more intuitive and practical.

Understanding Functions Through Pseudocode

In the previous sections, you have explored functions using real-world analogies such as vending machines and coffee makers. These examples helped to see how functions take input, process it, and return an output. Now, let us take this understanding one step further by breaking down functions in a structured way using pseudocode.

Understanding Pseudocode:

Pseudocode is a simple way to describe how a program works without worrying about the exact rules of a programming language. It blends programming logic with human language, making it easier to plan and understand code before actually writing it. Just like you used real-world examples to understand functions, pseudocode helps to visualize programming logic before you implement it in Python.

A Simple Function in Pseudocode:

Now, let us apply this idea to a function that adds two numbers. Instead of writing real Python code, you can describe it in an easy-to-read way using pseudocode:

Function `AddNumbers`:

- **Input**: Number1, Number2
- **Process**: Sum = Number1 + Number2
- **Output**: Return Sum

This follows the same input-process-output structure discussed earlier with vending machines and coffee makers:

1. **Input:** The function takes two numbers, similar to how a vending machine takes a selection or a coffee maker takes water and coffee grounds.
2. **Processing:** The function performs an action. In this case, adding the numbers. Just like a vending machine retrieves a product or a coffee maker brews coffee.
3. **Output:** The function gives back a result, similar to how a vending machine dispenses a snack or a coffee maker serves a cup of coffee.

Importance of Functions in Programming:

Functions simplify programming by allowing you to reuse code instead of repeating the same steps over and over. A function acts as a self-contained unit that can be used whenever needed. This improves efficiency, keeps code organized, and makes programs easier to manage.

As you move forward, functions will become even more powerful, handling different types of data, making decisions, and working with loops. However, the core idea remains the same: functions always follow the input → process → output model, making them a fundamental part of programming.

By practicing with pseudocode, you will develop a clear way of thinking about functions before writing them in Python. This step-by-step approach bridges the gap between understanding the logic behind functions and coding them in a real-world program.

The Concept of Functions in Programming

In the previous sections, you have explored how functions work by comparing them to real-world examples such as vending machines and coffee makers. Pseudocode was also introduced to break down how a function processes input and produces output. Now, let us focus on a key principle in programming: calling a function. Understanding how to call a function is essential because it allows you to execute the instructions you have defined within it.

Understanding Function Calls:

When you define a function, you are essentially creating a reusable set of instructions that perform a specific task. However, these instructions do not automatically run on their own. To make a function execute, you need to call it by name in your program. This calling action tells the computer to run the function's code at that moment.

Understanding the Execution of Function Calls:

When a function is called, the program temporarily jumps to the function and runs the instructions inside it. Once the function has completed its task, the program returns to the point where the function was called and continues running the rest of the code. This ability to move in and out of functions makes programs more organized, reusable, and efficient.

Example: Calling a Function in Pseudocode

To better understand function calls, let us look at a simple pseudocode example. Here, you will define a function called **`SayHello`**, which prints a message to the screen.

Defining a Function in Pseudocode:

```
Function SayHello
    Print "Hello, world!"
End Function
```

In this example, **`SayHello`** is a function with no inputs. It simply prints "**`Hello, world!`**" whenever it is executed. However, defining the function alone does not run it; you must explicitly call it for the message to appear.

Calling the Function in Pseudocode:

```
Call SayHello()
```

When the program reaches this line, it pauses its normal execution, jumps to the **`SayHello`** function, runs its instructions, and then returns to continue the program.

Importance of Function Calls

Functions make programming more efficient by allowing you to reuse code instead of writing the same instructions multiple times. Function calls activate these reusable blocks of code whenever needed, helping keep programs organized, readable, and easy to manage.

In the next sections, you will see how function calls work in Python, how to pass information to functions using parameters, and how to get results from functions using return values. Understanding function calls is the first step in writing clean, modular, and powerful programs.

Code Reusability

One of the biggest advantages of functions is reusability, which means you can write code once and use it multiple times. Instead of copying and pasting the same logic throughout a program, you can define a function and call it whenever needed. This saves time, reduces errors, and makes it easier to update the code.

For example, consider a simple function that greets a user:

```
Function SayHello:
    Input: UserName
    Process: Print "Hello, " + UserName
    Output: None
```

This function can be used in different parts of a program to greet users without rewriting the greeting logic each time. Whether welcoming a user to a website, sending a chat message, or displaying a notification, the **`SayHello`** function ensures consistency and prevents unnecessary repetition.

Improving Code Readability

Good programming is not just about writing code; it is about writing code that is easy to read and understand. Functions help by grouping related actions into clearly named blocks of code. Instead of looking at long, complicated lines of instructions, a well-structured program using functions gives a clear, high-level view of what it does.

For instance, calculating the area of a circle requires the formula $\pi \times \text{radius}^2$. Without a function, this formula would be repeated multiple times across the program. Instead, use a function like this:

```
Function CalculateAreaOfCircle:
    Input: Radius
    Process: Area = π * Radius²
    Output: Return Area
```

Now, whenever you need to calculate the area of a circle, simply call **`CalculateAreaOfCircle`**(radius). This makes the program cleaner, easier to maintain, and ensures that if you ever need to change the formula, it needs to be updated only in one place.

Simplifying Complex Problems

When solving a big problem, it is much easier to break it into smaller steps. Functions allow programmers to divide a large program into multiple smaller tasks, making it more structured and easier to understand.

For example, imagine writing a program to organize a party. Without functions, the code would be a long, complicated list of steps:

1. Send invitations
2. Prepare food
3. Arrange music

Instead, you can separate each task into its own function:

```
Function SendInvitations:
    ...

Function PrepareFood:
```

```
    ...

Function ArrangeMusic:
    ...
```

Now, the main program just calls each function in order:

```
Call SendInvitations
Call PrepareFood
Call ArrangeMusic
```

This simplifies the overall program, making it easier to read, debug, and modify. If you decide to change how to prepare food or arrange music later, you only need to update that specific function, rather than searching through the entire program.

As you move forward, you will explore how to define and use functions in Python, passing data through parameters and getting results using return values. Mastering functions will help you write smarter programs that are easy to maintain and expand.

Basic Structure of a Function

In the previous sections, you have explored why functions are important and how they help organize and simplify code. Now, let us look at how to define a function in Python. Understanding how to create a function is the first step toward writing reusable, well-structured programs.

Defining a Function

A function in Python is defined using the **def** keyword, followed by a function name, parentheses, and a colon. The actual code that runs inside the function is indented under the function definition.

```
def function_name():
    # Body of the function
    # Code to execute
```

This structure allows Python to recognize that a function has been declared.

Understanding the def Keyword:

The **def** keyword tells Python that you are about to define a function. After **def**, you provide a function name followed by parentheses. For now, these parentheses are empty, but later you will learn how to add parameters inside them.

Naming Conventions for Functions:

Choosing a good function name is important because it makes the code easier to read and understand. Here are a few key guidelines:

- Function names should clearly describe their purpose.
- Use snake_case (words separated by underscores) for function names, as this is the standard style in Python.
- Avoid using names that are already built-in Python functions (such as print or sum) to prevent unexpected behavior.

Example: A Simple Function

```
def greet():
    print("Hello, welcome to Python functions!")
```

Here, **greet()** is a function that simply prints a greeting message when called. The function name is clear and descriptive, making it easy to understand what the function does.

Another Example: Printing a Math Fact

Suppose you want to print an interesting mathematical fact using a function:

```
def print_math_fact():
    print("Did you know? 0.1 + 0.2 != 0.3 in most programming languages due to floating-point arithmetic!")
```

This function, **print_math_fact()**, is well-named because it clearly describes its purpose, printing a mathematical fact.

These examples show that all Python functions follow the same structure:

- The **def** keyword
- A descriptive function name
- Parentheses () (which may contain parameters later)
- A colon :
- An indented function body where the actual task is performed

Mastering this basic structure is the first step before learning how to pass data into functions using parameters and return values.

Function Parameters and Arguments

So far, you have defined functions that do not take any input. However, to make functions more flexible and useful, you need to allow them to accept data. This is where parameters and arguments come in.

Definition of Parameters and Arguments:

- Parameters are placeholders in a function definition. They specify what kind of input the function expects.
- Arguments are the actual values that are passed to the function when it is called.

In simple terms, parameters are like empty boxes, and arguments are the things you put inside those boxes when using the function.

Positional Arguments

Positional arguments are the most common way to pass data into functions. These arguments must be provided in the correct order, matching the function's parameters.

Example: Adding Two Numbers

```
def add_numbers(first_number, second_number):
    print(first_number + second_number)

add_numbers(5, 3)
```

Here is how the function works:

- The function **add_numbers()** has two parameters: **first_number** and **second_number**.
- When calling the function, you will provide two arguments: 5 and 3.
- These arguments are assigned to the corresponding parameters.

Since **first_number = 5** and **second_number = 3**, the function calculates 5 + 3 and prints 8.

Keyword Arguments

Keyword arguments allow you to specify which parameter each argument belongs to. This means that order does not matter as long as you name the arguments correctly.

Example: Introducing Yourself

```
def introduce_yourself(name, age):
    print(f"My name is {name}, and I am {age} years old.")

introduce_yourself(age=30, name="Alex")
```

Even though you passed **age=30** before **name="Alex"**, the function still correctly assigns values to the right parameters. Keyword arguments make code more readable and flexible.

Mixing Positional and Keyword Arguments

You can use both positional and keyword arguments in a function call, but positional arguments must come first.

Example: Creating a User Profile

```
def create_profile(name, age, country="Unknown"):
    print(f"Name: {name}, Age: {age}, Country: {country}")

create_profile("Jamie", 25, country="Canada")
```

In this function:

- "**Jamie**" and **25** are positional arguments (assigned in order).
- **country="Canada"** is a keyword argument, so its position does not matter.
- If the country argument was not provided, it would default to "**Unknown**."

Importance of Parameters and Arguments:

Understanding parameters and arguments makes functions much more useful. Instead of creating multiple versions of the same function for different values, you can pass in data dynamically and get different results with the same function.

By combining positional arguments, keyword arguments, and default values, you can create flexible and efficient functions that handle different inputs without modifying the function definition.

The Return Statement

In the previous sections, you learned how to define functions, pass data using parameters and arguments, and make your code more reusable and organized. Now, you will take a step further by exploring the return statement, which allows functions to send data back to the part of the program that called them.

Many functions do more than just perform actions such as printing to the console; they often calculate values, process data, and return results for further use. The return statement makes this possible by allowing a function to send back a value after execution.

Returning Values from Functions

When a function reaches a return statement, it stops execution and sends a value back to the place where the function was called. This returned value can then be:

- Stored in a variable for later use

- Used in calculations
- Passed into another function
- Included in conditions (if-else statements, loops, and so on)

Example: Adding Two Numbers and Returning the Result

```
def add_numbers(a, b):
    result = a + b
    return result

sum_value = add_numbers(5, 3)
print(sum_value)  # Outputs: 8
```

- The function **add_numbers(5, 3)** calculates 5 + 3.
- Instead of printing the result, it returns the value 8.
- The returned value is stored in **sum_value** and printed.

Unlike a function that only prints the result, a function with return can send back values to be used elsewhere in the program.

Understanding Void Functions

Not all functions need to return a value. Some functions are designed to perform actions instead, such as printing messages or modifying files.

In Python, if a function does not include a return statement, it automatically returns None. In other languages, such functions are sometimes called void functions because they do not return a meaningful value.

Example: A Function That Prints a Greeting Without Returning a Value

```
def print_greeting(name):
    print(f"Hello, {name}!")

print_greeting("Alice")  # Outputs: Hello, Alice!
```

This function prints a message but does not return anything. If you try to store its result in a variable, it will hold None.

```
greeting = print_greeting("Alice")
print(greeting)  # Outputs: None
```

Even though the function performed an action, it did not return a value that could be used elsewhere.

Returning Multiple Values

Python allows functions to return multiple values by grouping them into a tuple. These values can be unpacked into separate variables when calling the function.

Example: Returning Multiple Values from a Function

```
def get_user_data():
    name = "Alice"
    age = 30
    return name, age  # Returns a tuple (name, age)

user_name, user_age = get_user_data()
print(user_name, user_age)  # Outputs: Alice 30
```

- The function **get_user_data()** returns two values: "**Alice**"and **30**.
- These values are automatically stored as a tuple: (**"Alice", 30**).
- The caller unpacks the tuple into **user_name** and **user_age**, making them easy to use.

Importance of Return Statement:

The return statement makes functions more flexible and powerful. Instead of limiting functions to only performing actions, they can calculate results and send them back for further use.

- Functions that return values help keep code organized and modular, allowing different parts of the program to communicate with each other.
- Void functions (without return) are useful when a function's purpose is to perform an action, such as printing text or updating a file.

Mastering the return statement will allow you to write more advanced, efficient, and interactive programs. In the next section, you will explore default values and flexible arguments, which make functions even more adaptable.

Practical Exercise: Basic Calculator Function

Now that you understand functions, return statements, and function calls, let us apply this knowledge by building a simple calculator in Python. This exercise will show how to define functions, pass inputs, and return results while making the program interactive for the user.

Task Overview:

Create a Python program that acts as a basic calculator, capable of performing addition, subtraction, multiplication, and division. The program will:

1. Ask the user for two numbers
2. Ask for the desired operation (add, subtract, multiply, or divide)
3. Call the correct function to perform the operation
4. Display the result

This project will reinforce the importance of functions, making code cleaner, reusable, and easier to maintain.

Steps for the Exercise:

1. Define four functions, one for each arithmetic operation. Each function should take two parameters (the numbers to calculate) and return the result.
2. Get user input for two numbers and convert them to floats to allow decimal calculations.
3. Let the user choose an operation and use an if-elif-else statement to decide which function to call.
4. Display the result to the user.

```
# Function definitions
def add(a, b):
    return a + b

def subtract(a, b):
    return a - b

def multiply(a, b):
```

```
    return a * b

def divide(a, b):
    if b != 0:
        return a / b
    else:
        return "Error: Cannot divide by zero."

# User input
num1 = float(input("Enter the first number: "))
num2 = float(input("Enter the second number: "))
operation = input("Choose the operation (add, subtract, multiply, divide): ")

# Operation selection and result calculation
if operation == "add":
    result = add(num1, num2)
elif operation == "subtract":
    result = subtract(num1, num2)
elif operation == "multiply":
    result = multiply(num1, num2)
elif operation == "divide":
    result = divide(num1, num2)
else:
    result = "Invalid operation selected."

# Display the result
print(f"Result: {result}")
```

Understanding the Code:

This program wraps each arithmetic operation inside its own function, making it easy to reuse and organize.

- The four functions (add, subtract, multiply, and divide) each take two numbers and return the result.
- The if-elif-else statement determines which function to call based on user input.
- The divide function includes a condition to prevent division by zero, returning an error message instead.

This exercise highlights several key concepts:

Code Organization: Each operation is contained within its own function, making the main program simple and readable.

- **Reusability:** The functions can be used anywhere without rewriting code.
- **Return Statements:** Instead of just printing results, functions return values that can be stored and used later.
- **Handling User Input:** The program interacts with users and performs calculations dynamically.
- **Error Handling:** The division function ensures the program does not crash if the user enters zero as the denominator.

By applying functions in this way, you create a flexible and maintainable program that can be easily expanded with more features in the future.

In the next section, you will explore default values and flexible arguments, making functions even more adaptable to different scenarios.

Understanding Variable Scope

In the previous sections, you explored how functions help organize code by making it reusable and structured. Now, you need to understand variable scope, which determines where a variable can be accessed and modified in a program.

Scope defines the visibility of a variable, whether it can be used throughout the program or only within a specific function. Python uses two main types of variables: local variables (used inside functions) and global variables (accessible throughout the program). Understanding the difference between them is essential for writing clear and error-free code.

Local Variables

Local variables are defined inside a function and can only be used within that function. They are created when the function runs and are deleted once the function completes, meaning they cannot be accessed outside their function.

Using local variables prevents conflicts with other variables in the program and keeps the function's data self-contained.

Example: Local Variable in a Function

```
def greet():
    message = "Hello, Python!"  # Local variable
    print(message)

greet()  # Outputs: Hello, Python!
```

`print(message)` # This will cause an error because '**`message`**' is not accessible outside the function.

- The variable message only exists inside the **`greet()`** function.
- If you try to print message outside the function, Python raises an error because the variable is not recognized globally.

Local variables help keep functions independent, preventing accidental changes to variables in other parts of the program.

Global Variables

A global variable is defined outside any function and can be accessed by any part of the program, including functions.

Global variables are useful when multiple functions need to access or modify the same value. However, using too many global variables can make debugging difficult because changes to them can happen anywhere in the program.

Example: Using a Global Variable

```
user = "Alice"  # Global variable

def greet():
    print("Hello,", user)  # Accessing the global variable

greet()  # Outputs: Hello, Alice
```

- The variable user is defined outside the function, making it accessible inside the **`greet()`** function.

- Since user is global, it can be used anywhere in the program.

While global variables can be useful, they should be used carefully to avoid unexpected changes from different parts of the code.

Modifying Global Variables Inside a Function

By default, if you assign a value to a variable inside a function, Python treats it as a local variable, even if there is a global variable with the same name.

To modify a global variable inside a function, you need to explicitly tell Python to use the global variable using the global keyword.

Example: Using global to Modify a Global Variable

```
counter = 0  # Global variable

def increment_counter():
    global counter  # Access the global variable
    counter += 1  # Modify the global variable

increment_counter()
print(counter)  # Outputs: 1
```

- Without global, Python would create a new local variable instead of modifying counter.
- The **global** keyword tells Python not to create a new variable but to use the existing global variable.

While global variables can be useful, its excessive use can make debugging difficult. In most cases, it is better to pass variables as function parameters instead of modifying global variables inside functions.

Best Practices for Using Variables in Functions

- **Use local variables whenever possible**: They keep data inside functions, preventing unexpected changes in the program.
- **Use global variables sparingly**: Only when multiple functions need access to shared data.
- **Use the global keyword carefully**: It allows functions to modify global variables but can make code harder to track.
- **Prefer function parameters**: Instead of modifying global variables inside functions, pass values as arguments for better control and flexibility.

Understanding the difference between local and global variables helps create clean, efficient, and maintainable Python programs. In the next section, you will explore default parameter values and flexible arguments, making functions even more adaptable.

Practical Exercise: Tracking a High Score

Now that you understand the difference between local and global variables, let us apply this knowledge by building a simple program that tracks the highest score in a game. This exercise will show how global variables store persistent data across function calls, while local variables handle temporary calculations.

Task Overview:

Create a Python program that:

1. Stores the highest score using a global variable (**high_score**).
2. Allows the user to enter new scores and updates **high_score** if the new score is higher.

3. Uses a function to check and update the high score while demonstrating the use of the global keyword.
4. Runs in a loop, allowing users to enter scores until they choose to exit.

Steps for the Exercise

1. Initialize a global variable, **high_score = 0**, to store the top score.
2. Define a function **update_high_score(new_score)** that:
   a. Uses the global keyword to modify **high_score**.
   b. Compares **new_score** with **high_score** and updates it if the new score is higher.
3. Create a loop that allows users to enter new scores or exit the program.
4. Handle exit conditions: if the user enters "**exit**," the program stops.

```
# Global variable to track the highest score
high_score = 0

# Function to update the high score
def update_high_score(new_score):
    global high_score
    if new_score > high_score:
        high_score = new_score
        print(f"New high score: {high_score}")
    else:
        print(f"Current high score remains: {high_score}")

# Main loop to enter new scores
while True:
    score_input = input("Enter a new score (or type 'exit' to quit): ")

    if score_input.lower() == 'exit':
        print("Exiting. Final high score:", high_score)
        break
    else:
        new_score = int(score_input)
        update_high_score(new_score)
```

Understanding the Code:

This program demonstrates the interaction between global and local variables while tracking a high score.

- The global variable **high_score** keeps the highest score across multiple inputs.
- The function **update_high_score(new_score)**:
  - Uses global **high_score** to modify the global variable.
  - Compares **new_score** with **high_score** and updates if needed.
- The while loop continuously asks for new scores, allowing users to input scores until they type "**exit**."

Demonstrates global and local variable interaction, **high_score** remains persistent across function calls, while **new_score** is temporary.

- Uses the **global** keyword correctly to modify a global variable inside a function.
- Encapsulates logic in a function (**update_high_score**), keeping the main program clean and organized.

- Applies variable scope in a real-world scenario, showing how global variables are useful for tracking persistent data such as game scores.

This exercise highlights the advantages and risks of using global variables. While they allow data persistence, excessive use of global variables can make programs harder to debug. In most cases, passing values as function parameters is a better practice.

In the next section, you will explore default parameter values and flexible arguments, making functions even more adaptable.

Advanced Function Concepts

As you gain more experience with Python functions, you can make them more flexible and powerful using default parameter values and variable-length arguments. These features allow your functions to handle a wider range of input conditions, making them more adaptable and efficient.

Default Parameter Values

Sometimes, when calling a function, you may not always need to provide values for every parameter. In such cases, Python allows you to set default values for function parameters. If an argument is not provided when calling the function, the default value is used instead.

This feature makes functions easier to use by reducing the number of required arguments while still allowing customization when needed.

Example: Default Parameter Values

```
def print_greeting(name="World"):
    print(f"Hello, {name}!")

print_greeting()        # Outputs: Hello, World!
print_greeting("Alice") # Outputs: Hello, Alice!
```

- The function **`print_greeting`** has a parameter name with a default value of "**`World`**."
- If the function is called without an argument, it uses the default value.
- If an argument is provided (for example, "**`Alice`**"), it overrides the default value.

This approach makes functions more flexible while keeping them simple to use.

Variable-Length Arguments (*args and **kwargs)

Python allows functions to accept any number of arguments, making them more dynamic and adaptable. This is done using:

- **`*args`**: Allows a function to accept multiple positional arguments and stores them as a tuple
- **`**kwargs`**: Allows a function to accept multiple keyword arguments and stores them as a dictionary

These features make functions more adaptable, allowing them to handle different numbers of inputs without modifying the function definition.

Using *args (Multiple Positional Arguments)

If you do not know in advance how many values a user might pass, **`*args`** allows the function to accept any number of arguments.

Example: Summing Multiple Numbers

```
def sum_numbers(*args):
    total = sum(args)  # args is a tuple containing all provided numbers
    print(f"Sum: {total}")

sum_numbers(2, 4, 6)         # Outputs: Sum: 12
sum_numbers(10, 20, 30, 40) # Outputs: Sum: 100
```

- **`*args`** collects all extra arguments into a tuple.
- The function sums all numbers and prints the result.
- The function can handle any number of inputs without modifying its definition.

Using **kwargs (Multiple Keyword Arguments)

If you need to handle an unknown number of named parameters, **`**kwargs`** allows the function to accept multiple keyword arguments, which are stored as a dictionary.

Example: Describing a Pet

```
def describe_pet(name, **kwargs):
    print(f"Pet name: {name}")
    for key, value in kwargs.items():
        print(f"- {key}: {value}")

describe_pet("Fido", species="Dog", color="Brown", age=5)
```

Output:

```
Pet name: Fido
- species: Dog
- color: Brown
- age: 5
```

- The function **`describe_pet`** takes a required parameter (name) and any number of additional details using **`**kwargs`**.
- Each extra detail (species, color, age) is stored as a dictionary and printed dynamically.

Mixing *args and **kwargs

You can combine **`*args`** and **`**kwargs`** in the same function, allowing it to accept both positional and keyword arguments.

Example: Flexible Pet Description

```
def describe_pet(name, *args, **kwargs):
    print(f"Pet name: {name}")

    for attribute in args:
        print(f"- {attribute}")

    for key, value in kwargs.items():
        print(f"- {key}: {value}")

describe_pet("Fido", "dog", "friendly", color="Brown", age=5)
```

Output:

```
Pet name: Fido
- dog
- friendly
- color: Brown
- age: 5
```

- **`*args`** stores extra unnamed attributes ("dog," "friendly") as a tuple.
- **`**kwargs`** stores extra named attributes (color, age) as a dictionary.
- The function is highly flexible, allowing any number of inputs without modifying its definition.

Using default parameter values, **`*args`**, and **`**kwargs`** allows you to create more adaptable and dynamic functions.

- Default values make arguments optional, simplifying function calls.
- **`*args`** lets functions accept multiple positional arguments.
- **`**kwargs`** lets functions accept multiple keyword arguments.
- These techniques reduce redundant code and make functions more powerful.

Mastering these advanced function concepts, you can write more flexible, reusable, and scalable code for any programming project.

Practical Exercise: Customizable Greeting Card Generator

In the previous sections, you explored default parameter values, **`*args`**, and **`**kwargs`**, which make functions more flexible and adaptable. Now, let us put these concepts into practice by building a customizable greeting card generator. This project will show how functions can be designed to adjust to user input while providing useful defaults dynamically.

Task Overview

Create a Python program that generates a personalized greeting card message. The program will:

1. Define a function that accepts:
    a. A default occasion (for example, "**`Birthday`**")
    b. A recipient's name
    c. **`*args`** for additional wishes/messages
    d. **`**kwargs`** for extra details (for example, sender's name, date)
2. Ask the user for input to customize the greeting card.
3. Call the function with user-provided details.
4. Print the final greeting card message in a structured and friendly format.

```
# Function to create a customizable greeting card
def create_greeting_card(occasion="Birthday", recipient="Friend", *messages,
**details):
    print(f"\n Happy {occasion}, {recipient}!")

    # Print additional messages
    for message in messages:
        print(f"- {message}")
```

```
    # Print any extra details
    for key, value in details.items():
        print(f"{key.capitalize()}: {value}")

# Collect user input
recipient_name = input("Enter the recipient's name: ")
occasion_name = input("Enter the occasion (or press Enter for default
'Birthday'): ") or "Birthday"

# Allow the user to add multiple messages
print("Enter your greeting messages (type 'done' when finished):")
user_messages = []
while True:
    msg = input("- ")
    if msg.lower() == "done":
        break
    user_messages.append(msg)

# Allow the user to add extra details like sender's name and date
sender_name = input("Enter your name (optional): ")
greeting_date = input("Enter the date (optional): ")

# Prepare kwargs dictionary for extra details
extra_details = {}
if sender_name:
    extra_details["Sender"] = sender_name
if greeting_date:
    extra_details["Date"] = greeting_date

# Call the function with user input
create_greeting_card(occasion_name, recipient_name, *user_messages, **extra_
details)
```

Expected Output

If the user enters:

```
Enter the recipient's name: Alice
Enter the occasion (or press Enter for default 'Birthday'):
Enter your greeting messages (type 'done' when finished):
- Wishing you all the happiness in the world
- Hope you have a fantastic day!
- done
Enter your name (optional): Bob
Enter the date (optional): 2024-04-01
```

The output will be:

```
Happy Birthday, Alice!
- Wishing you all the happiness in the world
- Hope you have a fantastic day!
Sender: Bob
Date: 2024-04-01
```

Understanding the Code:

This program demonstrates how default parameters, ***args**, and ****kwargs** work together to create a highly flexible function.

- The function **create_greeting_card**:
  - Uses a default value "**Birthday**" for the occasion if none is provided.
  - Accepts an unlimited number of extra messages via ***args**.
  - Accepts extra details (such as sender name and date) via ****kwargs**.
- The program collects user input dynamically to:
  - Get the recipient's name and occasion.
  - Allow users to add multiple personalized messages.
  - Accept optional extra details (such as the sender's name and date).
- The loop for user messages allows the user to enter any number of wishes, stopping when they type "done."
- The function prints all details in a friendly, easy-to-read format.

Common Mistakes and Best Practices

When working with functions in Python, avoiding common mistakes and following best practices ensures clean, efficient, and error-free code.

Common Mistakes

Not Calling a Function: Simply defining a function does not execute it. If a function is not called, it will not run.

Mistake:

```
def greet():
        print("Hello!")
```

Fix:

```
def greet():
        print("Hello!")
greet()  # Function is now called
```

Forgetting the return Statement: If a function only prints a value instead of returning it, the result cannot be reused elsewhere.

Mistake:

```
def add(a, b):
        print(a + b)
```

Fix

```
def add(a, b):
        return a + b
```

Modifying Global Variables Incorrectly:

Mistake: Assigning a value to a global variable inside a function without using global creates a local variable instead.

Fix: Use global only when necessary to modify global variables.

Using Mutable Default Arguments:

Mistake: Default parameters should not be mutable objects, such as lists or dictionaries, as they persist across function calls.

Fix: Use None as a default and initialize inside the function.

Best Practices

- **Use Clear Function Names:** `calculate_area(radius)` instead of `do_stuff(x)`
- **Return Values Instead of Printing:** Makes functions more flexible and reusable
- **Keep Functions Small and Focused:** Each function should do one task efficiently
- **Use Default Parameters Wisely:** Helps avoid unnecessary argument passing
- **Limit Global Variables:** Prefer passing parameters over modifying global values

Following these principles makes your Python code efficient, readable, and maintainable.

Exercises and Challenges: Practice Problems and Solutions

Now that you have learned the fundamentals of Python functions, it is time to apply your knowledge to real-world programming tasks. These exercises will help strengthen your understanding of function definition, calling functions, handling parameters and return values, and using advanced function features, such as variable scope and flexible arguments.

Each challenge encourages problem-solving and logical thinking, helping you become more confident in writing Python code. Approach each problem systematically and test your solutions thoroughly to ensure they work correctly.

Practice Problem 1: Temperature Converter Function:

- **Task:** Create a function named `convert_temperature` that converts temperatures between Celsius and Fahrenheit. It should accept:
  - A temperature value
  - A unit ('C' for Celsius or 'F' for Fahrenheit)
- **Challenge:** Ensure your function correctly converts in both directions and test it with different temperature values.

Practice Problem 2: Prime Number Checker

- **Task:** Create a function called `is_prime` that determines whether a number is prime. It should return True if the number is prime and False otherwise.
- **Challenge:** A prime number is greater than 1 and is only divisible by 1 and itself. Optimize your function for larger numbers and test it against multiple inputs.

Practice Problem 3: Repeat String

- **Task:** Create a function named `repeat_string` that repeats a given string a specified number of times.
- **Challenge:** Use Python's string multiplication feature to implement this in one line. Ensure that it handles empty strings and zero repetitions correctly.

Practice Problem 4: Fibonacci Sequence Generator

- **Task:** Create a function called fibonacci that generates the Fibonacci sequence up to a given number n.
- **Challenge:** The Fibonacci sequence starts with 0 and 1, and each number is the sum of the previous two numbers. Ensure your function handles n = 0, 1, or negative numbers properly.

Practice Problem 5: Daily Step Goal Tracker

- **Task:** Create a function named **`track_daily_steps`** that updates a global variable, **`daily_steps`**, with the number of steps walked each day.
- **Challenge:**
    - o Set **`daily_steps = 0`** and **`step_goal = 10000`** outside the function.
    - o Use the **`global`** keyword to modify **`daily_steps`** inside the function.
    - o After updating **`daily_steps`**, check if the total meets or exceeds **`step_goal`**. If so, print "**`Congratulations! You have met your daily step goal`**!"
    - o Test the function with different step values to verify that it tracks progress correctly.

Practice Problem 6: Odd or Even Number Identifier

- **Task:** Create a function called **`identify_odd_even`** that determines whether a number is odd or even.
- **Challenge:**
    - o The function should take one parameter (num).
    - o Use conditional logic to check whether the number is even or odd.
    - o Utilize the modulo operator (%) to determine divisibility by 2.
    - o Call the function with both odd and even numbers to confirm the correct outputs.

Practice Problem 7: Factorial Calculator

- **Task:** Create a function named **`calculate_factorial`** to compute the factorial of a given number. The factorial of n is the product of all positive integers from 1 to n.
- **Challenge:**
    - o The function should take one argument (n) and return the factorial result.
    - o Remember that the factorial of 0 is always 1.
    - o Use a loop inside your function to calculate the factorial.
    - o Test your function with various numbers to confirm it produces accurate factorial calculations.

How to Approach These Problems:

- Understand the task clearly before writing any code.
- Break the problem into smaller steps and outline the logic.
- Write the function definition, ensuring it takes the correct parameters.
- Test your function with different inputs to check for correctness.
- Optimize where possible to make your code more efficient.

These exercises cover a variety of programming scenarios, from basic arithmetic operations to logic-based tasks and global variable tracking. Completing these challenges will reinforce key concepts and help you write better and more structured Python programs.

Solutions to Practice Problems

Here are the solutions to the practice problems presented earlier. Each solution includes a Python function definition, explanation, and testing examples to help you understand the logic and validate your own implementation.

Solution to Practice Problem 1: Temperature Converter Function

Defining the Function:

- Converts between Celsius and Fahrenheit
- Uses conditional logic to apply the correct formula
- Returns an error message if an invalid unit is provided

```
def convert_temperature(temp, unit):
    """Converts temperature between Celsius and Fahrenheit."""
    if unit == "C":
        return (temp * 9/5) + 32  # Celsius to Fahrenheit
    elif unit == "F":
        return (temp - 32) * 5/9  # Fahrenheit to Celsius
    else:
        return "Invalid unit. Use 'C' for Celsius or 'F' for Fahrenheit."

# Testing the function
print(convert_temperature(0, "C"))  # Outputs: 32
print(convert_temperature(32, "F"))  # Outputs: 0
print(convert_temperature(100, "C"))  # Outputs: 212
print(convert_temperature(212, "F"))  # Outputs: 100
```

Solution to Practice Problem 2: Prime Number Checker

Defining the Function:

- Checks if a number is greater than 1
- Loops from 2 to sqrt(n) + 1 to check divisibility
- Returns `True` if the number is prime, otherwise `False`

```
import math

def is_prime(number):
    """Checks if a number is prime."""
    if number <= 1:
        return False
    for i in range(2, int(math.sqrt(number)) + 1):
        if number % i == 0:
            return False
    return True

# Testing the function
print(is_prime(11))  # Outputs: True
print(is_prime(4))   # Outputs: False
print(is_prime(17))  # Outputs: True
print(is_prime(20))  # Outputs: False
```

Solution to Practice Problem 3: Repeat String

Defining the Function:

- Uses Python's built-in string multiplication feature
- Returns the string repeated n times
- Handles cases where the string is empty or n is zero

```
def repeat_string(s, n):
    """Repeats a given string 'n' times."""
    return s * n

# Repeating a simple greeting 3 times.
print(repeat_string("Hi! ", 3)) # Outputs "Hi! Hi! Hi! "
# Testing the function with an empty string and zero repetitions.
print(repeat_string("", 5)) # Outputs an empty string.
print(repeat_string("Python ", 0))  # Outputs: ""
print(repeat_string("!", 5))  # Outputs: "!!!!!"
```

Solution to Practice Problem 4: Fibonacci Sequence Generator

Defining the Function:

- Uses a loop to generate Fibonacci numbers up to n
- Returns an empty list for n <= 0
- Handles edge cases such as n = 1 and n = 2

```
def fibonacci(n):
    """Generates the Fibonacci sequence up to 'n' numbers."""
    if n <= 0:
        return []
    elif n == 1:
        return [0]

    sequence = [0, 1]
    while len(sequence) < n:
        sequence.append(sequence[-1] + sequence[-2])
    return sequence

# Testing the function
print(fibonacci(5))  # Outputs: [0, 1, 1, 2, 3]
print(fibonacci(1))  # Outputs: [0]
print(fibonacci(10))  # Outputs: [0, 1, 1, 2, 3, 5, 8, 13, 21, 34]
```

Solution to Practice Problem 5: Daily Step Goal Tracker

Defining the Function:

- Uses global variables **`daily_steps`** and **`step_goal`**
- Adds new steps to **`daily_steps`**
- Checks if **`daily_steps >= step_goal`**, then prints a congratulatory message

```
# Global variables
daily_steps = 0
step_goal = 10000

def track_daily_steps(steps):
    """Updates daily step count and checks if goal is met."""
    global daily_steps
    daily_steps += steps

    if daily_steps >= step_goal:
        print("Congratulations! You have met your daily step goal!")
    else:
        print(f"Great job! You need {step_goal - daily_steps} more steps.")
```

```
# Testing the function
track_daily_steps(3000)  # Outputs: "Great job! You need 7000 more steps."
track_daily_steps(4500)  # Outputs: "Great job! You need 2500 more steps."
track_daily_steps(3000)  # Outputs: "Congratulations! You have met your daily
step goal!"
```

Solution to Practice Problem 6: Odd or Even Number Identifier

Defining the Function:

- Uses the modulo operator (% 2) to check divisibility
- Prints "**Even**" if divisible by 2, otherwise "**Odd**"
- Tests with various numbers to ensure correctness

```
def identify_odd_even(num):
    """Checks if a number is odd or even."""
    if num % 2 == 0:
        print(f"{num} is Even.")
    else:
        print(f"{num} is Odd.")

# Testing the function
identify_odd_even(10)  # Outputs: "10 is Even."
identify_odd_even(7)   # Outputs: "7 is Odd."
identify_odd_even(0)   # Outputs: "0 is Even."
```

Solution to Practice Problem 7: Factorial Calculator

Defining the Function:

- Uses a loop to calculate n!
- Returns 1 for n = 0 (as per factorial definition)
- Prints an error message for negative numbers

```
def calculate_factorial(n):
    """Calculates the factorial of a given number."""
    if n < 0:
        return "Error: Factorial of a negative number doesn't exist."
    elif n == 0:
        return 1

    factorial = 1
    for i in range(1, n + 1):
        factorial *= i
    return factorial

# Testing the function
print(calculate_factorial(5))  # Outputs: 120 (5! = 5*4*3*2*1)
print(calculate_factorial(0))  # Outputs: 1 (0! = 1)
print(calculate_factorial(7))  # Outputs: 5040
print(calculate_factorial(-3)) # Outputs: "Error: Factorial of a negative
number doesn't exist."
```

By practicing these challenges, you will strengthen your problem-solving skills and write more efficient, reusable, and structured Python code. Keep practicing, and happy coding!

Conclusion

In this chapter, you have expanded your Python programming skills by creating and using functions, a key concept that helps make code structured, reusable, and efficient. Building on the logic and control structures from the previous chapter, where you learned to make decisions and repeat actions, you took the next step by encapsulating those actions into well-defined functions. Just as loops and conditionals made your programs more interactive and dynamic, functions allow you to organize and simplify your code, making it easier to manage and scale.

You have explored the fundamental structure of functions, learning how to define functions, pass parameters and arguments, and return useful results. You have also seen how local and global variables affect how data flows through programs, helping you manage data visibility and modification effectively.

In the next chapter, you will explore Python's data structures, including lists, tuples, dictionaries, and sets. These will help you store, access, and manipulate data efficiently, working alongside the functions you have learned to build even more powerful programs. The ability to organize and manage data is a crucial skill that will allow you to take your Python programming to the next level.

As you move from mastering individual functions to leveraging the aggregate power of data structures, keep calm and let us tame the Python!

Multiple-Choice Questions

1. What is the primary purpose of using functions in programming?
   a. To increase the speed of the program
   b. To minimize code readability
   c. To organize code into reusable blocks
   d. To use more memory
2. Which keyword is used in Python to define a function?
   a. function
   b. def
   c. func
   d. define
3. What type of variables can only be accessed within the function they are declared in?
   a. Global variables
   b. External variables
   c. Local variables
   d. Public variables
4. How can you pass data to functions in Python?
   a. Parameters
   b. Console input

   c. Using files
   d. Directly writing data inside the function
5. Which statement is used to return a value from a function?
   a. return
   b. output
   c. back
   d. result
6. What will happen if you try to use a local variable outside of its function?
   a. It will return a default value.
   b. It will cause an error.
   c. It will reset its value to zero.
   d. It will become a global variable.
7. Which of the following correctly declares a function with a default parameter in Python?
   a. `def my_func(x=5):`
   b. `def my_func(x): x=5`
   c. `def my_func(x==5):`
   d. `def my_func(x!=5):`
8. What does the global keyword do?
   a. It creates a new global variable
   b. It imports a global variable from another module
   c. It declares that the variable inside the function is global
   d. It exports a local variable to the global scope
9. What are `*args` and `**kwargs` used for in function definitions?
   a. `*args` is used for a single argument, and `**kwargs` for multiple
   b. `*args` gathers additional positional arguments, `**kwargs` gathers additional keyword arguments
   c. `*args` defines default parameters, and `**kwargs` defines required parameters.
   d. Both are used to specify variable names explicitly
10. In which scenario would you use a return statement in a function?
   a. When you need to print a value directly to the console
   b. When you need the function to exit and give a value back to the caller
   c. When you want to keep the function running indefinitely
   d. When you need to check if the function works correctly

Answers

1. c
2. b
3. c
4. a
5. a
6. b.
7. a
8. c
9. b
10. b

Points to Remember

- Python's **`def`** keyword defines functions, encapsulating reusable pieces of code for better program organization and management.
- Functions accept parameters and arguments, providing flexibility and functionality to your code.
- The return statement marks the end of a function's execution and outputs its value, allowing it to be integrated into program logic.
- Understanding variable scope is vital; local variables are limited to the function they are declared in, but global variables can be accessed throughout the program.
- The global keyword affects global variables inside a local scope, binding changes in a function to the entire program.
- Using default parameter values in function declarations improves flexibility by requiring fewer arguments.
- Variable-length arguments (**`*args`** for an arbitrary number of positional arguments and **`**kwargs`** for keyword arguments) enable functions to handle diverse inputs dynamically.
- Building practical projects, such as a calculator or greeting card generator, helps students comprehend functions through hands-on practice.
- Advanced function ideas, such as default values and variable-length parameters, prepare you for complicated programming tasks, allowing you to create adaptive and powerful functions.

Further Reading

For more in-depth exploration of Python functions, consider these resources:

1. **Python Functions – Real Python:**
   https://realpython.com/defining-your-own-python-function/
   A beginner-friendly guide to defining and using functions, with practical examples.
2. **Python Scope & Global Variables – W3Schools:**
   https://www.w3schools.com/python/python_scope.asp
   An easy-to-understand explanation of variable scope and how local and global variables work in Python.

CHAPTER 6
Organizing Data

Introduction

In the last chapter, you learned how to make decisions in programs and how to repeat actions when needed. This helped you write code that reacts to different situations and performs tasks efficiently. But what if you need to store a lot of information and manage it properly? That is where organizing data becomes important.

Think of this like cleaning up after a big event. If everything is scattered around, finding what you need becomes difficult. But if you put things in the right places, clothes in the wardrobe, books on the shelf, and dishes in the kitchen, then it is much easier to handle. The same happens in programming. If you store information properly, your programs become faster, smarter, and easier to work with.

In this chapter, you will explore the best ways to store, access, and manage information in Python. By the end, you will be able to keep your data neat and organized, making your programs run smoothly and efficiently.

Structure

In this chapter, the following topics will be covered:

- Introduction to Data and Data Structure
  - Understanding Data
  - Overview of Data Structures: Lists, Tuples, Dictionaries, Sets
- Lists
  - Understanding Lists and Their Characteristics
  - Creating and Accessing Lists
  - Manipulating Lists
  - Common Methods for Working with Lists
  - Practical Exercise: Task List Management
  - Advanced Topics in List Manipulation
- Tuples
  - Understanding Tuples and Their Characteristics
  - Creating and Accessing Tuples
  - Practical Exercise: Employee Record Management
  - Advanced Topics in Tuple Manipulation
- Dictionaries
  - Understanding Dictionaries and Their Characteristics
  - Creating and Using Dictionaries
  - Practical Exercise: Inventory Management System

- Sets
  - Understanding Sets and Their Characteristics
  - Creating and Using Sets
  - Practical Exercise: Event Guest List Management
- Common Mistakes and Best Practices
- Exercises and Challenges: Practice Problems and Solutions

Introduction to Data and Data Structure

Imagine your room is messy, with clothes, books, and toys scattered everywhere. Finding what you need would take a long time! But if everything is placed in the right spot, clothes in the wardrobe, books on a shelf, and toys in a box, you can find things quickly and easily. In programming, organizing data helps programs run faster and more smoothly.

Understanding Data

Data is just information. It could be your name, a phone number, a list of groceries, or even a photo. A program uses data just like you use information in real life to store, remember, and process things.

The Role of Data Structures:

A data structure is a smart way to store and organize data. Think of it like drawers in a cabinet. Each drawer holds something different, making it easy to find and use things when needed.

Real-Life Examples of Organizing Data:

- **A Library**: Books are placed on shelves by category, so you can find them quickly. In the same way, programs store data in an organized way.
- **Packing a Suitcase**: You keep clothes in one section, shoes in another, and toiletries in a small pouch. This is like using different data structures for different types of data.
- **A Music Playlist**: You do not scroll through thousands of songs to find your favorite. You organize them by artist or genre. That is what data structures do in programming. They help group similar data together so you can find it easily.

The Importance of Data Structures in Programming:

- **Saves Time**: Finding data quickly makes programs run faster.
- **Keeps Data Organized**: Structuring information properly makes programs easier to understand.
- **Handles Large Amounts of Data**: Just like a library can hold millions of books without confusion, good data structures help programs store and manage large amounts of information easily.

Just like organizing your room makes life easier, learning how to organize data properly will make you a better programmer. Let us dive in and learn how to store information the right way.

Overview of Data Structures: Lists, Tuples, Dictionaries, Sets

In the previous section, you have learned why organizing data properly is important and how it makes programs faster, easier to understand, and more efficient. Now, you will explore four powerful ways to store and manage data in Python: lists, tuples, dictionaries, and sets.

Each of these works like a different type of storage container, designed for specific needs. Think of this as a quick introduction. You do not need to fully understand them yet. As you move through this chapter, you will break them down step by step, using real-life examples and practical exercises to help you learn how to use them effectively.

Lists:

A list is like a playlist of songs. You can add, remove, or change tracks whenever you want. In programming, lists allow you to store multiple pieces of data in a specific order and modify them as needed.

When to Use a List:

- Keeping a to-do list where tasks can be added or removed
- Storing a shopping list that changes over time
- Managing a group of names for a team or event

Tuples:

A tuple is like a printed book. Once the pages are set, they cannot be changed. In Python, tuples store fixed sets of data that should not be modified.

Usage of a Tuple:

- Storing coordinates of a location (latitude, longitude) that do not change
- Keeping days of the week in a program since they are always the same
- Storing fixed settings or configuration values that should not be changed

Dictionaries:

A dictionary works like a phone book; you look up a person's name (key) to find their phone number (value). In Python, dictionaries store pairs of related information for quick and easy access.

Usage of a Dictionary:

- Looking up contact details based on a person's name.
- Storing student grades, where each student has a unique ID.
- Managing product prices in an online store.

Sets:

A set is like a club membership list. Every member is unique, and no duplicates are allowed. In Python, sets help store distinct values and perform fast comparisons between different groups of data.

Usage of a Set:

- Keeping a list of unique visitors to a website
- Removing duplicate items from a list automatically
- Comparing two groups of data to see what they have in common

If all of this feels a little overwhelming, do not worry! In the next sections, you will slowly break down each of these data structures, explaining exactly how they work and when to use them. You will use real-world examples and easy exercises so you can learn by doing.

Lists

In the previous section, you got a quick overview of different ways to store data in Python. Now, let us take a closer look at lists, one of the most commonly used data structures.

A list is like a grocery shopping list. You can add, remove, and change items as needed. It helps store multiple pieces of information in a specific order, making it easy to manage and update.

Understanding Lists and Their Characteristics

Lists are ordered and changeable, meaning you can arrange items in a specific order and modify them whenever needed.

- **Ordered**: Items are stored in a fixed order, and it is preserved unless you change it. Think of a to-do list where tasks appear in a specific sequence.
- **Mutable**: You can add, remove, or change items in a list. It is like a shopping list where you cross off bought items, add new ones, or swap one product for another.

Real-Life Example: Organizing a Bookshelf

Imagine organizing books on a shelf:

- **Ordered**: You arrange them by genre, author, or size, just like Python lists store items in a specific order.
- **Mutable:** You can add new books, remove old ones, or rearrange them anytime, just like updating a list in Python.

Lists in Python work the same way, making them flexible and easy to use in many situations.

Creating and Accessing Lists

To use lists effectively, you need to know how to create them and retrieve data from them.

Creating Lists in Python:

There are different ways to create a list, depending on what you need.

- An empty list:
  ```
  empty_list = []
  ```
  This starts with no items but allows adding elements later.
- A list with initial values:
  ```
  numbers = [1, 2, 3, 4, 5]
  fruits = ["apple", "banana", "cherry"]
  mixed_list = ["hello", 100, 15.5, True]
  ```
  Lists can store different types of data, including numbers, text, and even other lists.
- Using the **`list()`** constructor:
  ```
  string_to_list = list("hello")  # Converts a string into a list of characters
  range_to_list = list(range(5))  # Creates [0, 1, 2, 3, 4]
  ```
  The **`list()`** function converts other types of data (such as text or number sequences) into a list.

Accessing List Items Using Indexing and Slicing

Once a list is created, you can retrieve data from it using indexing and slicing.

- **Indexing (Accessing Individual Items):**

  Lists use index numbers to access elements. The first item starts at index 0.
  ```
  fruits = ["apple", "banana", "cherry", "date"]

  print(fruits[0])  # Outputs 'apple'
  print(fruits[2])  # Outputs 'cherry'
  print(fruits[-1])  # Outputs 'date' (negative index starts from the end)
  ```

Negative indexing is useful when accessing items from the end of the list.

- **Slicing (Accessing Multiple Items):**

  Slicing allows retrieving a portion of a list using a range of indexes.

```
numbers = [0, 1, 2, 3, 4, 5, 6, 7, 8, 9]

print(numbers[2:6])  # Outputs [2, 3, 4, 5] (items from index 2 to 5)
print(numbers[:3])  # Outputs [0, 1, 2] (first 3 elements)
print(numbers[4:])  # Outputs [4, 5, 6, 7, 8, 9] (everything from index 4
onward)
print(numbers[::-1])  # Outputs [9, 8, 7, 6, 5, 4, 3, 2, 1, 0] (reverses the
list)
```

  Slicing is powerful for working with parts of a list without modifying the original data.

Manipulating Lists

Python provides built-in functions to modify lists efficiently.

Adding Items to a List:

- Appending an item at the end:
  `fruits.append("date")`
- Inserting an item at a specific position:
  `fruits.insert(1, "blueberry")  # Adds "blueberry" at index 1`
- Extending a list with multiple items:

```
more_fruits = ["elderberry", "fig"]
fruits.extend(more_fruits)  # Adds multiple elements at once
```

Removing Items from a List:

- Removing a specific item:
  `fruits.remove("banana")  # Deletes 'banana' from the list`
- Removing an item by its **`index:CopyEdit`**
  `last_fruit = fruits.pop()  # Removes the last item and returns it`
- Clearing all items from the list:
  `fruits.clear()  # Now the list is empty []`

Changing Items in a List:

You can modify list elements by assigning new values to a specific index.

```
fruits[1] = "blackberry"  # Replaces 'banana' with 'blackberry'
```

Common Methods for Working with Lists

Python has additional useful functions for managing lists.

- Sorting items alphabetically or numerically:
  `fruits.sort()  # Sorts alphabetically`
- Reversing the order of items:
  `fruits.reverse()  # Reverses the list order`
- Counting occurrences of an item:
  `count = fruits.count("apple")  # Counts how many times 'apple' appears`

Importance of Lists:

Lists are one of the most flexible data structures in Python because they allow easy storage and modification of data. They are used in:

- To-do lists, where tasks need to be added, removed, or updated
- Managing user inputs in applications
- Storing dynamic data, such as real-time scores in a game

As you continue, you will explore other data structures such as tuples, dictionaries, and sets to see when they might be better choices than lists. Stay tuned!

Practical Exercise: Task List Management

In the previous section, you explored how lists allow you to store and modify data easily. Now, let us apply that knowledge by building a simple to-do list program. This exercise will show how lists can be used to add, remove, and display tasks, just like managing a daily planner.

Task Description:

Create a Python program that helps a user manage their to-do list. The program will allow users to:

- Add tasks to their list.
- Remove completed tasks from the list.
- View all tasks currently in the list.

This exercise will help practice list operations while making something useful!

Steps for the Exercise

1. **Start with an Empty List**: This will store all tasks.
2. **Create a Menu System**: Let users choose actions (add, remove, or view tasks).
3. **Add Tasks**: Allow users to input new tasks and store them in the list.
4. **Remove Tasks**: Users can delete a task, with a check to handle missing tasks.
5. **View Tasks**: Display all current tasks neatly.
6. **Enhance with List Comprehensions**: Allow filtering tasks based on specific criteria (optional).

Python Code for Task Management:

```
# Initialize the list of tasks
tasks = []

while True:
    # Display menu options
    print("\n1. Add a task")
    print("2. Remove a task")
    print("3. Show all tasks")
    print("4. Exit")

    # Get user's choice
    choice = input("Enter your choice: ")

    if choice == '1':
        # Adding a task
        task = input("What task would you like to add? ")
```

```
        tasks.append(task)
        print("Task added.")

    elif choice == '2':
        # Removing a task
        task = input("What task would you like to remove? ")
        if task in tasks:
            tasks.remove(task)
            print("Task removed.")
        else:
            print("Task not found.")

    elif choice == '3':
        # Viewing all tasks
        print("\nCurrent Tasks:")
        if tasks:
            for task in tasks:
                print(f"- {task}")
        else:
            print("No tasks in the list.")

    elif choice == '4':
        # Exiting the program
        print("Exiting program.")
        break

    else:
        # Handling invalid input
        print("Invalid choice. Please enter a valid option.")
```

Understanding the Code:

- **Using a List**: The tasks list stores all the user's to-do items.
- **Menu System**: The program runs in a loop, displaying a menu where the user can choose to add, remove, or view tasks.
- **Adding Tasks (`append()`)**: The program prompts the user to enter a task and adds it to the list.
- **Removing Tasks (`remove()`)**: The program checks if the task exists before removing it. If the task is not found, it displays an error message.
- **Displaying Tasks**: It neatly prints all current tasks, adding a message if the list is empty.
- **Loop and Exit Option**: The program keeps running until the user selects option 4 (Exit).

This is just the beginning! As you explore more list operations, you will learn how to sort, filter, and optimize data in Python to make programs even more powerful.

Advanced Topics in List Manipulation

In the previous section, you've learned how to create, access, and modify lists using simple methods like **`append()`**, **`remove()`**, and **`sort()`**. Now, you will take it a step further and explore more advanced techniques that can help you work with lists faster and more efficiently.

Two powerful concepts to be covered are:

- **Lists of Lists**: How to store and manage data in a multi-level structure, like a table.
- **List Comprehensions**: A shortcut for creating lists quickly and efficiently.

These techniques are useful when working with larger datasets or when writing code that needs to be clean and optimized.

Lists of Lists in Python:

Python allows lists to contain other lists, making it possible to store data in a structured way. This is useful for situations where data is organized in rows and columns, like a table or a game board.

Understanding Lists of Lists:

A list of lists is simply a list where each item is also a list. This is useful when organizing information that fits into a grid or table format.

Creating a List of Lists:

```
# A 3x3 matrix
matrix = [
    [1, 2, 3],
    [4, 5, 6],
    [7, 8, 9]
]

# A list representing a simple spreadsheet
spreadsheet = [
    ["Name", "Age", "City"],
    ["Alice", 30, "New York"],
    ["Bob", 27, "Los Angeles"]
]
```

- The matrix example represents a 3x3 grid, often used in math and programming.
- The spreadsheet example represents a table with rows and columns, just like a spreadsheet.

Accessing Data in a List of Lists:

To retrieve a specific value from a nested list, you use multiple indexes:

```
# Getting the first element of the first row
first_item = matrix[0][0]  # Outputs 1

# Getting the city of the second person in the spreadsheet
city = spreadsheet[1][2]  # Outputs "New York"
```

Each pair of square brackets [ ] zooms in deeper into the nested list.

Modifying Data in a List of Lists:

Just like normal lists, you can change the values inside a nested list:

```
# Changing an element in the matrix
matrix[0][0] = 10  # Now the first item is 10 instead of 1

# Updating the age of the second person in the spreadsheet
spreadsheet[1][1] = 31
```

This allows you to edit specific values while keeping the overall structure intact.

Usage of Lists of Lists:

- **Game Development**: Storing a game board (like tic-tac-toe or chess).
- **Data Science**: Organizing datasets for analysis.
- **Web Development**: Managing table-like data for websites.

While lists of lists are flexible and useful, they use more memory when handling large amounts of data. For high-performance tasks, special libraries such as NumPy provide more efficient solutions.

Using List Comprehensions:

List comprehensions are a shortcut for creating and modifying lists in a single line of code. They make code simpler, faster, and easier to read.

Basic Syntax of List Comprehensions

```
[expression for item in iterable]
```

- **Expression**: Defines what to do with each item
- **Item**: Represents each element in the sequence
- **Iterable**: The data collection being processed (such as a list or range).

Simple Examples of List Comprehensions: Creating a List of Squares

```
squares = [x**2 for x in range(10)]
print(squares)  # Outputs [0, 1, 4, 9, 16, 25, 36, 49, 64, 81]
```

Instead of using a loop, you can create a list of squares in one line.

Adding Conditional Logic:

List comprehensions can filter elements based on conditions.

- **Filtering Even Numbers**

  ```
  evens = [x for x in range(10) if x % 2 == 0]
  print(evens)  # Outputs [0, 2, 4, 6, 8]
  ```

  Only numbers that are divisible by 2 are included.

- **Filtering Words by Length**

  ```
  fruits = ["Apple", "Banana", "Cherry"]
  long_fruits = [fruit for fruit in fruits if len(fruit) > 5]
  print(long_fruits)  # Outputs ['Banana', 'Cherry']
  ```

  Only fruits with more than 5 letters are kept in the new list.

Nested Loops in List Comprehensions:

Sometimes, list comprehensions contain multiple loops.

Flattening a Nested List:

```
nested_list = [[1, 2], [3, 4], [5, 6]]
flat_list = [item for sublist in nested_list for item in sublist]
print(flat_list)  # Outputs [1, 2, 3, 4, 5, 6]
```

The inner loop extracts each item from sublists and stores it in a single list.

Usage of List Comprehensions:

- **Transforming Data**: Converting one list format into another
- **Filtering Data**: Selecting only the elements that meet a condition
- **Improving Readability**: Writing cleaner and more compact code

Usage of List Comprehensions:

- **Faster**: They execute faster than traditional loops.
- **More Readable**: They make code cleaner and easier to understand.
- **More Efficient**: They reduce the need for temporary lists and variables.

By mastering list comprehensions, you will be able to write Python code more effectively while keeping it short and readable.

Tuples

In the previous section, you have explored lists, which allow you to store and modify collections of data. However, not all data should be changeable. Sometimes, you will need to store information that should remain fixed. This is where tuples come in.

A tuple is like a sealed envelope. Once the contents are inside, they cannot be changed. This makes tuples ideal for storing important, unchangeable data while still keeping the ability to access and read it.

Understanding Tuples and Their Characteristics

Tuples have two main properties that make them different from lists:

- **Ordered**: Tuples store data in a fixed sequence, just like lists. Each item has a specific position (index).
- **Immutable**: Unlike lists, tuples cannot be changed after creation. If you need to modify a tuple, you must create a new one instead.

Real-Life Example: Passport Information

Imagine applying for a passport. When issued, your passport contains:

- **Ordered Information**: Your name, passport number, and nationality are always in the same order.
- **Immutable Data**: Once issued, the details cannot be changed. If there is an error, a new passport must be created.

Tuples work the same way in Python, making them perfect for storing unchangeable data, such as dates, coordinates, and configuration settings.

Creating and Accessing Tuples

Tuples are created just like lists, but instead of square brackets [], they use parentheses ().

Creating Tuples:

- **Using parentheses:**
  ```
  my_tuple = (1, 2, 3)
  ```
- **Without parentheses (tuple packing):**
  ```
  another_tuple = 'apple', 'banana', 'cherry'  # Python automatically treats
  this as a tuple
  ```
- **Single element tuple (requires a comma):**
  ```
  single_tuple = (4,)  # The comma is necessary; without it, Python treats it as
  a number
  ```
- **Using the `tuple()` constructor:**
  ```
  # Creating a tuple from a list
  list_to_tuple = tuple([5, 6, 7])

  # Creating a tuple from a string
  string_to_tuple = tuple("hello")  # Outputs ('h', 'e', 'l', 'l', 'o')
  ```

Accessing Tuple Elements:

Just like lists, tuples use indexing to access elements.

- **Retrieving an Element Using Indexing**

```
fruits = ("apple", "banana", "cherry")

print(fruits[1])  # Outputs 'banana'
```

  Tuples are zero-indexed, meaning the first item is at index 0, the second at 1, and so on.

- **Using Negative Indexing**

```
print(fruits[-1])  # Outputs 'cherry' (last element)
```

  Negative indexing starts from the end, with -1 referring to the last element.

Slicing a Tuple:

```
numbers = (0, 1, 2, 3, 4, 5)

print(numbers[:3])  # Outputs (0, 1, 2)
print(numbers[2:])  # Outputs (2, 3, 4, 5)
```

Slicing allows retrieving a portion of the tuple while keeping the original data unchanged.

Example: Working with a Date Tuple

Let us say you have a tuple representing a date:

```
date_tuple = (2023, 10, 5)  # (Year, Month, Day)

year = date_tuple[0]
day = date_tuple[2]

print("Year:", year)  # Outputs Year: 2023
print("Day:", day)  # Outputs Day: 5
```

Tuples are useful for grouping related data together, such as dates or database records.

Using Tuples Instead of Lists

Tuples are faster and safer than lists. Here is when you should use them:

- **Data That Should Not Change**: Example: Days of the week, months of the year, or configuration settings.
- **Performance Matters**: Tuples are faster than lists because they do not allow modifications.
- **Ensuring Data Integrity**: Prevents accidental changes to important data.

By mastering tuples, you will learn how to store and manage fixed data efficiently, making your programs more reliable and secure!

Practical Exercise: Employee Record Management

In the previous section, you explored how tuples store unchangeable data and why they are useful for keeping important information secure. Now, let us apply this concept to a real-world scenario, managing employee records.

In this exercise, you will create a simple employee database using tuples to store fixed employee details, such as name, position, and department. Using tuples ensures that employee data remains unchanged, just like in real HR systems, where certain records (such as employee IDs) should not be modified.

Task Description:

Build a Python program that:

- Stores employee details in tuples (ID, name, position, department)
- Keeps all employee records in a list for easy reference
- Retrieves and displays employee information based on their unique ID
- Uses tuple unpacking to neatly display employee details

Steps for the Exercise

1. **Create Employee Tuples**: Store each employee's details in a tuple
2. **Store Tuples in a List**: Maintain a list of all employees
3. **Retrieve Employee Data**: Allow users to search for an employee by their ID
4. **Display Employee Details**: Use tuple unpacking to present the data clearly

Python Code for Employee Management

```
# List to store employee tuples
employees = []

# Function to add an employee
def add_employee(emp_id, name, position, department):
    employee = (emp_id, name, position, department)  # Creating an employee
tuple
    employees.append(employee)  # Storing it in the list

# Function to display employee details
def display_employee(emp_id):
    for employee in employees:
        if employee[0] == emp_id:  # Checking if ID matches
            _, name, position, department = employee  # Unpacking tuple
            print("\nEmployee Details:")
            print(f"Name: {name}")
            print(f"Position: {position}")
            print(f"Department: {department}")
            break
    else:
        print("Employee not found.")

# Adding employees to the list
add_employee(1, "John Doe", "Software Developer", "Technology")
add_employee(2, "Jane Smith", "Project Manager", "Marketing")

# Displaying an employee's details
display_employee(1)
```

Understanding the Code:

- **Using Tuples for Secure Data Storage**: Each employee is stored in a tuple, ensuring that their ID, name, position, and department remain fixed.
- **Appending Tuples to a List**: The employees list acts as a storage system for multiple employee records.
- **Searching for an Employee**: The **`display_employee()`** function loops through the list, checks the ID, and retrieves details.

- **Tuple Unpacking**: The function extracts values from the tuple and displays them in a structured format.

Reasons for using Tuples for This Task:

- **Data Integrity**: Employee records should not be accidentally changed.
- **Efficiency**: Tuples consume less memory compared to lists.
- **Easy Retrieval**: Employees can be searched and displayed quickly.

This exercise demonstrates how tuples are useful for managing fixed data in real-world applications, ensuring data security, clarity, and efficiency.

Advanced Topics in Tuple Manipulation

In the previous section, you explored how tuples store unchangeable data and are useful for keeping information secure and organized. Now, let us look at some advanced ways to use tuples that can help make your programs more efficient and readable.

These topics are optional but can be useful if you want to write cleaner, more flexible code in complex programming scenarios.

Tuple Packing and Unpacking

Python allows packing multiple values into a tuple and unpacking them into individual variables. This makes working with multiple values easier and more organized.

- **Tuple Packing**

  Tuple packing allows grouping multiple values into a single tuple without explicitly defining a structure.

  ```
  # Packing multiple values into a tuple
  employee = "John Doe", "Engineering", "Software Engineer"
  ```

  The employee variable now holds three values in a single tuple.

- **Tuple Unpacking**

  Unpacking allows extracting each value from a tuple into separate variables.

  ```
  # Unpacking tuple values into individual variables
  name, department, position = employee

  print(name)       # Outputs: John Doe
  print(department) # Outputs: Engineering
  print(position)   # Outputs: Software Engineer
  ```

  This is useful when a function returns multiple values or when working with structured data.

Using Named Tuples for Better Readability

Python provides named tuples through the collections module, which makes it easier to refer to tuple elements by name instead of using index positions.

```
from collections import namedtuple

# Creating a named tuple class
Employee = namedtuple('Employee', ['name', 'department', 'position'])

# Creating an instance of a named tuple
emp = Employee(name="Jane Smith", department="Marketing", position="Manager")
```

```
# Accessing elements using attribute names
print(emp.name)       # Outputs: Jane Smith
print(emp.department) # Outputs: Marketing
print(emp.position)   # Outputs: Manager
```

Unlike regular tuples, named tuples improve code readability by allowing access to elements using names instead of index numbers.

Using Tuples in Functions

Tuples are commonly used in functions to:

- Return multiple values
- Handle variable-length arguments

Returning Multiple Values Using Tuples

A function can return multiple values as a tuple instead of using multiple return statements.

```
def get_dimensions():
    width = 10
    height = 5
    return width, height  # Returns a tuple

# Storing the returned tuple
dimensions = get_dimensions()

# Accessing values
print(f"Width: {dimensions[0]}, Height: {dimensions[1]}")
```

The function automatically packs values into a tuple, making it easy to return and retrieve multiple values.

Using Tuples for Variable-Length Arguments (`*args`)

Tuples can store any number of function arguments using **`*args`**.

```
def concat_strings(*args):
    return ' '.join(args)

result = concat_strings("Hello", "world", "!")
print(result)  # Outputs: "Hello world !"
```

`*args` collects all arguments into a tuple, making the function more flexible.

Tuple Comprehensions Using Generator Expressions

Python does not have tuple comprehensions, but you can create a tuple using generator expressions inside the **`tuple()`** constructor.

```
# Creating a tuple with squared numbers
numbers = tuple(x ** 2 for x in range(5))

print(numbers)  # Outputs: (0, 1, 4, 9, 16)
```

This approach saves memory compared to creating a full list first.

Importance of these Advanced Tuple Techniques

- **Tuple Packing and Unpacking**: Makes handling multiple values easier
- **Named Tuples**: Improve readability and make code more structured
- **Using Tuples in Functions**: Allows returning multiple values and handling variable-length arguments

- **Tuple Comprehensions**: Create optimized and memory-efficient tuples

By learning these techniques, you will write cleaner, faster, and more efficient Python code while taking full advantage of tuples in complex programming tasks.

Dictionaries

In the previous section, you explored tuples, which help store fixed, unchangeable data. However, in many cases, you will need a more flexible way to store and manage information. This is where dictionaries come in.

A dictionary is like a phone book. You look up a person's name (key) to find their phone number (value). This makes dictionaries perfect for storing and retrieving data quickly based on a unique key.

Understanding Dictionaries and Their Characteristics

Dictionaries are key-value pairs, meaning each piece of data is stored with a unique key that helps find it quickly.

- **Key-Value Pairs**: Instead of using index numbers (such as lists), dictionaries use keys to access data.
- **Unordered** (before Python 3.7): Before Python 3.7, dictionaries did not store elements in a fixed order. From Python 3.7 onwards, they maintain insertion order but should not be used for ordered operations.
- **Mutable**: You can add, remove, or change items in a dictionary after creating it.

Real-Life Example: Library Catalog

Imagine a library catalog where books are stored with ISBN numbers (unique keys) instead of their position on a shelf.

- **Key-Value Pairs**: Just like using an ISBN to find a book, dictionaries use keys to find values.
- **Unordered Storage**: The books may be physically arranged differently, but they are still easy to look up by ISBN.
- **Mutable Data**: You can add new books, update book details, or remove old books from the catalog.

Dictionaries work the same way, making them powerful for fast data lookup and management.

Creating and Using Dictionaries

Dictionaries store data by key instead of position. This makes them perfect for handling structured data.

Creating a Dictionary

- Using Curly Braces {} (Most Common Method)

  ```
  my_dict = {'name': 'John', 'age': 30, 'job': 'Developer'}
  ```

- Using the `dict()` Constructor

  ```
  # Creating a dictionary using keyword arguments
  another_dict = dict(name="Alice", age=25, job="Designer")

  # Creating a dictionary from key-value pairs
  pair_dict = dict([('name', 'Bob'), ('age', 20)])
  ```

Accessing Data in a Dictionary

Unlike lists, dictionaries do not use index numbers. Instead, you access values using keys.

- Retrieving a Value Using a Key
```
print(my_dict['name'])  # Outputs: John
```
- Using `.get()` to Avoid Errors
```
print(my_dict.get('age', 'Not Specified'))  # Outputs: 30
print(my_dict.get('city', 'Not Specified'))  # Outputs: Not Specified
```

`.get()` prevents errors if a key is missing by returning a default value instead.

Updating and Modifying Dictionary Data

Dictionaries allow you to update values, add new data, or remove existing data.

- **Updating an Existing Entry**
```
my_dict['age'] = 31  # Updates age to 31
```
- **Adding a New Entry**
```
my_dict['city'] = 'New York'  # Adds a new key-value pair
```
- **Using `.update()` to Modify Multiple Keys at Once**
```
my_dict.update({'age': 31, 'city': 'New York'})
print(my_dict)
# Outputs {'name': 'John', 'age': 31, 'job': 'Developer', 'city': 'New York'}
```

Example: Using a Dictionary for a Contact List

A dictionary can store a contact's details, such as name, email, and phone number.

```
contact_dict = {'name': 'Sarah', 'email': 'sarah@example.com', 'phone':
'123-456-7890'}

# Accessing data
print("Email:", contact_dict['email'])  # Outputs: sarah@example.com

# Updating phone number
contact_dict.update({'phone': '987-654-3210'})
print("Updated Phone:", contact_dict['phone'])  # Outputs: 987-654-3210
```

Fast and efficient for retrieving and updating structured data.

Powerful features of Dictionaries

- **Fast Lookups**: Finding an item by key is much faster than searching through a list.
- **Flexible and Dynamic**: Can store a mix of different data types.
- **Perfect for Large Datasets**: Great for handling large amounts of structured information.

Dictionaries are one of Python's most useful data structures, essential for organizing and managing information efficiently.

Practical Exercise: Inventory Management System

In the previous section, you explored how dictionaries store and manage structured data efficiently. Now, let us apply this knowledge by building a simple inventory management system.

This project will demonstrate how key-value pairs in dictionaries help you add, update, delete, and retrieve data efficiently, just like real-world inventory systems used in stores, warehouses, and online marketplaces.

Task Description:

Create a Python program that allows users to manage an inventory. Each product in the inventory will have:

- A unique product ID as the key.
- A dictionary of product details as the value (name, quantity, and price).

Steps for the Exercise

1. **Initialize the Inventory**: Start with an empty dictionary to store products.
2. **Add Products**: Create a function to add new products with details (ID, name, quantity, and price).
3. **Update Products**: Modify product details (such as quantity or price) using the product ID.
4. **Remove Products**: Delete products from the inventory based on their product ID.
5. **View Inventory**: Display all available products with their details.

Python Code for Inventory Management

```
# Initialize the inventory dictionary
inventory = {}

# Function to add a product
def add_product(product_id, name, quantity, price):
    inventory[product_id] = {'name': name, 'quantity': quantity, 'price':
price}
    print(f"Product {name} added successfully.")

# Function to update a product
def update_product(product_id, name=None, quantity=None, price=None):
    if product_id in inventory:
        if name:
            inventory[product_id]['name'] = name
        if quantity is not None:
            inventory[product_id]['quantity'] = quantity
        if price is not None:
            inventory[product_id]['price'] = price
        print(f"Product {product_id} updated successfully.")
    else:
        print("Product not found.")

# Function to remove a product
def remove_product(product_id):
    if product_id in inventory:
        del inventory[product_id]
        print(f"Product {product_id} removed successfully.")
    else:
        print("Product not found.")

# Function to view all products
def view_inventory():
    if not inventory:
        print("Inventory is empty.")
    else:
        print("\nCurrent Inventory:")
```

```
        for product_id, details in inventory.items():
            print(f"ID: {product_id}, Name: {details['name']}, Quantity:
{details['quantity']}, Price: ${details['price']:.2f}")

# Adding products
add_product(1, "Tea", 100, 1.99)
add_product(2, "Coffee", 50, 2.99)

# Updating a product
update_product(1, quantity=150)

# Viewing inventory
view_inventory()

# Removing a product
remove_product(2)

# Viewing inventory after removal
view_inventory()
```

Understanding the Code:

- **Using a Dictionary for Structured Data**: Stores inventory as a dictionary, where each product ID is a key, and the product details (name, quantity, price) are stored as values in a nested dictionary.
- **Adding Products (`add_product`)**: Adds a new product to the dictionary using its unique ID as the key
- **Updating Products (`update_product`)**: Allows modifying specific product details while keeping other details unchanged.
- **Removing Products (`remove_product`)**: Uses del to delete a product from the dictionary.
- **Viewing Inventory (`view_inventory`)**: Displays all products in a clear, structured format.

Reasons for using Dictionaries for This Task:

- **Fast Lookups**: Searching for a product by ID is much faster than searching through a list.
- **Easily Updatable**: Allows quick modifications and deletions.
- **Structured Data**: Stores multiple details about each product in an organized way.

This exercise demonstrates how dictionaries can efficiently manage structured data, making them perfect for real-world applications, such as inventory management, customer databases, and product catalogs.

Sets

In the previous section, you explored dictionaries, which allow you to store and manage data using key-value pairs. Now, let us look at sets, another powerful data structure that helps in managing unique collections of data efficiently.

A set is like a list, but without duplicates. It ensures that each item appears only once, making it ideal for removing duplicates, checking membership, and performing mathematical operations such as unions and intersections.

Understanding Sets and Their Characteristics

Sets have three important properties that make them different from other data structures:

- **Unique Elements**: A set automatically removes duplicate values, making it useful for storing distinct items.
- **Unordered**: Items in a set do not have a fixed order and cannot be accessed by index sch as lists.
- **Mutable**: You can add or remove elements after creating a set, but the individual items inside the set must be immutable (for example, numbers, strings, or tuples).

Real-Life Example: Social Media Tags

Imagine a social media platform where users tag posts with keywords.

- **Unique Elements**: If multiple users add the same tag, it should appear only once on the post.
- **Unordered**: The order of tags does not matter, just like in a Python set.
- **Mutable**: Users can add or remove tags, but duplicate tags are not allowed.

This is exactly how sets work; they store distinct items, making them perfect for eliminating duplicates and managing collections efficiently.

Creating and Using Sets

Sets can be created using curly braces {} or the **`set()`** function.

Creating a Set

```
# Using curly braces
fruits = {'apple', 'banana', 'cherry'}

# Creating a set from a list
more_fruits = set(['orange', 'melon', 'banana'])  # 'banana' is added only
once
```

Duplicate items are automatically removed when using sets.

Basic Set Operations

Sets support several operations that allow you to add, remove, and compare elements efficiently.

- **Adding an Element to a Set**

  ```
  fruits.add('date')
  print(fruits)  # Outputs something like {'banana', 'date', 'apple', 'cherry'}
  ```

  If the element already exists, the set remains unchanged.

- **Removing an Element from a Set**

  ```
  fruits.remove('banana')  # Removes 'banana' (raises an error if not found)
  fruits.discard('banana')  # Removes 'banana' (does nothing if not found)
  ```

  `.remove()` raises an error if the item is missing, while **`.discard()`** silently does nothing.

Set Theory Operations

Sets allow fast comparisons using mathematical operations, such as union, intersection, and difference.

- **Union (union() or |)**

  Combines elements from both sets, keeping only unique values.

  ```
  tropical = {'pineapple', 'mango'}
  new_set = fruits.union(tropical)  # or fruits | tropical
  print(new_set)  # Combines both sets
  ```

- **Intersection (intersection() or &)**

  Finds common elements between sets.

  ```
  more_fruits = {'watermelon', 'banana'}
  common_fruits = fruits.intersection(more_fruits)  # or fruits & more_fruits
  print(common_fruits)  # Outputs items that exist in both sets
  ```

- **Difference (difference() or -)**

  Finds elements that exist in one set but not the other.

  ```
  unique_fruits = fruits.difference(more_fruits)  # or fruits - more_fruits
  print(unique_fruits)  # Outputs elements in `fruits` that are not in `more_
  fruits`
  ```

Example: Checking Membership Renewals

Imagine you manage a club membership database and need to find members who have not renewed their membership this year.

```
last_year_members = {'John', 'Mary', 'Steve', 'Olivia'}
this_year_members = {'Mary', 'Steve', 'James'}

non_renewed_members = last_year_members.difference(this_year_members)  # Mem-
bers who did not renew
print(non_renewed_members)  # Outputs {'John', 'Olivia'}
```

This shows how sets quickly compare data to find missing items.

Importance of Sets

- **Fast Lookups**: Checking if an item exists is much faster in sets than in lists.
- **Removes Duplicates**: Automatically eliminates duplicate values.
- **Great for Comparisons**: Quickly finds common or missing elements.

By using sets effectively, you can write cleaner and more efficient programs that handle unique data easily!

Practical Exercise: Event Guest List Management

In the previous section, you explored how sets efficiently handle unique data and perform operations, such as unions, intersections, and differences. Now, let us apply these concepts to event planning by managing guest lists using sets.

This exercise will show how set operations can help track invitations, RSVPs, and actual attendance, ensuring smooth event management.

Task Description:

Create a Python program that:

- Stores a list of invited guests in a set
- Tracks RSVPs in a separate set

- Records attendance on event day in another set
- Uses set operations to determine:
  - Who RSVPed but did not attend
  - Who attended without RSVP
  - Who RSVPed and attended

Steps for the Exercise

1. **Create an Invitation Set**: Collects the names of all invited guests
2. **Manage RSVPs**: Stores names of guests who RSVP
3. **Track Attendance**: Records names of attendees on the event day
4. **Analyze Data Using Set Operations**: Identifies no-shows, unexpected guests, and confirmed attendees.

Python Code for Guest List Management

```
# Collecting guest details
invited = set(input("Enter invited guests (comma-separated): ").split(','))
rsvped = set(input("Enter guests who RSVP'd (comma-separated): ").split(','))
attended = set(input("Enter guests who attended (comma-separated):
").split(','))

# Cleaning up whitespace
invited = {guest.strip() for guest in invited}
rsvped = {guest.strip() for guest in rsvped}
attended = {guest.strip() for guest in attended}

# Guests who RSVP'd but did not attend
no_shows = rsvped - attended
print("\nRSVP'd but did not attend:", no_shows)

# Guests who attended without RSVP'ing
unexpected_guests = attended - rsvped
print("Attended without RSVP:", unexpected_guests)

# Guests who RSVP'd and attended
confirmed_guests = rsvped & attended
print("RSVP'd and attended:", confirmed_guests)
```

Understanding the Code

- **Using Sets for Guest Management**: The program uses three sets to store invited guests, RSVPs, and attendees.
- **Set Operations for Analysis**:
  - **`rsvped - attended`**: Finds guests who RSVP'ed but did not show up
  - **`attended - rsvped`**: Finds guests who attended without RSVP
  - **`rsvped & attended`**: Finds guests who RSVP'ed and attended
- **Trimming Whitespace: `strip()`** is used to clean up extra spaces from user input.

Reasons for using Sets for This Task

- **Fast Lookups**: Quickly checks if a guest attended or RSVP'ed
- **Automatic Deduplication**: Prevents duplicate names

- **Efficient Data Comparison**: Makes it easy to compare who attended versus who RSVP'ed

This exercise demonstrates how sets help organize data efficiently, making them useful in real-world applications, such as event management, membership tracking, and data analysis.

Common Mistakes and Best Practices

When working with **lists, tuples, dictionaries, and sets**, beginners often make common mistakes that can lead to errors or inefficiencies. The following are some **common mistakes** along with their **corrected approaches** to help you write better Python code.

Common Mistakes

Modifying a List While Iterating

Mistake:

```
numbers = [1, 2, 3, 4, 5]
for num in numbers:
        if num % 2 == 0:
        numbers.remove(num)  # Removing elements while iterating
```

Fix: Iterate over a copy of the list or use list comprehension.

```
numbers = [1, 2, 3, 4, 5]
numbers = [num for num in numbers if num % 2 != 0]
```

Forgetting the Comma in Single-Element Tuples

Mistake:

```
single_element_tuple = (5)  # This is just an integer, not a tuple
```

Fix: Add a trailing comma to define a tuple correctly.

```
single_element_tuple = (5,)
```

Using Unhashable Types as Dictionary Keys

Mistake:

```
my_dict = {['key1']: 'value1'}  # Lists cannot be used as dictionary
keys
```

Fix: Use immutable types like tuples as dictionary keys.

```
my_dict = {('key1',): 'value1'}
```

Assuming Set Elements Have a Fixed Order

Mistake:

```
my_set = {'apple', 'banana', 'cherry'}
print(my_set[0])  # Error: Sets do not support indexing
```

Fix: Convert the set into a list before accessing elements by index.

```
my_list = list(my_set)
print(my_list[0])
```

Best Practices for Working with Data Structures

- **Choose the Right Data Structure –** Use lists for ordered data, tuples for fixed data, dictionaries for key-value pairs, and sets for unique elements.
- **Use Dictionary `.get()` Method –** Prevent errors when accessing dictionary keys by using `get()`.

  ```
  value = my_dict.get('missing_key', 'Default Value')
  ```
- **Use Sets to Remove Duplicates –** Convert a list to a set to eliminate duplicates efficiently.

  ```
  unique_items = list(set(my_list))
  ```

By avoiding common mistakes and following best practices, you will write cleaner, more efficient Python code while working with data structures.

Exercises and Challenges: Practice Problems and Solutions

Now that you have explored lists, tuples, dictionaries, and sets, it is time to apply what you have learned through practical challenges. These exercises will help reinforce key concepts while improving your problem-solving skills.

Each challenge involves data structures along with basic programming concepts such as loops and conditionals, helping you think like a programmer.

Practice Problem 1: List Manipulations

Task:

Create a Python list of your favorite movies.

Challenge:

Write a program that:

- Asks the user to enter a movie name.
- If the movie is in the list, print: "That's one of my favorites, too!"
- If not, add it to the list and print: "I haven't seen that one, but I'll check it out!"

Practice Problem 2: Tuple Operations

Task:

Create a tuple containing the days of the week.

Challenge:

Write a program that:

- Asks the user to enter a day.
- Checks if it is a weekend (Saturday, Sunday) or a weekday.
- Prints "It's a weekend!" or "It's a weekday!" accordingly.

Practice Problem 3: Dictionary Lookup

Task:

Create a dictionary with programming languages as keys and their creators as values.

Challenge:

Write a program that:

- Prompts the user to enter a programming language.
- If the language is in the dictionary, print the creator's name.
- If not, ask for the creator's name and update the dictionary.

Practice Problem 4: Set Unions and Intersections

Task:

Create two sets:

- One with prime numbers under 10
- Another with odd numbers under 10

Challenge:

Write a program that:

Computes and prints the union and intersection of both sets.

Practice Problem 5: Comprehensive List Usage

Task:

Use list comprehension to generate a list of squares for numbers 1-10.

Challenge:

Extend the program to filter out only the odd squares and print them.

Practice Problem 6: Data Structure Conversion

Task:

Start with a list of numbers: [1, 2, 3, 1, 2, 3].

Challenge:

- Convert the list to a set to remove duplicates.
- Convert it back to a list and print the final result.

Practice Problem 7: Iterating Over Dictionaries

Task:

Create a dictionary where:

- Keys are music genres.
- Values are your favorite song in each genre.

Challenge:

- Write a program that iterates through the dictionary.
- Print each genre and song using this format:
- "In the [Genre] genre, I like [Song]."

Practice Problem 8: Nested Data Structures

Task:

Create a dictionary where:

- Keys are continents.
- Values are lists of countries inside each continent.

Challenge:

- Ask the user for a continent name.
- Print all countries from that continent.
- If the continent is not found, print "Continent not found."

By completing these exercises, you will gain confidence in using Python data structures while preparing for more advanced programming challenges.

Solutions to Practice Problems

The following are the solutions to the practice problems provided earlier. These solutions will help you validate your answers, fix mistakes, and understand better ways to use Python's data structures.

Solution to Practice Problem 1: List Manipulations

```
# Define the list of favorite movies
favorite_movies = ['Inception', 'The Matrix', 'Interstellar']

# Function to check and update movie list
def check_movie(movie_name):
    if movie_name in favorite_movies:
        print("That's one of my favorites too!")
    else:
        favorite_movies.append(movie_name)
        print("I haven't seen that one, but I'll check it out!")

# Test the function
check_movie('The Matrix')
check_movie('Avatar')
```

Solution to Practice Problem 2: Tuple Operations

```
Define the tuple of days
days_of_week = ('Monday', 'Tuesday', 'Wednesday', 'Thursday', 'Friday',
'Saturday', 'Sunday')

# Function to check the day type
def check_day(day):
    if day in days_of_week[5:]:
        print("It's a weekend!")
    elif day in days_of_week[:5]:
        print("It's a weekday!")
    else:
        print("Please enter a valid day of the week.")

# Test the function
check_day('Saturday')
check_day('Monday')
```

Solution to Practice Problem 3: Dictionary Lookup

```
# Define the dictionary
programming_languages = {'Python': 'Guido van Rossum', 'Java': 'James 
Gosling'}

# Function to get creator
def get_creator(language):
    return programming_languages.get(language, "Unknown language")

# Function to update dictionary if language is unknown
def update_language(language, creator):
    if get_creator(language) == "Unknown language":
        programming_languages[language] = creator
        print(f"Added {language} created by {creator} to the dictionary.")
    else:
        print(f"{language} was created by {get_creator(language)}.")

# Test the function
print(get_creator('Python'))
update_language('Ruby', 'Yukihiro Matsumoto')
```

Solution to Practice Problem 4: Set Unions and Intersections

```
# Define the sets
primes = {2, 3, 5, 7}
odds = {1, 3, 5, 7, 9}

# Union and intersection
union_set = primes.union(odds)  # or primes | odds
intersection_set = primes.intersection(odds)  # or primes & odds

print("Union:", union_set)
print("Intersection:", intersection_set)
```

Solution to Practice Problem 5: Comprehensive List Usage

```
# List comprehension for squares of numbers 1 through 10
squares = [x**2 for x in range(1, 11)]

# Filtering only odd squares
odd_squares = [x for x in squares if x % 2 != 0]

print("Squares:", squares)
print("Odd Squares:", odd_squares)
```

Solution to Practice Problem 6: Data Structure Conversion

```
python
CopyEdit
# Define the list with duplicates
numbers = [1, 2, 3, 1, 2, 3]

# Convert to set to remove duplicates and back to list
unique_numbers = list(set(numbers))

print("Unique numbers:", unique_numbers)
```

Solution to Practice Problem 7: Iterating Over Dictionaries

```
# Define the dictionary
music_genres = {'Rock': 'Bohemian Rhapsody', 'Pop': 'Thriller', 'Jazz': 'What a Wonderful World'}

# Function to display songs by genre
def display_songs():
    for genre, song in music_genres.items():
        print(f"In the {genre} genre, I like {song}.")

# Test the function
display_songs()
```

Solution to Practice Problem 8: Nested Data Structures

```
# Define the dictionary of continents and countries
world = {'Asia': ['China', 'India', 'Japan'], 'Europe': ['France', 'Germany', 'Italy']}

# Function to display countries in a continent
def display_countries(continent):
    countries = world.get(continent, "Continent not found")
    if isinstance(countries, list):
        print("Countries in", continent + ":", ', '.join(countries))
    else:
        print(countries)

# Test the function
display_countries('Asia')
display_countries('Africa')
```

By understanding these solutions, you will strengthen your Python skills and be more confident in writing efficient code.

Conclusion

As you conclude this chapter, you have explored the powerful world of Python data structures. Starting from the fundamentals such as lists, tuples, dictionaries, and sets, you have learned how to store, manage, and manipulate data effectively. These tools are essential for writing clean, efficient, and scalable programs.

Looking ahead, the next chapter will take you from structured data organization to Object-Oriented Programming (OOP). You will explore classes, objects, inheritance, and polymorphism, which are essential for building scalable and maintainable software. These concepts will expand your ability to structure code efficiently, making your programs more modular, reusable, and organized.

So, keep calm and let us tame the Python as you continue exploring Python, now equipped with a strong grasp of data structures and soon, the power of object-oriented programming.

Multiple-Choice Questions

1. What data type in Python is mutable and allows duplicate entries?

   a. Tuple

   b. Set

c. Dictionary

d. List

2. Which method is used to add an element to a set in Python?

    a. `append()`

    b. `add()`

    c. `insert()`

    d. `push()`

3. Which of the following data structures does NOT allow mutable items?

    a. Lists

    b. Tuples

    c. Dictionaries

    d. Sets

4. What method would you use to remove an item from a list by its value?

    a. `pop()`

    b. `discard()`

    c. `remove()`

    d. `delete()`

5. Which Python data structure uses key-value pairs for storing data?

    a. List

    b. Tuple

    c. Set

    d. Dictionary

6. In Python, which operation would you use to combine two sets?

    a. `append()`

    b. `union()`

    c. `join()`

    d. `merge()`

7. Which of the following is NOT a correct way to create a tuple in Python?

    a. x = (1, 2, 3)

    b. x = 1, 2, 3

    c. x = tuple([1, 2, 3])

    d. x = [1, 2, 3]

8. Which data structure would be most efficient for checking membership of an element?
    a. List
    b. Tuple
    c. Dictionary
    d. Set
9. If a dictionary is declared as d = {'a': 1, 'b': 2}, what will be the result of d['a']?
    a. 1
    b. {'a': 1}
    c. KeyError
    d. None
10. Which method can be used for safely removing an element from a set without causing an error if the element does not exist?
    a. `remove()`
    b. `discard()`
    c. `pop()`
    d. `clear()`

Answers

1. d
2. b
3. b
4. c
5. d
6. b
7. d
8. d
9. a
10. b

Points to Remember

- Python lists are mutable and ordered collections that can contain components of different kinds, making them useful for various programming tasks.
- The **`append()`**, **`delete()`**, and **`sort()`** methods provide dynamic list manipulation.
- Tuples are immutable and ordered, making them a dependable way to store data that should not be modified. This improves code safety and predictability.
- Dictionaries use key-value pairs for efficient retrieval, making them ideal for lookups and maintaining associative data.

- Sets include sophisticated mathematical operations such as **`union()`**, **`intersection()`**, and **`difference()`**, making them excellent for handling data that requires unique items.
- Set operations simplify collection comparisons and uniqueness checks, eliminating the need for loops or conditional logic.
- Choosing the appropriate data structure for your program can improve efficiency and simplicity.
- List comprehension and dictionary manipulation are advanced subjects that enable more concise and understandable code for collections. Each data format has distinct advantages in various contexts, and understanding them can help you make informed judgments when designing solutions to complicated problems.

Further Reading

To continue exploring Python data structures and improve your understanding, check out these helpful resources:

1. **Python Data Structures - W3Schools**
    - o https://www.w3schools.com/python/python_lists.asp
    - o https://www.w3schools.com/python/python_tuples.asp
    - o https://www.w3schools.com/python/python_dictionaries.asp
    - o https://www.w3schools.com/python/python_sets.asp

    A beginner-friendly guide covering lists, tuples, dictionaries, and sets with interactive examples.
2. **Real Python - Python Data Structures Tutorial**

    https://realpython.com/python-data-structures/

    A detailed tutorial explaining how and when to use different data structures effectively in real-world applications.

CHAPTER 7
Understanding OOP in Python

Introduction

In the last chapter, you learned how to store, organize, and manage data using Python's powerful built-in data structures such as lists, tuples, dictionaries, and sets. These structures helped you efficiently process large amounts of data, making your programs more structured and easier to work with.

Now, you are taking the next step toward writing well-organized programs by exploring Object-Oriented Programming (OOP). While Python's data structures allow you to store information effectively, OOP enables you to combine both data and behavior into a single entity called an object. This approach makes programs more reusable, scalable, and easier to maintain.

Think of it like organizing a team. So far, you have learned how to store and manage player names, scores, and rankings using lists and dictionaries. But what if you could group all the details of a player, such as name, score, team, and actions such as scoring a goal, into a single object? That is exactly what OOP allows you to do.

In this chapter, you will dive into the fundamentals of OOP by learning about classes and objects. You will also explore key concepts such as encapsulation, inheritance, polymorphism, and abstraction, which help you create structured, reusable, and efficient programs.

By the end of this chapter, you will understand how OOP transforms the way you write code, making it more modular and adaptable. Let us begin and discover how Object-Oriented Programming can help you build better Python programs!

Structure

In this chapter, the following topics will be covered:

- Introduction to Object-Oriented Programming (OOP)
- Core Principles of OOP Using Real-Life Analogies
    - Encapsulation: Keeping Data Safe Inside an Object
    - Inheritance: Passing Down Properties and Behaviors
    - Polymorphism: The Same Action, Different Outcomes
    - Abstraction: Hiding Complex Details to Simplify Usage
- Introduction to Classes and Objects
    - Connecting Classes and Objects to OOP Principles
    - Benefits of Object-Oriented Programming (OOP)
    - Creating Classes and Objects

Introduction to Object-Oriented Programming (OOP)

Since you have just started your programming journey, it can feel confusing. There are many rules, and sometimes the code looks complicated. Object-Oriented Programming (OOP) is a way to make things simpler and more organized.

Think of a messy room filled with different things. If you put similar items into separate boxes, such as books in one box and clothes in another, the room becomes neater and easier to use. OOP does the same for programming. It groups related data and actions into objects, making programs easier to manage.

For example, imagine a toy box filled with action figures. Each action figure has:

- Details (Attributes): such as its name and color.
- Actions (Methods): such as moving its arms or making a sound.

In OOP, each action figure is an object that stores both data (attributes) and functions (methods). This makes programming more natural because you now think about objects in real life in the same way.

One big reason for using OOP is reusability. Instead of writing the same code over and over, you can create one template (a class) and use it to make many objects, just like a school has many students who follow the same rules.

OOP also makes programs easier to update and work on as a team. If different people work on a project, they do not need to understand everything. Think of it just like teachers, students, and classrooms each have their own tasks in a school.

Real-Life Analogy: A School System

To understand OOP better, let us think about a school. A school has different parts, students, teachers, classrooms, and courses, and each has its own details and actions:

- Students have a name, grade, and enrolled courses. They attend class, submit assignments, and get grades.
- Teachers have a name, subject, and schedule. They teach lessons, grade work, and manage students.
- Classrooms have a room number and capacity. They host classes and provide space for learning.

- Courses have a name, number of credits, and a list of students. They let students enroll, update content, and assign grades.

Each of these things in a school works on its own, but they also work together. Students go to classes, teachers give lessons, and classrooms hold lectures.

In OOP, each of these are treated as an object, meaning:

- Each object has its own details (data).
- Each object has actions it can perform (functions).
- Objects interact with each other in an organized way.

This is why OOP is helpful. It breaks complex programs into smaller, manageable parts, just like a school organizes students, teachers, and classrooms efficiently.

A Friendly Reminder:

You will see words such as classes, objects, attributes, and methods. They might seem new and confusing at first, but do not worry. Think of them as puzzle pieces. As you go through this chapter, you will see how they fit together.

Every programmer starts by learning one step at a time. Keep going, and soon OOP will feel natural to you!

Core Principles of OOP Using Real-Life Analogies

Now that you have an idea of what Object-Oriented Programming (OOP) is, let us explore some of its core principles. These principles help organize code in a way that makes it easier to build, understand, and expand.

OOP is based on four key ideas:

- **Encapsulation**: Keeping data safe inside an object.
- **Inheritance**: Passing down properties and behaviors.
- **Polymorphism**: Allowing flexibility in how objects behave.
- **Abstraction**: Hiding unnecessary details to simplify usage.

Each of these principles helps you organize code better, making it easier to manage, reuse, and scale. To understand them, let us relate them to real-world examples, just like how you think about everyday objects.

Encapsulation: Keeping Data Safe Inside an Object

Encapsulation is like putting important things inside a secure box and only allowing certain ways to interact with them. It ensures that only necessary information is visible, while other details are kept hidden to prevent accidental changes.

Real-Life Analogy: A Coffee Machine

Imagine you have a coffee machine in your kitchen. You simply press a button, and it makes coffee. But do you see the entire process inside? No. You do not need to know how it grinds the beans, heats the water, or controls the pressure. You only interact with what is necessary, the buttons.

Encapsulation works the same way in programming. It hides complex details inside an object and only provides specific ways to interact with it. This makes programs safer, easier to use, and more organized, just like how a coffee machine makes brewing coffee simple without exposing its inner workings.

Inheritance: Passing Down Properties and Behaviors

Inheritance allows one thing to take features from another. Instead of creating everything from scratch, you can reuse and build upon existing structures.

Real-Life Analogy: A Family Tree

Think of how traits are passed down in a family. A child might inherit hair color, height, or facial features from their parents. Similarly, in OOP, a new object can inherit properties and behaviors from an existing one.

For example, if there is a general category such as "Bird," it might have common traits such as wings, feathers, and the ability to fly. A specific type of bird, such as a parrot, can inherit these traits while also having its own unique feature, such as talking.

Inheritance helps you reuse existing ideas while adding new ones. Instead of repeating code, you will create relationships between objects, just like how families share traits across generations.

Polymorphism: The Same Action, Different Outcomes

Polymorphism allows the same action to work in different ways. This makes programs more flexible because you can use one simple command for multiple things.

Real-Life Analogy: A Universal Remote

Imagine you have a universal remote that controls your TV, DVD player, and sound system. Even though the "power" button is the same, pressing it does different things depending on the device.

- If you press power while pointing at the TV, it turns the TV on.
- If you press power while pointing at the sound system, it turns the music on.
- If you press power while pointing at the DVD player, it starts the DVD.

In OOP, objects can respond differently to the same action, just like how the universal remote works differently for each device. This makes it easier to work with different objects using the same commands, reducing complexity and making the program more adaptable.

Abstraction: Hiding Complex Details to Simplify Usage

Abstraction helps you focus on what is important by hiding unnecessary details. This makes using objects easier and less confusing.

Real-Life Analogy: Driving a Car

When you drive a car, you do not need to understand how the engine works. You only need to know how to:

- Turn the key or press start to turn it on.
- Use the steering wheel to change direction.
- Press the pedals to accelerate or stop.

All the complex machinery inside the car is hidden from you, so you only interact with what matters.

In OOP, abstraction allows you to use objects without worrying about their internal complexity. This helps developers focus on high-level functionality instead of getting lost in details.

How These Principles Work Together:

Each of these principles plays an important role in making programs easier to write, maintain, and expand:

- Encapsulation keeps things organized and secure.
- Inheritance allows you to reuse and extend existing code.
- Polymorphism gives you flexibility by allowing the same action to work differently.
- Abstraction hides complexity, making objects easier to use.

By understanding these concepts, you can write better programs that are clean, structured, and scalable.

Introduction to Classes and Objects

Now that you have explored the core principles of Object-Oriented Programming (OOP) through real-life examples, let us take the next step and see how these concepts translate into Python.

In real life, you often use blueprints to build things. For example, a house blueprint shows the design of a house, including the number of rooms, the placement of doors and windows, and the kitchen layout. However, the blueprint itself is not a house; it is just a plan.

Similarly, in Python, a class acts as a blueprint for creating objects. A class defines what an object should look like and what it can do, but it is not an actual object. Instead, you can use the class to create objects, just like a house blueprint is used to construct real houses. Each object built from the same class may share the same structure but can have its own unique details.

Definition of Class:

A class is a template for creating objects. It defines what properties (attributes) an object will have and what actions (methods) it can perform.

Think of a cookbook. It provides recipes that describe how to make a dish, listing ingredients as attributes and steps as methods. But the cookbook itself is not food. It is just a guide. Similarly, a class is just a template for creating objects.

Definition of Object:

An object is an actual instance of a class. If a class is a blueprint, an object is the real thing built from that blueprint.

For example, if you have a class called "**`Car`**," it may define attributes such as color, model, and speed, along with methods such as **`start()`**, **`stop()`**, and **`accelerate()`**. But the class itself is not a car; it is just the template.

When you create an actual car object from the Car class, it will have specific values for its attributes:

- A red sports car with a speed of 200 km/h.
- A blue sedan with a speed of 150 km/h.

Each object created from the same Car class follows the same blueprint but can have its own unique properties.

Connecting Classes and Objects to OOP Principles

Now that you understand what classes and objects are, let us see how they relate to the four OOP principles:

- **Encapsulation**: A class groups related data (attributes) and actions (methods) inside a single unit, preventing direct access from outside. This protects data from being changed accidentally and ensures that objects manage their own behavior.

- **Inheritance**: A new class can inherit properties and behaviors from an existing class. This allows you to reuse code efficiently instead of writing the same thing multiple times. For example, a "`Vehicle`" class could have general features such as fuel capacity and weight, and subclasses such as "`Car`" and "`Truck`" could inherit these features while adding their own specific details.
- **Polymorphism**: Different objects can share the same method name but implement it in their own way. For example, if you have a "`Shape`" class with a `draw()` method, different subclasses such as "`Circle`," "`Square`," and "`Triangle`" can each implement `draw()` differently, but they can still be treated as the same type of object.
- **Abstraction**: Classes hide complex details and only expose necessary parts. For example, a "`Payment`" class might define a method `make_payment()`, but different payment types (CreditCard, PayPal, Bitcoin) can implement this method in their own way. This allows programmers to focus on what the object does rather than how it works internally.

Importance of Classes and Objects:

Classes and objects are the foundation of OOP. They allow you to write structured, reusable, and easy-to-manage programs. By understanding them, you can build more efficient software that mirrors real-world systems, just like you interact with objects in everyday life.

Benefits of Object-Oriented Programming (OOP)

Before diving into practice problems, let us quickly summarize why OOP is so powerful. Object-Oriented Programming helps you write clean, reusable, and scalable code. The following table highlights the key benefits of using OOP in Python:

Benefit	Explanation
Code Reusability	OOP allows the reuse of code through classes and inheritance, reducing duplication.
Better Code Organization	Objects group related data and behavior together, making code more structured.
Encapsulation	Protects data by keeping it inside a class and controlling access, preventing unintended modifications.
Modular and Scalable	Programs are easier to expand and modify without affecting existing code.
Polymorphism	The same function can behave differently for different objects, making code more flexible.
Inheritance	New classes can inherit properties from existing ones, reducing redundancy and promoting efficiency.
Improved Maintainability	Changes in one part of the program do not affect others, making debugging and updates easier.
Real-World Representation	Objects mirror real-world entities, making it intuitive and easier to model complex systems.

Table 7.1: *Benefits of OOP*

Creating Classes and Objects

Now that you understand what classes and objects are, let us explore how to create them in Python. This is an essential step in learning Object-Oriented Programming (OOP) because it allows you to start building real-world objects in code.

In this section, you will cover:

- **Defining a class**: Creating a blueprint for objects.
- **Creating an object**: Making real instances from a class.
- **Using attributes and methods**: Storing data and performing actions.

Let us keep things simple and focus on the fundamentals before moving on to more advanced topics such as constructors.

Creating a Class

A class in Python is defined using the class keyword, followed by the class name. The class name usually starts with a capital letter, following a naming style called CapWords (or CamelCase).

A class acts as a blueprint that defines attributes (data) and methods (actions) that objects created from it will have.

Let us look at an example of a basic class definition:

```
class Animal:
    # Class attribute (shared by all objects of this class)
    is_living = True

    # Method (an action that objects of this class can perform)
    def speak(self):
        return "This animal makes a sound"
```

Breaking it down:

- **`class Animal`:** Defines a class called Animal (such as a blueprint).
- **`is_living = True`:** A class attribute that applies to all animals (because all animals are living).
- **`speak(self)`:** A method that defines an action. Returning a message that says the animal makes a sound.

At this point, you have not created any animals yet, you have just defined what an animal should be like.

Creating an Object from a Class

A class is just a template, you will need to create an object to use it.

To create an object, you can simply call the class as if it were a function:

```
generic_animal = Animal()
```

What is happening here?

- **`Animal()`:** This creates a new object from the Animal class.
- **`generic_animal`:** This is now an instance of the Animal class, meaning it has all the properties and methods defined in Animal.

Using Object Attributes and Methods

Once you have an object, its attributes and methods can be accessed using dot notation (.).

```
print(generic_animal.is_living)   # Outputs: True
print(generic_animal.speak())     # Outputs: This animal makes a sound
```

What is happening here?

- `generic_animal.is_living`: This checks the `is_living` attribute, which is True for all animals.
- `generic_animal.speak()`: This calls the `speak()` method, which returns "This animal makes a sound."

This shows how objects store information (attributes) and perform actions (methods) based on the blueprint (class).

Why This Matters:

- **Classes provide structure**: They define how objects should behave.
- **Objects bring them to life**: You can use them to create real-world instances.
- **Attributes store data**: They define an object's properties.
- **Methods allow actions**: They define what an object can do.

Practical Exercise: Car Display System

Now that you know how to define classes and create objects, let us apply this knowledge by building a simple car display system. This exercise will help you understand how to work with class attributes and methods before you move on to more advanced topics such as constructors and instance-specific data.

Task Description:

Create a Car class that allows users to:

- **View car details**: Display the car's color and make.
- **Modify car attributes**: Change the car's color and make.
- **Use a menu system**: Let users interact with the program in a simple way.

Python Code for the Car Display System

```
# Define the Car class
class Car:
    # Class attributes (shared by all instances)
    color = 'White'
    make = 'Generic Make'

    # Class method to display car details
    @classmethod
    def display_info(cls):
        print(f"\nThe car is a {cls.color} {cls.make}.")

    # Class method to change car color
    @classmethod
    def change_color(cls, new_color):
        cls.color = new_color

    # Class method to change car make
    @classmethod
    def change_make(cls, new_make):
        cls.make = new_make


# Main interaction loop
```

```
while True:
    # Display the menu options
    print("\n1. Show car info")
    print("2. Change car color")
    print("3. Change car make")
    print("4. Exit")

    choice = input("Enter your choice: ")

    if choice == '1':
        Car.display_info()

    elif choice == '2':
        new_color = input("Enter the new color for the car: ")
        Car.change_color(new_color)
        print("Car color updated.")

    elif choice == '3':
        new_make = input("Enter the new make for the car: ")
        Car.change_make(new_make)
        print("Car make updated.")

    elif choice == '4':
        print("Exiting program.")
        break

    else:
        print("Invalid choice. Please choose a valid option.")
```

Understanding the Code:

- **Class attributes (`color` and `make`)**: These store the car's properties at the class level, meaning changes apply to all objects created from Car.
- **Class methods (`@classmethod`)**: These modify class attributes without requiring an object instance.
- **Menu system**: Allows users to view and modify car details interactively.

This example shows how class attributes work differently from instance attributes. Changes to class attributes affect all objects rather than just one.

Attributes and Methods

Now that you have seen how to create classes and objects, the next step is to understand how objects store information and perform actions. This is done using attributes and methods.

Attributes define what an object is, while methods define what an object can do. By learning how to use attributes and methods, you can make your objects more useful and closer to real-world entities.

Defining and Accessing Attributes

Attributes are variables associated with a class or an object. They store data that describes the state of an object.

There are two types of attributes in Python:

- **Class attributes**: Shared by all objects of the class.
- **Instance attributes**: Unique to each object and typically set in a constructor.

Example: Class and Instance Attributes

```
class Dog:
    # Class attribute (shared by all Dog objects)
    species = 'Canine'

    def __init__(self, name, age):
        # Instance attributes (specific to each Dog object)
        self.name = name
        self.age = age
```

How it works:

- **`species = 'Canine'`** is a class attribute because all dogs belong to the Canine species.
- **`self.name = name`** and **`self.age = age`** are instance attributes because they are unique for each dog.

Accessing Attributes:

You can retrieve an object's attributes using dot notation (.).

```
# Creating an object of the Dog class
my_dog = Dog("Buddy", 5)

# Accessing a class attribute
print(my_dog.species)  # Outputs: Canine

# Accessing instance attributes
print(my_dog.name)  # Outputs: Buddy
print(my_dog.age)   # Outputs: 5
```

What is happening?

- **`my_dog.species`** → Retrieves the class attribute, which is the same for all dogs.
- **`my_dog.name`** and **`my_dog.age`** → Retrieve instance attributes that are specific to Buddy.

Creating Methods

Attributes store what an object is, but methods define what an object can do.

A method is simply a function inside a class that can operate on the object's data.

Example: Defining and Using Methods

```
class Dog:
    def __init__(self, name, age):
        self.name = name
        self.age = age

    # Method to describe the dog
    def describe(self):
        return f"{self.name} is {self.age} years old."

    # Method to simulate the dog making a sound
    def speak(self, sound):
        return f"{self.name} says {sound}"
```

Now, you can call these methods on an object:

```
my_dog = Dog("Buddy", 5)

print(my_dog.describe())  # Outputs: Buddy is 5 years old.
print(my_dog.speak("Woof"))  # Outputs: Buddy says Woof
```

How it works:

- **`describe(self)`**: Returns information about the dog's name and age.
- **`speak(self, sound)`**: Allows you to pass a sound, making it flexible for different animals.

The `self` Parameter

When defining methods inside a class, you can use self as the first parameter.

self refers to the specific object that is calling the method. It ensures that the method is working with the correct instance's data.

Example: Using `self` to Modify Object Data

```
class Dog:
    def __init__(self, name, age):
        self.name = name
        self.age = age

    def speak(self, sound):
        return f"{self.name} says {sound}"

    def birthday(self):
        self.age += 1  # Increases the dog's age
        return f"Happy {self.age}th Birthday, {self.name}!"
```

Now, let us see it in action:

```
my_dog = Dog("Buddy", 5)

print(my_dog.birthday())  # Outputs: Happy 6th Birthday, Buddy!
```

What is happening?

- The **`birthday()`** method modifies the object's age using self.age += 1.
- This change is specific to the object calling the method.

Key Takeaways:

- Class attributes are shared across all objects of a class.
- Instance attributes store unique information for each object.
- Methods allow objects to perform actions.
- The self parameter ensures that methods modify the correct object.

With attributes and methods, objects can store information and perform actions, making them powerful building blocks in Object-Oriented Programming.

Practical Exercise: Simple Library System

Now that you have learned how attributes and methods work within a class, let us apply this knowledge to a real-world scenario. In this exercise, you will create a simple library system that allows users to manage a collection of books.

This project will help reinforce how to:

- Use class attributes to store shared information.
- Define methods to modify and interact with data.
- Implement a menu-driven system for user interaction.

This exercise will focus on class-level operations rather than individual object instances, making it a great introduction before you explore more advanced topics such as constructors and instance attributes.

Task Description:

Create a Book class that allows users to:

- **Add books**: Store book details (title and author).
- **Remove books**: Delete a book from the collection.
- **View available books**: Display a list of all stored books.

This will help you practice defining class attributes and methods while building a useful Python application.

Steps for the Exercise:

1. **Define the Book Class**: Store book data using class attributes.
2. **Create a Menu System**: Allow users to interact with the library system.
3. **Adding Books**: Prompt users to enter book details and store them.
4. **Removing Books**: Allow users to remove books by title.
5. **Viewing Books**: Display all books currently in the library.

Python Code for the Simple Library System

```
# Define the Book class
class Book:
    # Class attribute: Represents a shared book collection
    library_name = "Local Library"
    books = []  # A list to store all books

    # Class method to add a book
    @classmethod
    def add_book(cls, title, author):
        cls.books.append({'title': title, 'author': author})
        print(f"Book added: {title} by {author}")

    # Class method to remove a book
    @classmethod
    def remove_book(cls, title):
        for book in cls.books:
            if book['title'] == title:
                cls.books.remove(book)
                print(f"Book removed: {title}")
                return
        print("Book not found.")

    # Class method to display all books
    @classmethod
    def display_books(cls):
```

```
            if cls.books:
                print("\nListing all books:")
                for book in cls.books:
                    print(f"{book['title']} by {book['author']}")
            else:
                print("No books in the library.")

    # Main interaction loop
    while True:
        # Display menu options
        print("\n1. Add a book")
        print("2. Remove a book")
        print("3. Show all books")
        print("4. Exit")

        choice = input("Enter your choice: ")

        if choice == '1':
            title = input("Enter the title of the book: ")
            author = input("Enter the author of the book: ")
            Book.add_book(title, author)

        elif choice == '2':
            title = input("Enter the title of the book to remove: ")
            Book.remove_book(title)

        elif choice == '3':
            Book.display_books()

        elif choice == '4':
            print("Exiting program.")
            break

        else:
            print("Invalid choice. Please choose a valid option.")
```

Understanding the Code:

- **Class Attribute (books)**: Stores a list of all books in the library.
- **Class Methods (`@classmethod`)**: Allows interaction with the book collection without creating instances.
- **Menu System**: Provides a user-friendly interface to add, remove, and display books.

This approach shows how class attributes and methods can be used for data storage and manipulation, even without individual book objects.

Understanding Constructors

Now that you have seen how attributes and methods define the structure and behavior of objects, let us explore how objects are initialized with specific data when they are created.

In Python, this is done using a constructor, a special method that sets up an object's initial values when a new instance is created.

Defining a Constructor

A constructor is a method that runs automatically when an object is created. It initializes attributes, ensuring that each object starts with the necessary data.

In Python, the constructor is called **`__init__()`**.

Think of it like turning on a new device:

- When you buy a new phone, the first time you power it on, it asks for your language, Wi-Fi, and account details. This is like setting up an object with a constructor.
- Once set up, the phone is ready to use, just like an object in Python!

Usage of constructor:

- **Initialization**: Ensures that objects start with the correct data.
- **Flexibility**: Allows to create objects with different initial values.
- **Control**: Prevents objects from being created in an incomplete state.

Defining a Constructor in Python:

Here is how you can define a constructor inside a class:

```
class Book:
    def __init__(self, title, author):
        self.title = title  # Instance attribute for the book's title
        self.author = author # Instance attribute for the book's author
```

Breaking it down:

- **`__init__(self, title, author)`** is the constructor.
- **`self.title = title and self.author = author`** set up the instance attributes.
- Every time you create a **`Book`** object, it must have a title and author.

Using the Constructor to Create Objects:

Now, let us create a Book object:

```
my_book = Book("1984", "George Orwell")
```

What happens here?

- The constructor automatically assigns "**`1984`**" to **`self.title`** and "**`George Orwell`**" to **`self.author`**.
- Now, **`my_book`** is a fully initialized object, ready to be used.

Practical Example: Car Class with Constructor

Let us apply what you know to a more detailed example:

```
class Car:
    def __init__(self, make, model, year):
        self.make = make
        self.model = model
        self.year = year

    def display_info(self):
        return f"{self.year} {self.make} {self.model}"

# Creating an instance of Car
my_car = Car("Toyota", "Corolla", 2021)
print(my_car.display_info())  # Outputs: 2021 Toyota Corolla
```

What is happening?

- Car has a constructor that initializes make, model, and year.
- The **`display_info()`** method returns a formatted string with the car's details.
- **`my_car = Car("Toyota", "Corolla", 2021)`** creates an object with specific data.

This ensures that every Car object starts with valid details, preventing errors caused by missing data.

Practical Exercise: Simple Registration System Using Constructors

Now that you understand how constructors work within a class, let us apply this knowledge to a real-world scenario. You will practice using constructors by creating a participant registration system. This will allow to:

- Create participants with a name and email.
- Store them in a list.
- Remove participants when needed.
- View all registered participants.

Steps for the Exercise:

1. **Define the Participant Class**: Add a constructor to initialize participant details.
2. **Create a Menu System**: Allow users to add, remove, and view participants.
3. **Adding Participants**: Prompt users to enter a name and email.
4. **Removing Participants**: Let users remove participants by email.
5. **Viewing Participants**: Display the list of registered participants.

Python Code for the Simple Registration System

```
# Define the Participant class with a constructor
class Participant:
    def __init__(self, name, email):
        self.name = name
        self.email = email

    def __str__(self):
        return f"{self.name} ({self.email})"

# Initialize the list of participants
participants = []

# Main interaction loop
while True:
    print("\n1. Add a participant")
    print("2. Remove a participant")
    print("3. Show all participants")
    print("4. Exit")

    choice = input("Enter your choice: ")

    if choice == '1':
        name = input("Enter the participant's name: ")
        email = input("Enter the participant's email: ")
```

```
            participants.append(Participant(name, email))
            print("Participant added.")

        elif choice == '2':
            email = input("Enter the email of the participant to remove: ")
            found = False
            for participant in participants:
                if participant.email == email:
                    participants.remove(participant)
                    print("Participant removed.")
                    found = True
                    break
            if not found:
                print("Participant not found.")

        elif choice == '3':
            if participants:
                print("\nRegistered Participants:")
                for participant in participants:
                    print(participant)
            else:
                print("No participants registered.")

        elif choice == '4':
            print("Exiting program.")
            break

        else:
            print("Invalid choice. Please choose a valid option.")
```

Understanding the Code

- **Constructor (`__init__`())**: Ensures each Participant has a name and email.
- **List** (participants): Stores all registered participants.
- **Menu System**: Allows users to add, remove, and view participants interactively.

This system dynamically builds and manages objects, demonstrating how constructors make object creation easier.

Common Mistakes and Best Practices

As you work with Object-Oriented Programming (OOP), you may encounter some common mistakes. Following are a few pitfalls along with the best practices to avoid them.

Common Mistakes

Forgetting to Use self in Instance Methods:

Mistake: When defining methods inside a class, forgetting self as the first parameter causes errors.

```
class Car:
    def set_color(color):
        self.color = color  # Error: self is not defined
```

Fix: Always include self in instance methods to reference object attributes.

```
class Car:
    def set_color(self, color):
        self.color = color
```

Modifying Class Attributes Instead of Instance Attributes:

Mistake: Accidentally modifying a class attribute instead of an instance attribute affects all objects of the class.

```
class Dog:
    species = "Canine"
    def __init__(self, name):
       species = "Feline"  # This does not update the class attribute
```

Fix: Use `self.attribute_name` to ensure modifications apply to the specific object.

```
class Dog:
    species = "Canine"
    def __init__(self, name):
        self.species = "Feline"  # This modifies the instance attribute
```

Not Using Encapsulation Properly:

Mistake: Allowing direct access to attributes instead of using getter and setter methods.

```
class Account:
    def __init__(self, balance):
        self.balance = balance  # Exposes balance directly
```

Fix: Use private attributes (`__attribute`) and create methods to control class Account:

```
    def __init__(self, balance):
        self.__balance = balance  # Private attribute
    def get_balance(self):
        return self.__balance  # Getter method
```

Best Practices for Writing OOP Code

- **Use Meaningful Class and Method Names**
    - Class names should be nouns (Car and Dog).
    - Method names should describe an action (`drive()`, `bark()`).
- **Follow the DRY Principle (Don't Repeat Yourself):** Use inheritance to reuse common logic instead of duplicating code.
- **Use Polymorphism for Code Flexibility:** Instead of checking object types manually, design methods that work across different classes.
- **Encapsulate Data for Better Security:** Hide internal details using private attributes and provide getter and setter methods.
- **Use Constructors for Proper Object Initialization:** Always define an `__init__()` method to set up an object's initial state.

By following these best practices, you can write clean, maintainable, and efficient OOP code in Python.

Exercises and Challenges: Practice Problems and Solutions

Now that you have covered the fundamentals of Object-Oriented Programming (OOP) and implemented it in Python, it is time to test your understanding. These exercises will help you:

- Apply OOP concepts in real-world scenarios.
- Strengthen problem-solving skills through hands-on coding.
- Think critically about how OOP makes programs more structured and reusable.

Each exercise focuses on a specific OOP principle covered in this chapter.

Practice Problem 1: Modeling Real-World Objects

- **Task:** Identify objects in your daily environment that can be modeled with OOP.
- **Challenge**: Model three diverse objects around you using classes. Specify the classes, properties, and methods that these objects may have.

Practice Problem 2: Implementing Encapsulation

- **Task**: Create a class that encapsulates data.
- **Challenge**: Write a Python class. **`CoffeeMachine`** that conceals its internal state and just provides the method **`make_coffee(strength)`**, where strength can be 'light,' 'medium,' or 'strong.' The internal state should include attributes such as water level and beans.

Practice Problem 3: Simulating Inheritance

- **Task**: Use inheritance to extend class functionality.
- **Challenge**: Define a base class **`Vehicle`** with properties such as make and model. Then, construct two derived classes, **`Car`** and **`Bike`**, which inherit from Vehicle but add unique properties such as **`num_wheels`** and methods suited to their type.

Practice Problem 4: Exploring Polymorphism

- **Task**: Demonstrate polymorphism in a class structure.
- **Challenge**: Create an **`Animal`** class with a function called **`speak()`**. Derive the classes **`Dog`**, **`Cat`**, and **`Bird`** from Animal, with each overriding the **`speak()`** function to represent their respective noises (for example, bark for Dog and meow for Cat).

Practice Problem 5: Understanding Class and Object Relationships

- **Task**: Distinguish between a class and an instance.
- **Challenge**: Create explanations for the concepts "class" and "object." Then, create an object from a class you define and call one of its methods to show knowledge.

Practice Problem 6: Working with Attributes

- **Task**: Practice adding and using attributes in a class.
- **Challenge**: Create a class **`Book`** with the characteristics author and title. Add a means for printing a description of the book.

Practice Problem 7: Dynamic Method Creation

- **Task**: Develop methods that modify the state of an object.
- **Challenge**: In a **`Person`** class, provide methods for updating a person's name and age. Also, provide a method that displays the object's current state.

Practice Problem 8: Constructor Usage

- **Task**: Learn to use constructors effectively.
- **Challenge**: Write a **`Rectangle`** class with a constructor that initializes length and breadth. Include methods to calculate the area and perimeter.

Practice Problem 9: Deepening Constructor Understanding

- **Task**: Extend constructor functionality with default values.
- **Challenge**: Modify the **`Rectangle`** class so that length and breadth have default values of 1 if not specified.

Practice Problem 10: Practical Application of Constructors

- **Task**: Apply constructors to a practical scenario.
- **Challenge**: Create a **`UserProfile`** class in which the constructor sets attributes such as username, email, and location. Add mechanisms for updating the email and location.

These tasks enable you to apply what you have learned in a real situation, thereby improving your ability to think through problems utilizing Python's OOP principles.

Solutions to Practice Problems

Here are the solutions to the practice problems you gave. These answers will walk you through each process and help you validate your work. If you faced any issues, these answers will help you comprehend probable mistakes or alternate techniques.

Solution to Practice Problem 1: Modeling Real-World Objects

```
# Definition of classes for three everyday objects
# Class to represent a Chair with adjustable height
class Chair:
    # Constructor method to initialize a Chair object with material and
initial height
    def __init__(self, material, height):
        self.material = material  # Material of the chair, example, leather
        self.height = height      # Height of the chair in centimeters

    # Method to adjust the chair's height
    def adjust_height(self, new_height):
        self.height = new_height  # Update the chair's height to new_height

# Class to represent a Phone with calling functionality
class Phone:
    # Constructor method to initialize a Phone object with brand and model
    def __init__(self, brand, model):
        self.brand = brand  # Brand of the phone, example, Apple
        self.model = model  # Model of the phone, example, iPhone 13

    # Method to simulate making a call to a phone number
    def make_call(self, number):
        print(f"Calling {number}...")  # Output message simulating a call

# Class to represent a Lamp with adjustable brightness
class Lamp:
    # Constructor method to initialize a Lamp object with color and initial
brightness
```

```
    def __init__(self, color, brightness):
        self.color = color          # Color of the lamp, example, white
        self.brightness = brightness  # Brightness of the lamp in lumens

    # Method to adjust the lamp's brightness
    def change_brightness(self, new_brightness):
        self.brightness = new_brightness  # Update the lamp's brightness to
new_brightness

# Test the code by creating and using objects of the preceding classes

# Creating an object of Chair with 'leather' material and initial height of
120 cm
office_chair = Chair('leather', 120)
# Adjusting the chair's height to 125 cm
office_chair.adjust_height(125)
# Printing the adjusted height of the chair
print(f"Adjusted chair height to {office_chair.height}cm")

# Creating an object of Phone with 'Apple' brand and 'iPhone 13' model
mobile_phone = Phone("Apple", "iPhone 13")
# Simulating a call to the number "1234567890"
mobile_phone.make_call("1234567890")

# Creating an object of Lamp with 'white' color and initial brightness of 75
lumens
study_lamp = Lamp("white", 75)
# Changing the lamp's brightness to 80 lumens
study_lamp.change_brightness(80)
# Printing the new brightness of the lamp
print(f"Lamp brightness set to {study_lamp.brightness}%")
```

Solution to Practice Problem 2: Implementing Encapsulation

```
# Define a class named CoffeeMachine to simulate the behavior of a coffee machine.
class CoffeeMachine:
    # Constructor method for initializing a new CoffeeMachine instance
    def __init__(self):
        self.__water_level = 100  # Private attribute to store the water level
in the machine. Set to 100 units initially.

    # Method to make coffee with a specified strength
    def make_coffee(self, strength):
        # Check if the provided strength parameter is valid
        if strength not in ['light', 'medium', 'strong']:
            # If the strength is not one of the allowed values, inform the
user.
            print("Invalid strength. Choose 'light', 'medium', or 'strong'.")
            return  # Exit the method if the strength is invalid.

        # Check if there is enough water to make coffee
        if self.__water_level > 10:
            self.__water_level -= 10  # Reduce the water level by 10 units to
make a cup of coffee.
            # Inform the user that coffee is being made with the chosen
strength.
            print(f"Making {strength} coffee.")
        else:
```

```
            # If there is not enough water to make coffee, inform the user to
refill.
            print("Refill water.")

# Test the code by creating an instance of CoffeeMachine and making coffee.
machine = CoffeeMachine()  # Create an instance of CoffeeMachine named 'machine.'
machine.make_coffee('medium')  # Call the make_coffee method on the machine
instance to make medium strength coffee.
```

Solution to Practice Problem 3: Simulating Inheritance

```
# Define a base class named Vehicle to represent general characteristics of
vehicles.
class Vehicle:
    # Constructor method for initializing a new Vehicle instance with make and
model
    def __init__(self, make, model):
        self.make = make  # Assign the make of the vehicle (example, Toyota,
Trek)
        self.model = model  # Assign the model of the vehicle (example,
Corolla, Marlin)

# Define a subclass named Car that inherits from Vehicle
class Car(Vehicle):
    # Constructor method for initializing a new Car instance
    def __init__(self, make, model):
        super().__init__(make, model)  # Call the constructor of the base
class Vehicle
        self.num_wheels = 4  # Cars typically have 4 wheels, set this as a
default attribute

# Define a subclass named Bike that also inherits from Vehicle
class Bike(Vehicle):
    # Constructor method for initializing a new Bike instance
    def __init__(self, make, model):
        super().__init__(make, model)  # Call the constructor of the base
class Vehicle
        self.num_wheels = 2  # Bikes typically have 2 wheels, set this as a
default attribute

# Test the code by creating instances of Car and Bike and displaying their
details

# Create an instance of Car with make "Toyota" and model "Corolla"
my_car = Car("Toyota", "Corolla")
# Print out details about the car including make, model, and number of wheels
print(f"My car is a {my_car.make} {my_car.model} with {my_car.num_wheels}
wheels.")

# Create an instance of Bike with make "Trek" and model "Marlin"
my_bike = Bike("Trek", "Marlin")
# Print out details about the bike including make, model, and number of wheels
print(f"My bike is a {my_bike.make} {my_bike.model} with {my_bike.num_wheels}
wheels.")
```

Solution to Practice Problem 4: Exploring Polymorphism

```
# Define a base class named Animal with a generic method speak
class Animal:
    # Define a speak method that does nothing. This acts as a placeholder to be
overridden in subclasses.
    def speak(self):
        pass

# Define a subclass named Dog that inherits from Animal
class Dog(Animal):
    # Override the speak method to return a string specific to dogs
    def speak(self):
        return "Bark!"

# Define a subclass named Cat that inherits from Animal
class Cat(Animal):
    # Override the speak method to return a string specific to cats
    def speak(self):
        return "Meow!"

# Define a subclass named Bird that inherits from Animal
class Bird(Animal):
    # Override the speak method to return a string specific to birds
    def speak(self):
        return "Tweet!"

# Test the code by creating a list of animal objects and invoking their speak
method
animals = [Dog(), Cat(), Bird()]  # Create a list containing instances of Dog,
Cat, and Bird
for animal in animals:
    print(animal.speak())  # Iterate through the list and print the output of
the speak method for each animal
```

Solution to Practice Problem 5: Understanding Class and Object Relationships

```
# Define a class named MyClass
class MyClass:
    # Constructor method for initializing a new MyClass instance
    def __init__(self):
        self.message = "Hello, world!"  # Initialize an instance attribute
with the greeting message

    # Method that returns the greeting message stored in the instance attri-
bute
    def greet(self):
        return self.message

# Test the code by creating an instance of MyClass and using its greet method

# Create an instance of MyClass named 'my_object'
my_object = MyClass()
# Print the result of the greet method called on the my_object instance
print(my_object.greet())  # Outputs: "Hello, world!"
```

Solution to Practice Problem 6: Working with Attributes

```
# Define a class named Book
class Book:
    # Constructor method to initialize a new Book instance with an author and
a title
    def __init__(self, author, title):
        self.author = author  # Set the author attribute of the book
        self.title = title    # Set the title attribute of the book

    # Method to return a descriptive string that includes the book's title and
author
    def description(self):
        return f"{self.title} by {self.author}"

# Test the code by creating an instance of Book and printing its description

# Create an instance of Book with "George Orwell" as the author and "1984" as
the title
my_book = Book("George Orwell", "1984")
# Print the description of the book by calling the description method
print(my_book.description())  # Outputs: "1984 by George Orwell"
```

Solution to Practice Problem 7: Dynamic Method Creation

```
# Define a class named Person to represent an individual's basic information
class Person:
    # Constructor method to initialize a new Person instance with a name and age
    def __init__(self, name, age):
        self.name = name  # Set the name attribute of the person
        self.age = age    # Set the age attribute of the person

    # Method to update the name attribute of the person
    def update_name(self, new_name):
        self.name = new_name  # Update the person's name with the new name
provided

    # Method to update the age attribute of the person
    def update_age(self, new_age):
        self.age = new_age  # Update the person's age with the new age provided

    # Method to return a string that includes the person's name and age
    def display_info(self):
        return f"{self.name}, {self.age} years old"

# Test the code by creating an instance of Person and using its methods

# Create an instance of Person with the name "John Doe" and age 30
person = Person("John Doe", 30)
# Print the initial information of the person by calling the display_info method
print(person.display_info())  # Outputs: "John Doe, 30 years old"
# Update the name of the person instance to "Jane Doe"
person.update_name("Jane Doe")
# Update the age of the person instance to 31
person.update_age(31)
# Print the updated information of the person by calling the display_info
method again
print(person.display_info())  # Outputs: "Jane Doe, 31 years old"
```

Solution to Practice Problem 8: Constructor Usage

```
# Define a class named Rectangle to represent a rectangle's properties and
operations
class Rectangle:
    # Constructor method to initialize a new Rectangle instance with length
and breadth
    # Default values for length and breadth are set to 1
    def __init__(self, length=1, breadth=1):
        self.length = length  # Set the length attribute of the rectangle
        self.breadth = breadth  # Set the breadth attribute of the rectangle

    # Method to calculate and return the area of the rectangle
    def area(self):
        return self.length * self.breadth  # Multiply length by breadth to get
the area

    # Method to calculate and return the perimeter of the rectangle
    def perimeter(self):
        return 2 * (self.length + self.breadth)  # Calculate perimeter using
the formula 2*(length + breadth)

# Test the code by creating an instance of Rectangle and invoking its methods

# Create an instance of Rectangle with a length of 5 and a breadth of 3
rectangle = Rectangle(5, 3)
# Print the area of the rectangle by calling the area method
print(f"Area: {rectangle.area()}")  # Outputs: "Area: 15"
# Print the perimeter of the rectangle by calling the perimeter method
print(f"Perimeter: {rectangle.perimeter()}")  # Outputs: "Perimeter: 16"
```

Solution to Practice Problem 9: Deepening Constructor Understanding

```
# Define a class named Rectangle to represent the geometric shape rectangle
class Rectangle:
    # Constructor method to initialize a new Rectangle instance with optional
parameters for length and breadth
    # Default values for length and breadth are set to 1
    def __init__(self, length=1, breadth=1):
        self.length = length  # Initialize the length attribute of the rectangle
        self.breadth = breadth  # Initialize the breadth attribute of the
rectangle

    # Method to calculate and return the area of the rectangle
    def area(self):
        return self.length * self.breadth  # Area formula: length multiplied
by breadth

    # Method to calculate and return the perimeter of the rectangle
    def perimeter(self):
        return 2 * (self.length + self.breadth)  # Perimeter formula: 2 times
the sum of length and breadth

# Test the code by creating a default instance of Rectangle and invoking its
methods

# Create a default instance of Rectangle with no arguments passed
default_rectangle = Rectangle()
```

```
# Print the area of the default rectangle by calling the area method
print(f"Default Area: {default_rectangle.area()}")  # Outputs: "Default Area:
1" due to default dimensions being 1x1
# Print the perimeter of the default rectangle by calling the perimeter method
print(f"Default Perimeter: {default_rectangle.perimeter()}")  # Outputs:
"Default Perimeter: 4" calculated from the default dimensions
```

Solution to Practice Problem 10: Practical Application of Constructors

```
# Define a class named UserProfile to manage user profile information
class UserProfile:
    # Constructor method to initialize a new UserProfile instance with user-
name, email, and optional location
    def __init__(self, username, email, location="Not specified"):
        self.username = username  # Store the username of the profile
        self.email = email        # Store the email address of the profile
        self.location = location  # Store the location, with a default of "Not
specified"

    # Method to update the email address associated with the user profile
    def update_email(self, new_email):
        self.email = new_email  # Set the email attribute to the new email
provided

    # Method to update the location associated with the user profile
    def update_location(self, new_location):
        self.location = new_location  # Set the location attribute to the new
location provided

    # Method to return a formatted string that includes the user's profile
information
    def display_profile(self):
        return f"Username: {self.username}, Email: {self.email}, Location:
{self.location}"

# Test the code by creating an instance of UserProfile and using its methods

# Create an instance of UserProfile with a specific username and email
user_profile = UserProfile("john_doe", "john@example.com")
# Print the initial state of the user profile by calling the display_profile
method
print(user_profile.display_profile())  # Outputs: "Username: john_doe, Email:
john@example.com, Location: Not specified"

# Update the email address of the user profile instance
user_profile.update_email("new_john@example.com")
# Update the location of the user profile instance
user_profile.update_location("New York")
# Print the updated state of the user profile by calling the display_profile
method again
print(user_profile.display_profile())  # Outputs: "Username: john_doe, Email:
new_john@example.com, Location: New York"
```

These solutions showcase the practical use of constructors, methods, and attribute handling in Python. They should help solidify your understanding of how to structure classes, manage object data, and test functionality within a simple Python program.

Conclusion

In this chapter, you learned how to use Object-Oriented Programming (OOP) to structure and manage code more efficiently. You started with the fundamentals of OOP, understanding how to define classes and objects and how they help in organizing data and behavior together.

You explored constructors, which allow objects to be initialized with specific attributes, making them ready to use from the moment they are created. You also applied key OOP principles such as encapsulation, inheritance, polymorphism, and abstraction, which help in creating well-structured and reusable programs.

By mastering OOP, you have taken an important step toward writing structured, reusable, and scalable programs. In the next chapter, you will explore modules and packages, which help in organizing larger programs and reusing code efficiently. Understanding how to work with modules will allow you to break down complex programs into manageable parts and make your Python applications more modular and maintainable. Let us continue sharpening your skills as you dive into modular programming. Keep calm and let's tame the Python!

Multiple-Choice Questions

1. What does Encapsulation help to achieve in OOP?
    a. Speed up the program execution
    b. Allow classes to share their methods
    c. Protect sensitive data from outside interference
    d. Increase network security
2. Which principle of OOP is demonstrated by creating a new class that inherits attributes from an existing class?
    a. Polymorphism
    b. Encapsulation
    c. Inheritance
    d. Abstraction
3. What is Polymorphism in OOP?
    a. The ability to present the same interface for differing underlying forms (data types)
    b. The ability of a program to process objects differently depending on their data type or class
    c. The method of packaging data with methods that operate on that data
    d. Both A and B are correct
4. Which of the following is NOT a benefit of using OOP in programming?
    a. Reduced code maintenance
    b. Easy debugging and testing
    c. Increased code execution speed
    d. Improved data security

5. What does the self keyword represent in a Python class?
   a. The class itself
   b. An instance of the class
   c. The superclass
   d. The method being called
6. Which statement is true about constructors in Python classes?
   a. They must always return a value
   b. They are defined using the `__init__()` method
   c. They are optional for all classes
   d. They can only initialize instance attributes
7. Which of these is an example of an abstract class in Python?
   a. A class that cannot be instantiated and includes one or more abstract methods
   b. A fully implemented class with no abstract methods
   c. Any standard Python class
   d. A class with only constructors
8. How can you create a subclass that inherits from a superclass called Vehicle?
   a. `class Car(Vehicle): pass`
   b. `class Car: inherit Vehicle`
   c. `class Car(super): Vehicle`
   d. `class Car extends Vehicle: pass`
9. What is an instance attribute in Python OOP?
   a. An attribute that is shared across all instances of a class
   b. An attribute defined outside any class methods
   c. An attribute unique to each instance of a class
   d. An attribute that must be initialized in the constructor
10. What is the main purpose of method overriding in OOP?
    a. To speed up method execution
    b. To replace a superclass method's behavior in the subclass
    c. To overload a method within the same class
    d. To prevent subclasses from modifying a method

Answers

1. c
2. c
3. d
4. c
5. b
6. b
7. a
8. a
9. c
10. b

Points to Remember

- Classes define the structure and behavior of objects. Objects are instances of these classes, representing the defined characteristics and actions.
- Encapsulation protects data within classes by preventing external access to private properties and methods, represented by prefixes such as underscores.
- Inheritance allows for code reuse and hierarchical class relationships, simplifying application architecture.
- Polymorphism allows methods to be used for related objects, regardless of their underlying classes. This allows for the same interface to be used for different underlying forms, such as calling the same method on different classes with unique implementations.
- Abstraction simplifies complex systems by exposing just necessary components and hiding implementation details. This is commonly achieved using abstract classes and methods that define a framework and leave the exact implementation to derived classes.
- The self keyword represents the class instance and provides access to associated attributes and methods.
- The `__init__` method is essential for creating new object instances of a class and establishing their initial state based on specified parameters.

Further Reading

For further exploration of OOP in Python, consider these resources:

1. **Object-Oriented Programming in Python–Real Python**:

   https://realpython.com/python3-object-oriented-programming/

   A detailed, beginner-friendly guide to understanding and applying OOP in Python.

2. **Python Classes and Objects–W3Schools**:

   https://www.w3schools.com/python/python_classes.asp

   A structured introduction to defining and working with classes in Python.

CHAPTER 8
Using Modules and Packages

Introduction

In the last chapter, you explored Object-Oriented Programming (OOP) and learned how to structure code using classes and objects. Now, you will take another step forward by learning about modules and packages, which help you organize and manage code efficiently, just like how a book is divided into chapters to make it easier to read.

Think of modules as individual chapters in a book. Instead of writing all your code in one large file, you can break it into smaller, reusable parts called modules. Python already comes with many built-in modules that can instantly add powerful features to your programs. You will learn how to use these standard modules to expand the functionality of your code.

Next, you will create your own modules just like writing your own chapters in a book. This allows you to reuse code, making the programs cleaner and more manageable.

You will then move on to packages, which act like a collection of related chapters. A package groups multiple modules together, making it easier to organize large projects.

By the end of this chapter, you will know how to create, import, and use modules and packages to write better structured, scalable Python programs.

Structure

In this chapter, the following topics will be covered:

- Introduction to Modules
  - Understanding Modules
- Using Standard Modules
  - Key Standard Modules
  - Advantages of Using Standard Modules
  - Importing and Using Standard Modules
  - Practical Exercise: Area Calculator
- Creating Your First Module
  - Steps to Create a Simple Module
  - Using Your Module in Another Python Script
  - Practical Exercise: Simple Module for Basic Calculations

- Introduction to Packages
  - o Basic Structure of a Package
  - o Using Packages
  - o Practical Exercise: Contact Management System
- Common Mistakes and Best Practices
- Exercises and Challenges: Practice Problems and Solutions

Introduction to Modules

Imagine you are working on a big project that requires many tools. Instead of putting everything into one giant box, you organize them into smaller labeled boxes. One for screwdrivers, another for hammers, and another for wrenches. This way, you can quickly find the tool you need without searching through a cluttered box.

Python modules work the same way! Instead of writing all your code in one long file, you can break it into smaller, organized files called modules. These modules store functions, classes, and variables that can be reused in different programs, making your code cleaner and easier to manage.

Real-Life Example: A Library System

Think about how a kitchen is organized. You don't keep knives, spoons, and forks in one big drawer. You have separate drawers for each. When you need a knife, you go to the knife drawer, not the whole kitchen.

Similarly, if you are building a library management system, you might create separate modules:

- **`book_operations.py`**: Handles book-related actions such as adding, updating, and searching for books.
- **`member_operations.py`**: Manages library members, including adding new members, updating details, and tracking borrowed books.

With this setup, if you need to update book-related functions, you only modify **`book_operations.py`**, without touching other parts of your program.

Using modules keeps your code organized, efficient, and easy to work with, just like keeping tools or kitchen items in their proper places.

Understanding Modules

A module in Python is simply a file that contains reusable code. Think of it as a toolbox with different tools inside.

For example, a screwdriver box might have both Phillips and flathead screwdrivers. Similarly, a module might have multiple functions that perform related tasks, such as:

- File handling (reading and writing files)
- Math calculations (addition, subtraction, and multiplication)
- User input processing (taking input and formatting it)

Instead of writing the same functions in every new program, you can create a module once and reuse it whenever needed.

Example: A Math Operations Module

Suppose you often perform math operations in your programs. Instead of rewriting the same functions every time, you can create a module called **`math_operations.py`** that includes functions such as:

```
def add(a, b):
    return a + b

def subtract(a, b):
    return a - b

def multiply(a, b):
    return a * b

def divide(a, b):
    return a / b if b != 0 else "Error: Division by zero"
```

Now, whenever you need these functions in another program, you import the module and use them, just like grabbing the right tool from your toolbox!

Usage of Modules:

Using modules has many advantages:

- **Better Organization**: Just like sorting tools into labeled boxes, modules help keep your code neat and easy to manage.
- **Code Reusability**: Instead of rewriting the same code, you create it once and use it multiple times, just like reusing a screwdriver for different tasks.
- **Easier Maintenance**: If you need to update a function, you only update it in the module, not in every program that uses it.
- **Fewer Errors**: Keeping related functions together makes debugging easier and reduces mistakes.

Modules are like toolboxes for your Python programs. They help you organize, reuse, and simplify your code, making programming more structured and manageable.

Using Standard Modules

In the previous section, you learned how modules help organize and reuse code. Now, let us go further and explore Python's standard modules, which are pre-built tools that come with Python and are ready to use.

These modules allow you to perform common programming tasks without writing everything from scratch, making the code faster and more efficient.

Real-Life Example: Using Pre-Built Tools

Imagine you are baking a cake. Instead of grinding your own flour or making sugar from sugarcane, you buy ready-made ingredients such as flour, sugar, and baking powder. This lets you focus on baking instead of preparing everything from scratch.

Similarly, Python's standard modules provide pre-built tools so you don't have to rewrite basic functions. Just like using store-bought flour saves time in baking, using standard modules saves time in coding.

Understanding Standard Modules:

A standard module is a pre-written Python file that contains useful functions, classes, and data. These modules have been tested and optimized by Python developers to handle common programming tasks.

Instead of writing all the code yourself, you can import a module and use its features right away, just like using pre-made ingredients to start baking immediately.

Key Standard Modules for Beginners

- **Math**: Provides mathematical functions such as square roots, trigonometry, logarithms, and constants such as π (pi).
- **Random**: Generates random numbers, useful for games, simulations, and testing.

Example: Using Standard Modules

Let us see how standard modules can simplify coding tasks!

- **Calculating the Area of a Circle (Using `math` Module)**

```
import math

def calculate_circle_area(radius):
    return math.pi * math.pow(radius, 2)

area = calculate_circle_area(5)
print("The area of the circle is:", area)
```

  · Here, math.pi gives us the value of π (pi), and math.pow(radius, 2) calculates the square of the radius.

- **Simulating a Dice Roll (Using `random` Module)**

```
import random

def roll_dice():
    return random.randint(1, 6)

dice_result = roll_dice()
print("You rolled a:", dice_result)
```

  random.randint(1, 6) generates a random number between 1 and 6, just like rolling a real dice.

A Quick Note About import:

Do not worry if the import keyword is new to you! Think of it as Python's way of saying, "Bring in a toolbox I need." You will go into more detail about import in the upcoming sections, so just follow along for now.

Advantages of Using Standard Modules

Using Python's built-in modules saves time and effort because they are:

- **Efficient**: Optimized for performance.
- **Reliable**: Tested by the Python community for years.
- **Simple**: You can use powerful functions with just a few lines of code.

By incorporating standard modules into your projects, you unlock powerful functionality without writing complex code from scratch. Learning how to use them is an important step toward writing smarter and more professional Python programs!

Importing and Using Standard Modules

Now that you have explored Python's standard modules, let us learn how to import and use them in programs. Importing modules allows you to access powerful pre-built functions without writing them from scratch.

Using modules correctly will help keep your code organized, efficient, and easy to manage, just like using a recipe book instead of memorizing every recipe you need!

How to Import a Module:

To use a module in Python, you will need to import it into your script. This is done with a simple command at the beginning of the code.

Do not worry if the import keyword is new to you! Think of it as telling Python: "Hey, bring in this extra toolbox so I can use its tools." You will break it down step by step.

Example of Importing a Module:

```
import math
```

This command loads the math module, making all of its functions available in your program.

Using Imported Modules

Once you import a module, you can call its functions using dot notation (**`module_name.function_name`**).

Example: Using the `math` Module

```
area = math.pi * math.pow(5, 2)
```

- **`math.pi`** retrieves the π (pi) constant.
- **`math.pow(5, 2)`** calculates **5 squared** (5^2).

Example: Using the `random` Module

```
import random
dice_result = random.randint(1, 6)
```

`random.randint(1, 6)` generates a random number between 1 and 6, simulating a dice roll.

Tips for Importing Modules:

There are multiple ways to import modules depending on how you'd want to use them:

- **Selective Importing**: If you only need a few functions, you can import them directly instead of the entire module.

  ```
  from math import pi, pow
  area = pi * pow(5, 2)
  ```

  This way, you can use **`pi`** and **`pow()`** directly instead of writing **`math.pi`** or **`math.pow()`**.

- **Renaming a Module**: If a module's name is too long, you can assign it a shorter alias for convenience.

  ```
  import random as rnd
  dice_result = rnd.randint(1, 6)
  ```

Now, instead of writing **`random.randint()`**, you can use **`rnd.randint()`**.

- **Importing Multiple Functions**: You can import several functions at once to keep your code concise.

  ```
  from math import sqrt, sin, cos
  ```

  This lets you use **`sqrt()`**, **`sin()`**, and **`cos()`** without typing math every time.

Practical Exercise: Area Calculator

Let us apply what you have learned by creating a simple program that calculates the area of a circle using Python's math module.

Task Overview:

- Ask the user for a circle's radius.
- Use the math module to calculate the area.
- Display the result in a clear format.

Steps for the Exercise:

1. Import the math module.
2. Ask the user to enter a radius.
3. Use the formula $\pi \times radius^2$ to calculate the area.
4. Display the calculated area with two decimal places.

Python Code: Area Calculator

```
import math

def calculate_area(radius):
    return math.pi * radius ** 2

def main():
    user_input = input("Enter the radius of the circle: ")
    radius = float(user_input)
    area = calculate_area(radius)
    print(f"The area of the circle with radius {radius} is: {area:.2f}")

if __name__ == "__main__":
    main()
```

Understanding the Code

- **Importing the `math` Module**: **`math.pi`** is required for the π constant.
- **Defining `calculate_area()`**: Uses $\pi \times radius^2$ to compute the area.
- **Getting User Input**: Convert it to a float so you can perform calculations.
- **Displaying the Result**: The **`:.2f`** ensures the output is rounded to two decimal places.

Example Output:

```
Enter the radius of the circle: 5
The area of the circle with radius 5.0 is: 78.54
```

This is just one example of how Python's built-in modules make coding easier and more efficient. As you continue learning, you will see how importing modules helps you solve problems faster and write cleaner, reusable code!

Creating Your First Module

So far, you have explored Python's built-in modules such as math and random, which allow you to use predefined functions. Now, let us take it a step further and create your own module!

Building your own Python module allows you to:

- Reuse code across multiple programs.
- Keep projects well-structured and organized.
- Avoid rewriting the same functions over and over.

Let us walk through the process of creating, saving, and using a custom module just like you did with Python's built-in ones.

Real-Life Example: A Personalized Toolkit

Imagine you are a mechanic who often fixes cars. Instead of searching for tools every time, you organize them into a personalized toolbox that holds your most frequently used tools.

Similarly, a custom Python module is like a personalized coding toolbox. It stores functions that you can reuse in different projects whenever needed!

Definition of Custom Module:

A custom module is simply a Python script (`.py` file) that contains functions, variables, or classes that can be imported and used in multiple programs.

Instead of copying and pasting the same code over and over, you can write it once, save it as a module, and import it whenever needed, just like grabbing the right tool from your toolbox!

Steps to Create a Simple Module

1. **Define Your Module's Purpose**

   Create a module that contains functions to greet and say goodbye.

2. **Create a New Python File**

   Since a module is just a Python file, open a text editor or IDE and create a new file.

   Naming Tip: Choose a name that reflects what the module does. Let us call ours greetings.py.

3. **Add Functions to Your Module**

   Inside **`greetings.py`**, write the following code:

   ```
   def greet():
       print("Hello, welcome to our program!")

   def farewell():
       print("Goodbye, thank you for using our program!")
   ```

   - `greet()` will display a welcome message.
   - `farewell()` will display a goodbye message.

4. **Save Your Module**

   After writing the code, save the file with a **`.py`** extension. This makes it a Python module that can be imported into other scripts.

   `Filename: greetings.py`

Using Your Module in Another Python Script

Now that you have created greetings.py, let us learn how to import and use it in another script!

1. **Create a New Python Script**

   In the same directory as **`greetings.py`**, create another file and name it **`main.py`**.

2. **Import Your Custom Module**

   At the beginning of **`main.py`**, write:

   ```
   import greetings
   ```

This tells Python to load the greetings module so you can use its functions.

3. **Use Functions from Your Module**

   Now, in **main.py**, call the functions from **greetings.py**:

   ```
   greetings.greet()
   greetings.farewell()
   ```

   Python knows that **greet()** and **farewell()** exist in the **greetings** module, so you can access them using dot notation (**module_name.function_name**).

4. **Run Your Script**

   Save **main.py** and run it in your Python environment:

   ```
   python main.py
   ```

   If everything is set up correctly, you should see this output:

   ```
   Hello, welcome to our program!
   Goodbye, thank you for using our program!
   ```

   Congratulations! You have just created and used your own Python module!

Understanding Module Importation:

When you import a module, Python follows these steps:

- Checks the current directory to see if the module exists.
- If not found, it looks in Python's system path (**sys.path**).
- Executes the module's code once and makes its functions available for use.

Now that you know how to create and import your own module, you can start building your coding toolbox by storing useful functions to reuse in multiple projects.

Practical Exercise: Simple Module for Basic Calculations

In this exercise, you will create a custom Python module that performs basic arithmetic operations. This will help you understand how to construct and use your own modules, just like Python's built-in modules, such as math.

You will create a module containing functions for addition, subtraction, multiplication, and division, demonstrating how modules can be used in real-world programming.

Task Description:

Create a Python program that contains a custom module for basic arithmetic operations. The program will:

- Allow the user to enter two numbers.
- Ask the user to select an operation.
- Compute the result using the custom module.

Steps for the Exercise

1. **Create the Arithmetic Module**

   Create a new file called **arithmetic.py**. This file will serve as the custom module.

2. **Write Functions for Arithmetic Operations**

   Inside **arithmetic.py**, define the following functions:

```
def add(a, b):
    return a + b

def subtract(a, b):
    return a - b

def multiply(a, b):
    return a * b

def divide(a, b):
    return a / b if b != 0 else "Error: Division by zero"
```

   - Each function performs a basic mathematical operation and returns the result.
   - The **divide()** function ensures division by zero is handled gracefully.

3. **Save Your Module**

   Save the file as **arithmetic.py** so it can be imported into other scripts.

Using the Module in Another Python Script

Now that you have your arithmetic module, let us import it and use its functions.

1. **Create a New Python Script**

   Create another file called **main.py** in the same directory as **arithmetic.py**.

2. **Import Your Custom Module**

   At the beginning of **main.py**, import the arithmetic module:

```
import arithmetic
```

   This allows you to access functions from **arithmetic.py**.

3. **Get User Input and Perform Calculations**

   Inside **main.py**, write the following code:

```
def main():
    num1 = float(input("Enter the first number: "))
    num2 = float(input("Enter the second number: "))
    operation = input("Choose the operation (add, subtract, multiply, divide):
").lower()

    operations = {
        'add': arithmetic.add,
        'subtract': arithmetic.subtract,
        'multiply': arithmetic.multiply,
        'divide': arithmetic.divide
    }

    if operation in operations:
        result = operations[operation](num1, num2)
        print(f"The result is: {result}")
    else:
        print("Invalid operation selected!")

if __name__ == "__main__":
    main()
```

Understanding the Code

- **Importing the Module**: Import arithmetic allows you to use the functions from **`arithmetic.py`**.
- **Storing Functions in a Dictionary**: The operations dictionary maps user input ("add," "subtract," and so on) to the corresponding function in **`arithmetic.py`**.
- **Calling Functions Dynamically**: If the user selects "**add**," Python calls **`arithmetic.add(num1, num2)`**, performing the operation dynamically.
- **Handling Invalid Input**: If the user enters an unrecognized operation, an error message is displayed.

4. **Running the Script**

   Save **`main.py`**, then run it in your terminal:

   ```
   python main.py
   ```

   Example Output:

   ```
   Enter the first number: 10
   Enter the second number: 5
   Choose the operation (add, subtract, multiply, divide): multiply
   The result is: 50.0
   ```

Introduction to Packages

So far, you have learned how to create and use individual modules to keep your code organized and reusable. But as projects grow larger, managing multiple modules can become difficult.

To solve this, Python provides packages, which allow you to group related modules into a structured directory. Packages make it easier to:

- Organize large projects by keeping related modules in one place.
- Avoid naming conflicts between different modules.
- Improve code readability and maintainability.

Real-Life Example: Organizing Books in a Library

Think about a library. Books are categorized into sections such as Science, History, and Literature. Inside each section, books are further grouped by topics. For example, the Science section may include Physics, Chemistry, and Biology.

Similarly, in Python:

- Each book represents a function.
- Each section (for example, Science and History) represents a module.
- The library as a whole represents a package.

Just as a library directory helps people find books, a Python package helps programmers manage modules efficiently.

Understanding Python Packages:

A package in Python is a collection of related modules stored inside a directory. This allows you to:

- Group similar modules together.
- Use a single import statement to access multiple modules.
- Structure your projects logically.

Basic Structure of a Package

To create a package, follow these steps:

1. **Create a Package Directory**

   First, create a folder (directory) that will hold your package. The directory's name should describe its purpose.

2. **Add an `__init__.py` File**

   Inside the package directory, create a file called **`__init__.py`**. This special file tells Python that the directory is a package.

   Note: *The `__init__.py` file can be empty, but it can also contain initialization code or define which modules should be imported when using from package* **`import *`**.

Example: Creating a Mathematics Package

Let us say you want to group math-related modules into a package called mathematics.

1. **Create a directory named `mathematics/`**

```
mathematics/
│
├── __init__.py
├── arithmetic.py
└── geometry.py
```

2. **Add Modules Inside the Package**

   - **`arithmetic.py`** (handles basic math operations):

```
def add(a, b):
    return a + b

def subtract(a, b):
    return a - b
```

   - **`geometry.py`** (handles shapes and measurements):

```
def area_of_circle(radius):
    import math
    return math.pi * radius ** 2
```

   - **`__init__.py`** (can be empty or include package-level setup):

```
# This file makes 'mathematics' a package
```

Using Packages

Once the package is created, you can import modules from it using Python's dot notation:

```
from mathematics.arithmetic import add
result = add(10, 20)
print(result)  # Output: 30
```

Another Example: Creating a "`ScienceTools`" Package

Let us say you are building a package named **`ScienceTools`**, which includes modules for different scientific computations.

Package Structure:

```
ScienceTools/
│
├── __init__.py
├── physics.py
├── chemistry.py
└── biology.py
```

- **`physics.py`** (Physics formulas):

```
def force(mass, acceleration):
    return mass * acceleration
```

- **`chemistry.py`** (Chemistry calculations):

```
def calculate_molecular_weight(compound):
    # Assume a simple dictionary-based lookup
    molecular_weights = {'H2O': 18, 'CO2': 44}
    return molecular_weights.get(compound, "Unknown compound")
```

- Using the **`ScienceTools`** package in a script:

```
from ScienceTools.chemistry import calculate_molecular_weight

weight = calculate_molecular_weight('H2O')
print(f"The molecular weight of water is {weight}")
```

Expected Output:

```
The molecular weight of water is 18
```

Python packages help organize multiple modules into a structured directory, making large projects easier to navigate and manage.

Practical Exercise: Contact Management System

In this exercise, you will build a contact management system using a Python package. This will help you understand how to properly structure and use packages by organizing similar functionalities into separate modules.

By keeping related functions in different modules within a package, you can make the code cleaner, more modular, and easier to maintain.

Task Description

Create a Python package that manages contact information, allowing users to:

- Add a contact
- Update a contact
- Remove a contact
- Display all contacts

Each operation will be handled by a separate module inside a package named **`contact_manager`**.

Steps for the Exercise:

1. **Create the Package and Modules**

   First, create a directory called **`contact_manager/`**, which will serve as your package.

Inside this directory, create the following files:

```
contact_manager/
│
├── __init__.py
├── add_contact.py
├── update_contact.py
├── remove_contact.py
└── display_contacts.py
```

- **__init__.py** – This file makes **contact_manager** a Python package. It can be empty or contain initialization code.
- Each module will handle a specific function related to contact management.

2. **Implement Module Functionalities**

   - **add_contact.py**: Adds a new contact.

   ```
   def add_contact(contacts, name, phone):
       contacts[name] = phone
       print(f"Contact '{name}' added successfully.")
   ```

   - **update_contact.py**: Updates an existing contact.

   ```
   def update_contact(contacts, name, new_phone):
       if name in contacts:
           contacts[name] = new_phone
           print(f"Contact '{name}' updated successfully.")
       else:
           print(f"Contact '{name}' not found.")
   ```

   - **remove_contact.py**: Deletes a contact.

   ```
   def remove_contact(contacts, name):
       if name in contacts:
           del contacts[name]
           print(f"Contact '{name}' removed successfully.")
       else:
           print(f"Contact '{name}' not found.")
   ```

   - **display_contacts.py**: Displays all contacts.

   ```
   def display_contacts(contacts):
       if contacts:
           print("\nContact List:")
           for name, phone in contacts.items():
               print(f"{name}: {phone}")
       else:
           print("No contacts available.")
   ```

3. **Use the Package in Your Main Program**

   Now, let us create a main script (**main.py**) to use the package and handle user interactions.

   Structure of the Project

   ```
   contact_manager/
   │
   ├── __init__.py
   ├── add_contact.py
   ├── update_contact.py
   ├── remove_contact.py
   ├── display_contacts.py
   │
   main.py
   ```

- **`main.py`**: This script will import the package and interact with the user.

```
from contact_manager.add_contact import add_contact
from contact_manager.update_contact import update_contact
from contact_manager.remove_contact import remove_contact
from contact_manager.display_contacts import display_contacts

def main():
    contacts = {}

    while True:
        print("\n1. Add Contact\n2. Update Contact\n3. Remove Contact\n4.
Display Contacts\n5. Exit")
        choice = input("Enter your choice: ")

        if choice == '1':
            name = input("Enter contact name: ")
            phone = input("Enter contact phone: ")
            add_contact(contacts, name, phone)

        elif choice == '2':
            name = input("Enter contact name: ")
            new_phone = input("Enter new phone number: ")
            update_contact(contacts, name, new_phone)

        elif choice == '3':
            name = input("Enter contact name to remove: ")
            remove_contact(contacts, name)

        elif choice == '4':
            display_contacts(contacts)

        elif choice == '5':
            print("Exiting the program...")
            break

        else:
            print("Invalid choice, please try again.")

if __name__ == "__main__":
    main()
```

Understanding the Code:

- **Package Organization**: The **`contact_manager`** package contains separate modules for adding, updating, removing, and displaying contacts.
- **Modular Design**: Each function is encapsulated in its own module, making it easy to maintain and reuse.
- **Main Program Flow**: **`main.py`** imports functions from the package, prompting the user for input and executing the corresponding operation.

Running the Program:

Once everything is set up, run the **`main.py`** script:

```
python main.py
```

Example Output:

```
1. Add Contact
2. Update Contact
3. Remove Contact
4. Display Contacts
5. Exit
Enter your choice: 1
Enter contact name: Alice
Enter contact phone: 9876543210
Contact 'Alice' added successfully.

Enter your choice: 4
Contact List:
Alice: 9876543210
```

By structuring the contact management system as a package, you will ensure that:

- Each component is modular and reusable.
- The codebase is clean and scalable.
- Future updates are easy to implement.

Common Mistakes and Best Practices

When working with modules and packages, it is important to follow good coding practices to keep your projects organized and error-free. Following are some common mistakes and their solutions, along with best practices to ensure smooth development.

Common Mistakes

- **Mistake**: Forgetting to create an `__init__.py` file in a package directory.

  Fix: Always include an `__init__.py` file in a package to let Python recognize it as a package.
- **Mistake**: Using import * to import everything from a module.

  Fix: Instead of `from module import *`, import only the functions or classes you need to avoid conflicts and improve readability.
- **Mistake**: Naming a module the same as a built-in module (for example, `math.py`).

  Fix: Use unique names to prevent conflicts with standard Python modules.
- **Mistake**: Not specifying the full module path when importing from a package.

  Fix: Use `from package.module import function` to ensure Python can locate the correct module.

Best Practices

- **Keep modules focused:** Each module should handle a specific functionality to keep code maintainable.
- **Organize packages logically:** Group related modules into structured directories for better navigation.
- **Use absolute imports:** Avoid relative imports in larger projects to prevent confusion.
- **Document your modules:** Add comments and docstrings to explain module functionality for easy reference.

Following these practices will help you build well-structured, reusable, and scalable Python projects.

Exercises and Challenges: Practice Problems and Solutions

Practice Problem 1: Create a Utility Module

Task: Create a Python module with common utility functions.

Challenge: Create a module called utilities.py that has routines for converting temperatures between Celsius and Fahrenheit and vice versa. Include at least two functions: `celsius_to_fahrenheit` (Celsius) and `fahrenheit_to_celsius` (Fahrenheit).

Practice Problem 2: Math Operations Module

Task: Create a module for fundamental arithmetic operations.

Challenge: Create a module called `simple_math.py` that includes functions for adding, subtracting, multiplying, and dividing numbers. Ensure that your functions can gracefully handle division by zero and other unexpected problems.

Practice Problem 3: Python's os Module Exploration

Task: Use Python's os module to interact with your operating system.

Challenge: Create a script that uses the os module to list all files and directories in your current working directory, then locate and output all Python.py files.

Practice Problem 4: Working with the datetime Module

Task: Explore Python's datetime module.

Challenge: Use the datetime module to display the current year, the current month by name, and the current week of the year.

Practice Problem 5: Create a String Manipulation Package

Task: Create a Python library that can handle various string manipulations.

Challenge: Build a package named `string_tools` with modules that perform various string operations such as string reversal, word capitalization, and vowel counting.

Practice Problem 6: Utilizing Your String Manipulation Package

Task: Use your newly constructed string manipulation package in practical applications.

Challenge: Create a script that uses the `string_tools` package to manipulate a given sentence, applying numerous manipulations from different modules in the package.

Practice Problem 7: Numeric Operations Package

Task: Put together a package for doing various mathematical calculations.

Challenge: Create a `numeric_ops` package that includes modules for basic arithmetic, exponential operations, and logarithmic calculations. Each module should handle a different category of mathematics.

Solutions to Practice Problems

Here are the solutions to the practice problems you gave. These answers will walk you through each process and help you validate your work. If you face any issues, these answers will help you comprehend probable mistakes or alternate techniques.

Solution to Practice Problem 1: Create a Utility Module

Here is a full example of how to construct a custom utility module in Python, named **utilities.py**, that includes two basic functions for converting temperatures between Celsius and Fahrenheit.

utilities.py:

```
def celsius_to_fahrenheit(celsius):
    """Converts Celsius to Fahrenheit."""
    return (celsius * 9/5) + 32  # Formula to convert Celsius to Fahrenheit

def fahrenheit_to_celsius(fahrenheit):
    """Converts Fahrenheit to Celsius."""
    return (fahrenheit - 32) * 5/9  # Formula to convert Fahrenheit to Celsius
```

Using the utilities module: To use the functions described in your **utilities.py** module, build another Python script, possibly titled **main.py**, that imports and uses these functions.

main.py:

```
# Import the custom utilities module
from utilities import celsius_to_fahrenheit, fahrenheit_to_celsius
# Test the temperature conversion functions
# Convert 100 degrees Fahrenheit to Celsius
temp_in_celsius = fahrenheit_to_celsius(100)
print(f"100 degrees Fahrenheit is {temp_in_celsius:.2f} degrees Celsius.")
# Convert 37 degrees Celsius to Fahrenheit
temp_in_fahrenheit = celsius_to_fahrenheit(37)
print(f"37 degrees Celsius is {temp_in_fahrenheit:.2f} degrees Fahrenheit.")
```

This script shows how to construct and utilize a basic custom module to do common utility functions such as temperature conversion. The module **utilities.py** provides two functions for handling these conversions, which are subsequently imported and utilized in **main.py**. The result offers a plain demonstration of the functions' utility in practical circumstances.

Solution to Practice Problem 2: Math Operations Module

Here is how to make a custom module called **simple_math.py** for basic arithmetic operations. This module will have functions for addition, subtraction, multiplication, and division, dealing with edge circumstances such as division by zero.

simple_math.py:

```
def add(a, b):
    """Returns the sum of a and b."""
    return a + b

def subtract(a, b):
    """Returns the subtraction of b from a."""
    return a - b

def multiply(a, b):
    """Returns the product of a and b."""
    return a * b

def divide(a, b):
    """Returns the division of a by b, handling division by zero."""
```

```
    if b == 0:
        return "Error: Division by zero"
    else:
        return a / b
```

Using the **simple_math** module: To show the functionality of the **simple_math.py** module, build another script named **main.py** that imports and uses these arithmetic functions.

main.py:

```
# Import the simple_math module
import simple_math
# Test the arithmetic functions
# Addition of 15 and 23
result_add = simple_math.add(15, 23)
print(f"The sum of 15 and 23 is {result_add}.")
# Subtraction of 50 from 100
result_subtract = simple_math.subtract(100, 50)
print(f"100 minus 50 is {result_subtract}.")
# Multiplication of 8 by 12
result_multiply = simple_math.multiply(8, 12)
print(f"8 multiplied by 12 is {result_multiply}.")
# Division of 20 by 5
result_divide = simple_math.divide(20, 5)
print(f"20 divided by 5 is {result_divide}.")
# Attempt to divide by zero
result_divide_zero = simple_math.divide(10, 0)
print(f"Result of dividing 10 by 0 is {result_divide_zero}.")
```

This setup explains how to create and utilize a simple custom module for fundamental arithmetic operations while adhering to Python programming best practices. The module **simple_math.py** contains well-defined functions for performing fundamental mathematical operations, which are then imported and used in main.py to ensure the module works properly in a variety of contexts. The outputs are organized for clarity and offer rapid feedback on the actions completed.

Solution to Practice Problem 3: Python's os Module Exploration

For this practice issue, you will develop a script that uses Python's os module to communicate with the operating system, specifically to list files and directories in the current working directory and identify all Python.py files.

list_files.py:

```
# Script to list files and directories using os module
import os
# List all files and directories in the current directory
for item in os.listdir('.'):
    print(item)  # Print each item found in the directory
# Bonus: Find and print Python files
for item in os.listdir('.'):
    if item.endswith('.py'):
        print(f"Python file: {item}")  # Prints only Python files
```

Using the OS Module for Practical Tasks: This script begins by importing the os module, which provides a portable method of accessing operating system-specific functionality. It then completes the following tasks:

1. Use **os.getcwd()** to retrieve and print the current working directory.
2. Use **os.listdir()** to get a list of all files and folders in your current directory.
3. Filters and lists Python.py files based on their extension using **str.endswith()**.

This technique not only shows how to interface with the file system in Python but also presents certain common methods included in the os module that are especially useful for file and directory administration. The script's output provides clear and rapid feedback on the contents of the working directory, improving knowledge of both the os module's functionality and simple file operations in Python.

Solution to Practice Problem 4: Working with the datetime Module

For this practice issue, you will use Python's datetime module to display the current year, the current month by name, and the current week number in the year.

display_datetime.py:

```
# Script to display current date and time details using datetime module
from datetime import datetime
current_time = datetime.now()  # Get the current datetime
print(f"Current Year: {current_time.year}")  # Display the current year
print(f"Current Month: {current_time.strftime('%B')}")  # Display the name of
the current month
print(f"Current Week Number: {current_time.strftime('%U')}")  # Display the
current week number.
```

Using the datetime Module for Date and Time Information: This script begins by importing the datetime class from the datetime module, which is used to manage date and time data. It performs the following tasks:

1. Retrieve and print the current year using the year attribute of the **datetime.now()** instance.
2. Use the **strftime('%B')** method to format the date and display the current month's full name.
3. Use **strftime('%U')** to display the current week number of the year, beginning with the first Sunday as the first day of the week.

This practical application of the datetime module demonstrates how to obtain and format current date and time data in Python applications, simplifying operations such as scheduling, logging, and timestamping. The result is easy and clearly displays the utility of the datetime module for effectively managing date and time data.

Solution to Practice Problem 5: Create a String Manipulation Package

For this practice issue, you will construct a Python package entitled **string_tools** that has many modules for various string manipulation activities, such as reversing a string, capitalizing each word, and counting the number of vowels in a string.

Directory Structure:

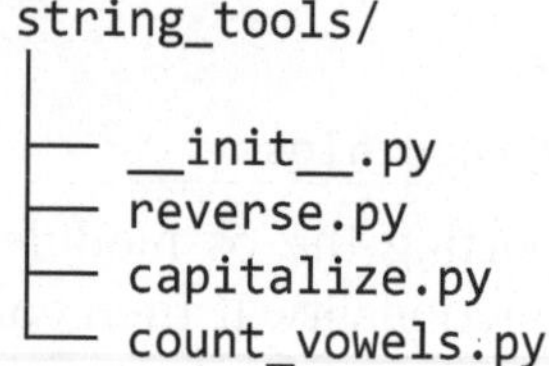

```
string_tools/
│
├── __init__.py
├── reverse.py
├── capitalize.py
└── count_vowels.py
```

reverse.py:

```
def reverse_string(s):
    """Return the reverse of the string."""
    return s[::-1]
```

capitalize.py:

```
def capitalize_words(s):
    """Capitalize each word in the string."""
    return ' '.join(word.capitalize() for word in s.split())
```

count_vowels.py:

```
def count_vowels(s):
    """Count the number of vowels in the string."""
    return sum(1 for char in s if char.lower() in 'aeiou')
```

Using the **string_tools** Package for String Manipulations: This package begins by defining many modules, each of which is responsible for a certain string action. It then completes the following tasks:

1. Reverse a String: Use **reverse.py**'s **reverse_string** method to reverse any string.
2. To capitalize words, use the capitalize.py module's **capitalize_words** function, which returns a new string with the first letter capitalized.
3. Count vowels: The **count_vowels.py** method calculates the number of vowels in a given string.

To use these modules in a Python script:

main.py:

```
# Import modules from the string_tools package
from string_tools.reverse import reverse_string
from string_tools.capitalize import capitalize_words
from string_tools.count_vowels import count_vowels
# Test the string manipulation functions
sample_text = "hello world"
# Reverse the text
reversed_text = reverse_string(sample_text)
print(f"Reversed Text: {reversed_text}")
# Capitalize the text
capitalized_text = capitalize_words(sample_text)
print(f"Capitalized Text: {capitalized_text}")
# Count vowels in the text
vowel_count = count_vowels(sample_text)
print(f"Number of vowels: {vowel_count}")
```

This script clearly shows how to organize a Python package to handle diverse string manipulations while keeping each functionality modular and reusable across multiple applications. The output offers direct feedback on the operations performed, demonstrating the applicability of the **string_tools** package in practical scenarios.

Solution to Practice Problem 6: Utilizing Your String Manipulation Package

For this practice issue, you will write a script that leverages the previously developed **string_tools** package to edit a given sentence using several manipulations from different modules within the package.

main.py:

```
# Import the string manipulation modules from the string_tools package
from string_tools.reverse import reverse_string
from string_tools.capitalize import capitalize_words
from string_tools.count_vowels import count_vowels
# Test the string manipulation functions with a sample text
sample_text = "hello world"
# Reverse the text using the reverse_string function
reversed_text = reverse_string(sample_text)
print(f"Reversed Text: {reversed_text}")
# Capitalize the text using the capitalize_words function
capitalized_text = capitalize_words(sample_text)
print(f"Capitalized Text: {capitalized_text}")
# Count the number of vowels in the text using the count_vowels function
vowel_count = count_vowels(sample_text)
print(f"Number of vowels: {vowel_count}")
```

Using the string tools Package for practical string manipulation: This script makes use of the **string_tools** package, which has specialized modules for string manipulation. It carries out the following tasks:

1. Reverse a string: The **reverse.py** module contains a function that reverses the given string. This is used to display the reverse of **sample_text**.
2. Capitalize Words: The script uses **capitalize.py** to capitalize each word in **sample_text**, demonstrating formatting capabilities.
3. Count vowels: The **count_vowels.py** module computes and displays the number of vowels in **sample_text**, demonstrating how to evaluate text content.

This Python script explains how the **string_tools** package's modules work together to alter and analyze text. The output clearly illustrates the consequence of each string manipulation, making it a useful tool for understanding the value of Python packages in organizing and carrying out related activities.

Solution to Practice Problem 7: Numeric Operations Package

For this practice problem, you will develop a package called **numeric_ops** that arranges several mathematical operations into discrete modules. This package will provide modules for fundamental arithmetic, exponential operations, and logarithmic calculations.

Directory Structure:

```
numeric_ops/
│
├── __init__.py
├── arithmetic.py
├── exponentials.py
└── logarithms.py
```

arithmetic.py:

```
# Module for basic arithmetic operations
def add(x, y):
    return x + y
def subtract(x, y):
    return x - y
def multiply(x, y):
```

```
        return x * y
    def divide(x, y):
        if y == 0:
            return "Error: Division by zero"
        else: return x / y
```

exponentials.py:

```
# Module for exponential operations
def power(base, exponent):
    return base ** exponent
def square_root(x):
    return x ** 0.5
```

logarithms.py:

```
# Module for logarithmic calculations
import math
def natural_log(x):
    if x > 0:
        return math.log(x)
    else:
        return "Error: Logarithm not defined for non-positive values"
def log_base_ten(x):
    if x > 0:
        return math.log10(x)
    else:
        return "Error: Logarithm not defined for non-positive values"
```

Using **Numeric_ops** Package for Mathematical Tasks: This package begins by categorizing various mathematical functions into distinct modules under **numeric_ops**. Each module focuses on a specific category of mathematics:

1. **Arithmetic Operations**: The **arithmetic.py** module supports basic operations such as addition, subtraction, multiplication, and division.
2. **Exponential Functions**: **Exponentials.py** defines functions such as power and **square_root** to do exponential calculations.
3. **Logarithmic functions**: The **logarithms.py** module uses Python's math library to conduct logarithmic computations and checks for valid input values.

To use these modules in a Python script:

main.py:

```
# Import modules from the numeric_ops package
from numeric_ops.arithmetic import add, divide
from numeric_ops.exponentials import power, square_root
from numeric_ops.logarithms import natural_log, log_base_ten
# Using the functions from the numeric_ops package
print(f"Addition: {add(10, 5)}")
print(f"Division: {divide(10, 0)}")
print(f"Power: {power(2, 3)}")
print(f"Square Root: {square_root(16)}")
print(f"Natural Log: {natural_log(-1)}")
print(f"Log Base Ten: {log_base_ten(100)}")
```

This script demonstrates how well the **numeric_ops** package's modules collaborate to accomplish various mathematical operations. The outputs are neatly formatted, displaying the results of each function and offering rapid feedback on the package's utility in practical circumstances.

Conclusion

In this chapter, you expanded your Python programming skills by learning about modules and packages, essential tools for structuring, reusing, and managing code efficiently. Building on the foundation of functions and object-oriented programming, you took the next step in organizing your code by working with modules, Python's way of grouping related functions together. You explored built-in modules, learned how to create your own, and understood how they improve modularity and code reusability.

You then moved on to packages, which help structure larger projects by grouping multiple modules into well-organized directories. Just as functions helped break down code into reusable parts, modules and packages allow for even better organization, making your Python programs more scalable and easier to maintain.

In the next chapter, you will move from modular programming to error handling, learning how to identify, catch, and manage errors gracefully. Understanding error handling is essential for building robust and reliable Python programs, ensuring they continue to run smoothly even when unexpected issues arise.

As you transition from structuring code with modules and packages to handling errors effectively, let us continue sharpening your Python skills and writing clean, efficient programs.

Till then, keep calm and let's tame the Python!

Multiple-Choice Questions

1. What is a Python module?
    a. A Python file containing executable code
    b. A compiled version of a Python script
    c. A special Python method
    d. None of the above
2. Which statement is true about Python packages?
    a. A package is a collection of Python scripts
    b. A package cannot contain sub-packages
    c. A package is a way to organize related modules
    d. A package does not require an __init__.py file
3. What is the purpose of an **__init__.py** file in a Python package?
    a. It prevents the folder from being included in git repositories
    b. It initializes the Python interpreter
    c. It tells Python that the directory should be treated as a package
    d. It compiles Python scripts

4. How can you import a function **`calculate_area`** from a module named geometry within a package **`math_tools`**?
   a. `import math_tools.geometry.calculate_area`
   b. `from math_tools import calculate_area`
   c. `from math_tools.geometry import calculate_area`
   d. `import calculate_area from math_tools.geometry`
5. Which of the following is a benefit of using modules in Python?
   a. Increased complexity of the code
   b. Reduced code readability
   c. Enhanced code reusability
   d. All of the above
6. When should you consider creating a custom module?
   a. When the code will be used once
   b. When the code does not relate to other parts of the project
   c. When the code needs to be reused across multiple projects
   d. Never
7. What command is used to import a module named utilities?
   a. import utilities
   b. #import utilities
   c. module utilities
   d. get utilities
8. Which Python statement is used to import a specific function from a module?
   a. import function from module
   b. from module import function
   c. import function, module
   d. get function from module
9. What is NOT a good practice when working with Python modules and packages?
   a. Importing only the required functions from a module
   b. Using absolute imports to avoid confusion
   c. Importing everything from a module to ensure availability
   d. Keeping the module and package names clear and concise
10. Which file is required to turn a directory into a Python package?
    a. `package.py`
    b. `__init__.py`
    c. `__main__.py`
    d. `__package__.py`

Answers

1. a
2. c
3. c
4. c
5. c
6. c
7. a
8. b
9. c
10. b

Points to Remember

- Modules are `.py` files that contain Python code. They may include functions, classes, and variables. A module is only loaded once per session by default, making it ideal for exchanging functions and classes between apps.
- Packages organize module namespaces using "dotted module names." A package is essentially a directory that contains a specific file called `__init__.py`, as well as other modules or sub-packages. They are used to divide enormous code bases into manageable and logical pieces.
- Importing Modules allows you to use the functionality of other Python modules. The import statement can be used in several ways to import entire modules, and individual properties, or even rename them for convenience in your code.
- The `__init__.py` file in a package directory tells Python to treat the directory as a package. This file can be left empty; however, it is frequently used to conduct package-specific initialization and import chores.
- To create a custom module, write Python code in a new file and import it using its name (without the `.py` extension). This enables you to reuse and share functionality across different portions of your application or projects.
- Using Python's built-in modules, which are optimized and tested, can save time and effort while writing code.

Further Reading

For further exploration of Python modules and packages, consider these resources:

1. **Python Modules - Real Python:**

   https://realpython.com/learning-paths/modules-and-packages/

   A comprehensive guide to understanding and working with modules and packages in Python.

2. **Python Modules and Packages - W3Schools:**

   https://www.w3schools.com/python/python_modules.asp

   A beginner-friendly introduction to creating and importing modules in Python.

CHAPTER 9
Error Handling

Introduction

In the previous chapter, you learned how to use modules and packages to keep your Python code organized and reusable. Modules help you structure your programs efficiently, but even the best-structured code is not immune to errors. Mistakes happen, whether it is a typo, a missing file, or unexpected user input. Instead of letting these errors crash your program, Python provides tools to catch and handle them.

Think of error handling like driving with a GPS. If you take a wrong turn, the GPS does not stop working. Instead, it reroutes you. Similarly, Python allows you to detect problems in your code and guide your program back on track.

In this chapter, you will explore common types of errors and how to handle them using Python's try, except, else, and finally blocks. These tools allow your programs to respond gracefully to mistakes instead of stopping unexpectedly. You will also learn how to debug issues using Visual Studio Code, making it easier to track down and fix problems in your code.

By the end of this chapter, you will be able to write more reliable programs that keep running smoothly, even when unexpected errors occur.

Let us dive in and learn how to make your Python programs error-resistant!

Structure

In this chapter, the following topics will be covered:

- Understanding Programming Errors
  - Types of Programming Errors
  - Practical Exercise: Find and Fix Errors in Python Code
- Catching Errors with try and except
  - Introduction to try and except Blocks
  - Practical Exercise: Catching Errors with try and except
- Using else and finally
  - Explanation of else and finally Clauses
  - Practical Exercise: Mathematical Operations Calculator
  - Visualizing try-except-else-finally with a Flowchart
- Raising Your Own Errors
  - Raising Exceptions Using the raise Keyword
  - Using raise to Stop Invalid Operations
  - Practical Exercise: Enforcing Input Range

- Introduction to Debugging
    - Step-By-Step Guide to Debugging Python with Visual Studio Code
- Common Mistakes and Best Practices
- Exercises and Challenges: Practice Problems and Solutions

Understanding Programming Errors

Programming errors are like the small mistakes you make in everyday life. Imagine leaving your house and realizing you forgot your keys, or trying to plug a charger into an outlet that does not fit. These mistakes interrupt what you are trying to do. Similarly, when coding, errors can stop a program from running correctly.

Types of Programming Errors

In Python, errors generally fall into two main categories:

- **Syntax Errors**: Mistakes in how the code is written.
- **Exceptions**: Issues that happen while the program is running, even if the code looks correct.

Syntax Errors: The Grammar Mistakes of Code

Think of syntax errors like grammar mistakes in a sentence. If a sentence is missing punctuation or words are in the wrong order, it might not make sense. Python follows strict rules for how code must be written. If something is missing or incorrect, Python would not understand what to do.

For example, look at this code:

```
if x > 0
print("x is greater than 0")
```

Python will show an error because the if statement needs a colon (:) at the end. It is like forgetting a period at the end of a sentence. Without it, the sentence feels incomplete.

Correct version:

```
if x > 0:
    print("x is greater than 0")
```

Exceptions: Errors That Happen While Running the Code

Exceptions are different from syntax errors. Even if the code is written correctly, something unexpected can still go wrong.

Imagine using the correct key for your house, but the lock is broken. You did everything right, but something outside your control is preventing the door from opening.

In Python, one common example is dividing by zero:

```
x = 5
y = 0
print(x / y)
```

Even though the syntax is correct, Python cannot divide by zero, just like you cannot open a broken lock. This causes an exception, which stops the program from running.

Practical Exercise: Find and Fix Errors in Python Code

Errors are a part of programming. Learning to identify and fix them is an important skill.

At this stage, you are manually identifying these mistakes, but later in this chapter, you will see how IDEs such as Visual Studio Code can automatically highlight syntax errors, making it easier to catch and correct them.

Let us look at some common mistakes in Python code and practice spotting and fixing them.

Syntax Errors (Code Would Not Run at All)

These errors occur when Python does not understand the code structure and refuses to execute it.

- **Code Snippet 1: Missing Colon in a Loop**

  ```
  for i in range(10)
  print(i)
  ```

  Identifying issues:

  The loop is missing a colon (:) at the end of the for statement.

  Real-life analogy: This is like writing a to-do list without checkboxes. You need them to show where each task begins.

  Fixed version:

  ```
  for i in range(10):
      print(i)
  ```

- **Code Snippet 2: Missing Colon in an If Statement**

  ```
  x = 10
  if x == 10
  print("x is ten")
  ```

  Identifying issues:

  The if statement is missing a colon (:) and the print statement needs indentation.

  Real-life analogy: This is like missing a step in a recipe. If you forget to preheat the oven, your cake would not bake properly!

  Fixed version:

  ```
  x = 10
  if x == 10:
      print("x is ten")
  ```

Exceptions (Code Runs but Crashes at a Certain Point)

These errors occur while the program is running and cause it to stop unexpectedly.

- **Code Snippet 3: Accessing a Non-Existent List Index**

  ```
  list = [1, 2, 3]
  print(list[3])
  ```

  Identifying issues:

  The list only has three items (list[0], list[1], and list[2]), but the code tries to access list[3], which does not exist.

Real-life analogy: This is like trying to pour a drink from an empty cup, there is nothing there!

Fixed version:

```
list = [1, 2, 3]
print(list[2])  # Accessing the last item correctly
```

Alternative Fix: If you need to check for valid indexes before accessing them, use this approach:

```
index = 3
if index < len(list):
    print(list[index])
else:
    print("Index out of range!")
```

- **Code Snippet 4: Mixing Strings and Numbers**

```
x = "two"
y = 2
print(x + y)
```

Identifying issues:

Python cannot add a string ("two") and a number (2) directly.

Real-life analogy: This is like trying to mix oil and water, they don't blend!

Fixed version:

```
x = "two"
y = 2
print(x + str(y))  # Convert the number to a string
```

Output:

```
two2
```

or

```
x = 2
y = 2
print(x + y)  # Keep both as numbers
```

Output:

4

By fixing these errors, you train your brain to recognize and correct mistakes quickly and efficiently. Later in this chapter, you'll learn how IDEs like Visual Studio Code can automatically highlight syntax errors, making it easier to spot and fix issues before running your code.

Catching Errors with `try` and `except`

In the previous section, you learned about syntax errors and exceptions, two common types of errors that can stop a program from running. While syntax errors must be fixed before a program can execute, exceptions occur while the program is running, causing it to crash if not handled properly.

Instead of letting an error stop the entire program, Python provides a way to handle exceptions gracefully. This is where try-except blocks come in. They allow you to catch errors when they happen and take the appropriate action, keeping the program running smoothly.

Introduction to `try` and `except` Blocks

Python's try and except blocks work together to handle errors smoothly:

- The try block contains the code that Python will attempt to run. If there are no errors, it executes normally.
- If an error occurs inside the try block, Python stops execution and moves to the except block, where the error is handled.

This allows you to control how the program responds to errors, rather than letting it crash unexpectedly.

Real-Life Analogy: Preparing for the Unexpected

Think of an outdoor event, such as a wedding or a picnic. You hope the weather stays clear, but just in case it rains, you have a backup plan such as a tent or an indoor space.

Similarly, in Python:

- The try block is like planning for good weather. If everything runs smoothly, no extra action is needed.
- The except block is like having an umbrella or moving the event indoors, a plan to handle the situation when things do not go as expected.

By using try and except, you ensure that your program does not stop working completely when it encounters an error. Instead, it switches to an alternative action, just like how an event planner smoothly adjusts to bad weather.

Writing a Basic `try-except` Block

Now that you have understood how try and except work, let us look at a basic example before moving to a more complex exercise.

Example: Handling User Input Errors

```
try:
    number = int(input("Enter a number: "))  # User inputs a number
    print(f"You entered: {number}")
except ValueError:
    print("Invalid input! Please enter a valid number.")
```

Understanding the code:

- The try block asks the user for a number.
- If the user enters text instead of a number, Python raises a ValueError, and the except block catches it and displays a message.
- This prevents the program from crashing and allows it to handle errors gracefully.

Now that you have seen a simple example, let us apply the try-except concept in a more practical scenario, creating a division calculator that prevents division by zero and incorrect input types.

Practical Exercise: Catching Errors with `try` and `except`

To gain a better grasp of Python's error-handling features, let us build a simple division calculator. This exercise will demonstrate how to use try and except blocks to handle errors that occur during division operations, such as division by zero or invalid input.

This is a great way to practice designing robust programs that can anticipate and gracefully handle errors during execution.

Task Description:

Create a Python program that:

- Asks the user to enter two numbers: a dividend and a divisor.
- Uses try and except to handle division errors.
- Displays the correct result if the division is successful.
- Shows an error message if something goes wrong.

Steps for the Exercise:

1. Prompt the user to enter two numbers: the dividend and the divisor.
2. Use try/except to handle division errors.
3. Perform the division and display the result if no errors occur.

Python Code Example:

```
def divide_numbers(dividend, divisor):
    try:
        result = dividend / divisor
        print(f"The result of dividing {dividend} by {divisor} is:
{result:.2f}")
    except ZeroDivisionError:
        print("Error: Division by zero is not allowed.")
    except ValueError:
        print("Error: Please enter valid numbers.")
    except Exception as e:
        print(f"An unexpected error occurred: {e}")

def main():
    try:
        num1 = float(input("Enter the dividend: "))
        num2 = float(input("Enter the divisor: "))
        divide_numbers(num1, num2)
    except ValueError:
        print("Invalid input. Please enter a valid number.")

if __name__ == "__main__":
    main()
```

Understanding the Code:

This program consists of two functions:

- **`divide_numbers(dividend, divisor)`**
  - Uses a try block to attempt division.
  - Handles **`ZeroDivisionError`** if the user tries to divide by zero.
  - Handles **`ValueError`** in case the user enters a non-numeric value.
  - Catches any other unexpected errors using a general Exception.
- **`main()` function**
  - Prompts the user for input **and ensures the values are converted to numbers.**
  - Handles incorrect input types **(for example, if the user enters text instead of numbers).**
  - Calls the **`divide_numbers()`** function **to perform the division.**

By handling these errors before they cause issues, you will ensure the program runs smoothly even when the user makes mistakes.

Your Turn!

Try running the code and test different inputs:

- Enter valid numbers (for example, 10 and 2).
- Try dividing by zero (10 and 0).
- Enter letters instead of numbers (a and b).

Observe how the program responds and handles these cases!

Using `else` and `finally`

In the previous section, you explored how try and except blocks help handle errors in Python, allowing programs to catch and manage exceptions gracefully. However, Python provides additional tools to control the execution flow, that is, else and finally blocks. These blocks help ensure structured error handling and allow you to manage both successful operations and necessary cleanup tasks.

Explanation of `else` and `finally` Clauses

Both else and finally serve different purposes in error handling, ensuring code remains organized and predictable.

The `else` Clause: Handling Successful Execution

The else block runs only if no exceptions occur in the try block. It allows you to define what should happen when everything goes as planned.

Real-life analogy: Imagine you are baking a cake. If everything goes smoothly. No spills, no incorrect measurements. You move on to decorating the cake. Similarly, the else block runs only when no errors are encountered in the try block.

Python Example:

```
try:
    number = int(input("Enter a number: "))
except ValueError:
    print("Invalid input! Please enter a valid number.")
else:
    print(f"You entered: {number}")
```

- If the user enters a valid number, the else block runs and prints the number.
- If the user enters text, the except block handles the error instead.

The `finally` Clause: Ensuring Cleanup

The finally block runs no matter what happens, whether an error occurs or not. It is often used for cleanup actions such as closing files or releasing resources.

Real-life analogy: No matter how the cooking process goes, you always clean the kitchen after baking. The finally block works the same way. It executes whether or not an error occurs.

Python Example:

```
try:
    file = open("sample.txt", "r")  # Attempt to open a file
    content = file.read()
    print(content)
except FileNotFoundError:
```

```
        print("File not found!")
    finally:
        print("Closing the file...")
        file.close()  # Cleanup action (executed regardless of success or failure)
```

- If the file exists, the content is displayed, and the file is closed.
- If the file does not exist, an error is shown, but the program still executes the cleanup action.

Practical Exercise: Mathematical Operations Calculator

To better understand else and finally in action, let us build a simple calculator that performs basic operations such as addition, subtraction, multiplication, and division. This exercise will demonstrate how else ensures successful execution and finally ensures proper cleanup actions.

Task Description:

Create a Python program that:

- Asks the user for two numbers and an operation (add, subtract, multiply, or divide).
- Uses try and except to handle errors, such as invalid input or division by zero.
- Uses else to display the result when no errors occur.
- Uses finally to print a completion message after execution.

Steps for the Exercise:

1. Prompt for user input: Ask the user for two numbers and the operation.
2. Implement error handling:
    - Use try to attempt the operation.
    - Use except to catch errors such as division by zero or invalid input.
    - Use else to display the result when the operation is successful.
    - Use finally to print a completion message, ensuring cleanup.
3. Process and display the result or handle errors accordingly.

Python Code Example:

```
def perform_operation(num1, num2, operation):
    try:
        if operation == 'add':
            result = num1 + num2
        elif operation == 'subtract':
            result = num1 - num2
        elif operation == 'multiply':
            result = num1 * num2
        elif operation == 'divide':
            result = num1 / num2
        else:
            raise ValueError("Invalid operation selected.")
    except ZeroDivisionError:
        print("Error: Division by zero is not allowed.")
    except ValueError as ve:
        print(f"Error: {ve}")
    else:
        print(f"The result of {operation} is: {result}")
    finally:
        print("Operation completed.")
```

```
def main():
    try:
        num1 = float(input("Enter the first number: "))
        num2 = float(input("Enter the second number: "))
        operation = input("Enter the operation (add, subtract, multiply, di-
vide): ").lower()
        perform_operation(num1, num2, operation)
    except ValueError:
        print("Invalid input. Please enter a valid number.")

if __name__ == "__main__":
    main()
```

Understanding the Code

This program follows a structured approach to error handling:

- **The try block**: Executes the selected mathematical operation.
- **The except block**: Handles:
    - `ZeroDivisionError` (when dividing by zero).
    - `ValueError` (if the user enters an invalid operation).
        - **The else block**: Runs only if no exceptions occur, displaying the result.
        - **The finally block**: Runs no matter what happens, ensuring a completion message is always printed.

By using else and finally, you will maintain structured, readable, and error-proof programs.

Your Turn!

Try running the program and test different inputs:

- Enter valid numbers with a correct operation (for example, 10, 5, add).
- Try dividing by zero (10, 0, divide).
- Enter an invalid operation (10, 5, square).
- Input letters instead of numbers (a, b, multiply).

Observe how the program responds in each case!

Visualizing try-except-else-finally with a Flowchart

So far, you have learned how Python handles errors using try and except and how you can add else and finally for better control. But how does Python decide which block to execute? The following flowchart shows the exact steps Python follows when running a try-except-else-finally structure:

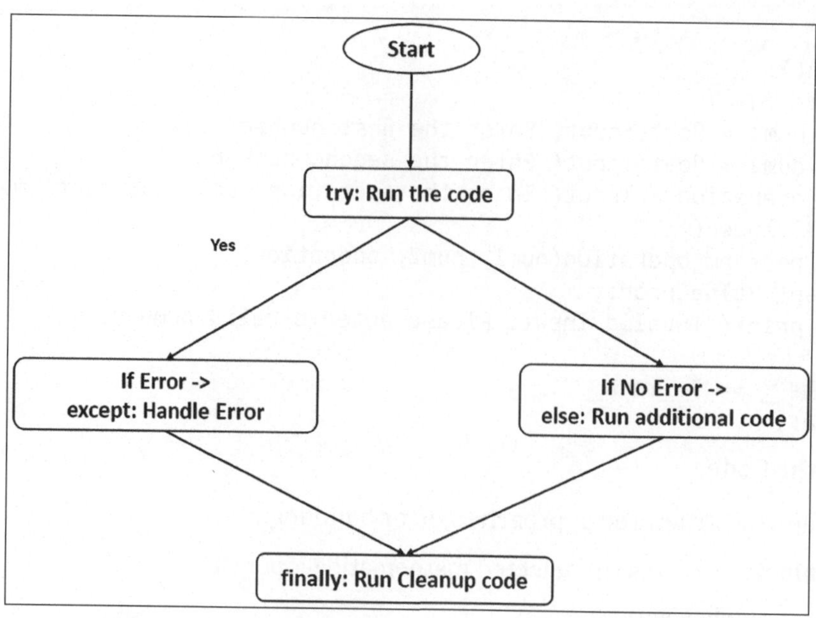

Figure 9.1: *Visualizing try-except-else-finally using Flowchart*

Explanation:

1. The program enters the try block and executes the code.
   - If no error occurs, Python moves to the else block (if present).
   - If an error occurs, Python skips else and goes to the except block to handle it.
2. Regardless of whether an error occurred or not, the finally block always executes.
3. After handling errors or cleanup, the program continues execution.

This structure ensures that Python programs handle errors gracefully while also allowing for necessary cleanup actions.

Raising Your Own Errors

In the previous sections, you have explored how Python handles predefined errors using try, except, else, and finally. However, not all errors are built into Python. Sometimes, you may need to create your own custom errors to enforce specific rules in your program.

This is where the raise keyword comes in; it allows you to intentionally trigger exceptions when certain conditions are not met. This helps make programs more reliable, prevents incorrect data from being processed, and makes debugging easier by providing clear error messages.

Raising Exceptions Using the `raise` Keyword

The raise keyword is an essential tool in Python for defining and enforcing specific conditions in a program. By raising exceptions, you can intentionally stop execution when something is wrong, ensuring that the program does not proceed with incorrect data.

Real-life analogy: Imagine you are filling out an online form, and you accidentally leave a required field empty. The form does not submit and instead displays an error message prompting you to enter the missing information. This is similar to how raise works in Python. It stops the program and informs the user about the issue.

Why Raise Exceptions?

- **Enforces rules in your program**: Ensuring that functions only process valid data.
- **Prevents invalid operations**: Such as performing calculations with incorrect inputs.
- **Improves debugging**: By providing specific error messages when something goes wrong.

For example, if you are building a system that processes user data, you may want to raise an exception if important information is missing. This prevents the program from running with incomplete or incorrect data.

Using `raise` to Stop Invalid Operations

The raise keyword is used to trigger built-in exceptions (such as **`ValueError`**, **`TypeError`**, and so on) or custom exceptions created by the programmer.

Example: Raising an Exception When a Condition is not Met

Imagine a function that calculates the square root of a number. Since the square root of a negative number is not defined in real numbers, you can use raise to prevent invalid input.

```
import math

def calculate_square_root(number):
    if number < 0:
        raise ValueError("Cannot calculate the square root of a negative number.")
    return math.sqrt(number)

def main():
    try:
        num = float(input("Enter a number to find the square root: "))
        result = calculate_square_root(num)
        print(f"The square root of {num} is {result:.2f}")
    except ValueError as error:
        print(error)

if __name__ == "__main__":
    main()
```

Understanding the Code:

- **`calculate_square_root()`** function:
  - o Checks if the number is negative.
  - o If so, it raises a **`ValueError`** to prevent invalid calculations.
  - o Otherwise, it returns the square root.
- **`main()`** function:
  - o Uses try to handle user input and call the function.
  - o Uses except to catch and display errors gracefully.

Now, if a user tries to calculate the square root of a negative number, they will see a clear error message instead of the program failing unexpectedly.

Practical Exercise: Enforcing Input Range

As you build more powerful Python applications, it is important to ensure that user inputs meet specific conditions. This exercise will teach you how to enforce input rules using raise.

In this task, you will require users to enter a positive number. If they enter a negative number or zero, an exception will be raised.

Task Description:

Create a Python program that:

- Asks the user to enter a positive number.
- Uses raise to enforce the positive number rule.
- Uses try and except to handle errors and display clear messages.

Steps for the Exercise:

1. Ask the user to enter a number.
2. Check if the number is positive using a conditional statement.
3. Raise an exception if the number is negative or zero.
4. Use a try-except block to handle errors and display user-friendly messages.

Python Code Example:

```
def get_positive_number():
    num = float(input("Enter a positive number: "))
    if num <= 0:
        raise ValueError("The number is not positive. Please enter a positive 
number.")
    return num

try:
    positive_number = get_positive_number()
    print(f"You entered: {positive_number}")
except ValueError as error:
    print(error)
```

Understanding the Code:

- **Function Definition:**
    - **`get_positive_number()`** prompts the user for input and converts it to a float.
    - If the input is not a positive number, it raises a **`ValueError`** with an explanation.
- **Condition Check and Exception Raising:** Ensures that only positive values are accepted.
- **Exception Handling:**
    - A try block attempts to get and process the user input.
    - An except block catches and displays error messages instead of crashing the program.

Your Turn!

Try running the program and test different inputs:

- Enter a positive number (for example, 5.5).
- Try entering zero (0).
- Enter a negative number (for example, -3).
- Try entering letters instead of numbers (hello).

Observe how the program responds in each case!

Introduction to Debugging

As you advance in Python programming, debugging becomes an essential skill. Debugging allows you to find and fix errors in your code efficiently, helping you understand how your program behaves and why certain issues occur.

In this section, you will explore how to use Visual Studio Code (VS Code) for debugging Python programs. Let us walk through the setup, breakpoints, inspecting variables, and using advanced debugging features, using a simple Python program as an example.

Debugging is the process of identifying and fixing errors (bugs) in a program. It helps:

- Find the exact location where the issue occurs.
- Inspect variable values and function calls.
- Fix problems to ensure the program runs correctly.

Real-life analogy: Debugging is like troubleshooting a broken remote control. You check if the batteries are inserted correctly, test different buttons, and eventually replace the batteries if needed. Similarly, in programming, debugging helps you test different parts of the code and fix errors systematically.

Step-by-Step Guide to Debugging Python with Visual Studio Code

In this section, you will use Visual Studio Code (VS Code) to explore debugging techniques that help identify and fix errors efficiently. In this section, you will learn how to:

- Use breakpoints to pause execution and inspect code behavior.
- Step through code to analyze how your program runs line by line.
- Inspect and modifying variables to understand and fix errors.
- Use the Debug Console to evaluate expressions and make quick changes.

By the end of this section, you will be able to debug Python programs efficiently using VS Code's built-in debugging tools.

1. **Setting Breakpoints**

   A breakpoint pauses the program at a specific line, allowing you to inspect values and control execution.

   Set a Breakpoint

   a. Open your Python file in VS Code.

   b. Click to the left of the line number where you want to stop execution.

   c. A red dot will appear, marking the breakpoint.

Example: Let us place a breakpoint inside the divide function at:

```
def divide(a, b):
    return a / b  # Place a breakpoint here
```

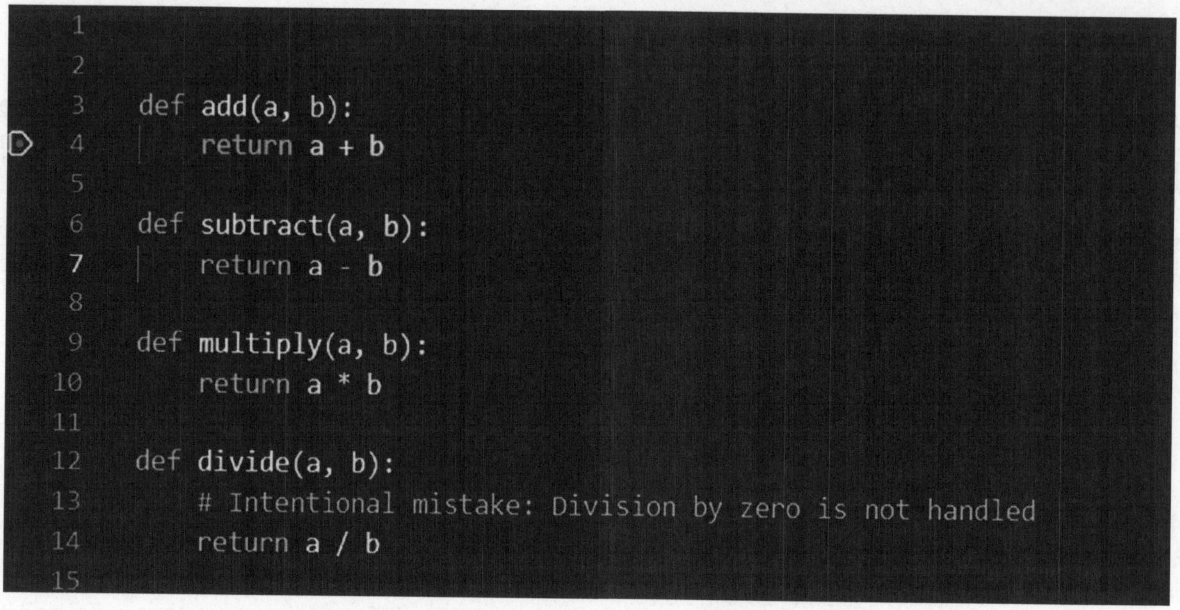

```
def add(a, b):
    return a + b

def subtract(a, b):
    return a - b

def multiply(a, b):
    return a * b

def divide(a, b):
    # Intentional mistake: Division by zero is not handled
    return a / b

```

Figure 9.2: *Setting breakpoint in Visual Studio Code*

2. **Running the Debugger**

   Once you have set your breakpoints, start debugging.

   Start Debugging

   a. Press F5 or click the green play button in the Debug panel.

   b. The program will pause at the first breakpoint, allowing you to inspect values.

   Example: Run the following calculator code and input values when prompted.

```
def add(a, b):
    return a + b

def subtract(a, b):
    return a - b

def multiply(a, b):
    return a * b

def divide(a, b):
    # Intentional mistake: Division by zero is not handled
    return a / b

def main():
    print("Simple Calculator!")
    a = int(input("Enter first number: "))
    b = int(input("Enter second number: "))
    operation = input("Choose the operation (+, -, *, /): ")

    if operation == '+':
        result = add(a, b)
    elif operation == '-':
        result = subtract(a, b)
    elif operation == '*':
        result = multiply(a, b)
    elif operation == '/':
        result = divide(a, b)
```

```
    else:
        print("Invalid operation!")
        return

    print("The result is:", result)

if __name__ == '__main__':
    main()
```

3. **Inspecting Variables**

   Once the program pauses at a breakpoint, you can examine values in the Variables panel.

   Inspect Variables

   a. Open the Debug sidebar (left panel in VS Code).

   b. Expand the '**`Variables`**' panel to see the values of all variables in the current scope.

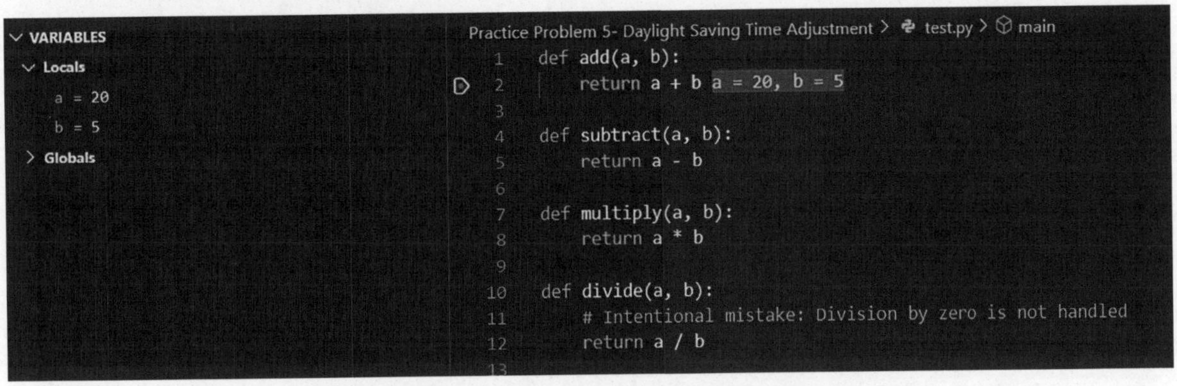

```
VARIABLES
  Locals
    a = 20
    b = 5
  Globals

Practice Problem 5- Daylight Saving Time Adjustment > test.py > main
def add(a, b):
    return a + b a = 20, b = 5

def subtract(a, b):
    return a - b

def multiply(a, b):
    return a * b

def divide(a, b):
    # Intentional mistake: Division by zero is not handled
    return a / b
```

***Figure 9.3:** Inspecting variables in Visual Studio Code*

   Example:

   - If execution is paused inside divide(a, b), check the values of a and b.
   - If b = 0, the program will crash on division, which you will fix later!

4. **Stepping Through Code**

   Instead of running the entire program at once, you can move through it step by step.

   Step Options in VS Code

   - Step Over (F10): Move to the next line without entering functions.
   - Step Into (F11): Enter a function to debug inside it.
   - Step Out (*Shift*+F11): Exit a function and return to the caller.

   Example:

   - Step into divide(a, b) using F11 to see what happens when b = 0.
   - Step over (F10) to continue execution line by line.

5. **Modifying Values During Debugging**

   You can change variable values while debugging to test different scenarios.

   Modify Variable Values

   a. Open the Variables panel in the Debug sidebar.

   b. Right-click a variable (for example, b) and select '**`Set Value.`**'

   c. Enter a new value (for example, change b = 0 to b = 1).

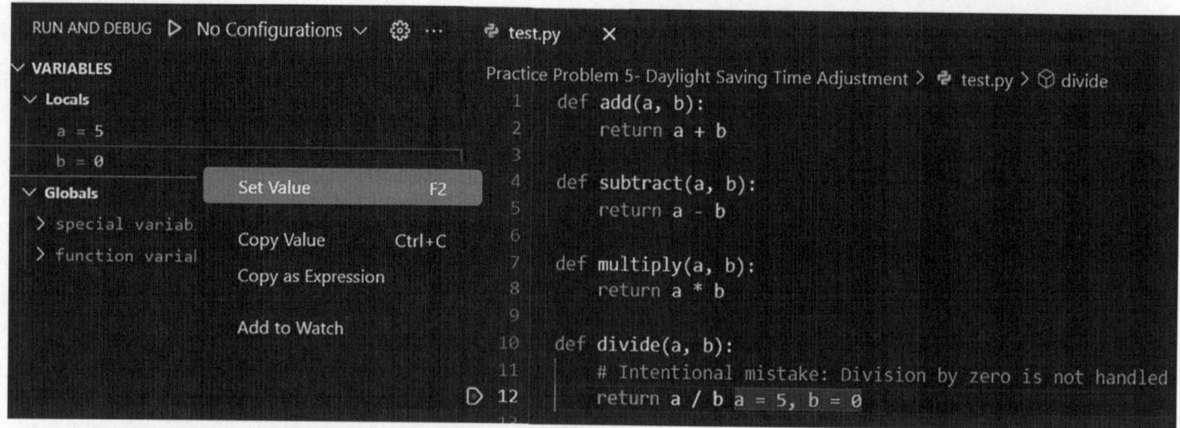

Figure 9.4: *Modifying variable values in Visual Studio Code*

Example:

- Change b = 0 to b = 1 before executing the division.
- This allows you to test how the program behaves with different inputs.

6. **Using the Debug Console**

The Debug Console lets you test expressions and change variables while debugging.

Use the Debug Console

a. Open the Debug Console in VS Code.

b. Type an expression (for example, a + b) and press *Enter* to evaluate it.

c. Modify variables by typing b = 1 before running an operation.

Example:

- Before executing the division, type b = 1 in the Debug Console.
- This prevents a division by zero error without modifying the code manually.

7. **Stopping and Restarting the Debug Session**

- Stop Debugging (*Shift*+F5): Ends the debugging session.
- Restart Debugging (*Ctrl*+*Shift*+F5): Restarts the program from the beginning.

8. **Adding Conditional Breakpoints**

Conditional breakpoints stop execution only when specific conditions are met.

Set a Conditional Breakpoint

a. Right-click a breakpoint and select "**`Edit Breakpoint`**."

b. Enter a condition (for example, b == 0).

c. The debugger will pause execution only when this condition is true.

Example: Inside the **`divide()`** function, add a conditional breakpoint:

```
def divide(a, b):
    if b == 0:  # Add a conditional breakpoint here
        raise ValueError("Cannot divide by zero!")
    return a / b
```

The program will only pause when b == 0, helping you debug division errors efficiently.

Importance of Breakpoint and Debugger:

- Breakpoints let you pause execution and inspect values.
- Stepping through code helps you understand program flow.
- The Debug Console allows you to modify values and test expressions.
- Conditional breakpoints make debugging more precise.

By following these steps, you will gain hands-on experience with debugging in VS Code, making it easier to identify and fix errors in your Python programs.

Your Turn!

Try running the debugger and experiment with:

- Valid operations (10, 2, +).
- Dividing by zero (10, 0, /).
- Changing values using the Debug Console.

Common Mistakes and Best Practices

Error handling is a crucial part of writing robust Python programs. Following are some common mistakes and best practices to follow when handling errors effectively.

Common Mistakes

- **Mistake**: Catching All Exceptions Without Specific Handling

```
try:
    result = 10 / 0
except:
    print("An error occurred.")
```

  Fix: Catch specific exceptions to handle different error types properly.

```
try:
    result = 10 / 0
except ZeroDivisionError:
    print("Error: Cannot divide by zero.")
```

- **Mistake**: Ignoring Errors Without Handling Them

```
try:
    file = open("nonexistent.txt", "r")
except FileNotFoundError:
    pass  # No action taken
```

  Fix: Log the error or inform the user instead of ignoring it.

```
try:
    file = open("nonexistent.txt", "r")
except FileNotFoundError:
    print("Error: The file was not found.")
```

- **Mistake**: Using a Generic Exception Message

```
try:
    num = int(input("Enter a number: "))
except ValueError:
    print("Something went wrong.")
```

Fix: Provide a clear error message to guide the user.

```
try:
    num = int(input("Enter a number: "))
except ValueError:
    print("Invalid input! Please enter a valid number.")
```

Best Practices for Error Handling

- **Use Specific Exceptions**: Catch only the exceptions you expect, instead of using a generic except.
- **Use else and finally Blocks**: Keep error-free logic in else and cleanup actions in finally.
- **Raise Custom Errors When Needed**: Use raise for better control over program flow.
- **Log Errors for Debugging**: Instead of printing errors, use Python's logging module to track issues.
- **Keep Try Blocks Short**: Only include the code that might fail inside the try block.

Following these practices will help you write cleaner, more predictable, and easier-to-debug Python programs!

Exercises and Challenges: Practice Problems and Solutions

Let us delve into a practical exercise aimed at enhancing your proficiency in Python error handling.

Practical Exercise: Fix the Code Using Error Handling

In this section, you will be shown ten Python code snippets that include common errors. Each sample contains basic error-handling structures such as try, except, else, and finally. Your objective is to alter each sample by improving or properly implementing these error handling blocks to guarantee the application handles faults gracefully.

Task Description:

Examine each code snippet for probable mistakes, then alter the try, except, else, and finally blocks to appropriately handle these errors. This will improve your ability to develop robust error handling in Python scripts.

Code Snippets for Error Handling:

1. **Incorrect Indentation Handling**

```
try:
    if True
        print("This will not run.")
except IndentationError:
    print("Caught an indentation error!")
```

2. **Handling Division by Zero**

```
try:
    num = 10 / 0
except ZeroDivisionError:
    print("Division by zero error.")
```

3. **Fixing Variable Name Mistakes**

```
try:
    print(age)
```

```
except NameError:
    print("Variable is not defined.")
```

4. **List Index Out of Range**

```
try:
    list = [1, 2, 3]
    print(list[5])
except IndexError:
    print("List index out of range.")
```

5. **Type Error While Adding String to Integer**

```
try:
    result = '100' + 100
except TypeError:
    print("Cannot add string and integer.")
```

6. **File Opening Error**

```
try:
    file = open('nonexistentfile.txt', 'r')
except FileNotFoundError:
    print("File not found.")
```

7. **Handling Improper Dictionary Key Access**

```
try:
    dict = {'key': 'value'}
    print(dict['nonexistentkey'])
except KeyError:
    print("Key does not exist in dictionary.")
```

8. **Handling ValueError in Number Conversion**

```
try:
    value = int('abc')
except ValueError:
    print("Cannot convert string to integer.")
```

9. **Incorrect Usage of Attribute**

```
try:
    list = []
    list.push(1)
except AttributeError:
    print("List object has no attribute 'push'.")
```

10. **Using Undefined Function**

```
try:
    undefined_function()
except NameError:
    print("Function is not defined.")
```

Instructions for Completion:

For each snippet, analyze the provided try and except blocks.

- Determine if exception handling is appropriate or contains errors.
- Improve error handling code to increase snippet robustness.
- Test the revised code to confirm it works as planned.

This exercise will help you understand not only basic programming errors, but also how to correctly use Python's error handling features to develop more robust and error-resistant applications.

Solutions to Practice Problems

Here are the corrected versions of the ten Python code snippets with explanations for each modification, ensuring robust error handling and program stability.

1. Incorrect Indentation Handling

```
# IndentationError cannot be caught by try-except because it is a syntax error that occurs before execution.
# Corrected version:
try:
    if True:  # Added colon
        print("This will run.")
except IndentationError:
    print("This line will never be reached.")
```

Explanation: To correct the syntax error, add a colon after if True. A try-except block cannot catch an indentation problem because it is a compile-time fault.

2. **Handling Division by Zero**

```
try:
    num = 10 / 0
except ZeroDivisionError:
    print("Handled division by zero error.")
```

Explanation: Added an exception handler for **ZeroDivisionError** to handle division by zero, a runtime issue.

3. **Fixing Variable Name Mistakes**

```
try:
    print(age)  # Assuming 'age' is not defined earlier
except NameError:
    print("Handled undefined variable.")
```

Explanation: Age is not defined; hence, a **NameError** is thrown. The unless block catches and handles the error.

4. **List Index Out of Range**

```
try:
    list = [1, 2, 3]
    print(list[5])
except IndexError:
    print("Handled list index out of range.")
```

Explanation: You attempted to access an index that did not exist in the list. Added an **IndexError** handler to manage this.

5. **Type Error While Adding String to Integer**

```
try:
    result = '100' + 100
except TypeError:
    print("Handled type error when adding string and integer.")
```

Explanation: You cannot add strings and numbers directly. This generates a **TypeError**, which is subsequently caught and managed.

6. **File Opening Error**

```
try:
    file = open('nonexistentfile.txt', 'r')
except FileNotFoundError:
    print("Handled file not found error.")
```

Explanation: Attempted to open a file that does not exist, causing a `FileNotFoundError`, which is properly detected.

7. **Handling Improper Dictionary Key Access**

```
try:
    dict = {'key': 'value'}
    print(dict['nonexistentkey'])
except KeyError:
    print("Handled missing key in dictionary.")
```

Explanation: Attempted to access a non-existent key in a dictionary. The generated `KeyError` is caught and handled.

8. **Handling `ValueError` in Number Conversion**

```
try:
    value = int('abc')
except ValueError:
    print("Handled value error when converting string to integer.")
```

Explanation: An attempt to convert a non-numeric string to an integer results in a `ValueError`. This exception was caught and handled.

9. **Incorrect Usage of Attribute**

```
try:
    list = []
    list.append(1)  # Correct method to add an element
except AttributeError:
    print("Handled attribute error.")
```

Explanation: Fixed push to append for list operations. If an improper method name is used, it will trigger an `AttributeError`.

10. **Using Undefined Function**

```
try:
    undefined_function()  # Assuming no function defined
except NameError:
    print("Handled undefined function error.")
```

Explanation: An attempt to call an undefined function resulted in a `NameError`. This error is detected and addressed.

These solutions demonstrate the correct implementation of error handling strategies in Python, which can help you find, repair, and manage mistakes successfully in your code.

Conclusion

In this chapter, you expanded your Python programming skills by learning about error handling, a crucial technique for writing reliable and robust programs. You explored different types of errors, from syntax errors to exceptions, and learned how to manage them gracefully using try, except, else, and finally blocks. These tools allow you to anticipate and handle potential issues, preventing unexpected crashes and improving the overall stability of your applications.

You also discovered how to raise custom exceptions, giving you more control over program execution and ensuring that invalid inputs or unexpected conditions are handled appropriately. Through practical exercises and real-world examples, you gained hands-on experience in identifying, catching, and debugging errors effectively.

In the next chapter, you will move from handling errors to working with files and strings in Python. You will learn how to read and write files, manipulate text, and manage file paths, essential skills for building applications that interact with external data. Understanding file handling and string operations will help you create dynamic and data-driven Python programs.

As you transition from debugging errors to handling files and text data, let us continue sharpening your Python skills and writing clean, efficient programs.

Till then, keep calm and let's tame the Python!

Multiple-Choice Questions

1. What is the purpose of the try block in Python?
   a. To define a block of code to be executed regardless of an error occurring
   b. To define a block of code to test for errors in its execution
   c. To declare variables
   d. To import necessary modules
2. Which statement is used to handle exceptions in Python?
   a. handle
   b. error
   c. except
   d. try
3. What does the finally block do?
   a. Executes code regardless of whether there is an error in the try block
   b. Executes code only if there is no error in the try block
   c. Checks for errors in its block of code
   d. None of the above
4. What type of errors does Python raise when the program has a fault that the code does not handle?
   a. Syntax errors
   b. Exceptions
   c. Logical errors
   d. Compilation errors
5. When would you typically use the raise keyword?
   a. When importing modules
   b. When you need to generate a specific exception manually

   c. When defining a function

   d. When testing for syntax errors

6. Which clause is used along with try and except to execute code only if no errors were raised?

   a. finally

   b. else

   c. continue

   d. pass

7. In the context of debugging, what is a breakpoint?

   a. A syntax error in the program

   b. A specific line of code where the debugger will pause execution

   c. An error generated by the IDE

   d. A point where the program exits

8. What will happen if an exception is raised but not handled in a try block?

   a. The program will exit or terminate unexpectedly

   b. The program will continue execution

   c. The exception will be ignored

   d. The program will rerun from the start

9. Which of the following is NOT a common use case for the finally block?

   a. Closing database connections

   b. Logging messages

   c. Raising exceptions

   d. Releasing external resources

10. Which of the following is a true statement about handling exceptions in Python?

    a. You can only handle one type of exception per try block

    b. You cannot handle multiple different exceptions with a single except statement

    c. You can specify which exception to handle right after an except keyword

    d. Exceptions are handled during the compile-time phase

Answers

1. b
2. c
3. a
4. b
5. b

6. b
7. b
8. a
9. c
10. c

Points to Remember

- Python errors are faults in the program that cause aberrant behavior or termination. Recognizing and managing these is critical for developing robust apps.
- Errors are divided into two categories: syntax errors and exceptions. Syntax errors occur when code violates Python's parsing rules, whereas exceptions occur when syntactically correct code finds an aberrant condition.
- The **`try`** block tests a block of code for mistakes, while the except block handles the errors. This structure is necessary to prevent your program from crashing due to unanticipated situations.
- Use the **`else`** block after the try and except blocks to declare code that will run if the try block does not throw an exception. It aids in neatly distinguishing successful code execution from error handling.
- The **`finally`** block will run after the other portions of **`try`**, **`except`**, and **`else`**, regardless of whether an exception was thrown, making it perfect for cleaning tasks like shutting files or releasing resources.
- The **`raise`** keyword is used to throw an exception when specified circumstances are met. This allows you to enforce certain limitations in your code, such as input validation or business logic requirements.

Further Reading

For further exploration of Python error handling, consider these resources:

1. **Python Exception Handling** – Real Python:

   https://realpython.com/python-exceptions/

   A detailed guide on handling exceptions in Python, with best practices and advanced techniques.

2. **Python Errors and Exceptions** – W3Schools:

   https://www.w3schools.com/python/python_try_except.asp

   A beginner-friendly introduction to handling errors using try and except in Python.

Chapter 10
File Handling and String Manipulation

Introduction

In the last chapter, you learned how to handle errors in Python and make your programs more reliable. Now you are ready to take the next step in your programming journey by working with text and files.

We interact with text every day, whether we are reading documents, saving information, or searching through data. As a programmer, knowing how to handle text and manage files is very important. This includes saving user input, processing data, or displaying well-formatted output.

In this chapter, you will learn how to work with strings in Python. You will explore how to create, change, and format text. You will also be introduced to regular expressions, which help you find patterns in text.

After learning about strings, you will move on to file handling. You will understand how to open files, read from them, write to them, and manage them properly. You will also learn good practices and how to handle errors when working with files.

By the end of this chapter, you will feel confident in working with both text and files using Python. Let's begin and unlock the power of these essential programming skills.

Structure

In this chapter, the following topics will be covered:

- Getting Started with File Handling and String Manipulation
    - Real-World Applications and Use Cases
- String Manipulation
    - Basic String Operations
    - String Methods
    - String Formatting
    - Regular Expressions (Regex)
    - Practical Exercise: Text Analyzer
- Working with Files
    - Opening and Closing Files
    - Different File Modes
    - Best Practices for Handling Files
    - Reading from Files
    - Writing to Files

- Error Handling in File Operations
  - Common File-Related Exceptions
  - Using try, except, and finally Blocks for Robust File Handling
  - Practical Exercise: Text File Manager
- Common Mistakes and Best Practices
- Exercises and Challenges: Practice Problems and Solutions

Getting Started with File Handling and String Manipulation

Programming often requires working with text and data, whether reading from files, writing reports, or processing information. Mastering file handling and string manipulation allows you, as a developer, to efficiently manage and analyze data across various applications. These skills are fundamental for tasks such as storing user input, processing logs, automating workflows, and formatting output. Here is why these skills matter:

- **Storing and Retrieving Data**: Files allow you to save data permanently. Unlike variables, which disappear when a program stops, files store information that you can access later. This is useful for saving settings, logs, or user data between program runs.
- **Processing Large Amounts of Data**: Many programs work with large text files, such as logs, configuration files, or CSVs. Knowing how to extract and modify text lets you analyze, clean, and structure data for reports and insights.
- **Sharing Data Between Systems**: Files act as a bridge between different programs and systems. For example, saving data in a CSV file makes it easier for other applications to read and process the information.
- **Automating Tasks**: Many automation scripts rely on file handling. Whether you need to process multiple text files, generate reports, or create backups, Python's file operations make it simple.
- **Manipulating Text Efficiently**: Strings are a fundamental part of programming. From formatting output, processing user input, or searching for patterns, strong string manipulation skills help you write cleaner and more powerful programs.

Real-World Applications and Use Cases

To see how these skills apply in real life, let us look at practical examples where file handling and string manipulation are essential:

- **Log File Analysis**: System administrators and developers analyze log files to troubleshoot errors. By scanning logs for specific messages, they can quickly find and fix problems.
- **Data Parsing and Transformation**: Many programs export raw data as text files. You can write Python scripts to clean, format, and store this data in a more structured format, such as databases or CSV files.
- **Configuration Management**: Applications often store settings in files. By reading these files at runtime, programs can adjust settings without modifying the code. Writing settings back to a file ensures persistent configurations.
- **Web Scraping**: Extracted data from websites is often saved into files for further processing. String manipulation helps clean and organize this text for analysis.
- **Text Processing and Natural Language Processing (NLP)**: In fields such as AI and data science, text is processed for search engines, chatbots, and sentiment analysis. Python's string tools

help in tokenization (splitting text into words), stemming (reducing words to their base form), and classification.

- **Automated Reporting**: Many businesses automate reports by extracting data, formatting it, and saving or emailing the results. This saves time and ensures accuracy in financial, sales, or operational reports.

Mastering file handling and string manipulation will open up new opportunities and make you a more versatile programmer. These skills will help you work with data efficiently, automate tasks, and improve the way your programs interact with the real world.

String Manipulation

In the previous section, you explored why text processing and file handling are crucial in programming. Now, let us take a deeper dive into string manipulation, which allows you to create, modify, and analyze text efficiently.

Python provides powerful tools for working with strings, making tasks such as formatting text, searching for patterns, and extracting information easier. In this section, you will cover:

- **Basic String Operations**: Creating, accessing, and slicing strings.
- **String Methods**: Built-in functions to modify text.
- **String Formatting**: Making output dynamic and readable.
- **Regular Expressions**: Searching for patterns in text.

These techniques will help you handle text efficiently in Python, whether you are cleaning up user input, processing files, or analyzing large datasets.

Basic String Operations

A string in Python is a sequence of characters, such as words or sentences. Since text is used everywhere, such as in file names, user input, and website data, Python provides powerful tools to work with strings efficiently.

Creating and Initializing Strings:

Strings in Python can be created in three simple ways:

```
# Single quotes
single_quote_string = 'Hello, World!'

# Double quotes
double_quote_string = "Hello, World!"

# Triple quotes for multi-line strings
multi_line_string = '''This is a
multi-line string.'''

# Creating an empty string
empty_string = ""
```

- Single or double quotes are used for short text.
- Triple quotes allow multi-line strings, such as paragraphs.
- An empty string is useful when you need a placeholder.

Now that you know how to create strings, let us explore how to access and manipulate them.

Accessing Characters and Slicing Strings:

Each character in a string has a position (index). Python allows you to access individual characters using their index number:

```
my_string = "Python"

# Accessing characters by positive index
first_char = my_string[0]  # 'P'
second_char = my_string[1]  # 'y'

# Accessing characters by negative index (counting from the end)
last_char = my_string[-1]  # 'n'
second_last_char = my_string[-2]  # 'o'
```

- Indexing starts at 0 (first letter) and goes up.
- Negative indexing starts from -1 (last letter) and moves backward.

To extract parts of a string, use slicing:

```
my_string = "Hello, World!"

# Slicing from index 0 to 4 (not including 5)
substring = my_string[0:5]  # 'Hello'

# Slicing with a step (every second character)
every_second_char = my_string[0:11:2]  # 'Hlo o'
```

- Slicing works like cutting text, allowing you to choose a starting point, an endpoint, and a step size.
- Omitting start or end automatically selects the beginning or end of the string.

Next, let us see how strings can be combined and repeated.

String Concatenation and Repetition:

Concatenation means joining two or more strings together. use the + operator:

```
string1 = "Hello"
string2 = "World"

# Concatenating strings
greeting = string1 + ", " + string2 + "!"  # 'Hello, World!'
```

The + operator combines text without spaces, so add "," to format the output.

To repeat a string multiple times, use *:

```
# Repeating strings
repeat_hello = "Hello" * 3  # 'HelloHelloHello'
```

The * operator multiplies the string, creating copies of it.

String Methods

In the previous section, you learned how to create, access, and manipulate strings using indexing and slicing. Now, let us explore Python's built-in string methods, which make it even easier to modify and process text.

Python provides many functions to help with changing case, removing spaces, replacing text, and more. Let us go through some of the most commonly used string methods.

Common String Methods:

Python's string methods allow you to modify and analyze text efficiently. Here are some of the most useful ones, along with examples.

- **Changing Letter Case**
  - **Convert text to uppercase:**

```
my_string = "Hello, World!"
upper_string = my_string.upper()
print(upper_string)  # 'HELLO, WORLD!'
```

  - **Convert text to lowercase:**

```
my_string = "Hello, World!"
lower_string = my_string.lower()
print(lower_string)  # 'hello, world!'
```

  `upper()` and `lower()` are useful when comparing text (for example, case-insensitive search).

- **Removing Unwanted Spaces and Characters**
  - **Remove extra spaces at the beginning and end:**

```
my_string = "    Hello, World!    "
stripped_string = my_string.strip()
print(stripped_string)  # 'Hello, World!'
```

  - **Remove specific characters from the beginning and end:**

```
char_string = "###Hello###"
stripped_char_string = char_string.strip("#")
print(stripped_char_string) # 'Hello'
```

  `strip()` is great for cleaning up text input, such as user data or filenames.

- **Replacing Parts of a String**
  - **Replace words inside a string:**

```
my_string = "Hello, World!"
replaced_string = my_string.replace("World", "Python")
print(replaced_string)  # 'Hello, Python!'
```

  `replace()` is useful for fixing typos, formatting text, or cleaning data.

- **Finding and Searching in Strings**
  - **Find the position of a word inside a string:**

```
my_string = "Hello, World!"
index = my_string.find("World")
print(index)  # 7
```

  `find()` returns the position (index) of the first match, or -1 if the word is not found.

- **Splitting and Joining Strings**
  - **Split a string into a list of words:**

```
my_string = "Hello, World!"
split_string = my_string.split(", ")
print(split_string)  # ['Hello', 'World!']
```

  - **Split text by spaces:**

```
whitespace_string = "Hello World"
split_whitespace_string = whitespace_string.split()
print(split_whitespace_string)  # ['Hello', 'World']
```

split() is useful for breaking down sentences, reading CSV data, or extracting words from text.

- **Join words back into a sentence:**

```
list_of_strings = ["Hello", "World"]
joined_string = ", ".join(list_of_strings)
print(joined_string)  # 'Hello, World'
```

join() is helpful for combining words into structured text, such as formatting file paths or CSV data.

- **Checking How a String Starts or Ends**
  - **Check if a string starts with a specific word:**

```
my_string = "Hello, World!"
starts_with_hello = my_string.startswith("Hello")
print(starts_with_hello)  # True
```

  - **Check if a string ends with a specific word:**

```
ends_with_world = my_string.endswith("World!")
print(ends_with_world)  # True
```

startswith() and **endswith()** are useful for validating user input, filtering file types, or checking URLs.

String Formatting

In the previous section, you have explored how to modify and manipulate strings using built-in methods. But what if you want to insert dynamic values into a string, such as a user's name or a calculated result?

Python provides several string formatting techniques that allow you to embed variables and expressions directly into text. These methods make it easy to customize output, create reports, and format data cleanly.

There are three main ways to format strings in Python:

- **The % Operator**: The traditional method, still used in older Python code.
- **The str.format() Method**: A flexible approach with named placeholders.
- **F-Strings**: The modern, fastest, and easiest way to format text.

Let us explore each method with examples.

- **Using the % Operator (Old Method)**

  The % operator is one of Python's earliest ways to format strings. It replaces placeholders (%s, %d, %f) with variable values.

```
name = "Alice"
age = 30
formatted_string = "Hello, %s! You are %d years old." % (name, age)
print(formatted_string)  # 'Hello, Alice! You are 30 years old.'
```

  - **Placeholders Explained:**
    - %s → for strings
    - %d → for integers
    - %f → for floating-point numbers (default: 6 decimal places)

- **Controlling Decimal Places in Numbers**

  You can limit decimal places by adding .precision before %f:

```
pi = 3.14159
formatted_pi = "The value of pi is %.2f" % pi
print(formatted_pi)  # 'The value of pi is 3.14'
```

Characteristics of % formatting:

- Simple for quick formatting in older Python versions.
- Less flexible for complex formatting.

- The **`str.format()`** Method (More Powerful and Flexible)

  The **`.format()`** method provides a more structured way to format strings. It replaces {} placeholders with values.

```
name = "Bob"
age = 25
formatted_string = "Hello, {}! You are {} years old.".format(name, age)
print(formatted_string)  # 'Hello, Bob! You are 25 years old.'
```

- Positional and Keyword Arguments

  You can reorder values using numbers inside {}:

```
formatted_string = "Hello, {0}! You are {1} years old.".format(name, age)
print(formatted_string)  # 'Hello, Bob! You are 25 years old.'
```

  You can also use named placeholders:

```
formatted_string = "Hello, {name}! You are {age} years old.".
format(name="Charlie", age=35)
print(formatted_string)  # 'Hello, Charlie! You are 35 years old.'
```

- Controlling Decimal Places

```
pi = 3.14159
formatted_pi = "The value of pi is {:.2f}".format(pi)
print(formatted_pi)  # 'The value of pi is 3.14'
```

Characteristics of `str.format()`:

- More readable and flexible than % formatting.
- Slightly more typing compared to F-strings (explained next).
- **F-Strings (The Modern and Recommended Approach)**

  Introduced in Python 3.6, F-strings (f"...") make string formatting faster, simpler, and more readable. They allow you to embed variables and expressions directly into text.

```
name = "Daisy"
age = 28
formatted_string = f"Hello, {name}! You are {age} years old."
print(formatted_string)  # 'Hello, Daisy! You are 28 years old.'
```

- **Mathematical Expressions Inside Strings**

```
value = 42
formatted_expression = f"Twice the value is {value * 2}"
print(formatted_expression)  # 'Twice the value is 84'
```

- **Controlling Decimal Places (Just Like `.format()`)**

```
pi = 3.14159
formatted_pi = f"The value of pi is {pi:.2f}"
print(formatted_pi)  # 'The value of pi is 3.14'
```

Characteristics F-Strings:

- Most readable and fastest formatting method.
- Supports expressions and calculations directly inside {}.
- Recommended for modern Python development.

Comparison of Formatting Methods:

Method	Pros	Cons
% Operator	Simple, used in older code	Less flexible, harder to read
str.format()	More powerful, supports ordering and named variables	Requires more typing than F-strings
F-Strings	Most readable, fastest, supports expressions	Requires Python 3.6+

***Table 10.1:** Different string formatting methods in Python*

Regular Expressions (Regex)

In the previous section, you learned how to modify and format text dynamically. But what if you need to search for patterns, extract specific data, or validate user input?

This is where regular expressions (regex) come in!

Regular expressions are a powerful tool that allow you to find, match, and manipulate text using patterns. Python provides a built-in module called re, which includes everything you will need to work with regex.

With regex, you can:

- Search for specific words or patterns in text.
- Extract information, such as phone numbers or emails.
- Replace text dynamically.
- Validate user input, like checking if an email address is correctly formatted.

Let us start by understanding how regex works.

Introduction to Regular Expressions (Regex):

A regular expression is a pattern that defines a search rule for text. You can use these patterns to find specific words, characters, or sequences in a string.

Here is a breakdown of key regex elements:

- **Literal Characters**: Matches exact characters in a string.
  - Example: The pattern abc matches only the string "abc."
- **Metacharacters: Special symbols that have** specific meanings:
  - . → Matches any character (except a newline).
  - * → Matches zero or more of the previous character.
  - ^ → Matches the start of a string.
  - $ → Matches the end of a string.
- **Character Classes**: A set of characters placed inside square brackets [ ]:
  - [a-z] → Matches any lowercase letter.
  - [0-9] → Matches any digit from 0 to 9.

Now, let us explore how to use regex in Python using the re module.

Using the re Module for Pattern Matching

Python's re module provides several functions for working with regex. Let us go through some of the most common ones.

- **Searching for a Pattern with `re.search()`**

  The **`re.search()`** function looks for the first occurrence of a pattern in a string.

```
import re

pattern = r"hello"
text = "hello world"
match = re.search(pattern, text)

if match:
    print("Match found:", match.group())  # 'hello'
else:
    print("No match found")
```

  - Returns a match object if found; otherwise, None.
  - **`.group()`** extracts the matched text.

- **Matching the Start of a String with `re.match()`**

  The **`re.match()`** function checks if the pattern appears at the beginning of the string.

```
match = re.match(pattern, text)

if match:
    print("Match found at the beginning:", match.group())  # 'hello'
else:
    print("No match found at the beginning")
```

  - If the text starts with "hello," it returns a match.
  - If "hello" appears later in the string, it would not match.

- **Finding All Matches with `re.findall()`**

  The **`re.findall()`** function returns a list of all occurrences of a pattern.

```
text = "hello world, hello universe"
matches = re.findall(pattern, text)
print("All matches:", matches)  # ['hello', 'hello']
```

  Useful for counting occurrences or extracting multiple values.

- **Replacing Text with `re.sub()`**

  The **`re.sub()`** function replaces all occurrences of a pattern with a new value.

```
text = "hello world"
new_text = re.sub(pattern, "hi", text)
print("Replaced text:", new_text)  # 'hi world'
```

  This is useful for modifying text dynamically.

- **Splitting Text with `re.split()`**

  The **`re.split()`** function splits a string at each occurrence of the pattern.

```
text = "hello world, hello universe"
parts = re.split(r"\s", text)  # Splitting by whitespace
print("Splitted text:", parts)  # ['hello', 'world,', 'hello', 'universe']
```

Similar to `.split()` for strings but with pattern-based flexibility.

Common Regex Patterns and Their Uses:

Now that you understand how to use regex, let us look at some common patterns and how they work.

- **Matching Digits (\d)**

  The pattern \d matches any digit (0-9).

```
pattern = r"\d+"
text = "The year is 2024"
matches = re.findall(pattern, text)
print("Digits found:", matches)  # ['2024']
```

  The + sign means one or more digits.

- **Matching Words (\w)**

  The pattern \w matches letters, numbers, and underscores (word characters).

```
pattern = r"\w+"
text = "Hello, world!"
matches = re.findall(pattern, text)
print("Words found:", matches)  # ['Hello', 'world']
```

  Splits text into individual words.

- **Matching Whitespace (\s)**

  The pattern \s matches spaces, tabs, and newlines.

```
pattern = r"\s+"
text = "Hello   world"
matches = re.findall(pattern, text)
print("Whitespace found:", matches)  # ['   ']
```

  Useful for detecting extra spaces in text.

- **Matching the Start (^) and End ($) of a String**
  - Match if the string starts with "hello."

```
pattern = r"^hello"
text = "hello world"
if re.match(pattern, text):
    print("String starts with 'hello'")
```

  - Match if the string ends with "world."

```
pattern = r"world$"
if re.search(pattern, text):
    print("String ends with 'world'")
```

- **Matching a Specific Number of Repetitions ({m,n})**

  This pattern matches between m and n repetitions of the previous character.

```
pattern = r"\d{2,4}"
text = "2024"
matches = re.findall(pattern, text)
print("Matches with 2 to 4 digits:", matches)  # ['2024']
```

  Useful for matching dates, ID numbers, and codes.

Regular expressions are a powerful tool for searching, extracting, and modifying text. They are commonly used in data validation, log analysis, and text parsing.

Now that you understand the basics of regex, you are ready to explore more advanced text-processing techniques!

Practical Exercise: Text Analyzer

Now that you have explored string manipulation techniques and regular expressions, let us apply them in a real-world scenario!

In this exercise, you will build a Text Analyzer that can:

- Count words, sentences, and characters in a text.
- Identify the most frequently used word.
- Extract email addresses using regular expressions.
- Display the results in a well-formatted report.

This project will help reinforce string operations, text analysis, and regex in a practical and interactive way.

Task Description

Create a Python program that processes a block of text entered by the user. The program will:

- Ask the user to enter text for analysis.
- Process the text using string operations.
- Use built-in string methods to modify and extract useful information.
- Format the output to display the results clearly.
- Use regular expressions to find email addresses in the text.
- Print a well-structured report with all the findings.

By the end of this exercise, you will have a useful tool that can analyze any given text and extract meaningful insights!

Python Code: Text Analyzer

```
import re
from collections import Counter

def analyze_text(text):
    # Basic String Operations
    words = text.split()
    num_words = len(words)
    num_characters = len(text)
    num_sentences = text.count('.') + text.count('!') + text.count('?')

    # String Methods
    word_frequencies = Counter(words)
    most_common_word = word_frequencies.most_common(1)[0][0] if words else
"None"

    # Regular Expressions - Finding Emails
    email_pattern = r'\b[A-Za-z0-9._%+-]+@[A-Za-z0-9.-]+\.[A-Z|a-z]{2,}\b'
    emails = re.findall(email_pattern, text)

    # String Formatting - Report Generation
    report = (
        f"\nText Analysis Report\n"
```

```
            f"{'-'*30}\n"
            f"Total Words: {num_words}\n"
            f"Total Characters: {num_characters}\n"
            f"Total Sentences: {num_sentences}\n"
            f"Most Frequent Word: {most_common_word}\n"
            f"Email Addresses Found: {', '.join(emails) if emails else 'None'}\n"
        )
        return report

    def main():
        user_text = input("Enter a block of text:\n")
        analysis_report = analyze_text(user_text)
        print(analysis_report)

    if __name__ == "__main__":
        main()
```

Understanding the Code:

Let us break down how this program works step-by-step.

- **Basic String Operations**
  - Splitting Text into Words: **`text.split()`** separates words into a list.
  - Counting Words and Characters: len(words) and len(text).
  - Counting Sentences: count the occurrences of . ! and ? to estimate the number of sentences.
- **String Methods**
  - Word Frequency Calculation: Counter(words) creates a dictionary-like object storing word counts.
  - Finding the Most Common Word: **`most_common(1)[0][0]`** returns the word that appears the most.
- **Regular Expressions (Regex) for Finding Emails**

  Define an email pattern using:

  ```
  email_pattern = r'\b[A-Za-z0-9._%+-]+@[A-Za-z0-9.-]+\.[A-Z|a-z]{2,}\b'
  ```

  `re.findall(email_pattern, text)` finds all email addresses in the text.
- **String Formatting for Report Output**

  The final output is a well-structured report using an f-string:

  ```
  report = (
      f"\nText Analysis Report\n"
      f"{'-'*30}\n"
      f"Total Words: {num_words}\n"
      f"Total Characters: {num_characters}\n"
      f"Total Sentences: {num_sentences}\n"
      f"Most Frequent Word: {most_common_word}\n"
      f"Email Addresses Found: {', '.join(emails) if emails else 'None'}\n"
  )
  ```

  This ensures that results are easy to read and well-organized.

Running the Program

When you run the program, it will prompt the user to enter a block of text.

Example Input:

```
Hello! My name is Alice. I love Python programming.
You can email me at alice@example.com for more info.
Python is great. Python is powerful!
```

Expected Output:

```
Text Analysis Report
------------------------------
Total Words: 17
Total Characters: 103
Total Sentences: 4
Most Frequent Word: Python
Email Addresses Found: alice@example.com
```

Now that you have built this Text Analyzer, you can expand it further by:

- Adding more regex patterns (for example, finding phone numbers).
- Filtering out common stop words (for example, "the," "and," "is").
- Saving the report to a file instead of printing it.

This hands-on practice will strengthen your understanding of text processing in Python

Working with Files

In the previous section, you explored how to analyze and manipulate text using Python. But what if you need to store data permanently instead of working with it temporarily?

This is where file handling comes in. Files allow you to store, retrieve, and manage data efficiently. Whether saving logs, processing reports, or handling user input, file operations are a fundamental part of programming.

In programming, files allow you to store and retrieve data for long-term use. Whether saving user preferences, processing reports, or handling large datasets, file operations are essential. In this section, you will cover:

- Opening and closing files
- Different file modes (read, write, append, and binary)
- Best practices for handling files efficiently

Opening and Closing Files

To work with files in Python, you will open a file, read or write data, and then close the file to free system resources.

Using **`open()`** and **`close()`**:

The **`open()`** function opens a file and returns a file object, which you can use to read or write data. After working with a file, it is important to close it using **`close()`**.

```
# Opening a file in read mode
file = open("example.txt", "r")

# Reading the file content
content = file.read()
print(content)
```

```
# Closing the file
file.close()
```

Always close files after use to prevent.

Different File Modes:

Python provides several modes for opening files, depending on whether you want to read, write, or append data.

- **Read Mode (`r`)**: Opens a file for reading. If the file does not exist, it raises an error.

```
file = open("example.txt", "r")
content = file.read()
file.close()
```

- **Write Mode (`w`)**: Opens a file for writing. Overwrites existing content or creates a new file if it does not exist.

```
file = open("example.txt", "w")
file.write("Hello, World!")
file.close()
```

- **Append Mode (`a`)**: Opens a file for writing but adds new content to the end instead of overwriting.

```
file = open("example.txt", "a")
file.write("Hello again!")
file.close()
```

- **Binary Read Mode (`rb`)**: Used for reading non-text files such as images or executables.

```
file = open("example.jpg", "rb")
content = file.read()
file.close()
```

- **Binary Write Mode (`wb`)**: Opens a file for binary writing, erasing existing content or creating a new file.

```
file = open("example.jpg", "wb")
file.write(b"\x00\x01\x02\x03")
file.close()
```

- **Binary Append Mode (`ab`)**: Appends data in binary mode instead of text mode.

```
file = open("example.jpg", "ab")
file.write(b"\x04\x05\x06\x07")
file.close()
```

Choosing the right mode ensures that your file operations work as expected.

Best Practices for Handling Files

To avoid errors and ensure proper resource management, always use the with statement when working with files. This automatically closes the file after the operation is complete.

```
with open("example.txt", "r") as file:
    content = file.read()
    print(content)  # File closes automatically after this block
```

- No need to call **`close()`** manually: Python handles it for you.
- Prevents resource leaks: Ensures files do not remain open accidentally.
- Makes code cleaner and easier to read.

Reading from Files

In the previous section, you learned how to open and close files in Python. Now, let us explore how to read data from files efficiently. Reading files is a common task in programming, whether you are working with logs, reports, or structured datasets.

Python provides multiple ways to read files depending on the use case:

- **`read()`**: Reads the entire file as a single string.
- **`readline()`**: Reads one line at a time.
- **`readlines()`**: Reads all lines and returns a list.

Let us go through each method with examples.

- **Reading the Entire File with `read()`**

  The **`read()`** method reads the entire file content as a single string.

  ```
  # Using 'with' ensures automatic file closure
  with open("example.txt", "r") as file:
      content = file.read()
      print(content)
  ```

  - Best for small files where you need all the data at once.
  - Not ideal for large files, as it loads everything into memory.

- **Reading Line by Line with `readline()`**

  If you want to process each line separately, use **`readline()`**.

  ```
  with open("example.txt", "r") as file:
      line = file.readline()
      while line:
          print(line.strip())  # strip() removes extra newline characters
          line = file.readline()
  ```

  - Useful for processing logs or structured data.
  - Efficient for large files, as it loads one line at a time.

- **Reading All Lines with `readlines()`**

  The **`readlines()`** method reads all lines into a list, where each line is a separate string.

  ```
  with open("example.txt", "r") as file:
      lines = file.readlines()
      for line in lines:
          print(line.strip())
  ```

  - Convenient if you need to store lines in a list for later processing.
  - Not memory-efficient for large files.

Comparison of Methods:

Method	Best For	Considerations
`read()`	Small files, reading full content at once	Loads entire file into memory, not efficient for large files
`readline()`	Processing line by line	Reads one line at a time, great for large files
`readlines()`	Storing lines as a list	Loads all lines into memory, not ideal for large files

Table 10.2: *Comparison of File reading Methods in Python*

Writing to Files

In the previous section, you've explored how to read data from files. Now, let's learn how to write data to files. Writing to files allows programs to store data permanently, making it useful for saving logs, storing user input, or generating reports.

Python provides multiple methods for writing files:

- **`write()`**: Writes a string to a file.
- **`writelines()`**: Writes multiple lines from a list.

Let us go through each method with examples.

- **Writing Data with `write()`**

  The **`write()`** method saves a string into a file.

  ```
  # Writing to a file using 'with' (ensures automatic file closure)
  with open("example.txt", "w") as file:
      file.write("Hello, World!\n")
      file.write("This is a new line.\n")
  ```

  - If the file does not exist, Python creates it.
  - If the file already exists, its content is overwritten.
  - Use write mode ("**w**") when you need to replace existing content.

- **Appending Data to a File ("a" mode)**

  To add new content without erasing existing data, use append mode ("**a**").

  ```
  with open("example.txt", "a") as file:
      file.write("Appending this line.\n")
  ```

  Use append mode ("**a**") when you want to add data without losing existing content.

- **Writing Multiple Lines with `writelines()`**

  The **`writelines()`** method allows writing multiple lines at once from a list.

  ```
  lines = [
      "First line.\n",
      "Second line.\n",
      "Third line.\n"
  ]

  with open("example.txt", "w") as file:
      file.writelines(lines)
  ```

  Best for writing structured data like logs or reports.

Comparison of Methods

Method	**Best For**	**Considerations**
`write()`	Writing single lines or small text	Overwrites file if in "w" mode
`writelines()`	Writing multiple lines from a list	Does not automatically add newlines
Append Mode ("a")	Adding content to an existing file	Ensures existing data is not lost

Table 10.3: *Comparison of File writing Methods in Python*

Error Handling in File Operations

Now that you have covered reading and writing files, it is important to handle errors gracefully to prevent crashes. When working with files, errors can occur due to missing files, lack of permissions, or disk issues.

Python provides exception handling using try, except, and finally blocks to make file operations more robust and error-free.

Common File-Related Exceptions

Here are some common file-related errors and how to handle them:

- **`FileNotFoundError`**: Raised when a file does not exist.

```
try:
    file = open("non_existent_file.txt", "r")
except FileNotFoundError as e:
    print(f"Error: {e}")
```

- **`PermissionError`**: Raised when trying to open a restricted file.

```
try:
    file = open("/restricted_access_file.txt", "r")
except PermissionError as e:
    print(f"Error: {e}")
```

- **`IsADirectoryError`**: Raised when trying to open a directory as a file.

```
try:
    file = open("/path_to_directory", "r")
except IsADirectoryError as e:
    print(f"Error: {e}")
```

- **`IOError`**: A general input/output error, such as hardware issues or full disk space.

```
try:
    file = open("file.txt", "r")
    content = file.read()
except IOError as e:
    print(f"Error: {e}")
```

Using `try`, `except`, and `finally` Blocks for Robust File Handling

You can prevent crashes by wrapping file operations inside a try-except-finally block.

```
try:
    file = open("example.txt", "r")
    content = file.read()
    print(content)
except FileNotFoundError as e:
    print(f"Error: File not found. {e}")
except PermissionError as e:
    print(f"Error: Permission denied. {e}")
except Exception as e:
    print(f"An unexpected error occurred: {e}")
finally:
    try:
        file.close()
```

```
    except NameError:
        pass  # File wasn't opened, so no need to close it
```

- **try** block: Attempts to open and read the file.
- **except** blocks: Handle specific errors (**FileNotFoundError**, **PermissionError**) and a general exception.
- **finally** block: Ensures the file is closed, preventing memory leaks.

Example: Writing Data with Error Handling

Here is a safe way to write data to a file while handling errors:

```
def write_data_to_file(filename, data):
    try:
        with open(filename, "w") as file:
            file.write(data)
        print("Data written successfully.")
    except PermissionError as e:
        print(f"Error: Permission denied. {e}")
    except IOError as e:
        print(f"Error: I/O error occurred. {e}")
    except Exception as e:
        print(f"An unexpected error occurred: {e}")

# Example usage
data = "Hello, World!"
write_data_to_file("output.txt", data)
```

- Uses with **open()** to automatically close the file.
- Handles specific exceptions (**PermissionError**, **IOError**).
- Catches unexpected errors for robustness.

By applying these techniques, you ensure your Python programs handle file-related errors smoothly, making them more reliable and user-friendly.

Practical Exercise: Text File Manager

Now that you have learned how to open, read, write, and handle errors in file operations, let us apply these skills by building a Text File Manager.

This program allows users to:

- Create new text files
- Write data to a file
- Read and display file content
- Handle common file-related errors

Task Overview

The Text File Manager will:

1. Create and open files using **open()**.
2. Write data using **write()** and **writelines()**.
3. Read files using **read()**, **readline()**, and **readlines()**.
4. Use try-except to handle file errors.
5. Provide a user-friendly menu for interaction.

Python Code: Text File Manager

```
def create_file(filename):
    """Creates a new file and writes an initial message."""
    try:
        with open(filename, "w") as file:
            file.write("This is a new file.\n")
        print("File created successfully.")
    except IOError as e:
        print(f"Error creating file: {e}")

def write_to_file(filename, data):
    """Appends user input to an existing file."""
    try:
        with open(filename, "a") as file:
            file.write(data + "\n")
        print("Data written successfully.")
    except IOError as e:
        print(f"Error writing to file: {e}")

def read_file(filename):
    """Reads and displays the content of a file."""
    try:
        with open(filename, "r") as file:
            content = file.read()
            print("File content:\n", content)
    except FileNotFoundError:
        print(f"Error: The file '{filename}' was not found.")
    except IOError as e:
        print(f"Error reading file: {e}")

def main():
    """Runs the text file manager with a menu-based system."""
    while True:
        print("\nText File Manager")
        print("1. Create a new file")
        print("2. Write to a file")
        print("3. Read from a file")
        print("4. Exit")

        choice = input("Enter your choice: ")

        if choice == '1':
            filename = input("Enter the filename: ")
            create_file(filename)
        elif choice == '2':
            filename = input("Enter the filename: ")
            data = input("Enter the data to write: ")
            write_to_file(filename, data)
        elif choice == '3':
            filename = input("Enter the filename: ")
            read_file(filename)
        elif choice == '4':
            print("Exiting the Text File Manager.")
            break
        else:
```

```
            print("Invalid choice. Please try again.")

if __name__ == "__main__":
    main()
```

Understanding the Code:

- Opening and Closing Files:
  - **`create_file()`** creates a file using with **`open(filename, "w")`** and writes an initial message.
  - **`write_to_file()`** appends user input to the file without overwriting existing content.
  - **`read_file()`** reads and prints the file's content.
- Reading and Writing Operations:
  - Uses **`read()`** to read full file content.
  - Uses **`write()`** to write strings and **`writelines()`** for multiple lines.
- Error Handling:
  - Handles missing files with **`FileNotFoundError`**.
  - Handles read/write errors with **`IOError`**.
- User Interaction:
  - The **`main()`** function presents a menu-based system, allowing users to choose actions.
  - Runs in a loop until the user selects "4" to exit.

Example Usage:

Creating a File:

```
Enter your choice: 1
Enter the filename: notes.txt
File created successfully.
```

Writing to a File:

```
Enter your choice: 2
Enter the filename: notes.txt
Enter the data to write: Python is great!
Data written successfully.
```

Reading from a File:

```
Enter your choice: 3
Enter the filename: notes.txt
File content:
This is a new file.
Python is great!
```

Handling Errors:

```
Enter your choice: 3
Enter the filename: missing.txt
Error: The file 'missing.txt' was not found.
```

This Text File Manager is a great foundation for larger projects, such as log managers, report generators, or data processors.

Common Mistakes and Best Practices

When working with file handling and string manipulation, it is easy to make small mistakes that lead to errors or inefficient code. Following are common mistakes along with their best practices to avoid them.

Common Mistakes and Fixes

- **Mistake**: Not Closing Files Properly

  ```
  file = open("example.txt", "r")
  content = file.read()
  # Forgot to close the file
  ```

  Fix: Use the with statement to automatically close files.

  ```
  with open("example.txt", "r") as file:
      content = file.read()
  ```

- **Mistake**: Overwriting Existing Files Accidentally

  ```
  file = open("data.txt", "w")  # 'w' mode overwrites the file
  file.write("New content")
  file.close()
  ```

  Fix: Use append mode ("**a**") to add content without deleting existing data.

  ```
  with open("data.txt", "a") as file:
      file.write("Appending new content\n")
  ```

- **Mistake**: Reading Large Files into Memory

  ```
  with open("large_file.txt", "r") as file:
      data = file.read()  # Loads entire file into memory (problematic for large
  files)
  ```

  Fix: Read line by line to handle large files efficiently.

  ```
  with open("large_file.txt", "r") as file:
      for line in file:
          print(line.strip())
  ```

- **Mistake**: Not Handling File Errors Properly

  ```
  file = open("missing.txt", "r")  # If file doesn't exist, the program crashes
  ```

  Fix: Use try-except to handle missing files gracefully.

  ```
  try:
      with open("missing.txt", "r") as file:
          content = file.read()
  except FileNotFoundError:
      print("Error: File not found!")
  ```

- **Mistake**: Using Inefficient String Concatenation in Loops

  ```
  text = ""
  for word in words:
      text += word  # Slow for large datasets
  ```

  Fix: Use join() for better performance.

  ```
      text = " ".join(words)
  ```

Best Practices

- Always use with **`open()`** to manage file operations and avoid forgetting to close files.
- Use appropriate file modes ("r," "w," "a," "rb," "wb") to prevent accidental data loss.
- Use try-except blocks to handle file-related errors gracefully.

- Read files efficiently using **`readline()`** or iteration for large files.
- Leverage built-in string methods (**`strip()`**, **`replace()`**, **`split()`**) for cleaner and optimized text processing.

Following these best practices ensures efficient, error-free, and maintainable code when working with files and strings in Python.

Exercises and Challenges: Practice Problems and Solutions

Practice Problem 1: String Manipulation - Case Conversion

Task: Create a Python application that transform a string between uppercase and lowercase.

Challenge: Write a script called **`case_converter.py`** that prompts the user to enter a string, converts it to uppercase and lowercase using the **`upper()`** and **`lower()`** methods, and shows the results.

Practice Problem 2: String Manipulation - Character Replacement

Task: Write a Python program that replaces all instances of a particular character in a string with another character.

Challenge: Write a script called **`char_replacer.py`** that prompts the user for a string, the character to be replaced, and the replacement character. The script should then display the updated string using the **`replace()`** technique.

Practice Problem 3: File Content Reader

Task: Write a Python program that reads and displays the contents of a text file.

Challenge: Make a script called **`file_reader.py`** that requests the user for the filename, reads the complete contents of the file using the **`read()`** method, and displays it. Handle potential errors, such as the file does not exist.

Practice Problem 4: Line-by-Line File Reader

Task: Write a Python program that reads and displays the contents of a text file line by line.

Challenge: Create a script called **`line_reader.py`** that prompts the user for the filename, reads the file line by line using the **`readline()`** method, and outputs each line. Ensure that the script handles problems such as file not found and permission errors.

Practice Problem 5: Text File Writer

Task: Create a Python software that writes user input to a text file.

Challenge: Write a script called **`file_writer.py`** that invites the user to enter text, writes it to a file using the **`write()`** method, and guarantees that the text is appended if the file already exists. Handle exceptions, including permission errors.

Solutions to Practice Problems

Practice Problem 1: String Manipulation - Case Conversion

```
# case_converter.py

def case_conversion():
    # Prompt the user to enter a string
    user_input = input("Enter a string: ")
```

```
    # Convert the string to uppercase
    upper_case = user_input.upper()
    # Convert the string to lowercase
    lower_case = user_input.lower()
    # Print the converted strings
    print(f"Uppercase: {upper_case}")
    print(f"Lowercase: {lower_case}")

# Execute the function if the script is run directly
if __name__ == "__main__":
    case_conversion()
```

Practice Problem 2: String Manipulation - Character Replacement

```
# char_replacer.py

def replace_char():
    # Prompt the user to enter a string
    user_input = input("Enter a string: ")
    # Prompt the user to enter the character to be replaced
    char_to_replace = input("Enter the character to replace: ")
    # Prompt the user to enter the replacement character
    replacement_char = input("Enter the replacement character: ")
    # Replace occurrences of the specified character with the replacement char-
acter
    modified_string = user_input.replace(char_to_replace, replacement_char)
    # Print the modified string
    print(f"Modified string: {modified_string}")

# Execute the function if the script is run directly
if __name__ == "__main__":
    replace_char()
```

Practice Problem 3: File Content Reader

```
# file_reader.py

def read_file():
    # Prompt the user to enter the filename
    filename = input("Enter the filename: ")
    try:
        # Attempt to open the file in read mode
        with open(filename, "r") as file:
            # Read the entire content of the file
            content = file.read()
            # Print the content of the file
            print(content)
    except FileNotFoundError:
        # Handle the case where the file does not exist
        print("Error: File not found.")
    except IOError as e:
        # Handle other I/O errors
        print(f"Error reading file: {e}")

# Execute the function if the script is run directly
if __name__ == "__main__":
    read_file()
```

Practice Problem 4: Line-by-Line File Reader

```
# line_reader.py

def read_file_line_by_line():
    # Prompt the user to enter the filename
    filename = input("Enter the filename: ")
    try:
        # Attempt to open the file in read mode
        with open(filename, "r") as file:
            # Read the first line from the file
            line = file.readline()
            # Loop through the file until the end is reached
            while line:
                # Print the line after stripping leading/trailing whitespace
                print(line.strip())
                # Read the next line from the file
                line = file.readline()
    except FileNotFoundError:
        # Handle the case where the file does not exist
        print("Error: File not found.")
    except IOError as e:
        # Handle other I/O errors
        print(f"Error reading file: {e}")

# Execute the function if the script is run directly
if __name__ == "__main__":
    read_file_line_by_line()
```

Practice Problem 5: Text File Writer

```
# file_writer.py

def write_to_file():
    # Prompt the user to enter the filename
    filename = input("Enter the filename: ")
    # Prompt the user to enter the text to write to the file
    data = input("Enter the text to write to the file: ")
    try:
        # Attempt to open the file in append mode
        with open(filename, "a") as file:
            # Write the user input to the file followed by a newline character
            file.write(data + "\n")
        # Inform the user that the data was written successfully
        print("Data written successfully.")
    except IOError as e:
        # Handle I/O errors
        print(f"Error writing to file: {e}")

# Execute the function if the script is run directly
if __name__ == "__main__":
    write_to_file()
```

Conclusion

In this chapter, you have expanded your Python programming skills by learning about file handling and string manipulation, essential techniques for working with text and managing data efficiently. You have explored various ways to create, read, write, and modify files, ensuring proper handling through best practices and error management.

You have also mastered string manipulation, from basic operations such as slicing and concatenation to more advanced topics such as string formatting and regular expressions. These tools allow you to process, search, and clean text data, making your programs more powerful and adaptable.

In the next chapter, you will shift focus to working with dates and times in Python. You will learn how to format, compare, and manipulate dates, a crucial skill for scheduling, logging, and managing time-sensitive data. Mastering these concepts will enable you to build applications that handle time efficiently across different time zones.

As you transition from handling text and files to working with time-based data, let us continue sharpening your Python skills and writing clean, efficient programs.

Till then, keep calm and let's tame the Python!

Multiple-Choice Questions

1. What method would you use to convert a string to all uppercase letters in Python?
   a. `upper_case()`
   b. `to_upper()`
   c. `upper()`
   d. `convert_upper()`
2. Which mode should you use to open a file for reading in binary format?
   a. r
   b. rb
   c. r+
   d. rb+
3. Which of the following methods reads all lines from a file and returns them as a list of strings?
   a. `read()`
   b. `readline()`
   c. `readlines()`
   d. `read_all()`
4. How can you safely ensure a file is properly closed after reading its contents?
   a. Using `file.close()`
   b. Using `try-finally`
   c. Using the `with` statement
   d. All of the above

5. What will be the output for the following code ?

```
text = "Python Programming"
print(text[0:6])
```

   a. Python Programming
   b. Python
   c. Pytho
   d. Program

6. Which string method would you use to remove leading and trailing whitespace from a string?
   a. `strip()`
   b. `trim()`
   c. `remove_whitespace()`
   d. `clean()`

7. In regular expressions, which character is used to match any single character except a new-line?
   a. *
   b. ?
   c. .
   d. ^

8. What exception will be raised if you try to open a file that does not exist?
   a. `IOError`
   b. `FileNotFoundError`
   c. `PermissionError`
   d. `ValueError`

9. Which method would you use to replace all occurrences of a substring within a string with another substring?
   a. `replace()`
   b. `sub()`
   c. `swap()`
   d. `change()`

10. How can you read a file line by line and process each line as you read it?
    a. `Using read()`
    b. `Using readlines()`
    c. `Using readline() inside a while loop`
    d. `Using read_all_lines()`

Answers

1. c
2. b
3. c
4. d
5. b
6. a
7. c
8. b
9. a
10. c

Points to Remember

- Any developer must be able to handle files and manipulate strings in order to process, store, and retrieve data efficiently.
- Common string operations include constructing and initializing strings, accessing characters, slicing strings, concatenation, and repeating. These serve as the foundation for text manipulation in Python.
- Common string operations like **`upper()`**, **`lower()`**, **`strip()`**, **`replace()`**, **`find()`**, **`split()`**, and **`join()`** are effective for changing and analyzing text data.
- String formatting techniques such as the % operator, **`str.format()`**, and f-strings enable dynamic and legible string production, which is required for user output and data presentation.
- Regular expressions (regex) are an extremely effective tool for pattern matching and text processing. Python's re module allows you to search, match, and alter strings using particular patterns.
- To open or close files, use the **`open()`** function and the **`close()`** method respectively. The with statement is recommended for managing file contexts and ensuring that files are properly closed following activities.
- Files can be opened in read (r), write (w), append (a), or binary mode (rb, wb, ab). Selecting the appropriate mode is critical for the planned file activity.
- Methods such as **`read()`**, **`readline()`**, and **`readlines()`** provide many ways to read data from files, depending on whether you require the entire content at once, line by line, or all lines as a list.
- The **`write()`** method writes a single string to a file, whereas **`writelines()`** writes a list of strings. Proper error handling guarantees that data is accurately written without damaging the file.
- Use the try, except, and finally blocks to handle file-related issues such as FileNotFoundError and IOError. This method ensures that your program can deal with unanticipated difficulties graciously.

Further Reading

For further exploration of Python file handling and text processing, consider these resources:

1. **Python File Handling – Real Python:**

   https://realpython.com/read-write-files-python/

   A comprehensive guide covering file operations and best practices.

2. **Python Strings and Regular Expressions – W3Schools:**

   https://www.w3schools.com/python/python_regex.asp

   A beginner-friendly introduction to string methods and regex.

CHAPTER 11
Dates and Times

Introduction

In the last chapter, you explored how to work with files and text in Python. Now, you will move on to another important topic, handling dates and times. Just like managing files and text, working with dates and times is essential for building reliable and user-friendly programs.

This chapter will teach you how to create and use dates and times in Python. You will learn how to find the current date and time, add or subtract days, and combine dates with time. You will also cover more advanced topics such as converting time zones and handling daylight saving time adjustments, useful for programs that operate across different regions.

Knowing how to handle dates and times is crucial for many real-world applications. Whether you are scheduling meetings, logging events, or managing deadlines, understanding how Python works with time will make your programs more accurate and efficient.

By the end of this chapter, you will have a strong grasp of Python's date and time features. You will be able to track time, format dates properly, and manage time zones so your programs work smoothly, no matter where they are used.

Structure

In this chapter, the following topics will be covered:

- Handling Dates and Times Effectively
    - Key Reasons for Proper Date and Time Management
    - Exploring Python's Datetime Module
- Working with Date Objects
    - Creating Date Objects
    - Accessing and Modifying Date Components
    - Formatting and Converting Date Strings
    - Practical Exercise: Creating and Modifying Date Objects
- Working with Time Objects
    - Creating Time Objects
    - Accessing and Modifying Time Components
    - Formatting and Converting Time Strings
    - Practical Exercise: Working with Time Components
- Performing Date and Time Calculations
    - Manipulating Dates with Arithmetic Operations
    - Calculating Differences Between Dates and Times

  - Using the timedelta Class for Time Durations
  - Practical Exercise: Performing Date and Time Calculations
- Combining Dates and Times
  - Creating and Using datetime Objects
  - Formatting and Parsing datetime Objects
  - Practical Exercise: Combining and Formatting Date and Time
- Managing Time Zones and Daylight Saving Time
  - Understanding Time Zones
  - Using pytz Library for Time Zone Conversions
  - Handling Daylight Saving Time (DST)
  - Practical Exercise: Time Zone Conversions
- Handling Date and Time in Different Formats
  - Understanding Timestamps
  - Converting Between Different Date and Time Formats
  - Using strptime() and strftime() Together
  - Practical Exercise: Parsing and Formatting Dates and Times
- Common Mistakes and Best Practices
- Exercises and Challenges: Practice Problems and Solutions

Handling Dates and Times Effectively

Managing dates and times correctly is crucial in many applications. Whether it is tracking deadlines, recording events, or handling time zones, accurate time management ensures programs function smoothly and reliably.

Key Reasons for Proper Date and Time Management

- **Ensuring Accurate Scheduling**: Many applications schedule events, set reminders, or manage tasks. Proper date and time handling ensures that these actions happen at the right moment.
- **Tracking and Analyzing Data**: Computers use timestamps to record events, such as log entries or transaction history. Accurate time records help analyze trends, detect errors, and troubleshoot problems efficiently.
- **Managing Global Time Zones**: Applications often serve users in different time zones. Converting time correctly prevents confusion and ensures a consistent user experience worldwide.
- **Meeting Industry Standards**: Fields such as finance, healthcare, and security have strict rules about date and time tracking. Proper time management helps meet legal and business requirements.
- **Improving User Experience**: Displaying dates and times in a familiar, localized format makes applications easier to use and prevents misinterpretation of time-based data.

Handling time correctly ensures that applications run smoothly, accurately, and reliably, no matter where or when they are used.

Exploring Python's Datetime Module

Since dates and times play a crucial role in many applications, Python provides a built-in solution to handle them efficiently. The datetime module is a powerful tool that allows programmers to work with dates, times, and time zones easily.

Key Components of the Datetime Module:

Main Classes

The datetime module provides several classes for handling date and time:

- `date`: Represents a calendar date, including year, month, and day.
- `time`: Represents a specific time of day, including hours, minutes, seconds, and microseconds.
- `datetime`: Combines both date and time into a single object.
- `timedelta`: Represents the difference between two dates or times, useful for date calculations.
- `tzinfo`: Stores time zone information, helping manage time differences across regions.

Commonly Used Functions

Python's datetime module also provides several useful functions for working with time:

- `today()`: Returns the current local date.
- `now()`: Returns the current local date and time.
- `utcnow()`: Retrieves the current Coordinated Universal Time (UTC) date and time.
- `strptime()`: Converts a date string into a datetime object using a specified format.
- `strftime()`: Formats a datetime object into a string based on a specified pattern.

By using the datetime module, programmers can accurately manage date and time values in Python. Whether it is storing timestamps, formatting date outputs, or performing date calculations, this module ensures accuracy and consistency, making applications more reliable.

Working with Date Objects

In the previous section, you explored Python's datetime module and its essential components. Now, let us focus on date objects, which help you represent and manipulate calendar dates in Python. Understanding how to create, modify, and format date objects is important for tasks such as scheduling events, logging activities, and organizing time-based data.

Creating Date Objects

Python provides the date class within the datetime module to represent a specific calendar date. A date object requires three values: year, month, and day.

Here is how to create a date object:

from datetime import date

```
# Creating a date object for July 1, 2024
my_date = date(2024, 7, 1)
print(my_date)  # Output: 2024-07-01
```

The date class uses the Gregorian calendar and allows you to store and manipulate date values easily.

Accessing and Modifying Date Components

Once a date object is created, you can extract its components such as year, month, and day.

- **Accessing Components**

```
# Extracting components of the date object
year = my_date.year
month = my_date.month
day = my_date.day

print(f"Year: {year}, Month: {month}, Day: {day}")  # Output: Year: 2024,
Month: 7, Day: 1
```

- **Modifying Components**

  Since date objects are immutable (unchangeable), modifications require creating a new date object using the **replace()** method.

```
# Modifying the date by creating a new date object
new_date = my_date.replace(year=2025)

print(new_date)  # Output: 2025-07-01
```

  The **replace()** method allows you to change specific parts of the date while keeping the rest unchanged.

Formatting and Converting Date Strings

Many applications require converting dates to readable text or parsing text into date objects. Python provides two methods for this:

  - **strftime()**: Converts a date object into a formatted string.
  - **strptime()**: Converts a string into a date object.

- **Formatting a Date as a String**

```
# Formatting a date object into a string
formatted_date = my_date.strftime("%B %d, %Y")

print(formatted_date)  # Output: July 01, 2024
```

  Here, **%B** represents the full month name, **%d** is the day, and **%Y** is the year.

- **Parsing a Date String into a Date Object**

```
from datetime import datetime
# Parsing a string into a date object
date_string = "July 01, 2024"
parsed_date = datetime.strptime(date_string, "%B %d, %Y").date()

print(parsed_date)  # Output: 2024-07-01
```

  The **strptime()** function interprets a string and converts it into a datetime object. Calling **.date()** extracts only the date portion.

Practical Exercise: Creating and Modifying Date Objects

Let us apply what you have learned by building a date manipulator program. This will help you practice creating, modifying, and formatting date objects in Python.

Task Description:

Create a Python program that:

- Creates a date object for a specific date.
- Extracts and prints its year, month, and day.
- Modifies the year while keeping other components unchanged.
- Formats the date into a readable string.

Python Code:

```
from datetime import date

# Step 1: Create a Date Object
my_date = date(2024, 7, 1)
print(f"Original Date: {my_date}")  # Output: 2024-07-01

# Step 2: Access Date Components
year = my_date.year
month = my_date.month
day = my_date.day
print(f"Year: {year}, Month: {month}, Day: {day}")  # Output: Year: 2024,
Month: 7, Day: 1

# Step 3: Modify Date Components
new_date = my_date.replace(year=2025)
print(f"Modified Date: {new_date}")  # Output: 2025-07-01

# Step 4: Format the Date
formatted_date = my_date.strftime("%B %d, %Y")
print(f"Formatted Date: {formatted_date}")  # Output: July 01, 2024
```

Understanding the Code:

- **Creating a Date Object**: Uses the date class to generate a specific date.
- **Accessing Date Components**: Extracts and prints year, month, and day values.
- **Modifying Date Components**: Uses the `replace()` method to change the year.
- **Formatting the Date**: Converts the date into a human-readable format.

Working with Time Objects

Previously, you have explored how to work with date objects in Python. Now, let us shift the focus to time objects, which help represent and manipulate time values such as hours, minutes, and seconds. Understanding how to create, modify, and format time objects is essential for tasks such as scheduling events, recording logs, and setting timers in applications.

Creating Time Objects

Python's datetime module includes the time class, which allows you to create time values. A time object consists of hours, minutes, seconds, and microseconds.

Here is how to create a time object:

```
from datetime import time

# Creating a time object for 14:30:00 (2:30 PM)
```

```
my_time = time(14, 30, 0)

print(my_time)  # Output: 14:30:00
```

The time class takes four optional parameters: hour, minute, second, and microsecond. If not provided, the values default to 0.

Accessing and Modifying Time Components

Once a time object is created, you can extract its individual components such as hour, minute, second, and microsecond.

- **Accessing Components**

```
# Extracting components of the time object
hour = my_time.hour
minute = my_time.minute
second = my_time.second
microsecond = my_time.microsecond

print(f"Hour: {hour}, Minute: {minute}, Second: {second}, Microsecond: {micro-
second}")
# Output: Hour: 14, Minute: 30, Second: 0, Microsecond: 0
```

- **Modifying Components**

  Since time objects are immutable, modifications require creating a new time object using the **replace()** method.

```
# Modifying the time by creating a new time object
new_time = my_time.replace(hour=16)

print(new_time)  # Output: 16:30:00
```

  The **replace()** method allows you to change specific parts of the time while keeping the rest unchanged.

Formatting and Converting Time Strings

Many applications require converting time to a readable format or parsing text into time objects. Python provides two key methods for this:

  - **strftime()**: Converts a time object into a formatted string.
  - **strptime()**: Converts a string into a time object.

- **Formatting a Time Object as a String**

```
# Formatting a time object into a string
formatted_time = my_time.strftime("%H:%M:%S")

print(formatted_time)  # Output: 14:30:00
```

  Here, %H represents the hour (24-hour format), %M is the minute, and %S is the second.

- **Parsing a Time String into a Time Object**

```
from datetime import datetime

# Parsing a string into a time object
time_string = "14:30:00"
```

```
parsed_time = datetime.strptime(time_string, "%H:%M:%S").time()

print(parsed_time)  # Output: 14:30:00
```

The **`strptime()`** function interprets a string and converts it into a datetime object. Calling **`.time()`** extracts only the time portion.

Practical Exercise: Working with Time Components

To practice working with time objects, let us build a time manipulator program that allows you to create, modify, and format time values.

Task Description:

Create a Python program that:

- Creates a time object for a specific time.
- Extracts and prints its hour, minute, second, and microsecond.
- Modifies the hour while keeping other components unchanged.
- Formats the time into a readable string.

Python Code:

```
from datetime import time

# Step 1: Create a Time Object
my_time = time(14, 30, 0)
print(f"Original Time: {my_time}")  # Output: 14:30:00

# Step 2: Access Time Components
hour = my_time.hour
minute = my_time.minute
second = my_time.second
microsecond = my_time.microsecond
print(f"Hour: {hour}, Minute: {minute}, Second: {second}, Microsecond: {micro-
second}")
# Output: Hour: 14, Minute: 30, Second: 0, Microsecond: 0

# Step 3: Modify Time Components
new_time = my_time.replace(hour=16)
print(f"Modified Time: {new_time}")  # Output: 16:30:00

# Step 4: Format the Time
formatted_time = my_time.strftime("%H:%M:%S")
print(f"Formatted Time: {formatted_time}")  # Output: 14:30:00
```

Understanding the Code:

- **Creating a Time Object**: Uses the time class to generate a specific time.
- **Accessing Time Components**: Extracts and prints hour, minute, second, and microsecond values.
- **Modifying Time Components**: Uses the **`replace()`** method to change the hour.
- **Formatting the Time**: Converts the time into a human-readable format.

Performing Date and Time Calculations

Now that you have understood how to work with date and time objects, let us explore how to perform arithmetic operations on them. In many applications, you will need to add or subtract days, calculate time differences, and work with durations. Python provides the **`timedelta`** class from the datetime module to make these calculations simple and efficient.

Manipulating Dates with Arithmetic Operations

The **`timedelta`** class allows you to modify date and time values easily. This is useful for calculating deadlines, schedules, and time-based events.

- **Adding Days to a Date**

```
from datetime import date, timedelta

# Creating a date object for July 1, 2024
my_date = date(2024, 7, 1)

# Adding 10 days to the date
future_date = my_date + timedelta(days=10)

print(f"Future Date: {future_date}")  # Output: 2024-07-11
```

- **Subtracting Days from a Date**

```
# Subtracting 10 days from the date
past_date = my_date - timedelta(days=10)

print(f"Past Date: {past_date}")  # Output: 2024-06-21
```

Calculating Differences Between Dates and Times

Sometimes, you need to find out how much time has passed between two dates. Python allows you to subtract one date from another to get the difference as a **`timedelta`** object.

Finding the Difference Between Two Dates

```
# Creating another date object for July 15, 2024
another_date = date(2024, 7, 15)

# Calculating the difference between two dates
difference = another_date - my_date

print(f"Difference: {difference}")  # Output: 14 days, 0:00:00
print(f"Difference in days: {difference.days}")  # Output: 14
```

The result is a **`timedelta`** object, which represents the number of days (and time, if applicable) between two dates.

Using the `timedelta` Class for Time Durations

The **`timedelta`** class represents a time duration and can be used to perform date and time calculations.

- **Creating a `timedelta` Object**

```
# Creating a timedelta object representing 10 days
ten_days = timedelta(days=10)
```

```
print(f"Timedelta: {ten_days}")  # Output: 10 days, 0:00:00
```

- **Adding and Subtracting `timedelta` Objects**

```
# Adding a timedelta to a date
future_date = my_date + ten_days
print(f"Future Date: {future_date}")  # Output: 2024-07-11

# Subtracting a timedelta from a date
past_date = my_date - ten_days
print(f"Past Date: {past_date}")  # Output: 2024-06-21
```

The **`timedelta`** class helps simplify date calculations, making it easy to schedule events, track deadlines, and manage time-based data efficiently.

Practical Exercise: Performing Date and Time Calculations

To practice date and time arithmetic, let us build a date calculator that performs basic calculations using **`timedelta.`**

Task Description:

Create a Python program that:

- Creates two date objects for specific dates.
- Adds and subtracts days from a date using **`timedelta`**.
- Calculates the difference between two dates.
- Displays all results clearly.

Python Code:

```
from datetime import date, timedelta

# Step 1: Create Date Objects
start_date = date(2024, 7, 1)
end_date = date(2024, 7, 15)

print(f"Start Date: {start_date}")  # Output: 2024-07-01
print(f"End Date: {end_date}")      # Output: 2024-07-15

# Step 2: Add and Subtract Dates
# Adding 10 days to the start date
future_date = start_date + timedelta(days=10)
print(f"Future Date: {future_date}")  # Output: 2024-07-11

# Subtracting 10 days from the start date
past_date = start_date - timedelta(days=10)
print(f"Past Date: {past_date}")      # Output: 2024-06-21

# Step 3: Calculate Differences Between Dates
date_difference = end_date - start_date
print(f"Difference: {date_difference}")  # Output: 14 days, 0:00:00
print(f"Difference in days: {date_difference.days}")  # Output: 14
```

Understanding the Code:

- **Creating Date Objects**: Uses the date class to generate specific date values.
- **Adding and Subtracting Dates**: Uses **`timedelta`** to shift dates forward or backward.
- **Calculating Date Differences**: Finds the number of days between two dates.
- **Displaying Results**: Prints all calculations clearly for easy interpretation.

Combining Dates and Times

So far, you have worked with dates and times separately, but in many real-world scenarios, you will need to combine them into a single object. Python's datetime class allows you to manage both date and time together, making it easy to store, manipulate, and format complete datetime values.

Creating and Using `datetime` Objects

The datetime class helps create objects that contain both date and time information.

- **Creating a datetime Object**

  ```
  from datetime import datetime

  # Creating a datetime object for July 1, 2024, at 14:30:00 (2:30 PM)
  my_datetime = datetime(2024, 7, 1, 14, 30, 0)

  print(my_datetime)  # Output: 2024-07-01 14:30:00
  In this example, the datetime object requires year, month, day, hour, minute,
  and second. The microsecond value is optional.
  ```

- **Accessing and Modifying datetime Components**

  Just like with date and time objects, you can extract and modify components from a datetime object.

  - **Accessing Components**

    ```
    # Extracting components from the datetime object
    year = my_datetime.year
    month = my_datetime.month
    day = my_datetime.day
    hour = my_datetime.hour
    minute = my_datetime.minute
    second = my_datetime.second

    print(f"Year: {year}, Month: {month}, Day: {day}, Hour: {hour}, Minute:
    {minute}, Second: {second}")
    # Output: Year: 2024, Month: 7, Day: 1, Hour: 14, Minute: 30, Second: 0
    ```

  - **Modifying Components**

    Since datetime objects are immutable, you cannot modify them directly. Instead, use the **`replace()`** method to create a new modified object.

    ```
    # Modifying the datetime by changing the year
    new_datetime = my_datetime.replace(year=2025)

    print(new_datetime)  # Output: 2025-07-01 14:30:00
    The replace() method lets us change specific parts of the datetime object
    while keeping the rest unchanged.
    ```

Formatting and Parsing datetime Objects

In many cases, you will need to convert datetime objects into readable strings or parse strings into datetime objects. Python provides two essential methods for this:

- **`strftime()`**: Converts a datetime object into a formatted string.
- **`strptime()`**: Converts a string into a datetime object.

- **Formatting `datetime` Objects**

```
# Formatting a datetime object into a string
formatted_datetime = my_datetime.strftime("%Y-%m-%d %H:%M:%S")

print(formatted_datetime)  # Output: 2024-07-01 14:30:00
```

Here is what the format codes mean:

- **`%Y`** – Year (four digits)
- **`%m`** – Month (two digits)
- **`%d`** – Day (two digits)
- **`%H`** – Hour (24-hour format)
- **`%M`** – Minutes
- **`%S`** – Seconds

- **Parsing Strings into datetime Objects**

```
# Parsing a string into a datetime object
date_string = "2024-07-01 14:30:00"
parsed_datetime = datetime.strptime(date_string, "%Y-%m-%d %H:%M:%S")

print(parsed_datetime)  # Output: 2024-07-01 14:30:00
```

The **`strptime()`** method reads a string representation of a date and time and converts it into a datetime object using a specified format.

Practical Exercise: Combining and Formatting Date and Time

Let us practice working with datetime objects by building a small date-time manipulator.

Task Description:

Create a Python program that:

- Generates a datetime object for a given date and time.
- Modifies the datetime object by changing the year.
- Formats the datetime object into multiple readable string formats.
- Displays the original, modified, and formatted datetime objects.

Python Code:

```
from datetime import datetime

def combine_and_format_datetime():
    # Step 1: Create a datetime Object
    original_datetime = datetime(2024, 7, 1, 14, 30, 0)
    print(f"Original datetime: {original_datetime}")
```

```
        # Step 2: Access and Modify Components
        year = original_datetime.year
        month = original_datetime.month
        day = original_datetime.day
        hour = original_datetime.hour
        minute = original_datetime.minute
        second = original_datetime.second

        # Create a new datetime object by modifying the year
        modified_datetime = original_datetime.replace(year=2025)
        print(f"Modified datetime: {modified_datetime}")

        # Step 3: Format the datetime Object
        formatted_original = original_datetime.strftime("%Y-%m-%d %H:%M:%S")
        formatted_modified = modified_datetime.strftime("%d/%m/%Y %I:%M %p")

        # Step 4: Display the Results
        print(f"Formatted original datetime: {formatted_original}")
        print(f"Formatted modified datetime: {formatted_modified}")

    # Execute the function if the script is run directly
    if __name__ == "__main__":
        combine_and_format_datetime()
```

Understanding the Code

- **Creating a `datetime` Object**: Uses the datetime class to generate a specific date and time.
- **Accessing and Modifying Components**: Extracts individual components and modifies the year.
- **Formatting the `datetime` Object**: Converts datetime into readable string formats using `strftime()`.
- **Displaying Results**: Prints both the original and modified datetime values.

Managing Time Zones and Daylight Saving Time

So far, you have worked with dates and times, but in many real-world applications, programs need to handle time zones and daylight saving time (DST). This is especially important for systems that operate in multiple regions and require accurate time calculations.

Python's **`pytz`** library provides an easy way to manage time zones, convert between different time zones, and account for DST changes automatically.

Understanding Time Zones

A time zone represents the local time of a region relative to Coordinated Universal Time (UTC). Each time zone has a standard offset from UTC, and some regions observe daylight saving time (DST), which shifts the clock forward or backward by one hour during specific seasons.

For example:

- UTC-5 (Eastern Standard Time) is 5 hours behind UTC.
- UTC-8 (Pacific Standard Time) is 8 hours behind UTC.
- UTC+1 (Central European Time) is 1 hour ahead of UTC.

Using pytz Library for Time Zone Conversions

Python's **pytz** library allows to work with different time zones and convert between them easily.

Installing pytz:

If you have not installed **pytz**, you can do so using:

```
pip install pytz
```

Converting Between Time Zones

You can use **pytz** to convert a UTC time to different time zones such as Eastern and Pacific.

```
from datetime import datetime
import pytz

# Define time zones
utc = pytz.utc
eastern = pytz.timezone('US/Eastern')
pacific = pytz.timezone('US/Pacific')

# Get the current time in UTC
utc_now = datetime.now(utc)
print(f"Current UTC time: {utc_now}")

# Convert UTC time to Eastern time
eastern_now = utc_now.astimezone(eastern)
print(f"Current Eastern time: {eastern_now}")

# Convert Eastern time to Pacific time
pacific_now = eastern_now.astimezone(pacific)
print(f"Current Pacific time: {pacific_now}")
```

- **datetime.now(utc)**: Returns the current UTC time.
- **astimezone(target_timezone)**: Converts a datetime object from one time zone to another.

This ensures that times remain accurate when displayed in different locations.

Handling Daylight Saving Time (DST)

Daylight Saving Time (DST) can make time calculations tricky, as the local time shifts forward or backward by an hour during certain months.

The **pytz** library automatically manages DST transitions when converting between time zones.

Working with DST Adjustments:

```
from datetime import datetime
import pytz

# Define the Eastern time zone
eastern = pytz.timezone('US/Eastern')

# Define a date during the DST transition period
dt = datetime(2024, 11, 3, 1, 30)  # November 3, 2024, at 1:30 AM

# Localize the time to Eastern time zone
```

```
dt_eastern = eastern.localize(dt, is_dst=True)
print(f"Localized time: {dt_eastern}")

# Convert to UTC
dt_utc = dt_eastern.astimezone(pytz.utc)
print(f"Converted to UTC: {dt_utc}")
```

- **`localize(dt, is_dst=True)`:** Converts a naive datetime into an aware datetime object in the specified time zone, automatically handling DST.
- **`astimezone(pytz.utc)`:** Converts local time to UTC while accounting for any DST shifts.

This ensures that Python programs display and store times correctly in regions that observe DST.

Practical Exercise: Time Zone Conversions

Let us build a time zone converter that transforms UTC time into different regional times.

Task Description:

Create a Python program that:

- Gets the current UTC time.
- Defines target time zones (Eastern and Pacific).
- Converts the UTC time into each time zone.
- Displays all results clearly.

Python Code:

```
from datetime import datetime
import pytz

def main():
    # Step 1: Get Current UTC Time
    utc_now = datetime.now(pytz.utc)
    print(f"Current UTC time: {utc_now}")

    # Step 2: Define Target Time Zones
    eastern = pytz.timezone('US/Eastern')
    pacific = pytz.timezone('US/Pacific')

    # Step 3: Perform Time Zone Conversions
    eastern_time = utc_now.astimezone(eastern)
    pacific_time = utc_now.astimezone(pacific)

    # Step 4: Display the Results
    print(f"Current Eastern time: {eastern_time}")
    print(f"Current Pacific time: {pacific_time}")

if __name__ == "__main__":
    main()
```

Understanding the Code:

- **Get Current UTC Time**: `datetime.now(pytz.utc)` retrieves the current time in UTC.
- **Define Target Time Zones**: `pytz.timezone('US/Eastern')` and `pytz.timezone('US/Pacific')` specify the target regions.
- **Convert Time Zones**: `astimezone()` shifts the UTC time to the target time zones automatically.

- **Display Results**: The program prints the original UTC time and its equivalents in different time zones.

Handling Date and Time in Different Formats

In many applications, date and time values need to be stored, processed, or displayed in different formats. Python's datetime module provides powerful tools to manage timestamps, format conversions, and parsing date-time strings into structured objects.

Understanding Timestamps

A timestamp represents the number of seconds that have passed since the Unix epoch (January 1, 1970, 00:00:00 UTC). Timestamps are widely used because they provide a precise, consistent way to record and compare time.

Creating and Converting Timestamps:

```
from datetime import datetime

# Get the current time as a timestamp
timestamp_now = datetime.now().timestamp()
print(f"Current timestamp: {timestamp_now}")

# Convert a timestamp back into a datetime object
dt_from_timestamp = datetime.fromtimestamp(timestamp_now)
print(f"Datetime from timestamp: {dt_from_timestamp}")
```

- **`timestamp()`**: Converts a datetime object into a timestamp (number of seconds since the epoch).
- **`fromtimestamp()`**: Converts a timestamp back into a datetime object.

Timestamps are especially useful in applications that require logging, sorting events, and calculating durations.

Converting Between Different Date and Time Formats

Dates and times often need to be converted between different formats, especially when dealing with user input, database storage, or API communication. Python provides two key methods for this:

- **`strptime()`**: Parses a date string into a datetime object.
- **`strftime()`**: Formats a datetime object into a readable string.

- **Parsing Strings into `datetime` Objects**

  When working with date-time data, you will often need to convert text-based date formats into structured datetime objects.

```
from datetime import datetime

# Date string and its expected format
date_string = "2024-07-01 14:30:00"
format_string = "%Y-%m-%d %H:%M:%S"

# Convert string to datetime object
parsed_date = datetime.strptime(date_string, format_string)

print(f"Parsed datetime: {parsed_date}")
```

- **`strptime(date_string, format_string)`**: Converts a date-time string into a datetime object.
- The format string specifies the structure of the date input.

- **Formatting `datetime` Objects into Strings**

  Once you have a datetime object, you may need to convert it into human-readable formats.

```
from datetime import datetime

# Get the current date and time
now = datetime.now()

# Convert datetime object to a formatted string
formatted_date = now.strftime("%B %d, %Y %I:%M %p")

print(f"Formatted date: {formatted_date}")
```

  `strftime(format_string)`: Converts a datetime object into a formatted string.

Common Date-Time Format Codes:

Format Code	Meaning	Example Output
%Y	Year (4 digits)	2024
%m	Month (2 digits)	7
%B	Full month name	July
%d	Day of the month	1
%H	Hour (24-hour format)	14
%I	Hour (12-hour format)	2
%M	Minute	30
%S	Second	0
%p	AM/PM	PM

Table 11.1: *Format codes for common Date-Time object*

Using `strptime()` and `strftime()` Together

The combination of parsing (**`strptime()`**) and formatting (**`strftime()`**) allows to work with flexible date-time conversions.

Example: Converting a Date String to Different Formats

```
from datetime import datetime

# Define a date string
date_string = "July 01, 2024 02:30 PM"
format_string = "%B %d, %Y %I:%M %p"

# Convert string to datetime object
parsed_date = datetime.strptime(date_string, format_string)
print(f"Parsed datetime: {parsed_date}")

# Convert datetime object to different formats
```

```
formatted_date1 = parsed_date.strftime("%Y-%m-%d %H:%M:%S")  # YYYY-MM-DD
HH:MM:SS
formatted_date2 = parsed_date.strftime("%d/%m/%Y")  # DD/MM/YYYY
formatted_date3 = parsed_date.strftime("%B %d, %Y")  # Month Day, Year
formatted_date4 = parsed_date.strftime("%d-%B-%Y %I:%M %p")  # Day-Month-Year
Hour:Minute AM/PM

# Print the formatted results
print(f"Formatted date 1: {formatted_date1}")
print(f"Formatted date 2: {formatted_date2}")
print(f"Formatted date 3: {formatted_date3}")
print(f"Formatted date 4: {formatted_date4}")
```

- **strptime()**: Converts a string into a datetime object.
- **strftime()**: Converts a datetime object into formatted strings.

This method is essential when working with data processing, logging, and displaying date-time values in user-friendly formats.

Practical Exercise: Parsing and Formatting Dates and Times

To practice working with different date-time formats, let us build a small date-time formatter program.

Task Description:

Create a Python program that:

- Parses a date string into a datetime object.
- Formats the datetime object into multiple readable string formats.
- Displays all results clearly.

Python Code:

```
from datetime import datetime

def main():
    # Step 1: Define a Date String
    date_string = "July 01, 2024 02:30 PM"
    format_string = "%B %d, %Y %I:%M %p"

    # Step 2: Parse the Date String
    parsed_date = datetime.strptime(date_string, format_string)
    print(f"Original date string: {date_string}")
    print(f"Parsed datetime: {parsed_date}")

    # Step 3: Format the datetime Object
    formatted_date1 = parsed_date.strftime("%Y-%m-%d %H:%M:%S")
    formatted_date2 = parsed_date.strftime("%d/%m/%Y")
    formatted_date3 = parsed_date.strftime("%B %d, %Y")
    formatted_date4 = parsed_date.strftime("%d-%B-%Y %I:%M %p")

    # Step 4: Display the Results
    print(f"Formatted date 1: {formatted_date1}")
    print(f"Formatted date 2: {formatted_date2}")
    print(f"Formatted date 3: {formatted_date3}")
    print(f"Formatted date 4: {formatted_date4}")
```

```
if __name__ == "__main__":
    main()
```

Understanding the Code:

- **Define a Date String**: Uses "July 01, 2024 02:30 PM" as input.
- **Parse the Date String**: Uses `strptime()` to convert it into a datetime object.
- **Format the `datetime` Object**: Uses `strftime()` to create four different string representations.
- **Display Results**: Prints the original string, parsed datetime, and formatted outputs.

Common Mistakes and Best Practices

Working with dates and times in programming can be tricky, and even small mistakes can lead to incorrect calculations, unexpected behavior, or bugs that are difficult to debug. This section covers common pitfalls to avoid and best practices for handling dates and times effectively in Python.

Avoiding Common Mistakes in Date and Time Handling:

- **Ignoring Time Zones**

  Pitfall: Assuming all date-time values are in the same time zone can lead to incorrect timestamps and misaligned schedules.

  Solution: Always specify time zones when working with datetime objects.

  ```
  from datetime import datetime
  import pytz

  # Create a timezone-aware datetime object
  utc = pytz.utc
  now_utc = datetime.now(utc)

  print(f"Current UTC time: {now_utc}")
  ```

- **Forgetting Daylight Saving Time (DST)**

  Pitfall: Failing to account for DST shifts can result in incorrect time calculations and scheduling errors.

  Solution: Use **pytz** to handle DST transitions automatically.

  ```
  from datetime import datetime
  import pytz

  # Define Eastern Time Zone
  eastern = pytz.timezone('US/Eastern')

  # A date during a DST change (November 3, 2024, at 1:30 AM)
  dt = datetime(2024, 11, 3, 1, 30)

  # Convert to timezone-aware datetime
  dt_eastern = eastern.localize(dt, is_dst=False)

  print(f"Localized Eastern Time: {dt_eastern}")
  ```

- **Using Naive datetime Objects for Time Comparisons**

  Pitfall: Comparing datetime objects without time zone information can lead to incorrect results, especially when dealing with multiple time zones.

Solution: Use timezone-aware datetime objects.

```
from datetime import datetime
import pytz

# Define timezone-aware datetime objects
dt1 = datetime(2024, 7, 1, 12, 0, tzinfo=pytz.UTC)
dt2 = datetime(2024, 7, 1, 8, 0, tzinfo=pytz.timezone('US/Eastern'))

# Always compare timezone-aware datetime objects
print(f"UTC Time: {dt1}, Eastern Time: {dt2}")
```

- **Misunderstanding `strftime()` and `strptime()` Format Codes**

  Pitfall: Using incorrect format codes can cause parsing errors or lead to improperly formatted strings.

  Solution: Refer to Python's documentation and verify format codes before using them.

```
from datetime import datetime

# Correctly parse a date string
dt = datetime.strptime("2024-07-01 14:30:00", "%Y-%m-%d %H:%M:%S")

# Format it correctly
formatted_date = dt.strftime("%B %d, %Y")

print(f"Formatted date: {formatted_date}")  # Output: July 01, 2024
```

  Common format mistakes:

  - Using %M for months instead of %m (uppercase %M is for minutes).
  - Using %I for a 24-hour format (use %H instead).
  - Forgetting %p when dealing with AM/PM times.

- **Not Using `timedelta` for Date Arithmetic**

  Pitfall: Manually adding days or calculating time differences can introduce errors.

  Solution: Use **`timedelta`** for reliable date arithmetic.

```
from datetime import datetime, timedelta

# Add 10 days to the current date
future_date = datetime.now() + timedelta(days=10)

print(f"Future Date: {future_date}")
```

Best Practices for Date and Time Manipulation in Python

- **Always Use Timezone-Aware `datetime` Objects**
  - Helps avoid time zone-related issues when working with multiple regions.
  - Convert to UTC for storage and only switch to local time zones when displaying values.
- **Use Reliable Libraries**
  - Use **`pytz`** for time zone handling.
  - Use **`dateutil`** for flexible date parsing.
- **Store Date-Times in UTC**
  - Keeping all timestamps in UTC avoids confusion and ensures consistency across different time zones.

- **Use ISO 8601 Format for Storage and Exchange**
  - The ISO 8601 format (YYYY-MM-DDTHH:MM:SSZ) is widely used in APIs and databases.

```
from datetime import datetime

# Format a datetime in ISO 8601 format
iso_date = datetime.now().isoformat()

print(f"ISO 8601 Format: {iso_date}")
```

- **Always Define Format Strings Explicitly**

  Avoid ambiguous date formats by specifying the expected format.

```
from datetime import datetime

# Define a format string explicitly
dt = datetime.strptime("2024-07-01 14:30:00", "%Y-%m-%d %H:%M:%S")

print(f"Parsed datetime: {dt}")
```

- **Keep Time Zone Data Updated**

```
pip install --upgrade pytz
```

- **Validate and Sanitize User Input**
  - Ensure date inputs are correctly formatted to prevent errors.
  - Handle invalid dates gracefully.
- **Document How Dates and Times Are Handled**

  Clearly document assumptions, conversions, and time zone handling to avoid confusion.

Exercises and Challenges: Practice Problems and Solutions

Practice Problem 1: Time Zone Conversion

Task: Convert the current time in UTC to Eastern and Pacific time zones.

Challenge: Write a script called **`timezone_converter.py`** that:

- Retrieves the current time in UTC.
- Converts this time to Eastern and Pacific time zones using the pytz library.
- Displays the original UTC time and the converted times.

Practice Problem 2: Date Arithmetic

Task: Calculate the date 10 days from today and the date 10 days before today.

Challenge: Write a script called **`date_arithmetic.py`** that:

- Retrieves the current date.
- Calculates the date 10 days in the future.
- Calculates the date 10 days in the past.
- Displays all three dates.

Practice Problem 3: Parsing and Formatting Dates

Task: Parse a given date string into a datetime object and format it into different string representations.

Challenge: Write a script called **`parse_format_dates.py`** that:

- Defines a date string in the format "July 01, 2024 02:30 PM."
- Parses this string into a datetime object.
- Formats the datetime object into "YYYY-MM-DD HH:MM," "DD/MM/YYYY," "Month Day, Year," and "Day-Month-Year Hour AM/PM."
- Displays the parsed datetime object and the formatted strings.

Practice Problem 4: Handling Timestamps

Task: Convert the current time to a timestamp and back to a datetime object.

Challenge: Write a script called **`timestamp_converter.py`** that:

- Retrieves the current time.
- Converts this time to a timestamp.
- Converts the timestamp back to a datetime object.
- Displays the original time, the timestamp, and the converted datetime object.

Practice Problem 5: Daylight Saving Time Adjustment

Task: Handle daylight saving time changes for a specific date and time in a given time zone.

Challenge: Write a script called **`dst_handler.py`** that:

- Defines a specific date and time in the "US/Eastern" time zone (for example, November 3, 2024, 1:30 AM).
- Localizes this time to the Eastern time zone considering DST.
- Converts this localized time to UTC.
- Displays the original date and time, the localized time, and the UTC time.

Solutions to Practice Problems

Practice Problem 1: Time Zone Conversion

`timezone_converter.py`

```
from datetime import datetime
import pytz

def timezone_conversion():
    # Get current UTC time
    utc_now = datetime.now(pytz.utc)
    print(f"Current UTC time: {utc_now}")

    # Define target time zones
    eastern = pytz.timezone('US/Eastern')
    pacific = pytz.timezone('US/Pacific')

    # Convert UTC time to Eastern and Pacific time zones
    eastern_time = utc_now.astimezone(eastern)
    pacific_time = utc_now.astimezone(pacific)

    # Display results
    print(f"Current Eastern time: {eastern_time}")
    print(f"Current Pacific time: {pacific_time}")
```

```
# Execute the function if the script is run directly
if __name__ == "__main__":
    timezone_conversion()
```

Practice Problem 2: Date Arithmetic

`date_arithmetic.py`

```
from datetime import datetime, timedelta

def date_arithmetic():
    # Get the current date
    today = datetime.now().date()
    print(f"Today's date: {today}")

    # Calculate the date 10 days from today
    future_date = today + timedelta(days=10)
    print(f"Date 10 days from today: {future_date}")

    # Calculate the date 10 days before today
    past_date = today - timedelta(days=10)
    print(f"Date 10 days before today: {past_date}")

# Execute the function if the script is run directly
if __name__ == "__main__":
    date_arithmetic()
```

Practice Problem 3: Parsing and Formatting Dates

`parse_format_dates.py`

```
from datetime import datetime

def parse_format_dates():
    # Define a date string
    date_string = "July 01, 2024 02:30 PM"
    format_string = "%B %d, %Y %I:%M %p"

    # Parse the date string into a datetime object
    parsed_date = datetime.strptime(date_string, format_string)
    print(f"Original date string: {date_string}")
    print(f"Parsed datetime: {parsed_date}")

    # Format the datetime object into different string representations
    formatted_date1 = parsed_date.strftime("%Y-%m-%d %H:%M:%S")
    print(f"Formatted date 1: {formatted_date1}")

    formatted_date2 = parsed_date.strftime("%d/%m/%Y")
    print(f"Formatted date 2: {formatted_date2}")

    formatted_date3 = parsed_date.strftime("%B %d, %Y")
    print(f"Formatted date 3: {formatted_date3}")

    formatted_date4 = parsed_date.strftime("%d-%B-%Y %I:%M %p")
    print(f"Formatted date 4: {formatted_date4}")

# Execute the function if the script is run directly
if __name__ == "__main__":
    parse_format_dates()
```

Practice Problem 4: Handling Timestamps

`timestamp_converter.py`

```
from datetime import datetime

def timestamp_converter():
    # Get the current time
    now = datetime.now()
    print(f"Current datetime: {now}")

    # Convert the current time to a timestamp
    timestamp = now.timestamp()
    print(f"Current timestamp: {timestamp}")

    # Convert the timestamp back to a datetime object
    dt_from_timestamp = datetime.fromtimestamp(timestamp)
    print(f"Datetime from timestamp: {dt_from_timestamp}")

# Execute the function if the script is run directly
if __name__ == "__main__":
    timestamp_converter()
```

```
Practice Problem 5: Daylight Saving Time Adjustment
```

`dst_handler.py`

```
from datetime import datetime
import pytz

def dst_handler():
    # Define a specific date and time in the US/Eastern time zone
    eastern = pytz.timezone('US/Eastern')
    dt = datetime(2024, 11, 3, 1, 30)

    # Localize the time to Eastern time zone considering DST
    dt_eastern = eastern.localize(dt, is_dst=False)
    print(f"Localized time: {dt_eastern}")

    # Convert the localized time to UTC
    dt_utc = dt_eastern.astimezone(pytz.utc)
    print(f"Converted to UTC: {dt_utc}")

# Execute the function if the script is run directly
if __name__ == "__main__":
    dst_handler()
```

Conclusion

In this chapter, you expanded your Python programming skills by learning how to manage dates and times effectively. You explored how to create and modify date and time objects, access their components, and format them into different string representations for better usability.

You also learned how to perform arithmetic operations with dates and times, including adding and subtracting time periods and calculating differences using the timedelta class. Understanding how to combine dates and times using datetime objects allowed you to handle timestamps more efficiently.

Handling time zones and daylight saving time (DST) can be complex, but you mastered Python's **`pytz`** library to ensure accurate time zone conversions. Additionally, you gained skills in working with timestamps and converting between various date-time formats using **`strptime()`** and **`strftime()`**.

By applying these techniques, you can build more reliable applications that handle scheduling, logging, and global time management efficiently. These skills are essential for developing Python programs that work accurately across different time zones and user environments.

In the next chapter, you will shift from handling dates and times to working with JSON and XML, two essential formats for storing and exchanging data in modern applications. You will learn how to parse, manipulate, and generate structured data efficiently, preparing you for tasks such as API development and data processing.

As you transition from managing time-related data to working with structured file formats, let us continue sharpening your Python skills and writing efficient, well-structured programs.

Till then, keep calm and let's tame the Python!

Multiple-Choice Questions

Test your understanding of the concepts covered in this chapter with the following multiple-choice questions.

1. Which method is used to parse a string into a datetime object?
   a. `strftime`
   b. `strptime`
   c. `fromtimestamp`
   d. `timestamp`
2. What is the output format of `datetime.now().timestamp()`?
   a. A formatted date string
   b. A datetime object
   c. The number of seconds since the Unix epoch
   d. A timedelta object
3. Which library is commonly used in Python for handling time zone conversions?
   a. timezone
   b. pytz
   c. datetime
   d. time
4. What is the function of the **`timedelta`** class in the datetime module?
   a. It formats datetime objects into strings
   b. It handles time zone conversions
   c. It represents the difference between two dates or times
   d. It converts timestamps to datetime objects

5. How do you convert a naive datetime object to a timezone-aware datetime object using `pytz`?
   a. `datetime.now(pytz.utc)`
   b. `datetime.localize()`
   c. `datetime.strftime()`
   d. `datetime.astimezone(pytz.utc)`
6. Which of the following format codes represents a 12-hour clock with AM/PM?
   a. %H
   b. %I
   c. %M
   d. %S
7. To handle daylight saving time changes automatically, which parameter should be set when localizing a datetime object with `pytz`?
   a. `is_dst=None`
   b. `is_dst=True`
   c. `is_dst=False`
   d. `is_dst=0`
8. What is the purpose of the `astimezone()` method in the datetime module?
   a. To parse a string into a datetime object
   b. To convert a naive datetime object to a timezone-aware datetime object
   c. To convert a datetime object to another time zone
   d. To format a datetime object into a string
9. Which strftime format code is used to represent the full month name?
   a. %b
   b. %B
   c. %m
   d. %M
10. What does the `fromtimestamp()` method in the datetime module do?
    a. Converts a datetime object to a timestamp
    b. Parses a string into a datetime object
    c. Converts a timestamp to a datetime object
    d. Represents the difference between two dates or times

Answers

1. b
2. c
3. b
4. c
5. b
6. b
7. a
8. c
9. b
10. c

Points to Remember

- Correct date and time handling is critical for scheduling, logging, and managing time-sensitive data in programming.
- Python's datetime module includes classes and functions for manipulating dates and times in both simple and advanced ways.
- Use the date class to generate date objects. Use the proper attributes and methods to access and edit components such as the year, month, and day.
- To format date objects into strings, use **`strftime`** and **`strptime`**. Always use correct format codes.
- Use the time class to generate time objects. Access and change hours, minutes, seconds, and microseconds.
- Use the **`timedelta`** class to do arithmetic operations such as adding and subtracting days. Use subtraction to calculate the differences between dates.
- Use the datetime class to build date/time objects. These objects are formatted and parsed using **`strftime`** and **`strptime`**.
- Time zones indicate local time relative to UTC. To ensure correct time comparisons and conversions, use timezone-aware datetime objects.
- The **`pytz`** package automates time zone conversions and DST modifications.
- When working with time zones, keep daylight savings time in mind. Pytz handles DST transitions when localizing time.
- Time stamps indicate the number of seconds since the Unix epoch. Use **`datetime.now().timestamp()`** returns the current timestamp and datetime. Use **`fromtimestamp()`** to convert timestamps back into datetime objects.
- Use **`strptime`** and **`strftime`** to convert between various formats. To ensure uniformity, use a standard format such as ISO 8601.
- Avoid common pitfalls like neglecting time zones, failing to account for DST, and using naive datetime objects for time comparison.

- Use timezone-aware datetime objects, rely on **pytz** libraries, maintain consistency in time zone handling, and keep libraries up to date. Document your codebase's handling of dates and times for clarity and maintenance.

Further Reading

For further exploration of Python date and time handling, consider these resources:

1. **Python Date and Time Handling - Real Python**:

   https://realpython.com/python-datetime/

   A comprehensive guide covering date and time manipulation, formatting, and best practices.

2. **Python Datetime Module - W3Schools**:

   https://www.w3schools.com/python/python_datetime.asp

   A beginner-friendly introduction to working with Python's datetime module.

Chapter 12
Working with JSON and XML

Introduction

In the last chapter, you explored how to work with dates and times in Python. Now, you will move on to another important topic, that is, handling structured data using JSON and XML. Just like working with dates and times helps build reliable applications, managing JSON and XML is essential for handling and exchanging data effectively.

This chapter will teach you how to read, write, and modify JSON and XML data in Python. You will start by understanding the differences between these formats and why they are widely used in modern applications. Then, you will see practical examples of how to use JSON and XML to store and exchange information efficiently.

You will begin with JSON, learning how to read data from files, modify it, and save it back. JSON is commonly used in APIs and web applications, making it a crucial skill for any programmer. Next, you will explore XML, a format used for organizing structured data, and you will learn how to parse, edit, and generate XML files.

By the end of this chapter, you will have a strong grasp of JSON and XML handling in Python. You will be able to work with structured data, making it easier to store, share, and process information across different applications. Let's get started!

Structure

In this chapter, the following topics will be covered:

- Introduction to JSON and XML
    - Overview of JSON
    - Overview of XML
    - Usage of JSON and XML
    - Real-World Examples
- Parsing and Generating JSON
    - Loading JSON Data
    - Parsing JSON Data
    - Generating JSON from Python Objects
    - Working with JSON Files
    - Handling Complex JSON Structures
    - Practical Exercise: Comprehensive JSON Data Handling

- Parsing and Generating XML
    - Loading XML Data
    - Parsing XML Data
    - Modifying XML Data
    - Generating XML Data
    - Working with XML Files
    - Handling Complex XML Structures
    - Practical Exercise: Comprehensive XML Data Handling
- Common Mistakes and Best Practices
- Exercises and Challenges: Practice Problems and Solutions

Introduction to JSON and XML

In the digital world, data needs to be stored, shared, and understood by different systems. Two of the most commonly used formats for this are JavaScript Object Notation (JSON) and Extensible Markup Language (XML). These formats help organize and exchange data in a structured way.

In this section, you will learn:

- **JSON and XML formats:** Usage of these formats and their applicability.
- **Key differences between JSON and XML**: When to use each format.
- **Real-world examples**: How they are used in applications.

Overview of JSON

JSON is a lightweight and easy-to-read format for storing and exchanging data. It is based on key-value pairs, similar to Python dictionaries. JSON is widely used in web applications and APIs because it is simple and efficient.

Key Features of JSON:

- **Easy to read and write**: JSON has a simple syntax that is user-friendly.
- **Structured like Python dictionaries**: Uses key-value pairs and supports data types such as objects, arrays, strings, numbers, booleans, and null.
- **Works across different programming languages:** JSON is language-independent, making it ideal for data exchange.
- **Common Uses**: Web development (APIs), configuration files, and databases (for example, MongoDB).

Example JSON Data:

```
{
  "name": "John Doe",
  "age": 30,
  "isStudent": false,
  "courses": ["Python", "Data Science"],
  "address": {
    "street": "123 Main St",
    "city": "Anytown"
  }
}
```

Overview of XML

XML is another format used to store and share data. Unlike JSON, XML uses tags to define data in a structured, hierarchical way. It is often used in configuration files, data exchange, and enterprise applications.

Key Features of XML:

- **Flexible**: Can store complex data structures.
- **Uses a tree-like structure**: Data is nested inside elements.
- **Self-descriptive**: Uses tags to define the structure and meaning of data.
- **Common Uses**: Configuration files, enterprise data exchange, and web services.

Example XML Data:

```
<person>
  <name>John Doe</name>
  <age>30</age>
  <isStudent>false</isStudent>
  <courses>
    <course>Python</course>
    <course>Data Science</course>
  </courses>
  <address>
    <street>123 Main St</street>
    <city>Anytown</city>
  </address>
</person>
```

JSON vs. XML: Key Differences

Feature	**JSON**	**XML**
Syntax	Simple and compact	More complex, uses tags
Structure	Key-value pairs (such as a dictionary)	Tree-like hierarchy with nested elements
Readability	Easier for humans to read	More detailed, less intuitive
Use Cases	APIs, config files, databases	Data exchange, enterprise applications

Table 12.1: *Differences between JSON and XML*

Usage of JSON and XML

JSON Use Cases:

- **Web APIs**: JSON is the standard format for REST APIs because it is simple and efficient.
- **Configuration Files**: Many software applications store settings in JSON.
- **Databases**: NoSQL databases such as MongoDB use JSON-like structures for data storage.

XML Use Cases:

- **Enterprise Applications**: XML is used in large-scale systems to store and transfer data.
- **System Configurations**: Many enterprise applications use XML for configuration files.
- **Hierarchical Data Storage**: XML is ideal for structured content such as HTML and XHTML.

Real-World Examples

Example: JSON in a Weather Application

Imagine you are creating a weather app that fetches real-time weather data from an API. The API sends data in JSON format, which your app reads and displays.

Example JSON Data from a Weather API:

```
{
  "location": {
    "city": "San Francisco",
    "country": "USA"
  },
  "current_observation": {
    "temperature": 68,
    "humidity": 60,
    "condition": "Clear"
  },
  "forecast": [
    {
      "day": "Monday",
      "high": 70,
      "low": 55,
      "condition": "Sunny"
    },
    {
      "day": "Tuesday",
      "high": 65,
      "low": 53,
      "condition": "Cloudy"
    }
  ]
}
```

Your Python application can parse this JSON and extract details such as temperature, humidity, and forecast to display them to users.

Example: XML in Enterprise Systems

Now, imagine you are working on a business application that shares configuration data with other systems. The configuration settings are stored in XML format, and your program needs to parse this data to apply the correct settings.

Example XML Configuration File:

```
<config>
  <system>
    <name>InventoryManagement</name>
    <version>2.1.3</version>
  </system>
  <settings>
    <setting>
      <key>maxItems</key>
      <value>500</value>
    </setting>
    <setting>
      <key>enableNotifications</key>
      <value>true</value>
```

```
      </setting>
      <setting>
        <key>notificationEmail</key>
        <value>admin@company.com</value>
      </setting>
    </settings>
  </config>
```

Your Python program can read this XML file and extract settings such as max items, notifications, and admin email to apply them correctly.

Importance of JSON and XML:

Understanding how to read and create JSON and XML will help you integrate your Python applications with APIs, databases, and enterprise systems. Whether you are retrieving real-time data or configuring software, these formats are crucial for modern programming.

Now that you have a solid foundation, let us move on to the practical part, where you will learn how to parse and generate JSON and XML in Python!

Parsing and Generating JSON

JSON is one of the most widely used formats for storing and exchanging data. To work with JSON in Python, you need to load JSON data, modify it, and convert Python objects back into JSON. In this section, you will learn how to parse, modify, and generate JSON data in Python using the JSON module.

Loading JSON Data

JSON data can come from two main sources:

- **A JSON string**: Data received from APIs or files.
- **A JSON file**: A stored file containing structured data.

Python provides two functions to handle these:

- **`json.loads()`**: Converts a JSON string into a Python dictionary.
- **`json.load()`**: Reads JSON data from a file and converts it into a Python dictionary.

Loading JSON from a String

Use **`json.loads()`** to convert a JSON string into a Python dictionary.

Example:

```
import json

# JSON string
json_string = '{"name": "John Doe", "age": 30, "isStudent": false}'

# Convert JSON string to Python dictionary
data = json.loads(json_string)

# Accessing values
print(data["name"])       # Output: John Doe
print(data["age"])        # Output: 30
print(data["isStudent"])  # Output: False
```

Explanation: **`json.loads()`** takes a JSON string and converts it into a dictionary. You can then access the data using dictionary keys.

Loading JSON from a File

When JSON data is stored in a file, use **json.load()** to read and convert it into a Python dictionary.

Example:

```
import json

# Open and read a JSON file
with open("data.json", "r") as file:
    data = json.load(file)

# Accessing values
print(data["name"])       # Output: John Doe
print(data["age"])        # Output: 30
print(data["isStudent"])  # Output: False
```

Explanation:

- The with **open()** statement ensures the file is properly closed after reading.
- **json.load(file)** reads the JSON data from the file and converts it into a Python dictionary.

Parsing JSON Data

Once JSON is loaded into Python, it is represented as dictionaries and lists. You can access the data using dictionary keys or list indexing.

Accessing JSON Data

Example:

```
import json

# JSON string
json_string = '''
{
  "name": "John Doe",
  "age": 30,
  "isStudent": false,
  "courses": ["Python", "Data Science"],
  "address": {
    "street": "123 Main St",
    "city": "Anytown"
  }
}
'''

# Convert JSON string to Python dictionary
data = json.loads(json_string)

# Accessing values
print("Name:", data["name"])
print("Age:", data["age"])
print("Is Student:", data["isStudent"])
print("Courses:", data["courses"])
print("City:", data["address"]["city"])
```

Key Takeaways:

- Use dictionary keys to access values (**`data["name"]`**).
- Use nested keys to access deeper values (**`data["address"]["city"]`**).
- Lists in JSON are converted to Python lists (**`data["courses"]`**).

Modifying JSON Data

You can modify JSON data just like you modify Python dictionaries. This includes:

- Updating existing values
- Adding new key-value pairs
- Deleting data

Example:

```
# Updating existing values
data["name"] = "Jane Doe"
data["age"] = 25

# Adding a new key-value pair
data["graduationYear"] = 2022

# Removing a key-value pair
del data["isStudent"]

# Printing the updated JSON
print(json.dumps(data, indent=4))
```

Explanation:

- Update values by assigning new data to existing keys.
- Add new data by setting a new key in the dictionary.
- Remove data using del.
- Format JSON output using **`json.dumps(data, indent=4)`**.

Generating JSON from Python Objects

Sometimes, you need to convert Python data back into JSON format. The **`json.dumps()`** function converts a Python dictionary into a JSON string.

Example:

```
import json

# Python dictionary
data = {
    "name": "John Doe",
    "age": 30,
    "isStudent": False,
    "courses": ["Python", "Data Science"],
    "address": {
        "street": "123 Main St",
        "city": "Anytown"
    }
}
```

```
# Convert dictionary to JSON string
json_string = json.dumps(data, indent=4)
print(json_string)
```

Key Takeaways:

- **`json.dumps(data)`** converts a Python dictionary into a JSON-formatted string.
- The **`indent=4`** argument makes the output more readable.

Working with JSON Files

Working with JSON files is common in data processing, API requests, and application settings.

Reading from a JSON File

Example:

```
import json

# Read JSON file
with open("data.json", "r") as file:
    data = json.load(file)

# Print data
print(data)
```

Explanation: The **`json.load(file)`** function reads JSON data from a file and converts it into a Python dictionary.

Writing to a JSON File

Example:

```
import json

# Sample data
data = {
    "name": "John Doe",
    "age": 30,
    "isStudent": False,
    "courses": ["Python", "Data Science"],
    "address": {
        "street": "123 Main St",
        "city": "Anytown"
    }
}

# Write JSON data to a file
with open("output.json", "w") as file:
    json.dump(data, file, indent=4)
```

Key Takeaways:

- **`json.dump(data, file)`** writes JSON data to a file.
- The **`indent=4`** argument makes the JSON file easy to read.

Handling Complex JSON Structures

Sometimes, JSON data contains nested lists and dictionaries. You can access and modify this data using indexing.

Example:

```
import json

# Complex JSON string
json_string = '''
{
  "employees": [
    {
      "name": "John Doe",
      "age": 30,
      "skills": ["Python", "Data Analysis"]
    },
    {
      "name": "Jane Smith",
      "age": 25,
      "skills": ["JavaScript", "Web Development"]
    }
  ],
  "company": {
    "name": "Tech Solutions",
    "location": "Silicon Valley"
  }
}
'''

# Convert JSON to Python dictionary
data = json.loads(json_string)

# Access nested data
company_name = data["company"]["name"]
employee_skills = data["employees"][0]["skills"]

print("Company Name:", company_name)
print("John Doe's Skills:", employee_skills)

# Modify nested data
data["employees"][1]["age"] = 26

# Print updated JSON
print(json.dumps(data, indent=4))
```

Explanation:

- JSON lists are accessed using **`data["employees"][0]`**.
- Nested keys retrieve deeper values (**`data["company"]["name"]`**).

Practical Exercise: Comprehensive JSON Data Handling

In this exercise, you will build a Python program that performs key JSON operations, including loading, parsing, modifying, generating, and handling complex JSON structures. This will help you apply everything you've learned in this section.

Task Overview:

Your program will:

- Load JSON data from a string and a file.
- Parse and access JSON data.
- Modify JSON data (update, add, and delete values).
- Convert Python objects into JSON format and write to a file.
- Handle nested JSON structures.

Step-by-Step Implementation

1. **Load JSON from a String**

   Use **`json.loads()`** to convert a JSON string into a Python dictionary.

```
import json

def load_json_from_string():
    json_string = '''
    {
        "name": "John Doe",
        "age": 30,
        "isStudent": false,
        "courses": ["Python", "Data Science"],
        "address": {
            "street": "123 Main St",
            "city": "Anytown"
        }
    }
    '''
    return json.loads(json_string)
```

2. **Load JSON from a File**

   Use **`json.load()`** to read JSON data from a file.

```
def load_json_from_file(file_path):
    with open(file_path, 'r') as file:
        return json.load(file)
```

3. **Access and Modify JSON Data**

   Access nested data, update values, and add/remove keys.

```
def access_and_modify_json(data):
    # Accessing data
    print(f"Name: {data['name']}")
    print(f"Courses: {data['courses']}")
    print(f"City: {data['address']['city']}")

    # Modifying data
    data['name'] = "Jane Doe"
    data['graduationYear'] = 2022
    del data['isStudent']

    return data
```

4. **Generate JSON from Python Objects**

   Use **`json.dumps()`** to convert a dictionary into a formatted JSON string.

```
def generate_json_string(data):
    return json.dumps(data, indent=4)
```

5. **Write JSON to a File**

   Save modified JSON data to a new file using **`json.dump()`**.

```
def write_json_to_file(data, file_path):
    with open(file_path, 'w') as file:
        json.dump(data, file, indent=4)
```

6. **Handle Complex JSON Structures**

   Work with nested objects and arrays.

```
def handle_complex_json(data):
    # Accessing nested data
    print(f"Company Name: {data['company']['name']}")
    print(f"First Employee's Skills: {data['employees'][0]['skills']}")

    # Modifying nested data
    data['employees'][1]['age'] = 26

    return data
```

Putting Everything Together (Main Function)

```
def main():
    # Load JSON from string
    data_from_string = load_json_from_string()
    print("Loaded JSON from string:")
    print(generate_json_string(data_from_string))

    # Load JSON from file
    file_path = 'data.json'  # Ensure this file exists with valid JSON data
    data_from_file = load_json_from_file(file_path)
    print("\nLoaded JSON from file:")
    print(generate_json_string(data_from_file))

    # Access and modify JSON data
    modified_data = access_and_modify_json(data_from_file)
    print("\nModified JSON data:")
    print(generate_json_string(modified_data))

    # Write modified JSON to a new file
    output_file_path = 'modified_data.json'
    write_json_to_file(modified_data, output_file_path)
    print(f"\nModified JSON data written to {output_file_path}")

    # Handling complex JSON structure
    complex_json_string = '''
    {
      "employees": [
        {
          "name": "John Doe",
          "age": 30,
          "skills": ["Python", "Data Analysis"]
```

```
            },
            {
              "name": "Jane Smith",
              "age": 25,
              "skills": ["JavaScript", "Web Development"]
            }
          ],
          "company": {
            "name": "Tech Solutions",
            "location": "Silicon Valley"
          }
        }
        '''
        complex_data = json.loads(complex_json_string)
        handled_complex_data = handle_complex_json(complex_data)
        print("\nHandled complex JSON data:")
        print(generate_json_string(handled_complex_data))

    if __name__ == "__main__":
        main()
```

Understanding the Code

- **Loading JSON**
  - **`load_json_from_string()`**: Reads JSON from a string using **`json.loads()`**.
  - **`load_json_from_file()`**: Reads JSON from a file using **`json.load()`**.
- **Parsing and Modifying JSON**
  - **`access_and_modify_json()`**: Reads, updates, and deletes values in JSON data.
- **Generating and Writing JSON**
  - **`generate_json_string()`**: Converts a Python dictionary into a formatted JSON string.
  - **`write_json_to_file()`**: Saves JSON data to a file using **`json.dump()`**.
- **Handling Complex JSON Structures**
  - **`handle_complex_json()`**: Works with nested objects and arrays, showing best practices.

Parsing and Generating XML

In the previous section, you learned how to work with JSON in Python. Now, you will explore Extensible Markup Language (XML), another widely used format for storing and exchanging structured data. Python's built-in **`xml.etree.ElementTree`** module makes it easy to parse, modify, and generate XML data.

Loading XML Data

You can load XML data from:

- A string: Data received from an API or a configuration file.
- A file: A stored XML document.

Python provides two functions for this:

- **`ET.fromstring()`** → Parses an XML string into an Element object.
- **`ET.parse()`** → Reads XML from a file and converts it into an ElementTree object.

Loading XML from a String

Use **ET.fromstring()** to convert an XML string into an Element object.

Example:

```
import xml.etree.ElementTree as ET

# XML string
xml_string = '''
<person>
  <name>John Doe</name>
  <age>30</age>
  <isStudent>false</isStudent>
  <courses>
    <course>Python</course>
    <course>Data Science</course>
  </courses>
</person>
'''

# Parse XML string
root = ET.fromstring(xml_string)

# Accessing data
print(root.find('name').text)  # Output: John Doe
print(root.find('age').text)   # Output: 30
```

Explanation:

- **ET.fromstring(xml_string)** converts the XML string into a structured Element object.
- **find('tag')** retrieves specific elements in the XML.

Loading XML from a File

Use **ET.parse()** to read XML data from a file.

Example:

```
import xml.etree.ElementTree as ET

# Parse XML file
tree = ET.parse('data.xml')
root = tree.getroot()

# Accessing data
print(root.find('name').text)  # Output: John Doe
print(root.find('age').text)   # Output: 30
```

Explanation:

- **ET.parse('data.xml')** reads the XML file and creates an **ElementTree** object.
- **getroot()** retrieves the root element of the XML tree.

Parsing XML Data

Once XML data is loaded, you can extract values using dictionary-like operations.

Example: Accessing XML Data

```
import xml.etree.ElementTree as ET

# Parse XML string
root = ET.fromstring(xml_string)

# Extract data
name = root.find('name').text
age = root.find('age').text
courses = [course.text for course in root.find('courses').findall('course')]

print(f"Name: {name}")
print(f"Age: {age}")
print(f"Courses: {courses}")
```

Key Takeaways:

- Use **find()** to locate a single element.
- Use **findall()** to retrieve multiple elements (for example, all **<course>** tags inside **<courses>**).

Modifying XML Data

You can update values, add new elements, and remove elements in XML.

Example: Updating XML Data

```
# Modifying existing data
root.find('name').text = "Jane Doe"
root.find('age').text = "25"

# Adding a new element
grad_year = ET.Element('graduationYear')
grad_year.text = "2022"
root.append(grad_year)

# Removing an element
root.remove(root.find('isStudent'))

# Displaying modified XML
print(ET.tostring(root, encoding='unicode'))
```

Key Takeaways:

- Modify existing values by updating text.
- Add new elements using **ET.Element()** and **append()**.
- Remove elements using **remove()**.

Generating XML Data

To create an XML document, use **ET.Element()** to define elements and build a tree structure.

Example: Creating an XML Document

```
import xml.etree.ElementTree as ET

# Create root element
root = ET.Element('person')
```

```
# Create child elements
name = ET.SubElement(root, 'name')
name.text = "John Doe"

age = ET.SubElement(root, 'age')
age.text = "30"

courses = ET.SubElement(root, 'courses')
ET.SubElement(courses, 'course').text = "Python"
ET.SubElement(courses, 'course').text = "Data Science"

# Convert to XML string
print(ET.tostring(root, encoding='unicode'))
```

Key Takeaways:

- Use **`ET.Element()`** to create a root element.
- Use **`ET.SubElement()`** to add child elements inside the root.
- Use **`ET.tostring()`** to convert XML into a readable format.

Working with XML Files

Working with XML files is common in configuration settings and data storage.

1. **Reading an XML File**

```
tree = ET.parse('data.xml')
root = tree.getroot()

print(root.find('name').text)  # Output: John Doe
```

2. **Writing to an XML File**

```
# Create an ElementTree object
tree = ET.ElementTree(root)

# Write to a file
tree.write('output.xml', encoding='unicode', xml_declaration=True)
```

Key Takeaways:

- **`tree.write()`** saves XML data into a file.
- **`xml_declaration=True`** ensures the XML file is properly formatted.

Handling Complex XML Structures

Some XML files contain nested elements and attributes. Use loops and indexing to navigate them.

Example: Parsing a Complex XML Document

```
import xml.etree.ElementTree as ET

# Complex XML string
xml_string = '''
<company>
  <employees>
    <employee id="1">
      <name>John Doe</name>
      <age>30</age>
```

```
        <skills>
          <skill>Python</skill>
          <skill>Data Analysis</skill>
        </skills>
      </employee>
      <employee id="2">
        <name>Jane Smith</name>
        <age>25</age>
        <skills>
          <skill>JavaScript</skill>
          <skill>Web Development</skill>
        </skills>
      </employee>
    </employees>
    <location>Silicon Valley</location>
  </company>
  '''

  # Parse XML string
  root = ET.fromstring(xml_string)

  # Accessing nested data
  employees = root.find('employees')
  for employee in employees.findall('employee'):
      name = employee.find('name').text
      age = employee.find('age').text
      skills = [skill.text for skill in employee.find('skills').findall('skill')]
      print(f"Name: {name}, Age: {age}, Skills: {skills}")

  # Modifying nested data
  employee_to_modify = employees.find("employee[@id='2']")
  employee_to_modify.find('age').text = "26"

  # Adding a new skill
  new_skill = ET.Element('skill')
  new_skill.text = "Project Management"
  employee_to_modify.find('skills').append(new_skill)

  # Display modified XML
  print(ET.tostring(root, encoding='unicode'))
```

Key Takeaways:

- Use loops to navigate multiple nested elements.
- Use [`@attribute`] to select elements by attributes (`id="2"`).
- Add new child elements dynamically.

Practical Exercise: Comprehensive XML Data Handling

So far you have learned how to parse and generate XML data using Python. Now, let us apply that knowledge in a hands-on exercise where you will build a real-world XML processing program.

Task Overview:

Your program will:

- Load XML data from a string and a file.
- Parse and access XML data.

- Modify XML data (update, add, and delete elements).
- Generate XML from Python objects.
- Write XML data to a file.
- Handle complex XML structures.

Step-by-Step Implementation

1. **Load XML from a String**

   Use **`ET.fromstring()`** to convert an XML string into an Element object.

```
import xml.etree.ElementTree as ET

def load_xml_from_string():
    xml_string = '''
    <person>
      <name>John Doe</name>
      <age>30</age>
      <isStudent>false</isStudent>
      <courses>
        <course>Python</course>
        <course>Data Science</course>
      </courses>
    </person>
    '''
    return ET.fromstring(xml_string)
```

2. **Load XML from a File**

   Use **`ET.parse()`** to read XML data from a file.

```
def load_xml_from_file(file_path):
    tree = ET.parse(file_path)
    return tree.getroot()
```

3. **Access and Modify XML Data**

   Retrieve, update, add, and remove XML elements.

```
def access_and_modify_xml(data):
    # Accessing data
    name = data.find('name').text
    courses = [course.text for course in data.find('courses').findall('course')]

    print(f"Name: {name}")
    print(f"Courses: {courses}")

    # Modifying data
    data.find('name').text = "Jane Doe"
    data.find('age').text = "25"

    # Adding a new element
    graduation_year = ET.Element('graduationYear')
    graduation_year.text = "2022"
    data.append(graduation_year)

    # Removing an element
    data.remove(data.find('isStudent'))

    return data
```

4. **Generate an XML Tree**

   Use **`ET.Element()`** and **`ET.SubElement()`** to create an XML structure.

```
def generate_xml_tree():
    root = ET.Element('company')

    employees = ET.SubElement(root, 'employees')

    # First Employee
    employee1 = ET.SubElement(employees, 'employee', id='1')
    ET.SubElement(employee1, 'name').text = "John Doe"
    ET.SubElement(employee1, 'age').text = "30"
    skills1 = ET.SubElement(employee1, 'skills')
    ET.SubElement(skills1, 'skill').text = "Python"
    ET.SubElement(skills1, 'skill').text = "Data Analysis"

    # Second Employee
    employee2 = ET.SubElement(employees, 'employee', id='2')
    ET.SubElement(employee2, 'name').text = "Jane Smith"
    ET.SubElement(employee2, 'age').text = "25"
    skills2 = ET.SubElement(employee2, 'skills')
    ET.SubElement(skills2, 'skill').text = "JavaScript"
    ET.SubElement(skills2, 'skill').text = "Web Development"

    ET.SubElement(root, 'location').text = "Silicon Valley"

    return root
```

5. **Convert to XML String**

   Use **`ET.tostring()`** to display the XML structure as a string.

```
def convert_to_xml_string(root):
    return ET.tostring(root, encoding='unicode')
```

6. **Write XML Data to a File**

   Save XML data using **`ET.ElementTree.write()`**.

```
def write_xml_to_file(root, file_path):
    tree = ET.ElementTree(root)
    tree.write(file_path, encoding='unicode', xml_declaration=True)
```

7. **Handle Complex XML Structures**

   Work with nested elements and attributes.

```
def handle_complex_xml():
    xml_string = '''
    <company>
      <employees>
        <employee id="1">
          <name>John Doe</name>
          <age>30</age>
          <skills>
            <skill>Python</skill>
            <skill>Data Analysis</skill>
          </skills>
        </employee>
        <employee id="2">
```

```
            <name>Jane Smith</name>
            <age>25</age>
            <skills>
              <skill>JavaScript</skill>
              <skill>Web Development</skill>
            </skills>
          </employee>
        </employees>
        <location>Silicon Valley</location>
      </company>
      '''

      root = ET.fromstring(xml_string)

      # Accessing nested data
      employees = root.find('employees')
      for employee in employees.findall('employee'):
          name = employee.find('name').text
          age = employee.find('age').text
          skills = [skill.text for skill in employee.find('skills').
findall('skill')]
          print(f"Name: {name}, Age: {age}, Skills: {skills}")

      # Modifying nested data
      employee_to_modify = employees.find("employee[@id='2']")
      employee_to_modify.find('age').text = "26"

      new_skill = ET.Element('skill')
      new_skill.text = "Project Management"
      employee_to_modify.find('skills').append(new_skill)

      return root
```

Putting Everything Together (Main Function)

```
def main():
    # Load XML from string
    data_from_string = load_xml_from_string()
    print("Loaded XML from string:")
    print(convert_to_xml_string(data_from_string))

    # Load XML from file
    file_path = 'data.xml'  # Ensure this file exists with valid XML data
    data_from_file = load_xml_from_file(file_path)
    print("\nLoaded XML from file:")
    print(convert_to_xml_string(data_from_file))

    # Access and modify XML data
    modified_data = access_and_modify_xml(data_from_file)
    print("\nModified XML data:")
    print(convert_to_xml_string(modified_data))

    # Write modified XML to a new file
    output_file_path = 'modified_data.xml'
    write_xml_to_file(modified_data, output_file_path)
    print(f"\nModified XML data written to {output_file_path}")
```

```
    # Generate and handle complex XML structure
    complex_data = handle_complex_xml()
    print("\nHandled complex XML data:")
    print(convert_to_xml_string(complex_data))

if __name__ == "__main__":
    main()
```

Understanding the Code

- **Loading XML**
  - `load_xml_from_string()`: Reads XML from a string using `ET.fromstring()`.
  - `load_xml_from_file()`: Reads XML from a file using `ET.parse()`.
- **Parsing and Modifying XML**
  - `access_and_modify_xml()`: Reads, updates, and deletes elements in XML data.
- **Generating and Writing XML**
  - `generate_xml_tree()`: Creates a structured XML document using ET.Element().
  - `write_xml_to_file()`: Saves XML data into a file.
- **Handling Complex XML Structures**
  - `handle_complex_xml()`: Works with nested elements and attributes, showing best practices.

Common Mistakes and Best Practices

In the previous sections, you learned how to work with JSON and XML in Python. Now, let us discuss some common mistakes to avoid and best practices to ensure efficient and reliable data handling.

Avoiding Common Mistakes when Working with JSON and XML

When dealing with JSON and XML, certain mistakes can cause errors or data inconsistencies. Here are key pitfalls to watch out for:

- **Invalid Data Formats**: Ensure JSON and XML follow the correct syntax to avoid parsing errors.
- **Incorrect Data Types**: Verify data types (for example, strings, numbers, booleans) when parsing or generating data.
- **Improper Encoding**: Use proper character encoding (for example, UTF-8) to handle special characters correctly.

Best Practices for Data Handling and Manipulation

To work efficiently with JSON and XML, follow these best practices:

- **Validate Data**: Use schema validation tools to ensure JSON and XML follow expected formats.
- **Maintain Consistency**: Keep a predictable structure for easy processing and manipulation.
- **Use Built-in Libraries**: Rely on Python's json and `xml.etree.ElementTree` modules for efficient data handling.
- **Improve Readability**: Format JSON/XML using indentation and line breaks for clarity.
- **Implement Robust Error Handling**: Gracefully handle parsing errors, incorrect data, and exceptions.

By following these principles, you can avoid common errors and improve the efficiency, reliability, and maintainability of your JSON and XML data handling.

Exercises and Challenges: Practice Problems and Solutions

Now that you have learned how to work with JSON and XML in Python, it is time to test your understanding through hands-on practice. The following exercises will help you reinforce key concepts, from basic data parsing to handling complex structures.

Practice Problem 1: Basic JSON Parsing and Modification

Task: Load JSON data from a string, parse it, edit some values, and then return it to a JSON string.

Challenge: Write a script called **`basic_json_parsing.py`** that:

- Loads JSON data from a specified string.
- Parses JSON data and displays original values.
- Changes some values in JSON data.
- Converts updated data to JSON string and prints it.

Practice Problem 2: Reading and Writing JSON Files

Task: Read JSON data from a file, edit it, and then save the revised data in a new file.

Challenge: Write a script called **`json_file_operations.py`** that:

- Reads JSON data from file **`input.json`**.
- Parses JSON data and prints values.
- Changes some values in JSON data.
- Saves the changed JSON data to a new file named **`output.json`**.

Practice Problem 3: Complex JSON Handling

Task: Load complex JSON data from a string, traverse across nested structures, and add new data.

Challenge: Write a script called **`complex_json_handling.py`** that:

- Loads complicated JSON strings with nested structures.
- Parses JSON data and navigates its hierarchical pieces.
- Adds new elements to JSON data.
- Converts updated data to JSON string and prints it.

Practice Problem 4: Basic XML Parsing and Modification

Task: Load XML data from a string, parse it, adjust some values, and then return it to an XML string.

Challenge: Write a script called **`basic_xml_parsing.py`** that:

- Loads XML data from a specified string.
- Parses XML data and displays original values.
- Changes values in XML data.
- Converts updated data to an XML string and prints it.

Practice Problem 5: Reading and Writing XML Files

Task: Read XML data from a file, edit it, and then save the revised data in a new file.

Challenge: Write a script called **xml_file_operations.py** that:

- Reads XML data from the input.xml file.
- Parses XML data and outputs values.
- Changes values in XML data.
- The revised XML data is written to a new file named output.xml.

Solutions to Practice Problems

Hopefully, you have attempted the practice problems before moving to this section. Now, let us go through the solutions step by step to understand the correct approach to parsing, modifying, and handling JSON data effectively. These examples will reinforce key concepts and help you compare your solutions with best practices.

Practice Problem 1: Basic JSON Parsing and Modification

basic_json_parsing.py

```
import json

def basic_json_parsing():
    # JSON string
    json_string = '{"name": "John Doe", "age": 30, "isStudent": false}'

    # Parse JSON string
    data = json.loads(json_string)
    print("Original JSON data:", data)

    # Modify JSON data
    data['name'] = "Jane Doe"
    data['age'] = 25
    data['graduationYear'] = 2022

    # Convert to JSON string
    modified_json_string = json.dumps(data, indent=4)
    print("Modified JSON data:", modified_json_string)

# Execute the function if the script is run directly
if __name__ == "__main__":
    basic_json_parsing()
```

Practice Problem 2: Reading and Writing JSON Files

json_file_operations.py

```
import json

def json_file_operations():
    # Read JSON data from file
    with open('input.json', 'r') as file:
        data = json.load(file)
    print("Original JSON data from file:", data)

    # Modify JSON data
    data['name'] = "Jane Doe"
    data['age'] = 25
    data['graduationYear'] = 2022

    # Write modified JSON data to a new file
```

```
        with open('output.json', 'w') as file:
            json.dump(data, file, indent=4)
        print("Modified JSON data written to output.json")

    # Execute the function if the script is run directly
    if __name__ == "__main__":
        json_file_operations()
```

Practice Problem 3: Complex JSON Handling

complex_json_handling.py

```
import json

def complex_json_handling():
    # Complex JSON string
    json_string = '''
    {
        "company": {
            "name": "Tech Solutions",
            "employees": [
                {
                    "name": "John Doe",
                    "age": 30,
                    "skills": ["Python", "Data Analysis"]
                },
                {
                    "name": "Jane Smith",
                    "age": 25,
                    "skills": ["JavaScript", "Web Development"]
                }
            ]
        }
    }
    '''

    # Parse JSON string
    data = json.loads(json_string)
    print("Original JSON data:", data)

    # Access and modify nested data
    data['company']['employees'][1]['age'] = 26
    new_skill = "Project Management"
    data['company']['employees'][1]['skills'].append(new_skill)

    # Convert to JSON string
    modified_json_string = json.dumps(data, indent=4)
    print("Modified JSON data:", modified_json_string)

# Execute the function if the script is run directly
if __name__ == "__main__":
    complex_json_handling()
```

Practice Problem 4: Basic XML Parsing and Modification

basic_xml_parsing.py

```
import xml.etree.ElementTree as ET

def basic_xml_parsing():
```

```
    # XML string
    xml_string = '''
    <person>
      <name>John Doe</name>
      <age>30</age>
      <isStudent>false</isStudent>
      <courses>
        <course>Python</course>
        <course>Data Science</course>
      </courses>
    </person>
    '''

    # Parse XML string
    root = ET.fromstring(xml_string)
    print("Original XML data:")
    print(ET.tostring(root, encoding='unicode'))

    # Modify XML data
    root.find('name').text = "Jane Doe"
    root.find('age').text = "25"
    graduation_year = ET.Element('graduationYear')
    graduation_year.text = "2022"
    root.append(graduation_year)
    root.remove(root.find('isStudent'))

    # Convert to XML string
    modified_xml_string = ET.tostring(root, encoding='unicode')
    print("Modified XML data:")
    print(modified_xml_string)

# Execute the function if the script is run directly
if __name__ == "__main__":
    basic_xml_parsing()
```

Practice Problem 5: Reading and Writing XML Files

xml_file_operations.py

```
import xml.etree.ElementTree as ET

def xml_file_operations():
    # Read XML data from file
    tree = ET.parse('input.xml')
    root = tree.getroot()
    print("Original XML data from file:")
    print(ET.tostring(root, encoding='unicode'))

    # Modify XML data
    root.find('name').text = "Jane Doe"
    root.find('age').text = "25"
    graduation_year = ET.Element('graduationYear')
    graduation_year.text = "2022"
    root.append(graduation_year)
    is_student = root.find('isStudent')
    if is_student is not None:
        root.remove(is_student)

    # Write modified XML data to a new file
```

```
        tree.write('output.xml', encoding='unicode', xml_declaration=True)
        print("Modified XML data written to output.xml")

    # Execute the function if the script is run directly
    if __name__ == "__main__":
        xml_file_operations()
```

Conclusion

In this chapter, you deepened your Python skills by learning how to work with JSON and XML, two essential formats for storing and exchanging structured data. You explored how to load, parse, modify, and generate both formats efficiently using Python's built-in libraries.

With these skills, you are now well-equipped to work with structured data in Python applications, making your programs more adaptable and efficient.

In the next chapter, the focus will be shifted to another important topic: Mathematics in Python. You will explore various mathematical operations and functions that Python provides, helping you perform calculations and solve numerical problems effectively.

Till then keep calm, and let's tame the Python!

Multiple-Choice Questions

Test your grasp of the concepts discussed in this chapter by answering the following multiple-choice questions.

1. Which method is used to parse JSON data from a string in Python?
   a. `json.dump()`
   b. `json.load()`
   c. `json.loads()`
   d. `json.dumps()`
2. Which function is used to write JSON data to a file in Python?
   a. `json.dumps()`
   b. `json.loads()`
   c. `json.dump()`
   d. `json.parse()`
3. In the `xml.etree.ElementTree` module, which method is used to parse XML data from a string?
   a. `ET.parse()`
   b. `ET.fromstring()`
   c. `ET.tostring()`
   d. `ET.load()`

4. Which method in the `xml.etree.ElementTree` module is used to write XML data to a file?
    a. `ET.write()`
    b. `ET.dump()`
    c. `ET.tostring()`
    d. `ET.save()`
5. What does the `json.dumps()` function do?
    a. Loads JSON data from a file
    b. Converts a Python object to a JSON string
    c. Parses JSON data from a string
    d. Writes JSON data to a file
6. Which of the following is a best practice when working with JSON and XML files?
    a. Avoid using indentation for readability
    b. Always handle character encoding properly
    c. Ignore schema validation
    d. Mix different data formats in the same file
7. What is the purpose of the `ET.Element()` function in the `xml.etree.ElementTree` module?
    a. To parse XML data from a file
    b. To create a new XML element
    c. To convert an XML element to a string
    d. To write an XML element to a file
8. Which method is used to read JSON data from a file in Python?
    a. `json.dumps()`
    b. `json.loads()`
    c. `json.load()`
    d. `json.read()`
9. In the `xml.etree.ElementTree` module, how do you access the root element of an XML tree?
    a. `tree.root()`
    b. `tree.getroot()`
    c. `tree.findroot()`
    d. `tree.accessroot()`
10. What is the output format of `ET.tostring`(root) in the `xml.etree.ElementTree` module?
    a. A formatted XML string
    b. A binary XML file
    c. A Python dictionary
    d. A list of XML elements

Answers

1. c
2. c
3. b
4. a
5. b
6. b
7. b
8. c
9. b
10. a

Points to Remember

- JSON and XML are commonly utilized for data interchange and storage in modern apps.
- To read JSON data from strings and files, use **`json.loads()`** and **`json.load()`**, while **`ET.fromstring()`** and **`ET.parse()`** may read XML data.
- Easily alter data using dictionary-like operations for JSON and element methods for XML.
- Customize JSON and XML structures to meet your needs.
- Use **`json.dumps()`** to convert Python objects to JSON, and **`ET.tostring()`** to convert XML components to strings.
- Save data with **`json.dump()`** for JSON and **`ET.write()`** for XML.
- Learn how to successfully manage complex JSON and XML formats.
- Validate data, use proper character encoding, and have a consistent structure for readability and maintainability.
- JSON and XML are essential for data exchange with online services, configuration management, and structured data handling in applications.

Further Reading

For further exploration of JSON and XML in Python, check out these resources:

1. **Working with JSON in Python – Real Python:**

   https://realpython.com/python-json/

   A comprehensive guide on how to load, parse, modify, and write JSON data in Python.

2. **Python XML Processing – W3Schools:**

   https://www.w3schools.com/xml/xml_parser.asp

   A beginner-friendly introduction to parsing and generating XML in Python.

CHAPTER 13
Math in Python

Introduction

In the last chapter, you have learned how Python can handle different types of data such as JSON and XML, which helps programs organize and share information clearly. Now, you will explore another important part of programming, that is, performing math in Python. Understanding how math works in Python is important because it helps you solve problems clearly, quickly, and accurately.

In this chapter, you will discover how Python can simplify math tasks, from basic calculations to more advanced topics. Think of Python as your friendly calculator, helping you solve mathematical problems step-by-step without mistakes.

You will start by understanding basic math operations, then move on to more complex topics such as working with precise decimal numbers, fractions, and random numbers. You will also learn how to perform statistical calculations, which are very helpful for analyzing data.

By the end of this chapter, you will feel confident solving math problems using Python, making your programs clearer, more reliable, and powerful. Let us dive into the world of math in Python and learn how to solve problems easily and accurately!

Structure

In this chapter, the following topics will be covered:

- Introduction to Math in Python
  - Importance of Math in Programming
  - Overview of Python's Math Capabilities
- Introduction to math Module
  - Basic Mathematical Operations
  - Exponentiation and Modulo Operations
  - Order of Operations (PEMDAS)
  - Practical Exercise: Basic Calculations
- Advanced Mathematical Functions
  - Functions for Powers and Logarithms
  - Trigonometric Functions
  - Practical Exercise: Using Advanced Math Functions
- Working with Complex Numbers
  - Basic Operations with Complex Numbers
  - Using the cmath Module for Complex Mathematics
  - Practical Exercise: Complex Number Calculations

- Statistics and Probability
  - Basic Statistical Calculations
  - Generating Random Numbers and Simulating Probabilities
  - Practical Exercise: Statistical Analysis and Randomness
- Working with Fractions and Decimals
  - Introduction to the fractions Module
  - Introduction to the decimal Module
  - Practical Exercise: Precision Arithmetic
- Linear Algebra
  - Introduction to the Numpy Library
  - Practical Exercise: Linear Algebra using NumPy
- Common Mistakes and Best Practices
- Exercises and Challenges: Practice Problems and Solutions

Introduction to Math in Python

Math is an essential part of programming, helping you perform calculations and solve problems easily and accurately. Python makes math tasks simple, clear, and quick, helping you create powerful programs.

Some math topics in this chapter might feel new or challenging at first, and that is completely okay! Don't worry or feel overwhelmed. The aim is to clearly show you how math in Python works, so you can comfortably use it according to your own needs and at your own pace.

Importance of Math in Programming

Math is the foundation of good programming. It helps you write better and clearer code, solve problems quickly, and understand how things work behind the scenes. Math helps you in different ways, such as:

- Doing simple and complex calculations clearly.
- Understanding and using step-by-step instructions (algorithms).
- Creating graphics and animations for games.
- Solving problems in Artificial Intelligence (AI) and Machine Learning (ML).
- Analyzing data clearly and showing results visually.

In short, math gives programmers the tools they need to solve different problems easily and clearly.

Overview of Python's Math Capabilities

Python is very good for math because it is easy to learn and has many built-in tools. Python helps you perform math tasks such as:

- Simple calculations such as addition, subtraction, multiplication, and division.
- Comparing numbers and making logical decisions.
- Doing advanced math with special Python tools.
- Working with data clearly and doing statistical calculations.
- Handling matrices and vectors, which are important in data science and AI.

Python's simple language and clear rules make math tasks easy, even for beginners. Python also offers extra libraries and tools that make working with math even simpler.

Introduction to `math` Module

Python has a special tool called the **`math`** module that helps you do different kinds of math easily. It provides ready-made functions for many types of math calculations.

Key Features of the math Module:

- **Basic Math:** Simple tasks such as finding square roots, rounding numbers, or getting absolute values (removing negative signs).
- **Powers and Logarithms:** Calculating powers (exponents) or logarithms easily.
- **Trigonometry:** Calculating angles and sides using functions such as sine (sin), cosine (cos), and tangent (tan).
- **Math Constants:** Common constants such as Pi ($\pi = 3.14159...$) and Euler's number ($e = 2.71828...$).

Using the math Module:

Before using the **`math`** module, you need to import it into your Python program:

```
import math

# Examples using math module
print(math.sqrt(16))    # Output: 4.0 (square root of 16)
print(math.ceil(4.2))   # Output: 5 (round up)
print(math.pi)          # Output: 3.141592653589793 (Pi value)
```

The math module simplifies math, so you can solve programming problems quickly and accurately.

Basic Mathematical Operations

Let us start with basic math operations commonly used in Python programming.

Addition, Subtraction, Multiplication, and Division:

Python uses simple operators (+, -, *, /) for basic calculations. The math module also provides extra functions for advanced calculations.

Example:

```
a = 10
b = 5

# Addition
print(a + b)  # Output: 15

# Subtraction
print(a - b)  # Output: 5

# Multiplication
print(a * b)  # Output: 50

# Division
print(a / b)  # Output: 2.0
```

Exponentiation and Modulo Operations

- **Exponentiation:** Raising numbers to powers (such as squaring or cubing). Use the ** operator or `math.pow()` function.
- **Modulo:** Finding the remainder after division, using %.

Example:

```
import math

    # Exponentiation
    print(math.pow(a, b))  # Output: 100000.0 (10 raised to the power of 5)

    # Modulo (Remainder)
    print(b % a)    # Output: 5 (remainder when 5 is divided by 10)
```

Order of Operations (PEMDAS)

When doing multiple operations, Python follows rules called PEMDAS:

- Parentheses first
- Exponents next
- Multiplication and Division (left to right)
- Addition and Subtraction (left to right)

Example:

```
result = 3 + 2 * 2 ** 2 - 4 / 2

# Step-by-step calculation:
# 2 ** 2 = 4
# 2 * 4 = 8
# 4 / 2 = 2
# Finally: 3 + 8 - 2 = 9

print(result)  # Output: 9
```

Understanding these math basics helps you write clear, accurate, and efficient Python code. The math module helps you easily perform even more advanced calculations when needed.

Practical Exercise: Basic Calculations

Let us put everything you have learned about mathematical operations and how to use the math module in practice. This exercise will help you understand how to use these operations in a real-world context.

Task Description:

Create a Python application that questions the user for two numbers and then does basic arithmetic operations (addition, subtraction, multiplication, division, exponentiation, and modulus). This practice reinforces your comprehension of these procedures and how to use the math module efficiently.

Steps for the Exercise:

1. **Prompt for User Input**: Prompt the user to enter two digits.
2. **Perform basic operations**: Using basic operators and the arithmetic module, including addition, subtraction, multiplication, division, exponentiation, and modulo.

3. **Display Results**: Provide the user with the results of each operation.

```
import math

def perform_calculations():
    # Prompt user for input
    num1 = float(input("Enter the first number: "))
    num2 = float(input("Enter the second number: "))

    # Perform operations
    addition = num1 + num2
    subtraction = num1 - num2
    multiplication = num1 * num2
    division = num1 / num2
    exponentiation = math.pow(num1, num2)
    modulo = num1 % num2

    # Display results
    print(f"Addition: {addition}")
    print(f"Subtraction: {subtraction}")
    print(f"Multiplication: {multiplication}")
    print(f"Division: {division}")
    print(f"Exponentiation: {exponentiation}")
    print(f"Modulo: {modulo}")

def main():
    perform_calculations()

if __name__ == "__main__":
    main()
```

Understanding the Code:

- **Function Definition:** The **perform_calculations** function provides essential functionality. It starts by inviting the user to enter two numbers, which are then converted into floats for numerical operations.
- **Basic Operations:** The function does addition, subtraction, multiplication, and division with basic operators. Exponentiation is performed using the **math.pow** function, while modulo operations are performed using the% operator.
- **Display results:** The outcomes of each operation are printed to the console, giving the user clear feedback.
- **Program execution:** The main function calls **perform_calculations**, and the standard if __ name__ equals "__main__": The check ensures that main runs when the script is invoked directly, but not when imported as a module.

This lesson teaches how to apply basic mathematical operations in practice, utilizing both basic operators and the math module. Completing it will give you a better grasp of how to conduct and apply these operations in Python programming.

Advanced Mathematical Functions

Now that you have practiced basic math operations clearly, let us move on to more advanced mathematical functions that Python offers. Python's math module gives you many useful functions to do advanced math clearly and easily. These functions are helpful in fields such as science, engineering, and data analysis. Let us explore some of these advanced functions step by step.

Functions for Powers and Logarithms

Python can help you easily calculate powers (exponents), roots, and logarithms:

- **`math.pow(x, y)`**: Calculates x raised to the power of y.
- **`math.sqrt(x)`**: Calculates the square root of x.
- **`math.exp(x)`**: Calculates e raised to the power of x (Euler's number).
- **`math.log(x, base)`**: Finds the logarithm of x with the chosen base. If no base is given, it calculates the natural log (base e).
- **`math.log10(x)`**: Finds the base-10 logarithm of x.

Example:

```
import math

x = 10
y = 2

print(f"{x} raised to {y}: {math.pow(x, y)}")  # Output: 100.0
print(f"Square root of {x}: {math.sqrt(x)}")  # Output: 3.1622776601683795
print(f"Exponential of {y}: {math.exp(y)}")   # Output: 7.3890560989306495
print(f"Natural log of {x}: {math.log(x)}")   # Output: 2.302585092994046
print(f"Base-10 log of {x}: {math.log10(x)}") # Output: 1.0
```

Trigonometric Functions

These functions help you work with angles and triangles, used often in physics, engineering, and computer graphics:

- **`math.sin(x)`**: Finds the sine of angle x.
- **`math.cos(x)`**: Finds the cosine of angle x.
- **`math.tan(x)`**: Finds the tangent of angle x.
- **`math.asin(x)`**: Finds the angle whose sine is x.
- **`math.acos(x)`**: Finds the angle whose cosine is x.
- **`math.atan(x)`**: Finds the angle whose tangent is x.

Example:

```
angle = math.pi / 4  # 45 degrees in radians

print(f"Sine of 45 degrees: {math.sin(angle)}")         # Output: 0.7071067811865475
print(f"Cosine of 45 degrees: {math.cos(angle)}")       # Output: 0.7071067811865476
print(f"Tangent of 45 degrees: {math.tan(angle)}")      # Output: 0.9999999999999999
print(f"Arc sine of 0.7071: {math.asin(0.7071)}")       # Output: 0.7853981633974483
```

Hyperbolic Functions

These functions are similar to trigonometric functions but are used for different types of curves called hyperbolas:

- **`math.sinh(x)`**: Finds the hyperbolic sine of x.
- **`math.cosh(x)`**: Finds the hyperbolic cosine of x.
- **`math.tanh(x)`**: Finds the hyperbolic tangent of x.
- **`math.asinh(x)`**: Finds the inverse hyperbolic sine of x.

- **`math.acosh(x)`**: Finds the inverse hyperbolic cosine of x.
- **`math.atanh(x)`**: Finds the inverse hyperbolic tangent of x.

Example:

```
x = 1

print(f"Hyperbolic sine of {x}: {math.sinh(x)}")    # Output: 1.1752011936438014
print(f"Hyperbolic cosine of {x}: {math.cosh(x)}")  # Output: 1.5430806348152437
print(f"Hyperbolic tangent of {x}: {math.tanh(x)}") # Output: 0.7615941559557649
print(f"Inverse hyperbolic sine of {x}: {math.asinh(x)}")  # Output:
0.881373587019543
print(f"Inverse hyperbolic cosine of 1.543: {math.acosh(1.543)}")  # Approximate
output: 1.0
print(f"Inverse hyperbolic tangent of 0.9: {math.atanh(0.9)}")    # Output:
1.4722194895832204
```

These advanced math functions let you perform many different types of calculations quickly, clearly, and accurately with Python.

Practical Exercise: Using Advanced Math Functions

In the previous part, you have looked at some of the more advanced mathematical functions available through Python's math module. Now, let us put these functions to use with an exercise that will help you understand these sophisticated computations.

Create a Python software that requests the user for a number and uses advanced mathematical functions to make several calculations. The software should have computations for powers, logarithms, trigonometric functions, and hyperbolic functions.

Steps for the Exercise:

1. Prompt the user to input a number.
2. Use the math module to do advanced calculations on input numbers, including square root, natural logarithm, sine, cosine, and hyperbolic sine.
3. Display the results of each calculation to the user.

```
import math

def perform_advanced_calculations():
    # Prompt user for input
    num = float(input("Enter a number: "))

    # Perform advanced calculations
    sqrt_result = math.sqrt(num)
    log_result = math.log(num)
    sin_result = math.sin(num)
    cos_result = math.cos(num)
    sinh_result = math.sinh(num)

    # Display results
    print(f"Square root of {num}: {sqrt_result}")
    print(f"Natural logarithm of {num}: {log_result}")
    print(f"Sine of {num} (in radians): {sin_result}")
    print(f"Cosine of {num} (in radians): {cos_result}")
    print(f"Hyperbolic sine of {num}: {sinh_result}")
```

```
def main():
    perform_advanced_calculations()

if __name__ == "__main__":
    main()
```

Understanding the Code

- **Function Definition:** The **perform_advanced_calculations** function provides basic functionality. It starts by inviting the user to enter a number, which is then converted into a float for numerical operations.
- **Advanced Calculations:** The function performs complex calculations using the math module, such as square root, natural logarithm, sine, cosine, and hyperbolic sine of the input value.
- **Display Results:** The results of each calculation are displayed on the console, providing direct feedback to the user.
- **Program Execution:** The main function invokes **perform_advanced_calculations**. The standard if __name__ == "__main__": check ensures that main executes when the script is evaluated directly, but not when imported as a module.

This assignment uses the math module to show how complex mathematical functions can be applied in practice. Completing it will give you a better grasp of how to conduct and use sophisticated computations in Python programming.

Working with Complex Numbers

Now that you are comfortable with advanced math functions, let us explore how Python handles another important area, complex numbers. Complex numbers are special numbers used often in fields such as engineering, physics, and mathematics. They have two parts: a real part and an imaginary part. Python makes it easy to work with these numbers using the complex type. In Python, the imaginary part is written with a j.

Example:

```
# Creating complex numbers
z1 = 2 + 3j
z2 = 4 - 2j

print(z1)  # Output: (2+3j)
print(z2)  # Output: (4-2j)
```

Basic Operations with Complex Numbers

Python lets you easily perform basic math operations on complex numbers, just like regular numbers:

Example:

```
# Basic operations with complex numbers
z1 = 2 + 3j
z2 = 4 - 2j

addition = z1 + z2
subtraction = z1 - z2
multiplication = z1 * z2
division = z1 / z2

print(f"Addition: {addition}")          # Output: (6+1j)
print(f"Subtraction: {subtraction}")    # Output: (-2+5j)
```

```
print(f"Multiplication: {multiplication}") # Output: (14+8j)
print(f"Division: {division}")         # Output: (0.2+0.7j)
```

Using the cmath Module for Complex Mathematics

Python provides a special module called **cmath** that helps you do advanced calculations with complex numbers easily. The **cmath** module includes helpful functions for complex number calculations, such as:

- **cmath.sqrt(z)**: Finds the square root of a complex number.
- **cmath.exp(z)**: Calculates e raised to a complex number.
- **cmath.log(z, base)**: Calculates logarithms for complex numbers.
- **cmath.sin(z), cmath.cos(z), cmath.tan(z)**: Performs trigonometric functions on complex numbers.
- **cmath.sinh(z), cmath.cosh(z), cmath.tanh(z)**: Calculates hyperbolic functions on complex numbers.

Example:

```
import cmath

z = 1 + 2j

sqrt_z = cmath.sqrt(z)
exp_z = cmath.exp(z)
log_z = cmath.log(z)
sin_z = cmath.sin(z)
cos_z = cmath.cos(z)
sinh_z = cmath.sinh(z)

print(f"Square root of {z}: {sqrt_z}")      # Output: (1.272019649514069+0.786
1513777574233j)
print(f"Exponential of {z}: {exp_z}")       # Output: (-1.1312043837568135+2.4
717266720048188j)
print(f"Natural log of {z}: {log_z}")       # Output: (0.8047189562170503+1.10
71487177940904j)
print(f"Sine of {z}: {sin_z}")              # Output: (3.165778513216168+1.959
6010414216063j)
print(f"Cosine of {z}: {cos_z}")            # Output: (2.0327230070196656-
3.0518977991517997j)
print(f"Hyperbolic sine of {z}: {sinh_z}")  # Output: (1.9596010414216063+3.16
5778513216168j)
```

Understanding complex numbers and using the **cmath** module will help you easily solve mathematical and engineering problems with Python.

Practical Exercise: Complex Number Calculations

Let us apply what you have learned about working with complicated numbers in Python. This exercise will allow you to obtain practical experience with basic operations using the **cmath** module for complex number calculations.

Task Description:

Create a Python program that invites the user to enter a complex number before performing several complex number calculations. The program should include operations such as as addition, subtraction, multiplication, division, and different functions of the **cmath** module.

Steps for the Exercise

1. Prompt the user to enter a complicated number.
2. Perform basic operations such as addition, subtraction, multiplication, and division with a predefined complex number.
3. Use **cmath** Module Functions to find the square root, exponential, logarithm, sine, cosine, and hyperbolic sine of a complex value.
4. Display the results of each calculation to the user.

```
import cmath

def perform_complex_calculations():
        user_input = '3+5j'
        z = complex(user_input)
        predefined_z = 3 + 4j

        # Perform basic operations
        addition = z + predefined_z
        subtraction = z - predefined_z
        multiplication = z * predefined_z
        division = z / predefined_z

        # Use cmath module functions
        sqrt_z = cmath.sqrt(z)
        exp_z = cmath.exp(z)
        log_z = cmath.log(z)
        sin_z = cmath.sin(z)
        cos_z = cmath.cos(z)
        sinh_z = cmath.sinh(z)

        # Display results
        print(f"Addition: {addition}")
        print(f"Subtraction: {subtraction}")
        print(f"Multiplication: {multiplication}")
        print(f"Division: {division}")
        print(f"Square root of {z}: {sqrt_z}")
        print(f"Exponential of {z}: {exp_z}")
        print(f"Natural logarithm of {z}: {log_z}")
        print(f"Sine of {z}: {sin_z}")
        print(f"Cosine of {z}: {cos_z}")
        print(f"Hyperbolic sine of {z}: {sinh_z}")

def main():
        perform_complex_calculations()

if __name__ == "__main__":
        main()
```

Understanding the Code

- Function Definition: The **perform_complex_calculations** method provides basic functionality. It starts by inviting the user to enter a complex number, which is then converted into a complex type.
- Basic Operations: The function adds, subtracts, multiplies, and divides a preset complex number (3 + 4j).

- Use **cmath** module functions: To calculate complex numbers, including square root, exponential, logarithm, sine, cosine, and hyperbolic sine.
- Display Results: The results of each calculation are displayed on the console, providing direct feedback to the user.
- Program execution: The main function calls **perform_complex_calculations**, and the standard is if __name__ == "__main__": The check ensures that main runs when the script is invoked directly, but not when imported as a module.

This exercise covers the practical use of complex number operations and Python's **cmath** module. Completing it will give you a better grasp of how to conduct and use sophisticated computations in Python programming.

Statistics and Probability

Now that you have learned about complex numbers, let us see how Python can help you easily perform statistics and probability tasks.

Understanding statistics and probability is important for analyzing data, machine learning, and science. Python provides simple ways to perform these calculations clearly using built-in modules.

Basic Statistical Calculations

Python's statistics module helps you calculate important statistics about your data easily. You can find:

- **Mean**: The average value.
- **Median**: The middle value.
- **Mode**: The most frequent value.
- **Variance**: Shows how data points vary from the average.
- **Standard Deviation**: Measures how spread out the data is around the average.

Example:

```
import statistics

data = [1, 2, 3, 4, 5, 6, 7, 8, 9, 10]

mean = statistics.mean(data)
median = statistics.median(data)
mode = statistics.mode(data)  # Be careful: raises error if there's no mode.
variance = statistics.variance(data)
std_deviation = statistics.stdev(data)

print(f"Mean: {mean}")                    # Output: 5.5
print(f"Median: {median}")                # Output: 5.5
# Mode might raise an error if no value repeats.
print(f"Mode: {mode}")
print(f"Variance: {variance}")            # Output: 9.166666666666666
print(f"Standard Deviation: {std_deviation}") # Output: 3.0276503540974917
```

Generating Random Numbers and Simulating Probabilities

Python also helps you perform random operations using the random module. This is very useful for probability, simulations, and choosing random samples.

Here are common random module functions:

- **`random.random()`**: Gives a random decimal number between 0.0 and 1.0.
- **`random.randint(a, b)`**: Chooses a random integer between two numbers, including both endpoints.
- **`random.choice(seq)`**: Picks a random item from a list.
- **`random.sample(population, k)`**: Picks a set of unique random items from a list.
- **`random.shuffle(seq)`**: Randomly mixes up items in a list.
- **`random.gauss(mu, sigma)`**: Picks a random number based on the Gaussian (normal) distribution.

Example:

```
import random

# Generate random numbers
random_float = random.random()
random_int = random.randint(1, 10)
random_choice = random.choice(['apple', 'banana', 'cherry'])
random_sample = random.sample(range(1, 100), 5)
numbers = [1, 2, 3, 4, 5]
random.shuffle(numbers)
random_gaussian = random.gauss(0, 1)

print(f"Random Float: {random_float}")      # Random float between 0.0 and 1.0
print(f"Random Integer: {random_int}")       # Random integer between 1 and 10
print(f"Random Choice: {random_choice}")     # Randomly chosen fruit from the list
print(f"Random Sample: {random_sample}")     # Random list of 5 unique numbers
print(f"Shuffled List: {numbers}")          # Shuffled list of numbers
print(f"Random Gaussian: {random_gaussian}") # Random number from Gaussian dis-
tribution
```

Learning how to use these statistical and probability functions makes it easy for you to analyze data clearly and run reliable simulations, making Python a great tool for scientific computing and analysis.

Practical Exercise: Statistical Analysis and Randomness

Building on your understanding of statistics and probability, this practical exercise will teach you how to use these principles with Python's statistics and random modules. You will run statistical tests on a dataset and create random numbers to simulate probabilities.

Task Description:

Create a Python application to evaluate a dataset, calculate statistical metrics, and produce random numbers for simulated probability scenarios.

Steps for the Exercise:

1. **Generate a Dataset**: Create a dataset of random numbers.
2. **Calculate statistical measures**: It involves computing mean, median, mode, variance, and standard deviation of the given dataset.
3. **Simulate Random Events**: Use the random module to generate random integers and run probability simulations.
4. **Display results**: Provide the findings of the statistical analysis and random simulations.

```
import random
import statistics

def generate_dataset(size):
    """Generate a dataset of random numbers."""
    return [random.randint(1, 100) for _ in range(size)]

def analyze_dataset(data):
    """Calculate statistical measures for the dataset."""
    mean = statistics.mean(data)
    median = statistics.median(data)
    try:
        mode = statistics.mode(data)
    except statistics.StatisticsError:
        mode = "No unique mode found"
    variance = statistics.variance(data)
    std_deviation = statistics.stdev(data)

    return mean, median, mode, variance, std_deviation

def simulate_randomness():
    """Simulate random events."""
    random_float = random.random()
    random_int = random.randint(1, 10)
    random_choice = random.choice(['apple', 'banana', 'cherry'])
    random_sample = random.sample(range(1, 100), 5)
    numbers = [1, 2, 3, 4, 5]
    random.shuffle(numbers)
    random_gaussian = random.gauss(0, 1)

    return random_float, random_int, random_choice, random_sample, numbers, random_
gaussian

def display_results(mean, median, mode, variance, std_deviation, randomness):
    """Display the results of the statistical analysis and randomness simulation."""
    print("Statistical Analysis of Dataset:")
    print(f"Mean: {mean}")
    print(f"Median: {median}")
    print(f"Mode: {mode}")
    print(f"Variance: {variance}")
    print(f"Standard Deviation: {std_deviation}")
    print("\nRandomness Simulation:")
    print(f"Random Float: {randomness[0]}")
    print(f"Random Integer: {randomness[1]}")
    print(f"Random Choice: {randomness[2]}")
    print(f"Random Sample: {randomness[3]}")
    print(f"Shuffled List: {randomness[4]}")
    print(f"Random Gaussian: {randomness[5]}")

def main():
    dataset = generate_dataset(100)
    mean, median, mode, variance, std_deviation = analyze_dataset(dataset)
    randomness = simulate_randomness()
    display_results(mean, median, mode, variance, std_deviation, randomness)

if __name__ == "__main__":
    main()
```

Understanding the Code:

- **Function Definitions:**
    - **generate_dataset(size):** Creates a dataset of random numbers from 1 to 100.
    - **analyze_dataset(data):** The function **analyze_dataset(data)** calculates the mean, median, mode, variance, and standard deviation of the dataset. Handles the situation in which no unique mode is detected.
    - **simulate_randomness():** The function **simulate_randomness()** generates random numbers and simulates randomness using random module functions.
    - **display_results:** The function **display_results(mean, median, mode, variance, std_deviation**, randomness) shows the results of statistical analysis and randomness simulation.
- **Main function:**
    - Creates a dataset of 100 random integers.
    - Analyzes data to calculate statistical metrics.
    - Simulates random events with the random module.
    - Displays results clearly and concisely.
- **Program Execution**: The main function orchestrates the entire process, and the if __name__ == "__main__": check makes sure that main runs when the script is executed directly.

This assignment gives you practical experience with statistical analysis and randomness simulation in Python, enhancing your comprehension of these important concepts.

Working with Fractions and Decimals

Now that you have learned about statistics and random numbers, let us see how Python can handle precise calculations using fractions and decimals.

Sometimes, your programs need very accurate calculations. Python helps you do these calculations easily and clearly using fractions and decimals.

Introduction to the `fractions` Module

Python has a special module called fractions that helps you work with fractions. Fractions clearly show numbers as ratios of two integers (such as ½ or ¾).

Example:

```
from fractions import Fraction

# Creating fractions
frac1 = Fraction(3, 4)
frac2 = Fraction(1, 2)

print(frac1)  # Output: 3/4
print(frac2)  # Output: ½
```

Math with Fractions

You can easily do arithmetic (addition, subtraction, multiplication, and division) with fractions in Python:

Example:

```
from fractions import Fraction

frac1 = Fraction(3, 4)
frac2 = Fraction(1, 2)

# Math operations with fractions
addition = frac1 + frac2
subtraction = frac1 - frac2
multiplication = frac1 * frac2
division = frac1 / frac2

print(f"Addition: {addition}")              # Output: 5/4
print(f"Subtraction: {subtraction}")        # Output: 1/4
print(f"Multiplication: {multiplication}") # Output: 3/8
print(f"Division: {division}")              # Output: 3/2
```

Introduction to the `decimal` Module

Python also has a decimal module that helps with calculations needing exact decimal values, which is important in finance or precise measurements.

Example:

```
from decimal import Decimal

# Creating decimals
dec1 = Decimal('0.1')
dec2 = Decimal('0.2')

print(dec1)  # Output: 0.1
print(dec2)  # Output: 0.2
```

Handling Precision with Decimals

The decimal module lets you control how accurate your calculations are by setting precision. You can use it to perform very accurate math:

Example:

```
from decimal import Decimal, getcontext

# Set precision to 6 decimal places
getcontext().prec = 6

dec1 = Decimal('1.123456')
dec2 = Decimal('2.654321')

# Math operations with decimals
addition = dec1 + dec2
subtraction = dec1 - dec2
multiplication = dec1 * dec2
division = dec1 / dec2

print(f"Addition: {addition}")              # Output: 3.77778
print(f"Subtraction: {subtraction}")        # Output: -1.53087
print(f"Multiplication: {multiplication}") # Output: 2.98408
print(f"Division: {division}")              # Output: 0.423074
```

Using fractions and decimals helps you get clear and precise results, which is essential in science, finance, and other areas where accuracy matters.

Practical Exercise: Precision Arithmetic

Building on your understanding of fractions and decimals, this practical exercise will teach you how to use these concepts to accomplish accurate arithmetic operations. This lesson will highlight the significance of using the fractions and decimal modules in Python for precise and accurate computations.

Task Description:

Create a Python program that uses the fractions and decimal modules to execute arithmetic operations. The program will emphasize the distinction between normal floating-point arithmetic and precision arithmetic.

Steps for the Exercise:

1. **Perform Basic Arithmetic with Floating-Point Numbers:** Use conventional float operations to examine results.
2. **Perform Arithmetic with Fractions:** Use the fractions module to execute arithmetic operations and compare results.
3. **Perform arithmetic with decimals:** Use the decimal module for precise operations.
4. **Display results:** Display the results of each arithmetic operation to show the differences.

```
from fractions import Fraction
from decimal import Decimal, getcontext

def float_arithmetic(a, b):
    addition = a + b
    subtraction = a - b
    multiplication = a * b
    division = a / b
    return addition, subtraction, multiplication, division

def fraction_arithmetic(a, b):
    frac1 = Fraction(a)
    frac2 = Fraction(b)
    addition = frac1 + frac2
    subtraction = frac1 - frac2
    multiplication = frac1 * frac2
    division = frac1 / frac2
    return addition, subtraction, multiplication, division

def decimal_arithmetic(a, b, precision):
    getcontext().prec = precision
    dec1 = Decimal(a)
    dec2 = Decimal(b)
    addition = dec1 + dec2
    subtraction = dec1 - dec2
    multiplication = dec1 * dec2
    division = dec1 / dec2
    return addition, subtraction, multiplication, division

def display_results(float_results, fraction_results, decimal_results):
    operations = ["Addition", "Subtraction", "Multiplication", "Division"]
```

```
    print("Floating-Point Arithmetic Results:")
    for op, result in zip(operations, float_results):
        print(f"{op}: {result}")
    print("\nFraction Arithmetic Results:")
    for op, result in zip(operations, fraction_results):
        print(f"{op}: {result}")
    print("\nDecimal Arithmetic Results (with specified precision):")
    for op, result in zip(operations, decimal_results):
        print(f"{op}: {result}")

def main():
    a = 1.123456
    b = 2.654321
    precision = 6

    float_results = float_arithmetic(a, b)
    fraction_results = fraction_arithmetic(a, b)
    decimal_results = decimal_arithmetic(str(a), str(b), precision)

    display_results(float_results, fraction_results, decimal_results)

if __name__ == "__main__":
    main()
```

Understanding the Code

- **Function Definitions:**
  - **`float_arithmetic(a, b)`**: The function **`float_arithmetic(a, b)`** performs fundamental arithmetic operations on standard float values.
  - **`Fraction_arithmetic(a, b)`**: Uses the fractions module to perform arithmetic operations on fractions.
  - **`Decimal_arithmetic(a, b, precision)`**: Uses the decimal module to perform arithmetic with a specific precision.
  - **`display_results`**: The **`display_results`** function compares arithmetic results (float, fraction, and decimal).
- **Main Function:**
  - Defines a and b for operations and specifies accuracy for decimal calculations.
  - Calls each arithmetic function and saves the results.
  - Display results with the **`display_results`** function.
- **Program Execution**: The main function manages the entire process, and the if __name__ == "__main__": check ensures that main is called when the script is run directly.

  This exercise uses the fractions and decimal modules to demonstrate how precision arithmetic can be applied in practice. After completing it, you will understand the significance of using these modules for precise and accurate computations in Python programming.

Linear Algebra

Now that you have learned how to handle precise calculations with fractions and decimals, let us explore linear algebra in Python, which is important in many scientific and technical fields.

Linear algebra is the study of vectors, matrices, and transformations. It is very useful in fields such as machine learning, computer graphics, and data analysis. Python makes working with linear algebra easy using the NumPy library.

Introduction to the numpy Library

NumPy is a powerful Python library that helps you easily work with large groups of numbers, such as vectors and matrices. NumPy makes calculations fast and simple.

First, you need to install NumPy:

```
pip install numpy
```

Working with Vectors and Matrices

In NumPy, vectors and matrices are represented as arrays. Here is how you create them clearly in Python:

Example:

```
import numpy as np

# Creating vectors
vector1 = np.array([1, 2, 3])
vector2 = np.array([4, 5, 6])

# Creating matrices
matrix1 = np.array([[1, 2, 3],
                    [4, 5, 6],
                    [7, 8, 9]])

matrix2 = np.array([[9, 8, 7],
                    [6, 5, 4],
                    [3, 2, 1]])

print("Vector 1:", vector1)
print("Vector 2:", vector2)
print("Matrix 1:\n", matrix1)
print("Matrix 2:\n", matrix2)
```

Basic Matrix Operations with NumPy

NumPy makes it easy to perform basic operations on matrices, such as addition, subtraction, multiplication, and transposition.

Example:

```
import numpy as np

# Creating matrices
matrix1 = np.array([[1, 2, 3],
                    [4, 5, 6],
                    [7, 8, 9]])

matrix2 = np.array([[9, 8, 7],
                    [6, 5, 4],
                    [3, 2, 1]])

# Matrix addition
matrix_addition = matrix1 + matrix2

# Matrix subtraction
matrix_subtraction = matrix1 - matrix2
```

```
# Element-wise multiplication
matrix_multiplication_elementwise = matrix1 * matrix2

# Dot product multiplication
matrix_multiplication_dot = np.dot(matrix1, matrix2)

# Matrix transposition
matrix_transpose = np.transpose(matrix1)

print("Matrix Addition:\n", matrix_addition)
print("Matrix Subtraction:\n", matrix_subtraction)
print("Element-wise Multiplication:\n", matrix_multiplication_elementwise)
print("Dot Product Multiplication:\n", matrix_multiplication_dot)
print("Matrix Transposition:\n", matrix_transpose)
```

Understanding linear algebra and how to use NumPy clearly helps you easily solve complex mathematical problems. These skills are valuable in data analysis, scientific research, and various technical areas.

Practical Exercise: Linear Algebra using NumPy

Building on your understanding of linear algebra and the numpy library, this practical exercise will teach you how to use these principles to execute various vector and matrix operations. This exercise will demonstrate numpy's capabilities for linear algebra computations.

Task Description:

Create a Python application that uses the numpy package to perform various linear algebra procedures. The program will feature vector operations, matrix addition, matrix multiplication, and matrix transposition.

Steps for the Exercise

1. **Create Vectors and Matrices:** Define vectors and matrices with NumPy.
2. **Perform Vector Operations:** Calculate the dot and cross products of two vectors.
3. **Matrix Operations:** Calculate sum, difference, element-wise product, and dot product between two matrices.
4. **Transpose a Matrix:** Calculate the transpose of a matrix.
5. **Display results:** Output the outcomes of each operation.

```
import numpy as np

def vector_operations(v1, v2):
    """Perform vector operations: dot product and cross product."""
    dot_product = np.dot(v1, v2)
    cross_product = np.cross(v1, v2)
    return dot_product, cross_product

def matrix_operations(m1, m2):
    """Perform matrix operations: addition, subtraction, element-wise
multiplication, and dot product."""
    addition = m1 + m2
    subtraction = m1 - m2
    elementwise_multiplication = m1 * m2
```

```
        dot_product = np.dot(m1, m2)
        return addition, subtraction, elementwise_multiplication, dot_product

    def transpose_matrix(matrix):
        """Transpose a matrix."""
        return np.transpose(matrix)

    def display_results(vector_results, matrix_results, transpose_result):
        """Display the results of the vector and matrix operations."""
        dot_product, cross_product = vector_results
        addition, subtraction, elementwise_multiplication, dot_product_matrix =
    matrix_results

        print("Vector Operations:")
        print(f"Dot Product: {dot_product}")
        print(f"Cross Product: {cross_product}")

        print("\nMatrix Operations:")
        print(f"Addition:\n{addition}")
        print(f"Subtraction:\n{subtraction}")
        print(f"Element-wise Multiplication:\n{elementwise_multiplication}")
        print(f"Dot Product:\n{dot_product_matrix}")

        print("\nMatrix Transposition:")
        print(f"Transpose:\n{transpose_result}")

    def main():
        # Define vectors
        vector1 = np.array([1, 2, 3])
        vector2 = np.array([4, 5, 6])

        # Define matrices
        matrix1 = np.array([[1, 2, 3], [4, 5, 6], [7, 8, 9]])
        matrix2 = np.array([[9, 8, 7], [6, 5, 4], [3, 2, 1]])

        # Perform operations
        vector_results = vector_operations(vector1, vector2)
        matrix_results = matrix_operations(matrix1, matrix2)
        transpose_result = transpose_matrix(matrix1)

        # Display results
        display_results(vector_results, matrix_results, transpose_result)

    if __name__ == "__main__":
        main()
```

Understanding the Code:

- **Function Definitions:**
    - **`vector_operations(v1, v2)`:** The function **`vector_operations(v1, v2)`** computes the dot and cross product of two vectors using numpy.
    - **`Matrix_operations(m1, m2)`:** Performs sum, difference, element-wise product, and dot product of two matrices with numpy.
    - **`transpose_matrix(matrix)`:** The function **`transpose_matrix(matrix)`** computes the transpose of a matrix using NumPy.

  - o **display_results**: The function **display_results(vector_results**, **matrix_results**, **transpose_result)** displays the results of vector and matrix operations.
- **Main Function:**
  - o Defines vectors (vector1, vector2) and matrices (matrix1, matrix2) for operations.
  - o Calls each operation function and saves the results.
  - o Display results with the **display_results** function.
- **Program Execution**: The main function manages the entire process, and the if __name__ == "__main__": check ensures that main is called when the script is run directly.

This lesson explains how to use linear algebra in practice using the numpy library. Completing it will provide you hands-on experience with vector and matrix operations, strengthening your understanding of linear algebra in Python programming.

Common Mistakes and Best Practices

When you do math in Python, it is easy to make some common mistakes that can lead to incorrect results. Let us look at these mistakes and learn how to avoid them.

Common Mistakes in Math Calculations

- **Floating-Point Precision Issues:**
  - o **Mistake**: Numbers with decimals can sometimes give small rounding errors because computers store them differently.
  - o **Solution**: Use Python's decimal module when you need exact calculations, especially in money-related tasks.
- **Integer Division Mistakes:**
  - o **Mistake**: Dividing two integers might give unexpected results, especially if you use older Python code (Python 2).
  - o **Solution**: Always use regular division (a/b) or clearly convert integers to decimals (float(a)/b) to get accurate results.
- **Overflow and Underflow Errors:**
  - o **Mistake**: Using numbers that are too big or too small for Python's default number types can lead to errors or incorrect results.
  - o **Solution**: Use libraries such as NumPy, which handle larger number ranges well and can warn you about these issues.

Best Practices for Accurate Math Calculations

Here are some important tips to make sure your math calculations in Python stay accurate:

- **Choose the right data type:**
  - o Use integers (int) for whole numbers.
  - o Use floats (float) for general numbers with decimals.
  - o Use Decimal from Python's decimal module for very precise calculations.
- **Set consistent precision:**
  - o When using decimals, always set precision clearly with **getcontext().prec** to keep your calculations accurate.

- **Don't hard-code constants:**
  - Avoid typing numbers such as Pi directly into your code. Instead, use built-in constants such as `math.pi`.
- **Handle math errors clearly:**
  - Use try and except blocks to catch errors, such as division by zero or overflow, so your program does not crash unexpectedly.
- **Always test your math calculations:**
  - Check your program with different inputs, including unusual cases, to make sure your calculations always produce correct results.

By knowing these common mistakes and best practices, you can write Python programs that perform math clearly, accurately, and reliably.

Exercises and Challenges: Practice Problems and Solutions

Now that you have learned how Python can help you easily handle many different types of math, it is time to practice your skills with these clear and useful exercises.

Practice Problem 1: Basic Vector Operations

Task: Perform basic vector operations using numpy.

Challenge: Write a script called `basic_vector_operations.py` that:

- Creates two vectors.
- Calculates the dot product of the vectors.
- Calculates the cross product of the vectors.

Practice Problem 2: Basic Matrix Operations

Task: Perform basic matrix operations using numpy.

Challenge: Write a script called `basic_matrix_operations.py` that:

- Creates two matrices.
- Performs matrix addition.
- Performs matrix subtraction.
- Performs element-wise multiplication of the matrices.
- Performs matrix multiplication (dot product) of the matrices.

Practice Problem 3: Working with Fractions

Task: Perform arithmetic operations with fractions.

Challenge: Write a script called `fraction_operations.py` that:

- Creates two fractions.
- Adds the fractions.
- Subtracts the fractions.
- Multiplies the fractions.
- Divides the fractions.
- Prints the results of each operation.

Practice Problem 4: Working with Decimals

Task: Perform precise arithmetic operations using the decimal module.

Challenge: Write a script called **`decimal_operations.py`** that:

- Sets the precision for decimal operations.
- Creates two decimal numbers.
- Adds the decimal numbers.
- Subtracts the decimal numbers.
- Multiplies the decimal numbers.
- Divides the decimal numbers.
- Prints the results of each operation with the specified precision.

Practice Problem 5: Statistical Analysis

Task: Perform basic statistical analysis on a dataset.

Challenge: Write a script called **`statistical_analysis.py`** that:

- Creates a dataset of random numbers.
- Calculates the mean, median, mode, variance, and standard deviation of the dataset.
- Prints the results of each statistical measure.

Solutions to Practice Problems

Now that you have attempted the practice problems, let us walk through the solutions.

Practice Problem 1: Basic Vector Operations

```
basic_vector_operations.py
import numpy as np

def basic_vector_operations():
    # Create two vectors
    vector1 = np.array([1, 2, 3])
    vector2 = np.array([4, 5, 6])

    # Calculate the dot product of the vectors
    dot_product = np.dot(vector1, vector2)
    print(f"Dot Product: {dot_product}")

    # Calculate the cross product of the vectors
    cross_product = np.cross(vector1, vector2)
    print(f"Cross Product: {cross_product}")

# Execute the function if the script is run directly
if __name__ == "__main__":
    basic_vector_operations()
```

Practice Problem 2: Basic Matrix Operations

```
basic_matrix_operations.py
import numpy as np

def basic_matrix_operations():
    # Create two matrices
```

```
        matrix1 = np.array([[1, 2, 3], [4, 5, 6], [7, 8, 9]])
        matrix2 = np.array([[9, 8, 7], [6, 5, 4], [3, 2, 1]])

        # Perform matrix addition
        addition = matrix1 + matrix2
        print(f"Matrix Addition:\n{addition}")

        # Perform matrix subtraction
        subtraction = matrix1 - matrix2
        print(f"Matrix Subtraction:\n{subtraction}")

        # Perform element-wise multiplication of the matrices
        elementwise_multiplication = matrix1 * matrix2
        print(f"Element-wise Multiplication:\n{elementwise_multiplication}")

        # Perform matrix multiplication (dot product) of the matrices
        dot_product = np.dot(matrix1, matrix2)
        print(f"Dot Product Matrix Multiplication:\n{dot_product}")

    # Execute the function if the script is run directly
    if __name__ == "__main__":
        basic_matrix_operations()
```

Practice Problem 3: Working with Fractions

```
fraction_operations.py
from fractions import Fraction

def fraction_operations():
    # Create two fractions
    frac1 = Fraction(3, 4)
    frac2 = Fraction(1, 2)

    # Perform arithmetic operations with fractions
    addition = frac1 + frac2
    subtraction = frac1 - frac2
    multiplication = frac1 * frac2
    division = frac1 / frac2

    # Print the results of each operation
    print(f"Addition: {addition}")
    print(f"Subtraction: {subtraction}")
    print(f"Multiplication: {multiplication}")
    print(f"Division: {division}")

# Execute the function if the script is run directly
if __name__ == "__main__":
    fraction_operations()
```

Practice Problem 4: Working with Decimals

```
decimal_operations.py
from decimal import Decimal, getcontext

def decimal_operations():
    # Set the precision for decimal operations
    getcontext().prec = 6

    # Create two decimal numbers
```

```
    dec1 = Decimal('1.123456')
    dec2 = Decimal('2.654321')

    # Perform arithmetic operations with decimals
    addition = dec1 + dec2
    subtraction = dec1 - dec2
    multiplication = dec1 * dec2
    division = dec1 / dec2

    # Print the results of each operation with the specified precision
    print(f"Addition: {addition}")
    print(f"Subtraction: {subtraction}")
    print(f"Multiplication: {multiplication}")
    print(f"Division: {division}")

# Execute the function if the script is run directly
if __name__ == "__main__":
    decimal_operations()
```

Practice Problem 5: Statistical Analysis

```
statistical_analysis.py
import random
import statistics

def statistical_analysis():
    # Create a dataset of random numbers
    dataset = [random.randint(1, 100) for _ in range(100)]

    # Calculate the mean, median, mode, variance, and standard deviation of 
the dataset
    mean = statistics.mean(dataset)
    median = statistics.median(dataset)
    try:
        mode = statistics.mode(dataset)
    except statistics.StatisticsError:
        mode = "No unique mode found"
    variance = statistics.variance(dataset)
    std_deviation = statistics.stdev(dataset)

    # Print the results of each statistical measure
    print(f"Mean: {mean}")
    print(f"Median: {median}")
    print(f"Mode: {mode}")
    print(f"Variance: {variance}")
    print(f"Standard Deviation: {std_deviation}")

# Execute the function if the script is run directly
if __name__ == "__main__":
    statistical_analysis()
```

Conclusion

In this chapter, you have learned how Python makes different kinds of math simple and clear. You started with basic calculations, then explored advanced math functions, complex numbers, and simple ways to perform statistical analysis. You also practiced accurate calculations with fractions and decimals and learned how to handle vectors and matrices using linear algebra with NumPy.

These new skills help you clearly and accurately solve math problems in Python, making your programming stronger and more reliable.

In the upcoming chapter you will learn how to install, update, and remove Python packages, manage project requirements, and organize your projects clearly using virtual environments.

Till then, keep calm and let's tame the Python!

Multiple-Choice Questions

Test your understanding of the concepts covered in this chapter with the following multiple-choice questions.

1. Which function is used to create a numpy array?
   a. `np.create()`
   b. `np.array()`
   c. `np.matrix()`
   d. `np.ndarray()`
2. What does the function `np.dot()` compute when applied to two vectors?
   a. Cross product
   b. Dot product
   c. Element-wise product
   d. Transpose
3. Which function in the `fractions` module creates a fraction from two integers?
   a. `Fraction.from_float()`
   b. `Fraction.create()`
   c. `Fraction()`
   d. `Fraction.convert()`
4. What is the output of Fraction(3, 4) + Fraction(1, 2)?
   a. 5/6
   b. 5/4
   c. 3/2
   d. 2/3
5. In the decimal module, which method sets the precision for decimal operations?
   a. `decimal.setprecision()`
   b. `decimal.precision()`
   c. `getcontext().prec`
   d. `Decimal.prec()`

6. What is the correct way to create a Decimal object for the number 1.23?
   a. Decimal(1.23)
   b. Decimal('1.23')
   c. Decimal([1, 2, 3])
   d. Decimal("1.23")
7. Which numpy function is used to calculate the cross product of two vectors?
   a. `np.dot()`
   b. `np.cross()`
   c. `np.prod()`
   d. `np.mul()`
8. How do you perform element-wise multiplication of two matrices in numpy?
   a. `np.dot(matrix1, matrix2)`
   b. `matrix1 * matrix2`
   c. `np.multiply(matrix1, matrix2)`
   d. `matrix1 + matrix2`
9. Which method in the statistics module calculates the mean of a dataset?
   a. `statistics.average()`
   b. `statistics.median()`
   c. `statistics.mean()`
   d. `statistics.mode()`
10. Which numpy function is used to transpose a matrix?
    a. `np.transpose()`
    b. `np.flip()`
    c. `np.rotate()`
    d. `np.switch()`

Answers

1. b
2. b
3. c
4. b
5. c
6. b
7. b

8. b
9. c
10. a

Points to Remember

- Programming requires understanding and applying mathematical procedures to solve issues and produce precise computations.
- The Python math module includes functions for basic operations such as addition, subtraction, multiplication, division, exponentiation, and modulo.
- Python's math module provides support for sophisticated functions such as logarithms, trigonometric, and hyperbolic.
- Python's `cmath` module enables complicated number operations, useful in domains such as engineering and physics.
- The statistics module calculates mean, median, mode, variance, and standard deviation. The random module generates random numbers and simulates probability.
- The fractions module enables accurate arithmetic with fractions, while the decimal module offers high precision calculations for financial applications.
- The `numpy` library is needed for performing vector and matrix operations such as addition, subtraction, element-wise multiplication, and dot product.
- Be mindful of floating-point precision concerns, integer division hazards, and overflow/underflow problems. To properly address these difficulties, use appropriate data formats and frameworks.
- Ensure precision settings are consistent, avoid hard-coding values, handle exceptions appropriately, and thoroughly test and validate mathematical computations.

Further Reading

For more learning, here are helpful resources you can explore:

1. **Python math module**: https://docs.python.org/3/library/math.html
2. **NumPy documentation**: https://numpy.org/doc/2.0/
3. **Python statistics module**: https://docs.python.org/3/library/statistics.html

CHAPTER 14
Managing Packages with PIP

Introduction

In *Chapter 8, Using Modules and Packages*, you learned how to structure your code effectively using Python modules and packages. You explored how to import built-in modules, create your own, and organize your projects using packages. Now, let us take the next step and learn how to efficiently manage these packages with PIP.

Understanding how to install and update packages is important because it helps keep your Python environment clean, organized, and up to date. Think of PIP as a helpful tool that allows you to quickly install the libraries you need, similar to adding new apps to your phone.

In this chapter, you will discover how to use PIP to install, upgrade, and remove Python packages. You will also learn how to manage project dependencies using a requirements file and how to work with virtual environments to keep different projects separate. You will also go over common mistakes and how to fix them so your projects run smoothly.

By the end of this chapter, you will feel confident managing Python packages and keeping your coding environment well-maintained. Let us dive into the world of PIP and learn how to handle Python packages efficiently!

Structure

In this chapter, the following topics will be covered:

- Introduction to PIP
    - Understanding PIP
    - Importance of Package Management
    - Overview of Python Package Index (PyPI)
- Installing PIP
    - Checking if PIP is Installed
    - Installing PIP if it is not Available
    - Upgrading PIP to the Latest Version
- Basic PIP Commands
    - Installing Packages
    - Uninstalling Packages
    - Upgrading Packages
    - Listing installed Packages

    - Showing Package Details
    - Practical Exercise: Using Basic PIP Commands
- Working with Requirements Files
    - Creating a Requirements File
    - Installing Packages from a Requirements File
    - Freezing Installed Packages to a Requirements File
    - Practical Exercise: Managing Requirements Files
- Virtual Environments
    - Introduction to Virtual Environments
    - Creating and Activating Virtual Environments
    - Managing Packages Within a Virtual Environment
    - Deactivating and Deleting Virtual Environments
    - Practical Exercise: Working with Virtual Environments
- Common Mistakes and Best Practices
    - Avoiding Common Mistakes When Using PIP
    - Using Virtual Environments for Project Isolation
    - Regularly Updating Packages
    - Checking for Package Vulnerabilities
    - Practical Exercise: Applying Best Practices
- Troubleshooting Common Issues
    - Common Installation Issues and Their Solutions
    - Resolving Dependency Conflicts
    - Handling Broken Installations
    - Practical Exercise: Troubleshooting PIP Issues
- Advanced PIP Usage
    - Customizing PIP Configuration
    - Using PIP with Private Repositories
    - Practical Exercise: Advanced PIP Techniques
- Exercises and Challenges: Practice Problems and Solutions

Introduction to PIP

In Python, you often need extra tools and libraries to help you build better programs. Instead of adding them manually, you can use PIP, which makes package management easy and fast. Let us explore what PIP is and why it is important.

Understanding PIP

PIP stands for "**Pip Installs Packages**." It is a tool that helps install and manage extra Python libraries that are not included by default. Think of it as an app store for Python, just like you download apps on your phone, PIP allows you to download useful tools for your Python projects. With just a simple command, you can install, update, or remove software packages without any hassle.

Importance of Package Management

Managing packages properly is essential because it keeps your projects organized, updated, and error-free. Here is why PIP is useful:

- **Easy to Use**: You can install a package with just one command, saving time and effort.
- **Keeps Everything Compatible**: PIP ensures you get the right version of a package, preventing conflicts between different tools.
- **Easy Updates**: You can quickly update packages to get new features and security fixes.
- **Handles Dependencies**: Some packages need other packages to work. PIP automatically installs everything needed, so you do not have to worry about missing pieces.

Overview of Python Package Index (PyPI)

The Python Package Index (PyPI) is a huge online collection of Python libraries. It is where PIP gets packages from when you install them. PyPI contains thousands of useful tools for web development, data analysis, machine learning, and more.

When you install a package using PIP, it downloads it directly from PyPI. This gives you access to a wide variety of pre-built libraries that make programming easier and more efficient.

Installing PIP

In the last section, you have learned that PIP is a powerful tool for managing Python packages. Before using it, you need to check if PIP is already installed on your computer. If it is missing, don't worry, you can install it easily. Let us go step by step!

Checking if PIP is Installed

First, let us see if PIP is already on your computer. You can check this by using the terminal in Visual Studio Code.

To open the terminal:

1. Click `View` menu at the top.
2. Select `Terminal`.

Once the terminal is open, type this command and press *Enter*:

```
pip --version
```

If PIP is installed, you will see a message showing its version number, as shown here:

```
pip 23.0.1 from C:\Users\<YourName>\AppData\Local\Programs\Python\Python39\
lib\site-packages\pip (python 3.9)
```

```
C:\Users>pip --version
pip 23.2.1 from C:\Users      AppData\Local\Programs\Python\Python311\Lib\site-packages\pip (python 3.11)

C:\Users>
```

***Figure 14.1**: PIP version check*

This means PIP is already installed, and you can skip to the Upgrading PIP section.

However, if you see an error message saying that the command is not recognized, it means PIP is not installed. In that case, follow the next steps to install it.

Installing PIP if it is not Available

If PIP is missing, you can install it in just a few steps:

1. **Download the PIP Installer**
   a. Open your web browser and go to the official PIP installation page.
   b. Download the file called **`get-pip.py`**.
2. **Run the Installer**
   a. Open Visual Studio Code and go to the terminal.
   b. Navigate to the folder where **`get-pip.py`** is saved.
   c. Type this command and press *Enter*:

```
python get-pip.py
```

```
C:\Users\Public>python get-pip.py
Collecting pip
  Downloading pip-24.1.2-py3-none-any.whl.metadata (3.6 kB)
Downloading pip-24.1.2-py3-none-any.whl (1.8 MB)
   ---------------------------------------- 1.8/1.8 MB 5.1 MB/s eta 0:00:00
Installing collected packages: pip
  Attempting uninstall: pip
    Found existing installation: pip 23.2.1
    Uninstalling pip-23.2.1:
      Successfully uninstalled pip-23.2.1
Successfully installed pip-24.1.2

C:\Users\Public>
```

Figure 14.2: *Installation of PIP*

This command runs the script, and PIP will be installed on your system.

Upgrading PIP to the Latest Version

To make sure PIP works properly, you should keep it updated. An updated version gives you new features and security fixes.

To upgrade PIP, type this command in the terminal and press *Enter*:

```
python -m pip install --upgrade pip
```

This tells Python to update PIP to the latest version.

```
C:\Users\Public>python -m pip install --upgrade pip
Requirement already satisfied: pip in c:\users\     \appdata\local\programs\python\python311\lib\site-packages (23.2.1)
Collecting pip
  Obtaining dependency information for pip from https://files.pythonhosted.org/packages/e7/54/0c1c068542cee73d8863336e97
4fc881e608d0170f3af15d0c0f28644531/pip-24.1.2-py3-none-any.whl.metadata
  Downloading pip-24.1.2-py3-none-any.whl.metadata (3.6 kB)
Downloading pip-24.1.2-py3-none-any.whl (1.8 MB)
   ---------------------------------------- 1.8/1.8 MB 5.3 MB/s eta 0:00:00
Installing collected packages: pip
  Attempting uninstall: pip
    Found existing installation: pip 23.2.1
    Uninstalling pip-23.2.1:
      Successfully uninstalled pip-23.2.1
Successfully installed pip-24.1.2
```

Figure 14.3: *Upgrading PIP*

Basic PIP Commands

Now that you have installed and updated PIP, let us explore some basic commands to manage Python packages. With these commands, you can install new packages, remove unnecessary ones, update existing packages, list installed packages, and view details about a package.

Installing Packages

The most common use of PIP is to install a package. You can do this with a simple command:

```
pip install package-name
```

For example, if you want to install the **pandas** library, you just need to type:

```
pip install pandas
```

```
(base) C:\Users\      >pip install pandas
Collecting pandas
  Downloading pandas-2.2.2-cp310-cp310-win_amd64.whl (11.6 MB)
     ---------------------------------------- 11.6/11.6 MB 21.1 MB/s eta 0:00:00
Collecting tzdata>=2022.7
  Downloading tzdata-2024.1-py2.py3-none-any.whl (345 kB)
     ---------------------------------------- 345.4/345.4 kB 22.3 MB/s eta 0:00:00
Requirement already satisfied: numpy>=1.22.4 in c:\users\      \anaconda3\lib\site-packages (from pandas) (1.23.5)
Requirement already satisfied: pytz>=2020.1 in c:\users\      \anaconda3\lib\site-packages (from pandas) (2022.7)
Requirement already satisfied: python-dateutil>=2.8.2 in c:\users\      \anaconda3\lib\site-packages (from pandas) (2.8.2)
Requirement already satisfied: six>=1.5 in c:\users\      \anaconda3\lib\site-packages (from python-dateutil>=2.8.2->pandas) (1.16.0)
Installing collected packages: tzdata, pandas
Successfully installed pandas-2.2.2 tzdata-2024.1
```

Figure 14.4: *Installing python package using PIP*

PIP will then download and install the latest version of pandas from PyPI, making it ready to use in your Python project.

Uninstalling Packages

If you no longer need a package, you can remove it using:

```
pip uninstall package-name
```

For example, if you want to remove pandas, run:

```
pip uninstall pandas
```

```
(base) C:\Users      >pip uninstall pandas
Found existing installation: pandas 1.5.3
Uninstalling pandas-1.5.3:
  Would remove:
    c:\users      \anaconda3\lib\site-packages\pandas-1.5.3.dist-info\*
    c:\users      \anaconda3\lib\site-packages\pandas\*
Proceed (Y/n)? y
  Successfully uninstalled pandas-1.5.3
```

Figure 14.5: *Uninstalling python package using PIP*

This command will delete the package from your system so it no longer takes up space or causes conflicts.

Upgrading Packages

To update a package to its latest version, use:

```
pip install --upgrade package-name
```

For example, if you want to update pandas to the newest version available, run:

```
pip install --upgrade pandas
```

```
(base) C:\Users\      >pip install --upgrade pandas
Requirement already satisfied: pandas in c:\users\      \anaconda3\lib\site-packages (1.5.3)
Collecting pandas
  Using cached pandas-2.2.2-cp310-cp310-win_amd64.whl (11.6 MB)
Requirement already satisfied: python-dateutil>=2.8.2 in c:\users\      \anaconda3\lib\site-packages (from pandas) (2.8.2)
Requirement already satisfied: numpy>=1.22.4 in c:\users\      \anaconda3\lib\site-packages (from pandas) (1.23.5)
Requirement already satisfied: pytz>=2020.1 in c:\users\      \anaconda3\lib\site-packages (from pandas) (2022.7)
Requirement already satisfied: tzdata>=2022.7 in c:\users\      \anaconda3\lib\site-packages (from pandas) (2024.1)
Requirement already satisfied: six>=1.5 in c:\users\      \anaconda3\lib\site-packages (from python-dateutil>=2.8.2->pandas) (1.16.0)
Installing collected packages: pandas
  Attempting uninstall: pandas
    Found existing installation: pandas 1.5.3
    Uninstalling pandas-1.5.3:
      Successfully uninstalled pandas-1.5.3
Successfully installed pandas-2.2.2
```

Figure 14.6: *Upgrading python package using PIP*

This ensures that your packages stay up to date with the latest features and security fixes.

Listing Installed Packages

If you want to see all the packages installed on your system, use:

```
pip list
```

```
(base) C:\Users\      >pip list
Package                       Version
----------------------------- ---------------
aiohttp                       3.8.5
aiosignal                     1.3.1
alabaster                     0.7.12
anaconda-client               1.11.2
anaconda-navigator            2.4.0
anaconda-project              0.11.1
annotated-types               0.5.0
anyio                         3.7.1
appdirs                       1.4.4
argon2-cffi                   21.3.0
argon2-cffi-bindings          21.2.0
arrow                         1.2.3
astroid                       2.14.2
astropy                       5.1
asttokens                     2.0.5
async-timeout                 4.0.3
```

Figure 14.7: *Listing python package using PIP*

This command will display a list of all installed Python libraries, along with their versions. It helps you keep track of what's already installed.

Showing Package Details

To get detailed information about a package, such as its version, author, and dependencies, use:

```
pip show package-name
```

For example, to check details about the **requests** library, type:

```
pip show requests
```

```
(base) C:\Users\      >pip show requests
Name: requests
Version: 2.32.3
Summary: Python HTTP for Humans.
Home-page: https://requests.readthedocs.io
Author: Kenneth Reitz
Author-email: me@kennethreitz.org
License: Apache-2.0
Location: c:\users\      \anaconda3\lib\site-packages
Requires: certifi, charset-normalizer, idna, urllib3
Required-by: anaconda-client, anaconda-project, chromadb, conda, conda-build,
_server, langchain, langsmith, openai, panel, pooch, posthog, requests-file,
```

Figure 14.8: *Showing python package details using PIP*

This command helps you understand what each package does and whether it has any dependencies on other libraries.

Managing Python Packages with Ease

These basic PIP commands will help you install, update, and remove packages effortlessly. By using PIP effectively, you can keep your Python environment clean, organized, and up to date. Next, you will learn how to manage multiple package dependencies using a requirements file.

Practical Exercise: Using Basic PIP Commands

Now it is your chance to try utilizing the fundamental PIP commands. The following instructions will guide you through installing, uninstalling, updating, and managing Python packages. For this example, you will use the pandas library.

Exercise Steps:

1. **Install a Package**
   a. Open the terminal in Visual Studio Code.
   b. Type the following command to install the requests library:
   ```
   pip install requests
   ```
   c. Observe the messages indicating that PIP is downloading and installing the package.
2. **Verify the Installation**
   a. To verify that the requests library has been installed, list all installed packages by typing:
   ```
   pip list
   ```
   b. Look for requests in the list of installed packages. You should see an entry like:
   ```
   requests      2.32.3
   ```

3. **Show Package Details**
   a. Get detailed information about the requests package by typing:
   ```
   pip show requests
   ```
   b. You will see details about the package, including its version, author, and dependencies.
4. **Upgrade a Package**
   a. Upgrade the requests package to ensure you have the latest version by typing:
   ```
   pip install --upgrade requests
   ```
   b. Observe the messages indicating the upgrade process.
5. **Uninstall a Package**
   a. To uninstall the requests package, type:
   ```
   PIP uninstall requests
   ```
   b. Confirm the uninstallation when prompted by typing y and pressing *Enter*.
6. **Verify the Uninstallation**
   a. To verify that the requests package has been uninstalled, list all installed packages again by typing:
   ```
   pip list
   ```
   b. Ensure that requests no longer appear in the list.

By completing these steps, you will feel more confident in using PIP to manage your Python packages. This hands-on practice will teach you how to efficiently handle package installations, upgrades, and removals in your projects.

Working with Requirements Files

In the previous section, you have learned how to manage individual packages using basic PIP commands. Now, let us take it a step further and learn how to handle multiple package dependencies efficiently using requirements files.

A requirements file is a simple way to list all the Python packages your project needs. This makes it easy to install the same packages on any computer without having to install them one by one.

Creating a Requirements File

A requirements file is just a text file that contains the names of all the packages your project needs. Each package is listed on a new line, and you can also include specific version numbers. Here is how to create one:

1. Open Visual Studio Code and create a new file named **requirements.txt**.
   ```
   requests==2.32.3
   scikit-learn==1.5.1
   tiktoken
   ```

- If you want a specific version of a package, use == followed by the version number (for example, requests==2.32.3).
- If you do not specify a version, PIP will install the latest version available.

Installing Packages from a Requirements File

Once you have a **`requirements.txt`** file, you can install all the listed packages at once using:

```
pip install -r requirements.txt
```

```
(base) C:\Users\     \Managing Packages with PIP>pip install -r requirements.txt
Requirement already satisfied: makefile in c:\users\     \anaconda3\lib\site-packages (from -r requirements.txt (line 1)) (1.1.0)
Requirement already satisfied: requests==2.32.3 in c:\users\     \anaconda3\lib\site-packages (from -r requirements.txt (line 2)) (2.32.3)
Collecting scikit-learn==1.5.1
  Downloading scikit_learn-1.5.1-cp310-cp310-win_amd64.whl (11.0 MB)
     ---------------------------------------- 11.0/11.0 MB 24.2 MB/s eta 0:00:00
Requirement already satisfied: tiktoken in c:\users\     \anaconda3\lib\site-packages (from -r requirements.txt (line 4)) (0.4.0)
Requirement already satisfied: urllib3<3,>=1.21.1 in c:\users\     \anaconda3\lib\site-packages (from requests==2.32.3->-r requirements.txt (line 2)) (1.26.14)
Requirement already satisfied: idna<4,>=2.5 in c:\users\     \anaconda3\lib\site-packages (from requests==2.32.3->-r requirements.txt (line 2)) (3.4)
Requirement already satisfied: certifi>=2017.4.17 in c:\users\     \anaconda3\lib\site-packages (from requests==2.32.3->-r requirements.txt (line 2)) (2022.12.7)
Requirement already satisfied: charset-normalizer<4,>=2 in c:\users\     \anaconda3\lib\site-packages (from requests==2.32.3->-r requirements.txt (line 2)) (2.0.4)
Requirement already satisfied: scipy>=1.6.0 in c:\users\     \anaconda3\lib\site-packages (from scikit-learn==1.5.1->-r requirements.txt (line 3)) (1.10.0)
Collecting joblib>=1.2.0
  Downloading joblib-1.4.2-py3-none-any.whl (301 kB)
     ---------------------------------------- 301.8/301.8 kB 19.4 MB/s eta 0:00:00
Requirement already satisfied: numpy>=1.19.5 in c:\users\     \anaconda3\lib\site-packages (from scikit-learn==1.5.1->-r requirements.txt (line 3)) (1.23.5)
Collecting threadpoolctl>=3.1.0
  Downloading threadpoolctl-3.5.0-py3-none-any.whl (18 kB)
Requirement already satisfied: regex>=2022.1.18 in c:\users\     \anaconda3\lib\site-packages (from tiktoken->-r requirements.txt (line 4)) (2022.7.9)
Installing collected packages: threadpoolctl, joblib, scikit-learn
  Attempting uninstall: threadpoolctl
    Found existing installation: threadpoolctl 2.2.0
    Uninstalling threadpoolctl-2.2.0:
      Successfully uninstalled threadpoolctl-2.2.0
  Attempting uninstall: joblib
    Found existing installation: joblib 1.1.1
    Uninstalling joblib-1.1.1:
      Successfully uninstalled joblib-1.1.1
  Attempting uninstall: scikit-learn
    Found existing installation: scikit-learn 1.2.1
    Uninstalling scikit-learn-1.2.1:
      Successfully uninstalled scikit-learn-1.2.1
Successfully installed joblib-1.4.2 scikit-learn-1.5.1 threadpoolctl-3.5.0
```

Figure 14.9: *Installing python package from requirements file*

This command tells PIP to read the requirements file and install everything listed inside it. This saves time and ensures that all team members use the same package versions.

Freezing Installed Packages to a Requirements File

If you already have packages installed and want to create a requirements file based on them, you can use the freeze command:

```
pip freeze > requirements.txt
```

This command generates a `requirements.txt` file that contains a complete list of all installed packages and their versions. This is useful if you want to share your project with others or set up the same environment on a different computer.

Managing Dependencies with Ease:

Using requirements files makes managing Python packages much easier. Instead of installing each package manually, you can install all dependencies at once, ensuring a consistent and error-free environment.

Practical Exercise: Managing Requirements Files

Now it is time to practice managing requirements files. Follow these steps to get hands-on experience.

Exercise Steps:

1. **Create a Requirements File**
   a. Open Visual Studio Code and create a new file named **`requirements.txt`**.

b. Add the following lines to the file:

```
makefile
requests==2.25.1
numpy==1.20.0
pandas==1.2.1
```

c. Save the file.

2. **Install Packages from the Requirements File**

a. Open the terminal in Visual Studio Code.

b. To install the packages indicated in requirements.txt, do the following command:

```
pip install -r requirements.txt
```

3. Freeze Installed Packages to a Requirements File

a. After installing packages, consider saving the current environment's packages to a new requirements file.

b. In the terminal, type:

```
pip freeze > new_requirements.txt
```

4. **Verify the Contents of the New Requirements File**

Open **`new_requirements.txt`** in Visual Studio Code to check for a list of installed packages and their versions.

Completing these steps will teach you how to efficiently build, use, and manage requirements files in Python applications. This expertise is necessary to ensure that your project dependencies are consistent and easily reproducible across diverse environments.

Virtual Environments

In the previous section, you have learned how to handle multiple dependencies using requirements files. Now, let us explore virtual environments, which help keep different Python projects separate and organized.

Introduction to Virtual Environments

A virtual environment is like a separate workspace for each Python project. It includes its own Python installation and installed packages, ensuring that each project uses the correct versions of dependencies without affecting other projects. This helps prevent version conflicts and makes it easier to manage different project requirements.

Creating and Activating a Virtual Environment

To create a virtual environment, you will use venv, a built-in Python module. Follow these steps:

1. **Create a Virtual Environment**

Open Visual Studio Code's terminal, navigate to your project folder, and run this command:

```
python -m venv myenv
```

This will create a new folder named **`myenv`**, which contains a Python installation and a copy of PIP.

2. **Activate the Virtual Environment**

   Before using the virtual environment, you need to activate it. The command depends on your operating system:

- **On Windows**:
  `myenv\Scripts\activate`
- **On macOS and Linux**:
  `source myenv/bin/activate`

After activation, you will see the virtual environment's name in your terminal prompt, indicating that it is now active.

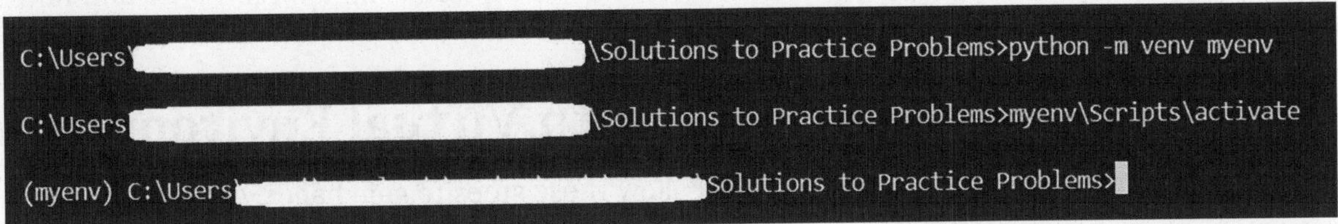

***Figure 14.10**: Creating and activating python virtual environment*

Managing Packages Inside a Virtual Environment

Once activated, you can use PIP to install packages just like before. However, these packages will only be available inside the virtual environment. Your global Python installation remains clean and unaffected.

```
pip install requests
```

You can also use commands such as **`pip list`** to see the installed packages and manage them as needed.

```
(myenv) C:\Users\ \Solutions to Practice Problems>pip list
Package            Version
------------------ --------
certifi            2024.7.4
charset-normalizer 3.3.2
idna               3.7
pip                23.2.1
requests           2.32.3
setuptools         65.5.0
urllib3            2.2.2
```

***Figure 14.11**: Listing python packages inside virtual environment*

Deactivating and Deleting Virtual Environments

Deactivating the Virtual Environment:

When you are done working in a virtual environment, you can exit it by running:

```
deactivate
```

This switches you back to the global Python environment.

Deleting a Virtual Environment:

If you no longer need the virtual environment, you can delete it by removing the folder:

- **On Windows:**
  ```
  rmdir /s /q myenv
  ```
- **On macOS and Linux:**
  ```
  rm -rf myenv
  ```

Keeping Your Projects Organized:

Using virtual environments ensures that each project has its own dependencies, avoiding conflicts and keeping your Python environment clean. Next, you will explore common PIP issues and how to troubleshoot them effectively.

Practical Exercise: Working with Virtual Environments

It is now time to try working in virtual settings. Follow these steps to gain hands-on experience.

Exercise Steps

1. **Create a Virtual Environment**
   a. Open Visual Studio Code's terminal and navigate to your project directory.
   b. Create a new virtual environment called **myenv** by typing:
   ```
   python -m venv myenv
   ```
2. **Activate the Virtual Environment**

   Activate the virtual environment by typing:

   a. **On Windows:**
   ```
   myenv\Scripts\activate
   ```
   b. **On macOS and Linux:**
   ```
   source myenv/bin/activate
   ```
3. **Install Packages within the Virtual Environment**

   With the virtual environment active, install the requests package by typing:
   ```
   pip install requests
   ```
4. **Deactivate the Virtual Environment**

   Deactivate the virtual environment by typing:
   ```
   Deactivate
   ```
5. **Delete the Virtual Environment**

   To eliminate the virtual environment, remove the **myenv** directory.

Completing these instructions will teach you how to establish, activate, manage, deactivate, and delete virtual environments in Python projects. This expertise is critical for keeping clean, segregated development environments.

Common Mistakes and Best Practices

In the previous sections, you have explored PIP, requirements files, and virtual environments to manage Python packages effectively. Now, let us discuss common mistakes people make while using PIP and the best practices to keep your projects running smoothly.

Avoiding Common Mistakes When Using PIP

Even though PIP makes package management easier, some mistakes can cause errors, conflicts, or security issues. Here are a few things to watch out for:

- **Not Using Virtual Environments**: Installing packages globally instead of inside a virtual environment can lead to version conflicts. Always use a virtual environment to keep each project's dependencies separate.
- **Ignoring Dependency Conflicts**: Some packages require specific versions of other packages to work correctly. Ignoring these dependencies can cause your project to break. PIP usually handles this, but if you see a warning, pay attention and resolve conflicts manually if needed.
- **Using Outdated Packages**: Older versions of packages may have security risks or missing features. Make it a habit to update your packages regularly to get the latest improvements and fixes.

Using Virtual Environments for Project Isolation

As discussed earlier, virtual environments help keep each project separate and organized. This ensures that one project's dependencies do not interfere with another.

To keep things simple, follow these steps:

1. Create a virtual environment for every new project.
2. Activate the virtual environment before installing packages.
3. Deactivate the virtual environment once you are done working.

This practice avoids conflicts and makes it easier to share and replicate your project on another machine.

Regularly Updating Packages

Keeping your packages up to date ensures you get the latest features, bug fixes, and security updates. To update a package, use:

```
pip install --upgrade package-name
```

If you have a requirements file, you can update all packages at once using:

```
pip install --upgrade -r requirements.txt
```

This ensures that all dependencies stay up to date and secure.

Checking for Package Vulnerabilities

Some packages may have security vulnerabilities that can put your project at risk. To check if your installed packages have any known security issues, you can use pip-audit.

How to Check for Security Issues

1. Install pip-audit (if not already installed):
   ```
   pip install pip-audit
   ```
2. Run pip-audit to scan for vulnerabilities:
   ```
   pip-audit
   ```

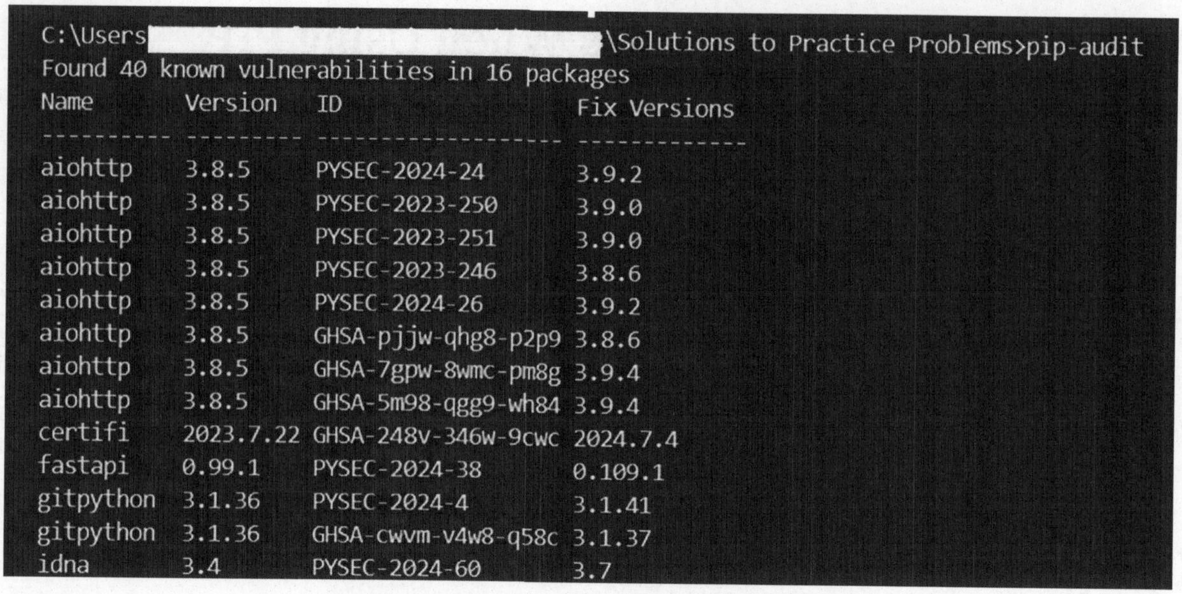

```
C:\Users\Solutions to Practice Problems>pip-audit
Found 40 known vulnerabilities in 16 packages
Name       Version   ID                  Fix Versions
---------- --------- ------------------- ------------
aiohttp    3.8.5     PYSEC-2024-24       3.9.2
aiohttp    3.8.5     PYSEC-2023-250      3.9.0
aiohttp    3.8.5     PYSEC-2023-251      3.9.0
aiohttp    3.8.5     PYSEC-2023-246      3.8.6
aiohttp    3.8.5     PYSEC-2024-26       3.9.2
aiohttp    3.8.5     GHSA-pjjw-qhg8-p2p9 3.8.6
aiohttp    3.8.5     GHSA-7gpw-8wmc-pm8g 3.9.4
aiohttp    3.8.5     GHSA-5m98-qgg9-wh84 3.9.4
certifi    2023.7.22 GHSA-248v-346w-9cwc 2024.7.4
fastapi    0.99.1    PYSEC-2024-38       0.109.1
gitpython  3.1.36    PYSEC-2024-4        3.1.41
gitpython  3.1.36    GHSA-cwvm-v4w8-q58c 3.1.37
idna       3.4       PYSEC-2024-60       3.7
```

Figure 14.12: *Checking for package vulnerabilities*

This tool will scan all installed packages and alert you if any have known security risks. Keeping your packages secure helps protect your project from potential threats.

Keeping Your Python Environment Safe and Efficient:

By following best practices, such as using virtual environments, resolving dependency conflicts, updating packages, and checking for security issues, you can ensure that your Python projects remain stable, secure, and well-organized.

Now that you have mastered package management, let us move on to troubleshooting common PIP issues and learning how to fix them effectively!

Practical Exercise: Applying Best Practices

Let us apply these best practices in a practical exercise.

Exercise Steps

1. **Create and Activate a Virtual Environment**
   a. Open Visual Studio Code's terminal and navigate to your project directory.
   b. Create a new virtual environment called **myenv** by typing:
      `python -m venv myenv`
   c. Activate the virtual environment by typing:
      - **On Windows**:
        `myenv\Scripts\activate`
      - **On macOS and Linux**:
        `source myenv/bin/activate`
2. **Install and Upgrade a Package**
   a. Install the requests package by typing:
      `pip install requests`
   b. Upgrade the requests package to the latest version by typing:
      `pip install --upgrade requests`

3. **Check for Vulnerabilities**
   a. Install the pip-audit tool by typing:
   ```
   pip install pip-audit
   ```
   b. Run pip-audit to check for vulnerabilities by typing:
   ```
   pip-audit
   ```

Following these recommended practices and completing the exercise will make you better suited to handle your Python projects efficiently and safely.

Troubleshooting Common Issues

Even when following best practices, you may still encounter problems with PIP while installing or managing packages. In this section, you will look at common installation errors, resolving dependency conflicts, and fixing broken installations.

Common Installation Issues and Their Solutions

Sometimes, installing packages with PIP may fail due to permissions, network issues, or outdated versions. Here is how to fix them:

- **Permission Errors**: If you get a permission denied error while installing a package, it means you do not have the right access. To fix this, install the package for your user only by running:
  ```
  pip install package-name --user
  ```
- **Network Issues**: If your internet connection is slow or unstable, PIP may fail to download packages. You can try increasing the timeout value or using a different package source:
  ```
  pip install package-name --index-url=https://pypi.org/simple/ --timeout=60
  ```
- **Outdated PIP**: If your PIP version is old, it may not work properly with newer packages. To update PIP, use:
  ```
  python -m pip install --upgrade pip
  ```

Resolving Dependency Conflicts

Sometimes, packages require different versions of the same dependency, causing conflicts. Here is how to fix it:

1. **Check Dependencies Using `pipdeptree`**

   You can check which packages depend on what using the **`pipdeptree`** tool. First, install it:
   ```
   pip install pipdeptree
   ```
   Then, run:
   ```
   pipdeptree
   ```

```
langchain==0.0.283
├── aiohttp [required: >=3.8.3,<4.0.0, installed: 3.8.5]
│   ├── aiosignal [required: >=1.1.2, installed: 1.3.1]
│   │   └── frozenlist [required: >=1.1.0, installed: 1.4.0]
│   ├── async-timeout [required: >=4.0.0a3,<5.0, installed: 4.0.3]
│   ├── attrs [required: >=17.3.0, installed: 22.1.0]
│   ├── charset-normalizer [required: >=2.0,<4.0, installed: 2.0.4]
│   ├── frozenlist [required: >=1.1.1, installed: 1.4.0]
│   ├── multidict [required: >=4.5,<7.0, installed: 6.0.4]
│   └── yarl [required: >=1.0,<2.0, installed: 1.9.2]
│       ├── idna [required: >=2.0, installed: 3.4]
│       └── multidict [required: >=4.0, installed: 6.0.4]
├── async-timeout [required: >=4.0.0,<5.0.0, installed: 4.0.3]
├── dataclasses-json [required: >=0.5.7,<0.6.0, installed: 0.5.14]
│   ├── marshmallow [required: >=3.18.0,<4.0.0, installed: 3.20.1]
│   │   └── packaging [required: >=17.0, installed: 24.1]
│   └── typing-inspect [required: >=0.4.0,<1, installed: 0.9.0]
│       ├── mypy-extensions [required: >=0.3.0, installed: 0.4.3]
│       └── typing_extensions [required: >=3.7.4, installed: 4.5.0]
```

Figure 14.13: *Resolving dependency conflicts*

This command will show a list of installed packages and their dependencies, helping you find conflicting versions.

2. **Specify Compatible Versions in Requirements Files**

   To avoid conflicts, specify package versions that work together in your **`requirements.txt`** file. For example:

   ```
   package-a==1.2.3
   package-b>=2.0,<3.0
   ```

   This ensures package-b will only install versions between 2.0 and 3.0, preventing version mismatches.

3. **Use Virtual Environments**

   The best way to avoid conflicts is by using virtual environments. This keeps each project isolated so that packages do not interfere with each other.

Handling Broken Installations

If a package stops working, it may be due to a broken or corrupted installation. Here is how to fix it:

1. **Reinstall the Package**: First, try removing and reinstalling the package:

   ```
   pip uninstall package-name
   pip install package-name
   ```

2. **Clear the PIP Cache**: If reinstalling does not work, clear the cache to remove any corrupted files:

   ```
   pip cache purge
   ```

3. **Check for Known Issues**: Some package issues might already have solutions online. Check the package's official website or issue tracker for known bugs and fixes.

Keeping Your Package Management Smooth:

By following these troubleshooting steps, you can fix common PIP issues quickly. Whether it is a failed installation, a dependency conflict, or a broken package, these solutions will help you keep your Python projects running smoothly.

Practical Exercise: Troubleshooting PIP Issues

Let us put these troubleshooting techniques into practice.

Exercise Steps

1. **Encounter and Fix a Permission Error**
   a. Try installing a package globally without using the `--user` flag:
      `pip install requests`
   b. If you encounter a permission error, resolve it by using:
      `pip install requests -user`
2. **Simulate a Network Issue and Use a Mirror**
   a. To simulate a network issue, disconnect the internet and try installing a package:
      `pip install requests`
   b. To address the issue, reconnect, and specify an alternative mirror:
      `pip install requests --index-url=https://pypi.org/simple/ --timeout=60`
3. **Resolve a Dependency Conflict**
   a. Install pipdeptree:
      `pip install pipdeptree`
   b. Run pipdeptree to visualize the dependency tree and identify conflicts:
      `pipdeptree`
   c. Update `requirements.txt` to identify compatible versions and reinstall packages.
4. **Handle a Broken Installation**
   a. To manually corrupt a package installation, delete its files from the site-packages directory.
   b. When attempting to utilize the package, you may experience errors.
   c. Reinstall the package to resolve the issue:

```
pip uninstall requests
pip install requests
```

Following these steps and utilizing these troubleshooting strategies will prepare you to tackle common issues that happen when using PIP and managing Python packages.

Advanced PIP Usage

So far, you have covered the basics of PIP, including installing packages, using requirements files, and fixing common issues. Now, let us explore some advanced PIP techniques, such as customizing PIP settings and working with private repositories.

Customizing PIP Configuration

You can customize how PIP works by modifying its configuration files. These files allow you to set default options, such as download timeouts, trusted repositories, and package sources.

1. **Locating PIP Configuration Files**

   PIP uses different configuration files depending on where the settings apply:

   - **Global (System-wide settings)**
     - Linux/macOS: `/etc/pip.conf`
     - Windows: `C:\ProgramData\pip\pip.ini`
   - **User-Specific settings** (Affects only your account)
     - Linux/macOS: `~/.pip/pip.conf`
     - Windows: `C:\Users\<username>\pip\pip.ini`
   - **Virtual Environment settings** (affects only one virtual environment)
     - `<virtualenv>/pip.conf`

2. **Common Configuration Options**

   Here are some useful settings you can add to your PIP configuration file:

   ```
   [global]
   timeout = 60
   index-url = https://pypi.org/simple/
   trusted-host = pypi.org
   ```

   - **`timeout`**: Sets a time limit (in seconds) for PIP downloads.
   - **`index-url`**: Defines the default package source (for example, PyPI).
   - **`trusted-host`**: Prevents SSL security warnings for trusted repositories.

3. **Creating a Configuration File**

   To create or edit a PIP configuration file, follow these steps:

   - On Linux/macOS, open the terminal and type:
     `nano ~/.pip/pip.conf`
   - On Windows, open Notepad and edit the file:
     `notepad C:\Users\<username>\pip\pip.ini`

After adding your preferred settings, save the file.

To view the current PIP settings, run:

```
pip config list
```

```
C:\Users>pip config list
:env:.user='no'
global.index-url='https://pypi.org/simple/'
global.timeout='60'
global.trusted-host='pypi.org'

C:\Users>
```

Figure 14.14: *Viewing PIP config file contents*

This will show all active PIP configurations.

Using PIP with Private Repositories

Sometimes, you may need to install packages from private repositories, such as company tools or proprietary software. PIP allows you to install such packages easily.

1. **Installing from a Private Repository with Authentication**

   If a package is stored in a private repository, you can install it by providing your username and password:

   ```
   pip install package-name --extra-index-url https://<username>:<password>@private-repo.com/simple
   ```

   This tells PIP to check the private repository for the package.

2. **Setting Up a Private Repository in PIP Configuration**

   If you frequently install packages from a private repository, you can set it as the default source in the PIP configuration file:

   ```
   [global]
   index-url = https://<username>:<password>@private-repo.com/simple
   ```

Figure 14.15: *Using PIP with private repositories*

This way, you do not need to enter your credentials every time you install a package.

Making PIP More Powerful:

By customizing PIP and using private repositories, you can automate installations, speed up downloads, and manage internal tools securely. These advanced features help developers work more efficiently, ensuring smooth package management for all types of projects.

Practical Exercise: Advanced PIP Techniques

Let us practice customizing PIP configuration and using private repositories.

Exercise Steps:

1. **Create and Customize a PIP Configuration File**

   a. Create a user-specific PIP configuration file:

      - On Linux and macOS:

        ```
        nano ~/.pip/pip.conf
        ```

      - On Windows:

        ```
        notepad C:\Users\<username>\pip\pip.ini
        ```

   b. Add the following settings to the file:

      ```
      [global]
      timeout = 60
      index-url = https://pypi.org/simple/
      trusted-host = pypi.org
      ```

   c. Save the file.

2. **Use a Private Repository**

   Assume you have access to a private repository. Try installing a package from this repository with authentication:

   ```
   pip install package-name --extra-index-url https://<username>:<password>@pri-
   vate-repo.com/simple
   ```

3. **Configure PIP to Use a Private Repository by Default**

   a. Update your PIP configuration file to utilize the private repository as default:

   ```
   [global]
   index-url = https://<username>:<password>@private-repo.com/simple
   ```

   b. Save the file.

Completing these steps will provide you expertise in customizing PIP configurations and using private repositories, boosting your ability to handle Python packages in more complicated contexts.

Exercises and Challenges: Practice Problems and Solutions

Practice Problem 1: Basic PIP Commands

Task: Practice using basic PIP commands to manage packages.

Challenge: Write a script called **`basic_pip_commands.py`** that:

- Installs the requests library.
- Lists all installed packages.
- Shows details for the requests library.
- Upgrades the requests library to the latest version.
- Uninstalls the requests library.

Practice Problem 2: Managing Requirements Files

Task: Work with requirements files to manage project dependencies.

Challenge: Write a script called **`manage_requirements.py`** that:

- Creates a `requirements.txt` file with the following packages: requests==2.25.1, numpy==1.20.0, pandas==1.2.1.
- Installs the packages from **`requirements.txt`**.
- Freezes the currently installed packages to a new file called **`new_requirements.txt`**.

Practice Problem 3: Working with Virtual Environments

Task: Create and manage virtual environments.

Challenge: Write a script called **`virtual_env_management.py`** that:

- Creates a virtual environment named **`myenv`**.
- Activates the virtual environment.
- Installs the requests package within the virtual environment.
- Deactivates the virtual environment.
- Deletes the **`myenv`** virtual environment.

Practice Problem 4: Troubleshooting PIP Issues

Task: Troubleshoot common PIP issues and resolve them.

Challenge: Write a script called **troubleshoot_pip_issues.py** that:

- Simulates a network issue by attempting to install a package without internet access, then retries with a different mirror.
- Installs pipdeptree and lists the dependency tree.
- Handles a broken installation by uninstalling and reinstalling the requests package.
- Clears the PIP cache.

Practice Problem 5: Advanced PIP Usage

Task: Customize PIP configuration and use private repositories.

Challenge: Write a script called **advanced_pip_usage.py** that:

- Creates a PIP configuration file (**pip.conf** or **pip.ini**) with the following settings:

  ```
  [global]
  timeout = 60
  index-url = https://pypi.org/simple/
  trusted-host = pypi.org
  ```
- Installs a package from a private repository using authentication.
- Updates the PIP configuration file to set the private repository as the default index URL.

Solutions to Practice Problems

Practice Problem 1: Basic PIP Commands

basic_pip_commands.py

```
import subprocess

def run_command(command):
    process = subprocess.Popen(command, shell=True, stdout=subprocess.PIPE, 
stderr=subprocess.PIPE)
    out, err = process.communicate()
    if process.returncode == 0:
        print(out.decode('utf-8'))
    else:
        print(f"Error: {err.decode('utf-8')}")

if __name__ == "__main__":
    # Install the requests library
    run_command('pip install requests')

    # List all installed packages
    run_command('pip list')

    # Show details for the requests library
    run_command('pip show requests')

    # Upgrade the requests library to the latest version
    run_command('pip install --upgrade requests')
```

```
    # Uninstall the requests library
    run_command('pip uninstall -y requests')
```

Practice Problem 2: Managing Requirements Files

manage_requirements.py

```
import subprocess

def run_command(command):
    process = subprocess.Popen(command, shell=True, stdout=subprocess.PIPE, 
stderr=subprocess.PIPE)
    out, err = process.communicate()
    if process.returncode == 0:
        print(out.decode('utf-8'))
    else:
        print(f"Error: {err.decode('utf-8')}")

if __name__ == "__main__":
    # Create a requirements.txt file with specified packages
    with open('requirements.txt', 'w') as file:
        file.write('requests==2.25.1\n')
        file.write('numpy==1.20.0\n')
        file.write('pandas==1.2.1\n')

    # Install the packages from requirements.txt
    run_command('pip install -r requirements.txt')

    # Freeze the currently installed packages to a new file
    run_command('pip freeze > new_requirements.txt')
```

Practice Problem 3: Working with Virtual Environments

virtual_env_management.py

```
import subprocess
import os
import shutil

def run_command(command):
    process = subprocess.Popen(command, shell=True, stdout=subprocess.PIPE, 
stderr=subprocess.PIPE)
    out, err = process.communicate()
    if process.returncode == 0:
        print(out.decode('utf-8'))
    else:
        print(f"Error: {err.decode('utf-8')}")

if __name__ == "__main__":
    # Create a virtual environment named myenv
    run_command('python -m venv myenv')

    # Activate the virtual environment
    activate_command = '.\\myenv\\Scripts\\activate' if os.name == 'nt' else 
'source myenv/bin/activate'
    run_command(activate_command)

    # Install the requests package within the virtual environment
```

```
    run_command('pip install requests')

    # Deactivate the virtual environment
    deactivate_command = 'deactivate' if os.name != 'nt' else '.\\myenv\\
Scripts\\deactivate'
    run_command(deactivate_command)

    # Delete the myenv virtual environment
    shutil.rmtree('myenv')
```

Practice Problem 4: Troubleshooting PIP Issues

troubleshoot_pip_issues.py

```
import subprocess

def run_command(command):
    process = subprocess.Popen(command, shell=True, stdout=subprocess.PIPE,
stderr=subprocess.PIPE)
    out, err = process.communicate()
    if process.returncode == 0:
        print(out.decode('utf-8'))
    else:
        print(f"Error: {err.decode('utf-8')}")

if __name__ == "__main__":
    # Simulate a network issue by attempting to install a package without
internet access, then retries with a different mirror
    print("Simulating network issue...")
    run_command('pip install requests --index-url=https://pypi.org/simple/
--timeout=60')

    # Install pipdeptree and list the dependency tree
    run_command('pip install pipdeptree')
    run_command('pipdeptree')

    # Handle a broken installation by uninstalling and reinstalling the
requests package
    run_command('pip uninstall -y requests')
    run_command('pip install requests')

    # Clear the PIP cache
    run_command('pip cache purge')
```

Practice Problem 5: Advanced PIP Usage

advanced_pip_usage.py

```
import subprocess
import os

def run_command(command):
    process = subprocess.Popen(command, shell=True, stdout=subprocess.PIPE,
stderr=subprocess.PIPE)
    out, err = process.communicate()
    if process.returncode == 0:
        print(out.decode('utf-8'))
    else:
        print(f"Error: {err.decode('utf-8')}")
```

```
if __name__ == "__main__":
    # Create a PIP configuration file with specified settings
    config_dir = os.path.join(os.path.expanduser("~"), ".pip")
    os.makedirs(config_dir, exist_ok=True)
    config_file = os.path.join(config_dir, "pip.conf")

    with open(config_file, 'w') as file:
        file.write("[global]\n")
        file.write("timeout = 60\n")
        file.write("index-url = https://pypi.org/simple/\n")
        file.write("trusted-host = pypi.org\n")

    # Print the configuration file content
    with open(config_file, 'r') as file:
        print(file.read())

    # Suppose you have access to a private repository, install a package from
this repository using authentication
    run_command('pip install package-name --extra-index-url https://<user-
name>:<password>@private-repo.com/simple')

    # Update the PIP configuration file to set the private repository as the de-
fault index URL
    with open(config_file, 'a') as file:
        file.write("index-url = https://<username>:<password>@private-repo.com/
simple\n")

    # Print the updated configuration file content
    with open(config_file, 'r') as file:
        print(file.read())
```

Conclusion

In this chapter, you explored how to manage Python packages effectively using PIP. You started by learning how to install, upgrade, and uninstall packages. Then, you saw how to use requirements files to keep track of project dependencies and how to set up virtual environments to keep different projects organized and conflict-free.

You also explored troubleshooting common PIP issues, such as installation errors and dependency conflicts. Finally, you explored advanced PIP features, including custom configurations and working with private repositories to manage internal tools.

Mastering these skills will help you manage Python projects efficiently, ensuring smooth development workflows, and well-structured environments.

In the next chapter, you will dive into Building Web Apps! You will learn how to create dynamic and interactive web applications using popular frameworks, such as Flask and Django. Get ready to apply your Python skills to real-world web development and build exciting projects.

So, keep calm and let us tame the Python!

Multiple-Choice Questions

Test your understanding of the concepts covered in this chapter with the following multiple-choice questions.

1. Which command is used to install a package using PIP?
   a. `pip get`
   b. `pip fetch`
   c. `pip install`
   d. `pip download`
2. Which file format is commonly used to list project dependencies in Python?
   a. `dependencies.txt`
   b. `requirements.txt`
   c. `packages.txt`
   d. `dependencies.cfg`
3. What command do you use to activate a virtual environment in Windows?
   a. `source myenv/bin/activate`
   b. `activate myenv`
   c. `myenv\Scripts\activate`
   d. `start myenv`
4. What does the pip freeze command do?
   a. Installs packages listed in a file
   b. Uninstalls all installed packages
   c. Lists installed packages and their versions
   d. Freezes the Python interpreter
5. Which of the following is NOT a benefit of using virtual environments?
   a. Isolating project dependencies
   b. Avoiding version conflicts
   c. Speeding up package installations
   d. Simplifying project management
6. How can you specify a package version in a requirements file?
   a. `package-name:version`
   b. `package-name (version)`
   c. `package-name==version`
   d. `package-name@version`

7. What command would you use to uninstall the requests library?
   a. `pip remove requests`
   b. `pip delete requests`
   c. `pip uninstall requests`
   d. `pip erase requests`
8. Where can you configure PIP settings globally on a Linux system?
   a. `/usr/local/pip.conf`
   b. `/etc/pip.conf`
   c. `~/.pip/pip.conf`
   d. `/opt/pip/pip.conf`
9. Which tool can you use to visualize the dependency tree of installed packages?
   a. `pip list`
   b. `pip show`
   c. `pipdeptree`
   d. `pipgraph`
10. What is the main advantage of using the **`--user`** flag with the pip install command?
    a. It installs packages for the current user without needing root permissions
    b. It speeds up the installation process
    c. It ensures compatibility with all Python versions
    d. It installs packages globally on the system

Answers

1. c
2. b
3. c
4. c
5. c
6. c
7. c
8. b
9. c
10. a

Points to Remember

- Proper package management is essential for preserving project dependencies and preventing conflicts.
- PIP is Python's standard package management, making it simple to install, upgrade, and remove packages.
- The requirements.txt file lists all project dependencies, making it easy to reproduce environments.
- Virtual environments segregate Python environments and prevent dependencies from interfering with each other.
- Updating packages on a regular basis ensures project security and includes the most recent features and fixes.
- Troubleshooting common PIP issues requires understanding error messages and resolving dependency conflicts and network concerns.
- Advanced PIP usage involves configuring setups and utilizing private repositories for proprietary or internal items.

Further Reading

For further learning, check out these resources:

1. **Official PIP Documentation**: https://pip.pypa.io/en/stable/
2. **Python Packaging User Guide**: https://packaging.python.org/
3. **Virtualenv Documentation**: https://virtualenv.pypa.io/en/stable/
4. **Python Package Index (PyPI)**: https://pypi.org/

Chapter 15
Building Web Apps

Introduction

In the previous chapter, you learned how to manage Python packages using PIP, making it easy to add new functionalities to your projects. Now, you will take the next step into web development, where you will learn how to build web applications using Python.

Web applications are a big part of everyday life. Whether you are booking a ticket, chatting with friends, or shopping online, you are using web apps. Python provides powerful tools that help you create these applications, and in this chapter, you will explore two of the most popular frameworks, Flask and Django.

You will start by understanding how web applications work and how Python helps in web development. Then, you will build simple web applications, learning how to display dynamic content and handle user input. Finally, you will explore how to make these applications available on the internet so that others can access them.

By the end of this chapter, you will have a solid foundation in building web applications with Python. With this knowledge, you will be ready to create your own web projects and bring your ideas to life on the internet.

Structure

In this chapter, the following topics will be covered:

- Overview of Web Development
    - Components of Web Applications
    - Client-Server Architecture
    - Making Development Easier with Web Frameworks
- Flask: A Beginner's Guide
    - Introduction to Flask
    - Getting Flask Ready for Development
    - Creating a Basic Flask App
    - Using Templates in Flask
    - Handling Forms and Input in Flask
    - Practical Exercise: Building a Simple Feedback Form
- Django: A Beginner's Guide
    - Introduction to Django
    - Setting Up Django
    - Building Your First Django App
    - Using Templates in Django

  - Handling Forms in Django
  - Practical Exercise: Building a Simple Contact Form
- Common Mistakes and Best Practices
- Exercises and Challenges: Practice Problems and Solutions

Overview of Web Development

Web development is the process of creating and managing websites and web applications. These applications are hosted on servers and accessed through web browsers, allowing you to interact with online services and content from anywhere.

Understanding Web Applications:

A web application is a software program that runs on the internet. Unlike traditional desktop applications that operate directly on a computer, web applications are accessed through a browser and can be used on any device with an internet connection. This makes them convenient and accessible across different platforms.

Components of Web Applications

A web application consists of several essential parts that work together to deliver functionality to you as the user.

- **Client**: This is your device, such as a computer, tablet, or smartphone, which interacts with the web application through a browser. When you click a button or submit a form, the client sends a request to the server.
- **Server**: The server runs the web application. It processes your requests, executes application logic, retrieves data when needed, and sends responses back to your device.
- **Database**: Most web applications use databases to store and manage information. While not all web apps require a database, they are commonly used to track user accounts, messages, transactions, and other stored data.
- **Network**: The network connects your device to the server, allowing communication between them. The internet is the most widely used network for web applications, using protocols such as HTTP (Hypertext Transfer Protocol) to transfer data.

Client-Server Architecture

Most web applications follow a client-server model, where your device interacts with the server to access and modify data. This process occurs in four steps.

1. **Request**: Your device sends a request to the server, such as when you fill out a form or click a link.
2. **Processing**: The server processes your request, executes the necessary operations, and retrieves any required data from the database.
3. **Response**: Once processing is complete, the server sends a response back to your device, usually in the form of an HTML page or structured data.
4. **Display**: Your browser displays the response, allowing you to interact with the application.

This model ensures efficiency and scalability, allowing the server to handle complex operations while your device provides a seamless experience.

Making Development Easier with Web Frameworks

Building a web application from scratch requires a lot of effort. To simplify this process, you can use web frameworks, which provide tools and libraries that handle common tasks.

- **Efficiency**: Frameworks automate repetitive tasks such as managing user sessions and handling request routing, allowing you to focus on core functionality.
- **Consistency**: By enforcing structured coding practices, frameworks make it easier for you and your team to collaborate and maintain projects over time.
- **Security**: Many frameworks include built-in protections against common vulnerabilities, helping you create more secure applications.
- **Scalability**: Web frameworks support applications of all sizes, making it easier for you to scale your project from a small personal app to a large enterprise system.

By using web frameworks, you can develop applications faster, reduce errors, and ensure your code remains well-structured and maintainable. In the next section, you will learn how Python simplifies web development with two powerful frameworks, Flask and Django.

Flask: A Beginner's Guide

In the previous section, you explored the fundamentals of web development and how web frameworks help simplify the process. Now, you are ready to dive into Flask, a powerful yet simple framework for building web applications with Python.

This section will introduce you to Flask and its key features. You will learn how to set up your development environment, create a basic Flask application, use templates to display dynamic content, and handle user input with forms. By the end of this section, you will have a solid foundation for building your own web applications using Flask.

Introduction to Flask

Now that you understand the basics of web development and the role of frameworks, it is time to explore one of the most popular Python frameworks: Flask. Flask makes it easy for you to develop web applications quickly without unnecessary complexity. Known for its simplicity and flexibility, it is an excellent choice if you are just getting started with web development.

Understanding Flask:

Flask is a micro-framework for web development. This means it provides only the essential tools needed to build a web application, without forcing you into a predefined structure. It was created by Armin Ronacher as part of the Pallets Projects, a collection of tools designed for Python web development.

Essential Features of Flask:

- **Lightweight and Minimal**: Flask has a small core but allows you to add only the features you need, making it easy to learn and use for small to medium-sized applications.
- **Flexibility**: Unlike larger frameworks that enforce a strict project structure, Flask gives you the freedom to organize your code as you like. You can start with a simple application and expand it as your project grows.
- **Extensibility**: Flask supports various extensions for adding features, such as database integration, authentication, and form handling. This means you do not have to build everything from scratch.

- Built-in Development Server; Flask comes with a built-in server that allows you to test your application during development. This lets you see changes in real-time without needing to deploy your app.

Reasons to Use Flask:

Flask is an excellent choice if you are looking for a simple yet effective way to build web applications. Here are some reasons why Flask might be the right framework for you:

- **Easy to Learn**: Flask has a simple and intuitive syntax, making it perfect if you are new to web development. You can create a basic web application with just a few lines of code.
- **Fast Prototyping**: If you want to test an idea quickly, Flask allows you to build prototypes with minimal effort. You can start small and gradually add more features as needed.
- **Strong Community Support**: Flask has an active community of developers who contribute to its growth. You will find plenty of tutorials, documentation, and third-party extensions to help you develop your application.

With its combination of simplicity and flexibility, Flask is a great choice whether you are building a small personal project or a larger web application.

Getting Flask Ready for Development

Before you can start building web applications with Flask, you need to set up your development environment. This section will guide you through installing Flask and creating your first project using Visual Studio Code.

Step 1: Creating a Project Directory

To keep your project files organized, create a new directory for your Flask project.

a. Open Visual Studio Code.

b. Open the integrated terminal by selecting `Terminal` > `New Terminal` from the menu.

c. In the terminal, run the following commands to create a new directory:

```
mkdir my_flask_app
cd my_flask_app
```

Step 2: Setting Up a Virtual Environment

A virtual environment allows you to manage dependencies for your project without affecting your system-wide Python installation. Run the following command in the terminal:

```
# Create a virtual environment
python -m venv venv
```

To activate the virtual environment:

- On Windows:

```
.\venv\Scripts\activate
```

- On macOS/Linux:

```
source venv/bin/activate
```

Once activated, your terminal prompt will update to indicate that you are inside the virtual environment.

Step 3: Installing Flask

With the virtual environment activated, install Flask using pip:

```
pip install Flask
```

To confirm that Flask is installed, check the version by running:

```
flask -version
```

```
[notice] A new release of pip is available: 23.2.1 -> 24.2
[notice] To update, run: python.exe -m pip install --upgrade pip
(flaskvenv) PS C:\Users\\Downloads\Book 3\code\242_14\my_flask_app> pip install Flask
Looking in indexes: https://pypi.org/simple/
Requirement already satisfied: Flask in c:\users\\downloads\book 3\code\242_14\my_flask_app\flaskvenv\lib\site-packages (3.0.3)
Requirement already satisfied: Werkzeug>=3.0.0 in c:\users\\downloads\book 3\code\242_14\my_flask_app\flaskvenv\lib\site-packages (from Flask) (3.0.3)
Requirement already satisfied: Jinja2>=3.1.2 in c:\users\\downloads\book 3\code\242_14\my_flask_app\flaskvenv\lib\site-packages (from Flask) (3.1.4)
Requirement already satisfied: itsdangerous>=2.1.2 in c:\users\\downloads\book 3\code\242_14\my_flask_app\flaskvenv\lib\site-packages (from Flask) (2.2.0)
Requirement already satisfied: click>=8.1.3 in c:\users\\downloads\book 3\code\242_14\my_flask_app\flaskvenv\lib\site-packages (from Flask) (8.1.7)
Requirement already satisfied: blinker>=1.6.2 in c:\users\\downloads\book 3\code\242_14\my_flask_app\flaskvenv\lib\site-packages (from Flask) (1.8.2)
Requirement already satisfied: colorama in c:\users\\downloads\book 3\code\242_14\my_flask_app\flaskvenv\lib\site-packages (from click>=8.1.3->Flask) (0.4.6)
Requirement already satisfied: MarkupSafe>=2.0 in c:\users\\downloads\book 3\code\242_14\my_flask_app\flaskvenv\lib\site-packages (from Jinja2>=3.1.2->Flask) (2.1.5)

[notice] A new release of pip is available: 23.2.1 -> 24.2
[notice] To update, run: python.exe -m pip install --upgrade pip
(flaskvenv) PS C:\Users\\Downloads\Book 3\code\242_14\my_flask_app> flask --version
Python 3.11.5
Flask 3.0.3
Werkzeug 3.0.3
(flaskvenv) PS C:\Users\\Downloads\Book 3\code\242_14\my_flask_app>
```

Figure 15.1: *Checking flask version*

Now that Flask is installed, you are ready to build your first web application!

Creating a Basic Flask App

Now that you have Flask set up, let us create a simple web application to test if everything is working correctly.

Step 1: Setting Up a New Python File

In Visual Studio Code, create a new file named **`app.py`** inside your project directory (**`my_flask_app`**). This file will contain the code for your Flask application.

Step 2: Writing Your First Flask Application

Open **`app.py`** and add the following code:

```
from flask import Flask

# Create an instance of the Flask class
app = Flask(__name__)

# Define a route for the homepage
@app.route('/')
def home():
    return 'Hello, Flask!'

# Run the app when the script is executed
if __name__ == '__main__':
    app.run(debug=True)
```

Understanding the Code

- **Importing Flask**: You first import the **`Flask`** class from the **`flask`** module.
- **Creating an App Instance**: You create an instance of the **`Flask`** class, which acts as the core of your application.
- **Defining a Route**: The **`@app.route('/')`** decorator tells Flask that when a user visits the homepage (/), the **`home()`** function should run and return the message **`"Hello, Flask!"`** to the browser.

- **Running the App**: The **`app.run(debug=True)`** command starts the Flask development server. Setting **`debug=True`** allows you to see errors and automatically reload changes during development.

Step 3: Running Your Flask Application

To start your Flask app, open the terminal in Visual Studio Code and enter:

```
python app.py
```

You should see output indicating that the Flask development server is running. It will appear as follows:

```
* Running on http://127.0.0.1:5000/ (Press CTRL+C to quit)
```

```
PS C:\Users\    \Downloads\Book 3\code\242_14\my_flask_app> python app.py
 * Serving Flask app 'app'
 * Debug mode: on
WARNING: This is a development server. Do not use it in a production deployment. Use a production WSGI server instead.
 * Running on http://127.0.0.1:5000
Press CTRL+C to quit
 * Restarting with watchdog (windowsapi)
 * Debugger is active!
 * Debugger PIN:
```

Figure 15.2: *Running flask*

Step 4: Viewing the Application in Your Browser

Open your web browser and go to:

```
http://localhost:5000
```

You should see the message:

```
Hello, Flask!
```

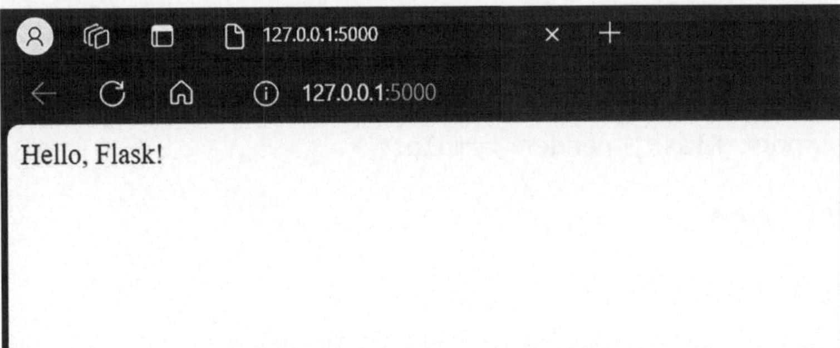

Figure 15.3: *Flask app output on browser*

Congratulations! You have successfully built and run your first Flask application. This simple program serves as a starting point for creating more advanced and interactive web applications in the next sections.

Using Templates in Flask

In the last section, you built a simple Flask application that displayed a basic message. However, most web applications need to show more dynamic content. Flask makes this possible by using Jinja2, a templating engine that allows you to generate dynamic HTML pages. In this section, you will learn how to use templates to create more complex web pages.

Understanding Templates:

Templates allow you to separate your web application's design from its logic. Instead of writing HTML directly inside your Flask routes, you can use templates to structure your web pages and insert dynamic content using variables. This makes your code more organized and easier to manage.

Creating a Template for Your Flask App

Step 1: Setting Up a Templates Directory

Flask looks for HTML templates inside a folder named templates. To set this up, create a new directory called templates inside your project folder. You can do this by running:

```
mkdir templates
```

Step 2: Creating a Template File

Inside the **`templates`** directory, create a new HTML file named **`index.html`**. Add the following code:

```
<!DOCTYPE html>
<html lang="en">
<head>
    <meta charset="UTF-8">
    <meta name="viewport" content="width=device-width, initial-scale=1.0">
    <title>Flask App</title>
</head>
<body>
    <h1>{{ title }}</h1>
    <p>Welcome to my Flask app! This content is rendered using a template.</p>
</body>
</html>
```

Understanding the Code:

Jinja2 Syntax: The {{ title }} syntax is part of Jinja2, Flask's templating engine. This placeholder allows Flask to insert dynamic content into the page when rendering the template.

Updating Your Flask Application to Use Templates

Modify the **`app.py`** file to use the **`index.html`** template instead of returning plain text.

```
from flask import Flask, render_template

app = Flask(__name__)

@app.route('/')
def home():
    return render_template('index.html', title='Hello, Flask!')

if __name__ == '__main__':
    app.run(debug=True)
```

Understanding the Code

Using `render_template`: Instead of returning a string, Flask now uses **`render_template('index.html', title='Hello, Flask!')`** to load the template and pass the title variable to it.

Running Your Flask App with Templates

Save the changes and restart your Flask application:

```
python app.py
```

Open your web browser and visit:

```
http://127.0.0.1:5000/
```

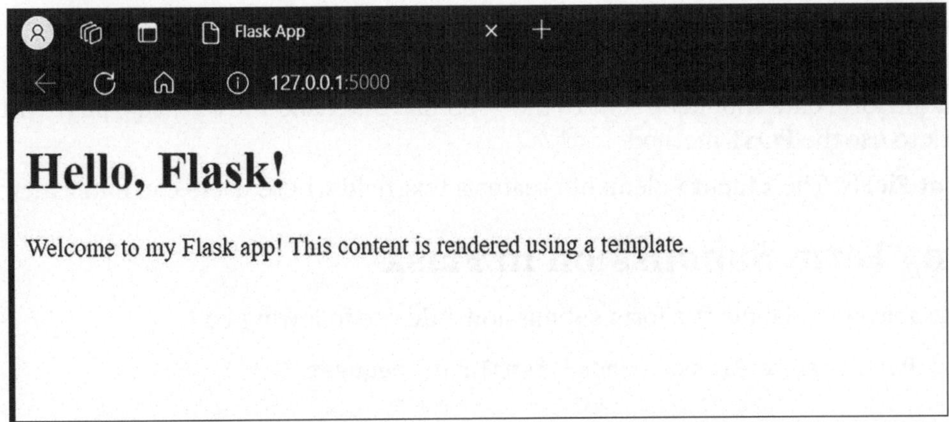

Figure 15.4: *Flask app (with template) output on browser*

You should see the message **"Hello, Flask!"** displayed as the page title, with the content rendered from your index.html template.

Flask generates dynamic HTML content using Jinja2, allowing you to insert variables into your HTML using {{ variable_name }} syntax. This makes it easy to build interactive and data-driven web applications while keeping your code structured.

In the next section, you will learn how to handle user input using forms.

Handling Forms and Input in Flask

Web applications often need to interact with users by collecting input, such as login details, sign-ups, or feedback. Flask makes it simple to handle form submissions and process user data. In this section, you will learn how to create and process forms in a Flask application.

Creating a Form in HTML

To begin, update the existing `index.html` template to include a basic form. Open **`index.html`** and modify it as follows:

```
<!DOCTYPE html>
<html lang="en">
<head>
    <meta charset="UTF-8">
    <meta name="viewport" content="width=device-width, initial-scale=1.0">
    <title>Flask App</title>
</head>
<body>
    <h1>{{ title }}</h1>
    <p>Welcome to my Flask app! This content is rendered using a template.</p>

    <form action="/submit" method="post">
        <label for="name">Name:</label>
        <input type="text" id="name" name="name" required>
        <br>
        <input type="submit" value="Submit">
    </form>
</body>
</html>
```

Understanding the Code:

- **Form Tag**: The <form> tag defines the form element. The **`action="/submit"`** attribute specifies that the form data should be sent to the /submit route, and the **`method="post"`** attribute tells Flask to use the POST method.
- **Input Fields**: The **`<input>`** element creates a text field where users can enter their name.

Handling Form Submission in Flask

Now, update **`app.py`** to handle the form submission. Add the following code:

```
from flask import Flask, render_template, request

app = Flask(__name__)

@app.route('/')
def home():
    return render_template('index.html', title='Hello, Flask!')

@app.route('/submit', methods=['POST'])
def submit():
    name = request.form.get('name')
    return f'Thank you, {name}, for submitting the form!'

if __name__ == '__main__':
    app.run(debug=True)
```

Understanding the Code:

- **Defining a New Route**: The **`@app.route('/submit', methods=['POST'])`** decorator creates a new route that handles form submissions using the POST method.
- **Retrieving Form Data**: **`request.form.get('name')`** retrieves the value entered in the form's name field.
- **Displaying User Input**: The server responds with a thank-you message that includes the user's name.

Testing the Form Submission:

Save the changes and restart your Flask application:

```
python app.py
```

Open your browser and visit:

```
http://127.0.0.1:5000/
```

Enter your name in the form and submit it. You should see a message, as illustrated here:

```
Thank you, John, for submitting the form!
```

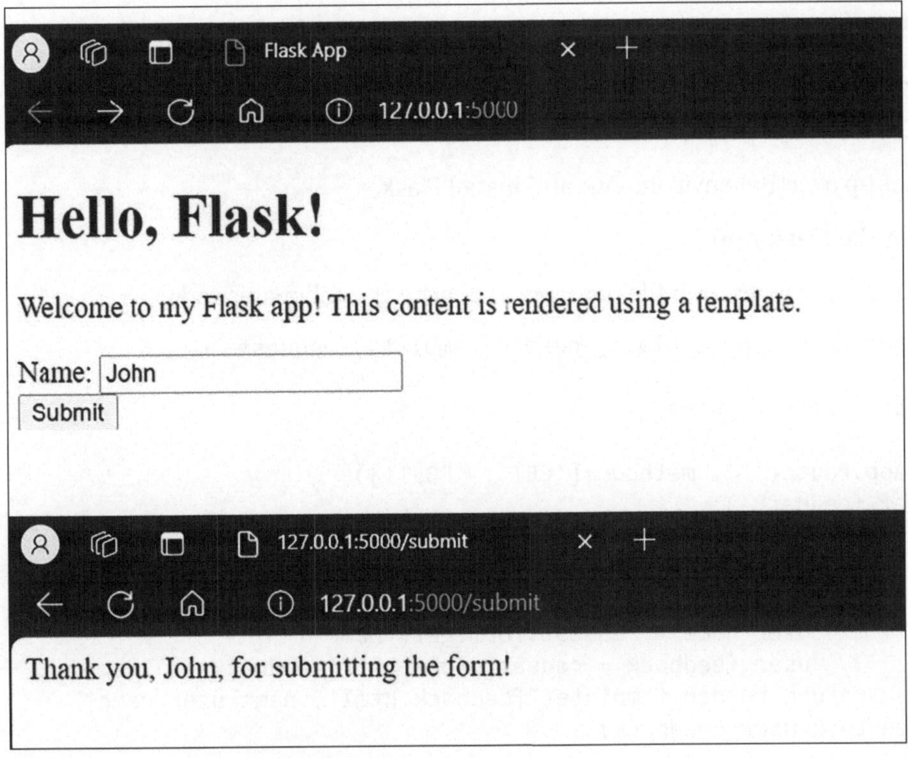

***Figure 15.5:** Flask app (with form) output on browser*

Expanding Form Handling in Flask:

Handling user input is essential for building interactive web applications. You can extend this functionality to handle multiple fields, validate inputs, and store form data in a database.

With Flask's simple form-handling approach, you can easily build applications that collect and process user input, making your web apps more interactive and user-friendly.

Practical Exercise: Building a Simple Feedback Form

In this exercise, you will use what you have learnt about Flask to create a simple feedback form web application. This exercise will help you improve your grasp of how to set up a Flask app, use templates for dynamic content, and manage form submissions.

Task Description:

Create a Flask web app that allows users to provide feedback via a form. When the user submits the form, the application should display a thank-you message that includes their name and feedback.

Real-life scenario:

Assume you are creating a website for a local community event. You want to get input from participants so that you can better future events. Your objective is to design a web page where people can leave their feedback, and then show a personalized thank-you message.

Steps for the Exercise

1. Start a new Flask project using a virtual environment.
2. Create a Flask app with routes to display feedback and manage form submissions.
3. Create a template for a feedback form with a personalized thank-you message.
4. Process form input with Flask's request handling.

Implementation Steps

1. **Set Up the Environment**
   a. Create a new project directory.
   b. Set up a virtual environment and install Flask.
2. **Create the Flask App**
   a. Create a new Python file (**app.py**) and write the following code:

```
from flask import Flask, render_template, request

app = Flask(__name__)

@app.route('/', methods=['GET', 'POST'])
def feedback():
    user_name = None
    user_feedback = None
    if request.method == 'POST':
        user_name = request.form.get('name')
        user_feedback = request.form.get('feedback')
    return render_template('feedback.html', name=user_name,
feedback=user_feedback)

if __name__ == '__main__':
    app.run(debug=True)
```

3. **Design the Template**
   a. Create a templates directory and add a **feedback.html** file with the following content:

```
<!DOCTYPE html>
<html lang="en">
<head>
    <meta charset="UTF-8">
    <meta name="viewport" content="width=device-width, initial-scale=1.0">
    <title>Event Feedback</title>
</head>
<body>
    <h1>Event Feedback Form</h1>
    <form method="post">
        <label for="name">Name:</label>
        <input type="text" id="name" name="name" required>
        <br>
        <label for="feedback">Feedback:</label>
        <textarea id="feedback" name="feedback" required></textarea>
        <br>
        <input type="submit" value="Submit">
    </form>

    {% if name and feedback %}
        <h2>Thank You!</h2>
        <p>Thank you, {{ name }}, for your feedback:</p>
        <blockquote>{{ feedback }}</blockquote>
    {% endif %}
</body>
</html>
```

4. **Test Your Application**
    a. Launch your Flask app in a web browser.
    b. Fill out the feedback form and submit it to receive a personalized thank-you note.

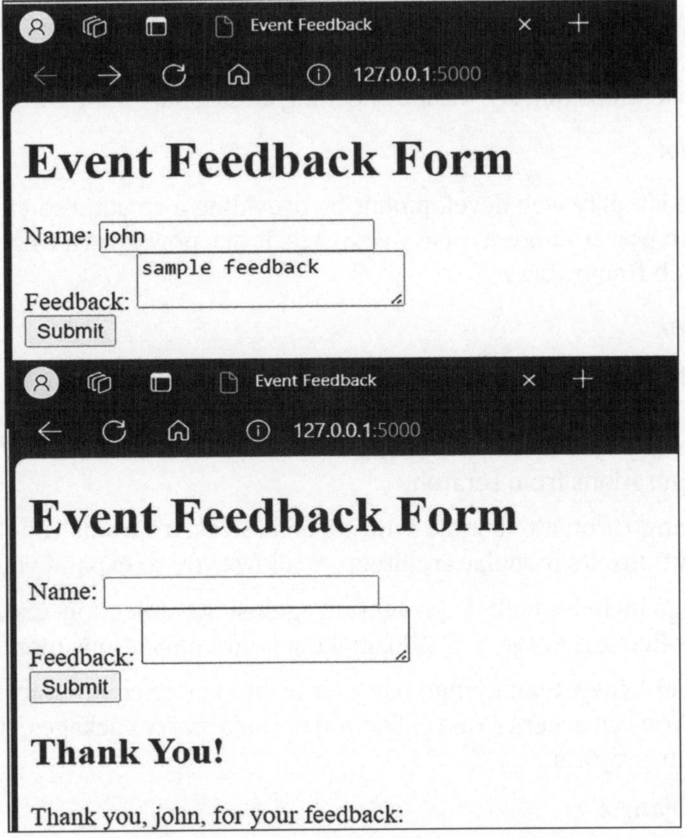

***Figure 15.6:** Flask app output on browser*

Understanding the Solution

- **Route Handling:** The `@app.route('/', methods=['GET', 'POST'])` decorator creates a route for displaying the form and accepting submissions. It supports both GET and POST requests.
- **Form Submission:** The `request.form.get()` method retrieves the user's name and feedback.
- **Template Rendering:** The template uses Jinja2 to dynamically display a thank-you message based on user input after form submission.

This exercise simulates a real-world scenario for gathering feedback, allowing you to use the Flask principles you studied in a practical setting. By completing this work, you will receive hands-on experience with Flask, templates, and form handling, which are key abilities for developing interactive online applications.

Django: A Beginner's Guide

After exploring Flask and understanding its lightweight approach to web development, you are now ready to learn Django, a more advanced and feature-rich framework for building web applications. Django is designed to help you quickly move projects from concept to completion by providing a variety of built-in tools and functionalities.

In this guide, you will get an introduction to Django and set up your development environment. You will create a basic Django project, use templates to generate dynamic content, and handle user input using forms. By the end of this section, you will have a strong foundation for building more complex and scalable web applications with Django while leveraging its extensive features.

Introduction to Django

Django is a high-level Python web framework that emphasizes fast development and clean, maintainable design. It follows the "batteries-included" philosophy, meaning it comes with many built-in tools that allow you to build applications quickly without needing additional configurations.

Understanding Django:

Django was created to simplify web development by providing a structured and organized approach. Originally developed to power content-heavy websites, it has now grown to become one of the most widely used Python web frameworks.

Key Features of Django:

- **Batteries-Included**: Django provides built-in functionality such as an Object-Relational Mapper (ORM) for database interactions, an admin panel, authentication support, and much more. This allows you to focus on building your application's unique features instead of setting up basic configurations from scratch.
- **Scalability**: Django is built to handle projects of all sizes, from small applications to large-scale enterprise solutions. Its modular architecture allows you to expand your application easily.
- **Security**: Django includes built-in protection against SQL injection, Cross-Site Scripting (XSS), and Cross-Site Request Forgery (CSRF), making your applications more secure by default.
- **Community and Ecosystem**: Django has a large and active community that contributes to its development. You can access a vast collection of third-party packages, tutorials, and resources to enhance your projects.

Advantages of Using Django:

Django is a great choice if you want to develop web applications efficiently while maintaining high quality and security. Some of its biggest advantages include:

- **Rapid Development**: Django simplifies common tasks such as user authentication, form handling, and database management, reducing the time required to build applications.
- **Clean and Maintainable Code**: Django follows the Model-View-Template (MVT) design pattern, which encourages structured and maintainable code, making it easier to manage projects in the long run.
- **Flexibility**: Django is versatile enough to be used for a wide range of projects, from simple websites to complex web applications.

With its power and flexibility, Django is an excellent choice for building scalable and maintainable web applications. The next step is to set up Django and build your first project using its rich features.

Setting Up Django

Before you can start developing web applications with Django, you need to set up your development environment. This section will guide you through the process of installing Django and setting up your project using Visual Studio Code.

Step 1: Installing Django

To begin, install Django in your development environment using Python's package manager, pip.

1. Open Visual Studio Code and launch the integrated terminal by selecting **`Terminal`** > **`New Terminal`** from the menu.
2. Create a new directory for your Django project and navigate into it:

```
mkdir my_django_app
cd my_django_app
```

3. Set up a virtual environment to manage project dependencies:

```
python -m venv venv
```

4. Activate the virtual environment:
   a. On Windows:

   ```
   .\venv\Scripts\activate
   ```

   b. On macOS/Linux:

   ```
   source venv/bin/activate
   ```

5. Install Django using pip:

```
pip install Django
```

6. Verify the installation by checking the Django version:

```
django-admin version
```

```
(venv) (base) C:\Users\      \Downloads\Book 3\code\242_14\my_django_app>django-admin version
5.1
```

Figure 15.7: *Checking Django version*

Once Django is installed, you are ready to create your first Django project.

Step 2: Creating Your First Django Project

Now that Django is installed, you can start a new Django project. A Django project is a collection of settings and configurations that define your web application.

- **Creating a Django Project**

  Run the following command to create a new Django project named **`myproject`**:

  ```
  django-admin startproject myproject
  ```

  This command will generate a new directory named **`myproject`**, which contains the following structure:

```
myproject/
    manage.py
    myproject/
        __init__.py
        settings.py
        urls.py
        wsgi.py
        asgi.py
```

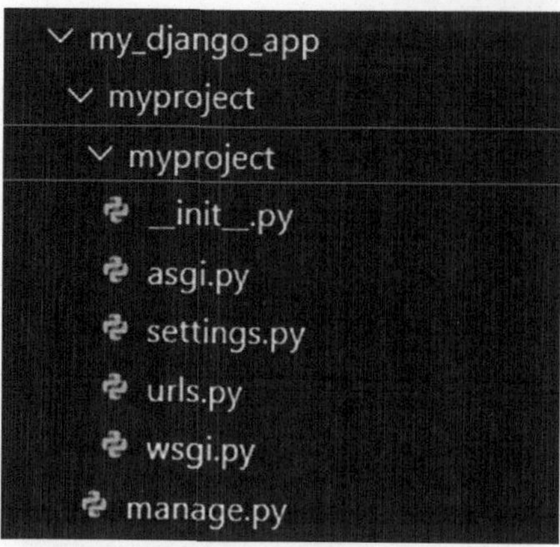

Figure 15.8: *Django folder structure*

Understanding the Project Structure

- **`manage.py`**: A command-line tool used for running Django commands such as starting the server or creating database migrations.
- **`settings.py`**: The configuration file that contains Django project settings such as database connections, security options, and installed applications.
- **`urls.py`**: The file that defines the URL patterns for your application, mapping URLs to specific views.
- **`wsgi.py`** and **`asgi.py`**: Entry points for web servers to serve your application.

- **Opening the Project in Visual Studio Code**

  Now, navigate into your project directory and open it in Visual Studio Code:

```
cd myproject
code .
```

  At this point, Django is installed, and your project structure is set up. You are now ready to build your first Django app.

Step 3: Running the Django Development Server

To test your setup, run Django's built-in development server. This server allows you to see your project in action without deploying it to a real web server.

- **Starting the Server**

  Inside the **`myproject`** directory, run the following command:

```
python manage.py runserver
```

  You should see output similar to this:

```
Watching for file changes with StatReloader
Performing system checks...

System check identified no issues (0 silenced).
March 15, 2025 - 12:34:56
Django version X.X.X, using settings 'myproject.settings'
Starting development server at http://127.0.0.1:8000/
Quit the server with CONTROL-C.
```

- Viewing Your Django Project in the Browser

  Open your web browser and go to:

```
http://127.0.0.1:8000/
```

You should see Django's default welcome page, confirming that your project is running successfully.

Django's development server provides a convenient way to test your application as you build it. However, for production use, you would need to deploy it to a more robust server.

Building Your First Django App

Now that your Django project is set up and running, you can begin creating an application within it. In the next section, you will learn how to build a simple Django app, use templates to generate dynamic content, and handle user input.

By following these steps, you will gain hands-on experience in developing Django applications and leveraging its built-in features to create powerful web applications.

Building a Basic Django App:

After setting up Django and creating a project, it is time to build a simple Django app. In this section, you will create an app within your Django project, define views, and configure URL routing to display a webpage. Each step will be explained so you can understand the purpose and process clearly.

Creating a Django App:

In Django, an app is a self-contained module that performs a specific function, such as handling a blog, managing user authentication, or processing database records. Apps are designed to be reusable and can be integrated into multiple projects. To structure your project efficiently, you need to create an app to manage different tasks.

Step 1: Creating an App in Django

a. Open Visual Studio Code and its terminal. Navigate to your project directory and run the following command to create a new app called **myapp**:

```
python manage.py startapp myapp
```

b. This command generates a new directory named **myapp** with the following structure:

```
myapp/
    __init__.py
    admin.py
    apps.py
    models.py
    tests.py
    views.py
```

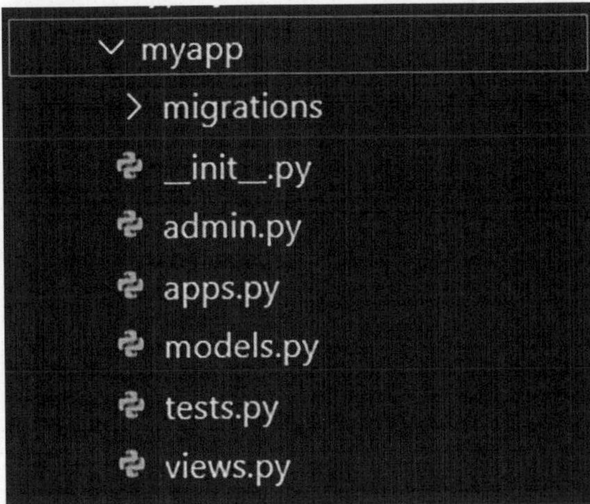

Figure 15.9: *Django folder structure*

Understanding the App Structure:

- **views.py**: Contains the logic for displaying content in your web application.
- **models.py**: Defines database models (not used in this example but essential for handling data).
- **admin.py, apps.py, and tests.py**: Provide additional functionality such as an admin interface and testing.

Step 2: Registering the App in Django

To let Django know about the new app, add it to the **INSTALLED_APPS** list in the **settings.py** file. Open **myproject/settings.py** and add '**myapp**' to the list:

```
INSTALLED_APPS = [
    'django.contrib.admin',
    'django.contrib.auth',
    'django.contrib.contenttypes',
    'django.contrib.sessions',
    'django.contrib.messages',
    'django.contrib.staticfiles',
    'myapp',  # Add your app here
]
```

Defining a View:

A view in Django is a function that handles a web request and returns a web response. This determines what happens when a user visits a specific URL.

Open **myapp/views.py** and add the following function:

```
from django.http import HttpResponse

def home(request):
    return HttpResponse("Hello, Django!")
```

- The home function specifies the logic for handling a request.
- When a user visits the assigned URL, Django returns an HTTP response with the message **"Hello, Django!"**.

Configuring URL Routing:

URL routing maps URL patterns to views, allowing Django to direct user requests to the appropriate functions.

Step 1: Creating a URL Configuration for the App

Inside the **myapp** directory, create a new file called **urls.py** and add the following code:

```
from django.urls import path
from . import views

urlpatterns = [
    path('', views.home, name='home'),
]
```

- This file defines the URL patterns for your app.
- The **path('', views.home, name='home')** line ensures that when a user visits the homepage (/), Django runs the home view.

Step 2: Connecting the App's URLs to the Project

To ensure Django recognizes the app's URLs, include them in the main project's **`urls.py`** file. Open **`myproject/urls.py`** and modify it as follows:

```
from django.contrib import admin
from django.urls import path, include

urlpatterns = [
    path('admin/', admin.site.urls),
    path('', include('myapp.urls')),  # Include the app's URLs
]
```

This step connects the app's URL patterns to the main project, allowing Django to direct user requests correctly.

Running the Django Development Server:

After completing the setup, you can run Django's development server to test your application.

Step 1: Starting the Server

In the terminal, run:

```
python manage.py runserver
```

```
August 16, 2024 - 20:24:44
Django version 5.1, using settings 'myproject.settings'
Starting development server at http://127.0.0.1:8000/
Quit the server with CTRL-BREAK.
```

Figure 15.10: *Running Django*

Step 2: Viewing the Application

Open your browser and go to:

```
http://localhost:8000
```

You should see the message **`"Hello, Django!"`** displayed on the webpage.

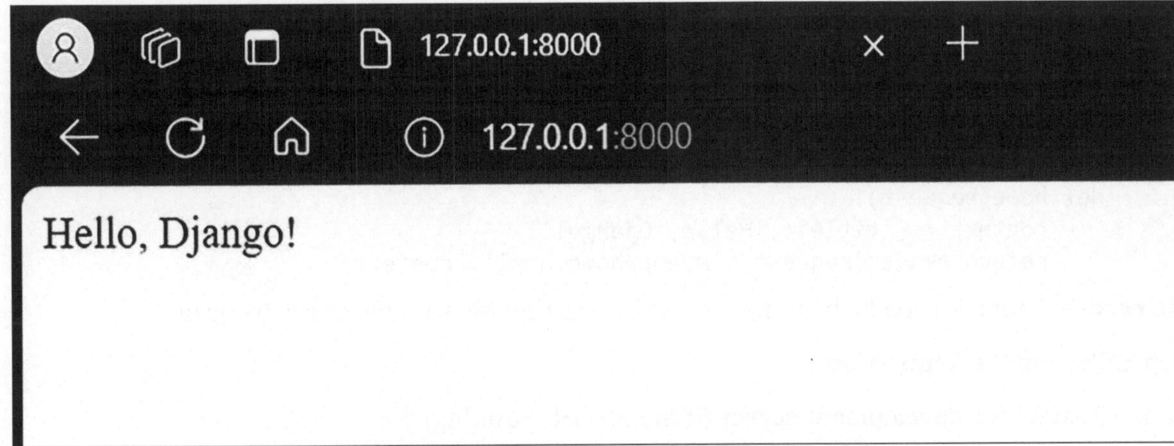

Figure 15.11: *Django output on browser*

Using Templates in Django

In the previous section, you built a basic Django app that displayed a simple message. To create more dynamic and interactive web pages, Django provides a templating engine. Templates allow you to separate your web application's design from its logic, making code easier to manage.

Understanding Templates:

Templates are HTML files that define the structure of a webpage while allowing dynamic content to be inserted using variables and expressions. Django's templating engine is similar to Jinja2, enabling you to insert dynamic content into your web pages.

Step 1: Creating a Templates Directory

Django searches for templates inside an app-specific **templates** directory. To organize your project properly, create the following structure:

```
cd myapp
mkdir templates
cd templates
mkdir myapp
```

This approach ensures that Django can locate templates unique to each app, preventing conflicts when multiple apps are used.

Step 2: Creating a Template File

Inside the **myapp/templates/myapp** directory, create a new HTML file called home.html and add the following code:

```
<!DOCTYPE html>
<html lang="en">
<head>
    <meta charset="UTF-8">
    <meta name="viewport" content="width=device-width, initial-scale=1.0">
    <title>My Django App</title>
</head>
<body>
    <h1>{{ title }}</h1>
    <p>Welcome to my Django app! This page is rendered using a template.</p>
</body>
</html>
```

The `{{ title }}` syntax allows Django to insert dynamic content into the template.

Step 3: Updating the View to Use Templates

Modify the home view in **myapp/views.py** to render the template instead of returning plain text:

```
from django.shortcuts import render

def home(request):
    context = {'title': 'Hello, Django!'}
    return render(request, 'myapp/home.html', context)
```

The **render()** function loads the template and passes the title variable to the webpage.

Step 4: Testing the Application

1. **Restart the development server (if not already running):**

   ```
   python manage.py runserver
   ```

2. **View the Application in your browser by going to:**

   ```
   http://localhost:8000
   ```

You should see the title **"Hello, Django!"** displayed on the webpage.

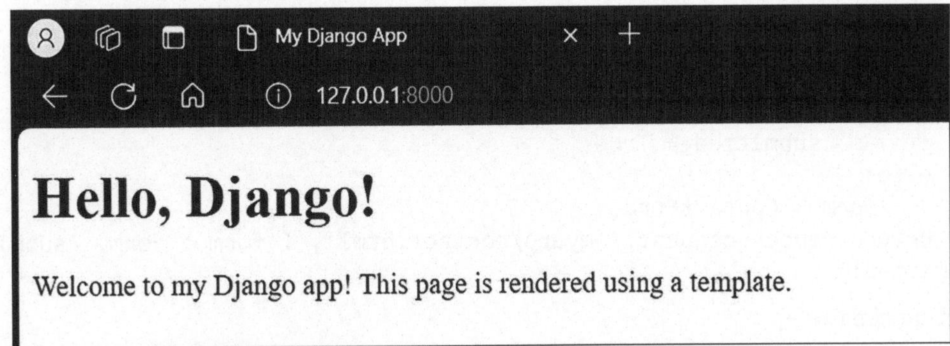

Figure 15.12: *Django output (with template) on browser*

Enhancing Your Django App:

Using Django's template engine, you can create dynamic and interactive web pages while keeping your application logic clean. Django allows you to manage complex pages efficiently and deliver personalized content to users.

In the next section, you will learn how to handle user input with forms, making your application more interactive.

Handling Forms in Django

Django forms are created as Python classes. Each form field is represented as a class attribute, and Django automatically generates the necessary HTML elements.

Step 1: Defining the Form

a. Open **`myapp/forms.py`** (create this file if it does not exist).

b. Add the following form class using Django's built-in form fields:

```
from django import forms

class ContactForm(forms.Form):
    name = forms.CharField(label='Your Name', max_length=100)
    message = forms.CharField(label='Your Message', widget=forms.Textarea)
```

Understanding the Code:

- **`name`** Field: A text input field for capturing the user's name.
- **`message`** Field: A textarea input field for capturing the user's message.
- Django will automatically generate the appropriate HTML input fields and handle validation.

Step 2: Creating a View to Handle the Form

To process the form, you need a view function that handles both displaying and processing user input.

Adding the View:

1. Open **`myapp/views.py`**.
2. Add the following function:

```
from django.shortcuts import render
from .forms import ContactForm

def contact(request):
    submitted = False
    if request.method == 'POST':
```

```
            form = ContactForm(request.POST)
            if form.is_valid():
                name = form.cleaned_data['name']
                message = form.cleaned_data['message']
                submitted = True
        else:
            form = ContactForm()
        return render(request, 'myapp/contact.html', {'form': form, 'submitted':
submitted})
```

Understanding the Code

- Handles Both GET and POST Requests:
    - If the request is GET, an empty form is displayed.
    - If the request is POST, Django validates the form and extracts the user's input.
- **`form.cleaned_data`**: Retrieves sanitized input data once validation is successful.
- **`submitted = True`**: Used to show a success message after submission.

Step 3: Creating a Template for the Form

You need a template to display the form and show a confirmation message after submission.

Creating the Template:

1. In the **`myapp/templates/myapp/`** directory, create a file named **`contact.html`**.
2. Add the following HTML code:

   html

   CopyEdit

```
<!DOCTYPE html>
<html lang="en">
<head>
    <meta charset="UTF-8">
    <meta name="viewport" content="width=device-width, initial-scale=1.0">
    <title>Contact Us</title>
</head>
<body>
    <h1>Contact Form</h1>
    {% if submitted %}
        <p>Thank you for your message, {{ form.cleaned_data.name }}!</p>
    {% else %}
        <form method="post">
            {% csrf_token %}
            {{ form.as_p }}
            <input type="submit" value="Submit">
        </form>
    {% endif %}
</body>
</html>
```

Understanding the Code:

- **`{% csrf_token %}`**: Protects against Cross-Site Request Forgery (CSRF) attacks.
- **`{{ form.as_p }}`**: Automatically generates form fields as paragraph elements.
- **Displays a Success Message**: If the form is submitted successfully, it shows a thank-you message.

Step 4: Configuring URL Routing

You need to define a URL pattern to make the contact form accessible in the application.

Updating URL Configuration:

1. Open **`myapp/urls.py`**.
2. Modify the file to include the new route:

```
from django.urls import path
from . import views

urlpatterns = [
    path('', views.home, name='home'),
    path('contact/', views.contact, name='contact'),
]
```

Understanding the Code:

- The URL pattern **`path('contact/', views.contact, name='contact'`**) maps the **`/contact/ URL`** to the contact view function.

Step 5: Testing the Contact Form

Once everything is set up, you can test your form.

- **Running the Development Server**

  If your server is not running, start it by running:

  `python manage.py runserver`

- **Accessing the Contact Form**

  Open your web browser and visit:

  `http://localhost:8000/contact/`

Enter a name and a message, then submit the form.

You should see a thank-you message displayed on the page.

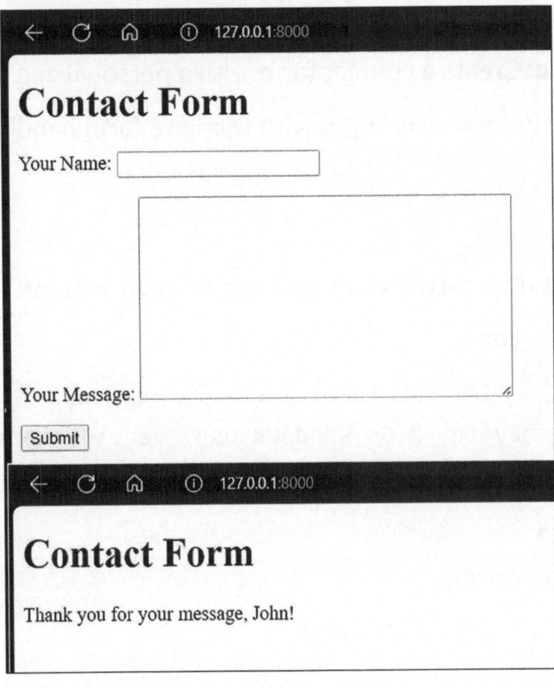

Figure 15.13: *Django output (with form) on browser*

Expanding Django Forms for Advanced Features

Django's form-handling framework simplifies user input validation and processing. You can extend this by:

- **Adding Email Fields**: To capture user email addresses.
- **Using Django ModelForms**: To save form data directly into a database.
- **Applying Custom Validation**: To enforce specific input rules.

With Django's form system, you can create interactive web applications that collect and process user data efficiently. In the next section, you will explore advanced Django features to enhance your applications further.

Practical Exercise: Building a Simple Contact Form

In this exercise, you will use what you have learned about Django to create a simple contact form web application. This exercise will help you improve your grasp of how to build up a Django project, use templates for dynamic content, and manage form submissions.

Task Description:

Create a Django web application that allows users to provide contact information via a form. When the user submits the form, the application should display a thank-you message that includes their name and message.

Real-Life Scenario:

Imagine you are creating a website for a small business. You want to give clients a method to contact thc company directly via the website. Your objective is to design a web page where users may submit their contact information and message, and then display a personalized thank-you message.

Steps for the Exercise:

1. **Set Up the Environment:** Start a new Django project with a virtual environment.
2. **Create the App:** Create a Django app with views to display the contact form and manage form submissions.
3. **Design the Template:** Create a contact form with a personalized thank-you message.
4. **Handle Form Input:** Process user input with Django's form handling system.

Implementation Steps:

Set Up the Environment:

1. Create a new project directory and set up a virtual environment:

   ```
   mkdir contact_form_app
   cd contact_form_app
   python -m venv venv
   source venv/bin/activate  # On Windows use `venv\Scripts\activate`
   ```

2. Install Django:

   ```
   pip install Django
   ```

3. Create a new Django project:

   ```
   django-admin startproject myproject
   cd myproject
   ```

4. Create a new Django app:

   ```
   python manage.py startapp contact
   ```

Create the Django App:

1. **Define the Form**: Create **`contact/forms.py`** and define a contact form:

   ```
   from django import forms

   class ContactForm(forms.Form):
       name = forms.CharField(label='Your Name', max_length=100)
       email = forms.EmailField(label='Your Email')
       message = forms.CharField(label='Your Message', widget=forms.Textarea)
   ```

2. **Create the View**: Open **`contact/views.py`** and add a view to handle the form:

   ```
   from django.shortcuts import render
   from .forms import ContactForm

   def contact_view(request):
       submitted = False
       if request.method == 'POST':
           form = ContactForm(request.POST)
           if form.is_valid():
               # Process the data in form.cleaned_data
               name = form.cleaned_data['name']
               submitted = True
       else:
           form = ContactForm()
       return render(request, 'contact/contact.html', {'form': form, 'submitted':
   submitted})
   ```

3. **Set Up URL Routing**: Open **`contact/urls.py`** and configure URL patterns:

   ```
   from django.urls import path
   from . import views

   urlpatterns = [
       path('', views.contact_view, name='contact'),
   ]
   ```

4. **Include the App's URLs in the Project**: Open **`myproject/urls.py`** and include the app's URLs:

   ```
   from django.contrib import admin
   from django.urls import path, include

   urlpatterns = [
       path('admin/', admin.site.urls),
       path('contact/', include('contact.urls')),
   ]
   ```

5. **Register the App**: Add '**`contact`**' to **`INSTALLED_APPS`** in **`myproject/settings.py`**:

   ```
   INSTALLED_APPS = [
       ...
       "contact",
   ]
   ```

Design the Template:

1. **Create the Template**: Create a directory **`contact/templates/contact/`** and add a **`contact.html`** file:

```
<!DOCTYPE html>
<html lang="en">
<head>
    <meta charset="UTF-8">
    <meta name="viewport" content="width=device-width, initial-scale=1.0">
    <title>Contact Us</title>
</head>
<body>
    <h1>Contact Form</h1>
    {% if submitted %}
        <p>Thank you, {{ form.cleaned_data.name }}, for your message!</p>
    {% else %}
        <form method="post">
            {% csrf_token %}
            {{ form.as_p }}
            <input type="submit" value="Submit">
        </form>
    {% endif %}
</body>
</html>
```

Test Your Application:

1. Run the Development Server:
   `python manage.py runserver`
2. View Your Application: Open your web browser and go to `http://localhost:8000/contact/`. Fill out the form and submit it to see the thank-you message.

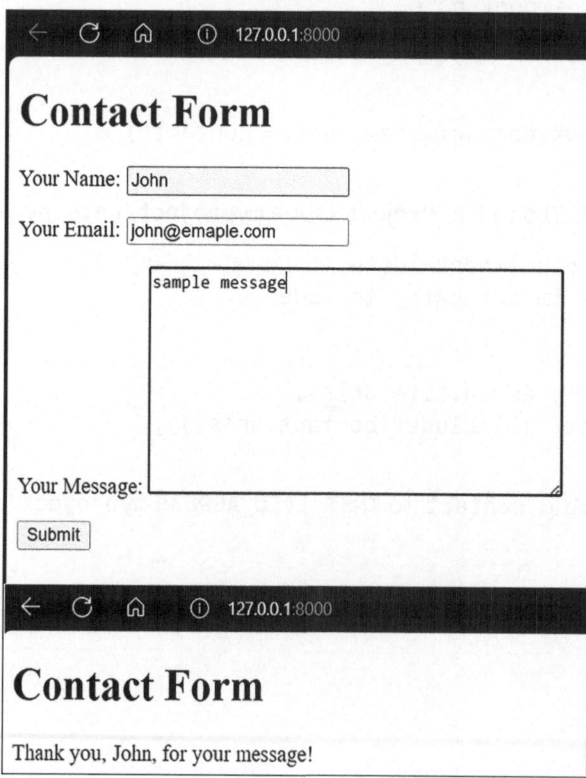

***Figure 15.14**: Django output on browser*

Understanding the solution:

1. The `ContactForm` class defines the form's fields and validation.
2. The `contact_view` function processes form submissions, validates input, and presents responses.
3. The template renders the form and displays a thank-you message for successful submission.

This exercise simulates a real-world scenario of answering user inquiries via a contact form, allowing you to use the Django ideas you have studied in a practical setting. By completing this work, you will receive hands-on experience with Django, templates, and form handling, which are vital abilities for developing interactive online apps.

Common Mistakes and Best Practices

When building web applications with Flask and Django, it is easy to run into common pitfalls. Being aware of these mistakes and following best practices will help you write better, more maintainable applications.

Common Mistakes

- **Not Using Virtual Environments**

  Many beginners install dependencies globally, which can lead to conflicts between projects. Always use a virtual environment to isolate dependencies.

- **Hardcoding HTML in Flask Views**

  Writing raw HTML inside Flask views using return "`<h1>Hello</h1>`" makes your code harder to manage. Instead, use templates to separate logic from presentation.

- **Forgetting CSRF Protection in Forms**

  Django and Flask provide built-in security measures against Cross-Site Request Forgery (CSRF) attacks. If you forget to include `{% csrf_token %}` in Django forms or enable CSRF protection in Flask, your forms may be vulnerable.

- **Ignoring Debug Mode in Production**

  Running your Flask or Django app with `debug=True` in a production environment can expose sensitive error messages. Always disable debug mode before deploying.

- **Not Defining URL Routes Properly**

  Many beginners define routes in multiple places incorrectly or forget to include their app's urls.py in Django's main urls.py. This results in broken links or inaccessible pages.

- **Using the Development Server for Deployment**

  The built-in Flask and Django development servers are not meant for production. Always use a proper WSGI server such as Gunicorn for Flask or Django's built-in deployment strategies for secure deployment.

Best Practices

- **Use Templates for Clean and Maintainable Code**

  Keep HTML templates separate from your views to improve readability and make your application easier to scale.

- **Follow Proper URL Routing Conventions**

  Organize your URL patterns efficiently using `include()` in Django and `url_for()` in Flask. This ensures modular and reusable code.

- **Implement Error Handling**

  Instead of returning generic error pages, use Flask's `@app.errorhandler` or Django's custom error templates (404.html, 500.html) to provide user-friendly messages.

- **Optimize Database Queries**

  Avoid inefficient queries in Django's ORM by using `select_related()` and `prefetch_related()` when dealing with related models. In Flask, use an ORM such as SQLAlchemy for efficient database interactions.

- **Use Environment Variables for Secrets**

  Never store API keys or database credentials directly in your code. Use environment variables and tools such as .env files to keep sensitive data secure.

- **Enable Logging for Debugging**

  Instead of using print statements for debugging, configure logging in both Flask and Django to track errors and application behavior.

By following these best practices and avoiding common mistakes, you will be able to develop more secure, scalable, and maintainable web applications.

Exercises and Challenges: Practice Problems and Solutions

Now that you have learned how to build web applications using Flask and Django, it is time to put your knowledge into practice. The following exercises will help you apply the concepts covered in this chapter and reinforce your understanding of web development.

Practice Problem 1: Flask Blog Post Submission

Task: Create a simple blog post submission application using Flask.

Challenge: Write a Flask application called **`blog_flask.py`** that allows users to submit and view blog posts.

- Set up a new Flask project and create a virtual environment.
- Develop a route to display the blog submission form and handle submissions.
- Store blog posts in a list in memory (no database required).
- Display the list of submitted blog posts on the main page.

Practice Problem 2: Flask Weather Checker

Task: Build a weather checker application using Flask and an external API.

Challenge: Write a Flask application called **`weather_flask.py`** that fetches and displays current weather information for a given city.

- Create a route to display a form where users can enter a city name.
- Use the OpenWeatherMap API (or a similar service) to fetch weather data.
- Display the current weather conditions for the entered city.
- Handle errors gracefully if the city is not found or the API request fails.

Practice Problem 3: Django Task Manager

Task: Develop a task management application using Django.

Challenge: Write a Django application called **task_manager** that allows users to create, update, and delete tasks.

- Set up a new Django project and create a task manager app.
- Define a model for tasks with fields for title, description, and completion status.
- Implement views to list tasks, create new tasks, and update or delete existing tasks.
- Use Django templates to render forms and task lists.

Practice Problem 4: Django Survey Application

Task: Create a survey application using Django where users can submit their responses to multiple-choice questions.

Challenge: Write a Django application called **survey_app** that allows users to participate in surveys.

- Define models for surveys and questions with multiple-choice options.
- Create a form for users to select answers to survey questions.
- Store user responses in a database.
- Display survey results and statistics after submission.

Solutions to Practice Problems

The solutions to the practice challenges for Flask and Django are listed here, with step-by-step implementations for each challenge.

Practice Problem 1: Flask Blog Post Submission

```
blog_flask.py
from flask import Flask, render_template, request, redirect, url_for

app = Flask(__name__)

# In-memory list to store blog posts
blog_posts = []

@app.route('/', methods=['GET', 'POST'])
def home():
    if request.method == 'POST':
        title = request.form.get('title')
        content = request.form.get('content')
        if title and content:
            blog_posts.append({'title': title, 'content': content})
            return redirect(url_for('home'))
    return render_template('home.html', blog_posts=blog_posts)

if __name__ == '__main__':
    app.run(debug=True)
home.html
<!DOCTYPE html>
<html lang="en">
<head>
    <meta charset="UTF-8">
    <meta name="viewport" content="width=device-width, initial-scale=1.0">
```

```
        <title>Flask Blog</title>
    </head>
    <body>
        <h1>Blog Post Submission</h1>
        <form method="post">
            <label for="title">Title:</label>
            <input type="text" id="title" name="title" required>
            <br>
            <label for="content">Content:</label>
            <textarea id="content" name="content" required></textarea>
            <br>
            <input type="submit" value="Submit">
        </form>
        <h2>Submitted Blog Posts</h2>
        <ul>
            {% for post in blog_posts %}
                <li><strong>{{ post.title }}</strong>: {{ post.content }}</li>
            {% endfor %}
        </ul>
    </body>
    </html>
```

Practice Problem 2: Flask Weather Checker

weather_flask.py

```
from flask import Flask, render_template, request
import requests

app = Flask(__name__)

# Replace 'your_api_key' with your actual API key from OpenWeatherMap
API_KEY = 'your_api_key'
BASE_URL = 'http://api.openweathermap.org/data/2.5/weather'

@app.route('/', methods=['GET', 'POST'])
def weather():
    weather_data = None
    error = None
    if request.method == 'POST':
        city = request.form.get('city')
        if city:
            try:
                response = requests.get(BASE_URL, params={'q': city, 'appid':
API_KEY, 'units': 'metric'})
                if response.status_code == 200:
                    weather_data = response.json()
                else:
                    error = 'City not found. Please try another city.'
            except requests.exceptions.RequestException:
                error = 'Failed to connect to the weather service. Please try
again later.'
    return render_template('weather.html', weather_data=weather_data,
error=error)

if __name__ == '__main__':
    app.run(debug=True)
```

weather.html

```
<!DOCTYPE html>
<html lang="en">
<head>
    <meta charset="UTF-8">
    <meta name="viewport" content="width=device-width, initial-scale=1.0">
    <title>Weather Checker</title>
</head>
<body>
    <h1>Weather Checker</h1>
    <form method="post">
        <label for="city">City:</label>
        <input type="text" id="city" name="city" required>
        <input type="submit" value="Check Weather">
    </form>
    {% if weather_data %}
        <h2>Weather in {{ weather_data.name }}</h2>
        <p>Temperature: {{ weather_data.main.temp }} °C</p>
        <p>Weather: {{ weather_data.weather[0].description }}</p>
    {% endif %}
    {% if error %}
        <p style="color:red;">{{ error }}</p>
    {% endif %}
</body>
</html>
```

Practice Problem 3: Django Task Manager

models.py

```
from django.db import models

class Task(models.Model):
    title = models.CharField(max_length=200)
    description = models.TextField(blank=True)
    completed = models.BooleanField(default=False)

    def __str__(self):
        return self.title
```

views.py

```
from django.shortcuts import render, redirect
from .models import Task
from .forms import TaskForm

def task_list(request):
    tasks = Task.objects.all()
    return render(request, 'tasks/task_list.html', {'tasks': tasks})

def add_task(request):
    if request.method == 'POST':
        form = TaskForm(request.POST)
        if form.is_valid():
            form.save()
            return redirect('task_list')
    else:
        form = TaskForm()
    return render(request, 'tasks/add_task.html', {'form': form})

def update_task(request, pk):
    task = Task.objects.get(id=pk)
```

```
    if request.method == 'POST':
        form = TaskForm(request.POST, instance=task)
        if form.is_valid():
            form.save()
            return redirect('task_list')
    else:
        form = TaskForm(instance=task)
    return render(request, 'tasks/update_task.html', {'form': form})

def delete_task(request, pk):
    task = Task.objects.get(id=pk)
    if request.method == 'POST':
        task.delete()
        return redirect('task_list')
    return render(request, 'tasks/delete_task.html', {'task': task})

forms.py
from django import forms
from .models import Task

class TaskForm(forms.ModelForm):
    class Meta:
        model = Task
        fields = ['title', 'description', 'completed']
urls.py
from django.urls import path
from . import views

urlpatterns = [
    path('', views.task_list, name='task_list'),
    path('add/', views.add_task, name='add_task'),
    path('update/<int:pk>/', views.update_task, name='update_task'),
    path('delete/<int:pk>/', views.delete_task, name='delete_task'),
]
task_list.html
<!DOCTYPE html>
<html lang="en">
<head>
    <meta charset="UTF-8">
    <meta name="viewport" content="width=device-width, initial-scale=1.0">
    <title>Task Manager</title>
</head>
<body>
    <h1>Task List</h1>
    <a href="{% url 'add_task' %}">Add New Task</a>
    <ul>
        {% for task in tasks %}
            <li>
                <strong>{{ task.title }}</strong> - {{ task.description }}
                {% if task.completed %}(Completed){% endif %}
                <a href="{% url 'update_task' task.id %}">Edit</a>
                <a href="{% url 'delete_task' task.id %}">Delete</a>
            </li>
        {% endfor %}
    </ul>
</body>
</html>
```

```
add_task.html
<!DOCTYPE html>
<html lang="en">
<head>
    <meta charset="UTF-8">
    <meta name="viewport" content="width=device-width, initial-scale=1.0">
    <title>Add Task</title>
</head>
<body>
    <h1>Add New Task</h1>
    <form method="post">
        {% csrf_token %}
        {{ form.as_p }}
        <input type="submit" value="Add Task">
    </form>
</body>
</html>
update_task.html
<!DOCTYPE html>
<html lang="en">
<head>
    <meta charset="UTF-8">
    <meta name="viewport" content="width=device-width, initial-scale=1.0">
    <title>Update Task</title>
</head>
<body>
    <h1>Update Task</h1>
    <form method="post">
        {% csrf_token %}
        {{ form.as_p }}
        <input type="submit" value="Update Task">
    </form>
</body>
</html>
delete_task.html
<!DOCTYPE html>
<html lang="en">
<head>
    <meta charset="UTF-8">
    <meta name="viewport" content="width=device-width, initial-scale=1.0">
    <title>Delete Task</title>
</head>
<body>
    <h1>Are you sure you want to delete this task?</h1>
    <form method="post">
        {% csrf_token %}
        <p>{{ task.title }} - {{ task.description }}</p>
        <input type="submit" value="Delete Task">
    </form>
</body>
</html>

admin.py
from django.contrib import admin
from .models import Task

admin.site.register(Task)
```

Folder structure of the project should be as follows:

```
task_manager/
 ├── manage.py
 ├── task_manager/
 │   ├── __init__.py
 │   ├── asgi.py
 │   ├── settings.py
 │   ├── urls.py
 │   ├── wsgi.py
 ├── tasks/
 │   ├── __init__.py
 │   ├── admin.py
 │   ├── apps.py
 │   ├── forms.py
 │   ├── migrations/
 │   │   ├── __init__.py
 │   │   └── 0001_initial.py
 │   ├── models.py
 │   ├── templates/
 │   │   └── tasks/
 │   │       ├── add_task.html
 │   │       ├── delete_task.html
 │   │       ├── task_list.html
 │   │       ├── update_task.html
 │   ├── urls.py
 │   ├── views.py
 └── venv/
     ├── bin/ (or Scripts/ on Windows)
     ├── include/
     ├── lib/
     └── ... (other virtual environment files)
```

Run the following script to apply migrations:

```
python manage.py showmigrations
python manage.py makemigrations tasks
python manage.py migrate
```

Practice Problem 4: Django Survey Application

models.py

```
from django.db import models

class Survey(models.Model):
    title = models.CharField(max_length=200)

    def __str__(self):
        return self.title

class Question(models.Model):
    survey = models.ForeignKey(Survey, on_delete=models.CASCADE)
    question_text = models.CharField(max_length=200)

    def __str__(self):
        return self.question_text

class Choice(models.Model):
    question = models.ForeignKey(Question, on_delete=models.CASCADE)
    choice_text = models.CharField(max_length=100)
```

```
    votes = models.IntegerField(default=0)

    def __str__(self):
        return self.choice_text
```

views.py

```
from django.shortcuts import render, redirect, get_object_or_404
from .models import Survey, Question, Choice
from .forms import SurveyResponseForm

def survey_list(request):
    surveys = Survey.objects.all()
    return render(request, 'survey/survey_list.html', {'surveys': surveys})

def survey_detail(request, survey_id):
    survey = get_object_or_404(Survey, id=survey_id)
    questions = survey.question_set.all()
    if request.method == 'POST':
        for question in questions:
            choice_id = request.POST.get(str(question.id))
            if choice_id:
                choice = Choice.objects.get(id=choice_id)
                choice.votes += 1
                choice.save()
        return redirect('survey_results', survey_id=survey.id)
    return render(request, 'survey/survey_detail.html', {'survey': survey,
'questions': questions})

def survey_results(request, survey_id):
    survey = get_object_or_404(Survey, id=survey_id)
    questions = survey.question_set.all()
    return render(request, 'survey/survey_results.html', {'survey': survey,
'questions': questions})
```

forms.py

```
from django import forms
from .models import Choice

class SurveyResponseForm(forms.Form):
    def __init__(self, *args, **kwargs):
        questions = kwargs.pop('questions')
        super(SurveyResponseForm, self).__init__(*args, **kwargs)
        for question in questions:
            choices = question.choice_set.all()
            self.fields[str(question.id)] = forms.ChoiceField(
                label=question.question_text,
                choices=[(choice.id, choice.choice_text) for choice in choices],
                widget=forms.RadioSelect,
                required=True
            )
```

urls.py

```
from django.urls import path
from . import views

urlpatterns = [
    path('', views.survey_list, name='survey_list'),
    path('<int:survey_id>/', views.survey_detail, name='survey_detail'),
    path('<int:survey_id>/results/', views.survey_results, name='survey_
```

```
results'),
]
```

survey_list.html

```
<!DOCTYPE html>
<html lang="en">
<head>
    <meta charset="UTF-8">
    <meta name="viewport" content="width=device-width, initial-scale=1.0">
    <title>Survey List</title>
</head>
<body>
    <h1>Available Surveys</h1>
    <ul>
        {% for survey in surveys %}
            <li><a href="{% url 'survey_detail' survey.id %}">{{ survey.title
}}</a></li>
        {% endfor %}
    </ul>
</body>
</html>
```

survey_detail.html

```
<!DOCTYPE html>
<html lang="en">
<head>
    <meta charset="UTF-8">
    <meta name="viewport" content="width=device-width, initial-scale=1.0">
    <title>{{ survey.title }}</title>
</head>
<body>
    <h1>{{ survey.title }}</h1>
    <form method="post">
        {% csrf_token %}
        {% for question in questions %}
            <fieldset>
                <legend>{{ question.question_text }}</legend>
                {% for choice in question.choice_set.all %}
                    <input type="radio" name="{{ question.id }}" value="{{
choice.id }}" required>
                    {{ choice.choice_text }}<br>
                {% endfor %}
            </fieldset>
        {% endfor %}
        <input type="submit" value="Submit">
    </form>
</body>
</html>
```

survey_results.html

```
<!DOCTYPE html>
<html lang="en">
<head>
    <meta charset="UTF-8">
    <meta name="viewport" content="width=device-width, initial-scale=1.0">
    <title>{{ survey.title }} Results</title>
</head>
<body>
    <h1>{{ survey.title }} Results</h1>
    <ul>
```

```
        {% for question in questions %}
            <li>
                <h2>{{ question.question_text }}</h2>
                <ul>
                    {% for choice in question.choice_set.all %}
                        <li>{{ choice.choice_text }}: {{ choice.votes }}
votes</li>
                    {% endfor %}
                </ul>
            </li>
        {% endfor %}
    </ul>
</body>
</html>
```

```
admin.py
from django.contrib import admin
from .models import Survey, Question, Choice

admin.site.register(Survey)
admin.site.register(Question)
admin.site.register(Choice)
```

Folder structure of the project should be as follows:

```
survey_app/
├── manage.py
├── survey_app/
│   ├── __init__.py
│   ├── asgi.py
│   ├── settings.py
│   ├── urls.py
│   ├── wsgi.py
├── survey/
│   ├── __init__.py
│   ├── admin.py
│   ├── apps.py
│   ├── forms.py
│   ├── migrations/
│   │   ├── __init__.py
│   │   └── 0001_initial.py
│   ├── models.py
│   ├── templates/
│   │   └── survey/
│   │       ├── survey_list.html
│   │       ├── survey_detail.html
│   │       ├── survey_results.html
│   ├── urls.py
│   ├── views.py
└── venv/
    ├── bin/ (or Scripts/ on Windows)
    ├── include/
    ├── lib/
    └── ... (other virtual environment files)
```

Run the following script to apply migrations:

```
python manage.py migrate
python manage.py showmigrations
```

```
python manage.py makemigrations survey
python manage.py migrate
```

Create Surveys

1. **Create a Superuser**

```
python manage.py createsuperuser

Username: admin
Email address: admin@example.com
Password: ********
Password (again): ********
```

2. **Access the Admin Interface**

```
http://127.0.0.1:8000/admin/
```

3. **Log In with Admin Credentials**
   - Once logged in, you can manage your data (such as adding surveys, questions, and choices) using the admin interface.
   - Navigate through the different sections such as Surveys, Questions, and Choices to add and modify entries.

Conclusion

In this chapter, you explored the fundamentals of building web applications using Flask and Django. You started by setting up your development environment and creating basic applications with both frameworks. You then learned how to use templates to generate dynamic content and how to handle user input through forms. By working through practical exercises, you applied these concepts to create functional web applications, strengthening your understanding of Python web development.

With these skills, you can now build interactive and dynamic web applications, setting the stage for more advanced web development projects. Your experience with Flask and Django will allow you to design flexible applications that can adapt to different user needs.

In the next chapter, you will learn about Python and databases. You will discover how to connect Python applications with databases using SQL, NoSQL, and web application integration. These skills will allow you to build data-driven applications and manage persistent data effectively in your projects.

So, keep calm and let us tame the Python!

Multiple-Choice Questions

Test your understanding of the concepts covered in this chapter with the following multiple-choice questions.

1. Which command is used to create a new Flask project?
   a. `flask init`
   b. `flask new`
   c. `flask create`
   d. `flask run`

2. In Flask, which function is used to render HTML templates?
   a. `render_html`
   b. `render_template`
   c. `render_page`
   d. `render_view`
3. Which templating engine does Flask use by default?
   a. Jinja2
   b. Mustache
   c. Handlebars
   d. Pug
4. In Django, which file is responsible for URL routing in an app?
   a. `views.py`
   b. `models.py`
   c. `urls.py`
   d. `settings.py`
5. What command is used to start a new Django project?
   a. `django-admin initproject`
   b. `django-admin startproject`
   c. `django-admin createproject`
   d. `django-admin newproject`
6. Which Django feature automatically creates a user interface for managing your application's data?
   a. Django ORM
   b. Django Views
   c. Django Templates
   d. Django Admin
7. Which of the following is a built-in field type for a Django model?
   a. `DateField`
   b. `FigureType`
   c. `ListField`
   d. `ObjectField`
8. In Flask, which decorator is used to define a route for a web page?
   a. `@flask.route`
   b. `@route`
   c. `@app.path`
   d. `@app.route`

9. Which of the following commands is used to run a Django development server?
   a. `django runserver`
   b. `python manage.py serve`
   c. `python manage.py runserver`
   d. `django-admin runserver`
10. What is the primary purpose of Django's **`settings.py`** file?
    a. Define URL patterns for the application
    b. Store configuration settings for the project
    c. Describe database models
    d. Render HTML templates

Answers

1. c
2. b
3. a
4. c
5. b
6. d
7. a
8. d
9. c
10. b

Points to Remember

- Flask and Django offer efficient tools for building web applications, allowing developers to focus on logic.
- Flask's simplicity and flexibility make it suitable for modest to medium-sized projects. It enables developers to select the components they require without imposing any limits.
- Django's built-in features, including an ORM, authentication, and admin interface, make it ideal for large projects that require rapid development and scalability.
- Flask (Jinja2) and Django use templating systems to create dynamic web pages by embedding Python-like expressions into HTML templates.
- In Flask and Django, routing maps URLs to view functions or methods, deciding how web requests are processed and returned.
- Forms are an essential component of web applications for gathering user input. Both frameworks include tools for creating, validating, and processing forms, which ensure data integrity and security.
- Django's ORM simplifies data administration by eliminating the need to write raw SQL.

- Both Flask and Django have built-in development servers that enable developers to test their apps locally, making it simple to iterate and troubleshoot.
- Django includes built-in security mechanisms to prevent XSS, CSRF, and SQL injection.
- Both Flask and Django have rich documentation and active communities, offering resources and assistance for developers at all skill levels.

Further Reading

For further learning, you can explore the following resources:

1. **Flask Documentation**: https://flask.palletsprojects.com/en/3.0.x/
2. **Django Documentation**: https://docs.djangoproject.com/
3. **HTML and CSS Basics**: https://developer.mozilla.org/en-US/docs/Learn/HTML

Chapter 16
Python and Databases

Introduction

In the previous chapter, you have explored how to build web applications using Python. Web apps allow users to interact with data dynamically, whether it is signing up for an account, posting a comment, or searching for information. But where does all this data go? How does a web app remember user details, store posts, or track changes? The answer lies in databases.

Databases are essential for storing and managing data in web applications and many other types of software. They allow programs to save information in an organized way, making it easy to retrieve, update, and scale as needed.

In this chapter, you will learn how Python interacts with different types of databases, including relational databases such as SQLite and NoSQL databases such as MongoDB. You will explore how to store, retrieve, and manipulate data efficiently, ensuring your applications can handle information smoothly and reliably.

By the end of this chapter, you will have the skills to integrate databases into your Python projects, whether you are working on a web app, a data-driven program, or a large-scale system. Understanding databases will make your applications more powerful, scalable, and efficient.

Structure

In this chapter, the following topics will be covered:

- Introduction to Databases
  - Overview of Databases
  - Types of Databases: Relational versus NoSQL
  - Importance of Databases in Programming
- Understanding Tables, Rows, and Columns in Relational Database
  - Data Organization in Relational Database
  - Tables versus Spreadsheets
  - Definition of Rows and Columns
- Working with Relational Databases
  - Introduction to SQLite
  - Setting Up SQLite
- CRUD Operations in a Relational Database
  - Creating tables
  - Inserting Data into Tables
  - Reading Data from Tables
  - Updating Data in a Table

  - Deleting Data from a Table
  - Practical Exercise: Building a Simple Contact Management System with SQLite
- Working with NoSQL Databases
  - Overview of MongoDB
  - Setting Up MongoDB
  - Practical Exercise: Storing and Querying JSON Data in MongoDB
- Common Mistakes and Best Practices
- Exercises and Challenges: Practice Problems and Solutions

Introduction to Databases

Prior to start working with databases in Python, it is important to understand what a database is, the different types available, and why they play a key role in programming. Let us begin with the basics.

Overview of Databases

A database is like a digital filing cabinet that helps store and organize information efficiently. Imagine you have a collection of books and want to track details such as titles, authors, and publication dates. Instead of writing everything on paper, you can save this information in a database.

With a database, you can easily add new data, search for specific details, update records, and delete information that is no longer needed. This makes databases a powerful tool for managing data effectively.

Types of Databases: Relational versus NoSQL

There are different types of databases, but the two most common categories are Relational Databases and NoSQL Databases.

Relational Databases:

- Store data in tables, similar to spreadsheets with rows and columns.
- Each row represents a record, and each column represents a field within that record.
- For example, a table for books might have columns for title, author, and publication date.
- Use SQL (Structured Query Language) to manage and retrieve data.
- Popular relational databases include MySQL, PostgreSQL, and SQLite.

NoSQL Databases:

- Do not use tables; instead, they store data in flexible formats such as documents, key-value pairs, or graphs.
- Ideal for handling large amounts of unstructured or semi-structured data.
- More flexible than relational databases, making them great for scalable and dynamic applications.
- Common NoSQL databases include MongoDB, Cassandra, and Redis.

Importance of Databases in Programming

Databases are essential because they provide a structured way to store, manage, and retrieve data. Here is why they matter:

- **Data Persistence:** Unlike temporary storage in memory, databases store data permanently, so information remains available even after the program stops running. This is useful for storing user accounts, product details, and more.
- **Efficient Data Management:** Databases are designed to handle large amounts of data efficiently, making it easy to search, filter, and analyze information quickly.
- **Scalability:** As applications grow, the amount of data increases. Databases can scale to manage large datasets and handle multiple requests simultaneously.
- **Data Integrity:** Databases help ensure data is accurate and consistent by using validation methods that prevent errors and maintain data quality.

Note: *Since this book focuses on Python, you won't dive deep into database theory. If you are new to databases, don't feel overwhelmed by the information here. It might seem a bit complex at first. Instead, focus on how Python interacts with databases, and take the time to explore more about database concepts as you progress in your learning journey.*

Understanding how databases work is a crucial skill for any programmer. Whether you are building a web app, a business application, or a data-driven system, working with databases allows you to create powerful and efficient programs.

Understanding Tables, Rows, and Columns in Relational Databases

Prior to start working with relational databases in Python, let us take a step back and understand how data is structured inside a relational database. If you are new to databases, this section will help you feel comfortable before moving on to writing SQL queries.

Note: *This section focuses on relational databases (such as SQLite, MySQL, and PostgreSQL), which store data in tables. If you later work with NoSQL databases (such as MongoDB), you will see that they use a different way of organizing data. For now, let us focus on how relational databases structure data.*

Data Organization in Relational Database

A relational database stores information in tables, similar to how a spreadsheet organizes data into rows and columns. Instead of saving data in random files or unstructured formats, databases provide a structured way to store and manage large amounts of information efficiently.

Each database can have multiple tables, and each table holds specific types of information.

For example, if you were creating a database for a library system, you could have different tables listed as follows:

- A Books table (to store book details)
- A Members table (to store member information)
- A BorrowedBooks table (to track which books are borrowed)

By organizing data in tables, retrieving, updating, and managing information becomes much easier.

Tables versus Spreadsheets

If you have worked with Excel or Google Sheets, you already have an idea of how relational databases work! A table in a relational database is very similar to a spreadsheet:

Spreadsheet Feature	Relational Database Equivalent
Spreadsheet Workbook	Database
Sheet	Table
Row	Record (Entry)
Column	Field (Attribute)

Table 16.1: *Tables versus Spreadsheets*

Just like in spreadsheets, each row in a table is a record, and each column represents a specific type of data.

Definition of Rows and Columns

A table in a relational database consists of rows and columns:

- **Rows (Records):** Each row represents a single entry in the table.
- **Columns (Fields):** Each column represents a specific attribute about that entry.

Let us look at an example of a Books table:

id	title	author	published_year
1	Python Basics	John Smith	2022
2	Web Development	Alice Johnson	2021
3	Data Science 101	Robert Brown	2023

Table 16.2: *Example of a Books table*

- Each row represents a book.
- Each column stores a different type of information (ID, Title, Author, and Published Year).

Understanding tables, rows, and columns is important before working with SQL, as these concepts form the foundation of relational databases. Once you grasp how data is organized, it will be much easier to create, retrieve, update, and delete records using Python and SQL.

Working with Relational Databases

Now that you have a basic understanding of relational databases and why they are important, let us move on to how Python works with them. In this section, you will learn how to use SQLite, a simple yet powerful relational database system. By the end of this section, you will know how to create and connect to an SQLite database.

Introduction to SQLite

SQLite is one of the most beginner-friendly database systems available. Unlike other databases that require a separate server, SQLite is lightweight and self-contained, meaning it works right out of the box with no extra setup. It is a great choice for learning databases and building small to medium-sized projects.

One of the best things about SQLite is that it comes built into Python, so you can start using it immediately, no need to install anything! It stores all data in a single file, making it easy to manage and move around. Despite its simplicity, SQLite supports transactions, data integrity, and basic SQL commands, making it a great tool for both learning and real-world applications.

Setting Up SQLite

Now that you know why SQLite is useful, let us set it up in Python.

1. **Importing the SQLite Module**

   To start working with SQLite in Python, you need to import the sqlite3 module. The good news? It is built into Python, so you do not have to install anything!

   Here is how to do it:

   ```
   import sqlite3
   ```

   Think of this like unlocking a toolbox. Once you import sqlite3, you have everything you need to work with databases in Python.

2. **Creating and Connecting to a Database**

   Once you have imported sqlite3, the next step is to connect to a database. If the database file does not exist, SQLite will automatically create one for you.

   Here is how to create and connect to a database:

   ```
   # Connect to SQLite database (or create it if it doesn't exist)
   connection = sqlite3.connect('example.db')

   # Create a cursor object to interact with the database
   cursor = connection.cursor()

   print("Database created and connected successfully")
   ```

Understanding the Code:

- **`sqlite3.connect('example.db')`:** Connects to a database file called **`example.db`**. If the file does not exist, SQLite creates it automatically.
- **`connection.cursor()`:** Creates a cursor object, which allows you to execute SQL commands. Think of it as a controller that helps you interact with the database.
- **`print("Database created and connected successfully")`:** Confirms that everything is working as expected.

3. **Closing the Connection**

   When you are done working with the database, always close the connection. This ensures that all changes are saved properly and prevents memory issues.

   Here is how to close the connection:

   ```
   # Close the database connection
   connection.close()

   print("Connection closed")
   ```

Importance of closing the connection:

- **`connection.close()`:** Closes the database connection, just like locking the door after leaving a room.
- **`print("Connection closed")`:** Confirms that the database was closed successfully.

By following these instructions, you have successfully installed SQLite in Python and connected to a database. You are now ready to begin building tables, entering data, and performing other database operations, which you will cover in the next sections. This configuration is the core of dealing with relational databases in Python, and learning it will allow you to properly handle data in your projects.

CRUD Operations in a Relational Database

In the last section, you have set up SQLite database and built the basic structure to organize data. Now, it is time to perform CRUD operations, which stand for Create, Read, Update, and Delete. These are the four essential operations used to manage data in any relational database.

You will start with the first step: creating tables, as it is the foundation of how data is structured in a database.

Definition of SQL:

Prior to start working with database operations, let us quickly understand Structured Query Language (SQL).

- SQL is the language used to communicate with relational databases, including SQLite, MySQL, and PostgreSQL.
- It allows you to store, retrieve, update, and delete data from databases using simple commands.
- Think of SQL as a set of instructions that help you tell the database what to do.

For example, if you want to create a table, you use the CREATE TABLE command. If you want to add new data, you use INSERT INTO.

You do not need to memorize everything at once! As you follow along, you will naturally get comfortable with SQL commands.

Creating Tables

Before storing data in a database, you will need to create a table to hold it. A table is like a spreadsheet, where:

- Rows represent individual records (entries).
- Columns define different types of information for each record.

For example, if you were managing a library database, you might need a Books table with details such as title, author, publication year, and genre.

Step 1: Defining the Table Structure

When creating a table, you need to define:

- **Column Names**: Each piece of data must have a name (for example, title, author).
- **Data Types**: Specify what type of data each column will hold (for example, TEXT for words, INTEGER for numbers).
- **Primary Key**: A unique identifier for each record (for example, **`book_id`**).

Step 2: Writing the SQL Command

Use the **`CREATE TABLE SQL`** command to set up the table. Here is how to create a Books table in SQLite:

```
import sqlite3

# Connect to the database (or create it if it doesn't exist)
connection = sqlite3.connect('library.db')
```

```
cursor = connection.cursor()

# Create a table for books
cursor.execute('''
    CREATE TABLE IF NOT EXISTS books (
        book_id INTEGER PRIMARY KEY,
        title TEXT NOT NULL,
        author TEXT NOT NULL,
        publication_year INTEGER,
        genre TEXT
    )
''')

print("Table 'books' created successfully")

# Commit and close the connection
connection.commit()
connection.close()
```

- **`CREATE TABLE IF NOT EXISTS books`:** Creates a books table if it does not already exist.
- **`book_id INTEGER PRIMARY KEY`:** Assigns a unique identifier for each book.
- **`title TEXT NOT NULL`:** Requires each book to have a title.

Step 3: Running the Code

Run the preceding Python script to create the table in your SQLite database. Do not forget to use **`commit()`** to save the changes!

Inserting Data into Tables

Once you have created a table, the next step is to add records to store useful information.

Step 1: Writing the SQL INSERT Command

To insert data, use the **`INSERT INTO SQL`** command. The basic format looks like this:

```
INSERT INTO table_name (column1, column2, column3, ...)
VALUES (value1, value2, value3, ...);
```

- **`table_name`** : The name of the table where data will be stored.
- **`Columns`** `(column1, column2, ...)`: The fields where data will be inserted.
- **`Values`** `(value1, value2, ...)`: The actual data to be added.

Step 2: Inserting a Single Record

Let us add a book to the Books table:

```
import sqlite3

# Connect to the database
connection = sqlite3.connect('library.db')
cursor = connection.cursor()

# Insert a new book record
cursor.execute('''
    INSERT INTO books (title, author, publication_year, genre)
    VALUES (?, ?, ?, ?)
''', ("To Kill a Mockingbird", "Harper Lee", 1960, "Fiction"))
```

```
print("Record inserted successfully")

# Commit the changes and close the connection
connection.commit()
connection.close()
```

- **INSERT INTO books (title, author, publication_year, genre)**: Specifies where to insert data.
- **VALUES (?, ?, ?, ?)**: Uses placeholders (?) for values.
- **Tuple** ("To Kill a Mockingbird", "Harper Lee", 1960, "Fiction"): The data to be inserted.

Step 3: Inserting Multiple Records at Once

To add multiple books in a single command, use **executemany()**:

```
import sqlite3

# Connect to the database
connection = sqlite3.connect('library.db')
cursor = connection.cursor()

# Insert multiple book records
books = [
    ("1984", "George Orwell", 1949, "Dystopian"),
    ("The Great Gatsby", "F. Scott Fitzgerald", 1925, "Fiction"),
    ("Moby Dick", "Herman Melville", 1851, "Adventure")
]

cursor.executemany('''
    INSERT INTO books (title, author, publication_year, genre)
    VALUES (?, ?, ?, ?)
''', books)

print("Multiple records inserted successfully")

# Commit the changes and close the connection
connection.commit()
connection.close()
```

- **executemany()**: Allows inserting multiple records at once.
- **List of tuples (books)**: Each tuple represents a book record.

In this section, you learned how to put data into an SQLite table with Python. Whether you are uploading a single record or several at once, the process is simple and efficient. These activities are critical in populating your database with the information you need to store and manage.

Reading Data from Tables

Now that you have added data to your SQLite tables, the next step is to retrieve, update, and delete data as needed. These operations allow you to access stored information, modify existing records, and remove unnecessary data efficiently.

Step 1: Writing the SQL SELECT Statement

The **SELECT** command retrieves data from specific columns in a table. The basic syntax is:

```
SELECT column1, column2, ...
FROM table_name;
```

- **`SELECT column1, column2, ...`**: Specifies which columns to retrieve.
- **`FROM table_name`** : Specifies the table from which data will be retrieved.
- Use * to select all columns.

Step 2: Retrieving All Records from a Table

Let us retrieve all records from the Books table:

```
import sqlite3

# Connect to the database
connection = sqlite3.connect('library.db')
cursor = connection.cursor()

# Select all records from the books table
cursor.execute('SELECT * FROM books')

# Fetch all the results
books = cursor.fetchall()

# Display the results
for book in books:
    print(f"ID: {book[0]}, Title: {book[1]}, Author: {book[2]}, Year:
{book[3]}, Genre: {book[4]}")

# Close the connection
connection.close()
```

- **`SELECT * FROM books`**: Retrieves all columns in the books table.
- **`cursor.fetchall()`**: Fetches all rows and stores them in a list of tuples.
- **Looping through results**: Each tuple represents a book, and print out its details.

Step 3: Retrieving Specific Columns

If you only need certain columns (for example, title and author), modify the **`SELECT`** statement:

```
cursor.execute('SELECT title, author FROM books')
books = cursor.fetchall()

for book in books:
    print(f"Title: {book[0]}, Author: {book[1]}")
```

`SELECT title, author FROM books`: Retrieves only the title and author columns.

Step 4: Filtering Data with `WHERE`

To retrieve specific records, use the **`WHERE`** clause. Let us find books published after 1950:

```
cursor.execute('SELECT title, author, publication_year FROM books WHERE publi-
cation_year > 1950')
books = cursor.fetchall()

for book in books:
    print(f"Title: {book[0]}, Author: {book[1]}, Year: {book[2]}")
```

`WHERE publication_year > 1950`: Filters results to include only books published after 1950.

Step 5: Sorting Results with `ORDER BY`

You can sort data using **`ORDER BY`**. For example, to list books by publication year (ascending order):

```
cursor.execute('SELECT title, author, publication_year FROM books ORDER BY
publication_year ASC')
books = cursor.fetchall()

for book in books:
    print(f"Title: {book[0]}, Author: {book[1]}, Year: {book[2]}")
```

`ORDER BY publication_year ASC`: Sorts by **`publication_year`** in ascending order. Use **`DESC`** for descending order.

Updating Data in a Table

Sometimes, you may need to modify existing data in a table. This is done using the **`SQL`** `UPDATE` command.

Step 1: Writing the `SQL UPDATE` Command

The syntax for updating a record is:

```
UPDATE table_name
SET column1 = value1, column2 = value2, ...
WHERE condition;
```

- **`SET column1 = value1`**: Specifies the new value for a column.
- **`WHERE`** condition: Ensures only specific rows are updated. (Without **`WHERE`**, all rows will be updated!)

Step 2: Updating a Record in Python

Let us update the genre of "**`To Kill a Mockingbird`**" to "**`Classic Fiction`**":

```
import sqlite3

# Connect to the database
connection = sqlite3.connect('library.db')
cursor = connection.cursor()

# Update the genre of a specific book
cursor.execute('''
    UPDATE books
    SET genre = ?
    WHERE title = ? AND author = ?
''', ("Classic Fiction", "To Kill a Mockingbird", "Harper Lee"))

print("Record updated successfully")

# Commit the changes and close the connection
connection.commit()
connection.close()
```

- **`UPDATE books SET genre = ?`**: Updates the genre column.
- **`WHERE title = ? AND author = ?`**: Ensures only "**`To Kill a Mockingbird`**" is updated.

Deleting Data from a Table

If a record is no longer needed, you can delete it using the SQL DELETE command.

Step 1: Writing the SQL DELETE Command

The basic syntax is:

```
DELETE FROM table_name
WHERE condition;
```

- **DELETE FROM table_name:** Specifies which table to delete from.
- **WHERE condition:** Ensures only specific records are removed. (Without **WHERE**, all rows will be deleted!)

Step 2: Deleting a Record in Python

Let us remove the book "**1984**" by **George Orwell**:

```
import sqlite3

# Connect to the database
connection = sqlite3.connect('library.db')
cursor = connection.cursor()

# Delete a specific book record
cursor.execute('''
    DELETE FROM books
    WHERE title = ? AND author = ?
''', ("1984", "George Orwell"))

print("Record deleted successfully")

# Commit the changes and close the connection
connection.commit()
connection.close()
```

DELETE FROM books WHERE title = ? AND author = ?: Removes the record for "**1984**" by **George Orwell**.

Practical Exercise: Building a Simple Contact Management System with SQLite

In this exercise, you will use the CRUD procedures you have covered to create a simple contact management system with SQLite. This practical exercise will lead you through creating, reading, updating, and removing contacts in your database, helping you strengthen your grasp of dealing with SQLite in Python.

Task Description:

Create an SQLite database to hold contact information, such as names, phone numbers, and email addresses. You will create a Python script that can add new contacts, display all contacts, edit existing contact information, and delete contacts.

Real-life Scenario:

Assume you are creating a tiny application to manage personal contacts. You want to maintain track of names, phone numbers, and email addresses, and you need to be able to add, update, view, and delete them as needed.

Steps for the Exercise:

1. **Set Up the SQLite Database**
    a. Create a Python script for managing your contact database.
    b. Create a contacts table with columns for names, phone numbers, and email addresses.
    c. Create a table in the SQLite database.
2. **Insert Sample Contacts:** Add a few contacts to your database using the `INSERT INTO` command.
3. **Read and Display Contacts:** Retrieve and display all contacts from the database using the `SELECT` command.
4. **Update Contact Information:** Update the phone number or email of an existing contact using the `UPDATE` command.
5. **Delete a Contact:** Remove a contact from the database using the `DELETE FROM` command.

Implementation Steps:

1. **Set Up the SQLite Database**
    a. Start by creating a new Python file (for example, **`contact_manager.py`**).
    b. Import the sqlite3 module and create a connection to a new database file named **`contacts.db`**.
    c. Define and create the contacts table:

```
import sqlite3
# Connect to the database
connection = sqlite3.connect('contacts.db')
cursor = connection.cursor()
# Create a table for contacts
cursor.execute('''
    CREATE TABLE IF NOT EXISTS contacts (
        contact_id INTEGER PRIMARY KEY,
        name TEXT NOT NULL,
        phone TEXT NOT NULL,
        email TEXT
    )
''')
print("Table 'contacts' created successfully")
# Commit the changes and close the connection
connection.commit()
connection.close()
```

2. **Insert Sample Contacts:**

Reopen the connection to the database and insert some sample contacts:

```
connection = sqlite3.connect('contacts.db')
cursor = connection.cursor()

# Insert sample contacts
contacts = [
    ("Alice Smith", "123-456-7890", "alice@example.com"),
    ("Bob Johnson", "987-654-3210", "bob@example.com"),
    ("Charlie Brown", "555-555-5555", "charlie@example.com")
]
cursor.executemany('''
```

```
    INSERT INTO contacts (name, phone, email)
    VALUES (?, ?, ?)
''', contacts)
print("Sample contacts inserted successfully")
connection.commit()
connection.close()
```

3. **Read and Display Contacts:**

   Write a function to retrieve and display all contacts:

```
connection = sqlite3.connect('contacts.db')
cursor = connection.cursor()
# Retrieve all contacts
cursor.execute('SELECT * FROM contacts')
all_contacts = cursor.fetchall()
# Display the contacts
print("Contact List:")
for contact in all_contacts:
    print(f"ID: {contact[0]}, Name: {contact[1]}, Phone: {contact[2]}, Email: 
{contact[3]}")
connection.close()
```

4. **Update Contact Information:**

   Write a function to update the phone number or email of a specific contact:

```
connection = sqlite3.connect('contacts.db')
cursor = connection.cursor()
# Update a contact's phone number
cursor.execute('''
    UPDATE contacts
    SET phone = ?
    WHERE name = ?
''', ("111-222-3333", "Alice Smith"))
print("Contact updated successfully")
connection.commit()
connection.close()
```

5. **Delete a Contact:**

   Write a function to delete a contact by name:

```
connection = sqlite3.connect('contacts.db')
cursor = connection.cursor()
# Delete a contact
cursor.execute('''
    DELETE FROM contacts
    WHERE name = ?
''', ("Charlie Brown",))
print("Contact deleted successfully")
connection.commit()
connection.close()
```

6. **Testing Your Contact Management System**

   a. Run the Python script to test the contact management system.

   b. Add new contacts, update old ones, and try deleting them.

   c. Check that all operations function properly by reviewing the contact list after each operation.

Understanding the Solution:

- **Database Setup:** Set up the contacts table with columns for name, phone number, and email address to store contact information.
- **CRUD Operations:** The CRUD operations (`Create`, `Read`, `Update`, and `Delete`) use Python functions and SQL commands.
- **Practical Application:** This exercise applies SQLite expertise to real-world contact management scenarios.

By completing this exercise, you will receive hands-on experience with performing CRUD operations in SQLite. These are vital abilities for any database-driven application.

Working with NoSQL Databases

As your applications grow more complex, you may find that a traditional relational database, such as SQLite, is not always the best fit for your data needs. In such cases, NoSQL databases provide a more flexible and scalable solution.

In this section, you will explore MongoDB, one of the most popular NoSQL databases. You will learn how to set up MongoDB in Python using PyMongo, and practice storing and retrieving data in a NoSQL environment.

Overview of MongoDB

MongoDB is a NoSQL database that stores data as JSON-like documents. Unlike relational databases that use tables, MongoDB uses collections to store documents, making it highly flexible for applications that deal with varied and evolving data structures.

Key Features of MongoDB:

- **Document-Oriented**: Stores data in BSON (Binary JSON) format, supporting complex structures such as arrays and nested documents.
- **Collections Instead of Tables**: Data is grouped into collections instead of tables, allowing documents to have different structures within the same collection.
- **Dynamic Schema**: Unlike SQL databases that enforce a strict schema, MongoDB allows documents to have different fields, making it flexible for applications that change over time.
- **Scalability**: MongoDB supports horizontal scaling, allowing it to handle large datasets and distribute data across multiple servers.

Setting Up MongoDB

To interact with MongoDB in Python, you will use the PyMongo package. Follow these steps to set up your environment:

Step 1: Install MongoDB and PyMongo

Before you begin, you need to install MongoDB and PyMongo.

a. **Install MongoDB**

   I. Download and install MongoDB Community Edition from:

      https://www.mongodb.com/try/download/community

   II. After installation, start the MongoDB server (Windows users can follow these steps):

i. Create a folder: **C:\data\db** (MongoDB stores its data here by default).

ii. Open Command Prompt, navigate to MongoDB's bin folder:

```
cd C:\Program Files\MongoDB\Server\<your_version>\bin
```

iii. Start the MongoDB server:

```
mongod
```

By default, MongoDB runs on port 27017.

b. **Install PyMongo**

Once MongoDB is running, install PyMongo using pip:

```
pip install pymongo
```

Step 2: Connect to MongoDB

Now, let us connect to MongoDB from Python:

```
from pymongo import MongoClient

# Connect to the MongoDB server
client = MongoClient('localhost', 27017)

# Access the 'library' database (it will be created if it doesn't exist)
db = client['library']

print("Connected to MongoDB successfully")
```

a. **MongoClient('localhost', 27017')**: Connects to MongoDB running locally on port 27017.

b. **client['library']:** Accesses (or creates) the library database.

Step 3: Create a Collection and Insert Data

In MongoDB, collections are used to store documents. Think of them as tables, but more flexible.

Let us create a books collection and insert a document:

```
# Create a collection called 'books'
books_collection = db['books']

# Insert a document into the 'books' collection
book = {
    "title": "To Kill a Mockingbird",
    "author": "Harper Lee",
    "publication_year": 1960,
    "genres": ["Fiction", "Classic"]
}

book_id = books_collection.insert_one(book).inserted_id
print(f"Book inserted with ID: {book_id}")
```

- **db['books']**: Creates (or accesses) the books collection.
- **insert_one(book)**: Inserts a single document (Python dictionary) into the collection.
- MongoDB assigns a **unique** _id to every document automatically.

Step 4: Querying Data in MongoDB

Just like SQL databases use SELECT, MongoDB allows you to retrieve data using the **find()** method.

a. **Find a Specific Document**

To retrieve a single document, use **find_one()**:

```
# Find a book by title
book = books_collection.find_one({"title": "To Kill a Mockingbird"})
print(book)
```

find_one({"title": "To Kill a Mockingbird"}): Retrieves the first document that matches the condition.

b. **Find All Documents by a Specific Author**

To find multiple documents, use **find()**:

```
# Find all books by a specific author
books_by_author = books_collection.find({"author": "Harper Lee"})

for book in books_by_author:
    print(book)
```

find({"author": "Harper Lee"}): Retrieves all books written by Harper Lee.

SQL versus NoSQL:

To quickly Summarize, the following table depicts the difference between SQL and NoSQL databases.

Feature	**SQL Databases (Relational)**	**NoSQL Databases (MongoDB)**
Data Structure	Tables (rows, columns)	Collections (documents)
Schema	Fixed, predefined	Flexible, dynamic
Relationships	Uses Foreign Keys	Embeds documents inside other documents
Query Language	SQL (SELECT, JOIN)	MongoDB Query Language (find(), aggregate())
Scalability	Vertical Scaling	Horizontal Scaling (easier for big data)

Table 16.3: SQL *versus* NoSQL

Key Takeaway: If your data is structured and follows a fixed format, a relational database such as SQLite is better. If your data structure is dynamic and constantly evolving, MongoDB is a great option.

MongoDB is a powerful tool for applications that need scalability, flexibility, and speed. In the next section, you will explore how to update and delete data in MongoDB!

Practical Exercise: Storing and Querying JSON Data in MongoDB

In this practical exercise, you will apply what you have learned to store and query JSON data in MongoDB.

Task Description:

Create a MongoDB database to store information about library books. You will save JSON-like documents with information such as the book title, author, publishing year, and genres. Then, you will create queries to retrieve and show this data.

Real-Life Scenario:

Assume you are developing a digital library application that allows users to explore books by various authors and genres. You must save book details in a versatile format that can support many types of information. MongoDB, with its document-based approach, is an excellent candidate for this task.

Steps for the Exercise:

1. **Set Up MongoDB:**
   a. Ensure MongoDB is running on your local machine.
   b. Create a Python script to connect to the MongoDB server and access a database.
2. **Create a Collection and Insert Data:**
   a. Create a books collection in your database.
   b. Insert multiple book documents with varying structures.
3. **Query the Data:**
   a. Retrieve and display books by a specific author.
   b. Retrieve and display all books published in a certain year.
   c. Retrieve and display all books in a specific genre.

Implementation Steps:

1. **Set Up MongoDB:**

```
from pymongo import MongoClient
# Connect to the MongoDB server
client = MongoClient('localhost', 27017)
db = client['digital_library']
print("Connected to MongoDB successfully")
```

2. **Create a Collection and Insert Data:**

```
# Create a collection called 'books'
books_collection = db['books']
# Insert multiple documents into the 'books' collection
books = [
    {
        "title": "1984",
        "author": "George Orwell",
        "publication_year": 1949,
        "genres": ["Dystopian", "Science Fiction"]
    },
    {
        "title": "Pride and Prejudice",
        "author": "Jane Austen",
        "publication_year": 1813,
        "genres": ["Romance", "Classic"]
    },
    {
        "title": "The Great Gatsby",
        "author": "F. Scott Fitzgerald",
        "publication_year": 1925,
        "genres": ["Classic", "Fiction"]
    }
]
books_collection.insert_many(books)
print("Books inserted successfully")
```

3. **Query the Data:**

```
# Find all books by George Orwell
books_by_orwell = books_collection.find({"author": "George Orwell"})
print("Books by George Orwell:")
for book in books_by_orwell:
    print(book)
# Find all books published in 1949
books_published_in_1949 = books_collection.find({"publication_year": 1949})
print("Books published in 1949:")
for book in books_published_in_1949:
    print(book)
# Find all books in the 'Classic' genre
classic_books = books_collection.find({"genres": "Classic"})
print("Classic genre books:")
for book in classic_books:
    print(book)
```

Understanding the Solution:

- **Flexible Data Storage:** MongoDB's flexibility is demonstrated by its ability to store book information as JSON-like documents with variable structures.
- **Powerful Queries:** MongoDB offers robust data retrieval capabilities by allowing queries based on multiple fields, even those nested within arrays.

This exercise simulates working with unstructured or semi-structured data and provides hands-on experience with NoSQL databases. This work will teach you the foundations of storing and accessing data in MongoDB, which is essential for managing modern, dynamic datasets.

Common Mistakes and Best Practices

While working with databases, whether relational (SQL) or NoSQL (MongoDB), can sometimes lead to errors if not handled carefully. Here are some common mistakes to avoid and best practices to follow when working with databases in Python.

Common Mistakes to Avoid

- **Not Closing the Database Connection:**

  Forgetting to close the connection after executing queries can lead to memory leaks and performance issues.

  Solution: Always call `connection.close()` (for SQLite) or let the database client handle connections properly (for MongoDB).

- **Executing Queries Without Committing Changes (SQL Databases)**

  If you insert, update, or delete records but forget to commit the transaction, your changes won't be saved.

  Solution: Always use `connection.commit()` after modifying data.

- **Using `DELETE` or `UPDATE` Without a `WHERE` Clause (SQL Databases)**

  Running DELETE FROM books; without specifying a condition will delete all records in the table!

  Solution: Always add a WHERE clause to ensure only specific records are modified or removed.

- **Not Handling Errors Properly**

  If the database connection fails or a query is incorrect, your program may crash.

Solution: Use try-except blocks to handle database errors gracefully.

```
try:
    connection = sqlite3.connect('library.db')
    cursor = connection.cursor()
    cursor.execute("SELECT * FROM non_existing_table")  # This will cause an
error
except sqlite3.Error as e:
    print(f"Database error: {e}")
finally:
    connection.close()
```

- **Hardcoding Values Instead of Using Placeholders**

  Directly inserting user input into SQL queries can lead to SQL injection attacks.

  Solution: Use parameterized queries (? in SQLite, {} in MongoDB) instead of hardcoding values.

```
cursor.execute("INSERT INTO books (title, author) VALUES (?, ?)", ("Python Ba-
sics", "John Doe"))
```

Best Practices for Working with Databases

- Use Indexing for Faster Queries (SQL and NoSQL)

  Indexes improve search speed in large datasets. For relational databases, use **`CREATE INDEX`**, and in MongoDB, use **`create_index()`**.

- Use Connection Pooling for Performance (SQL and NoSQL)

  Instead of opening and closing connections repeatedly, use a connection pool to manage multiple database connections efficiently.

- Backup Your Database Regularly

  Always keep a backup of your database, especially before performing bulk updates or deletions.

- Log Database Queries for Debugging

  Keep track of executed queries to debug issues and optimize performance.

- Understand When to Use SQL versus NoSQL
  - Use SQL when your data is structured and relational.
  - Use MongoDB (NoSQL) when your data is dynamic and needs flexibility.

Exercises and Challenges: Practice Problems and Solutions

Now that you have learned how to work with relational (SQL) and NoSQL databases in Python, it is time to put your skills to the test! These practice problems will help reinforce key concepts such as creating databases, managing records, retrieving data, and performing updates and deletions.

Practice Problem 1: Employee Records System with SQLite

Task: Develop an employee records management system using SQLite.

Challenge: Write a Python script called employee_records.py that manages employee information.

- Create an SQLite database with a table for storing employee information, such as name, ID, department, and pay.

- Add new employee records, obtain department details, amend salaries, and delete records.
- Improve the system by enabling users to generate a report on overall pay expenditure for each department.

Practice Problem 2: Task Tracker with MongoDB

Task: Create a task-tracking system using MongoDB to manage tasks and projects. **Challenge**: Write a Python script called **`task_tracker.py`** that helps users manage their tasks.

- Create a MongoDB database with a collection for task documents, including fields such as name, description, due date, and status (for example, "**`Pending`**," "**`Completed`**").
- Create functions for adding new tasks, updating statuses, retrieving due dates, and deleting completed tasks.
- Introduce a feature that allows users to assign tasks to projects, save project information in a separate collection, and link tasks to specific projects.

Practice Problem 3: Student Grades Management with SQLite and MongoDB

Task: Build a student grades management system using both SQLite and MongoDB. **Challenge**: Write a Python script called **`student_grades.py`** that manages student grades for a school or university.

- Create an SQLite database to store student information, such as name, ID, and enrolled courses.
- Use MongoDB to store grade information for each course as documents, including assessments such as examinations, quizzes, and assignments.
- Add new students, assign grades for specific courses, retrieve grade reports, and calculate average grades.
- Provide a report with the highest and lowest grades in each course, based on data from both databases.

Solutions to Practice Problems

The solutions to the practice challenges for working with SQLite and MongoDB are listed here, with step-by-step implementations for each challenge.

Practice Problem 1: Employee Records System with SQLite

```
employee_records.py
import sqlite3

# Connect to the SQLite database (or create it if it doesn't exist)
connection = sqlite3.connect('employee_records.db')
cursor = connection.cursor()

# Create a table for storing employee records
cursor.execute('''
    CREATE TABLE IF NOT EXISTS employees (
        employee_id INTEGER PRIMARY KEY,
        name TEXT NOT NULL,
        department TEXT NOT NULL,
        salary REAL
    )
''')

# Function to add a new employee
def add_employee(name, department, salary):
```

```
    cursor.execute('''
        INSERT INTO employees (name, department, salary)
        VALUES (?, ?, ?)
    ''', (name, department, salary))
    connection.commit()

# Function to retrieve employee details by department
def get_employees_by_department(department):
    cursor.execute('''
        SELECT * FROM employees WHERE department = ?
    ''', (department,))
    return cursor.fetchall()

# Function to update an employee's department or salary
def update_employee(employee_id, department=None, salary=None):
    if department:
        cursor.execute('''
            UPDATE employees SET department = ? WHERE employee_id = ?
        ''', (department, employee_id))
    if salary:
        cursor.execute('''
            UPDATE employees SET salary = ? WHERE employee_id = ?
        ''', (salary, employee_id))
    connection.commit()

# Function to delete an employee record
def delete_employee(employee_id):
    cursor.execute('''
        DELETE FROM employees WHERE employee_id = ?
    ''', (employee_id,))
    connection.commit()

# Example usage
add_employee('John Doe', 'Engineering', 75000)
add_employee('Jane Smith', 'Marketing', 65000)
print("Employees in Engineering:", get_employees_by_department('Engineering'))
update_employee(1, salary=80000)
delete_employee(2)
print("All Employees:", get_employees_by_department('Engineering'))

# Close the connection
connection.close()
```

This script sets up an SQLite database, creates a table for employee records, and provides functions to add, retrieve, update, and delete employee data.

Practice Problem 2: Task Tracker with MongoDB

task_tracker.py

```
from pymongo import MongoClient

# Connect to the MongoDB server
client = MongoClient('localhost', 27017)
db = client['task_tracker']
tasks_collection = db['tasks']

# Function to add a new task
def add_task(name, description, due_date, status="Pending"):
    task = {
```

```
        "name": name,
        "description": description,
        "due_date": due_date,
        "status": status
    }
    tasks_collection.insert_one(task)

# Function to update a task's status
def update_task_status(task_name, status):
    tasks_collection.update_one(
        {"name": task_name},
        {"$set": {"status": status}}
    )

# Function to retrieve all tasks due by a certain date
def get_tasks_due_by(due_date):
    return tasks_collection.find({"due_date": {"$lte": due_date}})

# Function to delete completed tasks
def delete_completed_tasks():
    tasks_collection.delete_many({"status": "Completed"})

# Example usage
add_task("Finish project", "Complete the final project deliverables", "2023-08-31")
add_task("Prepare presentation", "Prepare slides for the client meeting",
"2023-09-01", "In Progress")
update_task_status("Finish project", "Completed")
tasks_due = get_tasks_due_by("2023-09-01")
for task in tasks_due:
    print(task)
delete_completed_tasks()

# Close the connection
client.close()
```

This script connects to a MongoDB database, creates a collection for tasks, and provides functions to add tasks, update task status, retrieve tasks by due date, and delete completed tasks.

Practice Problem 3: Student Grades Management with SQLite and MongoDB

```
student_grades.py
import sqlite3
from pymongo import MongoClient

# SQLite setup for storing student information
sqlite_connection = sqlite3.connect('students.db')
sqlite_cursor = sqlite_connection.cursor()
sqlite_cursor.execute('''
    CREATE TABLE IF NOT EXISTS students (
        student_id INTEGER PRIMARY KEY,
        name TEXT NOT NULL,
        course TEXT NOT NULL
    )
''')

# MongoDB setup for storing grades
mongo_client = MongoClient('localhost', 27017)
```

```
grades_db = mongo_client['student_grades']
grades_collection = grades_db['grades']

# Function to add a student
def add_student(name, course):
    sqlite_cursor.execute('''
        INSERT INTO students (name, course)
        VALUES (?, ?)
    ''', (name, course))
    sqlite_connection.commit()

# Function to add a grade for a student
def add_grade(student_id, course, grade):
    grade_record = {
        "student_id": student_id,
        "course": course,
        "grade": grade
    }
    grades_collection.insert_one(grade_record)

# Function to retrieve a student's grades
def get_student_grades(student_id):
    return grades_collection.find({"student_id": student_id})

# Example usage
add_student("Alice Johnson", "Math 101")
add_grade(1, "Math 101", 95)
add_grade(1, "Math 101", 87)
grades = get_student_grades(1)
for grade in grades:
    print(grade)

# Close connections
sqlite_connection.close()
mongo_client.close()
This script integrates SQLite and MongoDB to manage student information and
grades, respectively. It provides functions to add students, assign grades,
and retrieve grade reports.
```

Conclusion

Databases play a crucial role in modern applications, enabling efficient storage, retrieval, and management of data. In this chapter, you explored both relational databases (SQLite) and NoSQL databases (MongoDB), understanding their differences and use cases.

You started with SQLite, where you learned how to create tables, insert records, and perform CRUD operations using Python. Then MongoDB, a flexible NoSQL database was introduced, that allows you to store data in JSON-like documents.

In the next chapter, you will shift focus to data analysis in Python. You will learn how to work with data manipulation, analysis tools, and visualization techniques to uncover meaningful insights from raw data.

So, keep calm and let us tame the Python!

Multiple-Choice Questions

Test your understanding of the concepts covered in this chapter with the following multiple-choice questions.

1. Which SQL command is used to create a new table in SQLite?
   a. `CREATE DATABASE`
   b. `CREATE TABLE`
   c. `INSERT INTO`
   d. `SELECT *`
2. In SQLite, which method is used to execute an SQL command in Python?
   a. `execute_sql`
   b. `run_query`
   c. `cursor.execute`
   d. `commit`
3. Which of the following is NOT a valid data type in SQLite?
   a. `TEXT`
   b. `INTEGER`
   c. `BOOLEAN`
   d. `FLOAT`
4. In SQLite, which clause is used to filter records in a query?
   a. `WHERE`
   b. `ORDER BY`
   c. `GROUP BY`
   d. `HAVING`
5. Which of the following is true about MongoDB?
   a. It is a relational database.
   b. It stores data in tables with rows and columns.
   c. It uses JSON-like documents to store data.
   d. It requires a fixed schema for all collections.
6. Which Python library is used to interact with MongoDB?
   a. Sqlalchemy
   b. Pandas
   c. PyMongo
   d. Sqlparse

7. Which of the following MongoDB operations is used to insert multiple documents into a collection?
   a. `insert_one`
   b. `insert_many`
   c. `insert_bulk`
   d. `insert_batch`
8. In MongoDB, which method is used to retrieve all documents that match a certain query?
   a. `find_one`
   b. `find_all`
   c. `find`
   d. `fetch_all`
9. Which command is used to start the MongoDB server on a local machine?
   a. `Mongos`
   b. `Mongod`
   c. `mongo-server`
   d. `start_mongo`
10. What is the primary advantage of using a NoSQL database such as MongoDB over a relational database?
    a. It always requires less storage space.
    b. It can handle unstructured and semi-structured data more efficiently.
    c. It provides stronger data integrity.
    d. It eliminates the need for indexes.

Answers

1. b
2. c
3. c
4. a
5. c
6. c
7. b
8. c
9. b
10. b

Points to Remember

- SQLite and MongoDB are capable Python data management technologies that serve distinct demands based on data type and application requirements.
- SQLite is a lightweight, serverless relational database management system ideal for small to medium-sized applications that require efficient storage, querying, and management of structured data.
- SQLite allows you to store data in tables and manage it using CRUD operations (Create, Read, Update, Delete). These activities are the foundation for dealing with relational databases.
- MongoDB, a NoSQL database, stores data in JSON-like documents, providing flexibility in data modeling. It is useful for processing unstructured or semi-structured data that does not fit neatly into rows and columns.
- MongoDB and other NoSQL databases are highly adaptable to changing requirements and data kinds, as they do not require a set structure. MongoDB's versatility makes it an excellent choice for applications that require scale and rapid iteration.
- PyMongo is a Python library for MongoDB that allows for straightforward document operations such as inserting, querying, updating, and deleting.
- MongoDB's collections enable dynamic data storage by grouping documents with different structures.
- MongoDB's CRUD operations (insert, find, update, and delete) provide efficient data management.
- While SQLite and MongoDB can be integrated into Python applications for data storage and retrieval, they serve distinct purposes. SQLite is best for structured data with a defined schema, whereas MongoDB is best for flexible, unstructured data.
- When deciding between SQLite and MongoDB, consider your application's specific needs, such as a defined schema versus flexibility, or lightweight local storage versus distributed data management.

Further Reading

For additional learning, explore the following resources:

1. **SQLite Documentation**: https://www.sqlite.org/docs.html
2. **PyMongo Documentation**: https://pymongo.readthedocs.io/en/stable/
3. **MongoDB Manual**: https://docs.mongodb.com/manual/
4. **NoSQL Databases Overview**: https://www.mongodb.com/resources/basics/databases/nosql-explained

CHAPTER 17
Analyzing Data

Introduction

In the previous chapter, you learned how Python works with databases, simplifying the process of storing and retrieving structured data. Now, let us move forward and focus on analyzing and understanding that data. Whether it is customer records, sales figures, or research data, raw information remains just numbers and text until it is properly analyzed and interpreted.

In this chapter, you will explore data analysis with Python, a valuable skill in today's data-driven world. With so much information available, knowing how to clean, organize, and extract insights from data is essential. Python makes this process simple, and we will start with Pandas, a powerful library designed for handling data efficiently. Using Pandas, you will work with DataFrames, a table-like structure that lets you store and manipulate data just like a spreadsheet.

By the end of this chapter, you will be able to confidently handle real-world datasets, turning raw data into meaningful insights. Whether for research, business, or personal projects, these skills will form the foundation for more advanced data analysis in the future.

Structure

In this chapter, the following topics will be covered:

- Introduction to Data Analysis
  - Importance of Data Analysis in Programming
  - Overview of Python Libraries for Data Analysis
  - Real-World Applications of Data Analysis
- Getting Started with Pandas
  - Introduction to the Pandas library
  - Setting Up Pandas in your Python Environment
  - Introduction to DataFrames
  - Creating DataFrames from Scratch
  - Loading Data into DataFrames
  - Basic Operations: Selecting, Filtering, and Sorting Data
  - Practical Exercise: Working with DataFrames
- Exploring Data
  - Descriptive Statistics
  - Grouping and Aggregating Data
  - Visualizing Data with Basic Plots
  - Practical Exercise: Exploring and Visualizing Data with Pandas
- Data Cleaning

- Identifying and Handling Missing Data
- Removing Duplicates
- Data Type Conversion
- Basic Data Transformation
- Practical Exercise: Cleaning a Dataset

- Common Mistakes and Best Practices
- Exercises and Challenges: Practice Problems and Solutions

Introduction to Data Analysis

Data analysis is the process of organizing, cleaning, and interpreting data to uncover patterns, make predictions, and support decision-making. In programming, data analysis allows to work with datasets efficiently, using algorithms, statistics, and specialized tools to find useful insights. This skill is essential in many fields, including business, healthcare, finance, and research, where decisions must be based on data-driven evidence rather than guesswork.

The process of data analysis generally follows these steps:

1. **Collecting Data**: Gathering information from different sources such as files, databases, or APIs.
2. **Cleaning Data**: Removing mistakes, missing values, and inconsistencies to ensure accuracy.
3. **Exploring Data**: Using summary statistics and visualizations to understand key patterns.
4. **Modeling Data**: Applying mathematical techniques to find relationships and make predictions.
5. **Interpreting Results**: Presenting meaningful insights in a clear and useful way.

Importance of Data Analysis in Programming

In today's world, data is everywhere, and making good decisions depends on understanding it. Whether you are designing a product, improving a website, or solving a technical issue, data analysis helps you make smart, fact-based choices instead of relying on guesses.

For programmers, data analysis is not just an extra skill, it is a powerful tool that improves the value of your work. Here is why it is so important:

- **Better Decision-Making**: Data helps programmers make informed choices rather than relying on intuition.
- **Efficiency and Optimization**: Analyzing trends can improve performance and simplify workflows.
- **Problem-Solving**: By examining logs, errors, and user behavior, programmers can find and fix issues faster.
- **Innovation**: Data insights allow developers to create new features and customized user experiences.

Overview of Python Libraries for Data Analysis

Python is one of the most popular languages for data analysis because of its simplicity and powerful libraries. Here are some key libraries that make data handling easier:

- **Pandas**: The most widely used library for working with structured data. It provides DataFrames, which are like spreadsheets, making it easy to filter, sort, and analyze data.

- **NumPy**: A foundational library for handling numerical data. It enables fast operations on large datasets using arrays and mathematical functions.
- **Matplotlib**: A visualization library that lets you create graphs and charts to explore patterns in data.
- **Seaborn**: Built on top of Matplotlib, Seaborn simplifies the creation of beautiful statistical visualizations.
- **SciPy**: Expands on NumPy with additional tools for scientific and technical computing, including functions for optimization, integration, and interpolation.

These libraries form the core of Python's data analysis toolkit, helping you manipulate, analyze, and visualize data efficiently.

Real-World Applications of Data Analysis

Data analysis is used in almost every industry to improve decision-making and drive innovation. Let us look at some real-world examples:

- **Healthcare**: Hospitals use data analysis to predict patient needs, optimize treatments, and manage resources efficiently. For example, predictive analytics can help estimate patient admission rates, improving staff scheduling.
- **Finance**: Banks and investment firms use data to detect fraud, assess loan risks, and automate trading strategies. Algorithms analyze market trends to make real-time financial decisions.
- **Retail**: Businesses analyze sales and customer behavior to manage inventory, optimize pricing, and create personalized marketing campaigns. This helps them increase profits while improving customer satisfaction.

These examples show how data analysis powers real-world decision-making. By working through this chapter, you will develop the skills to apply these techniques in practical situations.

Getting Started with Pandas

Now that you understand the basics of data analysis and how it is used in the real world, it is time to start working with Pandas, one of the most powerful tools for analyzing data in Python. Pandas makes it easy to organize, clean, and explore data, no matter how large or complex the dataset is.

Introduction to the Pandas Library

Pandas is a popular open-source Python library designed for working with structured data, such as tables. It provides efficient data structures that make data analysis simple and intuitive.

The two main data structures in Pandas are:

- **Series**: A one-dimensional labeled array (like a single column in a spreadsheet).
- **DataFrame**: A two-dimensional table with labeled rows and columns (like an entire spreadsheet).

With Pandas, you can easily load, clean, and manipulate data, making it an essential tool for anyone working with data in Python.

Setting Up Pandas in Your Python Environment

Before using Pandas, you need to install it in your Python environment. You can do this using the pip package manager:

1. Open your Command Prompt (Windows) or Terminal (Mac/Linux).

2. Run the following command:

   ```
   pip install pandas
   ```

Once the installation is complete, Pandas is ready to use in your Python scripts.

Introduction to DataFrames

A DataFrame is the core data structure in Pandas. It represents data in rows and columns, similar to an Excel spreadsheet or a SQL table. Each column can store different types of data, such as numbers, text, or dates.

Key features of DataFrames:

- **Labeled Axes**: Each row and column has labels, making it easy to access and modify data.
- **Automatic Alignment**: When merging data, Pandas aligns it based on labels rather than positions.
- **Powerful Operations**: You can quickly filter, sort, group, and modify data with simple commands.

Creating DataFrames from Scratch

Although you will often work with existing datasets (such as CSV or Excel files), you can also create DataFrames manually. This is useful for testing or small-scale data analysis.

Here is how you can create a DataFrame using a Python dictionary:

```
import pandas as pd

# Create a dictionary with sample data
data = {
    'Name': ['Alice', 'Bob', 'Charlie', 'David'],
    'Age': [24, 27, 22, 32],
    'City': ['New York', 'Los Angeles', 'Chicago', 'Houston']
}

# Convert dictionary into a DataFrame
df = pd.DataFrame(data)

# Display the DataFrame
print(df)
```

In this example, each dictionary key represents a column name, and the values are lists of data for that column. The **`pd.DataFrame()`** function converts this dictionary into a structured table.

Loading Data into DataFrames

Most of the time, you will work with external data sources, such as CSV files, Excel spreadsheets, or databases. Pandas makes it easy to load this data directly into a DataFrame.

For example, to load a CSV file:

```
import pandas as pd

# Load a CSV file into a DataFrame
df = pd.read_csv('customers.csv')

# Display the first few rows
print(df.head())
```

The **read_csv()** function loads the file, and **head()** lets you preview the first few rows. This is useful when working with large datasets.

Basic Operations: Selecting, Filtering, and Sorting Data

Once your data is in a DataFrame, you can start analyzing and modifying it. Let us look at some common operations:

Selecting Data:

To select a specific column, use its column name:

```
names = df['Name']
print(names)
```

Filtering Data:

To filter rows based on a condition (for example, selecting customers from a specific city):

```
filtered_data = df[df['City'] == 'New York']
print(filtered_data)
```

Sorting Data:

To sort data by a specific column, use **sort_values()**:

```
sorted_df = df.sort_values(by='Age')
print(sorted_df)
```

These basic operations help you explore and clean your data before moving to deeper analysis.

Practical Exercise: Working with DataFrames

You will practice building DataFrames from scratch, importing data from a CSV file into DataFrames, and carrying out simple tasks such as sorting, filtering, and choosing data in this activity. You will learn more about DataFrames and their capabilities through this practical experience, which takes place in the Visual Studio Code (VS Code) environment.

Task Description:

Before loading data from a CSV file into a DataFrame, you will first create a basic DataFrame from scratch. Following that, you will explore and change the data using a few simple procedures.

Real-Life Scenario:

Consider yourself a data analyst assigned to oversee a modest employee data set. To arrange this data, you must first establish a DataFrame, import more data from a CSV file, and then do some simple analysis to determine which employees are older and to arrange the data according to their pay.

CSV File Structure:

For this exercise, the CSV file you will be working with should have the following structure:

Name	Age	Department	Salary
John	28	HR	50000
Jane	34	Finance	60000
Emily	22	IT	45000

Michael	45	Marketing	75000
Laura	29	IT	52000

Table 17.1: CSV *file structure for Practical Exercise*

Each row represents an employee, with the following columns:

- Name: The employee's name.
- Age: The employee's age.
- Department: The department in which the employee works.
- Salary: The employee's salary.

You can either create a CSV file with this structure or use a similar file that you have.

Steps for the Exercise:

1. **Set Up Your Environment in VS Code**
    a. Get Visual Studio Code open.
    b. For this exercise, create a new Python file (**`dataframe_practice.py`**, for example).
    c. To improve code management and execution, make sure the Python extension is installed in Visual Studio Code.
2. **Create a DataFrame from Scratch**
    a. Start by importing Pandas into your newly generated Python file and constructing a DataFrame with a dictionary to represent employee data, which should include columns such as "**`Name`**," "**`Age`**," and "**`Department`**."
    b. To see the DataFrame and make sure it was built correctly, run your script in Visual Studio Code.
3. **Load Data into a DataFrame**
    a. Make use of the CSV file with the previously stated structure.
    b. In your Python script, load this CSV file into a Pandas DataFrame.
    c. To view the first few rows of the DataFrame and examine the data, run your script once more in Visual Studio Code.
4. **Perform Basic Operations on the DataFrame**
    a. Choose Particular Columns: From the DataFrame, pick the "**`Name`**" and "**`Salary`**" columns, then show them.
    b. Filter Rows: To see only employees over 30, filter the DataFrame.
    c. Sort Data: Arrange the DataFrame in decreasing order according to the "**`Salary`**" column.

Implementation Steps:

1. **Creating a DataFrame from Scratch in VS Code**
    a. Begin by importing Pandas and creating a DataFrame:

```
import pandas as pd
# Create a dictionary of employee data
data = {
    'Name': ['John', 'Jane', 'Emily', 'Michael'],
```

```
    'Age': [28, 34, 22, 45],
    'Department': ['HR', 'Finance', 'IT', 'Marketing']
}

# Create a DataFrame from the dictionary
df = pd.DataFrame(data)
# Display the DataFrame
print(df)
```

   b. Save your file and run the script in VS Code by right-clicking inside the file and selecting "**`Run Python File in Terminal`**." This will display the DataFrame in the terminal.

2. **Loading Data from a CSV File in VS Code**

   a. Load data from the CSV file into a DataFrame:

```
# Load the CSV file into a DataFrame
df = pd.read_csv('path_to_your_file.csv')
# Display the first few rows of the DataFrame
print(df.head())
```

   b. Save and run your script again in VS Code to see the first few rows of the DataFrame.

3. **Performing Basic Operations**

   a. **Select Specific Columns**:

```
# Select the "Name" and "Salary" columns
selected_columns = df[['Name', 'Salary']]
print(selected_columns)
```

   b. **Filter Rows:**

```
# Filter employees older than 30
older_than_30 = df[df['Age'] > 30]
print(older_than_30)
```

   c. **Sort Data:**

```
# Sort by "Salary" in descending order
sorted_df = df.sort_values(by='Salary', ascending=False)
print(sorted_df)
```

In this exercise, you loaded extra data from a CSV file, made a DataFrame from scratch to manage a tiny dataset, and used Visual Studio Code to carry out simple tasks such as selecting, filtering, and sorting data. These abilities are essential for using DataFrames and will form the basis of more complex data analysis methods.

Understanding the Solution:

- **Generating DataFrames**: You learned how to manually enter data and arrange it in an organized fashion by generating a DataFrame from a dictionary.
- **Loading Data**: One of the most frequent activities in data analysis is loading data from a CSV file into a DataFrame. You have now practiced this crucial ability.
- **Fundamental Operations**: Data selection, filtering, and sorting are essential processes that enable you to swiftly and effectively get valuable insights from your data.

You have developed a solid basis for dealing with DataFrames, which are the backbone of Pandas' data analysis, by finishing this task. As you proceed, you will discover how to use these potent tools to carry out increasingly intricate manipulations and analyses, all within the VS Code environment.

Exploring Data

In the previous sections, you learned how to load data into a Pandas DataFrame and perform basic operations such as sorting, filtering, and selecting data. Now, it is time to analyze your data in more depth. This section will introduce you to techniques for summarizing data, grouping and aggregating values, and visualizing trends. These techniques help uncover patterns and insights that might not be immediately visible in raw data.

Descriptive Statistics

Descriptive statistics help you summarize and understand data by providing key numerical values. Pandas makes it easy to compute these values for any dataset.

Some of the most commonly used statistics include:

- **Mean**: The average value of a dataset.
- **Median**: The middle value when the data is sorted.
- **Mode**: The most frequently occurring value in the dataset.
- **Standard Deviation**: Measures how spread out the data is.

Let us calculate these statistics in Pandas:

```
import pandas as pd

# Assuming df is your DataFrame

# Calculate mean of a column
mean_value = df['Salary'].mean()
print(f"Mean Salary: {mean_value}")

# Calculate median of a column
median_value = df['Salary'].median()
print(f"Median Salary: {median_value}")

# Calculate mode of a column
mode_value = df['Salary'].mode()[0]  # [0] to get the first mode
print(f"Mode Salary: {mode_value}")

# Calculate standard deviation of a column
std_dev = df['Salary'].std()
print(f"Standard Deviation of Salary: {std_dev}")
```

These summary statistics help understand the distribution of data and identify trends or anomalies.

Grouping and Aggregating Data

Often, you will need to summarize data based on categories. For example, you might want to find the average salary for each department or total sales for each product.

Pandas makes this easy using grouping and aggregation functions.

Here is how to group data and calculate the average salary per department:

```
# Group by 'Department' and calculate mean salary
grouped_data = df.groupby('Department')['Salary'].mean()
print(grouped_data)
```

You can also apply multiple calculations at once using **agg()**:

```
# Group by 'Department' and calculate multiple statistics
aggregated_data = df.groupby('Department').agg({
    'Salary': ['mean', 'max', 'min'],
})
print(aggregated_data)
```

Grouping and aggregating help summarize large datasets efficiently, making it easier to compare different groups.

Visualizing Data with Basic Plots

Data visualization allows to see patterns and trends that might not be obvious from numbers alone. Pandas makes it easy to create simple charts and graphs using Matplotlib.

Here are some useful visualizations:

- **Bar Plot – Comparing Categories**

  A bar plot is useful for comparing different groups, such as average salary by department.

  ```
  grouped_data.plot(kind='bar', title='Average Salary by Department')
  ```

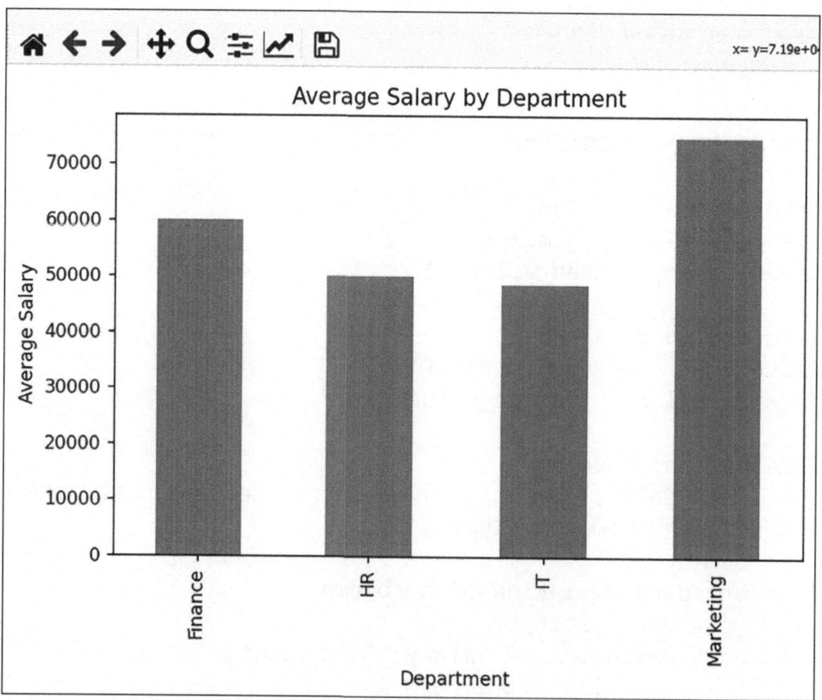

Figure 17.1: *Bar plot using Pandas and Matplotlib*

- **Line Plot – Showing Trends Over Time**

  A line plot helps visualize changes over time, such as salary growth over different years.

  ```
  df.plot(x='Date', y='Salary', kind='line', title='Salary Over Time')
  ```

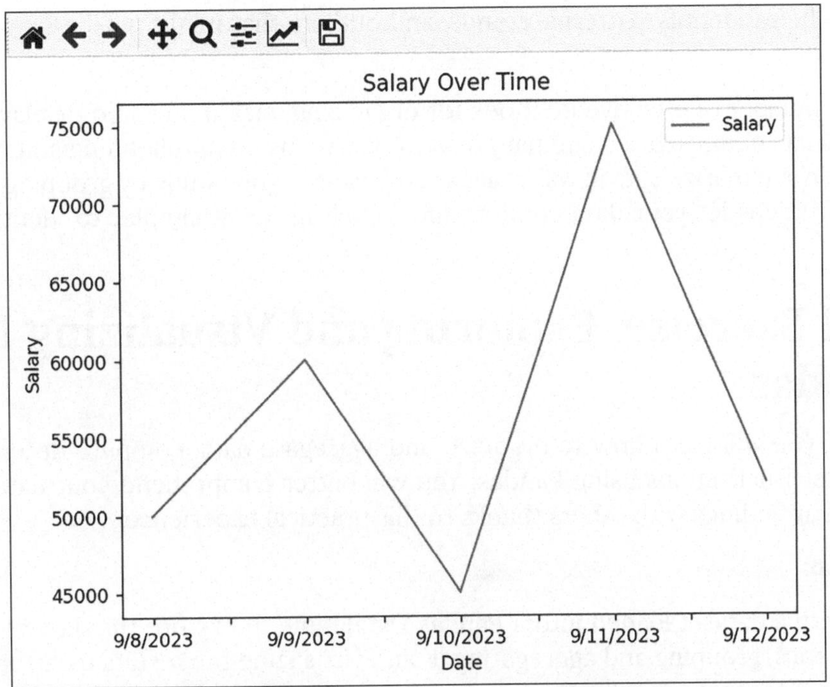

Figure 17.2: *Line plot using Pandas and Matplotlib*

- **Histogram – Understanding Distribution**

  A histogram shows how values are distributed within a dataset.

```
df['Salary'].plot(kind='hist', title='Salary Distribution')
```

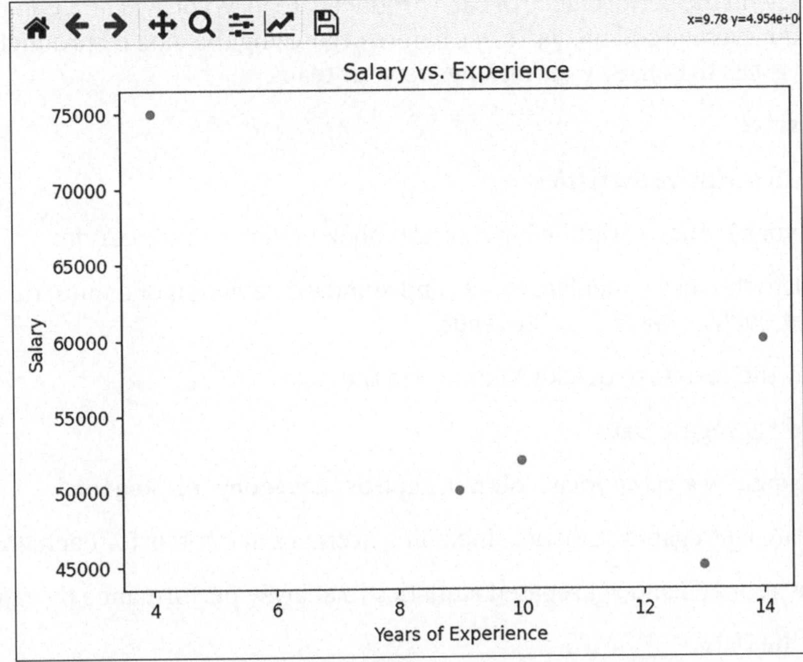

Figure 17.3: *Scatter plot using Pandas and Matplotlib*

- **Scatter Plot – Finding Relationships**

  A scatter plot is useful for showing correlations between two variables, such as experience vs. salary.

```
df.plot(kind='scatter', x='YearsExperience', y='Salary', title='Salary vs.
Experience')
```

Visualizing data helps identify patterns, trends, and outliers that might not be immediately obvious from raw numbers.

You looked at a number of effective methods for organizing, classifying, and displaying your data in this section. You can obtain a brief summary of your dataset by comprehending and using descriptive statistics. You can summarize data in ways that are relevant to your study by grouping and aggregating it. Lastly, visualizations let your data come to life, which makes it simpler to identify patterns and trends.

Practical Exercise: Exploring and Visualizing Data with Pandas

In this exercise, you will learn how to organize and aggregate data, compute descriptive statistics, and make simple visualizations using Pandas. You will better comprehend your data and be able to communicate your findings with others thanks to this practical experience.

Task Description:

You will work with a dataset loaded into a Pandas DataFrame to explore the data by calculating key descriptive statistics, grouping and aggregating it, and visualizing the results using basic plots. While this section introduces some visualizations, it relies on the Matplotlib library. To understand the syntax and capabilities of Matplotlib further, you can refer to its official documentation (https://matplotlib.org/stable/index.html) or other online resources.

Real-Life Scenario:

Imagine working for a company that requires you to analyze sales data and provide a summary report. In order to comprehend the performance of each product category, you will first compute fundamental statistics such as the average and median sales before organizing the data by product category. Lastly, you will produce visuals to convey your findings to your team.

Steps for the Exercise:

1. **Calculate Descriptive Statistics**
    a. Open your Python script or Jupyter notebook in Visual Studio Code.
    b. Calculate the mean, median, mode, and standard deviation of a numerical column in your dataset, such as "`Sales`" or "`Revenue`."
    c. Display the results to quickly summarize the data.
2. **Group and Aggregate Data**
    a. Group data by a categorical column, such as "`Category`" or "`Region`."
    b. Calculate aggregated statistics, including averages and totals for each group.
    c. Display grouped and aggregated statistics to analyze performance by category or region.
3. **Visualize the Data**
    a. Create a bar plot to compare average sales/revenue across categories.
    b. Use line plots to visualize trends over time, such as sales by month.
    c. Create a histogram to visualize the distribution of sales or other vital metrics.
    d. Create a scatter plot to analyze the relationship between two variables, such as sales and advertising spend.

Implementation Steps:

- **Import Libraries**

  Before starting, make sure to import both Pandas and Matplotlib:

  ```
  import pandas as pd
  import matplotlib.pyplot as plt
  ```

- **Calculate Descriptive Statistics**

  Start by importing Pandas and loading your dataset:

  ```
  import pandas as pd
  df = pd.read_csv('./data/sample_data_100_entries.csv')
  # Calculate and display statistics for 'Sales'
  print("Mean Sales:", df['Sales'].mean())
  print("Median Sales:", df['Sales'].median())
  print("Mode Sales:", df['Sales'].mode()[0])
  print("Standard Deviation of Sales:", df['Sales'].std())
  ```

- **Group and Aggregate Data**

  Group the data by a category and calculate aggregated statistics:

  ```
  # Group by 'Category' and calculate the mean sales for each category
  category_sales = df.groupby('Category')['Sales'].mean()
  print("\nAverage Sales by Category:\n", category_sales)
  # Group by 'Category' and aggregate multiple statistics
  aggregated_data = df.groupby('Category').agg({
      'Sales': ['mean', 'sum'],
      'Quantity': 'sum'
  })
  print("\nAggregated Data by Category:\n", aggregated_data)
  ```

- **Visualize the Data:**

  To visualize the data, Pandas integrates seamlessly with Matplotlib. While the following examples use Matplotlib, you can explore its documentation for further customization.

  - **Create a bar plot to compare average sales across categories:**

    ```
    # Bar plot: Average Sales by Category
    category_sales.plot(kind='bar', title='Average Sales by Category')
    plt.xlabel('Category')
    plt.ylabel('Average Sales')
    plt.tight_layout()
    plt.show()
    ```

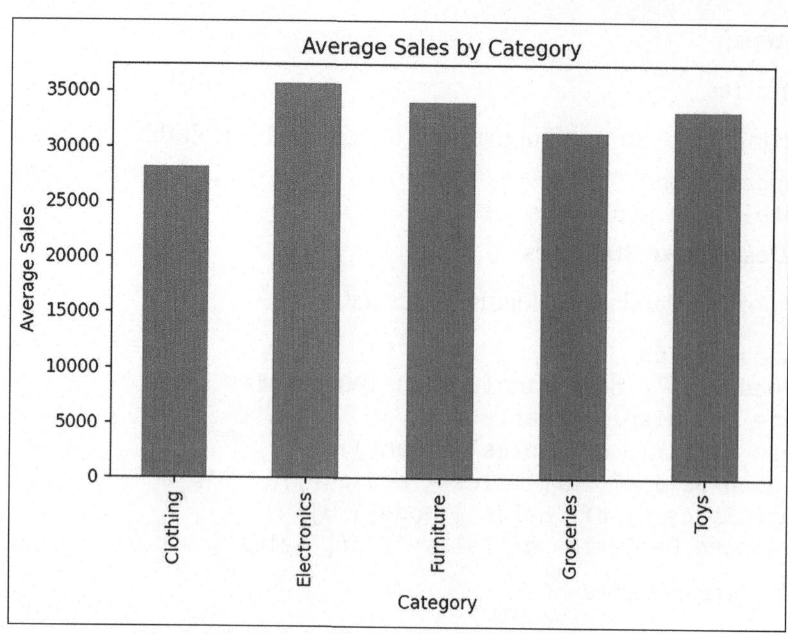

Figure 17.4: *Average Sales by Category*

- **Use a line plot to show sales trends over time:**

```
# Line plot: Sales Over Time
df.plot(x='Month', y='Sales', kind='line', title='Sales Over Time')
plt.xlabel('Month')
plt.ylabel('Sales')
plt.tight_layout()
plt.show()
```

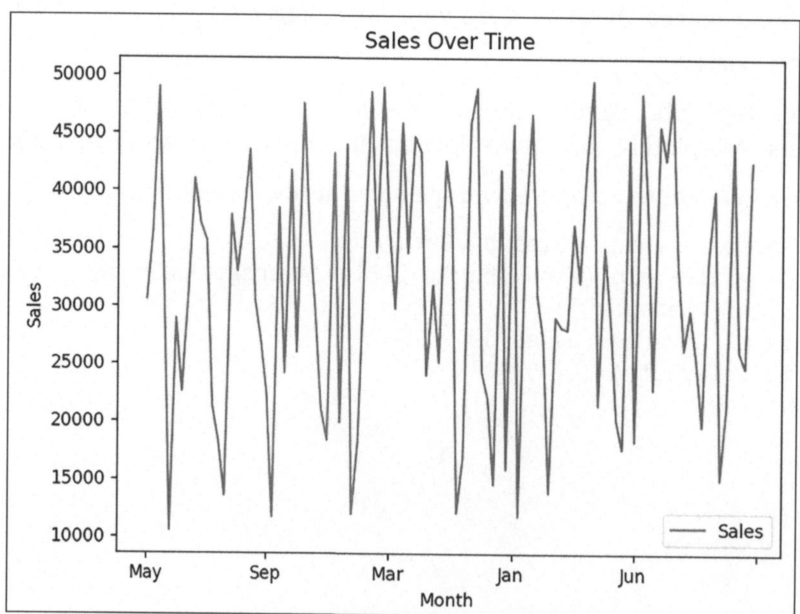

Figure 17.5: *Sales over Time*

- **Generate a histogram to visualize the distribution of sales:**

```
# Histogram: Sales Distribution
df['Sales'].plot(kind='hist', title='Sales Distribution', bins=10)
plt.xlabel('Sales')
plt.ylabel('Frequency')
plt.tight_layout()
plt.show()
```

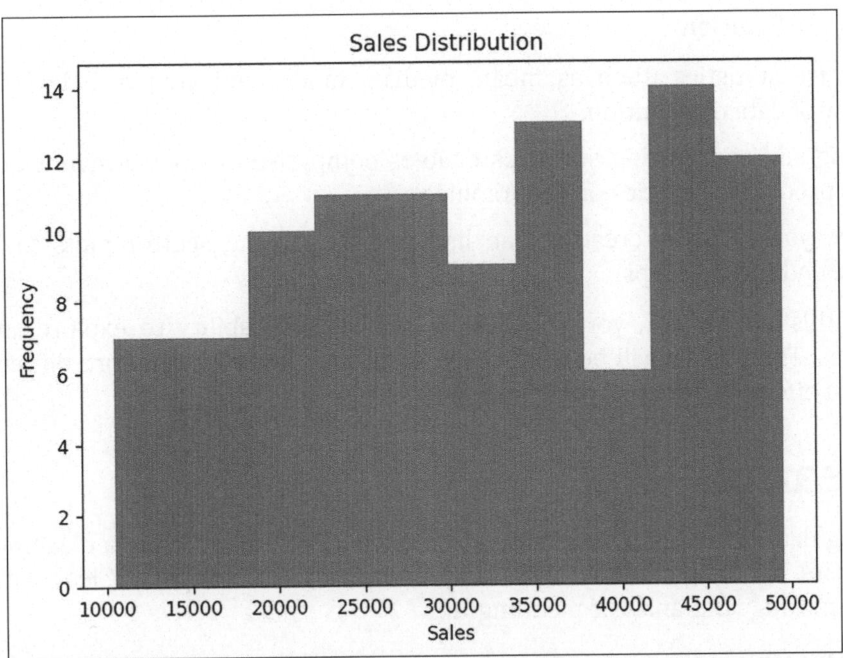

Figure 17.6: Sales distribution

- **Create a scatter plot to explore the relationship between sales and advertising spend:**

```
# Scatter plot: Sales vs. Advertising Spend
df.plot(kind='scatter', x='AdvertisingSpend', y='Sales', title='Sales vs.
Advertising Spend')
plt.xlabel('Advertising Spend')
plt.ylabel('Sales')
plt.tight_layout()
plt.show()
```

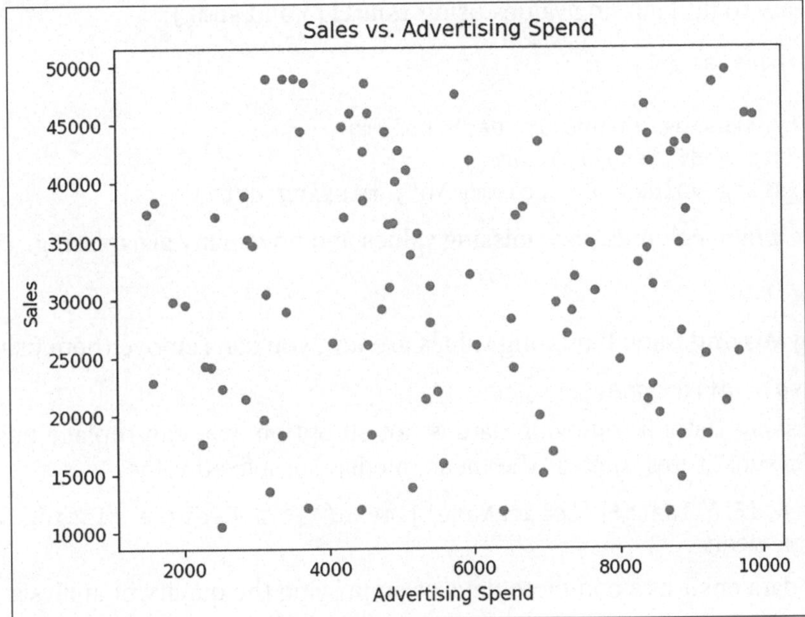

Figure 17.7: Sales distribution

In this exercise, you computed essential descriptive statistics to describe your data, grouped and aggregated it to detect trends and patterns, and generated visualizations to effectively explain your results. These stages are critical to interpreting your data and delivering your research in a clear and understandable way.

Understanding the Solution:

- Descriptive statistics, such as mean, median, mode, and standard deviation, provide an overview of data distribution.
- Grouping and aggregating statistics enables comparison of performance across segments, such as product categories or geographies.
- Visualize your data by creating bar, line, histogram, and scatter plots to identify trends, outliers, and relationships.

By completing this assignment, you will have improved your ability to explore and comprehend data with Pandas. These skills will be useful as you continue to work on more difficult data analysis assignments and effectively convey your findings.

Data Cleaning

Before analyzing data, it is crucial to ensure accuracy and consistency. Data cleaning is the process of removing errors, handling missing values, and structuring data properly. Clean data leads to more reliable results, making your analysis meaningful.

This section starts with handling missing data to ensure completeness, followed by removing duplicates to prevent inconsistencies. It then covers converting data types for accurate calculations and ends with basic transformations including renaming columns and reorganizing data for better usability.

Identifying and Handling Missing Data

Missing data is a common issue in real-world datasets. It occurs when some values are not recorded or lost. If not handled properly, missing data can lead to incorrect conclusions.

Checking for Missing Data:

Pandas makes it easy to find missing values using **`isnull()`** and **`sum()`**:

```
import pandas as pd

# Identify missing values in each column
missing_data = df.isnull().sum()
print("Missing values per column:\n", missing_data)
```

This helps you see which columns have missing values and how many are missing.

Handling Missing Data:

- **Removing Missing Data**: If missing values are few, you can remove them using **`dropna()`**:

  ```
  df_cleaned = df.dropna()
  ```

- **Filling Missing Data**: If removing data is not an option, you can replace missing values with meaningful substitutes, such as the mean, median, or a fixed value:

  ```
  df_filled = df.fillna(df['ColumnName'].mean())  # Replace missing values with
  the column mean
  ```

Handling missing data ensures a complete dataset, improving the quality of analysis.

Removing Duplicates

Duplicate records can skew analysis, especially when calculating averages, totals, or trends. Pandas provides easy ways to detect and remove duplicates.

- **Checking for Duplicates**

```
# Identify duplicate rows
duplicates = df.duplicated()
print("Duplicate rows:\n", df[duplicates])
```

- **Removing Duplicates**

```
# Remove duplicate rows
df_no_duplicates = df.drop_duplicates()
print("Data after removing duplicates:\n", df_no_duplicates)
```

Ensuring each record is unique prevents biased results and improves accuracy in data analysis.

Data Type Conversion

Data may not always be stored in the correct format. For example:

- Numbers might be stored as text, preventing calculations.
- Dates might be stored as plain strings, making analysis difficult.

Pandas allows easy conversion of data types to match analysis requirements.

Converting Data Types:

1. **Convert a column to an integer:**

```
df['ColumnName'] = df['ColumnName'].astype(int)
```

2. **Convert a column to datetime format:**

```
df['DateColumn'] = pd.to_datetime(df['DateColumn'])
```

Ensuring correct data types makes operations such as filtering, sorting, and calculations more efficient and accurate.

Basic Data Transformations

Sometimes, you need to rearrange or rename data to make it easier to work with.

- **Renaming Columns:**

```
df = df.rename(columns={'OldName': 'NewName'})
```

- **Setting a Column as Index:**

```
df = df.set_index('ColumnName')
```

- **Reordering Columns:**

```
df = df[['Column3', 'Column1', 'Column2']]
```

These transformations help organize data in a way that makes analysis simpler and more intuitive.

Practical Exercise: Cleaning a Dataset

Now that you have studied the fundamentals of data cleansing, it is time to put them into action. In this exercise, you will utilize a sample dataset to clean the data by dealing with missing values, deleting duplicates, converting data types, and performing fundamental data transformations.

Task Description:

You will begin with a raw dataset that includes missing values, duplicates, and poorly formatted data. Your task is to clean the data with the strategies you have studied.

Real-Life Scenario:

Assume you are creating a dataset for a report on employee performance. The data includes employee IDs, names, departments, salaries, and hire dates. However, the dataset is incomplete, with duplicates and formatting errors. Your responsibility is to clean the data so that it is ready for analysis.

Steps for the Exercise:

1. **Identify and Handle Missing Data**
   a. Identify missing values from the dataset.
   b. Decide if missing data should be dropped or filled with acceptable values (for exaample, mean or median).
2. **Remove Duplicates**
   a. Identify duplicate records in the dataset.
   b. Remove the duplicate records to ensure each entry is unique.
3. **Convert Data Types**
   a. Check the data types of each column.
   b. Convert any columns that are not in the correct format (for example, convert strings to integers, or strings to dates).
4. **Perform Basic Data Transformation**
   a. Rename columns to more meaningful names if necessary.
   b. Set an appropriate column as the index.
   c. Reorder columns to make the DataFrame easier to work with.

Implementation Steps:

1. **Load the Dataset**

```
import pandas as pd
# Load the dataset into a DataFrame
df = pd.read_csv('path_to_your_dataset.csv')
```

2. **Handle Missing Data**

```
# Identify missing values
print("Missing values in each column:\n", df.isnull().sum())
# Fill missing values with the mean (or drop rows with missing values)
df = df.fillna(df['Salary'].mean())
```

3. **Remove Duplicates**

```
# Identify and remove duplicates
df = df.drop_duplicates()
```

4. **Convert Data Types**

```
# Convert 'Salary' to integer and 'HireDate' to datetime
df['Salary'] = df['Salary'].astype(int)
df['HireDate'] = pd.to_datetime(df['HireDate'])
```

5. **Perform Basic Data Transformation**

```
# Rename columns and set 'EmployeeID' as the index
df = df.rename(columns={'EmpID': 'EmployeeID', 'Dept': 'Department'})
df = df.set_index('EmployeeID')
# Reorder columns
df = df[['Name', 'Department', 'Salary', 'HireDate']]
print(df)
```

This task required you to clean a dataset by finding and addressing missing data, deleting duplicates, converting data types, and executing fundamental data transformations. These steps are critical for preparing your data for analysis, ensuring that it is accurate, consistent, and in the correct format.

Understanding the Solution:

- **Handling Missing Data:** Decide whether to discard or fill missing numbers to ensure comprehensive and reliable data.
- **Removing Duplicates:** Using unique records reduces skewed analysis.
- **Correct Data Type Conversion**: Ensures precise calculations and analysis.
- **Basic Data Transformation:** Renaming, indexing, and reordering columns enhances DataFrame usability.

By finishing this exercise, you will gain practical experience cleaning data, which is an important skill in any data analysis endeavor. Clean data results in more accurate insights and improved decision-making.

Common Mistakes and Best Practices

Data analysis is a powerful tool, but small mistakes can lead to misleading results and incorrect conclusions. To ensure your analysis is accurate and efficient, it is important to be aware of common mistakes and follow best practices.

Common Mistakes in Data Analysis

- **Not Cleaning Data Before Analysis:**
  - **Mistake**: Jumping into analysis without checking for missing values, duplicates, or incorrect data types.
  - **Problem**: Leads to inaccurate results and flawed conclusions.
  - **Solution**: Always start with data cleaning, that is, handle missing data, remove duplicates, and ensure correct data types.
- **Ignoring Missing Data:**
  - **Mistake**: Proceeding with incomplete data without handling missing values.
  - **Problem**: Can lead to biased results or errors in calculations.
  - **Solution**: Identify missing data using `isnull().sum()` and decide whether to remove or fill missing values.
- **Using Incorrect Data Types:**
  - **Mistake**: Treating numbers as text or ignoring date formats.
  - **Problem**: Prevents calculations, sorting, and proper analysis.
  - **Solution**: Convert data using `.astype()` or `pd.to_datetime()` before performing operations.
- **Misinterpreting Descriptive Statistics:**
  - **Mistake**: Assuming that the mean always represents the data accurately.
  - **Problem**: Data with extreme values (outliers) can skew the mean, leading to false conclusions.
  - **Solution**: Always check median and standard deviation alongside the mean for a clearer picture.

- **Forgetting to Group or Aggregate Data**
  - **Mistake:** Analyzing individual records instead of summarizing data by relevant categories.
  - **Problem**: Hard to identify trends and key insights.
  - **Solution**: Use `groupby()` and `agg()` to summarize data by relevant groups.
- **Not Visualizing Data Before Drawing Conclusions**
  - **Mistake:** Relying only on numbers without plotting data.
  - **Problem**: Important patterns or outliers may be missed.
  - **Solution**: Use bar charts, histograms, and scatter plots to spot trends before making decisions.

Best Practices for Effective Data Analysis

- **Always Inspect Your Data First:**

  Before analysis, use `df.head()`, `df.info()`, and `df.describe()` to get an overview of your dataset.
- **Clean Your Data Thoroughly:**

  Handle missing values, correct data types, and remove duplicates to avoid errors in analysis.
- **Choose the Right Summary Statistics:**
  - Use mean when data is evenly distributed.
  - Use median when data has outliers.
  - Check standard deviation to understand variability.
- **Use Grouping and Aggregation for Better Insights:**

  Summarize data using `groupby()` and `agg()` to find trends across different categories.
- **Visualize Data Before Making Conclusions:**

  Create plots and graphs using Pandas and Matplotlib to identify patterns, trends, and outliers easily.
- **Document and Verify Your Analysis:**

  Keep clear notes on how data was cleaned and analyzed. Double-check results to avoid errors.

Exercises and Challenges: Practice Problems and Solutions

To solidify your understanding of the concepts covered in this chapter, here are a few practice problems that will challenge you to apply what you have learned. These exercises involve working with real-world data, cleaning it, performing analysis, and visualizing the results.

Practice Problem 1: Sales Data Analysis with Pandas

Task: Analyze sales data to gain insights into product performance.

Challenge: Write a Python script called `sales_analysis.py` that performs the following tasks:

- **Load**: Load a dataset containing sales information for a retail store, including columns such as `ProductID`, `ProductName`, `Category`, `QuantitySold`, `PricePerUnit`, and `TotalRevenue`.

- **Clean**: Identify and handle any missing data, remove duplicate records, and ensure that all data types are correctly formatted.
- **Analyze**: Calculate descriptive statistics such as the mean, median, and mode for key metrics such as `QuantitySold` and `TotalRevenue`.
- **Group and Aggregate**: Group the data by Category and calculate the average `TotalRevenue` for each category. Identify the best-performing product category.
- **Visualize:** Create visualizations to display the distribution of `TotalRevenue` and compare the average revenue across different product categories.

Practice Problem 2: Customer Feedback Analysis with Pandas

Task: Analyze customer feedback data to identify key trends.

Challenge: Write a Python script called `feedback_analysis.py` that helps a company understand customer sentiment.

- **Load**: Load a dataset containing customer feedback, with columns such as `CustomerID`, `FeedbackText`, `Rating`, and `Date`.
- **Clean**: Handle missing data in the Rating column by filling in the average rating. Remove any duplicate feedback entries.
- **Analyze**: Calculate the average rating and identify the most common keywords in the feedback text using basic text analysis techniques.
- **Group and Aggregate**: Group the feedback by Rating and analyze the frequency of different ratings. Identify the most common rating and the most frequent keywords associated with it.
- **Visualize**: Create a bar plot to show the distribution of ratings and a word cloud to visualize the most common keywords in the feedback.

Practice Problem 3: Employee Performance Analysis with Pandas

Task: Assess employee performance data to determine key performance indicators.

Challenge: Write a Python script called `employee_performance.py` that evaluates the performance of employees based on various metrics.

- **Load**: Load a dataset containing employee performance data, with columns such as `EmployeeID`, `Name`, `Department`, `ProjectsCompleted`, `HoursWorked`, and `PerformanceScore`.
- **Clean**: Identify and handle any missing data, ensure that all numeric data is correctly formatted, and remove any duplicates.
- **Analyze**: Calculate descriptive statistics for `ProjectsCompleted` and `PerformanceScore.` Determine the average number of projects completed by department and the average performance score.
- **Group and Aggregate**: Group the data by Department and calculate the total number of `HoursWorked` and `ProjectsCompleted` for each department. Identify the department with the highest performance score on average.
- **Visualize**: Create a bar chart to compare average performance scores across departments and a scatter plot to explore the relationship between `HoursWorked` and `PerformanceScore`.

Solutions to Practice Problems

Here are the solutions to the practice problems for working with Pandas. Each solution includes a step-by-step implementation to guide you through the process.

Practice Problem 1: Sales Data Analysis with Pandas

```
sales_analysis.py
import pandas as pd
# Load the dataset
df = pd.read_csv('./data/sales_data_sample.csv')
# Clean the data
df = df.dropna()  # Handle missing data by dropping rows with missing values
df = df.drop_duplicates()  # Remove duplicate records
# Analyze the data
mean_revenue = df['TotalRevenue'].mean()
median_revenue = df['TotalRevenue'].median()
mode_revenue = df['TotalRevenue'].mode()[0]
# Group and aggregate the data
category_revenue = df.groupby('Category')['TotalRevenue'].mean()

# Visualize the data
category_revenue.plot(kind='bar', title='Average Revenue by Category')
# Display results
print(f"Mean Revenue: {mean_revenue}")
print(f"Median Revenue: {median_revenue}")
print(f"Mode Revenue: {mode_revenue}")
print("Average Revenue by Category:")
print(category_revenue)
```

This script analyzes sales data by cleaning the dataset, calculating key statistics, and visualizing the performance of different product categories.

Practice Problem 2: Customer Feedback Analysis with Pandas

```
feedback_analysis.py
import pandas as pd
from wordcloud import WordCloud
import matplotlib.pyplot as plt

# Load the dataset
df = pd.read_csv('customer_feedback.csv')

# Clean the data
df['Rating'] = df['Rating'].fillna(df['Rating'].mean())  # Handle missing
ratings
df = df.drop_duplicates()  # Remove duplicate feedback entries

# Analyze the data
average_rating = df['Rating'].mean()
most_common_keywords = pd.Series(' '.join(df['FeedbackText']).lower().
split()).value_counts()[:10]

# Group and aggregate the data
rating_counts = df['Rating'].value_counts()

# Visualize the data
rating_counts.plot(kind='bar', title='Distribution of Ratings')
plt.figure(figsize=(10, 6))
wordcloud = WordCloud().generate(' '.join(df['FeedbackText']))
plt.imshow(wordcloud, interpolation='bilinear')
plt.axis('off')
plt.show()
```

```
# Display results
print(f"Average Rating: {average_rating}")
print("Most Common Keywords:")
print(most_common_keywords)
```

This script analyzes customer feedback by cleaning the dataset, performing basic text analysis, and visualizing the distribution of ratings and common keywords.

The following diagrams represents output from **`feedback_analysis.py`** - Distribution of Ratings in a column chart.

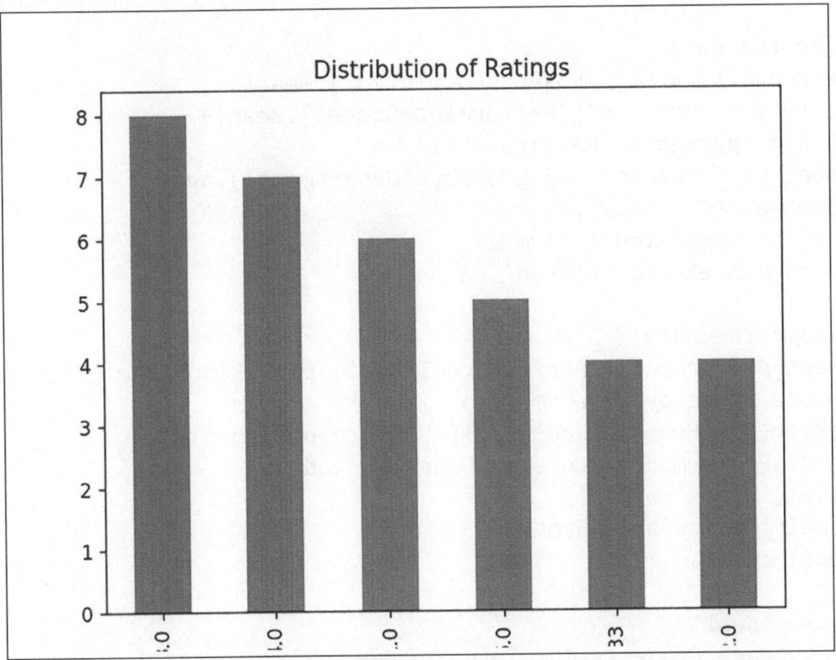

Figure 17.8: *output from feedback_analysis.py - Distribution of Ratings*

The following diagram represents output from **`feedback_analysis.py`** - Most Common Keywords.

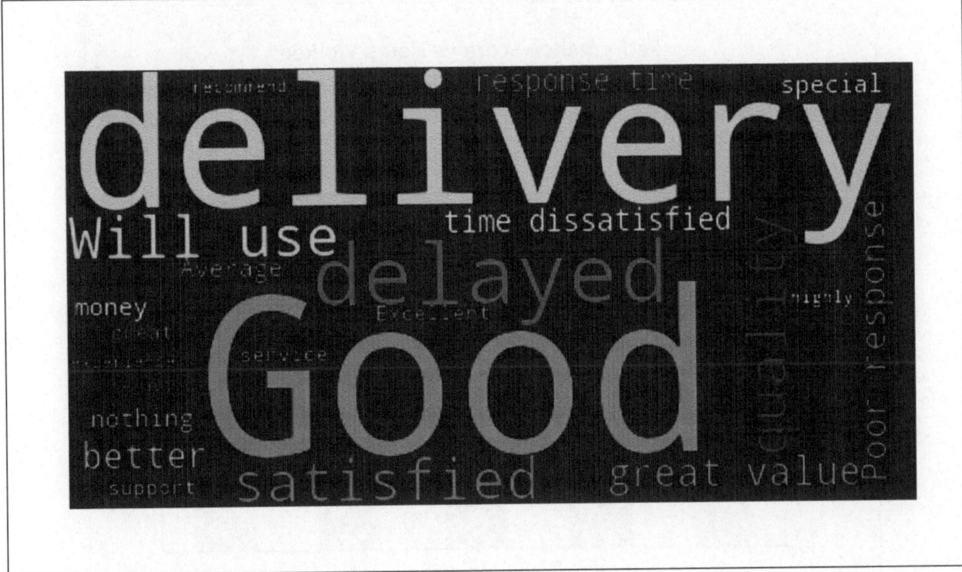

Figure 17.9: *output from feedback_analysis.py - Most Common Keywords*

Practice Problem 3: Employee Performance Analysis with Pandas

```
employee_performance.py
import pandas as pd
import matplotlib.pyplot as plt
# Load the dataset
df = pd.read_csv('employee_performance.csv')
# Clean the data
df = df.dropna()  # Handle missing data
df = df.drop_duplicates()  # Remove duplicates

# Analyze the data
average_projects = df['ProjectsCompleted'].mean()
average_performance = df['PerformanceScore'].mean()
# Group and aggregate the data
department_performance = df.groupby('Department').agg({
    'HoursWorked': 'sum',
    'ProjectsCompleted': 'sum',
    'PerformanceScore': 'mean'
})
# Visualize the data
department_performance['PerformanceScore'].plot(kind='bar', title='Average
Performance Score by Department')
plt.scatter(df['HoursWorked'], df['PerformanceScore'])
plt.title('Performance Score vs Hours Worked')
plt.xlabel('Hours Worked')
plt.ylabel('Performance Score')
plt.show()

# Display results
print(f"Average Projects Completed: {average_projects}")
print(f"Average Performance Score: {average_performance}")
print("Department Performance Summary:")
print(department_performance)
```

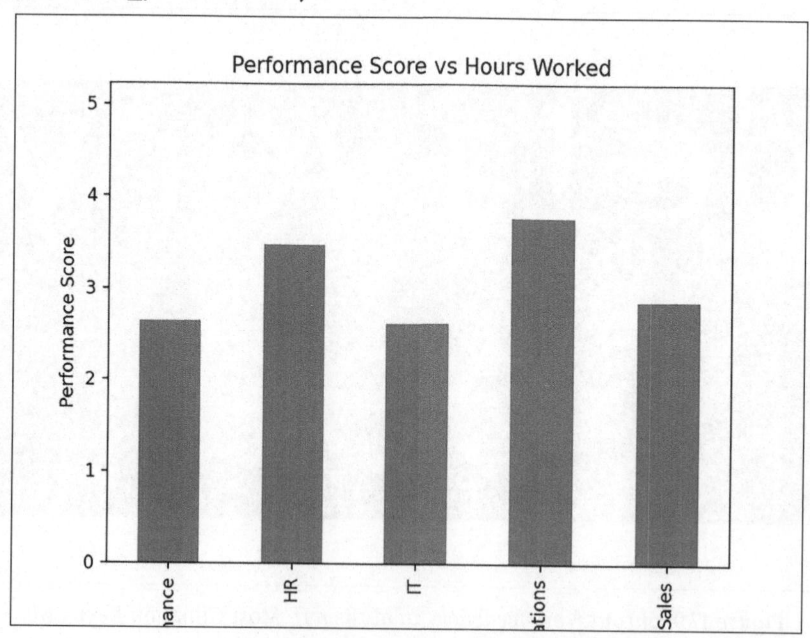

Figure 17.10: *output from employee_performance.py- Performance Score versus Hours Worked*

This script evaluates employee performance data by calculating key metrics, grouping data by department, and visualizing the relationship between hours worked and performance scores.

Conclusion

In this chapter, you explored the fundamentals of data analysis using Pandas, focusing on data cleaning, exploration, and visualization. You learned how to handle missing data, remove duplicates, group and aggregate information, and visualize trends. These techniques are essential for making sense of raw data and extracting meaningful insights.

A structured approach to data analysis ensures accuracy and efficiency, allowing to make informed decisions based on clean and well-organized data. By following best practices and avoiding common mistakes, you can ensure that the analysis is reliable and meaningful.

In the next chapter, you will explore how Python is used in Artificial Intelligence (AI). You will examine its role in machine learning and neural networks, where Python enables systems to learn from data and make intelligent decisions.

So, keep calm and let us tame the Python!

Multiple-Choice Questions

Test your understanding of the concepts covered in this chapter with the following multiple-choice questions.

1. Which function in Pandas is used to load a CSV file into a DataFrame?
   a. `pd.load_csv`
   b. `pd.read_csv`
   c. `pd.import_csv`
   d. `pd.get_csv`
2. Which method is used to remove duplicate rows from a DataFrame in Pandas?
   a. `dropna()`
   b. `drop_duplicates()`
   c. `remove_duplicates()`
   d. `clean_duplicates()`
3. In Pandas, which method is used to calculate the mean of a column?
   a. `mean()`
   b. `average()`
   c. `sum()`
   d. `median()`
4. Which of the following is a correct way to group data by a column and calculate the average in Pandas?
   a. `df.groupby('column').mean()`
   b. `df.group_by('column').average()`

c. `df.aggregate('column').mean()`

d. `df.group('column').mean()`

5. Which Matplotlib function is used to create a bar plot?

   a. `bar()`

   b. `plot.bar()`

   c. `plt.bar()`

   d. `plt.plot_bar()`

6. What does the `fillna()` function do in a Pandas DataFrame?

   a. Fills missing values with zeros.

   b. Fills missing values with a specified value.

   c. Removes rows with missing values.

   d. Adds new rows with NaN values.

7. Which of the following is NOT a valid way to visualize data using Pandas?

   a. `plot()`

   b. `scatter_matrix()`

   c. `line()`

   d. `hist()`

8. How can you change the data type of a column in Pandas?

   a. `df['column'].astype(new_type)`

   b. `df['column'].convert(new_type)`

   c. `df['column'].type(new_type)`

   d. `df['column'].change_type(new_type)`

9. Which function in Pandas can be used to display the first few rows of a DataFrame?

   a. `show()`

   b. `head()`

   c. `top()`

   d. `first()`

10. What is the primary purpose of using `groupby()` in Pandas?

    a. To filter data.

    b. To group data and perform aggregate functions.

    c. To plot data.

    d. To sort data by a column.

Answers

1. b
2. b
3. a
4. a
5. c
6. b
7. c
8. a
9. b
10. b

Points to Remember

- Pandas offers extensive tools for data manipulation and analysis, with DataFrames being essential for organizing and processing structured data efficiently.
- Data cleaning ensures accuracy and readiness for analysis by removing duplicates, addressing missing data, and converting data types.
- Pandas' descriptive statistics and grouping/aggregation algorithms help summarize data and discover relevant trends and patterns.
- Visualizing data with Matplotlib or Pandas' built-in plotting features enhances communication and insights.
- Best practices, such as comprehending data and recording processes, promote accurate and useful analysis.

Further Reading

For further learning, explore these resources:

1. **Pandas Documentation**: https://pandas.pydata.org/docs/
2. **Matplotlib Documentation**: https://matplotlib.org/stable/index.html
3. **Effective Data Cleaning Techniques**: https://www.geeksforgeeks.org/what-is-data-cleaning/
4. **Data Wrangling with Pandas**: https://www.geeksforgeeks.org/data-wrangling-in-python/

CHAPTER 18
Python in Artificial Intelligence

Introduction

Before you dive into this chapter, here is something important to keep in mind.

This is not a full-fledged chapter on AI and Python. Instead, think of it as a kickstart, a way to introduce you to the world of AI and machine learning. You don't need to worry if some of the concepts or terms seem complex at first. AI is a vast field, and no one learns it all in one go!

The goal of this chapter is to give you a basic understanding and help you take your first steps in AI using Python. You will learn key concepts, work through a simple hands-on example, and see how AI models are built. However, to go deeper, you will need to explore external resources, many of which are provided at the end of this chapter.

So, don't stress over technical jargon or unfamiliar terms! Just focus on getting a feel for how AI works and how Python helps in building machine learning models. Once you get comfortable, you can always explore further at your own pace.

Now, let us get started and have fun learning AI!

Structure

In this chapter, the following topics will be covered:

- Understanding Artificial Intelligence
  - Simple Definition of AI
  - Real-World Examples of AI
- Basic Concepts of Machine Learning
  - Introduction to Machine Learning
  - Types of Machine Learning
  - Common Terminology
- Python a Good Fit for AI and Machine Learning
  - Simplicity and Readability
  - Introduction to Scikit-Learn
- Getting Started with Scikit-Learn
  - Setting Up Scikit-Learn
  - Understanding the Basic Workflow
- Hands-On Example: Predicting House Prices with a Simple Model

Understanding Artificial Intelligence

Artificial Intelligence, or AI, is the ability of machines to mimic human intelligence. In simple terms, AI allows computers to perform tasks that usually require human thinking, such as recognizing objects in pictures, understanding speech, and making decisions based on large amounts of data.

Simple Definition of AI

Think of AI as a way to teach machines how to "think" and "learn." Instead of programming every single step manually, AI enables computers to analyze data, recognize patterns, and make decisions on their own. AI does not exactly copy human intelligence, but it helps automate and improve tasks that require logical thinking, allowing people to work faster and more efficiently.

A good way to imagine AI is to compare it to a human brain. Just like humans learn from experience, AI systems learn from data. Over time, they improve at making predictions or completing tasks more accurately. However, unlike humans, AI can process huge amounts of information extremely fast, making it better at some tasks that would take a person too long to do manually.

Real-World Examples of AI

To understand AI better, let us look at some examples of how it is used in everyday life:

- **Self-Driving Cars**

  One of the most well-known uses of AI is in self-driving cars. These cars use AI to analyze data from cameras, sensors, and other devices to understand their surroundings. The AI "sees" other vehicles, pedestrians, and traffic signs, making decisions on how to drive safely without human help. AI controls everything, from avoiding obstacles to stopping at red lights, making the car appear as if it "understands" the road.

- **Recommendation Systems**

  Have you ever noticed how YouTube or Netflix seem to know exactly what you want to watch next? That's AI at work! These recommendation systems analyze your past viewing history and compare it to millions of other users. Based on this data, AI predicts what you might like and suggests content. AI-powered recommendations aren't just used in movies. They are also found in social media, online shopping, and even music streaming apps such as Spotify to personalize your experience.

- **Virtual Assistants (Siri, Alexa, Google Assistant)**

  Voice assistants such as Siri, Alexa, and Google Assistant use AI to understand and respond to spoken commands. They can answer questions, play music, set reminders, and even control smart home devices. These assistants rely on Natural Language Processing (NLP), a type of AI that helps computers understand and interpret human language, making interactions feel more natural.

- **AI in Healthcare**

  AI is making a big impact in healthcare by helping doctors diagnose diseases faster and more accurately. For example, AI can analyze medical images such as X-rays or MRIs much quicker than a human specialist. In some cases, AI can even predict the risk of diseases before they happen, allowing doctors to take early preventive measures. By assisting medical professionals, AI improves patient care and helps make healthcare more efficient.

AI is Everywhere:

As you can see, AI is already a big part of daily life. Whether it is helping you find your next favorite movie, guiding you with smart navigation, or improving healthcare, AI is making things faster and easier. As you move forward, you will learn how Python plays a key role in building these AI systems and how you can start using it to create AI-powered programs yourself!

Note Before You Begin:

Before you dive into this chapter, here is something important to keep in mind:

- This is not a full-fledged chapter on AI and Python. Instead, think of it as a kickstart, a way to introduce you to the world of AI and machine learning. You don't need to worry if some of the concepts or terms seem complex at first. AI is a vast field, and no one learns it all in one go!
- The goal of this chapter is to give you a basic understanding and help you take your first steps in AI using Python. You will learn key concepts, work through a simple hands-on example, and see how AI models are built. However, to go deeper, you will need to explore external resources, many of which are provided at the end of this chapter.
- So, don't stress over technical jargon or unfamiliar terms! Just focus on getting a feel for how AI works and how Python helps in building machine learning models. Once you get comfortable, you can always explore further at your own pace.

Now, let us get started and have fun learning AI!

Basic Concepts of Machine Learning

Now that you have explored artificial intelligence and seen real-world examples, let us dive deeper into machine learning (ML), one of the most important parts of AI. Many AI applications rely on machine learning, which allows computers to learn from data and make decisions without you having to program them for every single task.

Introduction to Machine Learning

Machine learning is a branch of AI that teaches computers to learn from data instead of following fixed instructions. In traditional programming, you write specific rules for a computer to follow. However, in machine learning, data and algorithms help the computer find patterns on its own.

Think of it like teaching a child to recognize animals. Instead of giving them a strict definition of what a cat looks like, you show them many pictures of cats and non-cats. Over time, they learn the differences and can identify cats in new pictures. Similarly, machine learning models learn from examples and improve at recognizing patterns without needing your constant help.

For example, if you train a machine learning model with thousands of labeled pictures (some with cats, some without), the model learns what features make a cat unique. Once trained, it can correctly identify new cat images it has never seen before.

Machine learning is the foundation of many modern AI applications, such as image recognition, speech processing, and predictions. Thanks to Python's scikit-learn library, you can start building machine learning models with ease, even as a beginner.

Types of Machine Learning

There are different types of machine learning, but to keep things simple, let us focus on the most common one: supervised learning.

Supervised Learning:

In supervised learning, you train the machine using data that includes both inputs (features) and correct outputs (labels). This is like a teacher giving students example problems along with correct answers. The machine then learns to make predictions on new, unseen data.

For example, imagine you want a program to identify apples among other fruits. You provide a dataset of fruit images, each labeled as "apple" or "not apple." By studying these examples, the model learns to identify apples in new images.

Unsupervised Learning (Brief Mention for Context):

Unsupervised learning, unlike supervised learning, does not include labeled data. Instead, the model finds patterns on its own. One example is clustering, where AI groups similar data together, such as identifying different customer shopping behaviors.

Since supervised learning is easier and more commonly used, you will focus on it in this chapter. You will learn how to train a machine learning model using labeled data and how to build your own models using Python.

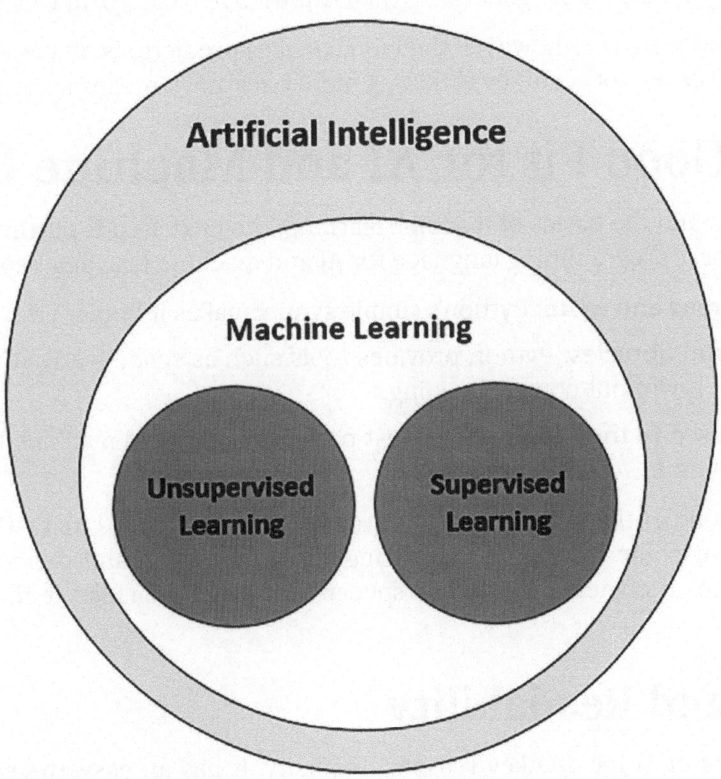

Figure 18.1: *The Framework of AI and Machine Learning Techniques*

Common Terminology

Before you start building models, let us go over some important terms you will come across in machine learning. Understanding these will make learning easier:

- **Dataset**: A dataset is a collection of data used for training the machine. Think of it like a table, where each row represents an example, and each column contains specific details.

  Example: If you are predicting house prices, a dataset might include details such as size, number of bedrooms, and location.

- **Features**: These are input variables that help the machine learn and make predictions.

  Example: In the house price dataset, the features might be square footage, number of rooms, and location.

- **Labels**: These are the output values that the model is trained to predict.

  Example: The house price in the dataset is the label because it is what you want to predict.
- **Model**: The final output of the machine learning process. Once trained, the model takes inputs and makes predictions based on what it has learned.

  Example: A trained model can predict home prices based on size and location.
- **Training**: This is the learning phase, where the machine studies patterns in the dataset. It adjusts itself until it finds the best way to make accurate predictions.

  Example: Just like you learn new concepts by practicing, machines learn by studying data.
- **Testing**: After training, you must test the model with new data it has never seen before. This ensures that it has actually learned rather than just memorizing the training data.

  Example: If you only memorize answers without understanding them, you might fail a new test. Similarly, models must generalize their knowledge to perform well on new data.
- **Accuracy**: This measures how well the model makes predictions. If a model correctly predicts 90 out of 100 cases, its accuracy is 90%. A higher accuracy means a better model.

Python a Good Fit for AI and Machine Learning

Now that you understand the basics of machine learning, the next step is putting it into practice. But how? Python is the best programming language for AI and machine learning because:

- **It is easy to read and write**: Python's simple syntax makes it beginner-friendly.
- **It has powerful libraries**: Python provides tools such as scikit-learn, which makes it easy to build AI models without complex coding.
- **It is widely used in the AI industry**: Most professional AI and machine learning applications are built in Python.

Python has become one of the most important programming languages in artificial intelligence (AI). It is widely used in machine learning, natural language processing, and neural networks. Python's popularity in AI is not a coincidence. It has special features that make it the best choice for AI developers like you.

Simplicity and Readability

Python is widely used in AI for one key reason: simplicity. It has an easy-to-read syntax, making it one of the most beginner-friendly programming languages. Whether you are just starting or already experienced, Python lets you focus on problem-solving instead of getting stuck on complicated programming rules.

Python's clean and readable code is another reason it is perfect for AI. Even if you didn't write the code yourself, you can understand it easily. This is especially helpful in AI projects, where you often work with a team or contribute to open-source communities. With Python, even complex AI algorithms can be written in a way that is simple and human-readable.

Another great advantage is Python's huge community. If you ever run into problems while working on AI projects, help is always available. You can find thousands of tutorials, guides, and forums where experienced developers share solutions, making it easier for you to learn and build AI models quickly.

In the next section, you will explore scikit-learn, a powerful Python library that makes machine learning simple. You will learn how to set it up and build your first AI model.

Let us move forward and start coding your first machine learning project!

Introduction to scikit-learn

One of the most powerful tools for AI development in Python is scikit-learn. This is a popular machine learning library that provides simple and efficient tools for data analysis and model building.

The best part is Scikit-learn makes AI easy. You do not need to be an expert in math or machine learning to get started. This library includes ready-to-use algorithms for both supervised and unsupervised learning, such as decision trees, linear regression, and clustering, all of which are essential for AI projects.

Scikit-learn also includes tools for:

- Preprocessing data (cleaning and preparing data for training)
- Splitting data into training and testing sets
- Evaluating model performance

Since most of the complex math is handled by scikit-learn, you can focus on using AI rather than understanding every mathematical detail.

With just a few lines of Python code, you can:

- Load a dataset
- Train a machine learning model
- Make predictions

Even if you have no prior AI experience, you can start building AI models right away. As you continue in this chapter, you will see how simple it is to use scikit-learn to create machine learning models, giving you a strong foundation for future AI projects.

Getting Started with scikit-learn

Now that you know why Python is perfect for AI, it's time to build your first machine learning model using scikit-learn. In this section, you will learn how to:

- Install scikit-learn
- Understand the basic workflow of machine learning
- Build a simple AI model step by step

By the end of this section, you will be able to create your own AI models in Python!

Setting Up scikit-learn

Installing scikit-learn is quick and easy. Since it is a Python library, you can install it using pip, Python's package manager.

Open your terminal or command prompt and type:

```
pip install scikit-learn
```

Once installed, you can start using scikit-learn in your Python environment. All the examples in this chapter can be run in your preferred IDE, such as Visual Studio Code, which was introduced in earlier chapters.

Understanding the Basic Workflow

Scikit-learn follows a structured approach to machine learning. If you understand this process, you can apply it to any AI model. The four main steps are:

1. Loading the Data
2. Preprocessing the Data
3. Training the Model
4. Evaluating the Model's Performance

Let us go through each step in detail.

Step 1: Loading the Data

The first step in any machine learning project is getting the data. Scikit-learn comes with built-in datasets, which are great for beginners. One of the most commonly used datasets is the Iris dataset, which is used for classification tasks.

Here is how you load the Iris dataset:

```
from sklearn.datasets import load_iris

# Load the Iris dataset
iris = load_iris()

# Extract features and labels
X = iris.data
y = iris.target

# Display sample data
print(f"Features: {X[:5]}")
print(f"Labels: {y[:5]}")
```

This dataset contains measurements of iris flowers, and your goal is to train a machine learning model to classify them based on their features.

Step 2: Preprocessing the Data

Before you train the model, you need to prepare the data. In real-world AI projects, data cleaning is very important. This can include removing missing values, standardizing data, and converting text into numbers.

For this example, you will split the data into training and testing sets. This ensures that the model learns from one portion of the data and is tested on unseen data to evaluate its accuracy.

```
from sklearn.model_selection import train_test_split

# Split data into training and testing sets (70% training, 30% testing)
X_train, X_test, y_train, y_test = train_test_split(X, y, test_size=0.3, ran-
dom_state=42)

print(f"Training data size: {X_train.shape}")
print(f"Testing data size: {X_test.shape}")
```

Now the training set will be used to teach the model, while the test set will be used to check how well it performs.

Step 3: Training the Model

Now that the data is ready, it is time to train your AI model.

For this example, you will use a Decision Tree Classifier, a simple but effective algorithm for classification tasks.

```
from sklearn.tree import DecisionTreeClassifier

# Create a Decision Tree model
model = DecisionTreeClassifier()

# Train the model
model.fit(X_train, y_train)

print("Model training completed!")
```

At this stage, your machine learning model has learned patterns from the training data and is ready to make predictions.

Step 4: Evaluating the Model's Performance

The final step is to test the model and check how accurately it makes predictions.

```
from sklearn.metrics import accuracy_score

# Make predictions with the test data
y_pred = model.predict(X_test)

# Evaluate accuracy
accuracy = accuracy_score(y_test, y_pred)

print(f"Model accuracy: {accuracy * 100:.2f}%")
```

The accuracy score tells you how often the model made correct predictions. While accuracy is just one way to measure performance, it is a good starting point.

If the accuracy is high, it means the model is good at predicting the correct flower type.

By following four simple steps, that is, loading data, preprocessing, training, and evaluating, you have successfully built your first AI model! Now, you can experiment with different datasets and machine learning algorithms in scikit-learn.

In the next section, you will work on a hands-on project where you will predict house prices using a linear regression model. This will give you even more practical experience in AI development.

Let us move on and build something exciting!

Hands-On Example: Predicting House Prices with a Simple Model

Machine learning is transforming industries by enabling data-driven decision-making. One of the most useful applications of machine learning is in real estate, where AI helps predict property prices based on key factors.

In this hands-on example, you will build a simple model to estimate house prices. This project is an excellent way to understand how machine learning works in action.

Understanding the Problem:

Imagine you are a real estate analyst trying to predict house prices. House prices depend on many factors, such as:

- Size of the house
- Number of bedrooms
- Location
- Neighborhood crime rate
- Property tax rate

Your goal is to use these factors to predict house prices.

To achieve this, you will use a regression model, which is ideal for predicting continuous values such as house prices. Specifically, you will use linear regression, a simple but powerful machine learning technique that finds the relationship between input features (for example, house size, number of rooms) and output values (house price).

You will walk through each step, from loading the data to evaluating the model's performance, using Python and scikit-learn.

Step-by-Step Code Implementation

Let us break down the process into simple steps.

Step 1: Load the Dataset

For this example, you will use the California Housing Dataset, which is included in scikit-learn. This dataset contains information about houses in California, such as the average number of rooms, crime rate, and property tax rate.

Your goal is to predict house prices using these features.

Here is how to load the dataset:

```
from sklearn.datasets import fetch_california_housing
import pandas as pd

# Load the California Housing dataset
california = fetch_california_housing()

# Convert dataset into a pandas DataFrame for easy visualization
california_df = pd.DataFrame(california.data, columns=california.feature_
names)

# Add the target (house prices) to the DataFrame
california_df['PRICE'] = california.target

# Display the first five rows of the data
print(california_df.head())
```

At this stage, you have loaded the dataset and displayed it in a table format, showing features (for example, average number of rooms) and the target value (house price).

Step 2: Preprocess the Data

Before training your model, you need to split the data into:

- **Training Set**: Used to train the model
- **Testing Set**: Used to evaluate how well the model performs on new data

You will use **train_test_split** from scikit-learn to separate the data.

```
from sklearn.model_selection import train_test_split

# Split data into features (X) and target variable (y)
X = california_df.drop('PRICE', axis=1)  # Features
y = california_df['PRICE']  # Target (house price)

# Split data into training (80%) and testing (20%) sets
X_train, X_test, y_train, y_test = train_test_split(X, y, test_size=0.2, ran-
dom_state=42)

print(f"Training data size: {X_train.shape}")
print(f"Testing data size: {X_test.shape}")
```

80% of the data is used to train the model, while 20% is reserved for testing its accuracy.

Step 3: Train the Model Using Linear Regression

Now that your data is ready, it is time to train a linear regression model.

Definition of Linear Regression

Linear regression fits a straight line through the data points in a way that minimizes the error between predicted and actual prices.

Here is how to train the model:

```
from sklearn.linear_model import LinearRegression

# Create a Linear Regression model
model = LinearRegression()

# Train the model using the training data
model.fit(X_train, y_train)

print("Model training completed!")
```

The model learns the relationship between the features (for example, house size, location) and the target (house price).

Step 4: Evaluate the Model's Performance

Once the model is trained, you need to test how well it performs on new data.

Measuring Performance:

- **Mean Squared Error (MSE)**: Measures the average squared difference between predicted and actual prices. A lower MSE means better predictions.
- **R-squared Score (R^2)**: Shows how well the model explains variations in house prices. A score close to 1 means a better model.

Here is how to evaluate the model:

```
from sklearn.metrics import mean_squared_error, r2_score

# Make predictions on the test data
y_pred = model.predict(X_test)

# Calculate performance metrics
mse = mean_squared_error(y_test, y_pred)
r2 = r2_score(y_test, y_pred)
```

```
print(f"Mean Squared Error: {mse:.2f}")
print(f"R-squared Score: {r2:.2f}")
```

- If the MSE is low, it means the model is making good predictions.
- If the R-squared score is high (close to 1), it means the model fits the data well.

Step 5: Understanding the Results

Now, let us interpret the model's performance.

- If the Mean Squared Error is low (e.g., 25.00), it means the predicted house prices are close to the actual values.
- If the R-squared score is 0.85, it means 85% of the variation in house prices is explained by the features in the model.

While this model is not perfect, it gives you a solid foundation for understanding how linear regression works.

Improvement scope for the Model:

- Add more relevant features (for example, nearby schools, transportation access)
- Use advanced algorithms such as random forests or neural networks
- Apply data preprocessing techniques to remove errors in data

Complete Annotated Code:

Here is the full annotated code for predicting house prices:

```
# Step 1: Load the dataset
from sklearn.datasets import fetch_california_housing
import pandas as pd
from sklearn.model_selection import train_test_split
from sklearn.linear_model import LinearRegression
from sklearn.metrics import mean_squared_error, r2_score

# Load the California Housing dataset
california = fetch_california_housing()
california_df = pd.DataFrame(california.data, columns=california.feature_
names)
california_df['PRICE'] = california.target

# Step 2: Split data into features (X) and target variable (y)
X = california_df.drop('PRICE', axis=1)
y = california_df['PRICE']
X_train, X_test, y_train, y_test = train_test_split(X, y, test_size=0.2,
random_state=42)

# Step 3: Train the model using Linear Regression
model = LinearRegression()
model.fit(X_train, y_train)

# Step 4: Evaluate the model's performance
y_pred = model.predict(X_test)
mse = mean_squared_error(y_test, y_pred)
r2 = r2_score(y_test, y_pred)

# Output the results
print(f"Mean Squared Error: {mse:.2f}")
print(f"R-squared Score: {r2:.2f}")
```

This project taught you the following:

- Load and preprocess data
- Train a machine learning model
- Evaluate model performance

This is just the beginning of your AI journey!

Now that you have built your first AI model, you can experiment with different datasets and algorithms to improve your skills.

Conclusion

In this chapter, you explored the fundamentals of AI and learned how Python plays a crucial role in building AI models. You started by understanding what AI is, looked at real-world examples, and then explored machine learning and its key concepts.

You also discovered why Python is an excellent choice for AI, thanks to its simplicity, readability, and powerful libraries such as scikit-learn. Additionally, you built a machine learning model, following a structured process of loading and preprocessing data, training the model, and evaluating its performance.

In the next and final chapter, you will review everything you have learned, discover additional learning resources, and explore certifications and future projects to continue your journey with Python.

Till then, keep calm and let's tame the Python!

Multiple-Choice Questions

1. What is the primary goal of AI?
    a. To make computers perform repetitive tasks.
    b. To enable machines to perform tasks that typically require human intelligence.
    c. To store and process large amounts of data.
    d. To automate manual coding tasks.
2. Which of the following is an example of AI in everyday life?
    a. A calculator performing arithmetic operations.
    b. A virtual assistant such as Siri responding to voice commands.
    c. A computer displaying an error message.
    d. A simple search algorithm returning results.
3. What is machine learning in the context of AI?
    a. A method of training computers to learn from pre-defined rules.
    b. A process of teaching machines to learn from data and make predictions.
    c. A programming language used to create AI systems.
    d. A tool for managing large datasets.

4. Which of the following is a type of supervised learning?
   a. Clustering
   b. Decision Trees
   c. Dimensionality reduction
   d. Association rule learning
5. What is the purpose of splitting data into training and testing sets?
   a. To ensure the model learns only from test data.
   b. To make the training process faster.
   c. To evaluate the model's performance on unseen data.
   d. To reduce the size of the dataset.
6. In the linear regression model, what does the model predict?
   a. Binary values (0 or 1)
   b. Continuous values such as house prices
   c. Categories such as "spam" or "not spam"
   d. Relationships between categorical variables
7. Which Python library did we use in this chapter to build machine learning models?
   a. NumPy
   b. Pandas
   c. Matplotlib
   d. Scikit-learn
8. What is Mean Squared Error (MSE) used for in evaluating a model?
   a. To measure how well the model explains variance in the data.
   b. To calculate the total error in the model.
   c. To measure the average squared difference between the predicted and actual values.
   d. To find the highest error in the model.
9. What function in scikit-learn is used to split a dataset into training and testing sets?
   a. `train_split()`
   b. `test_split()`
   c. `train_test_split()`
   d. `data_split()`
10. Which evaluation metric tells you how well a model fits the data, with values closer to 1 indicating a good fit?
    a. Accuracy score
    b. Precision score
    c. R-squared score
    d. Recall score

Answers

1. b
2. b
3. b
4. b
5. c
6. b
7. d
8. c
9. c
10. c

Points to Remember

- Artificial Intelligence (AI) enables machines to execute activities that need human intelligence, such as picture recognition and language comprehension.
- Machine Learning (ML) is a subset of AI that enables machines to learn from data and generate predictions without explicit programming.
- The most popular sort of machine learning is supervised learning, which involves using labeled data (input-output pairs) to predict new data.
- Python is a popular choice for AI and machine learning due to its user-friendly interface and rich libraries, facilitating model development and experimentation.
- The scikit-learn Python package offers sophisticated machine learning tools for beginners, allowing for easy model building with minimal coding.
- A typical machine learning workflow involves loading, preprocessing, training, and evaluating the model's performance.
- Linear Regression is a widely used supervised learning technique that predicts continuous quantities, such as property prices, using features.
- The Mean Squared Error (MSE) metric assesses regression model performance by calculating the average squared difference between predicted and actual data.
- The R-squared score measures how effectively a model explains variance in data. A value close to one implies a better fit.

Further Reading

If you want to explore further, here are some useful resources:

1. **Scikit-learn Documentation**: https://scikit-learn.org/stable/
2. **Machine Learning Mastery**: https://www.projectpro.io/article/top-10-machine-learning-projects-for-beginners-in-2021/397
3. **Python Data Science Handbook**: https://github.com/jakevdp/PythonDataScienceHandbook

CHAPTER 19
Conclusion and Next Steps

Introduction

You have come a long way in your Python journey! From writing your first lines of code to exploring functions, object-oriented programming, and even working with external data sources, you have built a strong foundation. Along the way, you have learned how to break down complex problems, write efficient code, and think like a programmer.

But learning Python does not end here. The true power of programming comes when you start applying your knowledge to real-world projects. This chapter is about what comes next, how to continue growing as a Python programmer, how to choose the right path based on your interests, and how to take your skills to the next level.

By the end of this chapter, you will have a clear direction on how to continue your Python journey, where to find the best resources, and how to become a confident, independent programmer.

Just as you have done throughout this book, the best way to move forward is to stay calm, experiment, and tame the Python step by step.

Structure

In this chapter, the following topics will be covered:

- The Importance of Applying Your Knowledge
- Exploring Different Paths in Python
- Building a Python Portfolio
- Python Certifications and Continuous Learning
- The Final Challenge: Independent Projects
- Keep Calm and Let's Tame the Python

The Importance of Applying Your Knowledge

Reading about Python and solving guided exercises is a great way to start, but real learning happens when you build things. Programming is a skill that improves with practice, and the best way to solidify your knowledge is by writing code regularly.

Instead of just focusing on learning more concepts, start using what you already know to build projects that interest you. The projects do not have to be complicated. Even a simple to-do list application or weather data scraper will help you develop problem-solving skills and reinforce what you have learned.

If you are unsure what to build, here are some ideas to help you get started:

- Automate a repetitive task on your computer.
- Create a small web application using Flask or Django.
- Analyze data using Pandas and Matplotlib.
- Write a script that interacts with an API, such as fetching weather data or news updates.
- Try solving problems on coding challenge platforms such as LeetCode, CodeWars, or HackerRank.

Programming is about experimentation, problem-solving, and continuous improvement. The more you build, the more confident you will become.

Exploring Different Paths in Python

Python is a versatile language with applications in various fields. Now that you have built a strong foundation, it is time to decide which area excites you the most. Here are some paths you can explore:

Web Development:

If you enjoy building interactive applications, consider learning Flask or Django to develop web applications. These frameworks allow you to create dynamic websites, work with databases, and handle user authentication.

Data Science and Machine Learning:

Python is widely used in data science and AI. Libraries such as Pandas, NumPy, and Matplotlib allow you to analyze and visualize data, while frameworks such as Scikit-Learn and TensorFlow help you build machine learning models.

Automation and Scripting:

If you want to automate repetitive tasks, Python is an excellent choice. You can use Selenium for web automation, BeautifulSoup for web scraping, or OS and subprocess modules to automate file and system tasks.

Cybersecurity and Ethical Hacking:

Python is heavily used in cybersecurity for writing penetration testing tools and security automation scripts. If this field interests you, explore libraries such as Scapy and Requests to interact with networks and APIs.

Game Development:

If you enjoy creating games, Python's Pygame library lets you design 2D games and interactive applications.

If you are unsure which path to take, try small projects in different fields and see what excites you the most.

Building a Python Portfolio

A strong portfolio can help showcase your skills to potential employers or collaborators. It not only demonstrates what you have built but also serves as a record of your progress and learning journey. Here is how you can start building your Python portfolio:

GitHub

Upload your projects to GitHub to share your code with the world. A well-maintained GitHub profile showcases your programming skills, version control knowledge, and ability to work on real-world projects. Recruiters and employers often check GitHub profiles when hiring developers, so having a few polished projects can make a difference.

Explore Other Repositories: Check out popular Python repositories to see how experienced developers write and structure their code. Some great repositories to follow include:

- **TheAlgorithms/Python:** A collection of Python-based algorithms: https://github.com/TheAlgorithms/Python
- **pandas-dev/pandas:** The official Pandas library repository: https://github.com/pandas-dev/pandas
- **realpython/materials:** Example code from Real Python tutorials: https://github.com/realpython/materials

Blogging

Writing about your learning journey, projects, and problem-solving techniques can help reinforce your understanding and establish you as a Python enthusiast. Platforms such as Medium, Dev.to, and Hashnode allow you to publish technical articles easily.

Check Out These Python Blogs:

- **Real Python:** High-quality Python tutorials and articles: https://realpython.com
- **Towards Data Science:** A great blog for data science enthusiasts: https://towardsdatascience.com
- **The Python Software Foundation Blog:** Official updates on Python: https://pyfound.blogspot.com

Following these blogs will keep you updated on Python trends, best practices, and new libraries.

YouTube Tutorials

If you enjoy teaching, consider creating YouTube tutorials where you explain Python concepts, walk through coding projects, or share debugging techniques. Teaching others is one of the best ways to solidify your knowledge while helping the community.

Check Out These YouTube Channels:

- **Corey Schafer:** Beginner to advanced Python tutorials: https://www.youtube.com/c/Coreyms
- **Tech With Tim:** Python projects, AI, and game development: https://www.youtube.com/c/TechWithTim
- **Programming with Mosh:** Beginner-friendly Python tutorials: https://www.youtube.com/c/programmingwithmosh

Watching tutorials from experienced programmers will expose you to different coding styles, industry standards, and best practices.

LinkedIn: Networking and Professional Growth

LinkedIn is an essential tool for building your professional brand, networking with industry experts, and showcasing your Python expertise.

Using LinkedIn Effectively as a Python Developer:

- **Share Your Learning Progress**: Post about the projects you are working on, interesting challenges you have solved, or new Python concepts you have learned.
- **Engage with Python Professionals**: Follow top developers, join Python-related groups, and comment on insightful posts.

- **Showcase Your Portfolio**: Add your GitHub profile, blog, or YouTube channel to your LinkedIn profile.
- **Apply for Python-Related Jobs**: Many companies use LinkedIn to find and hire developers, so keeping your profile updated can open job opportunities.

Follow Influential Python Developers on LinkedIn:

- Guido van Rossum (Creator of Python)
- Raymond Hettinger (Python Core Developer)
- Jake VanderPlas (Data Science and Machine Learning expert)

Building Your Own Footprint

While learning from others is essential, you should also focus on creating your own content. Whether it is uploading projects to GitHub, writing blog posts, making video tutorials, or engaging on LinkedIn, contributing to the Python community will help you stand out and stay motivated.

Your portfolio should reflect your learning journey, so do not hesitate to showcase small projects, experiments, and even challenges you have overcome. The key is consistency. Keep coding, keep sharing, and keep improving!

Would you like to start small? Try writing a short post about your favorite Python feature, recording a simple tutorial on a project you built, or connecting with other Python enthusiasts on LinkedIn. Over time, these small steps will build your confidence and help you grow as a Python developer.

Python Certifications and Continuous Learning

If you want to validate your skills, you can earn a Python certification. Certifications are useful for job applications and career advancement. Here are some of the most recognized Python certifications:

- PCEP – Certified Entry-Level Python Programmer (Python Institute)
- PCAP – Certified Associate in Python Programming (Python Institute)
- Google IT Automation with Python (Coursera)
- Microsoft Certified: Python for Data Science
- AWS Certified Machine Learning – Specialty

While certifications are not mandatory, they can help you stand out in the job market.

Continuing Your Learning

Python is constantly evolving, and there is always something new to learn. Here is how you can keep improving:

- Read Python blogs and follow developers on platforms such as Reddit and Twitter.
- Join online coding communities like Stack Overflow and Python Discord servers.
- Take specialized courses on topics like AI, web development, and cloud computing.

No matter how much you learn, the key is to stay curious and keep coding.

The Final Challenge: Independent Projects

Now that you have a solid foundation, it is time to apply your knowledge to real-world projects. The next chapter contains five project ideas, but without solutions. This is intentional, programming is about solving problems on your own, just like in real-world software development.

- These projects will require you to think critically and apply what you have learned.

- There are no single "correct" solutions. Be creative and experiment!
- If you get stuck, use the official Python documentation and other online resources.

This final challenge is your first step toward becoming an independent Python programmer. However, to help guide you in the right direction, the solutions to these problems will be made available on GitHub at a later point in time.

Stay Updated on GitHub:

The solutions will be uploaded to GitHub, so be sure to check back for updates. You can also try solving the problems yourself first, then compare your approach with the provided solutions.

Follow on GitHub for Solutions: https://github.com/ava-orange-education/Kickstarter-Python-Programming-Fundamentals

This is your opportunity to build, experiment, and reinforce your problem-solving skills. Take on the challenge and push your Python skills to the next level!

Keep Calm and Let's Tame the Python

Your Python journey does not end here, it is just beginning. Every great programmer started as a beginner, just like you. The more you practice, the more confident you will become. Some challenges will be frustrating, and some errors will take time to fix, but every problem you solve makes you a better coder.

Throughout this book, I have used the phrase "Keep Calm and Let's Tame the Python" as a guiding principle. It represents an approach to learning Python with patience and curiosity. Instead of feeling overwhelmed by errors or complex concepts, embrace them as opportunities to grow. Taming Python means understanding its quirks, solving problems step by step, and continuously improving your skills.

So, as you move forward in your journey, remember this:

- Keep coding, the best way to learn is by writing code.
- Keep experimenting, try new things and don't be afraid to make mistakes.
- Keep learning, Python is always evolving, and there is always more to discover.

Keep Calm and Let's Tame the Python!

Happy coding!

CHAPTER 20
Real-World Project

Introduction

Congratulations on reaching the final chapter of this book! You have learned Python step by step, from writing your first program to working with databases, web applications, and more. Now that you have a solid foundation, it is time to apply your knowledge to real-world projects.

This chapter presents five project ideas, but without solutions. This is intentional, programming is about solving problems on your own, just like in real-world software development. These projects will test your skills and help you think like a programmer.

- Each project requires you to apply multiple concepts from the book.
- There are no single "correct" solutions. Be creative and experiment.
- If you get stuck, review the relevant chapters or explore online resources.

This final challenge is your first step toward becoming an independent Python programmer. However, to help guide you in the right direction, the solutions to these problems will be made available on GitHub at a later point in time.

Structure

In this chapter, the following projects will be covered:

- Personal To-Do List Manager: A Task-Tracking Console Application
- Expense Tracker with Data Analysis: Log and Analyze Daily Expenses
- Student Report Card System: Store, Calculate, and Display Student Grades
- Flask Web App: Online Bookstore: Build a Book Catalog and Review System
- Library Management System: Track Book Inventory, Borrow and Return Books

Now, let us dive into the projects and put your Python skills to the test! Each project will guide you through a structured approach, ensuring that no topic from the book is left out.

Project 1: Personal To-Do List Manager (Console-Based Application)

Problem Statement:

Everyone needs a way to keep track of their daily tasks. In this project, you will create a To-Do List Manager that allows users to add tasks, mark them as complete, delete tasks, and save them for future use. This program will run in the console and help users stay organized.

Project Details:

- **Add tasks:** Users can enter tasks to add to the list.
- **View tasks:** Display all pending tasks.

- **Mark tasks as completed:** Users can check off finished tasks.
- **Delete tasks:** Remove tasks from the list.
- **Save and load tasks:** Store tasks in a file so they are not lost when the program is closed.

Steps to Solve the Problem

1. **Create a menu-based interface**: Let users choose actions (add, view, complete, delete tasks).
2. **Use a list to store tasks**: Keep track of tasks in memory.
3. **Implement file handling**: Save tasks to a file and reload them when the program starts.
4. **Use functions for different actions**: Keep the code organized by defining functions for each operation.
5. **Handle errors**: Prevent crashes if users enter incorrect inputs.

Reference Chapters:

- ***Chapter 5:*** *Creating Functions* (for organizing code into reusable functions).
- ***Chapter 6:*** *Organizing Data* (for managing tasks using lists).
- ***Chapter 10:*** *File Handling and String Manipulation* (for saving and loading tasks).
- ***Chapter 9:*** *Error Handling* (for managing invalid user input).

Extra Learning Suggestions

- Add a priority system so users can set high, medium, or low priority for tasks.
- Convert this program into a GUI-based app using Tkinter.

Project 2: Expense Tracker with Data Analysis

Problem Statement:

Many people struggle to keep track of their spending. You will create a program that lets users log their daily expenses and view spending insights. This program will store expense data in a file and help users analyze their spending habits.

Project Details:

- **Add expenses:** Users enter the amount and category (for example, food, transport, entertainment).
- **View past expenses:** Display expenses for a selected date range.
- **Summarize expenses:** Show total spending for each category.
- **Save data in a database:** Store expenses securely for future use.
- **Generate a spending report:** Display a summary of monthly spending trends.

Steps to Solve the Problem:

1. **Create a database**: Store expenses with details such as amount, category, and date.
2. **Build functions for adding and retrieving expenses**: Let users enter expenses and filter by category or date.
3. **Analyze spending trends**: Use Python to calculate total spending and show trends.
4. **Display reports**: Generate a summary of spending in different categories.
5. **Use error handling**: Prevent issues such as entering text instead of numbers.

Reference Chapters:

- ***Chapter 10:*** *File Handling and String Manipulation* (for storing expenses in a file).
- ***Chapter 16:*** *Python and Databases* (for saving and retrieving expense records).
- ***Chapter 17:*** *Analyzing Data* (for summarizing and analyzing spending habits).
- ***Chapter 13:*** *Math in Python* (for calculating totals and averages).

Extra Learning Suggestions:

- Add data visualization using Matplotlib to display spending graphs.
- Allow users to set a monthly budget and get alerts when they exceed it.

Project 3: Student Report Card System

Problem Statement:

Schools need a way to store and manage student grades. In this project, you will create a Student Report Card System that allows teachers to enter students' marks and generate report cards.

Project Details

- **Add student records:** Enter student names and their marks for different subjects.
- **Calculate total and average:** Compute the student's total and average marks.
- **Assign grades:** Convert marks into letter grades (A, B, C, etc.).
- **Store student records:** Save data in a database for later use.
- **Generate a report card:** Display student results in a readable format.

Steps to Solve the Problem:

1. **Create a dictionary to store student data**: Each student has a name, subjects, and marks.
2. **Allow teachers to enter marks**: Store subject-wise marks for each student.
3. **Calculate grades automatically**: Convert marks into grades using conditions.
4. **Use a database for record-keeping**: Save student records securely.
5. **Print a report card**: Format and display the student's marks, average, and grades.

Reference Chapters:

- ***Chapter 6:*** *Organizing Data* (for using dictionaries to store student records).
- ***Chapter 9:*** *Error Handling* (for handling missing or incorrect data).
- ***Chapter 16:*** *Python and Databases* (for storing student records).
- ***Chapter 13:*** *Math in Python* (for calculating grades and averages).

Extra Learning Suggestions

- Add a search feature to find student records quickly.
- Create a web-based version of the report card system.

Project 4: Flask Web App-Online Bookstore

Problem Statement:

Imagine building an online bookstore where users can browse books, leave reviews, and manage orders. This project will be a web application built using Flask.

Project Details:

- **Book listings:** Display books with details such as title, author, and price.
- **User reviews:** Users can submit and read reviews.
- **Database storage:** Store book details and reviews.
- **Error handling:** Prevent missing or incorrect data.

Steps to Solve the Problem:

1. **Set up a Flask app**: Configure routes and templates.
2. **Create a database for books and reviews**: Store data securely.
3. **Build book listing pages**: Use HTML and Jinja templates.
4. **Implement a review system**: Allow users to submit and view reviews.
5. **Handle errors gracefully**: Prevent invalid submissions.

Reference Chapters:

- ***Chapter 15***: *Building Web Apps* (for Flask development and routing).
- ***Chapter 16***: *Python and Databases* (for storing book and review data).
- ***Chapter 9***: *Error Handling* (for handling user input errors).

Extra Learning Suggestions:

- Add user authentication so only logged-in users can submit reviews.
- Allow users to buy books and process payments.

Project 5: Library Management System

Problem Statement:

Libraries need a way to manage books, track borrowed books, and handle returns. In this project, you will create a Library Management System that keeps a record of books, allows users to borrow books, and tracks return dates.

Project Details:

- **Book inventory:** Store a list of books with details such as title, author, and availability.
- **Borrow books:** Users can check out books, which updates the availability status.
- **Return books:** Users return books, updating the system accordingly.
- **Store book data:** Save book details in a database.
- **Track due dates:** Notify if a book is overdue.

Steps to Solve the Problem:

1. **Create a database of books**: Store details such as title, author, and status (available/borrowed).
2. **Implement a borrowing system**: Update the book's status when a user checks out a book.
3. **Handle book returns**: Change the status when a book is returned.
4. **Track due dates**: Record the return date and check if it is overdue.
5. **Display available books**: Show users a list of books they can borrow.

Reference Chapters

- ***Chapter 6:*** *Organizing Data* (for storing book details in lists or dictionaries).
- ***Chapter 10:*** *File Handling and String Manipulation* (for saving book records).
- ***Chapter 16:*** *Python and Databases* (for managing book inventory).
- ***Chapter 9:*** *Error Handling* (to prevent borrowing unavailable books).

Extra Learning Suggestions

- Add a search function to quickly find books by title or author.
- Implement a user login system so users can view their borrowed books.
- Convert this into a Flask web application with an online catalog.

Final Thoughts

These projects challenge you to apply every skill learned throughout this book. Completing them will give you hands-on experience in real-world Python programming, preparing you for advanced applications and career opportunities.

Remember, problem-solving is the key to mastery. If you get stuck, revisit the relevant chapters, research online, and experiment with different solutions. The best way to learn Python is by building with it!

Good luck and happy coding!

Index

Symbols

A

B

C

E

F

G

H

I

J

K

L